S0-BMX-850

Corrigenda to Mastronarde,
Introduction to Attic Greek (first printing)

p. 14, 6.d	read *diphthong* for *dipthong*
p. 40, 3.d., penultimate line	read *our* for *out*
p. 44, Ex. III.15	read ὁδόν for ὀδόν
p. 45, 8th line of paragraph A	read *vieille* for *vielle*
p. 59, line 10	read *They gave* for *The gave*
p. 71, 5.a.1, 4th line	read *U22.5* for *U22.6*
p. 77, 8th line from bottom	read *es findet sich* for *es sich findet*
p. 125, footnote 1 (twice)	read Σωκράτη for Σωκράτην
p. 147, 1st ex. under 3	read Σωκράτη for Σωκράτην
p. 155, 3, 2nd sentence	read The diphthong appears in nom. voc. sing. and dat. pl. of all types and also in the acc. sing. and pl. of nouns in αυ and ου.
p. 156, top paradigm, 3rd col., 4th row	read ναῦν for νῆα
p. 157, 5b, first example	read ἦν for ἦσαν
p. 170, 9th line	read διδω-, διδο- for δω-, δο-
p. 180, Ex. I.29	read προσεῖντο for προεῖντο
p. 213, Ex. I.3	read οὐχ for οὐκ
p. 239, footnote 1	read *particle* for *particile*
p. 254–55	(ἀτιμάζω should have been listed under a separate heading, apart from the contract verbs)
p. 258, top line	read *V* for *IV*
p. 278, Ex. II.6 end of 3rd line	read ὑμᾶς for ὑμὰς
p. 330, n. 1, line 4	read ἠῶ for ἠώ
p. 332, second impersonal example	read *We* [emphatic] for *We*
p. 352, top paradigm, 3rd col., 4th row	read ναῦν for νῆα
p. 372, aorist active imperative of ἵημι	read (ἄφ)ες, (ἄφ)ετον, (ἄφ)ετε for (ἀφ)ές, (ἀφ)έτον, (ἀφ)έτε
p. 391, entry ἵππος	delete accent on -ου
p. 404, entry "ask (a question)"	read (33) for (34)

Attica in the Classical Period

Introduction to Attic Greek

Donald J. Mastronarde

UNIVERSITY OF CALIFORNIA PRESS

BERKELEY   LOS ANGELES   LONDON

University of California Press
Berkeley and Los Angeles, California

University of California Press, Ltd.
Oxford, England

© 1993 by
The Regents of the University of California

Library of Congress Cataloging-in-Publication Data

Mastronarde, Donald J.
    Introduction to Attic Greek / D.J. Mastronarde
       p.   cm.
    Includes index.
    ISBN 0-520-07843-8 (alk. paper). — ISBN 0-520-07844-6 (pbk. : alk. paper)
    1. Attic Greek dialect   I. Title
PA522.M38 1993
480—dc20   92-21731
                                                  CIP

Printed in the United States of America

9 8 7 6 5 4 3 2

The paper used in this publication meets the minimum requirements
of American National Standard for Information Sciences—Permanence
of Paper for Printed Library Materials, ANSI Z39.48–1984. ⊗

Contents

Preface

There is no one best way to teach elementary Greek or to learn it. Any successful course will depend on a complex interaction among the classroom teacher, the textbook, and the students, with their varying learning-styles and differing degrees of dedication to a challenging project. The present book was inspired by frustration with a standard textbook and began several years ago as a typewritten manual prepared as part of an Undergraduate Instruction Improvement Project at the University of California, Berkeley. In my teaching I have worked with students of all levels and been keenly aware of the gaps and deficiencies with which many students arrive at advanced undergraduate and graduate courses. In writing this book, it was my desire to provide to the mature college student a reliable and relatively complete presentation of ancient Attic Greek. With a foundation comprising sufficient coverage of morphology and syntax, a substantial body of the central vocabulary (especially of verbs and their principal parts), and preliminary exposure to the reading of authentic connected passages, the student should be well prepared to face the transition to reading a continuous text with commentary and dictionary.

This book is adaptable to several formats of instruction. It is tailored primarily for a one-year college course in beginning Greek, in which the textbook may be covered in somewhat less than the full year and the remainder of the year may be devoted to reading some Xenophon or simple Plato or other straightforward Attic prose. Concomitant reading of a separate Greek text may indeed be assigned (time permitting) for Units 34 and beyond. I have myself normally taught from this book in more intensive courses, such as a two-quarter sequence covering the same material as a full-year (three-quarter) course, or (with more pressure and no time for reading from another book) in a one-semester version (counting at Berkeley as a double course). With very highly motivated students, the book should work well also at colleges where it is the custom to cover all or most of the textbook in a single semester-long course. I have not taught from it in a "workshop" setting (i.e., all of elementary Greek in six weeks) and do not claim that it is suited to that.

It should be emphasized that I have not aimed to make the units equal and that I do not think equal time should be spent on all units. I recommend a brisker pace through the first 10 or 11 units, which are relatively short, and in a two-semester course I would aim to complete either 24 or 22 units in the first semester. For the longer units, it is possible, with planning, to divide the material over several classes: one may, for instance, save some of the exercises of the previous unit (e.g., the reading selection in the later units) to be assigned while the students are studying the first half of the next unit, or one may at any time profitably give an assignment for vocabulary review or principal part memorization. If a class is pressed for time toward the end of the course, it is possible to move from Unit 35 to Unit 37 and Units 40–41 and advise the students to use the remaining units for reference when they begin reading Greek texts in their next course. In some courses there will not be time to assign and correct all the exercises, and the instructor should make a selection suitable to the goals of the particular class. There are other classes that want as many exercises as possible, and it is for these that I have expanded the exercises in this revision. I have striven to provide both a gradual buildup of knowledge and an alternation of material, emphasizing, for instance, now nouns and now verbs, now morphology and now syntax. I have tried to put as many fundamental features as possible as early as possible, but there have inevitably been compromises: not everything can come early.

My presentation is based on the belief that college students who are trying to learn Greek deserve full exposure to the morphology and grammar that they will encounter in real texts and full explanations of what they are asked to learn. To expect the student to learn such things as if by osmosis from annotated readings or to postpone a large portion of the more sophisticated concepts and constructions does not, in most cases, serve the long-range needs of the student. I believe that at least some students will find the conceptual or historical understanding of a linguistic phenomenon to be an aid to the chore of memorization which is unavoidable in beginning to master ancient Greek, and that the availability of such explanations need not be any obstacle to the other students. On the other hand, I have tried to indicate clearly what the student *must* learn as a necessary minimum, and the lengthier historical and grammatical explanations are intended for the students' information rather than memorization. I retain (and explain) many traditional terms (which the student will encounter anyway in commentaries and reference works), since provided that the book and the instructor lay emphasis on the true nature of each phenomenon the traditional terminology will be harmless. It is, of course, up to each instructor to gauge the abilities and level of motivation of his or her class, and to decide accordingly such questions as how far and when to press for accuracy in the use of accents, for which verbs the class must have the principal parts firmly committed to memory, how much of the vocabulary the students will be responsible for on a test, or how much emphasis to put on English-to-Greek exercises as compared to Greek-to-English.

The exercises are keyed to the grammar and vocabulary for which the student has been prepared by the units completed. Especially in the first half of the book I have tended to avoid introducing new words or constructions in a reading exercise, so that a student who has truly mastered the material to date should be well equipped to do the reading with a minimum of annotation or reference to the glossary. For this reason I refrain from introducing "genuine Greek" in the early units; but once the students' knowledge has been built to a certain point, many of the sentences are taken from Attic prose texts or patterned on sentences in such texts. In the later units, I emphasize reading from actual texts rather than made-up readings with untypically simple sentence-structure and artificially limited vocabulary. To ensure that the student begins with a sound grasp of what is prosaic or colloquial as opposed to poetic or recondite, I have avoided almost entirely poetic passages in the exercises. The vocabulary is intended to familiarize the student with a fairly large sample of basic and frequently occurring words, memorization of which will facilitate reading of all kinds of Greek as the student progresses.

Because this book treats concepts of language and grammar so thoroughly, there is not room in it for the cultural and anecdotal material that an experienced teacher of Greek brings to the classroom situation as an enrichment. It is my hope that instructors who use this book will provide such enrichment and that, even before the class reaches the reading selections in the later units, some items of vocabulary and sentences of the exercises may serve to inspire impromptu digressions on history, literature, mythology, society, or culture.

For the improvements made to this book over the years and for the encouragement to seek wider distribution I am grateful to a number of colleagues, graduate student instructors, and students in my own and others' classes. Many of the most user-friendly features of this book are due to their kind suggestions. I myself am responsible for all final decisions about inclusion and exclusion and ordering of material. Every user of the book will no doubt wish that this or that detail were handled differently or sooner or later, but I hope that there will be enough advantages to outweigh such irritations.

Finally, I would like to acknowledge here the meticulous care shown by my copy editor, Paul Psoinos, and the help provided by Mary Lamprech and other members of the staff of the University of California Press.

Introduction: The Ancient Greek Language and Attic Greek

1. Greek is an Indo-European tongue. Since the early nineteenth century linguists have demonstrated the existence of and studied a large family of European and Asian languages, ancient and modern, which are closely related to one another and not similarly related to languages outside the group. It is assumed that the kinship among Indo-European languages reflects a prehistoric kinship among the speakers of these tongues. A few of the language groups classified as Indo-European are Indic (Old Indic = Sanskrit), Slavic, Italic (including Latin), Germanic, and Greek. English, with its Germanic ancestry and admixture of Latinate elements via French, is also an Indo-European tongue.

2. Before about 2000 B.C.E. the inhabitants of the Balkan peninsula and the Aegean islands were probably non-Indo-European-speaking peoples. Among them were the Minoans on Crete, who had a script (as yet undeciphered) now known as Linear A; the Eteocypriots on Cyprus; and Pelasgians, Leleges, Tyrseni, and Carians on the mainland, the islands, and the coast of Asia Minor.

The Greek language inherited some words from these earlier inhabitants of the lands which became the Greek world. Many place names are thought to be non-Indo-European survivals: for example, those containing either *-nth-* (or its equivalent *-nd-* in the Ionic dialect) or *-ss-* (or its equivalent *-tt-* in the Attic dialect), such as Korinthos, Zakynthos, Aspendos, Parnassos, Halikarnassos, Hymettos; and those with a nasal ending, such as Athenai, Mykenai, Kalymna. Some personal names may also be survivals: for example, masculine names in *-eus* such as that of the hero Achilleus (Achilles) or feminine names in *-o* such as that of the poetess Sappho. A few basic items also seem to have names surviving from the pre-Greek period: for example, *plinthos* (brick), *kolossos* (statue), *thalassa* (sea).

1

3. Greek-speaking peoples migrated into the "Greek world" as we know it in two waves. An "Achaean" migration (from the north or east) took place between 2000 and 1500 B.C.E. (perhaps ca. 1900 B.C.E.). Mycenean civilization, which flourished from 1600 to 1200 or 1100, was one part of the "Achaean" culture. The Myceneans used an adaptation of Minoan Linear A in their written documents (clays tablets have survived); this script, called Linear B, was deciphered in 1952, revealing a Greek tongue (the earliest form known to us). The use of Linear B was probably limited to official documents and inventories and was apparently practiced only by a specially trained class of scribes within the palace societies of the time. Knowledge of Linear B seems to have died out ca. 1100 B.C.E., after the collapse of Mycenean civilization. The end of Mycenean civilization is somehow related to volcanic eruption and earthquakes and the influx of a new wave of Greek-speaking peoples (the "Dorians") ca. 1100. The exact details and chronology of the collapse are, however, variously reconstructed. The Greeks themselves remembered the Mycenean Age as an age of heroes and great warriors and associated its end with famous wars at Thebes and at Troy and with a "Dorian invasion."

4. Scholars have deduced that early Greek (ca. 1500 B.C.E.) had several characteristics not found in classical Greek in general or the Ionic-Attic dialect family in particular. "Open vowels," that is, those occurring together without an intervening consonant, were retained rather than contracted, as in many dialects of classical Greek. Etymologically original long vowel *a* still maintained itself in all contexts, whereas later a change of this vowel was characteristic of some dialects. The *w*-sound (vau or digamma) and the *h*-sound were still present, whereas most classical dialects had lost the *w* and some had lost the *h* as well. Semivocalic *i* (like English consonantal *y* in *you* or *beyond*) was still used after consonants, whereas in the later dialects other sounds developed from such combinations. There was not yet an aorist passive system based on the theta-suffix used in classical Greek, and there were more irregularities in declension of nouns.

Greek distinguished itself from other Indo-European tongues in several important ways. It had a tonal rather than a stress accent, and this provided for a better survival of inflectional endings than in some other languages. Initial Indo-European *s* developed into *h* in Greek, while initial semivocalic *i* became either *h* or Greek zeta. Of the original eight Indo-European cases for nouns, three (ablative, instrumental, locative) were lost in the development of classical Greek, and their uses were absorbed by other cases.

5. The classical period of the ancient Greek language extends from ca. 750 to ca. 350 B.C.E. Its beginning is marked by the spread of the Greek alphabet, the first surviving traces of which are from the second half of the eighth century B.C.E. Its end is marked by the dying out of many classical dialects and the development of a new common dialect (see §7 below). For the classical period numerous dialects can be documented thanks to the evidence of inscriptions, graffiti, and literary remains. The dialects often differed widely in spelling, accentuation, pronunciation, vocabulary, and even syntax, but their speakers still recognized each other as fellow Greek speakers.

The dialects of this period are shown on the map on the next page. There are three major dialect groups. The Ionic-Attic group includes the regions labeled 1–4. Regions 5–10 comprise the "Achaean" group (5–7 North Achaean; 8–10 South Achaean). These two groups are believed to correspond to the pre-Dorian layer of migrations. The third major group, Doric-NW Greek, corresponds to the Dorian migration and includes the regions labeled 11–23 (11–17 Doric; 18–19 NW Greek; 20–23 other). Not shown on the map are the Greek-speaking regions in Sicily, southern Italy, northern Africa, and the Black Sea region, colonized during the classical period.

6. The Attic dialect was that spoken by the natives of Attika, the peninsula jutting from the southeastern part of the mainland above the Peloponnesos. The major city and political center of Attika was Athens. The Greek taught in this book is basically Attic Greek of the fifth and fourth centuries B.C.E. It is the most convenient form of ancient Greek to master first. Knowledge of Attic makes accessible to the student both Attic drama and a vast amount of historical, oratorical, and philosophical prose. Once Attic is mastered, it is relatively simple to learn the variations to be found in the dialects of Homeric poetry, choral lyrics, Ionic prose, and pastoral poetry. It is even easier to move from Attic to the later Greek of the New Testament.

Attic shares with Ionic several features which distinguish Ionic-Attic from other dialects and shows other features which distinguish it in turn from Ionic. One of the most notable features (which you will find important already in Unit 4) is the development of original long vowel *a*: this sound has become a long *e*-vowel (eta) in all positions in Ionic and in all positions except after *e*, *i*, or *r* in Attic. Certain sequences of long vowel and short vowel in word endings have undergone an exchange of quantities (metathesis), that is, long-short has become short-long. The *w*-sound has disappeared in both Ionic and Attic; but in Ionic when vau has disappeared after *l*, *n*, or *r*, a short vowel in the preceding syllable has become long (compensatory lengthening), whereas

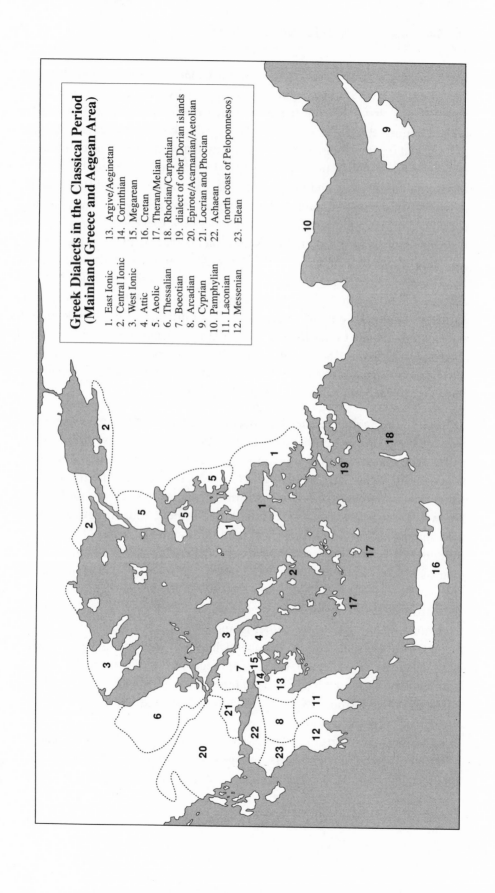

Greek Dialects in the Classical Period (Mainland Greece and Aegean Area)

1. East Ionic
2. Central Ionic
3. West Ionic
4. Attic
5. Aeolic
6. Thessalian
7. Boeotian
8. Arcadian
9. Cyprian
10. Pamphylian
11. Laconian
12. Messenian
13. Argive/Aeginetan
14. Corinthian
15. Megarean
16. Cretan
17. Theran/Melian
18. Rhodian/Carpathian
19. dialect of other Dorian islands
20. Epirote/Acarnanian/Aetolian
21. Locrian and Phocian
22. Achaean (north coast of Peloponnesos)
23. Elean

in Attic such a short vowel is unchanged (e.g., Attic *koros*, but Ionic *kouros* from original *korwos*). Ionic-Attic dialects add an optional *n* (nu ephelkus-tikon) to certain inflectional endings when the following word begins with a vowel (this is done to prevent "hiatus," the pronunciation of two vowels without intervening consonant). As opposed to other dialects, Ionic and Attic have the infinitive ending *-nai* (instead of *-menai*), *ei* for "if" (instead of *ai*), and the modal particle *an* (instead of *ke*). As opposed to Ionic, Attic has *-tt-* instead of *-ss-* and *-rr-* instead of *-rs-*, continues to use the dual number (rather than the plural) to refer to pairs of things, and in general preserves more irregular forms.

7. Because of the military, commercial, and intellectual prominence of Athens in the second half of the fifth century B.C.E., the use of Attic became more widespread. As it was used by more and more people outside of Attika, it lost some of its most peculiarly Attic features except among native Athenians. By the end of the fourth century, a new, "common" dialect had emerged: the Koine. This was the language that spread to Asia and Egypt with Alexander the Great and then underwent further modifications. From the mid-fourth century on, spoken Greek begins a long and gradual process of change affecting pronunciation, accentuation, vocabulary, and syntax, with the Koine eventually suppressing the old dialects. These changes in the language are also evident in nonliterary works written in Greek of the time, such as private letters, contracts, and writings without high cultural aspirations, including the Greek New Testament. But educated writers tried for centuries to stay as close as possible to classical Attic Greek, creating a split between the living spoken language and the artificial (mainly written) language of a cultural elite, a split which manifested itself even in modern times. For an excellent brief discussion of the development of Koine and later changes in the Greek language, see Robert Browning, *Medieval and Modern Greek* (London 1969).

The Alphabet; Pronunciation

---

1. *The Alphabet.* In the late ninth or early eighth century B.C.E. the Greeks borrowed a group of 22 letter symbols from the Phoenicians.[1] They reinterpreted symbols for sounds not present in Greek to serve as symbols for the vowel sounds (Phoenician, like other Semitic tongues, represented only consonants in writing). The earliest Greek alphabets included the letters vau ($_F$ or F), koppa (Ϙ), and san (an alternative to sigma that looked much like our capital M and followed Π in some alphabets). At this stage, the symbol H stood for the *h*-sound, and the letters xi, phi, chi, psi, and omega were not yet invented. The inherited forms (with san ignored) were originally arranged as follows:

Α Β Γ Δ Ε F Z H Θ I K Λ M N O Π Ϙ P Σ T Υ

In the early period there were many local variations in letter forms and even in correspondence of letter to sound, especially among the symbols added in some dialects to represent double consonants. For instance, X = *ks* in the west, whence it passed into the Latin and the modern "Roman" alphabet as *x*, whereas in the east (including Attic and Koine) X = *kh* (chi). The Attic alphabet before about 450 lacked omega, xi, and psi and still used H for the *h*-sound. The Ionians, however, had generally lost the *h*-sound and used the symbol H instead for a long open *e*-vowel; their alphabet had added omega (to represent a long open *o*-vowel) and the double-consonant symbols. From about 450 some of the Ionic letters were used sporadically in Athens, more often by private citizens than by the public secretaries who provided texts (of laws and decrees) for stonemasons to carve as inscriptions. In 403, the Athenian government officially made the transition to the Ionian alphabet (although use of the old system continued sporadically until about 350). During the

---

1. The date of the origin of the Greek alphabet is still debated. Some experts in alphabetic writing assign an earlier date, mainly on the basis of similarity of a few letter forms to Semitic forms known in the tenth or eleventh century. But the evidence on the Greek side favors the date given here.

fourth century the 24-letter Ionian/New Attic alphabet won acceptance throughout most of the Greek world and became the standard in Koine.

The ancient Greeks used only what we call capital letters (although after the fourth century there were more and less formal or cursive ways of writing them):

A B Γ Δ E Z H Θ I K Λ M N Ξ O Π Ρ Σ T Υ Φ X Ψ Ω

The lowercase letter forms of present-day Greek type-fonts are more or less closely derived from cursive letter forms of handwritten Greek used in the Middle Ages and Renaissance:

α β γ δ ε ζ η θ ι κ λ μ ν ξ ο π ρ σ τ υ φ χ ψ ω

Lowercase handwritten forms of some letters may differ slightly from those of the Greek font of this book. The instructor will demonstrate the handwritten forms for the class.

2. *Classification of Sounds.* [NOTE: the technical terminology introduced here is provided for the sake of explanation only and is not to be memorized by the student. The essential thing to learn is the recommended pronunciation, but some of the concepts in this section will turn out to be helpful in understanding features of morphology and word formation.]

The number of syllables in an utterance generally corresponds to the number of high points in a diagram of sonority or acoustic power. Sounds characteristically occurring at high points in the diagram are *vowels*. Those that occur at low points are *consonants*. A sound which can occur in both positions is a *semivowel*.

Vowels are classified in two important ways. (1) They are termed *front*, *central*, or *back* according to the areas of the tongue and palate involved in pronunciation. (2) They are termed *close*, *mid*, or *open* according to the degree of raising of the tongue, which determines the size of the passage through which air must pass during pronunciation of the sound. In addition, the quality of a vowel can be altered by *lip rounding* or by *nasalization* (the velum or soft palate is not raised, with the result that the nasal passages are open when the vowel is pronounced).

A *diphthong* is the coalescence of two vowel sounds within a single syllable. The speaker begins by articulating the first vowel, which is normally relatively more open, and glides into the articulation of the second vowel, which is normally relatively more close.

Vowels have *length* or *quantity*, *long* or *short* corresponding more or less to a greater or a lesser duration of pronunciation. Note that the vowels α, ι, and υ may be long or short, while ε and ο are short and η and ω are long.

The relations of the vowel sounds of classical Attic can be conveniently displayed on a vowel diagram:

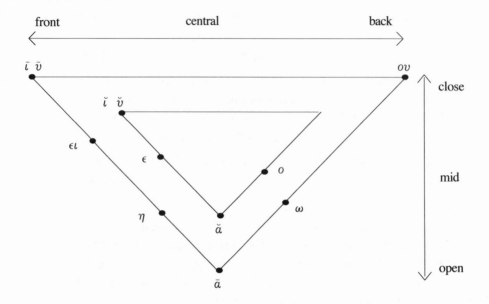

Consonants are classified in three important ways. First, according to whether or not the vocal cords draw together and vibrate, they are termed *voiced* or *voiceless*. To understand this distinction, pronounce *b*, then *p*, either with your ears closed or with a finger on your throat: you should hear or feel a vibration when the voiced consonant *b* is uttered, but not when the voiceless *p* is pronounced.

Secondly, according to the position or organ of articulation, consonants are described as follows:

labial or bilabial	lips
labio-dental	upper teeth and lower lip
dental	tongue-tip and upper teeth
alveolar	tongue-tip and upper gums
palatal	mid-tongue and hard palate
velar	back-tongue and soft palate

Thirdly, consonants are classified according to the manner in which air is released during pronunciation. When there is a complete closure of the speech organs, the sound is called a *stop*; when the stop is released suddenly, the consonant is termed a *plosive* (*p, b, t, d, k, g*). The nine classical Greek plosives may be arranged in a table as follows:

	voiced	voiceless	aspirated (voiceless)
labial	β	π	ϕ
velar	γ	κ	χ
dental	δ	τ	θ

When there is no complete closure of the speech organs, the sound is a *continuant*. One type of continuant is the *nasal*, pronounced with tongue or lips closed but air escaping through the nose (*m, n*). A second type of continuant is the *liquid* (a term taken over from the Latin grammarians, who thus translated the Greek grammarians' term *hugros*, which was probably in origin a metrical term): for example, *l*, a lateral continuant (air escapes on one side of the tongue); *r*, an alveolar continuant. If the air passage is so narrow as to create an audible effect, the continuant is termed a *fricative* (only *s* in classical Greek). The *aspirate* (*h*-sound) is also a continuant.

For further details on reconstructing the pronunciation of classical Attic, W. Sidney Allen, *Vox Graeca: A Guide to the Pronunciation of Classical Greek* (3rd ed., Cambridge 1987), is highly recommended.

3. *Recommended Pronunciations*

alpha

ᾰ	like the first *a* in English *aha* (or the first *a* in Italian *amare*); a short open central vowel
ᾱ	like the second *a* in English *aha* (or the second *a* in Italian *amare*); a long open central vowel
αι	like the vowel in English *high*; a diphthong
ᾳ (ᾱι)	generally pronounced by present-day students exactly like a plain long alpha; a so-called "long diphthong."[1] The practice of writing a small iota under the vowel ("iota subscript") was developed in the Middle Ages and has been followed in most printed texts, though you will also eventually meet texts with the iota written after the long vowel ("iota adscript"), which was the classical practice.
αυ	like the vowel in English *how*; a diphthong

---

1. The term "long diphthong" is slightly misleading: all diphthongs are normally long vowels, but the three "long diphthongs" ᾳ ῃ ῳ are formed from the combination of a long vowel and iota. In classical times these were true diphthongs (long alpha gliding into iota, eta gliding into iota, omega gliding into iota), but between the fourth and second centuries B.C.E. the iota weakened to a mere glide (like a consonantal *y*-sound) and then was not pronounced at all. Hence the modern pronunciation.

beta

β   like English *b*; a voiced labial plosive

gamma

γ   like hard *g* in *go*; a voiced velar plosive, except before γ, κ, χ, and
                           perhaps μ, where it is a velar nasal, like *n* in *ink* or *ng* in *song*

delta

δ   like French *d* (similar to English *d*, but English *d* tends to have a
                           slight aspiration absent in the Greek); a voiced dental plosive

epsilon[1]

ε   like *e* in English *pet*; a short front mid vowel

    ει   like the vowel of German *Beet* (similar to the vowel in English
                           eight); a digraph (two-letter symbol) representing a single sound
                           (monophthong); a long front close-mid vowel[2]

    ευ   a diphthong pronounced by combining ε with [u] (= *oo*) in one
                           syllable (cf. the vowel in English *feud*)

zeta

ζ   like [zd] in English *wisdom*; a monograph (single symbol) re-
                           presenting a double-consonant group. From about 350 B.C.E. on,
                           ζ came to be pronounced as a single fricative, [z] as in English
                           doze or *rose*, and you will often hear it pronounced that way.

eta[3]

η   like the *ê* in French *tête*; a long open vowel (similar to ει, but η is
                           more open and more central)

    η (ηι)   generally pronounced nowadays exactly like plain η, though this is
                           a postclassical practice; a "long diphthong" (see above on ᾳ)

    ηυ   a diphthong very similar in sound to ευ, made up of η gliding into
                           [u] (= *oo*); very hard for English speakers to distinguish from ευ,
                           and the Greeks themselves lost the distinction of sound in the
                           fourth century B.C.E.

theta

θ   pronounced by most people today like fricative *th* in English *thin*;
                           but pronounced in classical Attic like the *t* in English *top*, an

---

1. The classical Greeks called this letter εἶ; the Byzantines used the name ἒ ψιλόν = "plain *e*"
to distinguish ε from the letter pair αι, which in postclassical times became identical in
pronunciation to ε.

2. In earlier Attic ει represented a real diphthong (the sound of ε gliding into the sound of ι),
but the sound became single during classical times. The long vowel eventually represented by ει
also occurred in some words as a result of contraction or compensatory lengthening. In the
former places ει is (historically) a genuine diphthong, while in the latter it is traditionally
referred to as a "spurious" diphthong. This distinction will turn out to be significant in U29 and
elsewhere.

3. In western Greek alphabets and in early Attic, the letter H was heta, the *h*-sound. See §1
above.

aspirated voiceless dental plosive (i.e., an aspirated tau). The *th*-pronunciation arose in the Roman Imperial period (even earlier in some dialects) and is recommended in this course because it avoids confusion between τ and θ for English speakers.

iota

ῐ   like *i* in French *vite*; a short close front vowel, unrounded (the sound in English *bit* is similar, but more open)

ῑ   like *i* in French *vive*; a long close front vowel, unrounded

kappa

κ   like English *k* (but completely unaspirated); a voiceless velar plosive. In the preposition ἐκ kappa is assimilated in pronunciation to the following consonant: aspirated to [ekh] before θ or φ, or voiced to [eg] before β, δ, or λ.

lambda

λ   like a clear *l* in French or like English *l* before vowels; a liquid

mu

μ   like English *m*; a bilabial nasal

nu

ν   like *n* in English *net*; a dental nasal. Nu is often assimilated to the following consonant in compounds or in phrases pronounced as a unit: it is assimilated to the following consonant before λ, μ, ρ, σ; labialized to μ before labial plosives β, π, φ; converted to the velar nasal γ before velar plosives κ, γ, χ.

xi

ξ   like English *x* in *fox*; a double consonant [ks]

omicron[1]

ο   like *o* in German *Gott*; a short back mid vowel

οι   like the vowel in English *boy* or *coin*, a diphthong

ου   like *oo* in English *pool* or *ou* in French *rouge*, a digraph representing (during most of the classical period) a long close back vowel [u][2]

pi

π   like French *p* or non-initial *p* in English (that is, totally unaspirated); a bilabial voiceless plosive

rho

ρ   rolled *r* as in Italian or Scottish; a trilled alveolar liquid

---

1. Originally called by the Greeks οὖ; but the Byzantines called it ὂ μικρόν = "little *o*" when omega, ὦ μέγα = "big *o*," was no longer distinct from it in pronunciation.

2. As was the case with ει (see above), in earlier Attic ου represented a real diphthong ([ou], the sound of *o* gliding into the originally back sound of *υ*), but the sound became single during classical times. The long vowel eventually represented by ου also occurred in some words as a result of contraction or compensatory lengthening. In the former places ου is (historically) a genuine diphthong, while in the latter it is traditionally referred to as a "spurious" diphthong.

sigma

σ, ς, ϲ   like the English soft *s* in *mouse*; a voiceless fricative [s], except before the voiced consonants β, γ, δ, μ, when it is a voiced fricative [z], like the *s* in English *muse*. In most printed books, following an orthographic convention of late Byzantine times, sigma appears as σ at the beginning of a word or within it, but as ς at the end of a word. In some books you will also see the older letter form ϲ (lunate sigma) printed in all positions.

tau

τ   like French *t* or non-initial English *t* (totally unaspirated), a voiceless dental plosive

upsilon[1]

ῠ   like short French *u* or German *ü*, pronounced like the *u* in French *lune*; a short close front rounded vowel; in earlier Attic, a close back rounded vowel [u], the value it retained in diphthongs

ῡ   like long French *u* or German *ü*, pronounced like the *u* in French *ruse*; a long close front rounded vowel

υι   a diphthong combining the rounded vowel [ü] with semivocalic *i* = [y]. The full pronunciation was [üy] or [üyy], but in classical times the iota was weakened to a glide between vowels and sometimes omitted in spelling.[2]

phi

φ   pronounced by most people today as fricative *f* (as in English *foot*), but in classical times equivalent to an aspirated pi, like *p* in English *pot*, an aspirated voiceless bilabial plosive. Phi became fricative in postclassical times, and the *f*-pronunciation is recommended in this course because it avoids confusion between π and φ for English speakers.

chi

χ   pronounced like the *c* of English *cat* or like *ch* in Scottish *loch*; an aspirated voiceless velar plosive (aspirated kappa)

psi

ψ   like *ps* in English *lapse*; a monograph representing a double consonant [ps]

omega

ω   like *aw* in English *saw*; a long open central-back vowel (but you will also hear it pronounced like English long *o* in *go*)

---

1. The ancient Greeks called the letter ῦ, but by Byzantine times it shared the same pronunciation with οι and was given the name ῦ ψιλόν = "plain *u*" to distinguish it from "diphthong" οι.

2. Pronunciation like English *we* is sometimes heard, but is not correct.

ῳ (ωι)   a "long diphthong," generally pronounced nowadays exactly like plain ω, though this is a postclassical practice (see above on ᾳ)

Breathing Signs

῾   aspirate or rough breathing: a sign placed over an initial vowel or initial rho to indicate an initial *h*-sound. The sign derives from the use of the left half of H to indicate [h] after H had been converted to a vowel symbol.

᾿   smooth breathing: a sign placed over an initial vowel to indicate the absence of aspiration

4. *Punctuation and Capitalization.* The Greek comma (,) and period (.) are the same as are used in English. The Greek semicolon or colon is a single dot raised above the line (·). The Greek question mark looks like the English semicolon (;).

The Athenians of classical times used only capital letters and rarely punctuated; often they left no space between words. Punctuation was gradually introduced in books in postclassical times, but was consistently applied only in Byzantine and modern times. In printed editions of Greek, punctuation is used throughout, and lowercase letters are used except for the first letter of proper names or proper adjectives and sometimes for the first letter of a section, paragraph, or quoted speech.

5. *Elision and Crasis.* A short vowel at the end of a word (especially of certain relatively weak words, such as particles, adverbs, and prepositions) is usually eliminated (elided) before a following word beginning with a vowel. Elision is marked by an apostrophe ('), a symbol invented in postclassical times but applied consistently only in Byzantine and modern times. For example:

$$\grave{\alpha}\lambda\lambda\grave{\alpha}\ \dot{\omega}\phi\epsilon\lambda\acute{\eta}\sigma\omega \longrightarrow \grave{\alpha}\lambda\lambda' \ \dot{\omega}\phi\epsilon\lambda\acute{\eta}\sigma\omega$$
$$\pi\alpha\rho\grave{\alpha}\ \dot{\upsilon}\mu\hat{\omega}\nu \longrightarrow \pi\alpha\rho'\ \dot{\upsilon}\mu\hat{\omega}\nu$$

If the following word begins with a vowel that has rough breathing, then an unaspirated unvoiced plosive (π, τ, κ) at the end of the elided word is changed to the corresponding aspirated plosive (φ, θ, χ):

$$\dot{\upsilon}\pi\grave{o}\ \dot{\upsilon}\mu\hat{\omega}\nu \longrightarrow \dot{\upsilon}\phi'\ \dot{\upsilon}\mu\hat{\omega}\nu$$

Similar elisions and spelling changes occur in compound words formed with prepositional prefixes:[1]

---

1. But the final iota of περί is never elided.

$$\pi\alpha\rho\alpha\text{-} + \overset{\text{'}}{\alpha}\gamma\omega \longrightarrow \pi\alpha\rho\acute{\alpha}\gamma\omega$$
$$\kappa\alpha\tau\alpha\text{-} + \overset{\text{'}}{\iota}\sigma\tau\eta\mu\iota \longrightarrow \kappa\alpha\theta\acute{\iota}\sigma\tau\eta\mu\iota$$

In other cases a final vowel is not elided but undergoes contraction or
crasis ("mixing") with a following vowel: this occurs, for instance, with the
prefix $\pi\rho o$- and with the article. The symbol called *coronis* ("crown"),
identical to the smooth breathing sign ('), is usually placed over the vowel
formed by contraction:

$$\pi\rho o\acute{\epsilon}\delta o\sigma\alpha\nu \longrightarrow \pi\rho o\ddot{\upsilon}\delta o\sigma\alpha\nu$$
$$\tau\grave{o} \ \acute{\epsilon}\lambda\alpha\tau\tau o\nu \longrightarrow \tau o\ddot{\upsilon}\lambda\alpha\tau\tau o\nu$$

But when the first vowel in crasis is a form of the article with a rough breathing, the resulting vowel has a rough breathing rather than a coronis:

$$\acute{o} \ \alpha\grave{\upsilon}\tau\acute{o}s \longrightarrow \alpha\grave{\upsilon}\tau\acute{o}s$$
$$\acute{o} \ \overset{\text{'}}{\alpha}\nu\theta\rho\omega\pi os \longrightarrow \overset{\text{'}}{\alpha}\nu\theta\rho\omega\pi os$$

Finally, when the second vowel in crasis has a rough breathing, the aspiration
is transferred to any unaspirated consonant of the preceding syllable and the
coronis replaces the rough breathing:

$$\kappa\alpha\grave{\iota} \ \acute{o} \ \pi\acute{o}\nu os \longrightarrow \chi\grave{\omega} \ \pi\acute{o}\nu os$$
$$\tau\grave{\alpha} \ \acute{\iota}\mu\acute{\alpha}\tau\iota\alpha \longrightarrow \theta\alpha\acute{\iota}\mu\acute{\alpha}\tau\iota\alpha$$

6. *Some Typographic Conventions.* The following information is for
later reference. Not all of the phenomena described here will be seen in this
book, but students will meet them in reading Greek texts.

a. Diacritical marks (accents, breathings, coronis) belonging to a diphthong or vowel digraph are conventionally printed over the second of the
two vowels: $\alpha\grave{\upsilon}\tau\acute{o}s$, $o\mathring{\upsilon}\tau os$, $\pi\hat{\epsilon}\iota\rho\alpha$, $\eta\ddot{\upsilon}\rho o\mu\epsilon\nu$.
b. When such a word is capitalized, only the first vowel of the diphthong
is capitalized, and the diacritical marks remain on the second vowel: for
example, $\alpha\grave{\upsilon}\tau\acute{o}s \longrightarrow A\grave{\upsilon}\tau\acute{o}s$
c. When an initial single vowel is capitalized, its diacritical marks are
printed before it: $\overset{\text{'}}{\alpha}\nu\theta\rho\omega\pi os \longrightarrow \text{''}A\nu\theta\rho\omega\pi os$.
d. When a "long dipthong" is capitalized, the main vowel is printed as a
capital, lowercase iota is printed beside it, and diacritical marks are
placed before the capital: $\overset{\text{'}}{\alpha}\delta\eta s \longrightarrow \text{''}A\iota\delta\eta s$.
e. When two adjacent vowels that could form a diphthong are pro-
nounced as separate, the second vowel has a mark of separation
(*diaeresis*: two dots) printed over it: for example, $\gamma\rho\alpha\ddot{\iota}$, $\beta o\ddot{\iota}$ (two
syllables, not one).

WHAT TO STUDY

1. Learn to write the Greek alphabet, especially the lowercase forms.
2. Learn to recite the Greek alphabet.
3. Practice pronunciation by reading aloud the vocabulary words found in Units 3, 4, etc. It is recommended that you give a slight stress to the accented syllable. You may also want to begin memorizing the meanings of the words in Units 3 and 4.

UNIT TWO

Accentuation

---

1. Ancient Greek had a tonal accent or pitch accent, not a stress accent such as is found in Latin, English, and many European languages, including Modern Greek. The accent of a word or phrase consisted in a raising of the pitch of the voice at the accented syllable. The classical Greeks used no accent marks: they needed none since the language was their native tongue, and the tradition of writing and reading books was relatively young and the format not very "user-friendly." The practice of marking accents was initiated by literary scholars in Alexandria ca. 200 B.C.E. Accent marking was needed to help in the correct pronunciation of unfamiliar words in the great poetry of the past, to eliminate ambiguities which would be present in an unaccented text, to help in dealing with divergences between dialects, and perhaps to facilitate the teaching of Greek to foreigners. Accents were at first sporadically used and were especially applied to prevent ambiguities.

2. Gradually the Koine of the Hellenistic and Roman periods underwent a change in accentuation along with many other linguistic changes. By 400 C.E. a stress accent had fully supplanted the pitch accent. Subsequently, accent marking became even more necessary for dealing with the great literature of the past. In the ninth century C.E. Byzantine scholars modified the accent-marking system, producing the conventions we now follow.

3. Although scholars can deduce how the tonal accent worked on single words and short phrases that were treated as an accentual unit, there is no way to discover how the accents sounded in longer utterances, and it is therefore idle (as well as very difficult) for the beginner to attempt a tonal rendering of Greek accents. One approach to pronunciation by a modern student of the language is to ignore the accent; but for mnemonic purposes it is more practical and helpful to give a slight stress to the accented syllable (this practice will also be useful if you later learn Modern Greek). In writing and reading, however, accents should be used and attended to: although some accents are not of

crucial importance for understanding, there are also many which prevent ambiguities, and the accents do mirror important facts about the ancient language.

The beginner should not be worried if the rules for accentuation given here seem complicated and difficult to master. It takes time and practical application before a beginner starts to feel comfortable with accents; but it does not help to ignore them entirely at the beginning and try to repair the omission at a later stage. In learning accents, there should be a happy medium between insouciance and an obsession which detracts from the learning of other elements of the language.

Read this section carefully now, then tackle the succeeding units one by one, observing and learning the accentuation of various nouns and verbs. Review this unit after a few weeks and periodically thereafter until it makes sense to you.

4. *Contonation and Mora.* The apparently complex "rules" of Greek accentuation can be understood in terms of a single general principle involving the concepts of contonation and mora. *Contonation* is the combination of the rise of pitch generally thought of as the accent with the necessary return or fall to standard pitch which follows it. In the case of an acute accent, the contonation includes both the syllable on which the accent is written (and on which the pitch rises) and the entire following syllable (on which the pitch falls), if any, whether it counts as long or short. In the case of the circumflex accent, the contonation occurs on the one syllable on which the accent is written, for there are both a rise in pitch and a return to standard pitch on that syllable. A *mora* is the (theoretically assigned) "standard" length of a short vowel ($\breve{a}$, ϵ, $\breve{\iota}$, o, $\breve{\upsilon}$, and final $\alpha\iota$ and $o\iota$ in most cases). A long vowel ($\bar{a}$, $\epsilon\iota$, η, $\bar{\iota}$, $o\upsilon$, ω, $\bar{\upsilon}$) or a diphthong (except final $\alpha\iota$ and $o\iota$ in most cases) occupies (theoretically) a time span equivalent to two morae.

The general principle of Greek accentuation is that the contonation may be followed by no more than one mora before the end of the word (or phrase pronounced as one word unit). This principle is in many respects similar to rules in other languages (e.g., Latin) which constrain the position of accent according to the nature of the final syllables of a word. In Greek this principle limits the position of the acute and circumflex accents (see §6–9 below) and requires the addition of an extra accent in some phrases consisting of word + enclitic (see §12 below).

5. Only the last three syllables of a word may be accented. These syllables are traditionally referred to by terms derived from Latin: *ultima* = "the last syllable" (abbreviated in this book as *U*); *penult* = "almost last, second-to-

last syllable" (abbreviated here as *P*); and *antepenult* = "before the penult, third-to-last syllable" (abbreviated here as *A*). In what follows, the phrase "long ultima" ("long penult," etc.) will mean "ultima (penult, etc.) containing a long vowel or diphthong."

6. The *acute* accent (´) represents a simple rise in pitch over a short or long vowel. It may appear on *A, P,* or *U.*

The *circumflex* accent (ˆ, also ^ or ˜) represents a rise of pitch over the first mora of a long vowel followed by a return to standard pitch over the second mora. It cannot appear over a short vowel (a short vowel is too short to allow time for both rise and fall). It may appear on *P* or *U* (never on *A*).

The *grave* accent (`) occurs only on *U.* What it represented in terms of pitch in classical pronunciation is uncertain. In a connected utterance, the grave replaces an acute accent over *U* of a word not followed by punctuation (or an enclitic).

7. The ultima, if short and accented, has an acute when a word is written in isolation or occurs immediately before a pause (or an enclitic). In a connected context, a short accented ultima has the grave instead.

If long and accented, *U* may have a circumflex (whether in isolation or not) or an acute (in isolation or before punctuation [or enclitic]; otherwise a grave is substituted). In this case the type of accent must be learned for each word or particular form.

8. The penult, if short and accented, has the acute. If long and accented, then *P* has the acute if *U* is long, the circumflex if *U* is short.

9. The antepenult may be accented only if *U* is short and may receive only the acute.

10. *Examples of Accentuation*

ἀγαθός	short *U* accented with acute, in isolation (no mora follows the contonation on *U*)
ἀγαθὸς ἄνθρωπος	short *U* accented with grave in connected phrase (no mora follows the contonation on *U*)
ψυχή	long *U* accented with acute, in isolation (no mora follows the contonation on *U*)
ψυχὴ ἀνθρώπου	long *U* accented with grave in connected phrase (no mora follows the contonation on *U*)
ἀγαθοῦ	long *U* accented with circumflex, regardless of position (no mora follows the contonation on *U*)

λόγος, λόγου	short accented *P*, acute regardless of quantity of *U*
	(no mora follows the contonation on *P* + *U*)
δῶρον	long accented *P*, short *U*, circumflex
	(one mora follows the contonation on *P*)
δώρου	long accented *P*, long *U*, acute
	(no mora follows the contonation on *P* + *U*)
ἄνθρωπος	accented *A*, short *U*, acute
	(one mora follows the contonation on *A* + *P*)

11. *Proclitics.* Certain monosyllabic words normally lack their own accent and attach themselves in pronunciation to the following word to form a single word unit. These words are called *proclitics* (because they are considered to "lean forward" on the following word for their accent). Proclitics are normally written without an accent and do not affect the accentuation of the following word. In Attic the common proclitics (to be learned in later units) are the negative adverb οὐ, the conjunctions εἰ ("if") and ὡς ("as"), the prepositions εἰς, ἐν, ἐκ, and the nominative singular and plural masculine and feminine forms of the article (ὁ, ἡ, οἱ, αἱ). (A proclitic receives an acute accent when it is followed by an enclitic: see below.)

12. *Enclitics.* Certain words (mostly monosyllabic, a few disyllabic) normally lack their own accent and attach themselves in pronunciation to the preceding word to form a single word unit. These words are called *enclitics* (because they are considered to "lean upon" the previous word for their accent). In Attic the common enclitics (to be learned in later units) are the indefinite pronouns, indefinite adjectives, and indefinite adverbs, most present indicative forms of the irregular verbs εἰμί ("to be") and φημί ("to say"), certain particles, and certain unstressed forms of the personal pronouns. Enclitics sometimes affect the accent of the preceding word.

a. A word accented on *U* keeps its circumflex or acute (the acute is not changed to a grave, because it is no longer felt to be on the final syllable of its word unit).

Ex.   ἀγαθός τις, ἀγαθῷ τῳ

b. A word accented with an acute on *P* is unchanged in accent before a monosyllabic or disyllabic enclitic. But a disyllabic enclitic following such a word receives on its second syllable either an acute (in isolation or before punctuation) or a grave (in a connected context): that is, the word unit receives a second accent if more than one mora follows the contonation.

Ex.   λόγος τις, λόγῳ τινί, λόγῳ τινὶ καλῷ

c. A word accented with a circumflex on *P* or with an acute on *A* receives an extra accent on *U*. Again, this means that the word unit receives a second accent if more than one mora follows the contonation.

Ex.   δῶρόν <u>τι</u>, ἄνθρωπός <u>τις</u>

d. A proclitic followed by an enclitic receives an acute accent.

Ex.   εἴ <u>τις</u>, οὔκ <u>εἰσι</u>

13. For the student's information, the following terms, often used in traditional Greek grammars and in commentaries, are defined here, though they are not used in this book:

oxytone:	a word with acute on *U*
paroxytone:	a word with acute on *P*
proparoxytone:	a word with acute on *A*
perispomenon:	a word with circumflex on *U*
properispomenon:	a word with circumflex on *P*

WHAT TO STUDY AND DO

1. Read this unit carefully more than once. Return to review it every now and then during the course. (Further aids to accentuation will be given in later units.)
2. Continue to practice the alphabet.
3. Practice pronunciation by reading aloud the vocabulary words found in Units 3, 4, etc. It is probably best to give a slight stress to the accented syllable. You may also want to begin memorizing the meanings of the words in Units 3 and 4.
4. Do the exercises of this unit.

EXERCISES

I. For each of the following, identify the type of accent and the syllable on which it occurs, and give the length of *U*. Optional: tell which rule(s) given in §6–9 or §11–12 the example illustrates.

Ex.   ἄνθρωποι: acute accent on *A* (antepenult); *U* is short
                                              (recall that final - οι counts as short)
              Optional part: §9 (acute accent on *A* only when *U* is short)

1. ἀνέμου	4. ἀγορᾶς	7. πεῖρά τις
2. ψῆφος	5. ἀρχῶν	8. πόλεμός που
3. ψήφοις	6. τιμή	9. θάνατος

10. ποταμός   12. ἔπεμπε   14. ὁδός
11. ποταμὸς βαθύς   13. ψυχὴ ἀθάνατος   15. τιμαῖς

II. For each of the following, place the correct accent (acute, circumflex, or grave) on the indicated syllable.

Ex.   πεμπει   P: πέμπει
(*U* long, so accented *P* must have acute)

1. δωρᾰ   P   5. γλωττᾰν   P   9. παιδειᾳ   P
2. ἀνθρωπε   A   6. γλωττης   P   10. ἀνεμος   A
3. λαμβανει   P   7. λογον   P   11. ἀγαθον   U
4. βουλεται   A   8. λογους   P   12. καλον (*U*) δῶρον

UNIT THREE

Nouns: The O-Declension

PRELIMINARIES[1]

A. *The Parts of Speech.* The words of a language are commonly classi-fied, according to their function in a sentence, into categories called *parts of speech*. This categorization was developed in classical times in Greece (though similar classifications were developed, independently and contemporaneously, by Indian grammarians for Sanskrit), formalized by the Stoics in postclassical times, and passed via the Romans into modern linguistics.

The generally recognized parts of speech are noun, pronoun, adjective, article, verb, adverb, preposition, and conjunction. In Greek grammar certain connective and logical adverbs and conjunctions are also referred to as *par-ticles*. The parts of speech will be individually introduced in the appropriate units.

B. *Noun.* A noun [Greek ὄνομα, Latin *nomen*, both = "name"] is that part of speech which names or refers to a person, place, or thing. In the most obvious instances, the person, place, or thing is *concrete* and can be pointed out. But other nouns are used to "name" or refer to a quality or an action, something intangible or *abstract:*

> **Ex.**   intelligent: intelligence
>   to select: selection
>   to move: movement

---

1. The section called "Preliminaries" to be found at the beginning of some units is designed to provide the student with a review of (or introduction to) some basic terminology and concepts of grammar. It is impractical to study ancient Greek, a language rich in inflectional forms and permitting a highly variable word order, without an understanding of these concepts. References to other languages are given both for the purpose of comparison to benefit students who may have studied other languages and in order to demonstrate that English inflection and grammar are anomalous in their simplicity and that the richness and complexity of Greek are paralleled in many other languages.

of an individual creature, place, or thing (e.g., *Julia*
d is capitalized in English and many other lan-
eek by modern convention). A *common* noun is a
plied to many individuals (e.g., *chef, island*).
ther languages, nouns have *gender*. In many lan-
n the form of the noun (e.g., Italian *zio*, Spanish *tío*
anish *tía* = "aunt") and in the form of its modifiers.
glish is usually not related to the form (but cf. *actor*
al gender is significant only when a noun serves as
ronoun (such as *she, him, it*): nouns referring to
nine pronouns associated with them, those referring
sculine, and all others have neuter (unless there is
Greek, however, every noun has grammatical gen-
d to by masculine, feminine, or neuter nouns, and
male or female creatures. The gender of a Greek
and memorized when the noun itself is first learned.
many languages, including Greek. *Inflection* is the
f a word (in its suffix or stem or both) to indicate
iables is being employed. The inflection of a noun,
led *declension*. For a noun the variables are *number*

In most languages nouns have singular and plural *number* to distinguish between a reference to one person or thing and a reference to more than one. In English most plurals are formed by adding *s*, but there are also irregular formations: *day, days; woman, women*. Greek nouns have *singular*, *dual*, and *plural* numbers. The dual is used to refer to a pair of persons or things. In many dialects use of the dual died out before the classical period, but Attic preserved the dual, especially for natural pairs (like "hands" or "eyes") or inseparable pairs (like "the [two] goddesses" for Demeter and Kore). Even in Attic the plural is often used to refer to two persons or things, and an author may switch between dual and plural with no distinction in meaning in the same sentence or passage. The dual is so rare in proportion to the singular and plural that beginners are usually not required to learn it. Since students will soon meet the dual if they continue beyond this book, the dual forms are presented in paradigms in this book, always in parentheses, for information and reference. But dual forms are not used in the exercises.

In many languages, including Greek, nouns also are characterized by variation in *case*. Case identifies the grammatical function of the noun in its sentence or phrase. Nouns in Modern English show only vestiges of case declension: there are two cases in both singular and plural, an all-purpose form and a possessive form (e.g., *doctor, doctor's, doctors, doctors'*; *man, man's, men, men's*). In classical Attic there are five cases (Greek πτώσεις, Latin *casus* = "fallings [from a standard], modifications of ending"), which indicate functions such as subject, object, indirect object, or possession. The Greek cases are presented in detail in §2 of this unit. Since there are five cases and three numbers in Greek, each noun theoretically can be inflected into 15 forms; but in fact some forms serve more than one case, and most nouns have 9 endings to learn (or 11 if one includes the dual).

Another term often used to refer to nouns is *substantive*. Substantive is a more general term. It includes nouns, pronouns, verbal nouns, and any other noun-equivalent (e.g., *the ugly, the beautiful; the why and the wherefore*).

∷

1. Greek nouns are in general inflected according to three systems or *declensions*. Two of these are vowel declensions: the o-declension and the a-declension. The third declension is called the consonant declension, though this is in fact a grouping of various vowel and consonant declensions. Inflection is based on a noun stem, to which is added a series of case endings[1] to indicate each of the five cases in singular, dual, and plural. The stem of a Greek noun is always accurately obtained by removing the ending from the genitive singular form.

2. The five *cases* (see above) in Attic Greek are:

nominative: the subjective case, used for the subject of a finite verb and for predicate nouns after a finite form of the copula (this construction will be learned in Units 5 and 11). Abbreviated nom. or n.

genitive: the case used to indicate possession, source, origin, and many other relations (many of the uses will be learned in Units 10 and 29). A catch-all English translation for the genitive is a prepositional phrase with *of*. Abbreviated gen. or g.

dative: the case used for the indirect object (whence its name, from its frequent use with the verb *to give*) and for a variety of other relations (many of these will be learned in Units 10 and 29). A catch-all English translation for the dative is a prepositional phrase with *to* or *for*. Abbreviated dat. or d.

accusative: the case used for the direct object, the internal object, and a few other relations (these will be learned in Unit 17). Abbreviated acc. or a.

---

1. Sometimes these really consist of a combination of final stem-vowel and case ending.

vocative: the case used to address someone or call a person by name. For all types of Greek nouns the vocative plural is identical to the nominative plural. Abbreviated voc. or v.

3. Nouns whose stems end in *-o* belong to the o-declension (also called the "second" declension). Every case ending (except the voc. sing. of masculine and feminine nouns and the nom. acc. voc. pl. of neuter nouns) contains an *o*-sound (*o, ω, ου, οι,* or *ῳ*).

4. There are two groups of o-declension nouns.

a. *Masculine and feminine nouns with nominative in -ος.* (Genders are often abbreviated masc., fem., neut. [or m., f., n.].) The vast majority of nouns in this group are masc., but names in *- ος* of countries, cities, islands, trees, plants, and plant products are fem., as are a few isolated words such as ὁδός = "road" and *νόσος* = "sickness."

Ex.		"road" (f.)	"word" (m.)	"human being" (m.)	endings
sing.	nom.	ὁδός	λόγος	ἄνθρωπος	-ος
	gen.	ὁδοῦ	λόγου	ἀνθρώπου	-ου
	dat.	ὁδῷ	λόγῳ	ἀνθρώπῳ	-ῳ
	acc.	ὁδόν	λόγον	ἄνθρωπον	-ον
	voc.	ὁδέ	λόγε	ἄνθρωπε	-ε
(dual	n. a. v.	ὁδώ	λόγω	ἀνθρώπω)	(-ω)
	(g. d.	ὁδοῖν	λόγοιν	ἀνθρώποιν)	(-οιν)
plur.	n. v.	ὁδοί	λόγοι	ἄνθρωποι	-οι
	gen.	ὁδῶν	λόγων	ἀνθρώπων	-ων
	dat.	ὁδοῖς	λόγοις	ἀνθρώποις	-οις
	acc.	ὁδούς	λόγους	ἀνθρώπους	-ους

b. *Neuter nouns with nominative in -ον.* The paradigm is shown at the top of the next page. Three facts which apply to *all* neuter forms (o-declension nouns, consonant-declension nouns, and adjectival forms) should be noted: (1) the genitive and dative endings of all numbers are identical with those of masc. nouns of the same type; (2) the nom., acc., and voc. of each number have a single form; (3) the nom. acc. voc. plural ending is always *-ᾰ.*

5. *Accentuation.* The accentuation of all nouns and adjectives is *persistent*: that is, the same syllable tends to be accented in all forms except when the changing length of the ultima forces the contonation to move, either by the change of a circumflex on *P* to an acute or by the displacement of the acute

NEUTER NOUNS IN -ον

Ex.		"work" (n.)	"gift" (n.)	endings
sing.	nom.	ἔργον	δῶρον	-ον
	gen.	ἔργου	δώρου	-ου
	dat.	ἔργῳ	δώρῳ	-ῳ
	acc.	ἔργον	δῶρον	-ον
	voc.	ἔργον	δῶρον	-ον
(dual	n. a. v.	ἔργω	δώρω)	(-ω)
	(g. d.	ἔργοιν	δώροιν)	(-οιν)
plur.	n. v.	ἔργα	δῶρα	-ᾰ
	gen.	ἔργων	δώρων	-ων
	dat.	ἔργοις	δώροις	-οις
	acc.	ἔργα	δῶρα	-ᾰ

closer to the end of the word (from *A* to *P*). For example, the accent of ἄνθρωπος is persistent on *A*, except when *U* is long, forcing accentuation on *P* instead of *A*. Remember that final -οι in the nom. pl. masc. counts as short for the purposes of accentuation, hence ἄνθρωποι (but in the dat. pl. οι in -οις is not final, hence ἀνθρώποις). The accent of δῶρον is persistent on *P*, but changes from circumflex to acute (still on *P*) whenever the ultima is long. Since the accent is persistent, you should learn the position and type of accent of the nominative when you first learn a noun.

Special rule for accentuation of o-declension nouns: any noun of the o-declension with an accented ultima (acute on *U* in nom. sing.) has the circumflex on *U* in the gen. and dat. of all numbers (e.g., ὁδός above).

6. *Identification of Noun Forms.* When you learn a noun, you need to learn the nom. sing. form (including the accent), the gen. sing. form, the gender, and the English meaning.

Ex.   ἄγγελος, ἀγγέλου, m., "messenger"

When you are asked to identify a noun form, first specify the variables (case and number) and then give the "dictionary" information about the noun, namely, the nom. sing., gen. sing. (in full, or just the ending), and gender, and add one definition if the English meaning is requested.

Ex.   identify νόσοις and give one meaning
        answer: dat. pl. of νόσος, νόσου, f., sickness
                or dat. pl. of νόσος, -ου, f., sickness

WHAT TO STUDY AND DO

1. Learn the patterns of the two types of o-declension nouns.
2. Learn the vocabulary of this unit.
3. Do the exercises of this unit.

ADVICE ABOUT VOCABULARY AND EXERCISES

People differ in the ease with which they memorize and in the manner in which they do so most effectively. Some people have excellent visual memory and need only to look at paradigms and vocabulary repeatedly and carefully; others do better by repeatedly pronouncing and hearing the items to be memorized; others may find that writing out inflections and words helps memorization. Use whatever techniques suit you, and drill yourself (or collaborate with a fellow student), because in a college course there will never be time for enough in-class drill. The vocabulary is typed in separate columns to facilitate drill. A published set of ancient Greek flash cards is available[1] (there is a large degree of overlap between the words in the set and those assigned in this book). Or you may make your own drill cards: cut small index cards in half, write a Greek word on one side, the definition on the other. For inflections, make yourself set the paradigm aside after a while and try to write it out from memory. No matter what techniques you use, reciting and reading your Greek out loud are strongly recommended.

The exercises are designed to help the student put into use the vocabulary, inflections, and grammatical rules learned so far. Doing the exercises, however, is no substitute for the task of basic memorization which is necessary in the beginning stages of any language. There are several ways to complement the exercises given in the units if you need more practice:

1. Repeat the exercises after an interval (avoid writing the answers in the book).
2. Write paradigms.
3. Do an exercise in reverse, working back from the corrected answers.
4. Vary the given exercises by altering the instructions according to a fixed pattern (e.g., interchange singular and plural, active and middle/passive; transpose the case of a noun or the tense of a verb).
5. Apply a sequence of instructions to the words listed in the vocabulary (e.g., proceed through a list of nouns giving gen. pl. of the first, acc. sing. of the second, dat. pl. of the third, etc.).

---

1. *Vis-Ed Classical Greek Vocabulary Cards* (Visual Education Assn., Springfield, Ohio), often available in college bookstores.

VOCABULARY

In the vocabulary lists, English words derived from a Greek word (or from a closely related root) are given in square brackets after the definitions. The words in brackets are *not* definitions, but they may help you learn Greek vocabulary by association, and in any case will provide some enrichment of your English vocabulary, or occasionally amusement.

o-declension: masculine nouns

ἄγγελος, ἀγγέλου, m.　　　messenger, herald　[angel]
ἄνεμος, ἀνέμου, m.　　　　wind　[anemometer]
ἄνθρωπος, ἀνθρώπου, m.　human being, man (occasionally fem. = "woman")
　　　　　　　　　　　　　　　　[anthropology]
βίος, βίου, m.　　　　　　life, manner of living, livelihood　[biology]
ἥλιος, ἡλίου, m.　　　　　sun　[helium]
θάνατος, θανάτου, m.　　death　[euthanasia]
θεός, θεοῦ, m.[1]　　　　　god, divinity (occasionally fem. = "goddess")
　　　　　　　　　　　　　　　　[theology]
ἵππος, ἵππου, m.　　　　horse (also fem. = "mare")　[hippopotamus]
λόγος, λόγου, m.　　　　word, speech, tale, story; reckoning, account,
　　　　　　　　　　　　　　proportion; reason, rationality　[philology]
νόμος, νόμου, m.　　　　custom; law　[economic]
πόλεμος, πολέμου, m.　war　[polemic]

o-declension: feminine nouns

νόσος, νόσου, f.　　　　sickness, disease
ὁδός, ὁδοῦ, f.　　　　　road, path, way; journey　[odometer, method]
ψῆφος, ψήφου, f.　　　small stone, pebble (used in reckoning, in games, in
　　　　　　　　　　　　voting); vote　[psephologist]

o-declension: neuter nouns

βιβλίον, βιβλίου, n.　　book　[bibliophile]
δῶρον, δώρου, n.　　　gift　[Eudora]
ἔργον, ἔργου, n.　　　work, action, deed　[erg, energy]
μέτρον, μέτρου, n.　　measure, size, distance; moderate amount,
　　　　　　　　　　　　proportion　[meter]
παιδίον, παιδίου, n.　child　[pediatrics]

---

1. In classical Greek no vocative singular form is found; in postclassical Greek both θεός and θεέ are used as vocative.

EXERCISES

I.   Identify the following noun forms and give at least one meaning.

Ex.   ἔργα: nom. (or acc.) pl. of ἔργον, ἔργου, n., "work"

1. ἥλιον	9. νόμον	17. νόσους	25. πολέμῳ
2. πόλεμοι	10. ἀγγέλοις	18. ἄνεμε	26. θεοί
3. βιβλίοις	11, μέτρα	19. λόγου	27. βίον
4. παιδίου	12. δῶρα	20. ἔργοις	28. ἄγγελοι
5. θεῷ	13. βίων	21. δῶρον	29. παιδία
6. νόσοι	14. ὁδῶν	22. βιβλίου	30. θανάτων
7. ψήφῳ	15. ἵππου	23. ὁδοῖς	31. μέτρου
8. θανάτους	16. ἀνθρώπῳ	24. ψῆφοι	32. λόγους

II. Give the requested form of the Greek noun and indicate its gender.

Ex.   gen. pl. of wind: ἀνέμων, m.

1. nom. pl. of stone, vote
2. gen. sing. of war
3. acc. pl. of child
4. nom. sing. of sickness
5. acc. sing. of measure
6. nom. pl. of child
7. acc. sing. of gift
8. nom. sing. of sun
9. voc. pl. of god
10. dat. sing. of death
11. dat. pl. of deed
12. gen. pl. of man
13. dat. pl. of horse
14. dat. sing. of road
15. gen. pl. of word
16. acc. pl. of messenger
17. voc. sing. of life
18. acc. sing. of law
19. nom. sing. of story
20. gen. sing. of work
21. dat. pl. of gift
22. voc. pl. of law
23. nom. pl. of wind
24. gen. sing. of horse
25. acc. pl. of measure
26. dat. pl. of messenger
27. dat. sing. of child

III.   In the following list, the first of each pair of forms is the nominative singular of an o-declension noun. Following the principle of persistent accentuation, place the correct accent on the second form in each pair.

Ex.   κίνδυνος   κινδυνου
answer: κινδύνου
(length of *U* forces accent to move from *A* to *P*)

1. πλοῦτος	πλουτον	6. ποταμός	ποταμω
2. χρόνος	χρονοις	7. τρόπος	τροπων
3. στρατηγός	στρατηγε	8. λίθος	λιθοι
4. διδάσκαλος	διδασκαλου	9. στάδιον	σταδια
5. στρατόπεδον	στρατοπεδοις	10. υἱός	υἱων

UNIT FOUR

Nouns: The A-Declension I

1. Nouns whose stems end in alpha belong to the a-declension (or alpha-declension), also known as the "first" declension. The alpha-vowel appears in some form in almost all the cases of the dual and plural: ᾱ, ᾰ, αι, or ᾳ. In the singular, however, because of the vowel shift from long alpha to eta in the Ionic-Attic dialects (see Introd. §6), long alpha has been replaced by eta in the Attic case endings *except after* ε, ι, *or* ρ.

2. The nouns of the a-declension may be divided into three groups, each of which has two subgroups because of the alpha-eta vowel shift. The three groups differ in declension only in the singular. The dual and plural of all a-declension nouns have the same endings. The first group consists of the *long-vowel feminine nouns*: in these the vowel of the nom., acc., and voc. sing. is long.

a. *Alpha subgroup*: when the noun stem ends in ε, ι, or ρ, the vowel alpha appears throughout the singular and in most of the plural.

Ex.		*"goddess" (f.)*	*"education" (f.)*	*"land" (f.)*	*endings*
sing.	nom.	θεά	παιδεία	χώρα	-ᾱ
	gen.	θεᾶς	παιδείας	χώρας	-ᾱς
	dat.	θεᾷ	παιδείᾳ	χώρᾳ	-ᾳ
	acc.	θεάν	παιδείαν	χώραν	-ᾱν
	voc.	θεά	παιδεία	χώρα	-ᾱ
(dual	n. a. v.	θεά	παιδεία	χώρα)	(-ᾱ)
	(g. d.	θεαῖν	παιδείαιν	χώραιν)	(-αιν)
plur.	n. v.	θεαί	παιδεῖαι	χῶραι	-αι
	gen.	θεῶν	παιδειῶν	χωρῶν	-ῶν
	dat.	θεαῖς	παιδείαις	χώραις	-αις
	acc.	θεάς	παιδείας	χώρας	-ᾱς

b. *Eta subgroup*: when the noun stem ends in any other letter, eta appears in the singular endings, but alpha in most of the plural.

Ex.		*"opinion" (f.)*	*"flight" (f.)*	*endings*
sing.	*nom.*	γνώμη	φυγή	-η
	gen.	γνώμης	φυγῆς	-ης
	dat.	γνώμῃ	φυγῇ	-ῃ
	acc.	γνώμην	φυγήν	-ην
	voc.	γνώμη	φυγή	-η
(dual	*n. a. v.*	γνώμα	φυγά)	(-ᾱ)
	(g. d.	γνώμαιν	φυγαῖν)	(-αιν)
plur.	*n. v.*	γνῶμαι	φυγαί	-αι
	gen.	γνωμῶν	φυγῶν	-ῶν
	dat.	γνώμαις	φυγαῖς	-αις
	acc.	γνώμας	φυγάς	-ᾱς

3. *Accentuation.* There are two special rules for all nouns of the a-declension. (1) All a-declension nouns have a circumflex accent on the omega of the gen. pl. (the form was originally -άων and has been contracted to -ῶν). (2) Any noun of the a-declension with an accented ultima (acute on U in the nom. sing.) has the circumflex on U in the genitive and dative of all numbers (examples: θεά, φυγή).

4. The long alpha which appears in the acc. pl. has not shifted to eta in the second subgroup because the long alpha there is not original, but rather a product of *compensatory lengthening* which took place when ν was dropped from the original ending -ᾰνς. (The long alpha in the n. v. a. dual is a relatively recent analogical formation based on the o-declension and so did not undergo the vowel shift.)

5. Note the general similarities of case formation in the o- and a-declensions:

a. Nominative plural has iota-diphthong, counted as short: -οι, -αι.
b. Genitive plural has -ων.
c. Dative singular has a long stem-vowel with iota subscript: -ῳ, -ᾳ, -ῃ.
d. Dative plural has iota-diphthong with sigma: -οις, -αις.
e. Accusative singular has stem vowel plus nu: -ον, -ᾱν, -ην.
f. Accusative plural is derived from stem vowel plus νς: -ονς —> -ους, -ᾰνς —> -ᾱς.
g. If accented on U, these nouns have circumflex in genitive and dative of all numbers.

WHAT TO STUDY AND DO

1. Learn the patterns of the long-vowel feminine a-declension nouns.
2. Learn the vocabulary of this unit.
3. Do the exercises of this unit.

VOCABULARY

a-declension: long-vowel feminine nouns in α

ἀγορά, ἀγορᾶς, f.	assembly, place of assembly; marketplace [agoraphobia]
δημοκρατία, δημοκρατίας, f.	democracy
ἡμέρα, ἡμέρας, f.	day [ephemeral]
θεά, θεᾶς, f.	goddess
θύρα, θύρας, f. [ῠ][1]	door; (freq. pl.) double, folding doors
παιδεία, παιδείας, f.	education, training, culture [propaedeutic]
στρατιά, στρατιᾶς, f.	army [strategy]
συμφορά, συμφορᾶς, f.	event, happening, circumstance; unlucky event, misfortune
φιλία, φιλίας, f.	friendship [bibliophily]
χώρα, χώρας, f.	land, country; space, room, place [chorology]

a-declension: long-vowel feminine nouns in η

ἀρετή, ἀρετῆς, f.	excellence; valor; virtue [aretalogy]
ἀρχή, ἀρχῆς, f.	beginning; rule, office; realm, province [monarchy]
γνώμη, γνώμης, f.	faculty of judgment; opinion, decision, verdict [gnomic]
δίκη, δίκης, f.	justice, right; lawsuit; punishment (levied in a suit) [syndic]
ἡδονή, ἡδονῆς, f.	pleasure [hedonist]
νίκη, νίκης, f. [ῑ]	victory [epinician]
σκηνή, σκηνῆς, f.	tent, booth; stage building; stage [scene]
τῑμή, τιμῆς, f.	honor; esteem; price [timocratic]
φυγή, φυγῆς, f.	running away, flight; exile
φωνή, φωνῆς, f.	sound; voice [phonetic]
ψῡχή, ψυχῆς, f.	breath of life; life; soul [psyche]

---

1. The long or short quantity of α, ι, υ is sometimes indicated in the vocabulary, especially when the quantity must be known for correct accentuation (e.g., in this case, nom. pl. θύραι, not θῦραι). In general an unmarked vowel may be assumed to be short (e.g., δίκη has short ι). Long vowels in endings are marked only in the paradigm. The student need not use long marks when writing Greek.

EXERCISES

I. Give the requested form of the Greek noun and indicate its gender.

1. acc. sing. of friendship
2. nom. pl. of pleasure
3. gen. sing. of education
4. gen. pl. of flight
5. gen. sing. of honor
6. acc. pl. of opinion
7. gen. pl. of war
8. dat. pl. of justice
9. acc. pl. of tent
10. nom. pl. of door
11. voc. pl. of messenger
12. dat. sing. of sickness
13. voc. sing. of man
14. dat. pl. of road
15. gen. pl. of opinion
16. dat. sing. of voice
17. acc. pl. of day
18. nom. sing. of child
19. acc. sing. of justice
20. nom. pl. of day
21. gen. sing. of road
22. voc. sing. of soul
23. dat. pl. of pleasure
24. gen. sing. of army
25. voc. pl. of goddess
26. acc. sing. of honor
27. nom. pl. of word
28. dat. sing. of victory
29. acc. pl. of wind
30. gen. pl. of door

II. Identify the following noun forms and give at least one meaning.

1. ψυχῇ
2. στρατιάν
3. νίκη
4. ἀγοραῖς
5. τιμῶν
6. ἀρετάς
7. συμφοραί
8. θύρας
9. ἀρχήν
10. θεάς
11. δώροις
12. παιδείᾳ
13. λόγους
14. βιβλία
15. τιμή
16. συμφοραῖς
17. ἄγγελε
18. ἀγορῶν
19. θεόν
20. σκηνῆς
21. φωνῇ
22. δίκαι
23. φυγάς
24. νίκαις
25. ψυχήν
26. ἀρετῆς
27. ἡδοναί
28. ἀρχῶν
29. τιμαί
30. ἡμέραις

III. In the following list, the first of each pair of forms is the nominative singular of an a-declension noun. Following the principle of persistent accentuation and the special rules applying to such nouns, place the correct accent on the second form in each pair.

1. ἀνάγκη   ἀναγκην
2. μάχη   μαχαις
3. ἐπιθυμία   ἐπιθυμια
4. εἰρήνη   εἰρηνων
5. εὐχή   εὐχης
6. σοφία   σοφιαν
7. πληγή   πληγαι
8. ἐλευθερία   ἐλευθεριας
9. ἡσυχία   ἡσυχιᾳ
10. κεφαλή   κεφαλη

Nouns: The A-Declension II

1. The second group of a-declension nouns consists of *short-vowel feminine nouns*: in these the alpha in the nom., acc., and voc. sing. is short. The gen. and dat. sing. vary between long alpha and eta depending on the final letter of the stem. The dual and plural have alpha throughout (except gen. pl. -ῶν) and have the same endings as the long-vowel feminines learned in Unit 4.

a. *Alpha subgroup*: stems ending in ε, ι, or ρ

Ex.		"health" (f.)	"trial, attempt" (f.)	endings
sing.	*nom.*	ὑγίεια	πεῖρα	-ă
	gen.	ὑγιείας	πείρας	-ās
	dat.	ὑγιείᾳ	πείρᾳ	-ᾳ
	acc.	ὑγίειαν	πεῖραν	-ăν
	voc.	ὑγίεια	πεῖρα	-ă
(*dual*	*n. a. v.*	ὑγιεία	πείρα)	(-ā)
	(*g. d.*	ὑγιείαιν	πείραιν)	(-αιν)
plur.	*n. v.*	ὑγίειαι	πεῖραι	-αι
	gen.	ὑγιειῶν	πειρῶν	-ῶν
	dat.	ὑγιείαις	πείραις	-αις
	acc.	ὑγιείας	πείρας	-ās

b. *Eta subgroup*: stems ending in any other letter

Ex.		"sea" (f.)	"tongue" (f.)	endings
sing.	*nom.*	θάλαττα	γλῶττα	-ă
	gen.	θαλάττης	γλώττης	-ης
	dat.	θαλάττῃ	γλώττῃ	-ῃ
	acc.	θάλατταν	γλῶτταν	-ăν
	voc.	θάλαττα	γλῶττα	-ă

		"sea" (f.)	"tongue" (f.)	endings
(dual	n. a. v.	θαλάττα	γλώττα)	(-ā)
(g. d.		θαλάτταιν	γλώτταιν)	(-αιν)
plur.	n. v.	θάλατται	γλῶτται	-αι
	gen.	θαλαττῶν	γλωττῶν	-ῶν
	dat.	θαλάτταις	γλώτταις	-αις
	acc.	θαλάττας	γλώττας	-ᾱς

Note that the accentuation of the nom. sing. usually indicates a short-alpha noun: acute on *A* or circumflex on long *P* is possible only with the short alpha in *U*.

2. The third group of a-declension nouns consists of *masculine nouns*. These nouns have nominative singular in *-ᾱs* or *-ηs*, and the gen. sing. ending is *-ου*, borrowed from the o-declension. The dual and plural endings are the same as for all other a-declension nouns.

a. *Alpha subgroup*: stems ending in ε, ι, or ρ. The sing. endings other than nom. and gen. are like those of long-alpha feminines. Many proper names belong to this subgroup, but few common nouns.

b. *Eta subgroup*: stems ending in any other letter. The eta appears in nom. dat. acc. sing., but the voc. has -ă.

Ex.		(a) "young man" (m.)	endings (a)	(b) "soldier" (m.)	"judge" (m.)	endings (b)
sing.	nom.	νεανίας	-ᾱς	στρατιώτης	κριτής	-ης
	gen.	νεανίου	-ου	στρατιώτου	κριτοῦ	-ου
	dat.	νεανίᾳ	-ᾳ	στρατιώτῃ	κριτῇ	-ῃ
	acc.	νεανίαν	-ᾱν	στρατιώτην	κριτήν	-ην
	voc.	νεανία	-ᾱ	στρατιῶτα	κριτά	-ă
(dual	n. a. v.	νεανία)	(-ā)	(στρατιῶτα	κριτά)	(-ā)
(g. d.		νεανίαιν)	(-αιν)	(στρατιώταιν	κριταῖν)	(-αιν)
plur.	n. v.	νεανίαι	-αι	στρατιῶται	κριταί	-αι
	gen.	νεανιῶν	-ῶν	στρατιωτῶν	κριτῶν	-ῶν
	dat.	νεανίαις	-αις	στρατιώταις	κριταῖς	-αις
	acc.	νεανίας	-ᾱς	στρατιώτας	κριτάς	-ᾱς

3. Note that the rules for accentuation mentioned in U4.3 apply to *all* a-declension nouns.

WHAT TO STUDY AND DO

1. Learn the patterns of the short-vowel feminine and the masculine a-declension nouns.
2. Learn the vocabulary of this unit.
3. Do the exercises of this unit.

VOCABULARY

a-declension: short-vowel feminine nouns in α

ἀλήθεια, ἀληθείας, f.	truth; truthfulness [Alethea]
γέφῡρα, γεφύρας, f.	bridge
μοῖρα, μοίρας, f.	portion, lot; destiny, fate [Moira]
πεῖρα, πείρας, f.	attempt, trial [empirical]
ὑγίεια, ὑγιείας, f.	health, soundness [hygiene]

a-declension: short-vowel feminine nouns in η

γλῶττα, γλώττης, f.	tongue; language [isogloss, glottal][1]
δόξα, δόξης, f.	opinion; reputation [orthodoxy]
θάλαττα, θαλάττης, f.	sea [thalassocracy]
τράπεζα, τραπέζης, f.	table; money changer's table, "bank" [trapeze]

a-declension: masculine noun in α

νεᾱνίας, νεανίου, m.	young man [neologism (from base-root neo-)]

a-declension: masculine nouns in η

δεσπότης, δεσπότου, m.[2]	master, lord; absolute ruler [despot]
δικαστής, δικαστοῦ, m.	juryman, judge (in court)
κριτής, κριτοῦ, m.	judge (in a contest), umpire [critic]
ναύτης, ναύτου, m.	sailor [nautical]
ὁπλίτης, ὁπλίτου, m. [ῑ]	heavy-armed soldier, hoplite
ποιητής, ποιητοῦ, m.	maker, poet
πολίτης, πολίτου, m. [ῑ]	citizen [politics]
στρατιώτης, στρατιώτου, m.	soldier

---

1. Ionic and Koine have -σσ- where Attic has -ττ- (cf. Introd. §6), and in dictionaries such words are usually listed under the -σσ- form (γλῶσσα, θάλασσα).
2. The voc. sing. is accented δέσποτα.

EXERCISES

I. Give the requested form of the Greek noun and indicate its gender.

1. dat. pl. of citizen
2. gen. pl. of table
3. acc. sing. of truth
4. nom. pl. of fate
5. gen. sing. of juror
6. acc. pl. of umpire
7. nom. sing. of young man
8. dat. sing. of reputation
9. voc. sing. of poet
10. acc. sing. of sailor
11. acc. pl. of lawsuit
12. gen. pl. of wind
13. dat. pl. of faculty of judgment
14. dat. sing. of health
15. gen. sing. of sailor
16. acc. sing. of law
17. nom. pl. of land
18. nom. pl. of book
19. voc. sing. of hoplite
20. nom. pl. of goddess
21. gen. sing. of bridge
22. voc. pl. of master
23. dat. pl. of table
24. gen. sing. of health
25. voc. sing. of truth
26. acc. sing. of young man
27. nom. pl. of poet
28. dat. sing. of citizen
29. acc. pl. of soldier
30. gen. pl. of tongue

II. Identify the following noun forms and give at least one meaning.

1. ὁπλίτης
2. ὑγίειαν
3. θαλάττῃ
4. στρατιώτας
5. χώραις
6. γλωττῶν
7. πεῖραι
8. ἀρχῆς
9. φωνῇ
10. δόξας
11. γεφύρᾳ
12. πολῖται
13. δεσπότου
14. ναυτῶν
15. φυγαί
16. στρατιῶται
17. πολῖτα
18. ὑγιείᾳ
19. μοίρας
20. δεσπότας
21. δόξης
22. γλώτταις
23. ὁπλίτην
24. πεῖραν
25. ναῦται
26. ἡδονῶν
27. θαλάττας
28. νόσου
29. χώραις
30. κριτοῦ
31. ἀληθείᾳ
32. μοιρῶν

UNIT SIX

The Article; Prepositions I

PRELIMINARIES

A. *Articles.* An article (Latin *articulus*, Greek ἄρθρον = "joint, connecting word") is a small modifier placed before a noun or a noun phrase to limit, individualize, or give definiteness or indefiniteness to the application of the noun. English, like many modern languages, has both a *definite* article (*the*) and an *indefinite* article (*a, an*), and the English articles are not declined. In other languages the article is declined in number and gender to agree with the number and gender of the noun it accompanies (e.g., French *la femme*, Italian *il tempo*, Spanish *Los Angeles*), and in Greek, as in German, the article also is inflected in the cases in agreement with its noun. Greek has no indefinite article, and its definite article is used in ways (e.g., with abstract nouns and in a generic sense) that are paralleled in other languages but not in English.

B. *Prepositions.* A preposition (Greek πρόθεσις, Latin *praepositio* = "a word placed in front") is that part of speech which expresses a relation between a noun or pronoun (the *object* of the preposition) and some other word, with either adverbial or adjectival force. English has several dozen prepositions, such as *in*, *of*, *at*, *below*, *up*, *through*. Prepositions are in origin adverbs and are found in English and Greek (and other languages) also as adverbs more or less closely attached to the verb. Compare the following:

> *He went <u>down</u> the ladder.*   (preposition)
> *He knocked the door <u>down</u>.*   (adverb)

The word group consisting of the preposition and the noun or pronoun it governs is called a *prepositional phrase*. The object of a preposition is in a case other than the nominative (or "straight" case), that is, in an "oblique" case. Such case usage is evident in Greek as well as, for instance, German and Latin. English, like other languages, no longer distinguishes the objective case of nouns; but in formal English a pronoun that is the object of a preposition must be in the objective case: *to me, from whom, with us, before them*.

∵

1. The *definite article* (*the*) in Attic has masculine, feminine, and neuter forms whose endings are basically those of the o- and a-declensions. The stem of the article varies between τ- (found in almost all forms) and the *h*-sound, written as a rough breathing (found in the masc. and fem. nom. sing. and pl.).

		masc.	fem.	neut.
sing.	*nom.*	ὁ	ἡ	τό
	gen.	τοῦ	τῆς	τοῦ
	dat.	τῷ	τῇ	τῷ
	acc.	τόν	τήν	τό
(dual	*n. a.*	τώ	τώ	τώ)
	(g. d.	τοῖν	τοῖν	τοῖν)
plural	*nom.*	οἱ	αἱ	τά
	gen.	τῶν	τῶν	τῶν
	dat.	τοῖς	ταῖς	τοῖς
	acc.	τούς	τάς	τά

There is no vocative form of the article. The masc. and fem. nom. sing. and pl. forms are treated as proclitics (U2.11): they have no accent of their own.[1] Differentiated feminine dual forms in alpha (τά, ταῖν) also existed in the fourth century B.C.E. and perhaps earlier.

2. *Concord.* (Concord will be discussed more fully in U7.) The article agrees with its noun in gender, number, and case. It does *not necessarily* agree with its noun *in ending.* Examples: τὴν γνώμην, τῷ λόγῳ, but also τοὺς ναύτας, ταῖς ὁδοῖς.

3. *Some Uses of the Article*

a. The Greek article may individualize or make definite the noun it modifies, just as the English article *the* does. This is the *particular* article. In Greek the particular article is often used with proper names.

Ex. πoιητής   *poet, a poet*
ὁ πoιητής   *the poet*
ὁ Σόλων   *Solon*

---

1. This difference in treatment of the nom. case of the article is actually a postclassical graphic convention designed to distinguish the masc. and fem. nom. of the article from the same forms of the relative pronoun (which look the same but are accented). In fact, all cases of the definite article, when used as straightforward article, were probably proclitic within their word groups.

b. The Greek article, in the context of a sentence, often has the force of an English possessive adjective (*my, our, your, his, her, its, their*). The proper English translation is obvious from the context (normally the subject of the sentence is the possessor).

Ex.   ὁ στρατιώτης <u>τὸν</u> ἵππον ἄγει.
           The soldier is leading <u>his</u> horse.

c. Abstract nouns and abstract substantives are often accompanied by the definite article in Greek, a use found in other languages, but not in English (cf. French *la beauté*, German *die Schönheit*, English *beauty*).

Ex.   ἡ ὑγίεια   *health*
           ἡ ἀλήθεια   *truthfulness*
           τὸ καλόν   *beauty, the beautiful*

d. Substantives that refer to an entire class and make a general statement usually are accompanied by the definite article in Greek. The *generic* article is found in other languages as well, but rarely in English except with proper names (cf. Italian *l'uomo*, Spanish *la mujer*).

Ex.   ὁ ἄνθρωπος   *man, mankind,*
           or οἱ ἄνθρωποι   *men in general*

Note that in English a noun with the indefinite article *a(n)* sometimes refers to a class and is equivalent to the generic definite article in Greek: contrast (indefinite) *A poet visited out class* with (generic) *A poet ought to speak piously of the gods.*

4. The nom. sing. forms of the article are often used in Greek dictionaries and vocabulary lists instead of the abbreviations m., f., and n. to indicate the gender of a noun: for instance, ὁδός, ὁδοῦ, ἡ is the same as ὁδός, ὁδοῦ, f.

5. *Some Prepositions.* Greek prepositions were in origin adverbs which were optionally added to a sentence to reinforce a grammatical relationship already conveyed by the case of a noun. By classical times, the use of these words became standard in spoken Greek and prose, while verse sometimes still reflected the older custom of letting the case of a noun act on its own. The words themselves acquired a fixed position in front of the noun they reinforced.

Greek prepositions govern one or more of the three "oblique" cases (gen., dat., acc.). When a preposition can govern more than one case, there is usually a clear distinction in meaning conveyed by the difference. In general, the genitive with a preposition often conveys *motion away from*; the dative often conveys *static position*; the accusative often conveys *motion toward*. The follow-

ing definitions are only rough indications of some of the most common uses of
the various prepositions. The finer distinctions of usage can be perceived only
after some experience in reading Greek. Note that the prepositions ἐκ, ἐν, and
εἰς are proclitics (U2.11).

ἀπό + gen.	away from, from
ἐκ + gen. (ἐξ before vowels)	out of, forth from
ἐν + dat.	in, within, on, at, among
εἰς or ἐς + acc.	into, to, toward
σύν + dat.	together with, with
μετά + gen.	among, with
μετά + acc.	into the middle of; in pursuit of; after
διά + gen.	through (of space or time); through, by (of agent or means)
διά + acc.	by aid of, by reason of, on account of
ἐπί + gen.	upon; in the time of
ἐπί + dat.	upon, over; next to; in addition to
ἐπί + acc.	onto, up to, toward; against
παρά + gen.	from the side of, from (usually with a person as object)
παρά + dat.	by the side of, at the house of
παρά + acc.	to the side of; beside; past, beyond
πρός + gen.	from, proceeding from
πρός + dat.	near, beside; in addition to
πρός + acc.	to, toward; against; in respect to, regarding

6. *Examples of Usage of These Prepositions*

ἀπὸ τῆς γεφύρας	(movement or distance) *away from the bridge*
ἀπὸ τῆς σκηνῆς	(movement) *away from (the vicinity) of the tent*
ἀπὸ ταύτης τῆς ἡμέρας	*from this day (onward)*
ἐκ τῆς σκηνῆς	(movement) *out from (the inside of) the tent*
ἐκ τῆς θαλάττης	*out of the sea*
ἐξ ἀρχῆς[1]	*from the beginning*

1. The article is omitted in this phrase because it is an old expression, predating the development of the article.

ἐκ τούτων	as a result of or after these things
ἐν τῇ χώρᾳ	in (within) the land
ἐν τῇ σκηνῇ	in (within) the tent
ἐν τοῖς θεοῖς	among the gods
ἐν Κερκύρᾳ	at Corcyra
ἐν δίκῃ	in justice = justly
εἰς τὴν σκηνήν	into the tent
εἰς τὴν θάλατταν	into or toward the sea
εἰς παιδείαν	with respect to training
σὺν τοῖς στρατηγοῖς	with the generals
σὺν πόνῳ	with toil
σὺν δίκῃ	with justice = justly
μετὰ τῶν κριτῶν	(in the midst of and so) among, with the umpires
μετὰ τοῦ παιδίου	with the child
μετὰ φθόνου	with envy = enviously
μετὰ τοὺς ὁπλίτας	(movement) in pursuit of or after the hoplites
μετὰ τὸν πόλεμον	(temporal) after the war
μετὰ ταῦτα	(temporal) after these things
διὰ τῆς χώρας	(movement) through the land; (location) throughout the land
διὰ τούτου τοῦ χρόνου	throughout this period of time
διὰ βίου	throughout life
δι᾽ ἀγγέλων	through or by means of messengers
διὰ γλώττης	by means of the tongue
διὰ τοὺς θεούς	by aid of or thanks to the gods
διὰ τὸν φόβον	because of or by reason of fear
διὰ τὴν δόξαν	because of the reputation
διὰ τὴν νόσον	because of or on account of the sickness
ἐπὶ τῆς τραπέζης	upon the table [superposition]
ἐπὶ Καλλίου	in the time of (the archon) Callias
ἐφ᾽ ἵππου	upon a horse, on horseback
ἐπὶ τῇ θαλάττῃ	(position) by or next to the sea
ἐπὶ τοῖς στρατιώταις	over, i.e., in charge of the soldiers
ἐπὶ τούτοις	in addition to these things
ἐπὶ τὸν ποταμόν	up to the river

ἐπὶ πολὺν χρόνον	*(up to the limit of,* i.e.*) for a long time*
ἐπὶ τοὺς Πέρσας	(warlike campaign) *against the Persians*
παρὰ Κύρου	*from Cyrus's presence* or *from the vicinity of Cyrus*
παρὰ Κύρῳ	*in Cyrus's presence* or *with Cyrus* or *on Cyrus's side*
παρὰ πᾶσιν ἀνθρώποις	*among* or *in the eyes (judgment) of all men*
παρὰ Κῦρον	*to* or *into Cyrus's presence*
παρὰ τὸν ποταμόν	(movement or extension) *alongside the river*
παρὰ δόξαν	*beyond* or *contrary to expectation*
πρὸς τῶν πολιτῶν	(e.g., hear, receive) *from the citizens*
πρὸς τῷ ποταμῷ	(position) *near the river*
πρὸς τούτοις	*in addition to these things*
πρὸς τὴν γέφυραν	(direction) *toward the bridge*
πρὸς τοὺς στρατιώτας	(fighting, war) *against the soldiers*
πρὸς τοὺς πολίτας	(speak) *to the citizens*; (behave in a certain way) *with regard to the citizens*

WHAT TO STUDY AND DO

1. Learn the declension of the article.
2. Study the examples of prepositional usage presented above.
3. Learn as vocabulary the prepositions presented above in §5 and the words presented below.
4. Do the exercises of this unit.

VOCABULARY

further masculine o-declension nouns

πλοῦτος, πλούτου, m.	wealth, riches [plutocrat]
πόνος, πόνου, m.	hard work, toil; suffering [geoponics]
ποταμός, ποταμοῦ, m.	river [Mesopotamia]
στρατηγός, στρατηγοῦ, m.	general [strategic]
τρόπος, τρόπου, m.	turn; way, manner, fashion; habits, character [tropics, heliotrope]
ὕπνος, ὕπνου, m.	sleep [hypnotism]
φθόνος, φθόνου, m.	envy, jealousy
φόβος, φόβου, m.	fear [phobia, Phobos]
χρόνος, χρόνου, m.	time; period of time [chronology]

EXERCISES

I. Give the requested form of the Greek noun with the article.

Ex.   dat. sing of the road   τῇ ὁδῷ

1. acc. pl. of (the) fear
2. gen. sing. of the general
3. dat. pl. of (the) character
4. nom. pl. of (the) jealousy
5. gen. pl. of the toil
6. acc. sing. of (the) sleep
7. dat. sing. of the hoplite
8. nom. sing. of the gift
9. gen. pl. of the day
10. nom. pl. of the citizen
11. acc. pl. of the wind
12. gen. sing. of the honor
13. dat. pl. of the table
14. nom. pl. of the juryman
15. gen. pl. of the door
16. acc. sing. of the poet
17. dat. sing. of the god
18. nom. sing. of the office
19. gen. pl. of the measure
20. nom. pl. of the horse
21. acc. pl. of the vote
22. dat. pl. of the road

II. Write out the declension of "the sickness" in the singular only, of "the sailor" in the plural only, and of "the book" in both singular and plural.

III. Translate the following into English.

1. ἀπὸ τῆς θαλάττης
2. σὺν τοῖς ὁπλίταις
3. ἐπὶ τοὺς στρατιώτας
4. μετὰ τὰ παιδία
5. ἐν τῇ ἀγορᾷ
6. πρὸς τῶν δικαστῶν
7. ἐκ τῆς φιλίας
8. παρὰ τοῦ στρατηγοῦ
9. διὰ τὸν φθόνον
10. ἐπὶ τοῖς δώροις
11. εἰς τὸν ἥλιον
12. ἐκ τῆς χώρας
13. μετὰ τῶν δικαστῶν
14. ἐν τῷ ποταμῷ
15. εἰς τὴν ὁδόν
16. ἐπὶ τῶν τραπεζῶν
17. παρὰ τὴν ὁδόν
18. πρὸς τοῖς δώροις

IV. Translate the following prepositional phrases into Greek. (For some expressions there is more than one correct rendering.)

1. on account of the hard work
2. in the house of the children
3. beside the doors
4. from the general
5. in pursuit of the soldier
6. toward the sea
7. among the gods
8. regarding the Fates
9. next to the table
10. upon the horse
11. beyond reason
12. out of the land
13. by means of the voice
14. with fear

Vowel-Declension Adjectives;
Attribution and Predication

PRELIMINARIES

A. *Adjectives*. An adjective (Greek ἐπίθετον, Latin *adiectivum* = "word added to [a noun]") is that part of speech which modifies (or describes or qualifies) a noun. Examples: the *large* book; The food is *good*.

In many languages adjectives are inflected to mark *concord* (see below) with the nouns they modify. English has no inflection showing gender, number, and case of adjectives (*the large house, the large men*), but inflection in number and gender occurs, for instance, in Spanish, French, and Italian (e.g., French *un vieux livre* vs. *la vielle nourrice*). In Greek, as in Latin or German, adjectives are inflected to indicate not only gender and number, but also case.

Another characteristic of adjectives is that they have three degrees. The *positive* degree is the standard form. The *comparative* degree is used to compare one noun with another in regard to their possession of the same quality: for example, English *stronger*, *more virtuous*. The *superlative* degree is used to mark an excess or supremacy in the possession of a quality: for instance, English *strongest*, *most virtuous*. The formation of the comparative and superlative degrees is sometimes called "comparison of adjectives" (Unit 30).

B. *Concord*. Concord is the agreement in various grammatical categories between words which are associated in the grammar of a sentence or in the logic of an extended passage.

There may be agreement in number. The singular noun *farmer* agrees in number with the verb form *plows* in the sentence *The farmer plows*, whereas the plural *farmers* agrees with the verb form *plow* in *The farmers plow*. Or the plural pronoun *they* is used to refer to *the farmers*, while the singular *he* refers to *the farmer*. These types of concord are also evident in Greek.

There may be agreement in gender. The feminine pronoun *she* is used to refer to a feminine noun such as *actress*, whereas the neuter *it* is used to refer to a neuter noun like *car*. This type of concord is also evident in Greek.

There may be agreement in case as well, although this is rarely evident in English (cf. however *I expect the winner to be him.*). In a highly inflected language like Greek, agreement in case is widespread. The most common type is the agreement of an article or an adjective with its noun in gender, number, and case.

C. *Phrases and Clauses.* A *clause* is a group of words which contains a subject and a finite verb (to be discussed in detail in Unit 8). A *phrase* is a group of grammatically or semantically associated words that does not contain a subject–finite verb group.

A noun, taken by itself, is used only to refer to, to identify, or to specify a person or thing. Without departing from this function of *referring*, a noun may have associated with it an article and/or adjectival elements (adjective, adjectival prepositional phrase, participle, relative clause). The resulting group of words may be called a *noun phrase*. The adjectival elements in such a phrase are said to be *attributive* (or are called *attributes*). The speaker's application of these adjectival elements is called *attribution*. Attribution simply makes the act of referring more detailed and precise.

Ex.

man		no attribute
the man		article
the tall man		article, adjective
the tall man	*by the window*	art., adj., prep. phrase
the dancing figure	*by the window*	art., participle, prep. phrase
the young man	*now leaving the room*	art., adj., participial phrase
the old man	*who left the room*	art., adj., relative clause

In noun phrases the word order varies in different languages. In English, adjectives come between the article and the noun, participles precede or follow the noun, and relative clauses follow the noun. In German, attributive adjectives and adjectival phrases are placed between article and noun. In French, Spanish, or Italian, most attributive adjectives immediately follow their nouns. In Greek, attributive words accompanying a noun that has the article are restricted to a couple of positions, but an attributive word accompanying a noun without the article is less restricted. Inflection clarifies most grammatical relationships in Greek, so that, in general, word order in Greek is freer than in less inflected tongues.

In order to utter a complete and meaningful sentence or clause (in written English or formal spoken English), a speaker must not only *refer* (by means of a noun or other substantive) to a person or thing which is the *subject* or topic of his or her utterance, but also *predicate* something of that subject, that is, the speaker must comment on the given topic, must assert or affirm an action or a state of being as applicable to the subject. The main verb of a sentence or clause carries the force of *predication*, and the *predicate* of a sentence or clause includes the verb itself and all its modifiers and/or complements. Whereas a reference can be successful or unsuccessful (if we don't understand to what the speaker is trying to refer), a predication has a truth value: what the speaker asserts is either true or false.

D. *Predicate Nouns and Adjectives.* Verbs that express a state of being (such as *be, seem, look, smell, sound*) often serve to link the subject noun either to another noun in the predicate (which is identified with the subject or otherwise asserted to apply to it) or to an adjective in the predicate. In the traditional terminology used in many Greek grammars and commentaries, such a verb is called a *copula* (Latin for "link").

Ex.

predicate nouns:	That man *is* <u>my father</u>.
	She *was* <u>an astronaut</u>.
	The students *became* <u>experts</u> in Greek.
predicate adjectives:	The man *is* <u>tall</u>.
	This *seems* <u>correct</u>.
	The restaurant *smelled* <u>fishy</u>.
	She *looked* <u>tired</u>.

Note the difference between a phrase containing an attributive adjective and performing the function of reference only and a sentence in which the adjective is in the predicate and (along with the verb) is essential to the act of predication:

the blue book	(reference only, attributive adjective)
The book is blue.	(reference and predication, predicative adj.)

∵

1. *Adjective Declension.* Greek adjectives are inflected in two general classes: the vowel-declension adjectives (also called "first-and-second-declension" adjectives), and the consonant-declension adjectives (also called "third-declension" adjectives). The latter will be treated in Unit 22. The vowel-declension adjectives, treated in this unit, have a single stem to which masc., fem., and neut. endings are added to form all the cases and numbers. The masculine endings are the same as those of o-declension nouns in -ος (learned in U3). The feminine endings are the same as those of the long-vowel feminine

nouns of the a-declension (learned in U4): in the *singular* long alpha appears when the stem ends in ε, ι, or ρ; eta appears when the stem ends in any other letter. The neuter endings are the same as those of the o-declension neuter nouns in *-ον* (learned in U3).

Ex.

a. *with alpha-type feminine singular:* ἄξιος = *"worthy"*

		masc.	fem.	neut.
sing.	*nom.*	ἄξιος	ἀξία	ἄξιον
	gen.	ἀξίου	ἀξίας	ἀξίου
	dat.	ἀξίῳ	ἀξίᾳ	ἀξίῳ
	acc.	ἄξιον	ἀξίαν	ἄξιον
	voc.	ἄξιε	ἀξία	ἄξιον
(dual	*n. a. v.*	ἀξίω	ἀξία	ἀξίω)
	(g. d.	ἀξίοιν	ἀξίαιν	ἀξίοιν)
plur.	*n. v.*	ἄξιοι	ἄξιαι	ἄξια
	gen.	ἀξίων	ἀξίων	ἀξίων
	dat.	ἀξίοις	ἀξίαις	ἀξίοις
	acc.	ἀξίους	ἀξίας	ἄξια

b. *with eta-type feminine singular:* ἀγαθός = *"valorous, good"*

		masc.	fem.	neut.
sing.	*nom.*	ἀγαθός	ἀγαθή	ἀγαθόν
	gen.	ἀγαθοῦ	ἀγαθῆς	ἀγαθοῦ
	dat.	ἀγαθῷ	ἀγαθῇ	ἀγαθῷ
	acc.	ἀγαθόν	ἀγαθήν	ἀγαθόν
	voc.	ἀγαθέ	ἀγαθή	ἀγαθόν
(dual	*n. a. v.*	ἀγαθώ	ἀγαθά	ἀγαθώ)
	(g. d.	ἀγαθοῖν	ἀγαθαῖν	ἀγαθοῖν)
plur.	*n. v.*	ἀγαθοί	ἀγαθαί	ἀγαθά
	gen.	ἀγαθῶν	ἀγαθῶν	ἀγαθῶν
	dat.	ἀγαθοῖς	ἀγαθαῖς	ἀγαθοῖς
	acc.	ἀγαθούς	ἀγαθάς	ἀγαθά

2. *Accentuation.* The accentuation of adjectives (like that of nouns) is *persistent* (see U3.5): that is, the same syllable tends to be accented in all forms except when the changing length of the ultima forces a change. The special rule that applied for nouns of the o- and a-declensions with accented ultima also applies to the adjectives of this class: an adjective of this type with acute on *U* in the masc. nom. sing. has the circumflex in the gen. and dat. of all

numbers and genders (example: ἀγαθός). Note, however, that the fem. gen. pl. of adjectives of this class is not treated like the gen. pl. of the corresponding nouns: the nouns *always* have -ῶν, but in the adj. the accentuation is assimilated to that of the masc. gen. pl. (thus -ῶν appears only if the ultima is accented, as in ἀγαθός, not in adjs. accented like ἄξιος).[1]

3. *Attributive Adjectives.* The simplest form of noun phrase in Greek consists of a noun without the article and an adjective agreeing with it in gender, number, and case (*concord*). The adjective is normally adjacent to the noun, but the order is variable.

πολίτης ἄξιος	*a worthy citizen*
μικραὶ ἡδοναί	*small pleasures*

More common is the noun phrase with definite article. The position of an adjective in relation to the definite article and the noun serves to mark it as an attribute: an attributive adjective is *inside* the article-noun group. Three possible attributive positions are found:

a. (most common) article — modifier — noun
b. (less common) article — noun — article (repeated) — modifier
c. (uncommon) noun — article — modifier

The attributive modifier may be not only an adjective, but also a prepositional phrase or a participle or (occasionally) even an adverb or certain dependent genitives.

Ex.	ὁ ἀγαθὸς βίος	*the good life*
	ὁ ἐν τῇ ἀγορᾷ στρατιώτης	*the soldier in the marketplace*
	οἱ ἄνθρωποι οἱ τότε	*the people of that time*
	οἱ δικασταὶ οἱ δίκαιοι	*the just jurymen*

4. *Substantive-creating Force of the Article.* A frequent idiomatic use of the Greek article is the creation of a substantive by placement of any type of modifier in attributive position with the article but with no noun expressed.[2] The modifier can thus become a masc., fem., or neut. substantive when used with the appropriate form of the article. For instance, the masc. sing. article plus attribute may form a singular substantive referring to a male (e.g., ὁ

---

1. The contrast in accentuation is semantically important when a fem. noun in -ία coexists with an adjective in -ιος -ία -ιον from the same root: e.g., ἀξιῶν, ὁσιῶν, φιλιῶν, gen. pl. of fem. nouns ἀξία, ὁσία, φιλία vs. ἀξίων, ὁσίων, φιλίων, gen. pl. of any gender, including feminine, of adjectives from the same root.

2. In some contexts an adjective may be used without the article as an indefinite substantive: e.g., κακόν = "a bad thing, harm."

σοφός = "the wise man" or "a wise man" [in general]); the fem. pl. may form a
plural substantive referring to women (e.g., αἱ δίκαιαι = "[the] just women");
or a neuter sing. may form an abstract substantive (e.g., τὸ καλόν = [literally]
"the beautiful thing" = "beauty" or "that which is beautiful"). Compare also
the following:

οἱ τότε	the people of that time
οἱ πρὸς τῇ θαλάττῃ	the people near the sea
τὰ χαλεπά	(the) difficult things
τὰ δίκαια	the just things = just deeds = what is just

5. *Predicate Adjective.* When an adjective falls outside the article-noun
unit it is *predicative* rather than attributive. In Greek (especially in poetry, in
proverbial sayings, and on any occasion of concise utterance) a nominative
noun plus an agreeing adjective in predicate position may form a sentence
without the appropriate form of the copula *be* being expressed:

   ὁ δικαστὴς δίκαιος.   *The juryman is just.* (predication)

(Contrast ὁ δίκαιος δικαστής = *the just juryman* [attribution].)

Because ancient Greek is so highly inflected, the word order is not rigid. The
subject-predicate relationship is sufficiently clear from the forms of the noun
and adjective. The order of words may be altered to suit stylistic goals or to
affect the emphasis:

| non-emphatic adj.: | ὁ δικαστὴς δίκαιος. | *The juryman is just.* |
| emphatic adj.: | δίκαιος ὁ δικαστής. | *The juryman is just [not unjust].* |

6. *Predicate Noun.* Another simple form of sentence consists of subject
noun and predicate noun linked by the copula *be*. As with the predicate-
adjective construction, the verb is sometimes omitted in Greek. A predicate
noun in Greek must agree with its subject noun in *case*. Usually the subject
noun is accompanied by the definite article and the predicate noun is without
the article.

Ex.

| ὁ δικαστὴς ναύτης. | *The juryman is a sailor.* |
| ποιητὴς ὁ στρατηγός. | *The general is a poet.* |

(Note the case: nominative subject, predicate noun is also nominative. Because
this is the most frequent construction, a predicate noun is sometimes called
"predicate nominative.")

7. *Possessive Genitive.* The genitive of a noun (with its article and other modifiers, if any) may be placed in attributive position to express possession. (More details about this construction will be learned in U10.)

ἡ τοῦ στρατηγοῦ σκηνή	*the general's tent* or
	the tent of the general
τὸ τοῦ δικαίου δικαστοῦ βιβλίον	*the just juror's book* or
	the book of the just juror

8. *Identification of Adjective Forms.* When you learn an adjective, you need to learn all the nom. sing. forms (including the accent), and the English meaning.

Ex. δίκαιος, δικαία, δίκαιον, *just*

When you are asked to identify an adjective form (or article), first specify the three variables (case and number and gender) and then give the "dictionary" information about the word, namely, the nom. sing. forms (either all in full, or the masc. in full and the other endings abbreviated), and tell what noun the adjective modifies, specifying it as attributive or predicative (or say that the adj. is used as a substantive if it does not modify an expressed noun).

Ex. identify the adj. in τῇ μακρᾷ ὁδῷ
answer: dat. sing. fem. of μακρός, μακρά, μακρόν
(or μακρός, -ά, -όν), attributive modifying ὁδῷ

WHAT TO STUDY AND DO

1. Learn the declension of vowel-declension adjectives.
2. Learn the vocabulary of this unit.
3. Do the exercises of this unit.

VOCABULARY

vowel-declension adjectives

ἀγαθός, ἀγαθή, ἀγαθόν	good; well-born; brave [Agatha]
αἰσχρός, αἰσχρά, αἰσχρόν	ugly; shameful, base
ἄξιος, ἀξία, ἄξιον	worth; worthy, deserving of (takes a genitive complement: ἄξιος τιμῆς = "worthy of honor") [axiom]
δῆλος, δήλη, δῆλον	clear, manifest [psychedelic]
δίκαιος, δικαία, δίκαιον	just
κακός, κακή, κακόν	bad; evil; low-born [cacophony]

καλός, καλή, καλόν   beautiful; fine, noble   [calligraphy]
μακρός, μακρά, μακρόν   long, tall, large; far   [macroscopic]
μῑκρός, μῑκρά, μῑκρόν   small, little   [microscopic, microcomputer]
πονηρός, πονηρά, πονηρόν   worthless; knavish; evil, base
σοφός, σοφή, σοφόν   skilled, clever, wise   [sophomore]
φίλιος, φιλία, φίλιον   friendly; beloved
χαλεπός, χαλεπή, χαλεπόν   difficult, hard; harsh, cruel

some vowel-declension adjectives often used substantivally

ἱερός, ἱερά, ἱερόν   holy, consecrated   [Hieronymus = Jerome,
                                 hierarchy]
    τὸ ἱερόν   holy place, shrine
    τὰ ἱερά   offerings; omens; sacred rites
πεζός, πεζή, πεζόν   on foot, on land
    ὁ πεζός   infantry
    οἱ πεζοί   foot soldiers
πλούσιος, πλουσία,   wealthy, rich   [cf. πλοῦτος]
    πλούσιον
    οἱ πλούσιοι   rich men
πολέμιος, πολεμία,   hostile; belonging to war
    πολέμιον
    οἱ πολέμιοι   the enemy
φίλος, φίλη, φίλον   beloved, dear
    ὁ φίλος, ἡ φίλη   (male) friend, (female) friend

EXERCISES

I.   Give the requested form of each phrase in Greek.

1. shameful deeds (dat.)   6. the wealthy umpires (acc.)
2. the harsh misfortune (acc.)   7. a beautiful river (gen.)
3. the base men (nom.)   8. a good portion (dat.)
4. a clear measure (gen.)   9. the consecrated roads (gen.)
5. the friendly messenger (dat.)   10. the just manner (acc.)

II.   For each sentence or phrase (a) translate into English; (b) identify fully all adjective forms; (c) specify the use of the adjective (either attributive modifying which noun, or predicative modifying which noun, or used as a substantive).

Ex.   ὁ χαλεπὸς πόλεμος
          (a) the cruel war; (b) χαλεπὸς is nom. sing. masc. of χαλεπός, -ή, -όν; (c) attributive modifying πόλεμος.

1. πρὸς τὸν δίκαιον λόγον   2. μικρὰ τὰ παιδία.

3. διὰ τῶν μακρῶν θυρῶν
4. ὁ δίκαιος ἄξιος τῆς ἀρχῆς.
5. μετὰ τῶν καλῶν θεῶν
6. ἡ παρὰ τὸν ποταμὸν ὁδὸς χαλεπή.
7. ἄξιοι κακῶν οἱ πονηροί.
8. εἰς τὴν τοῦ στρατηγοῦ σκηνήν
9. ὁ τοῦ νεανίου φθόνος οὐ [= not] μικρός.
10. πρὸς τὴν πολεμίαν στρατιάν
11. σὺν τοῖς ἀνθρώποις τοῖς ἀγαθοῖς
12. διὰ τὸ αἰσχρόν
13. σοφὴ ἡ γνώμη ἡ τῶν ἐφ᾿ ἵππων στρατηγῶν.
14. ἡ πρὸς τῶν θεῶν μοῖρα δήλη.
15. πολέμιοι οἱ πρὸς τῇ θαλάττῃ.
16. ἱερὰ τὰ βιβλία τὰ τῶν κριτῶν.

III. Translate the following phrases and sentences into Greek.

1. upon the small bridge
2. because of the valor of the foot soldiers
3. next to the holy books
4. throughout the long life
5. with the small children of the messenger
6. The poet's exile is disgraceful.
7. The deeds of wise men are worthy of honor.
8. Good books are worthy friends.
9. The soldiers in the tent are handsome.
10. The envy of the young men is shameful.

Ω-Verbs: Present Active Indicative

PRELIMINARIES

A. *Verbs.* A verb (Greek ῥῆμα, Latin *verbum* = "that which is said, predicate") is that part of speech which affirms or predicates (see U7 Prelim. C) by expressing an action or a state of being.

The inflection of a verb is called *conjugation.* The *finite forms* of a verb are those whose inflectional ending defines precisely the *person* and *number* of the subject, or, in an uninflected or slightly inflected language like English, those which combine with a subject to form a clause: for example, *we see, they saw, the man is walking.* There are also two important *non-finite forms* of a verb: verbal noun (infinitive [e.g., *to see*] and/or gerund [e.g., *seeing*]) and verbal adjective (participle: e.g., *seeing, seen*). Finite and non-finite forms share such features as tense and voice and the ability to govern objects and be modified by adverbs. Non-finite forms, however, cannot serve as the predicate of a clause and carry no distinction of person.

B. *Finite verb forms* have five important variable features:

1. *Person* expresses the relation of the verb's subject to the speaker and listener of the utterance.

   first person: the subject is the speaker or a group including the speaker (*I, we*).
   second person: the subject is the listener or listeners (*you*).
   third person: the subject is a person or thing other than the speaker or listener (*he, she, it, they*).

   Most English verbs now show distinction of person only in third person singular present forms (*walks, has* vs. *walk, have*), and thus the person must be expressed in English by a subject noun or a *personal pronoun* separate from the verb itself.

2. *Number* marks whether the verb's subject is singular or plural. The subject and the verb are in *concord.* Again, most English verbs now distinguish

number only in the case of the third person present forms: *she goes, they go* vs. *I go, we go*. And again, the number is made clear in English by the necessary presence of the subject noun or pronoun. (Greek has not only singular and plural verb forms, but also dual, as for nouns. The dual is rare, and beginning students are not usually required to learn it. In this book the dual forms are given in parentheses and are not used in exercises or reading; but students who go on in Greek will soon meet dual forms.)

3. *Tense* expresses the time distinction of the verbal action (present, past, future: for instance, *I teach, she taught, they will teach*). In Greek as in some other languages tense also conveys a distinction in verbal *aspect*, sometimes even to the exclusion of a distinction in time. Aspect will be discussed in detail in Unit 20. The seven Greek tenses (present, imperfect, future, aorist, perfect, pluperfect, future perfect) will be discussed separately in the units in which they are learned.

4. *Voice* expresses the relationship of the subject of the verb to the action expressed by the verb. The *active* voice is used when the subject is the doer of the action (or the one who experiences a state of being). Some active verbs, called *transitive*, express actions which are carried through to a recipient or object, while others, called *intransitive*, are used absolutely, without such a complement. Transitive verbs can also be used in the *passive* voice, in which the scheme *doer–action–recipient of action* is reversed so that the recipient of the action becomes the subject, the verb is made passive, and the doer is left unexpressed or is expressed in a subordinate element of the sentence (in English in a prepositional phrase with *by*).

Ex.	*The man <u>walks</u>.*	active (intransitive)
	The boy <u>throws</u> the ball.	active (transitive)
	The cavalry <u>lost</u> the battle.	active (transitive)
	The ball <u>is thrown</u> by the boy.	passive
	The battle <u>was lost</u>.	passive

Greek has a third voice, the *middle*, which is lacking in English and many other languages. The middle is used when the subject is the doer of the action but acts upon itself or for itself. The middle will be discussed in detail in Unit 11.

5. *Mood* expresses the manner in which the action or state of being denoted by the verb is conceived by the speaker, namely, whether as fact, as assumption, as wish, or the like. Greek has four moods, three of which are paralleled in English:

indivative*indicative*: for the assertion of fact (as in English)

   subjunctive: for mere assumption or possibility (as opposed to assertion); often used in subordinate clause constructions. (The English subjunctive is now largely defunct, replaced by the indicative or by verb phrases using modal helper verbs; but cf. *It is necessary that he go now.*)

optative: originally for expression of a wish, but also used for expression of a possibility and in subordinate clause constructions. (There is no English equivalent, nor is there such a separate mood in Latin, German, French, etc.)

imperative: for expressing a command (as in English)

C.   The *principal parts* of a verb are those forms from which the major tense stems can be derived and from which, thereby, all the conjugational forms of a verb can (in theory) be generated. The number of principal parts varies from language to language. English verbs have three: present, simple past, and past (passive) participle (e.g., *go, went, gone; break, broke, broken; bake, baked, baked*). The normal Greek verb has six principal parts (to be learned as they arise in future units).

::

1. *μι-Verbs and ω-Verbs*. There are two basic systems of conjugation in Greek, and the distinction is readily apparent in the present tense. A limited number of very basic verbs are conjugated in certain tense systems, including the present, by the addition of personal endings directly to the verb stem: these are known as μι-verbs (because the first person singular ending is -μι) or athematic verbs (because the ending is added directly to the stem). Other verbs (the ω-verbs or the thematic verbs) are conjugated with a theme vowel intervening between the verb stem and the personal endings.

2. *The Present System*. The present system consists of all forms which can be generated from the first principal part, including the present active and middle/passive indicative, subjunctive, optative, imperative, participle, and infinitive, and the imperfect active and middle/passive indicative. All these forms contain the present stem, which is obtained by removing the ending -ω from the first principal part (the form in which the verb is listed in a dictionary). The present system of ω-verbs features the theme vowel o/ϵ, that is, it shows two *grades* or variable forms, o and ϵ (and also lengthened forms ω and η).

3. *Present Active Indicative*. Any Greek verb form can be analyzed into a tense stem (consisting of a form of the verb stem plus prefixed or suffixed tense signs), prefixes, and suffixes (indicating, e.g., mood, voice, person, and number for a finite form). The present active indicative consists of present

stem plus theme vowel plus personal endings. The theme vowel o/ϵ appears as o when the first letter of the personal ending is μ or ν, and as ϵ otherwise. Because of linguistic developments, it is more difficult to separate theme vowel from personal ending in many forms of the present active than in some other tenses. Therefore, the beginner should simply learn the combined ending (theme vowel plus personal ending).

Ex. *"release," principal part:* λύω, *stem:* λυ- + o/ϵ *endings*

sing.	*1st pers.*	λύω	*I release*	-ω
	2nd pers.	λύεις	*you (s.) release*	-εις
	3rd pers.	λύει	*he (she, it) releases*	-ει
(dual	*2nd pers.*	λύετον)		(-ετον)
	(3rd pers.	λύετον)		(-ετον)
plur.	*1st pers.*	λύομεν	*we release*	-ομεν
	2nd pers.	λύετε	*you (pl.) release*	-ετε
	3rd pers.	λύουσι(ν)	*they release*	-ουσῐ(ν)

Ex. *"send," principal part:* πέμπω, *stem:* πεμπ- + o/ϵ *endings*

sing.	*1st pers.*	πέμπω	*I send*	-ω
	2nd pers.	πέμπεις	*you (s.) send*	-εις
	3rd pers.	πέμπει	*he (she, it) sends*	-ει
(dual	*2nd pers.*	πέμπετον)		(-ετον)
	(3rd pers.	πέμπετον)		(-ετον)
plur.	*1st pers.*	πέμπομεν	*we send*	-ομεν
	2nd pers.	πέμπετε	*you (pl.) send*	-ετε
	3rd pers.	πέμπουσι(ν)	*they send*	-ουσῐ(ν)

4. *English Equivalents.* The present indicative of Greek is equivalent to the English simple present (*I send*), the progressive present (*I am sending*), and the present emphatic (*I do send*, more commonly used in the negative, *I don't send*, or in interrogative form, *Do I send?*). Context and English idiom determine which equivalent is appropriate in any given case. Note that the Greek finite verb form indicates number and person by itself and may be used without an explicit pronoun subject (cf. Latin and Italian). When a pronoun subject is expressed, it is emphatic.

λέγω   *I say*   ἐγὼ λέγω   *I say*

5. *Nu Movable.* The third person plural of the present active indicative may have nu added when the verb occurs at the end of a clause or when it is followed by a word beginning with a vowel (or in verse when it is more con-

venient to the poet to add it). The optional nu was added to avoid *hiatus*, the pronunciation of two vowels in succession, a phenomenon often avoided in everyday speech and almost completely eliminated by the fussiest Greek prose stylists (such as the orator and teacher of rhetoric Isocrates). (Another term used for this optional nu is *nu ephelkustikon,* "attracted, suffixed nu.")

6. *Accentuation.* The accent of all *finite* forms of the Greek verb is *recessive*. That is, it falls as far from the end of the word as is permitted by the general rules of accentuation: acute on *A* when *U* is short, acute on *P* when *U* is long. The circumflex accent appears only when a contraction is involved (some verbs with contraction will be learned in Unit 13) or in a two-syllable form with long *P* and short *U*. For the present active indicative, it turns out that the accent falls on the last (or only) syllable of the stem in every form.

7. *Negation.* Indicative verbs in main clauses and in most dependent clauses are normally negated with the adverb οὐ, and a simple unemphatic negative usually precedes the verb it negates. When the word following οὐ begins with a vowel, οὐ takes the form οὐκ (before an unaspirated vowel) or οὐχ (before an aspirated vowel).

οὐ μένω	*I do not remain*
οὐκ ἐθέλω	*I am not willing*
οὐχ ἁρπάζω	*I am not seizing*

8. *Concord.* As one would expect, a Greek verb agrees with its subject in person and number (see U7, Prelim. B). But when the subject is a neuter plural noun or pronoun, the Greek verb is normally third person *singular* rather than plural, apparently because the neuter plural was originally felt to express a single collective concept.

9. *Direct and Indirect Objects.* As mentioned in connection with voice in Preliminaries of this unit, *transitive* verbs are those which express an action that is carried through to a recipient of the action (person or thing) or to an enduring effect or result of the action. The recipient of the action may in general be called the *direct object* of the verb. In English the direct object is expressed in the objective case, which is noticeable only in pronouns. In Greek the direct object is expressed in the accusative case (the principal use of this case). Examples:

He trained <u>the children</u>.   *The man <u>whom</u> we saw . . .*
She wrote <u>this poem</u>.   *We built <u>a house</u>.*
The general sent <u>them</u>.

ὁ στρατηγὸς <u>τοὺς στρατιώτας</u> εἰς τὴν ἀγορὰν πέμπει.
The general sends <u>the soldiers</u> into the marketplace.

οὐ λείπετε τὴν χώραν;
Are you not leaving the country?

Some transitive verbs also govern a secondary object of the person (much less often the thing) more indirectly affected by the action than is the direct object. This is the *indirect object*. In English it is again in the objective case (noticeable only in pronouns) and either follows the verb immediately or is governed by the preposition *to* or *for*. In Greek the indirect object is expressed by the dative case without a preposition. Examples:

They gave *the boy* some money.   They gave *him* some money.
The gave some money *to the boy*.   Tell *me* a story.

τὰ βιβλία τῷ ποιητῇ οὐκ ἐπιτρέπουσιν.
They are not entrusting the books to the poet.

10. *Word Order.* The word order of a Greek sentence is very flexible. In a majority of sentences in which no special emphasis is being sought, the normal order is subject (if expressed), direct object (if any), indirect object (if any), verb. But in fact speakers and writers are more often than not trying to convey some special emphasis, and adjust the word order to suit. The first word or phrase normally carries the greatest emphasis:

τῷ ποιητῇ τὰ βιβλία οὐκ ἐπιτρέπουσιν.
They are not entrusting the books to the poet.

Here *the poet* is emphasized in contrast to some other person or persons whom they find more trustworthy: English uses stress on the word or phrase more often than a shift of word order to convey such emphasis.

11. *Identification of Verb Forms.* When identifying a finite verb form, specify the five variable features (person, number, tense, voice, mood) and give the first principal part of the verb, and add the definition if it is requested.

Ex.   ἔχετε: 2nd pl. pres. act. ind. of ἔχω, to have

WHAT TO STUDY AND DO

1. Learn the conjugation of the present active indication of ω-verbs.
2. Learn the vocabulary of this unit. For now, you are presented with only the first principal part of each verb. If your instructor prefers that you begin to memorize the first three principal parts from this unit onward, consult the Appendix to U18 or Appendix 2 for the other principal parts.
3. Do the exercises of this unit.

VOCABULARY

Vocabulary-building Hints. Greek has a very large vocabulary, but this richness is in large part due to the readiness with which the same root manifests itself in several shapes and the frequency with which words are formed by compounding of familiar elements. Knowledge of the relationships between roots can make the acquisition of new vocabulary much easier. Two observations can be made about some words in the very limited vocabulary presented up to this point. (1) Different vowel grades within the same root are common. One of the basic variations is between ε and ο grades. The "say" root produces ο-grade noun λόγος and ε-grade verb λέγω. The same relationship exists with τρόπος and ἐπιτρέπω, and (if we consider some words not yet learned) νόμος and νέμω, φόρος and φέρω, πομπή and πέμπω. A different vowel variation is seen in φυγή and φεύγω. (2) A root of the same form may also appear with various suffixes or compounding elements. For instance, the root στρατ- = "army" forms the collective noun στρατιά with the common suffix -ια (cf. φιλία, δημοκρατία), the individual noun στρατιώτης with a form of the -της suffix, meaning "person who does X" (cf. πολίτης, ναύτης, δικαστής, etc.), and the compound noun στρατηγός, in which -ηγος is a form of the root of ἄγω = "lead" (the lengthening of the vowel in composition is common). Later you will also meet στρατός, στρατόπεδον, στρατεύω, στράτευμα.

ω-verbs

ἄγω	lead; carry [pedagogy]
ἀποθνήσκω (ἀπο)[1]	die
ἄρχω	begin (+ gen.);[2] rule, be leader of (+ gen.) [monarchy]
γράφω	scratch; inscribe; write [graphic]
ἐθέλω	be willing, wish
ἐλαύνω	drive, set in motion; (intrans.) ride, march [elastic]
ἐπιτρέπω (ἐπι)	turn over to, entrust
ἔχω	have, hold [echeneis]
λαμβάνω	take, grasp; receive [narcolepsy]
λέγω	say, speak; recount
λείπω	leave, abandon [ellipsis]

---

1. Compound verbs are indicated by addition of the prepositional prefix in parentheses. It will become apparent in later units (e.g., U16.2) why one needs to know that a verb is a compound.

2. When a verb takes a complement other than the usual accusative object, that fact will be mentioned in the vocabulary. Here, for instance, where English uses an ordinary direct object in *They begin the war* or *He rules the land*, the Greek verb governs the genitive: τοῦ πολέμου ἄρχουσι. τῆς χώρας ἄρχει.

λύω [ῡ]   loosen, release   [analysis]
μένω   remain, stay; wait for, wait
πείθω   persuade, urge
πέμπω   send   [pomp]
φέρω   bear, carry, bring; endure   [pheromones, euphoria]
φεύγω   flee, be in exile

negative adverb

οὐ, οὐκ, οὐχ   not (for negation of statements)   [Utopia]

EXERCISES

I. Give the requested Greek verb form.

     Ex.   we are dying   answer: *ἀποθνῄσκομεν*

1. they do persuade   16. you (pl.) entrust
2. she is sending   17. you (sing.) are dying
3. you (pl.) are speaking   18. he is not urging
4. they rule   19. I send
5. I am entrusting   20. we are speaking
6. you (sing.) have   21. you (pl.) rule
7. we are remaining   22. she is entrusting
8. he is releasing   23. it has
9. it carries   24. I do not receive
10. you (sing.) are leaving   25. they abandon
11. I wish   26. he leaves
12. they are willing   27. you (pl.) drive
13. we march   28. you (sing.) are in exile
14. she is writing   29. we do not endure
15. they are leading   30. she says

II. Translate the following verb forms into English.

     Ex.   λέγετε   you (pl.) are saying

1. ἐλαύνεις   10. ἄγομεν   19. ἄρχεις
2. φέρομεν   11. οὐκ ἔχω   20. λέγει
3. γράφω   12. φεύγουσι   21. λύομεν
4. λαμβάνει   13. λύεις   22. οὐ μένω
5. μένουσι   14. φέρει   23. ἐθέλετε
6. ἔχεις   15. ἐπιτρέπομεν   24. ἔχουσιν
7. πείθω   16. οὐ πέμπετε   25. ἐλαύνετε
8. φεύγομεν   17. λείπουσι   26. λείπω
9. πέμπει   18. λαμβάνω   27. ἄρχομεν

28. ἐθέλουσι	33. μένεις	38. οὐκ ἄγει
29. ἄρχετε	34. ἐλαύνει	39. οὐ λαμβάνετε
30. λέγεις	35. ἀποθνῄσκουσι	40. φέρεις
31. λείπει	36. ἄγω	
32. ἐπιτρέπετε	37. ἔχομεν	

III. (a) Translate each sentence into English. Then (b) give a full identification of any underlined word(s), and, if the word is a noun, explain its case (why is it in the case it is in?).

> **Ex.**   ὁ στρατηγὸς τοὺς ἀγαθοὺς <u>ὁπλίτας</u> εἰς τὴν τῶν πολεμίων <u>χώραν</u> πέμπει.
>
> (a) *The general is sending the brave hoplites into the land of the enemy.*
> (b) ὁπλίτας is acc. pl. of ὁπλίτης, -ου, m.; it is acc. because it is the direct object of πέμπει. χώραν is acc. sing. of χώρα, -ας, f.; it is acc. because it is object of the preposition εἰς.

1. τὰς <u>Μοίρας</u> οὐ πείθουσιν οἱ θεοί.
2. οἱ σοφοὶ τὴν <u>ἀλήθειαν</u> λέγουσιν.
3. ἡ θεὰ ἐλαύνει τοὺς <u>πεζοὺς</u> ἐκ τοῦ ἱεροῦ.
4. διὰ τὸ ἀγαθὸν ἔργον ὁ δικαστὴς τὸν κακὸν <u>λύει</u>.
5. οἱ ἄνθρωποι τοὺς πόνους παρὰ τῶν <u>θεῶν</u> ἔχουσι.
6. οἱ νεανίαι τὰ δῶρα τοῖς <u>ἀξίοις</u> φέρουσιν.
7. οἱ πολῖται τοὺς νόμους μετὰ γνώμης <u>σοφῆς</u> γράφουσι.
8. λείπουσι παρὰ τῇ γεφύρᾳ τοὺς τῶν στρατιωτῶν <u>ἵππους</u> οἱ πολέμιοι.
9. λέγουσιν οἱ ἄγγελοι τὰς τῆς στρατιᾶς συμφορὰς τοῖς ἐν τῇ ἀγορᾷ <u>πολίταις</u>.

IV. Render the following sentences into Greek.

> **Ex.**   The goddesses do not receive the offerings.
>
> *The goddesses* is subject of the sentence, so will be nominative plural (αἱ θεαί). The verb *receive* is third person plural present active indicative, with negative adverb (οὐ λαμβάνουσι). The direct object of *receive* is *the offerings*, which will thus be in the accusative case (τὰ ἱερά). Therefore, a correct answer is:
>
> αἱ θεαὶ τὰ ἱερὰ οὐ λαμβάνουσι. (other word orders are possible)

1. The horses are dying because of the disease.
2. The wicked men are not persuading the jurors.
3. The general is leading his soldiers toward the sea.
4. The citizens entrust their laws to the judges.
5. You (pl.) are not leading the children of the poet out of the large tent.

Infinitive; Adjectives with Two Endings

PRELIMINARIES

The *infinitive*, a non-finite form of the verb (see U8 Prelim.), is a verbal noun. As a verb form it has tense and voice and can govern noun complements and adverbial modifiers. As a noun, it can serve as subject, object, and the like. In English the infinitive (formed with *to* plus the verb) shares the job of verbal noun with the *gerund* (formed from the present stem of a verb plus *-ing*). In Greek there is only the infinitive to fulfill the verbal noun function.

> **Ex.** *To see* is *to believe*.
> *Seeing* is *believing*.
> *Learning* Greek is not difficult.

In addition to functioning as a noun in these simple uses, the infinitive is used (1) as a complement to many verbs and (2) in dependent phrases which are transformations of simple sentences embedded in a more complex sentence.

You like to swim.	(complementary infinitive)
They are willing to lead.	(complementary infinitive)

Wilson is president.	(simple sentence, finite verb)
They want Wilson to be president.	(embedded sentence, infinitive)
They chose Wilson to be president.	(embedded sentence, infinitive)
They believe Wilson to be president.	(embedded sentence, infinitive)

∴

1. *Present Active Infinitive.* The present active infinitive is formed by adding -ειν to the present stem. (-ειν is a contraction of the theme vowel ε and the infinitival ending -εν.)

> **Ex.** ἄγω —> ἄγειν = to lead; πείθω —> πείθειν = to persuade

Accentuation: the non-finite forms of the verb do *not* have recessive accentuation (U8.6). The accentuation of each type of infinitive and participle must be learned separately. The present infinitive of ω-verbs is always accented on the final syllable of the stem.

2. *Some Uses of the Greek Infinitive*

a. The *complementary* infinitive is used to complete the meaning of a variety of verbs, such as those expressing will or desire, request, permission, choice, command, and the like. In the simplest examples the verb has no other complement:

ἐθέλουσι μένειν.   *They are willing to stay.*
οὐκ ἐθέλετε φέρειν τὸν πόνον.   *You are not willing to endure the toil.*

Some verbs (e.g., those of asking, commanding, persuading) take an accusative object (of the person who is to do the action of the infinitive) plus the complementary infinitive:

τοὺς συμμάχους μένειν πείθομεν.   *We are urging the allies to remain.*
κελεύω τὴν στρατιὰν ἐλαύνειν.   *I am ordering the army to march.*

b. The infinitive, as a verbal noun, often serves as the subject of a sentence, usually with a predicate adjective (the copula *is* being sometimes expressed and sometimes omitted) or with an impersonal verb. In English this usage is somewhat concealed by the use of the expletive *it* (a "filler" or apparent subject):

It is just <u>to take</u> the horses.   (expletive—copula—pred. adj.—inf.
                                                    phrase)
= *<u>To take</u> the horses is just.*   (inf. phrase—copula—pred. adj.)
= *<u>Taking</u> the horses is just.*   (gerund phrase—copula—pred. adj.)

δίκαιον λαμβάνειν τοὺς ἵππους.   (pred. adj.—inf.—direct obj. of inf.)

ἄρχειν χαλεπόν.   *It is difficult to lead.*
                                 = *To lead is difficult.*

Note that the infinitive as noun is considered neuter singular: thus the predicate adj. is neuter singular nom. to agree with the subject infinitive.

Impersonal verbs are verbs normally used only in the third person singular with an unspecifiable subject *it* (e.g., *it is raining*) or with an expletive *it* with an infinitive as the true subject:

<u>δεῖ</u> πέμπειν δῶρα.   *It is necessary to send gifts.*
                                 = *To send gifts is necessary.*

οὐ <u>πρέπει</u> δῶρα λαμβάνειν.   *It is not seemly to take gifts (bribes).*
                                 = *To take bribes is not seemly.*

What is expressed in Greek idiom by an impersonal verb and infinitive is often idiomatically conveyed in English by a personal construction with a modal verb using *must*, *should*, or *ought*. For example, δεῖ πέμπειν δῶρα may also be translated *One must (should, ought to) send gifts*.

c. The substantival force and case usage of an infinitive used as a noun are sometimes marked more strongly by the use of the neuter singular definite article to introduce the infinitive phrase (*articular infinitive*). The article *must* be used when the infinitive functions as a substantive in the genitive or dative or as the object of a preposition. In the nominative and many uses of the accusative, either the articular infinitive or the bare infinitive (as exemplified in a and b above) is allowed.

nom.	τὸ ἄρχειν πόνον φέρει.	<u>*To rule*</u> *brings toil.*
gen.	ἐκ τοῦ φεύγειν	*as a result of* <u>*fleeing*</u>
dat.	πρὸς τῷ δῶρα λαμβάνειν	*in addition to* <u>*taking bribes*</u>
acc.	πρὸς τὸ ἐλαύνειν τὰς ἵππους	*with regard to* <u>*driving*</u> *the mares*

3. *Negation.* The negative adverb μή is used to negate an infinitive in any of the above uses.

πρέπει δῶρα μὴ λαμβάνειν.   *It is fitting not to take bribes.*

4. *Subject of Infinitive.* When the subject of the action expressed by the infinitive is expressed in Greek, it is normally in the *accusative* case unless it is the same person or thing as the subject of the finite verb (there are further exceptions to be learned later).

οὐ δίκαιον τοὺς πολίτας λείπειν τὰ παιδία.
It is not right for the citizens to leave the children.
(It is not right that the citizens leave the children.)

δεῖ τοὺς ἀνθρώπους πόνους φέρειν.
It is necessary for men to endure toil.
or (personal form) *Men must endure toil.*

ἐκ τοῦ τὸν κακὸν ναύτην ἄρχειν
as a result of the bad sailor's being leader
(as a result of the fact that the bad sailor is leader)

Note that in English the subject of an infinitive is often expressed in a prepositional phrase with *for* or as the possessive with a gerund, or that English idiom may prefer a personal construction (like *men must*). In other cases the infinitive phrase of Greek may be equivalent to a *that*-clause in English with subject and finite verb.

5. *Dative of Reference.* The person to whose case a statement is limited or in whose opinion a statement is true is expressed in the dative case. Such a *dative of reference* is often used in sentences with infinitive phrase as subject.

τῷ σοφῷ ὁ βίος οὐ χαλεπός.
For a wise man life is not difficult.

οὐ καλὸν τῷ ἀγαθῷ πολίτῃ φεύγειν.
Being in exile is not a fine thing for the good citizen.

(Compare the slightly different emphasis of:
οὐ καλὸν τὸ τὸν ἀγαθὸν πολίτην φεύγειν.
It is not a fine thing that a good citizen be in exile.)

6. *Vowel-declension Adjectives with Two Endings.* Some vowel-declension adjectives (usually ones formed by compounding two roots, or prefix and root) have no separate feminine endings, the "masculine" endings serving as endings for a common non-neuter gender. Thus in ἄδικος πολίτης the adjective is masculine, but in ἄδικος γνώμη the same form is feminine. These adjectives thus have only two endings: masc./fem. and neuter.

Ex.	"unjust"		masc./fem.	neuter
sing.		*nom.*	ἄδικος	ἄδικον
		gen.	ἀδίκου	ἀδίκου
		dat.	ἀδίκῳ	ἀδίκῳ
		acc.	ἄδικον	ἄδικον
		voc.	ἄδικε	ἄδικον
(dual		*n. a. v.*	ἀδίκω	ἀδίκω)
		(g. d.	ἀδίκοιν	ἀδίκοιν)
plur.		*n. v.*	ἄδικοι	ἄδικα
		gen.	ἀδίκων	ἀδίκων
		dat.	ἀδίκοις	ἀδίκοις
		acc.	ἀδίκους	ἄδικα

7. *Alpha Privative.* The commonest negative compounding element in Greek is the prefix ἀ- (or ἀν- before a vowel): compare the English derivatives *atypical* and *anhydrous* and the corresponding negative prefixes *in-* and *un-* in English. Many compound adjectives meaning "not X" or "without X" are formed from the root X and the alpha-privative prefix, and many of these are vowel-declension adjs. of two endings.

WHAT TO STUDY AND DO

1. Study the formation and uses of the infinitive.

2. Learn the declension of two-ending adjectives of the vowel declension.
3. Learn the vocabulary of this unit.
4. Do the exercises of this unit.

VOCABULARY

ω-verbs

βλάπτω	harm, damage
κελεύω	order, command (+ acc. of person + inf.)
κόπτω	strike, chop, beat [syncope]
τάττω[1]	marshal, draw up (troops); arrange; appoint [tactics, syntagmatic]

impersonal verbs

δεῖ	it is necessary, it is needful (for one to do something) (+ acc. of person + inf.) (often to be translated with *ought to*, *must*, *should* in a personal construction) [deontology]
δοκεῖ	it seems good, it seems best (+ dat. of person + inf.)
ἔξεστι	it is permitted, it is possible (+ acc. or dat. of person + inf.)
πρέπει	it is fitting, becoming, seemly (+ acc. or dat. of person + inf.)
χρή[2]	it is necessary (+ acc. of person + inf.) (often to be translated with *ought to*, *must*, *should* in a personal construction)[3]

negative adverb

μή	not (for negation of most infinitives, individual words, many types of subordinate clauses)

vowel-declension adjectives

ὅσιος, ὁσία, ὅσιον	hallowed; pious, pure
ῥᾴδιος, ῥᾳδία, ῥᾴδιον	easy

---

1. Non-Attic τάσσω (cf. Intro. §6).

2. This word was in origin a noun, with the copula omitted, but the Greeks came to treat it as an impersonal verb form. The infinitive of χρή is χρῆναι, a contraction of χρή with εἶναι, the infinitive of εἰμί (U10.4).

3. χρή and δεῖ are sometimes used synonymously, but in classical Attic there is a tendency for χρή to denote an obligation related to internal constraints of an ethical nature and δεῖ to imply external constraints. Compare τί χρὴ δρᾶν; = *What should I do?* (in an ethically ambiguous situation) with τί δεῖ λέγειν; = *Why should I mention?* (the matter being so obvious) or δεῖ φέρειν τὰ τῶν θεῶν = *One must endure what the gods give.*

vowel-declension adjectives with two endings

ἄδικος, ἄδικον	unjust
ἀθάνατος, ἀθάνατον	undying, immortal
ἀνόσιος, ἀνόσιον	unholy, profane
βάρβαρος, βάρβαρον	non-Greek-speaking, foreign; (pejorative) barbarian
οἱ βάρβαροι	foreigners, esp. the Persians
σύμμαχος, σύμμαχον	fighting along with, allied with
οἱ σύμμαχοι	allies

EXERCISES

I. Write in Greek.

1. to lead
2. you (pl.) order
3. we are not harming
4. to arrange
5. as a result of speaking
6. they strike
7. to loosen
8. to persuade
9. she rules
10. I ride

II. Translate the following sentences.

1. τὴν στρατιὰν μένειν πείθετε.
2. ὁ ναύτης τοὺς στρατιώτας τὰς ἵππους λείπειν κελεύει.
3. ἐπιτρέπειν ἐθέλει τὰ χαλεπὰ ἔργα τοῖς καλοῖς νεανίαις.
4. οὐκ ἐθέλω ἀποθνῄσκειν ἐν τῇ θαλάττῃ.
5. μὴ βλάπτειν τοὺς πλουσίους πολίτας κελεύεις τοὺς ὁπλίτας.
6. ὁ θεὸς οὐκ ἐθέλει κόπτειν τὴν θεάν.
7. δοκεῖ τοῖς σοφοῖς τὴν ἀλήθειαν λέγειν.
8. τοὺς ἀνοσίους δεῖ ἐλαύνειν ἀπὸ τῆς τῶν παιδίων σκηνῆς.
9. οἱ σύμμαχοι τοὺς βαρβάρους τὴν ἀγορὰν λαμβάνειν κελεύουσιν.
10. οἱ ἀθάνατοι μὴ λέγειν ἀνόσια τοὺς ἀνθρώπους πείθουσιν.
11. διὰ τὸ τοὺς πολεμίους ἐν τῇ χώρᾳ μένειν φεύγουσιν οἱ πολῖται.
12. τοῖς ἀγαθοῖς ῥᾴδιον νόμους γράφειν.
13. τοὺς ναύτας χρὴ ἄνεμον καλὸν μένειν.
14. τοὺς πολεμίους βλάπτειν ἔξεστι τοῖς στρατηγοῖς.

III. Render the following sentences into Greek.

> **Ex.**   It is unseemly for an unjust person to rule the just (people).
>   οὐ πρέπει   τὸν ἄδικον   τῶν δικαίων ἄρχειν.

1. With friends it is easy to endure evils.
2. The general of the enemy army is marshaling his hoplites.
3. The poet urges the citizens to entrust their fate to the gods.
4. It is impossible for the immortal gods to feel [= have] jealousy.

5. It is possible for a wicked man not to have a bad reputation.
6. It isn't wise to damage one's health.
7. Because of their wealth the rich are permitted to flee difficult tasks. [Hint: convert to impersonal form: "it is permitted…"]
8. A poet ought to be unwilling [= not + be willing] to say bad things.
9. In addition to honor, ruling brings envy.

Present Indicative of εἰμί;
Some Uses of the Genitive and Dative

1. *The Verb "to be."* One of the most commonly used words in the language, the Greek verb *to be* shows irregularities of conjugation in all dialects. The Attic forms of the present active indicative are:

sing.	1st pers.	εἰμί	I am
	2nd pers.	εἶ	you (s.) are
	3rd pers.	ἐστί(ν)	he (she, it) is
(dual	2nd pers.	ἐστόν)	
	(3rd. pers.	ἐστόν)	
plur.	1st pers.	ἐσμέν	we are
	2nd pers.	ἐστέ	you (pl.) are
	3rd pers.	εἰσί(ν)	they are

Note that the third person sing. and pl. forms may take nu movable (see U8.5).

2. *Accentuation.* All forms of the present indicative of εἰμί except second singular εἶ (and the third singular in some uses: §3) are *enclitic* (see U2.12). This is traditionally indicated in paradigms by the use of the acute on the ultima. The enclitic forms are accented with acute or grave on *U* when the preceding word has acute on *P*: πολίτης ἐστί; ὁ πολίτης ἐστὶ καλός. In other circumstances, the enclitic forms have no accent, but they may affect the accent of the previous word (review the rules given in U2.12): ἄνθρωποί ἐσμεν; δῶρόν ἐστι; κακοί εἰσι; τῶν στρατιωτῶν ἐστιν ἡ σκηνή.

3. *Emphatic* ἔστι. When used emphatically, that is, placed at the beginning of the sentence, the third person singular form is accented on *P*: ἔστι(ν). This form is also used when the proclitic οὐκ, εἰ (*if*), or ὡς (*as, that*) or the conjunction καί (*and*) or ἀλλά (*but*) or the demonstrative τοῦτ' (*this*) immediately precedes. Emphatic ἔστι may stress existence ("there is . . . ") or may be used with an infinitive subject in the same sense as the compound ἔξεστι ("it is possible to X").

4. *Infinitive* εἶναι. The present active infinitive of εἰμί is εἶναι. When an infinitive phrase with εἶναι includes a predicate noun or predicate adjective, the word in the predicate must agree in case with the subject of the infinitive. Since the subject of an infinitive is normally accusative, the predicate noun or adjective will normally be accusative.

> **Ex.** ἐκ τοῦ τοὺς πολίτας δικαίους εἶναι
> *as a result of the fact that the citizens are just*
>
> χαλεπὸν ἀγαθὸν εἶναι.
> *It is difficult to be brave.*

(The unexpressed subject of εἶναι, "one," "a man," or whatever, is felt to be acc., so the adjective is acc.)

Occasionally the predicate adj. will be in another case:

> **Ex.** οὐκ ἔξεστι τῷ δικαίῳ ἀνοσίῳ εἶναι.
> *It is not possible for the just man to be unholy.*

5. *Some Uses of the Genitive.* The genitive in general limits the meaning of the substantive, adjective, adverb, or verb on which it depends. The Latin name *genitivus* is a translation of the Greek γενική (πτῶσις) = "the case denoting the class [to which something belongs]."

a. *Genitive of Possession.* Like the English possessive or prepositional phrase with *of*, the genitive may denote ownership, possession, or the like.

(1) *Attributive Use.* The genitive of a noun or of a demonstrative or reflexive pronoun placed in attributive position (i.e., within article–noun phrase)[1] may denote possession. (Personal pronouns denoting possession fall outside of the article–noun group: see U22.6.)

> οἱ τῶν Ἀθηναίων νόμοι   *the Athenians' laws*
> τὸ βιβλίον τὸ τοῦ παιδίου   *the child's book*
> τὰ τῶν ναυτῶν   *the affairs, possessions,*
>   or *deeds of the sailors* (see U7.4)

An attributive genitive of possession may also be attached to a noun that is not accompanied by the article:

> Αἰσώπου λόγοι   *fables of Aesop*

(2) *Predicate Use.* The genitive of a noun or pronoun in the predicate may denote possession.

> ἡ ἵππος ἐστὶ τοῦ δικαστοῦ.
> *The mare belongs to the juryman.* (*The mare is of the juryman.*)

---

1. This is the normal position, but the gen. of possession is occasionally found outside the article–noun group.

τοῦ σοφοῦ ἐστι φέρειν πόνους.
It is characteristic of the wise man to endure toils.
[literally, *To endure toils is of, belongs to, the wise man.*]

b. *Partitive Genitive.* The genitive is used to denote the whole, a part of which is expressed by the noun it limits. This genitive takes the predicate position, that is, it falls outside the article–noun group.

οἱ πλεῖστοι τῶν συμμάχων   *most of the allies*

c. *Subjective and Objective Genitive.* When a noun expresses a verbal notion, the subject of the action referred to by the noun may be expressed by the *subjective genitive* (often in attributive position).

clause form: *The unjust man committed perjury.*   (subject–verb)
verbal noun form: *the unjust man's perjury*
                    ἡ τοῦ ἀδίκου ἐπιορκία   (verbal noun with gen.)

clause form: *The foreigners are afraid.*   (subject–verb)
verbal noun form: *the foreigners' fear*
                    ὁ τῶν βαρβάρων φόβος   (verbal noun with gen.)

(The subjective genitive is easily confused with the possessive genitive and in many cases such confusion makes no difference.)

The object of the action referred to by a noun expressing a verbal notion may be expressed by the *objective genitive* (normally in predicate position).

verb–object form: *to desire pleasures*
verbal noun form: *the desire of (for) pleasures*
                    ἡ ἐπιθυμία τῶν ἡδονῶν   (verbal noun with gen.)

verb–object form: *to be afraid of the Athenians*
verbal noun form: *fear of the Athenians*
                    φόβος τῶν Ἀθηναίων   (verbal noun with gen.)

6. *Some Uses of the Dative.* The Greek dative (δοτική, Latin *dativus,* case of "giving to") has instrumental and locative uses (Greek having lost these cases at an early stage: see Introd. §4) as well as uses belonging to the dative proper.

a. *Dative of Indirect Object.* See U8.9.

b. *Dative of Interest.* The dative is used to denote the person for whom something is or is done. Several uses of the dative are classified under this general heading:

(1) *Dative of Possession.* With verbs meaning *to be, to become, to be available*, and the like, the dative may be used to denote the possessor.

> τῷ δικαίῳ παρὰ τῶν θεῶν δῶρά ἐστιν.
> *There are gifts from the gods for the just man.*
>
> or   *The just man has gifts from the gods.*
>
> τοῖς Ἀθηναίοις σύμμαχοι ἀγαθοί εἰσιν.
> *There are brave allies for the Athenians.*
>
> or   *The Athenians have brave allies.*

The dative of possession emphasizes having vs. not having something; the genitive of possession, on the other hand, emphasizes that something belongs to X and not to anybody else.

ἔστι βιβλία τῷ ποιητῇ.	*The poet has books.*
οὐκ ἔστι βιβλία τῷ ποιητῇ.	*The poet has no books.*
τὰ βιβλία ἐστὶ τοῦ δικαστοῦ, οὐ τοῦ ποιητοῦ.	*The books belong to the juryman, not to the poet.*

(2) *Dative of Advantage or Disadvantage.* The dative is used to denote the person or thing for whose advantage or disadvantage something is or is done.

> τὰ παιδία αἴτια πόνων τοῖς ἀνθρώποις.
> *Children are a cause of toil for mankind.*
>
> ὁ ἀγαθὸς πλούσιός ἐστι τοῖς πολίταις, οὐχ ἑαυτῷ.
> *The virtuous man is rich for (in the interest of, to the advantage of) his fellow citizens, not for himself.*

(3) *Dative of Reference.* See U9.5.

c. *Dative of Means (or Instrument).* The dative is used to denote that by which or with which an action is done (instrument, means, or cause).

> βάλλουσι τὸν στρατηγὸν λίθοις.
> *They strike the general with stones.*
>
> δώροις πείθει τοὺς δικαστάς.
> *He persuades the jurymen by means of bribes.*

d. *Dative of Time When.* The dative is used to denote the point in time when or at which an action occurred.

> τῇ προτέρᾳ ἡμέρᾳ   *on the previous day*

WHAT TO STUDY AND DO

1. Learn the present of εἰμί.
2. Study the uses of the genitive and dative.
3. Learn the vocabulary of this unit.
4. Do the exercises of this unit.

VOCABULARY

verbs

βάλλω	throw, strike [ballistics]
εἰμί	be [ontology (from the participial stem)]
εὑρίσκω	find, find out, discover [heuristic, Eureka]
πάσχω	have (something) done to one, experience; suffer [sympathy]
πράττω[1] [ā]	effect, accomplish, do; experience (a certain fortune), fare [practical]

nouns

ἀνάγκη, ἀνάγκης, f.	force, constraint, necessity
ἀνάγκη (ἐστί)	(impersonal expression) it is necessary (compulsory, unavoidable)[2] (+ dat. or acc. of person + inf.) (often to be translated with *must* in a personal construction)
εἰρήνη, εἰρήνης, f.	peace; peace treaty [Irene]
ἐπιθυμία, ἐπιθυμίας, f.	desire, yearning
ἐπιορκία, ἐπιορκίας, f.	false swearing, perjury
λίθος, λίθου, m.	stone [monolith]
(as fem.)	a particular variety of stone, e.g., magnet, crystal
μάχη, μάχης, f.	battle, combat [Titanomachy]

adjectives

Ἀθηναῖος, Ἀθηναία, Ἀθηναῖον	Athenian
οἱ Ἀθηναῖοι	the Athenians
αἴτιος, αἰτία, αἴτιον	responsible; responsible for, cause of (+ objective gen.) [aetiology]
πλεῖστος, πλείστη, πλεῖστον	most, greatest, largest; (often with art.) the greatest number, the most [pleistocene]
οἱ πλεῖστοι	the majority, the greatest part (of a group)

---

1. Non-Attic πράσσω (or Ionic πρήσσω): cf. Intro. §6.

2. ἀνάγκη in this use connotes strong external constraint, whereas δεῖ and χρή connote needfulness, propriety, moral obligation, and the like.

πρότερος, προτέρα,   former, earlier, previous   [hysteron proteron]
  πρότερον
ὕστερος, ὑστέρα, ὕστερον   latter, later, next

EXERCISES

I. Translate the following short sentences.

1. ἀθάνατοί εἰσι.   6. πονηρὸς εἶ.
2. οὐκ ἀγαθοί ἐστε.   7. οὐ σοφοί ἐσμεν.
3. ἄδικόν ἐστι.   8. σοφή ἐστιν.
4. φίλος εἰμί.   9. χαλεπόν ἐστι.
5. δῆλόν ἐστι.   10. ὅσιαί ἐστε.

II. Render the following sentences into Greek, using the appropriate form of
εἰμί. Think carefully about the accentuation and review the rules if necessary.

      Ex.   *I am harsh.*   χαλεπός εἰμι.   or   χαλεπή εἰμι.

1. It is worthy.   6. You (sing.) are pious.
2. The Athenians are responsible. 7. You (pl.) are just.
3. The battle is long.   8. Perjury is not just.
4. We are immortal.   9. She is responsible.
5. I am a sailor.   10. The pebble is small.

III. (a) Translate the following sentences. Then (b) name the case of the underlined word and give the reason for the case.

      Ex.   τῷ σοφῷ βιβλία ἐστίν.
              (a) *The wise man has books.*   (b) dative of possession

1. οἱ πλεῖστοι τῶν πολιτῶν εἰσι δίκαιοι.
2. τῷ πονηρῷ οἱ νόμοι οὔκ εἰσι[1] καλοί.
3. ἡ ἐπιθυμία τοῦ πλούτου τοὺς ἀνθρώπους κακὰ πάσχειν πείθει.
4. τῇ ὑστέρᾳ ἡμέρᾳ εἰρήνην γράφουσιν.
5. οἱ ἀθάνατοί εἰσιν αἴτιοι τῶν ἀγαθῶν τοῖς ἀνθρώποις.
6. τῶν Ἀθηναίων ἐστὶν ἡ νίκη.
7. οἱ ἀνόσιοι τὸ ἱερὸν λίθοις βάλλουσιν.
8. οὐ δεῖ λέγειν τὸν τῶν πολεμίων φόβον.
9. ἔστι τὸ καλόν.
10. ἐν τῇ προτέρᾳ μάχῃ οἱ πλεῖστοι τῶν ὁπλιτῶν οὐ φεύγουσιν.

IV. Render into Greek.

1. By means of difficult toils the allies are taking the marketplace.

---

1. Remember that a proclitic followed by an enclitic receives an acute accent (U2.12d).

2. It is necessary for men to do what is just [= just things].
3. After the battle the soldiers flee into the land of the Athenians.
4. The desire for peace persuades the citizens not to harm the enemy's messengers.
5. The jurors are discovering the majority of the unjust deeds.
6. It is characteristic of wise men to discover the fine pleasures.
7. On account of the war against the foreigners the citizens must suffer.
8. It does not befit a virtuous man to be unjust.
9. In the eyes of the majority pleasure is not the measure of virtue.

UNIT ELEVEN

Ω-Verbs: Present Middle/Passive Indicative

---

1. *Middle and Passive.* At an early stage Greek had two sets of personal endings which served to mark two *voices* (cf. U.8 Prelim.): active and middle. In the active voice the subject is the agent. In the middle voice the subject is agent but acts with some special reference to himself/herself, or to his/her possessions or own interest (*to* or *for* or *within himself/herself* or the like).

The middle sometimes has a reflexive or reciprocal meaning:

γυμνάζομαι	*I exercise myself.* (direct reflexive)
παρασκευάζομαι τὴν σκηνήν.	*I prepare the tent for myself.*
	or *I prepare my tent.*
	(indirect reflexive)
οἱ στρατιῶται παρακελεύονται.	*The soldiers encourage one*
	another. (reciprocal)

From the reflexive force of the middle there developed the passive use of the middle form, so that in classical Greek most middle forms also serve as passive (that is, the subject is acted upon by some other agent). The development may be thought of as follows:

πείθομαι: *I persuade myself.* —> *I get myself persuaded.* —> *I am persuaded (by someone else).*

φέρεται: *It carries itself.* —> *It gets itself carried.* —> *It is carried.*

(Compare reflexive formations in other languages that are translated by the English passive, such as French *il se trouve* or German *es sich findet* = "it is located" or Italian *mi chiamo* = "I am called.")

In the context of a Greek sentence, a middle/passive verb will usually be identifiable as *either* middle *or* passive in sense; but in isolation these forms are referred to in this book as middle/passive.

When a Greek verb is used in the passive, the personal agent, if mentioned, is usually expressed in a prepositional phrase with ὑπό + gen. (equivalent to English *by someone*).

2. *Present Middle/Passive Indicative.* This is formed from the present stem plus the theme vowel o/ϵ (o before μ or ν, ϵ before other sounds) plus the middle/passive personal endings (-μαι, -σαι, -ται, [-σθον, -σθον,] -μεθα, -σθε, -νται). The personal endings are clearly recognizable except in the second person singular, where the elimination of intervocalic sigma[1] in -εσαι allows contraction of -εαι to -ῃ.

| **Ex.** | | "ransom," "be released" | "obey," "be persuaded" | *theme vowel* |
	present stem:	λυ- + o/ϵ	πειθ- + o/ϵ	*+ ending*
sing.	*1st pers.*	λύομαι	πείθομαι	-ομαι
	2nd pers.	λύῃ	πείθῃ	-ῃ[2]
	3rd pers.	λύεται	πείθεται	-εται
(dual	*2nd pers.*	λύεσθον	πείθεσθον)	(-εσθον)
(3rd pers.		λύεσθον	πείθεσθον)	(-εσθον)
plur.	*1st pers.*	λυόμεθα	πειθόμεθα	-ομεθα
	2nd pers.	λύεσθε	πείθεσθε	-εσθε
	3rd pers.	λύονται	πείθονται	-ονται

Note that the *accentuation* is recessive, as for all finite forms. In the present middle/passive indicative it turns out that the accent is on the verb stem in all forms except the first person plural, where the number of syllables in the ending forces the accent to move to the theme vowel.

3. *Present Middle/Passive Infinitive.* The middle infinitive ending is -σθαι. When this is added to the present stem with theme vowel ϵ, the result is the present middle/passive infinitive. Like the present active infinitive, it is accented on the final syllable of the verb stem: for example, λύεσθαι = "*to ransom*" or "*to be released.*"

4. *Deponent Verbs.* Many Greek verbs are found only in middle/passive forms and have no active forms. Such verbs are called *deponent* (a not very helpful term coined by Latin grammarians). You will recognize deponent

---

1. Sigma "between vowels" (intervocalic) was lost in the development of many Greek forms, and in Attic this loss usually resulted in the contraction of the vowels.

2. From about 350 B.C.E. the second person singular middle/passive ending was often spelled (and pronounced) -ει rather than -ῃ in Attic, and the form in -ει will be found in modern editions of some Greek authors (either under the influence of the manuscripts or because the editor believes the particular author originally used this form). Note that such middle/passive forms as λύει, πείθει look exactly like the third sing. active form; but in the context of a sentence there is usually no ambiguity.

verbs in vocabulary lists or a dictionary because the first principal part is the first person singular present middle/passive form (-ομαι instead of -ω).

Ex. γίγνομαι *I become, I am born*
βούλομαι *I desire, I want*
αἰσθάνομαι *I perceive*

5. *Idiomatic Meanings of the Middle.* It takes time for the student to get an adequate sense of the range of implications conveyed by the middle voice. Here are some examples of common verbs to illustrate shifts in meaning noticeable between active and middle.

ἔχω + acc. *I have, hold*
ἔχομαι + gen. *I hold on to, cling to*

γράφω *I write*
γράφομαι *I indict, bring a suit against* (literally, *I get X['s name] recorded by the magistrates*)

φέρω *I carry*
φέρομαι *I carry off for myself, I win (a prize)*

δικάζω *I (as a judge) decide a suit*
δικάζομαι *I (as a plaintiff) conduct a suit*

σπένδω *I pour a libation*
σπένδομαι *I make a truce* (solemnized by a libation)

λύω *I release*
λύομαι *I ransom*

βουλεύω *I plan*
βουλεύομαι *I deliberate*

πολιτεύω *I am a citizen*
πολιτεύομαι *I behave like a citizen, I participate in public affairs, I am a politician*

πείθω + acc. *I persuade, urge*
πείθομαι + dat. *I obey, trust, believe (a person)*

As can be seen, the middle usually implies that the subject is more closely involved or interested in the action. The middle is common when emphasis is laid on mental or perceptual activities (note the deponent αἰσθάνομαι and several verbs of intellectual activity which lack a future active but possess a future middle [U18.9]).

WHAT TO STUDY AND DO

1. Learn the conjugation of the present middle/passive indicative and the formation of the present middle/passive infinitive.
2. Study the idiomatic meanings of the middle (§5).
3. Learn the vocabulary of this unit.
4. Do the exercises of this unit.

VOCABULARY

ω-verbs

ἀκούω	hear (usually with acc. of thing heard + gen. of person from whom it is heard, usually with prep. ἀπό, ἐκ, etc.) [acoustics]
ἀποκτείνω (ἀπο)	kill, put to death
βουλεύω	plan, devise; (mid.) take counsel, deliberate [probouleutic]
γυμνάζω	train (naked), exercise; (mid.) exercise oneself, be in training [gymnastics, gymnasium]
δικάζω	judge; serve as judge or juror; (mid.) plead a case, participate in a suit
παρασκευάζω (παρα)	prepare, provide, procure; (mid.) prepare for oneself, make preparations
πολῑτεύω	be a citizen; have a certain form of government; (mid.) live or behave as a free citizen; participate in politics
σπένδω	pour a libation;[1] (mid.) exchange libations, make a truce, make peace [spondaic]

deponent verbs

αἰσθάνομαι	perceive, sense, understand [esthetics]
βούλομαι	want, desire, wish (+ complementary inf.)[2]
γίγνομαι	come into being, be born, become [genus]
ἔρχομαι	come, go
μάχομαι	fight (+ dat. of the enemy person or + prep. phrase)
οἴομαι or οἶμαι[3]	think, suppose, believe

---

1. In Greco-Roman antiquity a "libation" was a ritual offering of liquid to the gods; it was made by pouring the liquid on an altar or on the ground. The liquid could be wine, milk, honey, oil, or a mixture.

2. In poetry βούλομαι and ἐθέλω may be synonymous, but in classical prose there is often a clear distinction between active desire (βούλομαι) and willingness or consent (ἐθέλω).

3. οἶμαι is a contracted form of οἴομαι. The remaining forms of the present are normal: οἴῃ, οἴεται, etc., inf. οἴεσθαι.

παρακελεύομαι   exhort, encourage (+ dat. of person, sometimes +
                                     inf.)

πυνθάνομαι   learn, hear; learn by inquiry, inquire

EXERCISES

I. Give a complete identification of each verb form and translate it precisely.

   Ex.   παρασκευαζόμεθα: 1st pl. pres. mid/pass. ind. of παρασκευάζω,
              we are making preparations

1. σπένδομεν	11. λέγεται	21. φέρονται
2. μάχῃ	12. οἴεσθε	22. βλάπτετε
3. κόπτομαι	13. πάσχετε	23. βάλλεται
4. γράφονται	14. εἰσί	24. ἄγῃ
5. λαμβάνεις	15. πολιτεύεσθαι	25. παρακελεύεσθε
6. γίγνεται	16. βούλεται	26. πυνθάνονται
7. πράττειν	17. δικάζουσι	27. δικάζεται
8. βουλεύομαι	18. σπενδόμεθα	28. ἀκούομεν
9. ἔρχονται	19. ἀποκτείνει	29. λείπεται
10. ἔχῃ	20. αἰσθάνῃ	30. γίγνονται

II. Render into Greek.

1. we are going	16. they are fighting
2. he serves as judge	17. you (s.) suppose
3. you (pl.) cling to	18. it is being led
4. they desire	19. we are indicting
5. you (s.) are making preparations	20. they become
6. he is pleading a case	21. we are being ruled
7. they pour a libation	22. to learn by inquiry
8. you (pl.) are deliberating	23. I am not willing
9. you (s.) exhort	24. to prepare
10. we inquire	25. she supposes
11. she is ransoming	26. we are
12. they hear	27. to be
13. you (pl.) are being marshaled	28. he is being stricken
14. to be in training	29. to be carried
15. I participate in politics	30. you (pl.) are finding

III. Translate.

1. ἐν τῷ πρὸς τοὺς βαρβάρους πολέμῳ ἀγαθοῖς πολεμίοις μάχονται οἱ
   Ἀθηναῖοι.
2. τοὺς στρατηγοὺς χρὴ βουλεύεσθαι.
3. τοὺς ὁπλίτας κελεύουσι τάττεσθαι παρὰ τὸν ποταμόν.

4. οὐ φεύγειν ἐθέλουσιν οἱ πλεῖστοι τῶν στρατιωτῶν.
5. χαλεποῖς ἔργοις νίκη τοῖς Ἀθηναίοις γίγνεται.
6. σπένδονται τῇ ὑστέρᾳ ἡμέρᾳ.
7. ἔχεσθαι χρὴ τῆς τιμῆς.
8. ὑπὸ [= by] τῶν πολεμίων οὐ βλάπτεσθε.
9. οὐκ ἔξεστι τοῖς παιδίοις τοῖς θεοῖς σπένδειν.
10. οἱ ναῦται πρὸς τὴν τῶν βαρβάρων χώραν τοῖς ἀνέμοις ἐλαύνονται.

UNIT TWELVE

Adverbs; Conjunctions; Prepositions II; Relative Pronoun

PRELIMINARIES

A. *Adverbs*. An adverb (Greek ἐπίρρημα, Latin *adverbium* = "word added to the verb") is that part of speech which modifies (qualifies, limits) a verb, an adjective, or another adverb. Adverbs usually express ideas of manner or degree or time or place.

They walk <u>quickly</u>.	(modifying verb *walk*)
The pitcher is <u>fairly</u> good.	(modifying adj. *good*)
The house is <u>very</u> poorly constructed.	(modifying adverb *poorly*)

In many languages a large number of the adverbs are derived from adjectives by the addition of a standard suffix. In English the suffix is *-ly* (cf. German *-lich*, French *-ment*, Spanish and Italian *-mente*).

B. *Sentences and Clauses.* A *simple sentence* contains one subject–verb unit (although subject or verb or both may be multiple). It consists of a single *independent* or *main* clause (a clause that can stand by itself).

Ex. *The sailor leaves the marketplace.*
The sailor picks up his gear and leaves.
The sailor and the merchant leave the marketplace.
The woman and her daughter hug and kiss.

A *compound* sentence consists of two (or more) independent clauses joined together (though each clause is capable of standing on its own).

Ex. *The woman waves, and her daughter waves back.*

A *complex* sentence consists of an independent or main clause and one or more *dependent* or *subordinate* clauses, that is, clauses which do not by themselves form a sentence and cannot be uttered in isolation. In the following examples the subordinate clauses are underlined:

<u>*When the sailor arrived*</u>, *they called a meeting.*

83

The messenger <u>who came yesterday</u> told a different story.

C.   *Conjunctions.* A conjunction (Greek σύνδεσμος, Latin *coniunctio* = "bond, joining") is that part of speech which joins together two or more words, phrases, or clauses. There are two kinds of conjunctions. A *coordinating* conjunction links two elements (words, phrases, clauses) which are on an equal footing. A *subordinating* conjunction links a dependent clause to a clause of more independent standing (either an actual independent clause or another dependent clause which is grammatically superordinate). For instance,

the boy <u>and</u> his dog	(coordinating two nouns)
in the city <u>or</u> in the country	(coordinating two phrases)
He knocked, <u>but</u> nobody answered.	(coordinating two independent clauses)

<u>If</u> he is found guilty, he will pay a large fine.
(subordinating the conditional clause to the main clause *he will pay a large fine*)

The truce which was concluded <u>after</u> Cleon died lasted more than a year.
(subordinating the temporal clause *after Cleon died* to the relative clause *which was concluded*, which is itself subordinate to the main clause *the truce lasted*)

A number of common Greek conjunctions and adverbs with connective and emphatic force are traditionally termed *particles.* In a beginning course a student is exposed to only a few particles, but they are an important part of Greek idiom and should be studied in detail in conjunction with the student's later reading of Greek texts.

D.   *Pronouns.* A pronoun (Greek ἀντωνυμία, Latin *pronomen* = "substitute for a noun") is that part of speech which takes the place of a noun already used or obvious from the context. The noun which a pronoun replaces (or the person or thing to which it is understood to refer) is its *antecedent.*

Jane called Jim, <u>who</u> had called <u>her</u> earlier.
(The antecedent of *who* is *Jim*; the antecedent of *her* is *Jane*.)

Like nouns, pronouns have gender (*he, she, it; who, which*), number (*I, we*), and case (*she, her, hers; who, whom, whose*). Normally, a pronoun has the same gender and number as its antecedent, but its case is determined by its function in its own sentence or clause.

There are seven types of pronouns: personal, demonstrative, relative, interrogative, indefinite, reflexive, and reciprocal. The relative pronoun is presented in this unit; the others will be considered in detail in later units.

E.   *Relative Clauses.* A dependent clause which serves as an adjective modifying a noun is called a *relative* clause and is introduced by a *relative pronoun* (*who, which, that*) or a *relative adverb* (*where, when*). These words are called *relative* because while introducing a subordinate clause they refer back to (relate to) an element of the main (or other superordinate) clause.

Ex.   The man <u>whom we saw</u> looked familiar.
          (*whom* is masculine and singular to agree with its antecedent *man*, but it is in the objective case because it is the object of the verb *saw* in its own clause)
          This is the thing <u>that bothers me</u>.
          Leave it in the place <u>where you found it</u>.

Note that in English the relative pronoun may be omitted (*The man <u>we saw</u> looked familiar*), but that other languages, including Greek, require that it always be expressed.

∷

1. *Formation of Adverbs.* Adverbs expressing *manner* are formed from adjectival stems by the addition of the adverbial ending -ωs (in origin an ablative case ending). The stem of vowel-declension adjectives is obvious from the nominative singular forms. The accentuation of the adverb always follows the pattern of the gen. pl. form of the adjective.

Ex.

adjective	(gen. pl.)	adverb	
καλός	(καλῶν)	καλῶς	*nobly, beautifully, well*
κακός	(κακῶν)	κακῶς	*badly, poorly, ill*
ἄξιος	(ἀξίων)	ἀξίως	*worthily*
ῥᾴδιος	(ῥᾳδίων)	ῥᾳδίως	*easily*

Although adverbs can be formed in this way from virtually any adjective in Greek, no -ωs adverb is formed from ἀγαθός in classical Greek, the adverb εὖ (= *well*) being used instead.

2. *Coordinating Conjunctions.* There are five common coordinating conjunctions in Greek.

a. καί = *and*, joining words, phrases, or clauses. In addition to the simple use as a conjunction, there are other uses of καί to note:

καὶ X καὶ Y = <u>both</u> X *and* Y

adverbial καί: καί was in origin an adverb meaning *also*, and is often still
used as adverb adding emphasis to the word or phrase that follows it. In
its adverbial use, καὶ X may be translated *even X, X too, X also*, or in
English one may simply give extra emphasis to X in pronunciation.

Ex.   ἀνάγκη καὶ τῷ σοφῷ πάσχειν κακά.
            It is necessary that even the wise man suffer hardships.
            or *The wise man, too, must suffer hardships.*

   b. τε = *and*, an enclitic *postpositive* conjunction joining clauses, phrases,
or single words. A postpositive is a word which cannot be placed first in its
clause or phrase but normally follows the first word of its clause or phrase.
This conjunction is etymologically related to and similar in usage to Latin
-que. τε may be used alone or in combination with καί. (τε is elided to τ'
before a vowel with smooth breathing or to θ' before a vowel with rough
breathing.)

Ex.   X Y τε = *X and Y*
            ὅσιος δίκαιός τε = *pious and just*

            X τε Y τε = *both X and Y*
            ἡδονή τε τιμή τε = *both pleasure and honor*

            X τε καὶ Y = *both X and Y*
            ἔχει τε καὶ ἔχεται = *she (both) holds and is held*

   c. δέ = *and, but*, a postpositive conjunction most often found joining
clauses, but occasionally linking phrases or single words. δέ can be either neu-
trally connective (*and*) or adversative in sense (*but*); the context normally
helps decide which English equivalent is appropriate. (δέ is elided to δ' before
a vowel.)

   d. X μέν ... Y δέ. A very important use of δέ, and one which is especially characteristic of Greek thought and idiom, is its use in combination with
the postpositive particle μέν to create a contrast between antithetic elements
(or sometimes simply an emphatic link between enumerated elements). The
force of μέν is to anticipate an antithesis by marking its beginning; the second
element is most often joined by δέ. The contrasted elements may be single
words, parallel phrases, or entire clauses. A common, but clumsy, English
translation of μὲν ... δέ is *on the one hand ... on the other hand*; often it is
more idiomatic to convey the antithesis by emphasis in pronunciation or by
turning one of the paired clauses into an English subordinate clause introduced
by *while* or *whereas*.

Ex. ὁ μὲν στρατηγὸς ἀποθνήσκει, οἱ δὲ στρατιῶται φεύγουσιν.
The <u>general</u> is dying, but the <u>soldiers</u> are fleeing.

οἱ μὲν Ἀθηναῖοι πείθονται τοῖς νόμοις, οἱ δὲ βάρβαροι τῷ δεσπότῃ.
The Athenians obey their laws, whereas the Persians obey their master.

(Note the position of the postpositives in these sentences: words like τε, μέν, and δέ often intervene between an article and its noun or between a preposition and its object; less commonly, the postpositive may be placed after the phrase unit, for instance, after article–noun unit.)

e. γάρ = *for, because*, a postpositive joining clauses (be careful to distinguish between English *for* as a conjunction and as preposition).

Ex. τὸν δικαστὴν ἐξελαύνειν βουλόμεθα· δῶρα γὰρ λαμβάνει.
We want to drive out the judge, for he is taking bribes.

f. ἀλλά = *but, but rather*, a strong adversative joining clauses or less often phrases or words, usually following a stated or implied negative. (ἀλλά is elided to ἀλλ᾽ before a vowel.)

Ex. οὐκ ἔστι ποταμός, ἀλλὰ θάλαττα.
It is not a river, but rather the sea.

3. *Pronominal Use of the Article.* The Attic article ὁ, ἡ, τό was originally a demonstrative pronoun (this is the usual function of the word in Homeric Greek and other early poetry). The pronominal use survives in classical Attic in certain restricted circumstances: namely, preceding μέν and δέ when they are paired, or preceding δέ used alone. With μέν . . . δέ the pronominal article usually means *the one . . . the other . . .* or (plural) *some . . . others . . .*; with δέ alone, the pronominal article usually makes a change of grammatical subject from the previous sentence and may be translated by *he, she, it, they*. The pronominal article may be used in any of the three genders, agreeing in gender and number with its antecedent.

Ex. <u>τοὺς μὲν</u> ἀποκτείνουσι, <u>τοὺς δ᾽</u> ἄγουσιν.
They kill <u>some</u> and carry off <u>others</u>.

<u>αἱ μὲν</u> μένουσιν, <u>αἱ δὲ</u> φεύγουσιν.
<u>These women</u> are staying, but <u>the other women</u> are fleeing.

τὸν ποιητὴν βουλεύεσθαι πείθομεν· <u>ὁ δ᾽</u> οὐκ ἐθέλει.
We are urging the poet to take counsel, but <u>he</u> is unwilling to do so. (note change of subject from *we* to *he*)

4. *Prepositions II*

ἀνά + acc.	up, up along, throughout
ἀντί + gen.	instead of, in place of, in return for
κατά + gen.	down from, down upon; against (the interests of a person); concerning
κατά + acc.	down along, over, throughout; in accordance with
περί + gen.	about, concerning; above, beyond
περί + dat.	around (position); about (an object for which one struggles)
περί + acc.	around (motion); about, concerning
πρό + gen.	in front of; in defense of; before (of time or preference)
ὑπέρ + gen.	over, above (of motion or position); in defense of; concerning
ὑπέρ + acc.	over, across, beyond (of motion or position)
ὑπό + gen.	from under, under; by (agent with passive verb or expression)
ὑπό + dat.	under; under the power of
ὑπό + acc.	under; during, in the course of

5. *Examples of Usage of These Prepositions*

ἀνὰ τὸν ποταμόν	*up (upstream) along the river*
ἀν᾽ Ἑλλάδα	*throughout Greece*
ἀντὶ τούτων	*in return (exchange) for these things*
ἀντ᾽ ἀγαθῶν	*instead of good men* (they have become bad men)
κατὰ τῆς κεφαλῆς	(something poured) *down upon the head*
κατ᾽ Ὀλύμπου	*down from Olympus*
κατὰ τοῦ στρατηγοῦ	(speak, accuse) *against the general*
κατὰ τῶν βαρβάρων	(speak) *about, concerning the foreigners*
κατὰ τὸν ποταμόν	*down (downstream) along the river*
κατὰ τὴν χώραν	*throughout the land*
κατὰ τὸν πρότερον πόλεμον	*all during the previous war*
κατὰ μοῖραν	*in accordance with destiny*
κατὰ λόγον	*in accordance with reason*
περὶ τῆς ἀρετῆς	*concerning virtue*
περὶ πάντων τῶν ἄλλων	(superiority) *above all others*

περὶ τῇ κεφαλῇ	(a crown) *around one's head*
περὶ τῇ τιμῇ	(compete) *over, concerning honor*
περὶ Πελοπόννησον	(a fleet sailing) *around the Peloponnese*
περὶ τὴν ἀρετήν	*in relation to, concerning virtue*
πρὸ τῶν θυρῶν	*in front of the doors*
πρὸ τῆς χώρας	*on behalf of the land*
πρὸ τοῦ πολέμου	*before the war*
ὑπὲρ τοῦ ποταμοῦ	(position) *over, across the river*[1]
ὑπὲρ τῶν παιδίων	*on behalf of, in defense of the children*
ὑπὲρ τὸν Ἑλλήσποντον	(motion or position) *across, beyond the Hellespont*
ὑπὲρ μοῖραν	*beyond (in violation of) fate*
ὑπὸ γῆς	(position) *under the earth*
ὑπὸ τῶν πολιτῶν (πέμπεσθαι)	(personal agent) *(to be sent) by the citizens*
ὑπὸ τοῖς Ἀθηναίοις	(be ruled, controlled, enslaved, etc.) *under the power of the Athenians*
ὑπὸ γῆν	(motion) *under the earth*
ὑπὸ τὸν αὐτὸν χρόνον	*during the same period of time*

6. *Relative Pronoun.* The Attic Greek relative pronoun has the stem *h-* (that is, rough breathing) and is inflected in all three genders with the vowel-declension endings. The declension of ὅς, ἥ, ὅ, *who, which, that,* is as follows:

	singular				plural		
	masc.	*fem.*	*neut.*		*masc.*	*fem.*	*neut.*
nom.	ὅς	ἥ	ὅ		οἵ	αἵ	ἅ
gen.	οὗ	ἧς	οὗ		ὧν	ὧν	ὧν
dat.	ᾧ	ᾗ	ᾧ		οἷς	αἷς	οἷς
acc.	ὅν	ἥν	ὅ		οὕς	ἅς	ἅ

(dual, all genders	nom. acc.	ὥ)
	(gen. dat.	οἷν)

Note that the fem. sing. nom. and masc. and fem. pl. nom. are different from the same forms of the article only in that these forms of the article are conventionally written without accents. Similarly the masc. sing. nom. article ὁ is distinguished from neut. sing. nom. relative ὅ by the accent.

---

1. For this sense, the accusative is also found in phrases like ὑπὲρ τὸν ποταμόν, esp. in postclassical Greek.

7. *Use of the Relative Pronoun.* Relative pronouns serve as subordinating conjunctions introducing adjectival clauses. The relative pronoun agrees with its antecedent in gender and number; but the case of the relative pronoun is usually determined by its use in its own clause (an idiomatic exception will be learned later, in U38).

Ex.   *The soldier <u>whom</u> the general is striking is a coward.*
(antecedent of *whom* is *soldier*; *whom* is dir. obj. of *is striking*)
ὁ στρατιώτης <u>ὃν</u> ὁ στρατηγὸς κόπτει κακός ἐστιν.
(ὃν is masc. sing. because antecedent στρατιώτης is masc. sing.; it is acc. because it is direct object of κόπτει)

We do not want to abandon the woman with <u>whom</u> we are fleeing.
οὐ βουλόμεθα λείπειν τὴν ἄνθρωπον μεθ᾽ <u>ἧς</u> φεύγομεν.
(ἧς is fem. sing. because antecedent ἄνθρωπον is fem. sing.; it is gen. because it is object of preposition μετὰ = *with*)

WHAT TO STUDY AND DO

1. Learn the formation of adverbs and declension of the relative pronoun.
2. Study the examples of usage of the conjunctions and prepositions presented above.
3. Learn as vocabulary the conjunctions and prepositions and relative pronoun presented above (§2, 4, 6) and the remaining words presented below.
4. Do the exercises of this unit.

VOCABULARY

ω-verb

τύπτω	strike, beat	[tympanum]

adverbs not formed from adjectives

ἀεί (early Attic + poetic αἰεί, also poetic αἰέν)	always
αὖ	again; in turn
αὖθις	again; in turn; hereafter, in the future
αὐτίκα	at once, immediately
εἶτα	then, next; accordingly, therefore
ἔπειτα	then, next; therefore
ἐνθάδε	here, there
εὖ	well

ἤδη	already; immediately; actually, now
μάλα	very, exceedingly
νῦν	now, presently
τότε	at that time, then

EXERCISES

I.   Translate the following phrases.

1. πρὸ τῶν σκηνῶν
2. ὑπὸ τῷ ἀνοσίῳ δεσπότῃ
3. κατὰ τὴν τοῦ δικαστοῦ γνώμην
4. περὶ τῆς τῶν ᾿Αθηναίων τιμῆς
5. ὑπὲρ τῶν φίλων
6. ὑπὸ τοῖς πολεμίοις
7. ἀνὰ τὴν ὁδόν
8. κατὰ τὴν προτέραν ἡμέραν

9. ἀντὶ τῶν πόνων
10. ὑπὲρ τὴν θάλατταν
11. ὑπὸ τὴν σκηνήν
12. περὶ τὴν ἀγοράν
13. κατὰ τῶν κριτῶν
14. πρὸ τῆς μάχης
15. ἀντὶ τοῦ πλούτου
16. περὶ τῇ νίκῃ

II.   Translate.

1. οἱ μὲν σοφοὶ εὖ πράττουσιν, οἱ δὲ κακοὶ οὔ.[1]
2. οὐ πόλεμον βουλόμεθα ἔχειν ἀλλ᾿ εἰρήνην.
3. οἱ πολῖται σπένδουσι τοῖς θεοῖς οἳ μάχονται ὑπὲρ τῆς χώρας· αἴτιοι γάρ εἰσι τοῦ καλῶς πράττειν.
4. καλὴ ἡ χώρα ἡ ὑπὲρ τοῦ ποταμοῦ εἰς ἣν τὰ παιδία ἔρχεται.
5. ὑπὸ τῶν τ᾿ ᾿Αθηναίων καὶ τῶν συμμάχων ἤδη δικαίως βλάπτονται οἱ βάρβαροι.
6. τὸ δίκαια πράττειν χαλεπὸν μὲν τοῖς πλείστοις, ῥᾴδιον δὲ τοῖς σοφοῖς.
7. τοῖς πολίταις παρακελεύεται ὁσίοις εἶναι καὶ νῦν καὶ αὖθις.[2]
8. οἱ ἀγαθοὶ τὴν τιμὴν ἀντὶ τοῦ πλούτου ἔχειν ἀεὶ βούλονται.

III.   Render into Greek.

1. wisely, shamefully, badly, easily, unjustly
2. on behalf of the allies
3. in accordance with the laws of the foreigners
4. concerning democracy
5. The hoplites to whom we are entrusting the children are both just and pious.
6. One is telling the truth; the other is not.

---

1. Note that a proclitic receives an acute accent when it precedes a pause at a mark of punctuation, as here.
2. For the agreement of the predicate adj. here, review U10.4.

7. The sailors are going up (along) the river with difficulty, for they are being pelted with stones by the enemy.
8. The mares about which you are speaking belong not to the citizens, but to the gods.
9. One must always deliberate exceedingly wisely on behalf of the citizens.
10. It is not easy to obey a harsh law.

Contract Verbs in -έω;
Demonstratives

---

1. *Contract Verbs.* A large number of Greek verbs have present stems which end in one of the three vowels a, ϵ, o. The present-tense forms of these verbs have personal ending preceded by the theme vowel, preceded in turn by the final vowel of the stem. In Attic, as in several other dialects, the final a, ϵ, or o of the stem contracts with the theme vowel (or theme vowel plus personal ending, where these have coalesced).

2. *Verbs in* -έω. These are the most common type. The Attic contractions which are relevant to the present indicative are:

$\epsilon + \epsilon \quad \longrightarrow \epsilon\iota$ $\epsilon + o \quad \longrightarrow ov$ $\epsilon + \omega \quad \longrightarrow \omega$

$\epsilon + \epsilon\iota \quad \longrightarrow \epsilon\iota$ $\epsilon + ov \quad \longrightarrow ov$ $\epsilon + \eta \quad \longrightarrow \eta$

(Fuller general schemes for contraction are set out in Appendix 1.)

In the following paradigm the uncontracted form is illustrated in parentheses next to the contracted form which results from it in Attic:

Ex. ποιέω, *"make"*

		present active ind.		present middle/passive ind.	
sing.	*1st*	(ποιέω)	ποιῶ	(ποιέομαι)	ποιοῦμαι
	2nd	(ποιέεις)	ποιεῖς	(ποιέῃ)	ποιῇ
	3rd	(ποιέει)	ποιεῖ	(ποιέεται)	ποιεῖται
[*dual*	*2nd*	(ποιέετον)	ποιεῖτον	(ποιέεσθον)	ποιεῖσθον]
	[*3rd*	(ποιέετον)	ποιεῖτον	(ποιέεσθον)	ποιεῖσθον]
plur.	*1st*	(ποιέομεν)	ποιοῦμεν	(ποιεόμεθα)	ποιούμεθα
	2nd	(ποιέετε)	ποιεῖτε	(ποιέεσθε)	ποιεῖσθε
	3rd	(ποιέουσι)	ποιοῦσι(ν)	(ποιέονται)	ποιοῦνται

The present active infinitive ends in -εῖν (e.g., ποιεῖν from ποιέειν); the present middle/passive infinite ends in -εῖσθαι (e.g., ποιεῖσθαι from ποιέεσθαι).

Accentuation: the uncontracted forms of the indicative have the recessive accentuation that is normal in finite forms of the verb (in the infinitive the accent of the uncontracted form is on the last syllable of the stem, as for other ω-verbs). In contraction a circumflex accent results when the first of the two original vowels has the acute (as happens in all the forms above except 1st plural middle/passive -εόμεθα). An acute accent results when the second of the two original vowels has the acute (as in ποιούμεθα). When the two original vowels are both unaccented, the resulting vowel is also unaccented: this does not occur in the present, but you will encounter it in the imperfect in U16.

3. *Demonstratives.* Demonstratives are words which refer with extra emphasis, as if by pointing (hence the name): in English, *this, that, these, those.* Demonstratives function either as pronouns (standing alone, with an antecedent expressed or implied) or as adjectives (modifying a noun). The pronoun which became the Attic article was originally a demonstrative. There are three demonstratives in Attic.

a. ὅδε, ἥδε, τόδε = *this* or *that*, referring to something near, usually present or in sight. In some contexts it refers *forward* and may be translated as *the following.* ὅδε consists of the old demonstrative ὅ that became the Attic article plus an indeclinable demonstrative suffix -δε. The fact that -δε was originally a separate enclitic element accounts for the accentuation of forms like ἥδε or τούσδε, which are apparent exceptions to the rule that long accented *P* followed by short *U* must have the circumflex.

		masc.	*fem.*	*neut.*
sing.	nom.	ὅδε	ἥδε	τόδε
	gen.	τοῦδε	τῆσδε	τοῦδε
	dat.	τῷδε	τῇδε	τῷδε
	acc.	τόνδε	τήνδε	τόδε
(dual	n. a.	τώδε	τώδε	τώδε)
	(g. d.	τοῖνδε	τοῖνδε	τοῖνδε)
plural	nom.	οἵδε	αἵδε	τάδε
	gen.	τῶνδε	τῶνδε	τῶνδε
	dat.	τοῖσδε	ταῖσδε	τοῖσδε
	acc.	τούσδε	τάσδε	τάδε

b. οὗτος, αὕτη, τοῦτο = *this, the nearer*. When contrasted with ἐκεῖνος, οὗτος means *the latter* vs. *the former*. When contrasted with ὅδε, οὗτος refers backward (*the foregoing* vs. *the following*). When used by itself, οὗτος may refer either backward or forward. Note two oddities of declension: (1) the stem of most forms begins with tau, but the masc. and fem. nom. sing. and pl. have initial rough breathing (*h-*) instead (the same forms have *h-* instead of tau in the article); (2) the diphthong of the stem varies between *av* and *ov* depending on whether there is an *a*-vowel or *o*-vowel in the ending (phonetic assimilation): hence *av* appears in most of the fem. and in the neut. pl. nom. and accusative.

		masc.	*fem.*	*neut.*
sing.	nom.	οὗτος	αὕτη	τοῦτο
	gen.	τούτου	ταύτης	τούτου
	dat.	τούτῳ	ταύτῃ	τούτῳ
	acc.	τοῦτον	ταύτην	τοῦτο
(dual	n. a.	τούτω	τούτω	τούτω)
	(g. d.	τούτοιν	τούτοιν	τούτοιν)
plural	nom.	οὗτοι	αὗται	ταῦτα
	gen.	τούτων	τούτων	τούτων
	dat.	τούτοις	ταύταις	τούτοις
	acc.	τούτους	ταύτας	ταῦτα

c. ἐκεῖνος, ἐκείνη, ἐκεῖνο = *that one there, the more distant*. When contrasted with οὗτος, ἐκεῖνος means *the former* vs. *the latter*. It is declined like a normal vowel-declension adjective except that the neuter sing. nom./acc. have the ending -*o*, not -*ov* (also, dual forms of the fem. are the same as the masc.).

		masc.	*fem.*	*neut.*
sing.	nom.	ἐκεῖνος	ἐκείνη	ἐκεῖνο
	gen.	ἐκείνου	ἐκείνης	ἐκείνου
	dat.	ἐκείνῳ	ἐκείνῃ	ἐκείνῳ
	acc.	ἐκεῖνον	ἐκείνην	ἐκεῖνο
(dual	n. a.	ἐκείνω	ἐκείνω	ἐκείνω)
	(g. d.	ἐκείνοιν	ἐκείνοιν	ἐκείνοιν)
plural	nom.	ἐκεῖνοι	ἐκεῖναι	ἐκεῖνα
	gen.	ἐκείνων	ἐκείνων	ἐκείνων
	dat.	ἐκείνοις	ἐκείναις	ἐκείνοις
	acc.	ἐκείνους	ἐκείνας	ἐκεῖνα

4. *Position of Demonstrative Adjectives.* When a demonstrative is used as an adjective, the noun modified by the demonstrative has the definite article and the demonstrative is placed in the predicate position (outside the article–noun group). If a regular attributive adjective modifies the same noun, it has its usual position inside the article–noun group.

Ex. ταύτῃ τῇ ἡμέρᾳ or τῇ ἡμέρᾳ ταύτῃ *on this day*

   οἱ ναῦται ἐκεῖνοι or ἐκεῖνοι οἱ ναῦται *those sailors*

   πρὸς τῇδε τῇ μακρᾷ σκηνῇ or
   πρὸς τῇ μακρᾷ σκηνῇ τῇδε *next to this long tent*

WHAT TO STUDY AND DO

1. Learn the present indicative and infinitives of verbs in -έω.
2. Learn the declension and use of the demonstratives.
3. Learn as vocabulary the demonstratives presented above and the remaining words presented below.
4. Do the exercises of this unit.

VOCABULARY

Vocabulary-building Hints. A great many of the verbs in -έω are *denominative* verbs, that is, verbs formed from noun or adjective roots, meaning *to do* or *to be* whatever the root conveys. In this unit, note φιλέω from φίλος, φοβέω from φόβος, νοσέω from νόσος, ἀδικέω from ἄδικος.

contract verbs in -έω[1]

ἀδικέω	be unjust, do wrong; harm, do wrong to (someone [acc.])
αἱρέω	take, grasp, seize; (mid.) choose, elect [heresy]
ἀφικνέομαι (ἀπο)	arrive at, come to, reach
δέω[2]	lack, be in need of (+ gen.) (rare outside of certain fixed idioms)
δεῖ	it is necessary (already learned in U9)
δέομαι	want, be in need of (+ gen.) (more common than the active); beg, ask for (+ gen. of person + inf.)

---

1. In dictionaries and vocabulary lists contract verbs are traditionally listed under the uncontracted form, because this makes clear the stem of the verb (and the non-Attic forms). In the readings and exercises of this course the student should of course use the contracted forms.

2. Verbs in -έω with a monosyllabic stem, such as δέω, suffer contraction only when the theme vowel plus personal ending begins with ε. Thus the present active is, e.g., δέω, δεῖς, δεῖ, δέομεν, δεῖτε, δέουσι; present middle/passive δέομαι, δέῃ, δεῖται, δεόμεθα, δεῖσθε, δέονται.

δεῖται	(impersonal) there is need of (+ dat. of person and gen. of thing needed)
δοκέω	(commonly) seem (sometimes + dat. of person + inf.); (rarely in prose) think, suppose
δοκεῖ	it seems best (already learned in U9)
κρατέω	be strong; rule over (+ gen.); conquer (+ acc. or gen.) [democratic]
νοσέω	be sick
οἰκέω	inhabit, settle; manage (a house or a government); dwell, live [economy, ecology]
ποιέω	make, produce; do [poet]
φιλέω	love, like
φοβέω	put to flight; terrify, frighten
φοβέομαι	be afraid, be afraid of
ὠφελέω	help, aid

adverbs formed from demonstratives

ὧδε	in this way, thus, so very
οὕτω, (before vowel) οὕτως	in this manner, thus, so
ἐκεῖ	in that place, there

EXERCISES

I. Write in Greek.

1. we seem
2. they fear
3. you (s.) help
4. she arrives
5. he likes
6. I conquer
7. it is inhabited
8. we desire
9. they are sick
10. you (pl.) make a truce
11. to be afraid
12. they terrify
13. it is being produced
14. to seem
15. we are being aided

16. they order
17. I like
18. to be harmed
19. you (s.) become
20. you (pl.) seize
21. she is wronged
22. they are being led
23. they arrive
24. to be in need of
25. we make
26. you (s.) indict
27. you (s.) choose
28. it seems
29. I help
30. we are afraid

II. Translate each form precisely and give a complete identification of any
     ten of the forms.

1. νοσεῖτε   11. ἀδικεῖσθε   21. κρατοῦσι
2. δέονται   12. ἀφικνεῖται   22. οἰκοῦνται
3. δοκεῖν   13. φοβεῖν   23. αἱρούμεθα
4. φιλοῦμαι   14. ποιεῖς   24. φιλεῖτε
5. αἱροῦμεν   15. φοβούμεθα   25. πολιτεύῃ
6. ὠφελεῖ   16. πυνθάνεται   26. ἄρχετε
7. ἀφικνεῖσθαι   17. ἀκούεις   27. ποιεῖται
8. κρατῇ   18. εὑρίσκῃ   28. δοκεῖς
9. δοκοῦσι   19. ἀδικεῖν   29. ὠφελοῦμαι
10. οἰκῶ   20. δεῖ   30. γιγνόμεθα

III. Render each phrase into Greek in the designated case.

1. the following brave Athenians (acc.)   6. the former bad reputation (nom.)
2. that worthless ally (dat.)   7. these wealthy people (acc.)
3. this noble victory (nom.)   8. this hostile army (dat.)
4. these harsh toils (gen.)   9. those evil misfortunes (gen.)
5. those beloved children (acc.)   10. that clever deed (acc.)

IV. Translate.

1. οἱ βάρβαροι οὓς ἐκεῖνοι κρατοῦσιν ἐπὶ τῇ θαλάττῃ οἰκοῦσιν.
2. αὗται μὲν τὰ παιδία φοβοῦσιν, ἐκεῖναι δὲ φοβοῦνται.
3. ταύτῃ τῇ ἡμέρᾳ δοκεῖ τοῖς πολίταις εἰρήνην ποιεῖσθαι πρὸς τοὺς
   πολεμίους· νοσοῦσι γὰρ οἱ πλεῖστοι τῶν στρατιωτῶν.
4. ἐκεῖνοι τοὺς μὲν ἀγαθοὺς ἀδικοῦσι, τοὺς δὲ κακοὺς ὠφελοῦσιν.
5. τῷ σοφῷ στρατηγῷ δεῖται, οἶμαι, τῶνδε· τοῦ καλῶς βουλεύεσθαι πρὸ
   τῆς μάχης καὶ τοῦ εὖ πράττειν ἐν τῇ μάχῃ.
6. οὗτος ῥᾳδίως τιμὴν φέρεται· οὕτω δίκαιος καὶ σοφὸς τοῖς πολίταις δοκεῖ
   διὰ τοὺς καλοὺς νόμους οὓς γράφει.

V. Render into Greek.

1. This country is inhabited both by the Persians and by the Athenians.
2. Because of the earlier peace treaty the general is not permitted to help the
   people in the temple of the goddess.
3. Base men rule over most people, for good men are always unwilling to
   hold office [use ἄρχειν].
4. As a result of doing wrong but seeming virtuous, the unjust man wins for
   himself wealth and honor.
5. Of the young men, some are now arriving, others are already in training.

Consonant-Declension Nouns I

1. *Consonant Declension.* The consonant declension (also referred to as the *third* declension) is so termed because most of its nouns have stems ending in a consonant. But it is actually a diverse family of declension types (including some vowel stems) that share certain case endings. The consonant declension shows much more variety than the o- and a-declensions because some of its nouns have variable stems, with different forms of the stem appearing in different sets of cases, and some feature contraction of vowels in the endings. The various types will be learned over the course of several units. In the consonant declension it is essential to know *both* the nominative singular *and* the genitive singular in order to understand to which family a particular noun belongs and what form or forms of stem to use in the declension.

CONSONANT-DECLENSION ENDINGS

		masc./fem.	*neuter*
sing.	*nom.*	— or -ς	—
	gen.	-ος	-ος
	dat.	-ῐ	-ῐ
	acc.	-ᾰ or -ν[1]	—
	voc.	— or -ς	—
(dual	*n. a. v.)*	(-ε)	(-ε)
	(g. d.)	(-οιν)	(-οιν)
plur.	*nom./voc.*	-ες	-ᾰ
	gen.	-ων	-ων
	dat.	-σῐ(ν)	-σῐ(ν)
	acc.	-ᾰς	-ᾰ

---

1. The alternative masc./fem. acc. sing. endings are in origin the same (a zero-grade *n*-sound), but have developed to vowel -α or consonant -ν depending on the context.

The case endings shown on the previous page are historically valid, but in Attic Greek may appear in somewhat different forms because of various phonetic developments. In general, students need to pay special attention for each type of noun to the nom., acc., and voc. in the sing. and to the dat. pl. For instance, when the nom./voc. sing. ending -ς or the dat. pl. ending -σι is added to a stem ending in a consonant, the sigma may combine with the previous consonant to form ψ or ξ or may produce a more extensive change. When there is no case ending added to the stem (as for some nouns in nom. and voc. sing.), the stem may lose its final consonant because in ancient Greek it is a phonetic law that words must end either in a vowel or in ν, ρ, or ς.

2. *Labial and Velar Plosive Stems* (On plosives [also called mutes], see U1.2.) Nouns of this type, all masculine or feminine, have stems ending in π, β, or φ (*labial plosives*) or in κ, γ, or χ (*velar plosives*). The original case endings are all well preserved. The nom. and voc. sing. have -ς; the acc. sing. has -ă. In the nom./voc. sing. and the dat. pl., the final plosive of the stem combines with sigma to form either ψ (labial) or ξ (velar).

Ex.		*"thief" (m.)*	*"guard" (m.)*
	stem:	κλωπ-	φυλακ-
sing.	nom.	κλώψ	φύλαξ
	gen.	κλωπός	φύλακος
	dat.	κλωπί	φύλακι
	acc.	κλῶπα	φύλακα
	voc.	κλώψ	φύλαξ
(dual	n. a. v.	κλῶπε	φύλακε)
	(g. d.	κλωποῖν	φυλάκοιν)
plural	n. v.	κλῶπες	φύλακες
	gen.	κλωπῶν	φυλάκων
	dat.	κλωψί(ν)	φύλαξι(ν)
	acc.	κλῶπας	φύλακας

Accentuation: as for other nouns, the accent is persistent. But there is a special rule for all *monosyllabic-stem* nouns of the consonant declension: monosyllabic stems (e.g., κλωπ-) have the ultima accented in the gen. and dat. of all numbers (acute on short *U*, circumflex on long *U*: e.g., κλωπί, κλωπῶν), while in the nom., acc., and voc. the accent falls on the first or only syllable (acute on any short vowel or on a long vowel in the nom. and voc. sing.; circumflex on a long vowel in acc. sing. or nom., acc., and voc. pl.).

4. *The Suffix -μaτ-*. A large number of neuter nouns of the consonant declension are formed from verb stems by adding the suffix -μaτ- (nom. sing. -μa). The usual meaning of such a noun is "thing created by the action X."

Ex.

βουλεύω	*to plan*	βούλευμα	*plan, proposal*
πράττω	*to do*	πρᾶγμα	*action, event,*
(root πραγ-)			*circumstance, thing*
ποιέω	*to make*	ποίημα	*creation; poem*
γράφω	*to write*	γράμμα	*writing, letter*

WHAT TO STUDY AND DO

1. Learn the various consonant-declension patterns presented above.
2. Learn the vocabulary of this unit.
3. Do the exercises of this unit.

VOCABULARY

consonant-declension nouns

labial or velar plosive stems

θώραξ, θώρακος, m.	breastplate; breast, trunk (of the body) [thoracic]
κλώψ, κλωπός, m.	thief [kleptomania]
φάλαγξ, φάλαγγος, f.	line of battle; line of hoplites [phalanx, Falangist]
φύλαξ, φύλακος, m.	guard, sentinel [prophylactic]

masc. and fem. dental plosive stems

ἀσπίς, ἀσπίδος, f.	shield [aspidistra]
Ἑλλάς, Ἑλλάδος, f.	Hellas, Greece [Helladic]
ἐλπίς, ἐλπίδος, f.	hope, expectation
ἔρις, ἔριδος, f.	strife, quarrel, rivalry [eristic]
ὄρνις, ὄρνιθος, m. or f.	bird; omen [ornithology]
πατρίς, πατρίδος, f.	fatherland [patriotic]
χάρις, χάριτος, f.	grace, beauty; favor, kindness; gratitude [charisma, Eucharist]

dental plosive stems in *ντ*

γέρων, γέροντος, m.	old man [geriatrics]
γίγας, γίγαντος, m.	earth-born monster, giant [gigantic, gigabyte]
λέων, λέοντος, m.	lion
ὀδούς, ὀδόντος, m.	tooth [orthodontist]

neuter dental plosive stems

βούλευμα, βουλεύματος, n.	plan; proposal, resolution

γράμμα, γράμματος, n.   line, picture; letter (of alphabet); piece of writing
                              [grammatical, grammatology]
ποίημα, ποιήματος, n.   work, product; poem
πρᾶγμα, πράγματος, n.   deed, action; event, circumstance, thing; (pl.) toil,
                              trouble   [pragmatic]
τέρας, τέρατος, n.   portent, sign, marvel; monster   [teratogenesis]
ὕδωρ, ὕδατος, n.   water   [hydrofoil]
φῶς, φωτός, n.[1]   light   [photon, photograph]

EXERCISES

I. Write in Greek the requested form of each noun.

1. voc. sing. of favor
2. dat. pl. of old man
3. acc. sing. of water
4. gen. pl. of poem
5. nom. pl. of lion
6. dat. sing. of tooth
7. voc. pl. of hope
8. gen. sing. of phalanx
9. dat. sing. of omen
10. acc. pl. of strife
11. gen. pl. of giant
12. nom. pl. of thief
13. nom. sing. of event, action
14. dat. sing. of Greece
15. dat. pl. of sentinel
16. gen. sing. of shield
17. acc. pl. of fatherland
18. voc. pl. of portent, monster
19. nom. sing. of piece of writing
20. gen. pl. of plan
21. dat. sing. of breastplate
22. acc. sing. of bird
23. voc. sing. of giant
24. dat. pl. of piece of writing
25. acc. sing. of light
26. gen. pl. of water
27. nom. pl. of bird
28. dat. sing. of gratitude
29. voc. pl. of guard
30. gen. sing. of portent, monster

II. Give a complete identification of each of the following forms.

1. θωράκων
2. λέουσιν
3. φωτί
4. ὀδόντας
5. βουλεύματα
6. φάλαγγος
7. ἐλπίδες
8. ὄρνιν
9. φύλακι
10. ἔριδος
11. πατρίς
12. ἀσπίσι
13. κλῶπες
14. ποιήμασι
15. πρᾶγμα
16. χάριν
17. Ἑλλάδα
18. φάλαγξι
19. ὑδάτων
20. γίγαντας
21. γερόντων
22. ὀδοῦσιν
23. φωτός
24. ὕδατι

---

1. The non-Attic form is φάος; in Attic the stem is contracted and treated like a monosyllabic stem *except* in the gen. pl., which is accented φώτων.

III. Sentences for reading. (From this point on it is recommended that the student cease to write out translations of Greek sentences. In order to learn to *read* Greek rather than decipher it, one must practice translating mentally or orally from the text.)

1. διὰ τὰς καλὰς ὄρνιθας οὐ φοβούμεθα τὸν πρὸς ἐκείνους πόλεμον.
2. κακὸν λείπειν τὴν ἀσπίδα, ἀλλ᾽ ἀγαθὸν σῴζειν [save] τὴν ψυχήν.
3. μετὰ ταῦτα ὕδωρ φέρουσιν οἱ γέροντες τοῖς νεανίαις οἳ ὑπὲρ τῆς πατρίδος μάχονται.
4. οἱ φύλακες οὓς οἱ πολέμιοι αἱροῦσιν ἀποθνήσκουσιν.
5. δεῖ τὸν Ἡρακλῆ [Heracles, acc. case] κρατεῖν τόν τ᾽ ἐν Νεμέᾳ λέοντα τούς τε γίγαντας τά τε καθ᾽ Ἑλλάδα τέρατα.

Consonant-Declension Nouns II; Interrogative Pronoun

1. *Consonant Stems Ending in Liquid* (λ, ρ) *or Nasal* (ν). Almost all nouns in this group are masculine or feminine. The nom. and voc. sing. may have no case ending (and the nom. then has a strong-vowel form of the stem, e.g., ω for ο in ῥήτωρ and δαίμων) or -ς (e.g., ἅλς). Acc. sing. has -ἄ. Stems with final ν do not exhibit it in the dat. pl., but there is no compensatory lengthening in (e.g.) δαίμοσι.[1]

Ex.		*"orator" (m.)*	*"divinity" (m.)*	*"contest" (m.)*[2]	*"salt" (m.)*
	stem:	ῥητορ-	δαιμον-	ἀγων-	ἁλ-
sing.	nom.	ῥήτωρ	δαίμων	ἀγών	ἅλς
	gen.	ῥήτορος	δαίμονος	ἀγῶνος	ἁλός
	dat.	ῥήτορι	δαίμονι	ἀγῶνι	ἁλί
	acc.	ῥήτορα	δαίμονα	ἀγῶνα	ἅλα
	voc.	ῥῆτορ	δαῖμον	ἀγών	—
(dual	n. a. v.	ῥήτορε	δαίμονε	ἀγῶνε	ἅλε)
	(g. d.	ῥητόροιν	δαιμόνοιν	ἀγώνοιν	ἁλοῖν)
plur.	n. v.	ῥήτορες	δαίμονες	ἀγῶνες	ἅλες
	gen.	ῥητόρων	δαιμόνων	ἀγώνων	ἁλῶν
	dat.	ῥήτορσι(ν)	δαίμοσι(ν)	ἀγῶσι(ν)	ἁλσί(ν)
	acc.	ῥήτορας	δαίμονας	ἀγῶνας	ἅλας

2. *Irregular Stems in* ρ. Three important words have variable stems ending in ρ: a strong-vowel form in -τηρ, a normal grade with short vowel -τερ, and a weak grade realized as -τρ- (or -τρα- in dat. pl.). The strong-vowel

---

1. This form may derive from a dat. pl. ending -ασι borrowed from another type of noun (cf. §2 below), but with the vowel assimilated to that of the other cases.

2. Note the accentuation of stems in -ων- with accent on the final syllable of the stem (ἀγών): acute in nom. and voc. sing., circumflex in most other forms, because an accented long *P* followed by short *U* must have a circumflex.

form appears in the nom. sing, the weak form in gen. and dat. sing. and dat. pl., the normal grade in the rest of the cases. The common noun ἀνήρ is similar, but the Attic forms have δ inserted before ρ in all but nom. and voc. singular.

Ex.		*"father" (m.)*	*"mother" (f.)*	*"daughter" (f.)*	*"man" (m.)*
	stems:	πατ(ε)ρ-	μητ(ε)ρ-	θυγατ(ε)ρ-	ἀνερ-, ἀνδρ-
sing.	*nom.*	πατήρ	μήτηρ	θυγάτηρ	ἀνήρ
	gen.	πατρός	μητρός	θυγατρός	ἀνδρός
	dat.	πατρί	μητρί	θυγατρί	ἀνδρί
	acc.	πατέρα	μητέρα	θυγατέρα	ἄνδρα
	voc.	πάτερ	μῆτερ	θύγατερ	ἄνερ
(dual	*n. a. v.*	πατέρε	μητέρε	θυγατέρε	ἄνδρε)
	(g. d.	πατέροιν	μητέροιν	θυγατέροιν	ἀνδροῖν)
plur.	*n. v.*	πατέρες	μητέρες	θυγατέρες	ἄνδρες
	gen.	πατέρων	μητέρων	θυγατέρων	ἀνδρῶν
	dat.	πατράσι(ν)	μητράσι(ν)	θυγατράσι(ν)	ἀνδράσι(ν)
	acc.	πατέρας	μητέρας	θυγατέρας	ἄνδρας

Note the variations in *accentuation* of these nouns. The voc. sing. of πατήρ has recessive accentuation, as do both the nom. and voc. sing. of μήτηρ and θυγάτηρ. Elsewhere the accent of these three words falls on the stem-ending -ερ- (or -ρα- in dat. pl.) or on the case ending (in the gen. and dat. sing., where the rule about monosyllabic stems applies normally to μήτηρ and πατήρ, while θυγάτηρ is treated similarly by analogy). The accentuation of ἀνήρ follows the rule for monosyllabic stems of the consonant declension (U14.2), except that nom. sing. and dat. pl. (based on disyllabic stem) are accented on the second syllable of the stem and the voc. sing. has recessive accentuation.

3. *Stems in Sigma.* Many sigma-stems originally ended in -εσ-: this is still visible in the voc. sing. of masc. and fem. nouns (e.g., τριῆρες, Σώκρατες), and is present in a long-vowel form -ης in nom. sing. (τριήρης, Σωκράτης). In a large group of *neuter* nouns the -εσ- ending appears in the *o*-grade form -ος in nom. acc. voc. sing. (e.g., γένος). In the other cases the sigma of -εσ- has dropped out between vowels and contraction has taken place. The acc. pl. of masc./fem. nouns in -ης, however, is assimilated to the nominative rather than based on the usual ending -ᾰς. A few sigma-stem neuters have final -ασ- (e.g., γέρας): again, whenever the sigma drops out, contraction takes place. In the paradigms on the next page, the uncontracted forms (sometimes found in poetry and in other dialects) are shown in parentheses after the Attic prose forms.

Ex.		*"trireme"* (f.)		*"kind, race"* (n.)	
	stem:	τριηρε(σ)-		γενε(σ)-	
sing.	nom.	τριήρης		γένος	
	gen.	τριήρους	(τριήρεος)	γένους	(γένεος)
	dat.	τριήρει	(τριήρεϊ)	γένει	(γένεϊ)
	acc.	τριήρη	(τριήρεα)	γένος	
	voc.	τριῆρες		γένος	
[dual	n. a. v.	τριήρει	(τριήρεε)	γένει	(γένεε)]
[g. d.		τριήροιν	(τριηρέοιν)	γενοῖν	(γενέοιν)]
plur.	n. v.	τριήρεις	(τριήρεες)	γένη	(γένεα)
	gen.	τριήρων	(τριηρέων)	γενῶν	(γενέων)
	dat.	τριήρεσι(ν)	(τριήρεσσι)	γένεσι(ν)	(γένεσσι)
	acc.	τριήρεις		γένη	(γένεα)

		"prize, honor" (n.)	
	stem:	γερα(σ)-	
sing.	nom.	γέρας	
	gen.	γέρως	(γέραος)
	dat.	γέραι or γέρᾳ	(γέραϊ)
	acc.	γέρας	
	voc.	γέρας	
[dual	n. a. v.	γέρᾱ	(γέραε)]
[g. d.		γερῶν	(γεράοιν)]
plur.	n. v.	γέρᾱ	(γέραα)
	gen.	γερῶν	(γεράων)
	dat.	γέρασι(ν)	(γέρασσι)
	acc.	γέρᾱ	(γέραα)

Note that the accent of the contracted form of the gen. pl. (and gen. dat. dual) of τριήρης is assimilated to that of the other cases and does not derive from the uncontracted form. For proper names in -ης like Σωκράτης, the voc. is accented recessively, on A (Σώκρατες).

4. *Interrogative Pronoun.* (On pronouns in general, see U12 Prelim. D.) Interrogative pronouns are pronouns used to introduce questions. In English the interrogative pronouns are *who, which, what*. Note that *who* and *which* are also used as relative pronouns and that *which* and *what* can also be used with a noun as *interrogative adjectives*.

Ex.	<u>Who</u> *is winning the prize for boxing?*	personal (masc./fem.)
	<u>Whom</u> *are they selecting as general?*	personal (objective)

<u>*What*</u> *are you doing?*   impersonal (neuter)
<u>*Which*</u> *is the just citizen?*   pronoun
<u>*Which*</u> *daughter is the sailor marrying?* interrogative adj.

The Greek interrogative pronoun/adjective τίς, τί, equivalent to all three English interrogatives, has a nasal consonant stem (τιν-) in most cases and a simple *i*-stem in the masc./fem. nom. sing. form and the neuter nom. acc. sing. form. Like some consonant-declension adjectives (to be learned in U22), the interrogative has a common *personal* gender that serves as masculine and feminine. In such a declension, the gen. and dat. forms are identical for all three genders, and the neuter is distinguished from the masc./fem. only in nom. and acc. (and voc., if any).

	singular				*plural*	*neuter*
	masc./fem.		*neuter*		*masc./fem.*	
nom.	τίς		τί		τίνες	τίνα
gen.	τίνος	(τοῦ)	τίνος	(τοῦ)	τίνων	τίνων
dat.	τίνι	(τῷ)	τίνι	(τῷ)	τίσι(ν)	τίσι(ν)
acc.	τίνα		τί		τίνας	τίνα

(*dual, all genders: nom. acc.* τίνε, *gen. dat.* τίνοιν)

Note that there are alternative forms for the gen. and dat. sing. (shown in parentheses). These are *o*-stem forms and look just like the corresponding forms of the article.

Accentuation: because of the interrogative intonation (and perhaps also to distinguish the forms from similar indefinite enclitic forms), the interrogative is accented with the acute on its first (or only) syllable, and this acute never changes to a grave even though the one-syllable interrogative is normally followed by another word without pause. (The alternative forms in gen. and dat. sing. have the circumflex, just like the article; in context, the interrogative and articular uses are usually easily distinguishable.)

Ex. τίνα βλάπτομεν;   *Whom are we hurting?*
        τίς ἔρχεται;   *Who is coming?*
        τῷ ἐπιτρέπεις τὰ παιδία;   *To whom are you entrusting the children?*
        τίνα στρατηγὸν πέμπει;   *Which general is he sending?*

WHAT TO STUDY AND DO

1. Learn the various consonant-declension patterns presented above.
2. Learn the interrogative τίς, τί.

3. Learn the vocabulary of this unit.
4. Do the exercises of this unit.

VOCABULARY

consonant-declension nouns: liquid and nasal stems

ἀγών, ἀγῶνος, m.   contest, struggle; assembly, national games
                             [agony, agonistic]

ἅλς, ἁλός, m.   salt, grain of salt   [halides]
ἅλς, ἁλός, f.   (poetic) sea

ἀνήρ, ἀνδρός, m.   man, male; warrior; husband; "real man," "man" (in
                             contexts emphasizing sexist or macho traits)[1]
                             [android, androgynous]

δαίμων, δαίμονος, m. or f.   god, divinity; tutelary divinity, the power controlling
                             an individual's destiny; one's destiny, lot [demon]

Ἕλλην, Ἕλληνος, m.   a Greek (man), Hellene   [Hellenic]
θυγάτηρ, θυγατρός, f.   daughter
μήτηρ, μητρός, f.   mother   [metropolis, metronymic]
πατήρ, πατρός, m.   father   [patriarchy]
ῥήτωρ, ῥήτορος, m.   speaker, orator   [rhetoric]

consonant-declension nouns: sigma-stems

Δημοσθένης, Δημοσθένους,   Demosthenes (Athenian orator and politician, 4th
m.   cent. B.C.E.)

Σωκράτης, Σωκράτους, m.   Socrates (Athenian philosopher, teacher of Plato)

τριήρης, τριήρους, f.   trireme (a military vessel with three banks of oars)
                             [trierarch]

γένος, γένους, n.   race, stock; offspring; class, sort, kind   [genocide,
                             genealogy]

γέρας, γέρως, n.   gift of honor, privilege
γῆρας, γήρως, n.   old age   [geriatrics]
ἔτος, ἔτους, n.   year   [etesian]
κράτος, κράτους, n.   strength, power; victory   [timocratic]
μέρος, μέρους, n.   share, portion; part; one's turn   [meroblastic,
                             penthemimeral]

πλῆθος, πλήθους, n.   multitude; the masses, the majority; quantity; size
                             [plethora]

τεῖχος, τείχους, n.   wall   [teichoscopy]

---

1. Contrast ἄνθρωπος, which refers to human beings as a species. Herodotus (7.120) commented on the repelling of numerous Persian forces by the few Spartan defenders of Thermopylae that it showed πολλοὶ μὲν ἄνθρωποί εἰσιν, ὀλίγοι δ᾽ ἄνδρες.

τέλος, τέλους, n.   fulfillment, completion; end, finish; authority; (pl.)
                                 service, duty; offerings, rites; taxes
                                 [teleological]

interrogative pronoun/adjective

τίς, τί   (pronoun) who? which? what?; (adj.) which? what?

EXERCISES

I. Give a complete identification of each of the following.

1. ἔτει	11. μερῶν	21. τίνων
2. Σωκράτους	12. γήρᾳ	22. ἄνδρας
3. τείχη	13. τριήρεσι	23. πάτερ
4. πατρός	14. ἀνδρί	24. τριήρη
5. Ἕλληνι	15. ἅλα	25. γήρως
6. δαιμόνων	16. ἀγῶνα	26. τίνα
7. ῥήτορσιν	17. Δημόσθενες	27. κράτει
8. μητέρας	18. γέρα	28. δαίμονες
9. θύγατερ	19. πλήθους	29. ἀγῶσιν
10. κράτη	20. τέλος	30. τίσι

II. Render into Greek.

1. what portion? (nom.)
2. the unjust orators (dat.)
3. most (acc.) of the triremes
4. which Greeks? (gen.)
5. a small privilege (gen.)
6. evil strife (acc.)
7. large teeth (nom.)
8. during that year
9. the wise plan (dat.)
10. what hopes? (nom.)
11. this multitude (gen.)
12. after the contest
13. which mothers? (dat.)
14. toward that wall
15. with the husband

III. Sentences for reading.

1. τίς ἐστιν ὁ ῥήτωρ; Δημοσθένης, ὃς τὸ πλῆθος πείθει τὰς τριήρεις τοῖς πλουσίοις ἐπιτρέπειν καὶ τέλη εἰσφέρειν.[1]
2. τί χρὴ ποιεῖν; οἱ μὲν γὰρ τῶν Ἑλλήνων ἐν τῇ τῶν βαρβάρων χώρᾳ μάχεσθαι φοβοῦνται, οἱ δὲ τῷ τῶν Ἀθηναίων στρατηγῷ πείθεσθαι οὐκ ἐθέλουσιν.
3. ὁ πατὴρ καὶ ἡ μήτηρ τήν τε θυγατέρα φιλοῦσι καὶ ὑπ᾽ ἐκείνης φιλοῦνται.

---

1. Compound of φέρω and εἰς, "into (the public treasury)."

4. τίν᾿ ἀγῶνα παρασκευάζουσιν οἱ κριταί; τίνες νεανίαι γέρα φέρονται;

5. ἀνόσιόν ἐστι μὴ ἔχειν χάριν τῶν ἀγαθῶν ἔργων ἃ ὑπὲρ τῆς δημοκρατίας ἐκεῖνοι πράττουσιν.

IV. Render into Greek.

1. The men have breastplates and shields, but are not brave.
2. Being just and telling the truth are parts of virtue for the race of men.
3. This year is the beginning of a long and difficult war.
4. We await the end of the court case [= suit], for the thief is responsible for the fact that the citizens do not fare well.
5. From those walls the mother of Socrates hears the voice of the speaker in the marketplace.

Ω-Verbs: Imperfect Indicative

1. *Secondary Tenses.* The tenses of the indicative which refer to present or future time are called the *primary* tenses, while those which refer to past time are called *secondary* tenses. The distinction between the two types is apparent in three ways. (1) The personal endings of secondary tenses differ in some persons and numbers from those of primary tenses. (2) Secondary tenses show *augment* (explained in §2 below). (3) In many forms of complex sentence, the mood used in the subordinate clause may differ according to whether the main verb is primary or secondary (sequence of moods, presented in U31.5). The primary tenses are the present, future, perfect, and future perfect (also for some purposes the gnomic aorist, U20.5c); the secondary tenses are the imperfect, aorist, and pluperfect (also for some purposes the historical present, U20.5b).

2. *Augment.* Augment is a modification of the beginning of a tense stem which marks an indicative verb as referring to past time. Augment is found in the imperfect indicative (presented below), in the aorist indicative (U19), and in the pluperfect indicative (U41). Augment takes one of two forms:

a. *Syllabic augment* is the addition of the syllable ἐ- to the beginning of a tense stem that begins with a consonant.

Ex.

present stem	*imperfect stem*
πεμπ-	ἐπεμπ-
βουλ-	ἐβουλ-
ταττ-	ἐταττ-

Note that a few stems which begin with a vowel in classical Greek originally began with a consonant (e.g., initial sigma or vau [U1.4]) and so have syllabic augment, but the vowel ἐ- has contracted with the following vowel after the disappearance of the intervening consonant. For instance, from ἔχω with its present stem ἐχ- based on original *σεχ- is derived the imperfect stem εἰχ- (by way of *ἐσεχ- —> *ἐεχ-).[1]

b. *Temporal augment* is the lengthening of the initial vowel or diphthong of a stem that begins with a vowel. If the stem already begins with a long vowel or a "long" diphthong or ου, no change is made; but otherwise the vowel is changed as follows: ᾰ —> η, ε —> η, ῐ —> ῑ, ο —> ω, ῠ —> ῡ, αι —> ῃ, ει —> ῃ, αυ —> ηυ, ευ —> ηυ, οι —> ῳ.[2]

Ex.

present stem	imperfect stem	
ἀγ-	ἠγ-	
αἰρε-	ᾐρε-	
οἰκε-	ᾠκε-	
ὠφελε-	ὠφελε-	(no change)

Augment is applied directly to the verb stem. Consequently, in compounds consisting of prepositional prefix and verb stem, the augment appears between the preposition and the verb stem, often with elision of the final vowel of a two-syllable preposition (for elision review U1.5):

Ex.

present stem	imperfect stem
ἀπο/κτειν-	ἀπ/ε/κτειν-
ἐπι/τρεπ-	ἐπ/ε/τρεπ-
παρα/κελευ-	παρ/ε/κελευ-
ἀφ/ἱκνε-	ἀφ/ῑκνε-

3. *Imperfect Indicative.* The Greek imperfect indicative refers to action in the past which is incomplete (hence the name, from the Latin for "unfinished"), in progress, or repeated or customary. It corresponds to the English past progressive (*I was sending*), verb phrases with *used to* (*I used to send*), and in some contexts the English simple past (*I sent*).

The imperfect is formed from the imperfect stem (= present stem with augment) plus theme vowel ο/ε plus *secondary* personal endings. Recall that theme vowel ο is used before μ or ν; otherwise ε is used. The secondary endings are worth memorizing, as they will reappear in later units. Note that the second person singular middle/passive ending -σο, when combined with theme vowel ε, loses the intervocalic sigma, and the remaining ο contracts

---

1. An asterisk (*) placed before a form indicates that the form is a reconstructed historical precursor of a known form and is not actually found in surviving Greek documents.

2. Outside of Ionic/Attic, ᾰ —> ᾱ instead of η and αι —> ᾳ instead of ῃ. In postclassical Greek there are two verbs beginning with υι-, and the augmented form is also υι-.

with ϵ to form ov (just as in the second person singular primary ending in the present middle/passive: $-\eta$ from $-\epsilon(\sigma)\alpha\iota$).

SECONDARY PERSONAL ENDINGS

		active	*middle/passive*
sing.	*1st*	$-\nu$	$-\mu\eta\nu$
	2nd	$-\varsigma$	$-\sigma o$
	3rd	—	$-\tau o$
(dual	*2nd*	$-\tau o\nu$	$-\sigma\theta o\nu)$
	(3rd	$-\tau\eta\nu$	$-\sigma\theta\eta\nu)$
plur.	*1st*	$-\mu\epsilon\nu$	$-\mu\epsilon\theta\alpha$
	2nd	$-\tau\epsilon$	$-\sigma\theta\epsilon$
	3rd	$-\nu$	$-\nu\tau o$

CONJUGATION OF IMPERFECT ACTIVE

Ex.	stem:	*"send"* $\dot{\epsilon}\pi\epsilon\mu\pi- + o/\epsilon$	*"lead"* $\dot{\eta}\gamma- + o/\epsilon$	*theme vowel* + *pers. ending*
sing.	*1st*	$\ddot{\epsilon}\pi\epsilon\mu\pi o\nu$	$\mathring{\eta}\gamma o\nu$	$-o\nu$
	2nd	$\ddot{\epsilon}\pi\epsilon\mu\pi\epsilon\varsigma$	$\mathring{\eta}\gamma\epsilon\varsigma$	$-\epsilon\varsigma$
	3rd	$\ddot{\epsilon}\pi\epsilon\mu\pi\epsilon(\nu)$	$\mathring{\eta}\gamma\epsilon(\nu)$	$-\epsilon(\nu)$
(dual	*2nd*	$\dot{\epsilon}\pi\dot{\epsilon}\mu\pi\epsilon\tau o\nu$	$\ddot{\eta}\gamma\epsilon\tau o\nu)$	$(-\epsilon\tau o\nu)$
	(3rd	$\dot{\epsilon}\pi\epsilon\mu\pi\acute{\epsilon}\tau\eta\nu$	$\dot{\eta}\gamma\acute{\epsilon}\tau\eta\nu)$	$(-\epsilon\tau\eta\nu)$
plur.	*1st*	$\dot{\epsilon}\pi\acute{\epsilon}\mu\pi o\mu\epsilon\nu$	$\ddot{\eta}\gamma o\mu\epsilon\nu$	$-o\mu\epsilon\nu$
	2nd	$\dot{\epsilon}\pi\acute{\epsilon}\mu\pi\epsilon\tau\epsilon$	$\ddot{\eta}\gamma\epsilon\tau\epsilon$	$-\epsilon\tau\epsilon$
	3rd	$\ddot{\epsilon}\pi\epsilon\mu\pi o\nu$	$\mathring{\eta}\gamma o\nu$	$-o\nu$

CONJUGATION OF IMPERFECT MIDDLE/PASSIVE

sing.	*1st*	$\dot{\epsilon}\pi\epsilon\mu\pi\acute{o}\mu\eta\nu$	$\dot{\eta}\gamma\acute{o}\mu\eta\nu$	$-o\mu\eta\nu$
	2nd	$\dot{\epsilon}\pi\acute{\epsilon}\mu\pi o\upsilon$	$\ddot{\eta}\gamma o\upsilon$	$-o\upsilon\ [-\epsilon(\sigma)o]$
	3rd	$\dot{\epsilon}\pi\acute{\epsilon}\mu\pi\epsilon\tau o$	$\ddot{\eta}\gamma\epsilon\tau o$	$-\epsilon\tau o$
(dual	*2nd*	$\dot{\epsilon}\pi\acute{\epsilon}\mu\pi\epsilon\sigma\theta o\nu$	$\ddot{\eta}\gamma\epsilon\sigma\theta o\nu)$	$(-\epsilon\sigma\theta o\nu)$
	(3rd	$\dot{\epsilon}\pi\epsilon\mu\pi\acute{\epsilon}\sigma\theta\eta\nu$	$\dot{\eta}\gamma\acute{\epsilon}\sigma\theta\eta\nu)$	$(-\epsilon\sigma\theta\eta\nu)$
plur.	*1st*	$\dot{\epsilon}\pi\epsilon\mu\pi\acute{o}\mu\epsilon\theta\alpha$	$\dot{\eta}\gamma\acute{o}\mu\epsilon\theta\alpha$	$-o\mu\epsilon\theta\alpha$
	2nd	$\dot{\epsilon}\pi\acute{\epsilon}\mu\pi\epsilon\sigma\theta\epsilon$	$\ddot{\eta}\gamma\epsilon\sigma\theta\epsilon$	$-\epsilon\sigma\theta\epsilon$
	3rd	$\dot{\epsilon}\pi\acute{\epsilon}\mu\pi o\nu\tau o$	$\ddot{\eta}\gamma o\nu\tau o$	$-o\nu\tau o$

Note the similarities and differences between the secondary endings (plus theme vowel) and the primary endings (plus theme vowel), which are most obvious in the middle/passive.

Accentuation: the accent is recessive, as for all finite forms. An apparent exception arises in compounds of verbs with monosyllabic stems that begin with a vowel. It is a rule that when a Greek verb has more than one preverb (prefixed element: e.g., augment or prepositional prefix) the accent cannot precede the first preverb element (namely, the augment). For instance, from ἀπέχω = *to be distant* is derived the imperfect ἀπεῖχον (not ἄπειχον, because the accent cannot precede the augment contained in ει), and from παράγω = *to lead astray* is derived the imperfect παρῆγον (not πάρηγον, because the accent cannot precede the augmented vowel η).

The imperfect indicative is part of the present-stem system of the verb (which consists of all forms derived from the first principal part). You will learn later how the present infinitive and participle sometimes serve to convey "imperfect" meanings.

4. *Imperfect of Verbs in* -έω. Review the possible contractions of -έω verbs and the explanation of their accentuation presented in U13.2. Here is an example of the imperfect indicative of a verb in -έω (οἰκέω = *inhabit*). In the following paradigm the uncontracted form is illustrated in parentheses next to the contracted form which results from it in Attic:

		active		*middle/passive*	
sing.	1st	ᾤκουν	(ᾤκεον)	ᾠκούμην	(ᾠκεόμην)
	2nd	ᾤκεις	(ᾤκεες)	ᾠκοῦ	(ᾠκέου)
	3rd	ᾤκει	(ᾤκεε)	ᾠκεῖτο	(ᾠκέετο)
[dual	2nd	ᾠκεῖτον	(ᾠκέετον)	ᾠκεῖσθον	(ᾠκέεσθον)]
	[3rd	ᾠκείτην	(ᾠκεέτην)	ᾠκείσθην	(ᾠκεέσθην)]
plur.	1st	ᾠκοῦμεν	(ᾠκέομεν)	ᾠκούμεθα	(ᾠκεόμεθα)
	2nd	ᾠκεῖτε	(ᾠκέετε)	ᾠκεῖσθε	(ᾠκέεσθε)
	3rd	ᾤκουν	(ᾤκεον)	ᾠκοῦντο	(ᾠκέοντο)

5. *Imperfect of* εἰμί

	singular	*(dual)*	*plural*
1st	ἦν or ἦ		ἦμεν
2nd	ἦσθα	(ἦστον)	ἦτε or ἦστε
3rd	ἦν	(ἤστην)	ἦσαν

6. *Imperfect of* χρή *and* οἴομαι. The imperfect *it was necessary* has the form χρῆν or ἐχρῆν. The former is a contraction of χρή (noun) + ἦν (imperfect of εἰμί); the latter is χρῆν with augment added on the analogy of ordinary imperfect forms. The imperfect of οἴομαι has both the regular forms (ᾠόμην, etc.) and a contracted first sing. ᾤμην (like the present form οἶμαι).

WHAT TO STUDY AND DO

1. Learn the imperfect active and middle/passive indicative.
2. Learn the imperfect of the irregular verb εἰμί.
3. Learn the vocabulary of this unit.
4. Do the exercises of this unit.

VOCABULARY

consonant-stem nouns

ἡγεμών, ἡγεμόνος, m.	leader, guide [hegemony]
θήρ, θηρός, m.	beast of prey, wild animal
θηρίον, θηρίου, n.	wild animal [theriomorphic, megatherium]
παῖς, παιδός, m. or f.[1]	child, boy, girl; slave, servant [pedagogy]

adjectives

ἀρχαῖος, ἀρχαία, ἀρχαῖον	ancient, old; old-fashioned [archaeology]
βλαβερός, βλαβερά, βλαβερόν	harmful
δεινός, δεινή, δεινόν	fearful, terrible; wondrous; clever, skillful
δεινὸς λέγειν	clever at speaking
κοινός, κοινή, κοινόν	common, public [Koine, epicene]
τὸ κοινόν	public authority, state, league
τὰ κοινά	public affairs; public funds
φανερός, φανερά, φανερόν	visible, manifest

verbs

αἰτέω	ask for (+ acc. of person and acc. of thing or inf.)
ἀπάγω (ἀπο)	lead away; arrest, carry off to prison
ἀπέχω (ἀπο)	hold off; (intrans.) be away from, be distant from
ἐπαινέω (ἐπι)	approve, praise
ἐπιθῡμέω (ἐπι)	long for, desire (+ gen. of object desired)
ζητέω	seek, seek for; examine, investigate

---

1. The vocative singular is παῖ; the genitive plural is accented παίδων.

ἡγέομαι	lead, guide (usually + dat. of person); command, rule (usually + gen. of person); consider, think
κωλύω [ῡ]	hinder, prevent (+ acc. + inf.)
παράγω (παρα)	lead by; lead astray, mislead; bring forward, introduce
παρέχω (παρα)	furnish, supply, afford
τρέπω	turn, direct; change; put to flight (in battle) [trophy]
φυλάττω[1]	guard, defend; watch for; (mid.) be on one's guard (against)

EXERCISES

I.   Translate each form precisely and give a complete identification of any ten.

1. ἠτεῖσθε	15. ἠδικεῖτε	29. ὠφελεῖσθε
2. ἀπῆγε	16. ἠσθανόμην	30. φέρεται
3. ἀπέχεις	17. γίγνῃ	31. ἐπέτρεπον
4. ἐπῄνουν	18. ἔδει	32. ποιοῦμαι
5. ἐπιθυμεῖν	19. ἐδόκουν	33. ἐζήτει
6. ἐζητοῦμεν	20. ᾠκεῖτο	34. κωλύεσθαι
7. ἡγοῦντο	21. παρεκελευόμην	35. ἀπήγοντο
8. ἐκωλύετο	22. πυνθάνονται	36. ἐγίγνετο
9. ἦν	23. ἔσπενδες	37. αἰτεῖσθαι
10. παράγεσθαι	24. ἔφευγε	38. ἐβουλόμεθα
11. παρεῖχε	25. ἐφοβούμην	39. ἐνόσουν
12. ἐτρέπομεν	26. ἐπράττετο	40. ἐπυνθάνου
13. ἡγοῦνται	27. ἦσαν	41. ᾤου
14. ἐφυλάττου	28. ἐταττόμεθα	42. ἐλαμβάνομεν

II.   Write in Greek.

1. it was being carried
2. we were afraid
3. to be loved
4. I was helping
5. they used to suffer
6. you (s.) were fighting
7. to march
8. you (pl.) were
9. he was leading away
10. they used to arrive
11. you (pl.) were guiding
12. they were being misled
13. we are seeking
14. she was perceiving
15. I was inquiring
16. we used to seem
17. it is being made
18. she used to say
19. you (pl.) were leaving
20. you (s.) supposed
21. they were remaining
22. I desired

---

1. Non-Attic φυλάσσω.

23. I hindered
24. to be furnished
25. you (s.) are on your guard
26. it is distant from

27. it was being written
28. we used to harm
29. it is being heard
30. you (s.) were finding

III. Reading.

1. ἐνθάδε οἱ μὲν καλοὶ καὶ ἀγαθοὶ τὴν πατρίδα βλάπτειν καὶ πλοῦτον λαμβάνειν οὐκ ἤθελον, ἀλλὰ μὴ ἀδικεῖσθαι ὑπὸ τῶν πονηρῶν ἐβούλοντο· τοῖς δὲ πονηροῖς, οἳ ἀεὶ ἀρχῆς τε καὶ πλούτου ἐπεθύμουν, τότε ἐξῆν τῆσδε τῆς χώρας κρατεῖν· τοὺς μὲν γὰρ στρατηγοὺς ἀποκτείνουσι, τοὺς δὲ ῥήτορας εἰς τὸ ἱερὸν ἀπάγουσι καὶ ἐκεῖ φυλάττουσιν. ἔπειτα τὸ πλῆθος περὶ τῶν πραγμάτων βουλεύεσθαι ἐκώλυον.

2. ταῦτα τὰ δεινὰ ἐκ τοῦ γέροντος αἱ τοῦ Δημοσθένους θυγατέρες ἀκούουσι καὶ αὐτίκα τοὺς νεανίας ᾔτουν ἡγεῖσθαι ἐκ τῆς χώρας ἐκείνης, ἐν ᾗ ἦσαν θῆρές τε καὶ ὄρνιθες βλαβεροί.

3. ἔπειτα ὁ Παυσανίας[1] τοῖς Ἀθηναίοις παρεκελεύετο κήρυκας πέμπειν περὶ τῆς εἰρήνης· οἱ δὲ ἐπείθοντο.

4. ἐπεὶ [when] δὲ ἦσαν ἐπὶ ταῖς θύραις ταῖς Τισσαφέρνους,[2] οἱ μὲν στρατηγοὶ εἰς τὴν σκηνὴν ἔρχονται, οἱ δὲ στρατιῶται ἐπὶ ταῖς θύραις ἔμενον. μετὰ δὲ οὐ μακρὸν χρόνον ἐκεῖνοί τε ᾑροῦντο καὶ οὗτοι ἐκόπτοντο. ἔπειτα δὲ οἱ βάρβαροι διὰ τοῦ πεδίου [plain] ἤλαυνον καὶ τοὺς Ἕλληνας ἀπέκτεινον.

---

1. Pausanias, king of the Lacedaemonians at the end of the Peloponnesian War.
2. Gen. of Τισσαφέρνης, Tissaphernes, a Persian governor.

Indefinite τις; Uses of the Accusative

1. *The Greek Indefinite.* Indefinite pronouns and indefinite adjectives refer to an unspecified, uncertain, or vague person or thing or portion of a group of persons or things. In English the indefinite words include pronouns *any, some, anyone, someone, anything, something*, and adjectives *any, some*. The idiomatic use of *a certain* or *certain* (with plural noun), by which the speaker refers to someone definite without making the identification precise, is also equivalent to use of an indefinite adjective. The Greek indefinite pronoun/ adjective τις, τι is identical in form to the interrogative pronoun/adjective (learned in U15.4), except that the indefinite is an enclitic, whereas the interrogative always has the acute on its first syllable.

	singular				plural		
	masc./fem.		neuter		masc./fem.	neuter	
nom.	τις		τι		τινές	τινά	(ἄττα)
gen.	τινός	(του)	τινός	(του)	τινῶν	τινῶν	
dat.	τινί	(τῳ)	τινί	(τῳ)	τισί(ν)	τισί(ν)	
acc.	τινά		τι		τινάς	τινά	(ἄττα)

(*dual, all genders: nom. acc.* τινέ, *gen. dat.* τινοῖν)

Remember that in paradigms disyllabic enclitics are shown with an accent on the second syllable, though they will not always have an accent in actual use. The use of the circumflex on the second syllable of τινῶν may be an orthographic convention rather than a reflection of classical pronunciation. Note the alternative forms given in parentheses for the gen. and dat. sing. (as for the interrogative) and also for the neuter nom. and acc. pl. (ἄττα is not treated as an enclitic and usually follows an adjective with its neuter pl. -ᾰ elided).[1]

---

1. ἄττα actually derives from adjective ending in -ᾰ plus enclitic *τya redivided (e.g., δεινά τya ——> δείν' ἄττα (y = semivocalic iota). (Note that the accent on *P* in δείν' is the result of elision: when a final vowel accented with a grave is elided, an acute accent is placed on *P*.)

2. *Accentuation of the Indefinite.* Review U2.12 on the accentuation of enclitics and be sure that you understand the accentuation of the indefinite in the following examples:

ἀνήρ τις	*a certain man*
λόγῳ τινί	*by a certain account*
ἄνθρωποί τινες	*some people*
πεῖρά τις	*any attempt*
μητέρων τινῶν	*of some mothers*

An additional peculiarity in the accentuation of enclitics occurs when two or more enclitics appear in a series. In such a series, the convention is usually that every enclitic except the last in the series receives an acute on its final syllable.

Ex. βάλλει τίς τινά τῳ.
Someone is striking someone with something.
εἴ τί τινα βλάπτεις, . . .
If you are doing any harm to anyone, . . .

Recall [U2.12d] that a proclitic that precedes an enclitic receives an acute, as εἴ in the second example here.

3. *Uses of the Accusative Case.* The accusative case (Greek αἰτιατικὴ πτῶσις, "case of effect," misleadingly translated as *accusativus* by Latin grammarians because of the ambiguity of the Greek word αἰτία) in general serves to define or qualify the action expressed by a verb.

a. *Accusative of the Object of a Verb.* The use of the accusative to express the direct object of a transitive verb was introduced in brief in U8.9. It is now time to learn the finer details of grammar related to objects of a Greek verb.

(1) *External object*, object of the thing affected, or "direct object": a person or thing existing prior to an action and directly affected by the action is normally expressed in the accusative case.

βάλλει τὸν λίθον.	*He throws the stone.*
βάλλει τὸν ἄνδρα.	*He strikes the man.*
τίνα βλάπτομεν;	*Whom are we hurting?*

(2) *Object of the thing effected*, accusative of result, or (loosely) "direct object": a thing (often but not always concrete) which is brought into existence, produced, or effected by an action and which continues to exist as a temporary or enduring result is expressed in the accusative case.

ποιήματα γράφει.	*She writes poems.*

ἀσπίδας ποιεῖ.	*He makes shields.*
φόβον ποιοῦσιν.	*They create (cause) fear.*

(3) *Internal object*, internal accusative, "cognate" object or accusative, accusative of the content:[1] an abstract thing (usually a noun of action) which is brought into existence by an action and the existence of which is coextensive with the action (that is, the object has no existence external to the action of the verb) is expressed in the accusative case. The internal accusative is sometimes etymologically related (*cognate*) to the verb itself, but is often a noun of related meaning or a neuter pronoun or neuter adjective (a noun of related meaning being understood). Stylistically, the motivation for using an internal object is often the desire to attach adjectives to the internal-object noun.

> He <u>lived</u> a long and peaceful <u>life</u>.
> You <u>ran</u> a very fast <u>race</u>.
> He <u>struck</u> several <u>blows</u> upon the boy's back.

διπλῆν πληγὴν ἔπληττε.	*He was striking a double stroke.*
διπλῆν πληγὴν ἔτυπτε.	*He was striking a double blow.*
εὔχομαι τὴν εὐχὴν τήνδε.	*I pray the following prayer.*
φόρον φέρουσιν.	*They pay tribute.*
τί βλάπτομεν;	*What harm are we doing?*
[in English we cannot idiomatically say *What (harm) are we harming?*]	
ἀγαθὰ ποιεῖς.	*You do good (doings).*
	= You do good things.
	= You benefit . . . [someone].
κακὰ ποιεῖ.	*She does bad (doings).*
	= She does bad things.
	= She harms . . . [someone].

---

1. As the lists of terms show, there is considerable variety in the terminology used by grammarians to describe the different types of accusative object. Note that type (2) shares some characteristics of both type (1) and type (3). The object of the thing effected, type (2), may be considered an "external object" (in a wider sense) because the object is something which exists after the action has ceased and so is "external" to it; cf. type (1). On the other hand, type (2) shares with type (3) the characteristic that the object does not exist prior to the action and is thus, in origin, "internal" to the action. Moreover, an object of the thing effected can be "cognate" with its verb just as type (3) is: ποιήματα ποιεῖ. But type (2) again sides with type (1) in the distinction between transitive and intransitive verbs: verbs with objects of these two types are transitive, they need the object to complete the sense of the verb. Intransitive verbs, on the other hand, may have only an internal object, type (3): this object is either dispensable to the sense or present only to make possible the use of a modifier qualifying the action.

τοῦτο εὔχομαι.	*I pray this prayer.* *= I make this prayer.*

A transitive verb may have both an internal accusative (double underline below) and a direct object (single underline) at the same time:

τοὺς πολίτας ἀγαθὰποιεῖς.	*You do good doings (to) the citizens.* *= You benefit the citizens.*
τοὺς πατέρας κακὰἐποίουν.	*They were doing bad doings (to) their* * fathers.* *= They were harming their fathers.*
τί ἐκείνας βλάπτομεν;	*(In) what are we harming those women?* *= What harm are we doing to those* * women?*

Verbs that normally govern a complement in the genitive or dative may take an internal accusative:

> κατηγορῶ τοῦ στρατηγοῦ.
> *I accuse the general.* (gen. complement)
> τοῦτο κατηγορῶ τοῦ στρατηγοῦ.
> *I make this accusation against the general.*
> * (I accuse the general this accusation.)*

> ἐπείθεσθε τοῖς Ἀθηναίοις. *You used to obey*
> * the Athenians.* (dat. complement)
> ταῦτα ἐπείθεσθε τοῖς Ἀθηναίοις.
> *You used to obey the Athenians in these matters.*
> * (You used to obey the Athenians these obeyings.)*

The internal accusative construction is much more at home in Greek idiom than in English. Note that it is often convenient or necessary to translate a Greek verb with internal accusative other than literally. In some cases it is best to use the English catch-all verbs *make* or *do* and express the verbal action in a noun (*What harm are we doing? I make this accusation.*); in others, a prepositional phrase (esp. with *in* or *in respect to*) may be appropriate (*I obey them in this*).

  b. *Internal Accusative with Adjectives.* Verb phrases consisting of copula (*to be*) and predicate adjective sometimes take an internal accusative, and this usage is also extended sometimes to the adjective alone used outside such a copula phrase.

> σοφός ἐστιν.   *He is wise.*
> σοφός ἐστι τὴν τῶν ποιητῶν σοφίαν.
> *He is wise in the wisdom of the poets.*

ὁ ταύτην τὴν σοφίαν σοφὸς εὖ πράττει.
The man who is wise in this wisdom fares well.

c. *Accusative of Extent of Space or Duration of Time*

(1) The *space over which* a motion takes place or the *extent of space* (how far?) is expressed in the accusative case.

ἄγει τὴν στρατιὰν στενὰς ὁδούς.
He leads the army along (over) narrow roads.
ἄγει τὴν στρατιὰν στάδια ὀκτώ.
He leads the army eight stades (= one mile).
ὁ ποταμὸς δέκα στάδια ἀπεῖχε.
The river was ten stades (= 1.25 miles) away.

(2) *Duration of time* (how long?) is expressed in the accusative case.

ἐνταῦθα μένουσιν ἑπτὰ ἡμέρας.
They remain there (for) seven days.

d. *Accusative of Respect or Specification.* The accusative case is used to express the thing in respect to which an adjective or verb phrase denoting a state is applicable.

οἱ Ἀθηναῖοι διαφέρουσι τὴν σοφίαν.   *The Athenians excel in cleverness.*
πόδας ὠκύς   *swift in respect to the feet, swift-footed*
ποταμὸς Κύδνος ὄνομα   *a river Kydnos by name*

e. *Adverbial Accusative.* Some words and phrases originally used as internal accusatives became frozen as abverbial forms, and this usage is known as the adverbial accusative. Here are some typical, idiomatic examples:

τί;   *why?* (neuter sing. acc. of interrogative)
τοῦτον τὸν τρόπον   *in this manner, in this way*
τέλος   *finally, at last*
τὸ ἀρχαῖον   *formerly, in the old days*

f. *Accusative Subject of Infinitive.* This use was presented in U9.4.

4. *Two Accusatives.* In various circumstances there may be two accusative complements with one verb.

a. Some verbs have both an internal and an external (direct) object, as illustrated in §3a(3) above.

b. Certain verbs (e.g., of asking, concealing, reminding) take two direct objects, one a person and one a thing. (English idiom will have only one object and a prepositional phrase for the other noun.)

τὸν παῖδα τὸν τῆς μητρὸς θάνατον ἔκρυπτον.
They concealed from the boy his mother's death.

χρήματα αἰτεῖ τοὺς πολίτας.
He asks the citizens for money.

c. Verbs meaning *to appoint, to choose, to consider, to make, to render,* or the like may take both a direct object (single underline below) and a predicate accusative (either predicate noun or predicate adjective: double underline).[1]

τοῦτον τὸν <u>πολίτην</u> <u>στρατηγὸν</u> ᾑροῦντο.
They were choosing (electing) this citizen (as, to be) general.

<u>ἀγαθοὺς</u> ποιεῖτε <u>τοὺς στρατιώτας</u>.
You are making the soldiers brave.

WHAT TO STUDY AND DO

1. Study the indefinite pronoun τις, τι.
2. Study the uses of the accusative.
3. Learn the adverbial phrases under §3e above and the vocabulary of this unit.
4. Do the exercises of this unit.

VOCABULARY

o-declension nouns

διδάσκαλος, διδασκάλου, m.	teacher; trainer of a chorus, producer of a play [Didaskalia, didactic]
στάδιον, σταδίου, n. alternative plural στάδιοι, σταδίων, m.	stade (unit of length, about 600 ft. or 1/8 mile); race course, single course (without a turn) [stadium]
στρατόπεδον, στρατοπέδου, n.	camp (of an army)
φόρος, φόρου, m.	payment, tribute

---

1. A construction of this kind may be considerd a transformation and embedding of a subject/copula/predicate-noun (or adj.) clause with the copula suppressed. In fact, in Greek the infinitive εἶναι is sometimes expressed in this construction, just as *to be* may appear in English versions.

Socrates is general.	ὁ Σωκράτης στρατηγός ἐστιν.
They choose Socrates to be general.	αἱροῦνται τὸν Σωκράτην στρατηγὸν εἶναι.
They elect Socrates general.	αἱροῦνται τὸν Σωκράτην στρατηγόν.

a-declension nouns

εὐχή, εὐχῆς, f.   prayer, vow
πληγή, πληγῆς, f.   blow, stroke   [paraplegic]
σοφία, σοφίας, f.   cleverness, skill; intelligence, wisdom, learning
                                            [philosophy]

consonant-declension nouns

ὄνομα, ὀνόματος, n.   name   [synonym, onomatopoeia]
πούς, ποδός, m.[1]   foot   [octopus, podiatrist]
χρῆμα, χρήματος, n.   thing, matter, affair; (pl.) goods, property, money
                                            [chrematistic]

verbs

διαφέρω (δια)   carry across; endure; differ, excel (+ gen. of person
                                            or thing compared; sometimes + acc. of respect)
εὔχομαι   pray, pray for; profess openly, boast
κατηγορέω (κατα)   speak against, accuse (+ gen. of person accused)
                                            [category]
κρύπτω   hide, cover, conceal   [cryptographer]
πλήττω[2]   strike   [apoplexy]

adjectives, etc.

ἰσχυρός, ἰσχυρά, ἰσχυρόν   strong, forceful, violent
στενός, στενή, στενόν   narrow; close, confined   [stenography]
τις, τι   (enclitic) (pron.) any, some, anyone, someone,
                                            anything, something; (adj.) any, some, (a) certain
ἑπτά   (indeclinable)[3] seven   [heptagon]
ὀκτώ   (indeclinable) eight   [octopus]
δέκα   (indeclinable) ten   [decade]
πότε   when? (interrogative)
        ποτε   (enclitic) at any time, ever; (idiomatically
                                            reinforces a preceding interrogative: e.g., τίς ποτε
                                            = who *in the world*?)
        οὔποτε, μήποτε   never
ποῦ   where? (interrogative)
        που   (enclitic) somewhere, anywhere; to some degree,
                                            perhaps
πῶς   how? (interrogative)
        πως   (enclitic) somehow, in any way, at all

---

1. The dat. pl. of πούς is ποσί(ν); the voc. sing. is πούς.

2. Non-Attic πλήσσω.

3. "Indeclinable" means that the word does not vary with case: the same form can accompany any case of a noun.

EXERCISES

I.   Write in Greek. Remember that an enclitic cannot be placed first in a sentence or isolated phrase: thus *a certain measure* by itself should be μέτρον τι, in that order (within a sentence one might find τι μέτρον, *provided* some other element of the sentence precedes).

1. any leaders (dat.)
2. a certain daughter (gen.)
3. certain Greeks (nom.)
4. a certain clever soldier (acc.)
5. some small power (nom.)
6. because of a certain one of the prayers
7. in return for a certain blow
8. next to a certain narrow road
9. some (acc.) of the hoplites
10. in the presence of any teacher
11. with some goddesses
12. in a certain one of the tents

II.   Reading.

1. ὁ τῶν Ἑλλήνων στρατηγὸς ἐν ἐκείνῃ τῇ χώρᾳ δέκα ἡμέρας μένει καὶ χρήματα λαμβάνει παρὰ τῶν βαρβάρων οἳ ἐπὶ τῇ θαλάττῃ οἰκοῦσιν. ἐφοβοῦντο δ᾽ οἱ γέροντες καὶ αἱ μητέρες ὑπὲρ τῶν παίδων, ἀλλ᾽ ὁπλῖταί τινες ἀγαθοὶ τοὺς ναύτας κακόν τι ποιεῖν ἐκείνους ἐκώλυον.

2. μετὰ ταῦτα ἡ στρατιὰ ἐλαύνει ἑπτὰ στάδια καὶ ἀφικνεῖται εἰς ποταμὸν Χάλον ὄνομα καὶ εἰς γέφυράν τιν᾽ ἀρχαίαν· ἣν ἐφύλαττε πλῆθος ἀνδρῶν ἰσχυρῶν.

3. κατηγόρει μὲν ὁ διδάσκαλος, ἔφευγε[1] δ᾽ ὁ κλώψ, ἐδίκαζον δ᾽ οἱ πλούσιοι.

4. τὸ μὲν πρότερον βούλευμα οὕτως γίγνεται, τὸ δ᾽ ὕστερον ὧδε· τὸ πλῆθος τῷ Δημοσθένει ἐπείθετο.

5. ἐζήτουν οἱ γέροντες τὰ ἀρχαῖα γράμματα, ἀλλ᾽ ὑπὸ παιδίων τινῶν ἐκρύπτετο.

III.   Render into Greek.

1. Who must excel in this wisdom? A teacher.
2. At that time you (pl.) were making those dreadful accusations against the guide.
3. Somebody was guiding the soldiers away from the enemy's camp along a narrow road.
4. He wanted to conceal his feet somehow, but his (tutelary) divinity always used to prevent (it).
5. They are asking the beast [i.e., Chiron, the only just and wise centaur] for water, for he is in a certain way friendly to human beings.
6. How and where must one seek the truth?

---

1. Here φεύγω is used in a legal idiom, "flee a charge," so "be a defendant (in a court case)."

Ω-Verbs: Future Active and Middle Indicative

1. *Future Principal Part.* The second principal part of a Greek verb is the first person singular future active indicative form (or if the active is lacking, the first person singular future middle indicative form). This form provides the tense stem from which are formed the future indicative, optative, infinitive, and participle in both active and middle voices.

2. *Formation of Future Stem.* The safest way to recognize or to be able to form the future of a given verb is to know the principal parts of the verb. But it is also useful to know some of the basic patterns involved in formation of the future stem, as this helps in learning principal parts and helps in interpreting future forms you come across for the first time in reading.

The future stem is commonly formed by the addition of sigma to a simple form of the verb stem (the verb stem is not always obvious from the present: further discussion of this in U19.8).

Ex.	*present*	*stem + σ*	*future stem*
	ἄγω	ἀγ- + σ	ἀξ-
	ἀκούω	ἀκου- + σ	ἀκουσ-
	βλάπτω	βλαβ- + σ	βλαψ-
	πείθω	πειθ- + σ	πεισ-
	πράττω	πραγ- + σ	πραξ-
	ποιέω	ποιε- + σ	ποιησ-
	φιλέω	φιλε- + σ	φιλησ-

Note that stems ending in labial (β, π, φ) or velar (γ, κ, χ) plosives form a double consonant (ψ, ξ) in the future stem, whereas stems ending in a dental (δ, θ) plosive lose the dental before the sigma of the future. In verbs in -έω it is normal for the ε of the stem to be lengthened to η in the formation of the other principal parts, though there are a few verbs which show no lengthening (e.g., ἐπαινέω, ἐπαινέσω).

Under the influence of verbs in -έω, a number of verbs which do not have
ε in the present stem nevertheless have η (i.e., lengthened ε) inserted before the
sigma of the future (and in some other principal parts as well):

μανθάνω	μαθ- + ε + σ	μαθησ-
βούλομαι	βουλ- + ε + σ	βουλησ-
γίγνομαι	γεν- + ε + σ	γενησ-
ἐθέλω	ἐθελ- + ε + σ	ἐθελησ-

3. *Conjugation of Future Indicative.* The future is conjugated by the addition of theme vowel ο/ε and primary personal endings to the future stem.
Primary endings are used because the future refers to future time or to intention in present time. The combinations of theme vowel plus personal endings
are thus *exactly* the same as in the present indicative (only the *stem* differs).
The accent is recessive, as usual for finite forms. The English equivalent of the
future uses the modal verb *shall* or *will*, as in *I shall lead, you will go,* and so
on.

FUTURE INDICATIVE OF ἄγω AND ἀκούω

		active	*middle*
sing.	*1st*	ἄξω	ἀκούσομαι
	2nd	ἄξεις	ἀκούσῃ
	3rd	ἄξει	ἀκούσεται
(dual	*2nd*	ἄξετον	ἀκούσεσθον)
	(3rd	ἄξετον	ἀκούσεσθον)
plur.	*1st*	ἄξομεν	ἀκουσόμεθα
	2nd	ἄξετε	ἀκούσεσθε
	3rd	ἄξουσι(ν)	ἀκούσονται

4. *Future Infinitives.* The future active and future middle infinitives have
the same endings as the corresponding present infinitives (-ειν, -εσθαι), and
the accent again falls on the final syllable of the stem.

future active	ind.: ἄξω	inf.: ἄξειν
	ind.: γράψω	inf.: γράψειν
future middle	ind.: ἄξομαι	inf.: ἄξεσθαι
	ind.: ἀκούσομαι	inf.: ἀκούσεσθαι

The uses of the future infinitive will be learned later. When the future infinitive is used in isolation in an exercise, it is convenient to translate it with the
paraphrase *about to X* (λέξειν = *about to say*).

5. *Contract Futures.* Some verbs, especially those whose stems end in a liquid (λ, ρ) or nasal (μ, ν), have ε inserted between the verb stem and the tense suffix sigma. In this case the ε was not lengthened and (as often happens in the development of Greek forms) the intervocalic sigma dropped out and (in Attic) the remaining vowels suffered contraction. The resulting endings are the same as those of the present of verbs in -έω.

present	*stem* + ε + σ	*future stem*
(ἀπο)θνῄσκω	θαν + ε + (σ)	θανε-
βάλλω	βαλ- + ε + (σ)	βαλε-
μένω	μεν- + ε + (σ)	μενε-
μάχομαι	μαχ- + ε + (σ)	μαχε-
πίπτω	πεσ- + ε + (σ)	πεσε-

FUTURE OF βάλλω AND ἀποθνῄσκω

		active ind.	*middle ind.*
	stem:	βαλε-	ἀποθανε-
sing.	*1st*	βαλῶ	ἀποθανοῦμαι
	2nd	βαλεῖς	ἀποθανῇ
	3rd	βαλεῖ	ἀποθανεῖται
(dual	*2nd*	βαλεῖτον	ἀποθανεῖσθον)
	(3rd	βαλεῖτον	ἀποθανεῖσθον)
plur.	*1st*	βαλοῦμεν	ἀποθανούμεθα
	2nd	βαλεῖτε	ἀποθανεῖσθε
	3rd	βαλοῦσι(ν)	ἀποθανοῦνται
infinitive		βαλεῖν	ἀποθανεῖσθαι

6. *Attic Futures.* In certain verbs the future involves contraction in Attic and some other dialects, but not in Koine. Later grammarians called this class of futures the *Attic future* because they encountered it most often in Attic literature. There are two types of Attic future:

a. A few verbs with stems ending in ε or α lose the sigma of the future and undergo contraction. The α-type will be learned later (U29). The most common word of the ε-type is καλέω, present stem καλε-, future stem καλε- + (σ) = καλε- (for this verb the present and future forms end up looking identical in Attic).

b. Verbs of more than two syllables with present-tense suffix -ίζω have an alternative future-tense suffix σε- (instead of σ).[1] ζ was eliminated before the future suffix, the sigma dropped out, and contraction took place. For instance, νομίζω —> fut. *νομισέω —> νομιέω —> νομιῶ (inflected like βαλῶ).

7. *Note on Terminology.* The future middle is called "middle" rather than "middle/passive" because there is a separate future form, based on a different tense stem, that has traditionally been termed "future passive" by grammarians (to be learned in U35). In fact the future "middle" is a middle/passive form and in many verbs it can be translated as a passive:

Ex.   ὁ δίκαιος τοὺς πολίτας ὠφελεῖν ἀεὶ λέξεται.
        The just man will always be said to benefit his fellow citizens.

8. *Future of* εἰμί *and* χρή. εἰμί has a future middle, with stem ἐσ-; the future middle inf. is ἔσεσθαι.

	singular	(dual)	plural
1st	ἔσομαι		ἐσόμεθα
2nd	ἔσῃ	(ἔσεσθον)	ἔσεσθε
3rd	ἔσται	(ἔσεσθον)	ἔσονται

Note the elimination of theme vowel ε in 3rd sing. ἔσται. The future of χρή is χρῆσται = *it will be necessary*, a contraction of χρή (noun) + ἔσται (fut. of εἰμί).

WHAT TO STUDY AND DO

1. Learn the various types of future conjugation presented above.
2. Learn the future principal parts of the verbs learned to date (these are compiled in the Appendix at the end of this unit). Note that in this book the future principal part is always given in its uncontracted form for the sake of clarity; in many books and dictionaries only the contracted form is listed.
3. Learn the vocabulary of this unit.
4. Do the exercises of this unit.

---

1. This alternative suffix produces variant futures in a few other verbs: e.g., φεύγω has future middle (future active lacking) φεύξομαι (with normal suffix) or φευξοῦμαι (from φευξέομαι, from the suffix σε-).

VOCABULARY

Studying the principal parts of the verbs learned to date will be a major assignment in the next two units as well. You may wish to begin learning the third principal part along with the second as you study the list in the appendix of this unit, and from this unit on the first three principal parts are given for new verbs in the Vocabulary.

ω-verbs

καλέω, καλέω, ἐκάλεσα call, summon; call by name, name [ecclesiastic]

μανθάνω, μαθήσομαι, learn; perceive; understand [mathematics]
 ἔμαθον[1]

μέλλω, μελλήσω, be destined to, be likely to (+ inf.); be about to (+ fut.
 ἐμέλλησα[2]   inf.); delay (+ pres. inf.)

νομίζω, νομιέω, ἐνόμισα have as a custom; acknowledge, consider as; believe,
   think (+ inf. of indirect discourse [U20])
   [numismatics]

πίπτω, πεσέομαι, ἔπεσον fall [peripety]

negative conjunctions

οὐδέ, μηδέ and not, but not; (adverb) not even

οὔτε . . . οὔτε, neither . . . nor
 μήτε . . . μήτε

particle

ὦ o! (exclamatory particle that often accompanies
   vocatives, often best left untranslated in English)

EXERCISES

I. Translate each form precisely.

1. καλεῖσθαι	7. βαλεῖν	13. ἀποθανεῖσθε
2. μαθησόμεθα	8. εὔξεσθε	14. κόψεται
3. νομιοῦσι	9. δεήσομαι	15. ἔξεσται
4. πεσοῦνται	10. διοίσεις	16. παρακελεύσεται
5. ἀδικήσει	11. λείψω	17. ἐπιθυμήσω
6. αἰτήσετε	12. οἰήσεται	18. κρύψῃ

---

1. Note that many verbs with active forms in the present have only middle forms in the future (with the same meaning as the active). This is often true of verbs of perception or mental activity (ἀκούσομαι, μαθήσομαι), but is also found in other verbs (φεύξομαι, λήψομαι, etc.).

2. This verb sometimes shows *double* augmentation: imperfect ἤμελλον as well as ἔμελλον, aorist ἠμέλλησα as well as ἐμέλλησα.

19. σχήσειν	23. ἔσῃ	27. λήψονται
20. ἀφέξομεν	24. φευξοῦμαι	28. φοβήσειν
21. ἀποκτενεῖς	25. πέμψειν	29. λέξετε
22. ἀφίξῃ	26. πείσεσθαι	30. ἐπαινέσει

II. Render into Greek.

1. we shall not fare well
2. they will make a truce
3. he will not fear
4. about to be on one's guard
5. you (pl.) will be
6. I shall be in training
7. we shall throw
8. you (pl.) will be in need of
9. it used to seem
10. about to have as a custom
11. you (s.) will prevent
12. they will guide
13. it will be written
14. we shall be wronged
15. she will carry
16. I shall never fall
17. you (pl.) will turn
18. they will obey
19. it will be possible
20. he will suppose

III. Reading.

1. Δαρείου καὶ Παρυσάτιδος [gen. of Parysatis, wife of Dareios II, king of Persia 423–404 B.C.E.] γίγνονται παῖδες δύο [two]. ἐπεὶ [when] δ᾽ ὁ Δαρεῖος ἔμελλε ἀποθανεῖσθαι, ἐβούλετο τοὺς παῖδας παρεῖναι [be present, from παρα + εἰμί]. ἀγγέλους δὲ πέμπει οἳ καλοῦσι Κῦρον, ὁ δ᾽ ἀφικνεῖται παρὰ τὸν πατέρα. ὕστερον δ᾽ ὁ Κῦρος περὶ τῇ ἀρχῇ πρὸς τὸν ἀδελφὸν [brother] ἀδίκως μαχεῖται καὶ οὔτ᾽ εὖ πράξει οὔτε νίκην οἴσεται, ἀλλ᾽ ἐν τῇ μάχῃ πεσεῖται. τέλος δ᾽ ὁ ἀδελφὸς ἄρξει ἀντ᾽ ἐκείνου.

2. οὔποτε μαθήσῃ, ὦ πονηρέ, οὐδ᾽ ἐκεῖνα τὰ μικρά· καλὸν γὰρ δόξει τοῖς πολίταις μὴ πείθεσθαι ταῦτα λέγειν μήτε χρήμασι μήτε[1] πληγαῖς.

3. Κέφαλος, ὁ τοῦ Λυσίου [gen. of Lysias] πατήρ, πείθεται μὲν ὑπὸ Περικλέους [gen. of Pericles] εἰς τὴν τῶν Ἀθηναίων χώραν ἔρχεσθαι, χρόνον δὲ μακρὸν ἐκεῖ οἰκεῖ καὶ πλούσιος γίγνεται.

IV. Render into Greek.

1. The Greeks will choose the Athenians to be leaders.
2. This thing which I am about to say is wondrous, but I shall not conceal the truth.
3. Neither the sailor nor the juror will ever do any harm to any of those rich citizens.
4. The fact that not even the children are afraid will aid the army.
5. For the duration of those years we had ten triremes.

---

1. μήτε . . . μήτε is here to be translated as *either . . . or*. Formal English does not tolerate double negatives; but Greek idiom often employs multiple negatives within a sentence for emphasis.

APPENDIX TO UNIT EIGHTEEN

The following list presents all the verbs learned in Units 8–20 with their present, future, and aorist principal parts. The number preceding each verb indicates the lesson in which it was first introduced. Use this list while studying Units 18–20 to learn the principal parts. A long dash indicates that the verb lacks a principal part and has no forms for that tense system. Contract futures, like contract presents, are given in uncontracted form.

19	announce	ἀγγέλλω	ἀγγελέω	ἤγγειλα
8	lead	ἄγω	ἄξω	ἤγαγον
13	do wrong	ἀδικέω	ἀδικήσω	ἠδίκησα
13	seize	αἱρέω	αἱρήσω	εἷλον (stem ἑλ-)
11	perceive	αἰσθάνομαι	αἰσθήσομαι	ᾐσθόμην
16	ask for	αἰτέω	αἰτήσω	ᾔτησα
11	hear	ἀκούω	ἀκούσομαι	ἤκουσα
16	lead away	ἀπάγω (ἀπο): see ἄγω		
16	be distant	ἀπέχω (ἀπο): see ἔχω		
8	die	ἀποθνήσκω (ἀπο)	ἀποθανέομαι	ἀπέθανον
11	kill	ἀποκτείνω (ἀπο)	ἀποκτενέω	ἀπέκτεινα
8	lead	ἄρχω	ἄρξω	ἦρξα
13	arrive	ἀφικνέομαι (ἀπο)	ἀφίξομαι	ἀφῑκόμην
10	throw	βάλλω	βαλέω	ἔβαλον
9	harm	βλάπτω	βλάψω	ἔβλαψα
11	plan	βουλεύω	βουλεύσω	ἐβούλευσα
11	desire	βούλομαι	βουλήσομαι	——
11	become	γίγνομαι	γενήσομαι	ἐγενόμην
19	recognize	γιγνώσκω	γνώσομαι	ἔγνων (U24)
8	write	γράφω	γράψω	ἔγραψα
11	exercise	γυμνάζω	γυμνάσω	ἐγύμνασα
9	be necessary	δεῖ: see δέω		
13	lack	δέω	δεήσω	ἐδέησα
17	excel	διαφέρω (δια): see φέρω		
11	judge	δικάζω	δικάσω	ἐδίκασα
9	seem best	δοκεῖ: see δοκέω		
13	seem	δοκέω	δόξω	ἔδοξα
8	be willing	ἐθέλω	ἐθελήσω	ἠθέλησα
19	saw			εἶδον: see ὁράω
10	be	εἰμί	ἔσομαι	——
19	said			εἶπον: see ἐρέω

8	drive	ἐλαύνω	ἐλάω (U29)	ἤλασα
19	hope	ἐλπίζω	ἐλπιέω	ἤλπισα
9	be possible	ἔξεστι (ἐξ): see εἰμί		
16	praise	ἐπαινέω (ἐπι)	ἐπαινέσω	ἐπήνεσα
16	desire	ἐπιθῡμέω (ἐπι)	ἐπιθῡμήσω	ἐπεθύμησα [ῡ]
8	entrust	ἐπιτρέπω (ἐπι): see τρέπω		
19	say	[no present in Attic]	ἐρέω	εἶπον or εἶπα (stem εἰπ-)
11	go	ἔρχομαι	ἐλεύσομαι	ἦλθον (stem ἐλθ-)
10	find	εὑρίσκω	εὑρήσω	ηὗρον
17	pray	εὔχομαι	εὔξομαι	ηὐξάμην
8	have	ἔχω	ἕξω and σχήσω	ἔσχον
16	seek	ζητέω	ζητήσω	ἐζήτησα
16	lead, believe	ἡγέομαι	ἡγήσομαι	ἡγησάμην
18	call	καλέω	καλέω	ἐκάλεσα
17	accuse	κατηγορέω (κατα)	κατηγορήσω	κατηγόρησα
9	order	κελεύω	κελεύσω	ἐκέλευσα
9	beat	κόπτω	κόψω	ἔκοψα
13	be strong	κρατέω	κρατήσω	ἐκράτησα
17	hide	κρύπτω	κρύψω	ἔκρυψα
16	prevent	κωλύω [ῡ]	κωλύσω [ῡ]	ἐκώλῡσα
8	take	λαμβάνω	λήψομαι	ἔλαβον
8	say	λέγω	λέξω	ἔλεξα
8	leave	λείπω	λείψω	ἔλιπον
8	release	λύω [ῡ]	λύσω [ῡ]	ἔλῡσα
18	learn	μανθάνω	μαθήσομαι	ἔμαθον
11	fight	μάχομαι	μαχέομαι	ἐμαχεσάμην
18	be about to	μέλλω	μελλήσω	ἐμέλλησα
8	remain	μένω	μενέω	ἔμεινα
18	believe	νομίζω	νομιέω	ἐνόμισα
13	be ill	νοσέω	νοσήσω	ἐνόσησα
13	dwell	οἰκέω	οἰκήσω	ᾤκησα
11	suppose	οἴομαι or οἶμαι	οἰήσομαι	— —
19	see	ὁράω (U28)	ὄψομαι	εἶδον (stem ἰδ-)
16	lead astray	παράγω (παρα): see ἄγω		
11	exhort	παρακελεύομαι (παρα): see κελεύω (use middle forms)		
11	prepare	παρασκευάζω (παρα)	παρασκευάσω	παρεσκεύασα
16	furnish	παρέχω (παρα): see ἔχω		
10	suffer	πάσχω	πείσομαι	ἔπαθον

8	*persuade*	πείθω	πείσω	ἔπεισα
8	*send*	πέμπω	πέμψω	ἔπεμψα
18	*fall*	πίπτω	πεσέομαι	ἔπεσον
17	*strike*	-πλήττω	-πλήξω	-έπληξα
13	*make*	ποιέω	ποιήσω	ἐποίησα
11	*be a citizen*	πολῑτεύω	πολῑτεύσω	ἐπολίτευσα [ῑ]
10	*do*	πράττω [ᾱ]	πράξω [ᾱ]	ἔπρᾱξα
9	*be fitting*	πρέπει	— —	— —
11	*inquire*	πυνθάνομαι	πεύσομαι	ἐπυθόμην
11	*pour libation*	σπένδω	σπείσω	ἔσπεισα
9	*arrange*	τάττω	τάξω	ἔταξα
16	*turn*	τρέπω	τρέψω	ἔτρεψα and ἔτραπον[1]
12	*strike*	τύπτω	τυπτήσω	— —
8	*bear*	φέρω	οἴσω	ἤνεγκον and ἤνεγκα (stem ἐνεγκ-)
8	*flee*	φεύγω	φεύξομαι and φευξέομαι	ἔφυγον
20	*say*	φημί	φήσω	ἔφησα
13	*love*	φιλέω	φιλήσω	ἐφίλησα
13	*frighten*	φοβέω	φοβήσω	ἐφόβησα
16	*guard*	φυλάττω	φυλάξω	ἐφύλαξα
9	*be necessary*	χρή[2]	χρῇσται	— —
13	*help*	ὠφελέω	ὠφελήσω	ὠφέλησα

1. The second aorist is poetic and intransitive in sense; in prose the second aorist middle is used with the intransitive meaning "fled."
2. Imperf. χρῆν or ἐχρῆν, inf. χρῆναι.

Ω-Verbs: Aorist Active and Middle Indicative

1. *Aorist Principal Part.* The third principal part of a Greek verb is the first person singular aorist active indicative form (or if the active is lacking, the first person singular aorist middle indicative form). This form provides the tense stem from which are formed the aorist indicative, subjunctive, optative, imperative, infinitive, and participle in both active and middle voices.

2. *Formation of Aorist Stem.* The safest way to recognize or to be able to form the aorist of a given verb is to know the principal parts of the verb. But it is also useful to know some of the basic patterns involved in formation of the aorist stem, as this helps in learning principal parts and helps in recognizing aorist forms you come across for the first time in reading.

There are two types of aorist stem and two corresponding schemes of aorist conjugation.

a. *Strong aorist*, traditionally called *second aorist*. This is the more primitive type of inflection and is found in many of the most common and basic verbs. (Cf. "irregular" verbs in modern languages, such as English *break, broke; teach, taught; bring, brought.*) The strong aorist stem is usually a simple form of the verb stem itself with a weak-grade vowel, such as ᾰ, ε, ῐ, ῠ.

Ex.

present	aorist stem
βάλλω	βαλ-
λαμβάνω	λαβ-
γίγνομαι	γεν-
πίπτω	πεσ-
λείπω	λιπ-
πάσχω	παθ-
φεύγω	φυγ-
say (no pres.)	εἰπ-
see (no pres.)	ἰδ-

present	aorist stem
ἄγω	ἀγαγ-
ἔχω	σχ-
φέρω	ἐνεγκ-
ἔρχομαι	ἐλθ-

The root form of a verb is not always obvious from the present principal part (see further details on stem formation in §8 below). A few verbs (*to see, to say*) have no present stem from the same root in Attic Greek. For a few verbs a full conjugation is created by using etymologically distinct roots in different principal parts: for instance, three separate roots in φέρω, οἴσω, ἤνεγκον; two separate roots in ἔρχομαι, ἐλεύσομαι, ἦλθον. A few primitive verbs show *reduplication* (repetition of an identical or nearly identical syllable) in the formation of the strong aorist: for instance, ἀγαγ- from root ἀγ- of ἄγω; ἐνεγκ- from root *ἐγκ-/*ἐνεκ-.

b. *Weak aorist*, traditionally called *first aorist*. This is the (historically) more recent type of inflection and is found in "younger" and derivative verbs. (Cf. "regular" verbs in modern languages, such as English *narrate, narrated; walk, walked; type, typed*.) The weak aorist stem commonly consists of a simple form of the verb stem with sigma added, whence it is also sometimes called *sigmatic aorist*. In some forms, however, the sigma has disappeared or its presence has caused some modification in the verb stem. In particular,

(1) stems ending in labial (β, π, φ) or velar (γ, κ, χ) plosives form a double consonant (ψ, ξ) in the aorist stem;
(2) stems ending in a dental (δ, θ) plosive or in ζ lose the consonant before the sigma of the aorist;
(3) stems ending in a liquid (λ, ρ) or nasal (μ, ν) lose the sigma, but the vowel of the preceding syllable is lengthened in compensation;
(4) in verbs in -έω it is normal for the ε of the stem to be lengthened to η in the formation of the aorist (as of other principal parts), though there are a few verbs which show no lengthening (e.g., ἐπαινέω, aorist ἐπήνεσα).

Ex.

present	stem + σ	aorist stem
ἀκούω	ἀκου- + σ	ἀκουσ-
λύω	λυ- + σ	λυσ-
βλάπτω	βλαβ- + σ	βλαψ-
πράττω	πραγ- + σ	πραξ-
πείθω	πειθ- + σ	πεισ-
νομίζω	νομιζ- + σ	νομισ-

present	stem + σ	aorist stem
μένω	μεν + σ	μειν-
ἀγγέλλω	ἀγγελ- + σ	ἀγγειλ-
ποιέω	ποιε- + σ	ποιησ-

Note that in some cases the aorist stem turns out to be identical to the future stem (the actual conjugated forms will nevertheless almost always be distinct).

When you know a verb's principal parts, you know the aorist stem: to obtain it, simply remove the augment and remove the ending.

3. *Conjugation of Aorist Indicative.* The aorist indicative is more or less equivalent to the English simple past tense and so is a *secondary* tense in Greek. Accordingly the aorist indicative has augment, like the imperfect, and the personal endings are secondary endings. The accent is recessive, as usual for finite forms.

a. The *strong aorist* indicative is formed by adding syllabic or temporal augment to the front of the aorist stem and adding theme vowel o/ϵ and secondary personal endings at the end of the stem. The combinations of theme vowel plus personal endings are thus *exactly* the same as those found in the imperfect indicative, but the tense stem differs.

STRONG AORIST INDICATIVE

aorist stem:		active of λείπω λιπ-	middle of γίγνομαι γεν-
sing.	1st	ἔλιπον	ἐγενόμην
	2nd	ἔλιπες	ἐγένου[1]
	3rd	ἔλιπε(ν)	ἐγένετο
(dual	2nd	ἐλίπετον	ἐγένεσθον)
	(3rd	ἐλιπέτην	ἐγενέσθην)
plural	1st	ἐλίπομεν	ἐγενόμεθα
	2nd	ἐλίπετε	ἐγένεσθε
	3rd	ἔλιπον	ἐγένοντο

b. The *weak aorist* indicative is formed by adding syllabic or temporal augment to the front of the aorist stem and by adding tense vowel ᾰ and secondary personal endings at the end of the stem. The tense vowel appears in all forms except the third person singular active, where ϵ appears (with no per-

----

1. From *ἐγένε(σ)ο.

sonal ending, but nu movable may be added). The personal endings are the same as those learned in U16.3, *except* for the first person singular active (where nothing is added to ἄ). In the second person singular middle, the sigma is dropped from -ἄσο, and -ἄο contracts in Attic to -ω.

WEAK AORIST INDICATIVE

		λύω, aorist stem: λῡσ-			
		active	*endings*	*middle*	*endings*
sing.	*1st*	ἔλυσα	-ἄ	ἐλυσάμην	-ἄμην
	2nd	ἔλυσας	-ἄς	ἐλύσω	-ω [*-ἄ(σ)ο]
	3rd	ἔλυσε(ν)	-ε(ν)	ἐλύσατο	-ἄτο
[dual	*2nd*	ἐλύσατον	(-ἄτον)	ἐλύσασθον	(-ἄσθον)]
	[3rd	ἐλυσάτην	(-ἄτην)	ἐλυσάσθην	(-ἄσθην)]
plur.	*1st*	ἐλύσαμεν	-ἄμεν	ἐλυσάμεθα	-ἄμεθα
	2nd	ἐλύσατε	-ἄτε	ἐλύσασθε	-ἄσθε
	3rd	ἔλυσαν	-ἄν	ἐλύσαντο	-ἄντο

4. *Aorist Infinitives*

a. The strong aorist infinitives are formed by adding to the aorist stem (N.B. *no augment*) the active ending -ειν (= theme vowel ε + εν) or the middle ending -εσθαι (= theme vowel ε + σθαι) and accenting the theme vowel (producing a circumflex in the contracted active form). Accentuation of the theme vowel is a distinguishing trait of strong aorist infinitives and participles.[1]

Ex.   (active)   λιπεῖν, ἰδεῖν, ἀγαγεῖν, σχεῖν
             (middle) γενέσθαι, ἀγαγέσθαι

b. The weak aorist infinitives are formed by adding to the aorist stem (N.B. *no augment*) the active ending -αι or the middle ending -ασθαι (= tense vowel ἄ + σθαι) and accenting the final syllable of the stem (the accent of the active inf. will be a circumflex if it falls on a long vowel, since final -αι counts as short).

Ex.   (active)   λῦσαι, βουλεῦσαι, νομίσαι, βλάψαι
             (middle) λύσασθαι, βουλεύσασθαι

The uses of the aorist infinitive will be learned later. When the aorist infinitive is used in isolation in an exercise, it should be translated in the same way as the present, *to X* (λέξαι = *to say*).

---

1. And as will be seen later (U41) also in a very few imperative forms.

5. *Translation of Aorist Indicative.* The aorist indicative corresponds in general to the English simple past: ἔλυσα = *I released*, ἐλυσάμην = *I ransomed*. A more detailed discussion of aorist aspect and possible translations will be presented in U20.

6. *Note on Terminology.* The aorist middle is called "middle" rather than "middle/passive" because there is a separate aorist passive form, based on a different tense stem (to be learned in U35). In fact, strong aorist middle forms are sometimes found with passive meaning in early poetry and early prose, but in classical Attic usage this passive use of the aorist middle form is confined to ἐσχόμην, from ἔχω (and compounds). The weak aorist middle is sometimes used intransitively or reflexively, but it cannot be used with a passive meaning.

7. *Two Aorists of* φέρω *and* εἶπον. From the earliest period of classical Greek there already existed weak aorist alternative forms for ἤνεγκον (aorist of φέρω) and εἶπον, namely ἤνεγκα and εἶπα. For instance, εἶπας, and not εἶπες, was the normal second singular form in Attic. In postclassical Greek prose the α-endings also appear sometimes in other strong aorist verbs (e.g., ἔπεσαν for ἔπεσον in Polybius).

8. *The Formation of Tense Stems.* This section contains optional information for the curious student. It may make the variety of Greek principal parts somewhat more understandable and learnable.

a. *Present stems* are derived from verb roots in a variety of ways:

(1) simple root without suffix: e.g., λύω, μένω, πείθω, ποιέω;
(2) labial plosive stems with present suffix τ: e.g., βλάπτω from βλαβ-, κόπτω from κοπ-, κρύπτω from κρυφ-;
(3) with present suffix semivocalic iota (*y*), which has always disappeared while producing euphonic changes (changes made for the sake of ease of pronunciation):
(a) added to dental stems, such as κομίζω from κομιδ-, ἐλπίζω from ἐλπιδ- [but note that -ιζω and -αζω were productive suffixes in their own right, as in νομίζω from νόμος or παρασκευάζω from σκευή];
(b) added to stems in γ, such as ἁρπάζω from ἁρπαγ-;
(c) added to velar plosive stems, producing Attic -ττ- and non-Attic -σσ-, e.g., φυλάττω (φυλακ-), πράττω (πραγ-), τάττω (ταγ-);
(d) added to stems in liquid or nasal, producing either a doubling of λ or a compensatory lengthening and alteration of the vowel preceding ν: e.g., ἀγγέλλω (ἀγγελ-), βάλλω (βαλ-), φαίνω (φαν-), κτείνω (κτεν-);

(4) with present suffix ending in ν, often involving the insertion of μ or ν within the present-tense verb stem (*nasal infix*): e.g., λαμβάνω from λαβ- (suffix αν, infix μ), ἐλαύνω from ἐλα-, πυνθάνομαι from πυθ- (suffix αν, infix ν), μανθάνω from μαθ- (suffix αν, infix ν);

(5) with present suffix -σκω or -ισκω (usually with *inceptive* meaning, i.e., "beginning to X, becoming X," or the like): e.g., θνῄσκω from root θνη- (a variant of root θαν-), γιγνώσκω from root γνω-, πάσχω from root παθ- (*παθσκω —> πάσχω by elimination of θ and transference of its aspiration to κ [assimilation]).

b. *Reduplication* (repetition of the initial sound) occurs in some tense stems. In the perfect stem reduplication with the vowel ε is regular, as will be seen in U37 (e.g., λέλοιπα, γέγονα). Some present stems feature iota-reduplication: for instance, γίγνομαι from root γ(ε)ν-, γιγνώσκω from root γνω-, πίπτω from root π(ε)τ- (alternative form πεσ-), and several μι-verbs (to be learned in U23). As mentioned above (§2a), a few aorist stems are formed by reduplication (ἤγαγον, ἤνεγκον).

c. Variation in *vowel grade* is common in the different tense stems from the same root. The consonants of the root stay the same, but the central vowel shifts in quality or quantity (cf. in English *sink, sank, sunk; eat, ate*). For example, λείπω (strong ε-grade), ἔλιπον (weak grade), perfect λέλοιπα (strong o-grade); λαμβάνω, λήψομαι (strong grade), ἔλαβον; γίγνομαι (zero grade γν), ἐγενόμην (ε grade), perfect γέγονα (o grade). In some verbs the shift in quantity of the vowel is accompanied by a shift in position of the consonants (*metathesis*): weak grade θαν- in future and aorist, strong grade θνη- in present and perfect; weak grade καλ- in present, future, and aorist, strong grade κλη- in perfect.

d. The verb ἔχω has interesting variations of stem. The root was *σεχ- (with zero grade σχ-, still evident in the aorist). Initial sigma before a vowel normally disappeared in Greek, replaced by the *h*-sound. But the expected root *ἐχ- does not appear in the present because of a phonetic rule (Grassmann's law): normally in Greek when two successive syllables contain an aspiration, one of the aspirations is lost (dissimilation). Thus the present is ἔχω, but in the future, where the aspiration of the χ is lost in its combination with suffix σ, the initial aspiration survives in ἕξω. The alternative future of ἔχω is formed from the root σχ- with ε (lengthened) added before the suffix σ: σχήσω.

WHAT TO STUDY AND DO

1. Learn the two types of aorist conjugation presented above.

2. Learn the aorist principal parts of the verbs learned to date (these are compiled in the Appendix of Unit 18).
3. Learn the vocabulary of this unit.
4. Do the exercises of this unit.

VOCABULARY

ω-verbs

ἀγγέλλω, ἀγγελέω, ἤγγειλα	bear a message, announce, report
γιγνώσκω, γνώσομαι, ἔγνων[1]	come to know, get to know; perceive; think, judge [agnostic]
εἶδον (stem ἰδ-), fut. ὄψομαι[2]	(aorist) saw [optics]
εἶπον (stem εἰπ-), fut. ἐρέω[3]	(aorist) said
ἐλπίζω, ἐλπιέω, ἤλπισα	expect; hope for, hope

adjective/pronouns

ἄλλος, ἄλλη, ἄλλο[4]	another, other [allomorph, allegory]
ἕτερος, ἑτέρα, ἕτερον	one of two, the other of two [heterodox]
ἑκάτερος, ἑκατέρα, ἑκάτερον	each of two
ἕκαστος, ἑκάστη, ἕκαστον	each (of more than two)
ἑκάστοτε	(adv.) on each occasion, each time

EXERCISES

I. Translate each form precisely.

1. ἀγγελεῖν	11. ηὕρομεν	21. ἐκρύψατε
2. ἀγγεῖλαι	12. ἡγήσατο	22. διήνεγκον
3. ἤγαγες	13. μενεῖν	23. εἵλομεν
4. ἐλέσθαι	14. μένειν	24. γυμνάσω
5. ᾐσθόμεθα	15. παρεκελεύσω	25. ἐγυμνάσω
6. παρέσχον	16. ἐσπείσαντο	26. ζητῆσαι
7. ἔβαλες	17. ἐμάχου	27. ἦλθεν
8. ἔβαλλες	18. ἀποσχήσω	28. μαχέσασθαι
9. ἠνέγκετε	19. παρασχεῖν	29. ἐπύθου
10. ἔδοξε	20. ἐγένετο	30. μαθεῖν

---

1. A μι-verb aorist, to be learned in U24; for now simply learn the principal part.

2. Present (from another stem) ὁράω, to be learned in U29; you may wish to learn this now as first principal part.

3. No present from these roots in Attic; for present system λέγω or φημί is used.

4. Note the pronominal ending -ο instead of -ον in the neuter nom. acc. voc. sing.

31. ἀπέθανε	33. εἰπεῖν	35. ἐφυλάξαντο
32. ἠλπίσατε	34. ἦμεν	36. ἤρξαμεν

II. Render into Greek.

1. to provide (aor.)
2. we fell
3. to bear (aor.)
4. we fled
5. you (sing.) saw
6. they led astray
7. they were leading astray
8. to acquire [= aor. of *to have*]
9. they announce
10. about to have as a custom
11. she said
12. you (pl.) became
13. to summon (aor.)
14. we arrived
15. we deliberated
16. she will hear
17. to prevent (aor.)
18. they participated in a lawsuit

19. about to kill
20. to choose (aor.)
21. she died
22. you (sing.) throw
23. I shall hope
24. we saw
25. they led away
26. to entrust (aor.)
27. it was necessary
28. we learned by inquiry
29. I shall fall
30. to hope (aor.)
31. it was possible
32. to praise (aor.)
33. to ransom (aor.)
34. you (sing.) went
35. I shall excel
36. we wrote

III. Reading.

1. οἱ ἐπὶ τῇ θαλάττῃ τὰ μὲν ἄλλα εὖ ἔπραττον, κακῶς δὲ ἔπασχον ὑπό τινων τῶν πολεμίων οἳ τὴν χώραν ἀεὶ ἔφερον καὶ ἦγον.[1]

2. ὁ Κέφαλος καὶ οἱ παῖδες ἔτη τριάκοντα [30] ἐκεῖ ᾤκησαν καὶ δίκην οὔτε ἐδικάσαντό ποτε οὔτε ἔφυγον·[2] οὔτε γὰρ ἐκεῖνοι τοὺς ἄλλους κακὰ ἐποίησαν οὔτε οἱ ἄλλοι ἐκείνους ἠδίκησαν. ἐπεὶ [when] δὲ οὗτοι οἱ πονηροὶ τὴν ἀρχὴν εἷλον, τὸν μὲν Πολέμαρχον διὰ τὰ χρήματα ἀπέκτειναν, ὁ δὲ Λυσίας χαλεπῶς τὴν χώραν ἔλιπεν. ἀλλὰ τέλος οἱ τῆς δημοκρατίας σύμμαχοι ἐκράτησαν καὶ ἐκεῖνος τῶν ἀνοσίων κατηγορήσατο· δεινὸς γὰρ ἦν λέγειν.

3. πρὸς τὸν στρατηγὸν ἦλθεν ὁ ἄγγελος καὶ εἶπεν· "εἶδον τοὺς πολεμίους πρὸς ταῖς ἑπτὰ πύλαις [gates]. τίς ἐν ἑκάστῃ[3] τῇ πύλῃ ὑπὲρ τῶν πολιτῶν μαχεῖται; τίσι θεοῖς κελεύσω τὰς μητέρας εὔχεσθαι; πῶς νίκη γενήσεται; τί χρὴ ποιεῖν;" ὁ δὲ εἶπεν· "οὐ δεῖ φοβεῖσθαι· σοφῶς γὰρ τοὺς στρατιώτας περὶ τὰ τείχη ἔταξα."

---

1. Idiom φέρειν καὶ ἄγειν = *plunder*.

2. For the idiom δίκην ἔφυγον, cf. U17 Ex. II.3.

3. ἕκαστος as adjective may be used either with a noun without the article or in predicate position with a noun with the article, as here.

UNIT TWENTY

Tense and Aspect; Indirect Discourse

---

1. *Time versus Aspect*. Greek tense stems convey time distinctions in most uses of the indicative and in a few uses of the infinitive and participle. But the fundamental distinction conveyed by Greek tense stems is one of *aspect*, that is, of the type of action or state of being denoted in terms of completion vs. noncompletion, customary action vs. single occurrence, general truth vs. a specific occurrence, or some similar distinction.

Aspectual distinctions of the type of action denoted by a verb are especially clear in the case of certain verbs which are used exclusively or predominantly with one kind of aspect or which have noticeably different senses in different tense systems. Certain actions by their very nature must take place over an extended period of time (the occurrence cannot be fixed at one point on a time line) or do not include conceptually the intended completion of the action. Other actions by their very nature must take place at an instant (at one point on a time line), or they include conceptually the intended completion of the action. For illustration, consider the contrasts between the following pairs of verbs:

to seek	*to find*
to look	*to perceive, to see*
to believe	*to realize, to learn*
to go, to travel	*to arrive, to depart*
to urge	*to persuade, to convince*
to be	*to become*
to cry	*to burst into tears*
to be dying	*to die*

The type of action exemplified by the left-hand column is that expressed by the present stem; some verbs with such meanings have a present stem but no aorist stem (εἰμί, ἔρχομαι). The type of action exemplified by the right-hand column is that expressed by the aorist stem; some verbs with such meanings have an aorist stem but no present stem (εἶδον, ἦλθον), or the aorist may show most clearly the verbal root while the present stem is formed secondarily by the addition of reduplication and/or a suffix that marks the change in aspect (ἐγενόμην vs. γίγνομαι, ἔμαθον vs. μανθάνω, ἀπέθανον vs. ἀποθνῄσκω).

2. *Present-stem Aspect.* The present stem has the aspect of action not yet completed, or in progress, repeated, customary, or pertaining to general truth:

λέγω
I am talking (action in progress)
πείθω
I am urging (persuasion, the intended effect of the action on the speaker, is not yet complete)
πολλάκις δῶρα φέρω.
I often bring gifts. (repeated action)
οἱ βάρβαροι τοῖς πατράσι πείθονται.
The foreigners obey their fathers. (customary action)
ὁ σοφὸς τὴν ἀλήθειαν ζητεῖ.
A wise man (always, in general) pursues the truth. (general truth)

This force of the present stem is evident throughout the present system, not just in the present indicative. The imperfect is a past tense with the aspect of continuous or incomplete or repeated or customary action:

ταῦτα ἔλεγον.
I was saying these things (at a particular moment).
πολλάκις δῶρα ἔφερον.
I often used to bring gifts.
ἑκάστοτε τὸν στρατηγὸν ἐπῄνουν.
On each occasion they praised the general.

Likewise the present infinitive in most uses has aspect meaning rather than time meaning: it refers to continuous or customary action:[1]

οἱ πολῖται ἀγαθοὶ εἶναι βούλονται.
The citizens want to be brave (on all occasions, in general).
χαλεπὸν τὸ φεύγειν.
It is difficult to be in exile. (exile is a lasting state, not isolated at one point in time)

Because the present stem implies action not yet completed, its meaning is often *conative*, that is, it expresses an action begun, attempted, or intended (often translated into English with the phrase *try to X*):

---

1. Thus, some of the examples of inf. usage in the exercises of earlier units were not fully idiomatic, for in some cases real Greek would have used an aorist infinitive, which the student was then not yet ready to use: e.g., in Ex. I.4 of U9, idiom actually requires aorist ἀποθανεῖν.

ταῦτα τοῖς στρατιώταις δίδωμι.

I give/offer the soldiers these things.

(In the proper context, if it is unclear whether the soldiers will accept the gift, the verb is better translated with *try to give* or *offer* [conative present].)

τοὺς παῖδας ἔπειθε.

He was trying to persuade the children.

(If it is unclear whether the children will be convinced, the verb is best translated with *was trying to persuade* or *was urging* [conative imperfect].)

3. *Aorist-stem Aspect.* The aorist stem conveys an action which is instantaneous and includes conceptually its completion. In the indicative, since the aorist carries no suggestion of duration or of permanent results of the action, it is used to refer to simple, unique occurrence in the past (for instance, for the statement of historical fact):

οἱ Ἀθηναῖοι τὸν Σωκράτην ἠδίκησαν.

The Athenians wronged Socrates.

ἀπέθανον ἐν τῇ μάχῃ ἑπτὰ ὁπλῖται.

Seven hoplites died in the battle.

Outside the indicative the aorist stem normally has aspect meaning only and does not refer to past time. The aorist infinitive, for example, in most of its uses refers to a self-complete, instantaneous, or unique occurrence:

οἱ πολῖται ἀγαθοὶ γενέσθαι ἐν ταύτῃ τῇ μάχῃ βούλονται.

The citizens want to be (become, prove themselves, show themselves) brave in this battle.

ἔδοξε τοῖς Ἀθηναίοις ἐπαινέσαι τὸν Δημοσθένη.

The Athenians resolved to praise Demosthenes (on some particular occasion).

Verbs which denote a state of being or an action which by its nature is usually continuous may require a somewhat different English translation in the aorist, which refers to action at a single moment in time. Often the aorist of such verbs refers to the single moment in time at which the subject enters into the state of being or begins the continuous action (*ingressive* or *inceptive* aorist):

present stem	aorist
ἔχω, εἶχον, *I have, I had*	ἔσχον, *I came to have, I acquired, I got*
βασιλεύω, *I am king*	ἐβασίλευσα, *I became king*
δακρύω, *I am crying*	ἐδάκρυσα, *I began to cry, I burst into tears*
νοσῶ, *I am ill*	ἐνόσησα, *I became ill, I fell ill*

4. *Perfect-stem Aspect.* The distinction between present and aorist aspect is by far the most important in Greek idiom, but there is a third significant variety of verbal aspect, that of the perfect stem. The Greek perfect stem conveys a completed action with results that continue in the present, and the Greek perfect is a primary tense, like the present. For instance, μεμάθηκα = *I have learned (and now know),* βεβούλευμαι = *I have deliberated (and am now resolved).* Further illustration and discussion of perfect aspect will be provided in U37, when the conjugation of the perfect is learned.

5. *Exceptions to Aspect*

a. The *future stem* conveys no distinction of aspect; that is, it may convey either continuous/repeated action in future time or unique/instantaneous action in future time.[1] (For the rare occasions when the Greeks wanted to convey a perfect aspect in future time, there was a separate future perfect, to be learned in U41.) Because the future stands outside the aspect system, Greek had no use for a future imperative or subjunctive, and the future optative is of quite restricted use compared to the present and aorist optative. Similarly, the future infinitive is rarely used for complementary or articular or other substantival purposes, since the present and aorist infinitives sufficiently serve these functions: the future infinitive is thus found mainly in indirect discourse and occasionally as a complementary infinitive with μέλλω (where it is "hypercharacteristic," that is, "overdoes" the marking of futurity, which could have been conveyed with a present or aorist complementary infinitive).

b. In historical narrative the present indicative is sometimes used without its usual aspect to convey historical fact, as a stylistic variation on the aorist of historical narrative. This use is called the *historical* present (and the student has already seen it in exercises, e.g., U16 Ex. III.1 or U18 Ex. III.3), and it may be translated in English with a similar present or with a past tense.

c. In poetry and proverbs, the aorist indicative is sometimes used to express a "timeless" general truth, translated in English as a present tense. This use is called the *gnomic* aorist. Example: (Pindar) βία καὶ μεγάλαυχον ἔσφαλεν ἐν χρόνῳ, *in time violence trips up even a supremely confident man.*

---

1. In *some* uses of the futures of ἔχω there appears to be a distinction of aspect between ἕξω, formed from the root of the present stem, "will have, will possess" (present aspect), and σχήσω, formed from the root of the aorist stem, "will acquire, will stop (hold)" (aorist aspect). But this distinction is not absolute. Some grammarians formerly suggested that there was an aspectual distinction between future middle forms used with passive meaning and future passive forms (based on an aorist stem), but this is not borne out by Greek usage.

6. *Indirect Discourse.* Indirect discourse is the embedding of a thought or of an actual statement as a subordinate element in an independent sentence. The most common form of indirect discourse in English is the subordinate noun-clause introduced by *that.* The English indirect discourse construction is a clause because it contains a subject and a finite verb; it is subordinate because it cannot stand on its own and must depend on an independent clause; it is a *noun* clause because the whole clause performs the function of a noun in the main sentence, whether as object, subject, or appositive to a noun (as in the phrase *the fact that ...*).

Ex. (direct quotation) *"The soldier is ill."*
(indirect) *He says that the soldier is ill.*
(indirect) *I believe that the soldier is ill.*

Note that the subject of the statement sometimes changes *person* in the transformation from direct to indirect form:

(direct) *"<u>I</u> am ill," says Bill.*
(indirect) *Bill says that <u>he</u> is ill.*

Furthermore, in English, the verb of the statement sometimes changes tense in the transformation from direct to indirect form:

(direct) *"There <u>are</u> no seats."*
(indirect) *The man said that there <u>were</u> no seats.*
(direct) *"He <u>will come</u>."*
(indirect) *They believed he <u>would come</u>.*[1]

7. *Indirect Discourse with the Infinitive.* In Greek there are three indirect discourse constructions: with infinitive; with participle (U28); with ὅτι or ὡς and a finite verb (U33). The choice among these three is determined by the type of verb introducing the indirect discourse and by idiom (some verbs may take two of the three constructions).

The infinitive construction for indirect discourse is found with certain verbs of saying, thinking, believing, hoping, swearing, promising, and the like (e.g., φημί, οἴομαι, νομίζω, ἡγέομαι, ἐλπίζω). In this construction the subject–finite verb unit of the direct form is converted into an infinitive phrase with subject either unexpressed or expressed in the accusative case.

direct   ὁ στρατιώτης νοσεῖ.
             The soldier is ill.

---

1. Note that English is not always consistent or unambiguous in these changes: sometimes a present tense of the direct form remains present in the indirect form; moreover, the indirect form of *There were no seats* would also be *The man said that there were no seats.*

indirect	τὸν στρατιώτην οἶμαι νοσεῖν.
	I believe that the soldier is ill.
direct	οἱ δικασταὶ δῶρα λαμβάνουσι.
	The jurymen are taking bribes.
indirect	τοὺς δικαστάς φησι δῶρα λαμβάνειν.
	He says that the jurymen are taking bribes.

In the transformation from direct to indirect form, the finite verb of the state-ment or thought is *always* changed to the infinitive *of the same tense* (or same tense stem: imperfect ind. of direct becomes present inf. of indirect) *and same voice*. The subject of the statement or thought is left unexpressed if it is the same as the subject of the main verb (of saying, believing, etc.) but is other-wise expressed in the accusative (as usual for the subject of a Greek infinitive).

> direct (imperfect indicative)
> τότε ἦρχεν ὁ Ξέρξης.
> *Xerxes was then ruler.*

> indirect (present infinitive; different subject)
> τότε ἄρχειν φασὶ τὸν Ξέρξην.
> *They say that Xerxes was then ruler.*

> direct (future indicative)
> κρατήσω τοὺς πολεμίους.
> *I'll conquer the enemy.*

> indirect (future infinitive; same subject)
> κρατήσειν φημὶ τοὺς πολεμίους.
> *I say that I'll conquer the enemy.*
> κρατήσειν ἔφην τοὺς πολεμίους.
> *I said that I would conquer the enemy.*

> direct (aorist indicative)
> ὁ κλὼψ τὰ χρήματα ἔλιπε.
> *The thief left the money.*

> indirect (aorist infinitive; different subject)
> ἡγεῖται τὸν κλῶπα τὰ χρήματα λιπεῖν.
> *She believes that the thief left the money.*
> ἐνόμιζον τὸν κλῶπα τὰ χρήματα λιπεῖν.
> *They believed that the thief (had) left the money.*

In the indirect discourse construction, the infinitive is negated with οὐ (where-as in its other uses it is negated with μή):

> τὸν στρατηγὸν οὐκέτι νοσεῖν ἡγοῦνται.
> *They believe that the general is no longer ill.*

8. *Predicate Nouns and Adjectives in Indirect Discourse with Infinitive.* Nouns or adjectives in the predicate after an infinitive copula in indirect dis-

course follow the usual rules of concord (cf. U10.4). A predicate noun must be in the same case as its subject; a predicate adjective must agree with its subject noun in gender, number, and case. Thus, if the subject of the indirect statement is expressed in the accusative, the predicate noun or adjective will also be accusative; if the subject is unexpressed because it is the same as that of the main verb, the predicate noun or adjective will be nominative, agreeing with the subject of the main verb (of saying, etc.).

δίκαιον τὸν ἄνδρα φαμὲν εἶναι.
We say that the man is just.

ὁ Σωκράτης οὐκ οἴεται σοφὸς εἶναι.
Socrates does not believe that he is wise.

οἱ Ἀθηναῖοι δίκαιοι εἶναι ἡγοῦνται.
The Athenians believe that they are just.

9. *The Verb* φημί. The verb φημί, *say*, normally takes the infinitive of indirect discourse and (like εἰμί) has enclitic forms in the present active indicative (except 2nd sing. φῄς). The present system (stems φᾰ-, φη-, inf. φάναι) is conjugated as follows (the future φήσω and aorist ἔφησα are regular):

		present active	*imperfect active*
sing.	*1st*	φημί	ἔφην
	2nd	φῄς	ἔφησθα or ἔφης
	3rd	φησί(ν)	ἔφη
(dual	*2nd*	φατόν	ἔφατον)
	(3rd	φατόν	ἐφάτην)
plural	*1st*	φαμέν	ἔφαμεν
	2nd	φατέ	ἔφατε
	3rd	φᾱσί(ν)	ἔφασαν

Note that the other common verbs of saying, λέγω and εἶπον, are not normally used with the indirect-discourse infinitive construction in Attic prose.

WHAT TO STUDY AND DO

1. Study the examples of aspect meaning and study indirect discourse with the infinitive.
2. Learn the present system of φημί.
3. Study again the first three principal parts of all verbs learned to date (use the list in the Appendix of Unit 18).
4. Do the exercises of this unit.

EXERCISES

I. Translate each form precisely.

1. ἐσπεισάμεθα	8. λέξαι	15. φατέ
2. ἐπλήττοντο	9. μαθήσεσθαι	16. ἐνόσησας
3. ἤγγειλαν	10. γιγνώσκεις	17. ηὐχόμην
4. διοίσετε	11. καλεῖται	18. ἐβουλεύσασθε
5. λαβεῖν	12. ἤρχομεν	19. ἀφίξεται
6. ἐλπιοῦσιν	13. ἔβλαψας	20. ἔσῃ
7. ἔφασαν	14. ἔπαθε	21. φιλῶ

II. Render into Greek.

1. we are leading
2. you (pl.) threw
3. it will be necessary
4. I praised
5. about to guide
6. they say
7. we used to dwell
8. you (s.) perceived
9. she wanted
10. they used to seem
11. we shall say
12. I was ordering
13. he learned
14. they make preparations
15. you (s.) will die
16. to write (aor.)
17. you (pl.) were
18. they pray
19. it will be concealed
20. you (s.) will remain
21. we urged
22. to find (aor.)

III. Reading.

1. Ἐρατοσθένης, ὃς δίκην φόνου [murder] ἔφευγε,[1] τάδ᾽ εἶπε τοῖς δικασ-
ταῖς· "ἐξ ἀρχῆς λέξω τὰ πράγματα καὶ οὐκ ἀποκρύψομαι."[2] οὕτω γὰρ
ἡγεῖτο πείσειν τοὺς πολίτας μὴ ἀποκτεῖναι ἑαυτόν [him(self), acc.],
ἀλλὰ λῦσαι τῆς αἰτίας [charge].[3]

2. πῶς οὐ θεῶν τις τὴν τούτου γνώμην ἔβλαψεν, ὃς ἔλεγε μὲν ἀνόσια περὶ
τοῦ θ᾽ ἡλίου τῶν τ᾽ ἀνέμων καὶ τῶν ἄλλων μετεώρων [celestial phenom-
ena], ἐποίει δὲ πλεῖστα κακὰ τὰ ἱερὰ τὰ τῶν Ἑλλήνων;

3. "καὶ οὔποτ᾽ ἐρεῖ οὐδείς [no one, nom. sing.], ὦ ἄνδρες στρατιῶται, ὡς
[that] Ἕλληνας ἤγαγον εἰς τοὺς βαρβάρους καὶ ἔπειτα ἔλιπον μὲν τοὺς
Ἕλληνας, τὴν δὲ τῶν βαρβάρων φιλίαν εἱλόμην. ἀλλ᾽ ἐπεὶ [since] ἐμοὶ
[me, dat.] οὐκ ἐθέλετε πείθεσθαι, πείσομαι ὑμῖν [you, dat. pl.]." ταῦτ᾽
εἶπεν ὁ Κλέαρχος. ἐνόμιζε γὰρ τοὺς στρατιώτας ἑαυτῷ [him(self), dat.]

---

1. For the idiom δίκην ἔφευγε, cf. U17, Ex. II.3.

2. You should be able to guess the meaning of this ἀπο- compound; the sense is here middle,
not passive.

3. The reflexive pronoun ἑαυτόν is better translated in this sentence (and sentence 3) simply as
English *him*. The gen. αἰτίας here expresses separation, *from*.

εἶναι καὶ[1] πατρίδα καὶ φίλους καὶ συμμάχους. οἱ δὲ στρατιῶται οἵ τ᾽ ἐκείνου καὶ οἱ ἄλλοι ταῦτ᾽ ἐπῄνεσαν.

4. ὁ γέρων τοὺς κλῶπας ἔφη μέλλειν τὰ χρήματα ἀπάξειν, ἀλλὰ τὸν φύλακα κωλῦσαι.

5. τοὺς θεοὺς οἴῃ ὠφελήσειν τοὺς δικαίους ἐν τῷ πολέμῳ;

6. τοῦτον τὸν κήρυκα νίκην ἀγγελεῖν ἐλπίζομεν.

IV. Render into Greek. (Hint: when translating indirect discourse from English into Greek, always determine first what is the direct form of the thought or statement and use the direct form to decide the tense of the Greek infinitive. Remember that an English past tense may represent a present tense in direct discourse, indirect *would* may represent direct *will*, indirect *had Xed* may represent a direct simple past [aorist].)

1. One must not obey those orators in these matters, but one must deliberate well and justly and seek the truth.
2. We used to believe that <u>different</u> men excelled in <u>different</u> things [use ἄλλος].
3. The young men resolved [use impersonal δοκεῖ] to marry [use middle of ἄγω] the daughters of the chorus trainer, for they hoped that each one would be both beautiful and wealthy.
4. Do you suppose that the Greeks will choose the Athenians to be leaders?
5. They did not believe that an orator must excel in this wisdom.
6. This woman said that the soldiers had led the jurymen away to the shrine next to the walls.

---

1. This καὶ introduces the series of three coordinate nouns, πατρίδα, φίλους, and συμμάχους. The first καὶ in the series can be omitted in English or translated as *both*. In a series of coordinate words, Greek style usually prefers a conjunction between each pair of words, whereas English often has a conjunction only between the final pair of words.

Consonant-Declension Nouns III; Pronoun αὐτός

PRELIMINARIES

Personal Pronouns. The pronouns which refer without special demonstrative emphasis to persons or things are *personal* pronouns. For the concept of person, review U8 Prelim.; for pronouns in general, U12 Prelim. D. Personal pronouns occur in all three persons: (1st) *I, me, we, us*; (2nd) *you*; (3rd) *he, him, she, her, it, they, them*. In English (as in some other languages), the personal pronouns are very common, because English verbs must have either a noun subject or an explicit pronoun as subject; but there are also other uses of the personal pronouns. Greek verbs normally do without an explicit pronoun subject, but a personal pronoun may be used as subject for purposes of emphasis, and there are other uses for the oblique cases.

∴

1. *Third-declension Vowel Stems*. Some nouns of the consonant or third declension have stems ending in a vowel. The case endings are the same as for other consonant-declension nouns, but in many forms contraction has taken place with the final vowel of the stem or the quantities of two consecutive vowels have been exchanged (short–long becoming long–short by *quantitative metathesis*). Many of these nouns also show a variation in stem vowel.

2. *Stems in ι or υ*. There are two types:

a. Nouns in which stem vowel ι or υ appears only in nom., acc., and voc. sing., but an alternative stem vowel ε appears in the other cases. The paradigm is shown on the next page. Note that the gen. sing. form derives from an alternative stem with strong vowel η (e.g., πολη-), the ending -ηος becoming -εως by quantitative metathesis *without change of accent* (the accent is still on A despite the long vowel in U). The unusual accent in the gen. pl. is by analogy with the gen. sing. Contraction has occurred in dat. sing. and also in masc./fem. nom pl. and nom. acc. dual (ε + ε —> ει) and in the neuter nom. acc. pl. (ε + ᾰ —> η). The masc./fem. acc. pl. is probably borrowed from the nom. pl. (some explain it instead as derived from *-ενς).

Ex.		*"city" (f.)*	*"forearm" (m.)*	*"town" (n.)*
	stems:	πολι-, πολε-	πηχυ-, πηχε-	ἀστυ-, ἀστε-
sing.	*nom.*	πόλις	πῆχυς	ἄστυ
	gen.	πόλεως	πήχεως	ἄστεως
	dat.	πόλει	πήχει	ἄστει
	acc.	πόλιν	πῆχυν	ἄστυ
	voc.	πόλι	πῆχυ	ἄστυ
(dual	*n. a. v.*	πόλει	πήχει	ἄστει)
	(g. d.	πολέοιν	πηχέοιν	ἀστέοιν)
plur.	*n. v.*	πόλεις	πήχεις	ἄστη
	gen.	πόλεων	πήχεων	ἄστεων
	dat.	πόλεσι(ν)	πήχεσι(ν)	ἄστεσι(ν)
	acc.	πόλεις	πήχεις	ἄστη

b. Nouns in which ι or υ appears in all forms. These are not common, and since pure ι-stems are especially rare, only the υ-stem is demonstrated here, with the example ἰχθύς, *fish* (m.) (stem: ἰχθυ-).

singular		*(dual)*		*plural*	
nom.	ἰχθύς or -ῦς	*(n. a. v.*	ἰχθύε)	*n. v.*	ἰχθύες
gen.	ἰχθύος	*(g. d.*	ἰχθύοιν)	*gen.*	ἰχθύων
dat.	ἰχθύϊ[1]			*dat.*	ἰχθύσι(ν)
acc.	ἰχθύν			*acc.*	ἰχθῦς
voc.	ἰχθύ				

In this noun the υ is short in trisyllabic cases, long in the disyllabic cases (in poetry sometimes short in acc. sing.). The accentuation of the nom. sing. is uncertain (and the acc. sing. is also sometimes written ἰχθῦν). The acc. pl. ending is from *-υνς.

3. *Stems in* ευ, αυ, ου. In this type, too, the stem vowel varies (paradigm on next page). The diphthong appears in nom. acc. voc. sing. and dat. pl. (and also in acc. pl. of nouns in αυ or ου). In the remaining cases there is found an alternative stem: namely, ευ is replaced by ε or strong vowel η in ἱππεύς, αυ by ᾱ or η (or ε) in γραῦς and ναῦς, ου by ο in βοῦς.

---

1. Recall that the mark over the iota (*diaeresis*) indicates that the υ and ι are in separate syllables and do not form a diphthong: cf. U1.6e.

stems:	"cavalry-man" (m.) ἱππευ-, ἱππη-, ἱππε-	"old woman" (f.) γραυ-, γρα-	"ship" (f.) ναυ-, νη-, νε-	"ox" (m., f.) βου-, βο-
sing. nom.	ἱππεύς	γραῦς	ναῦς	βοῦς
gen.	ἱππέως	γρᾱός	νεώς	βοός
dat.	ἱππεῖ	γρᾱΐ	νηΐ	βοΐ
acc.	ἱππέᾱ	γραῦν	νῆα	βοῦν
voc.	ἱππεῦ	γραῦ	ναῦ	βοῦ
(dual n. a. v.	ἱππῆ	γρᾶε	νῆε	βόε)
(g. d.	ἱππέοιν	γρᾱοῖν	νεοῖν	βοοῖν)
plur. n. v.	ἱππῆς, -εῖς	γρᾶες	νῆες	βόες
gen.	ἱππέων	γρᾱῶν	νέων	βοῶν
dat.	ἱππεῦσι(ν)	γραυσί(ν)	ναυσί(ν)	βουσί(ν)
acc.	ἱππέᾱς	γραῦς	ναῦς	βοῦς

Quantitative metathesis is apparent in several forms (e.g., ἱππέως, νεώς, ἱππέᾱ from ἱππῆος, νηός, ἱππῆᾰ). The nom. pl. ending of -εύς nouns was -ῆς in the fifth century, but in the course of the fourth century this was replaced by -εῖς. Note the shifting accentuation of the nouns with monosyllabic stems (review U14.2).

4. *Some Irregular Nouns*

		"woman" (f.)	"hand" (f.)	"son" (m.)
sing.	nom.	γυνή	χείρ	υἱός or υός
	gen.	γυναικός	χειρός	υἱέος or υέος
	dat.	γυναικί	χειρί	υἱεῖ or υεῖ
	acc.	γυναῖκα	χεῖρα	—
	voc.	γύναι	χείρ	—
(dual	n. a. v.	γυναῖκε	χεῖρε	υἱεῖ or υεῖ)
	(g. d.	γυναικοῖν	χεροῖν	υἱοῖν or υοῖν)
plur.	n. v.	γυναῖκες	χεῖρες	υἱεῖς or υεῖς
	gen.	γυναικῶν	χειρῶν	υἱέων or υέων
	dat.	γυναιξί(ν)	χερσί(ν)	υἱέσι(ν) or υέσι(ν)
	acc.	γυναῖκας	χεῖρας	υἱεῖς or υεῖς

Note the unusual accentuation of *U* in the gen. and dat. forms of γυνή. In poetry the two stems of *hand* (χειρ-, χερ-) are used as variants in all cases to suit metrical requirements. The noun *son* has o-declension inflection (υἱός, υἱοῦ, etc. or υός, υοῦ etc.) as well as the consonant-declension inflection shown above. Only the o-declension forms υἱόν and υἱέ are found for the acc. and voc. sing. In addition, the iota of the initial diphthong υι was usually so weakened in pronunciation that the word was often spelled without it.

5. *Pronoun αὐτός.* The pronoun αὐτός, αὐτή, αὐτό is declined like ἐκεῖνος (that is, like a vowel-declension adj. except for pronominal neuter -ο in place of adjectival -ον). It has several uses.

a. In origin this pronoun is reflexive (*himself, herself, itself, myself, yourself,* etc., according to context) and is used in conjunction with the personal pronouns to form reflexive pronouns (to be learned in U25).

b. When used in agreement with a noun in any case or when used in the nominative in agreement with the subject pronoun implied in the personal ending of the verb, it is *emphatic* or *intensive.* In this use it must be in predicate position (outside the article–noun group).

τὰ βιβλία ἦσαν αὐτοῦ τοῦ διδασκάλου.
The books belonged to the teacher <u>himself</u>.
(pred. position, agrees with διδασκάλου)

ταύτην τὴν συμφορὰν αὐτὴ εἶδον.
I <u>myself</u> saw this disaster. (woman speaking; with a man speaking, αὐτός)
(agrees with implied [fem. sing. nom.] subject)

c. When placed in attributive position (with article), αὐτός is adjectival and means *the same, the very.*

ὁ αὐτὸς μάντις εἶπεν . . .   *<u>The same</u> prophet said . . .*
ἔπεμψε τοὺς αὐτοὺς ἱππέας.   *He sent <u>the same</u> cavalrymen.*

d. The oblique cases (that is, all except the nominative) are used in Attic as the personal pronoun of the third person (*him, her, it, them*).

ἀπέκτειναν αὐτόν.   *They put <u>him</u> to death.*
τὰ παιδία αὐτῆς ληψόμεθα.   *We'll seize <u>her</u> children.*

Note that when used as possessive (as in the second example above) the genitive of αὐτός takes predicate position. Do not confuse αὐτή (*herself*) with αὕτη (*this woman*), or αὐταί (fem. *themselves*) with αὗται (*these women*): both breathing and accent are different.

WHAT TO STUDY AND DO

1. Learn the various declensional patterns presented above.
2. Study the uses of pronoun αὐτός.

3. Learn the vocabulary of this unit.
4. Do the exercises of this unit.

VOCABULARY

Vocabulary-building Hints. With this unit you learn the declensional patterns used with two very productive suffixes. (1) The suffix -εύς, -έως (m.) is added to many noun roots to form a noun meaning "person who is involved with or works with X": so ἱερεύς for the person involved with sacred rites and sacrifices (ἱερά), ἱππεύς for the person involved with horses, χαλκεύς for the person who works with χαλκός, so *bronzesmith*, and so forth. (For many of these nouns there are corresponding verbs in -εύω, like βασιλεύω, ἱππεύω, and the -εύω suffix also forms verbs for which there is no -εύς noun, like πολιτεύω.) (2) The suffix -σις, -σεως (f.) is added to verbal roots to form an abstract noun of action: for instance, ποίησις from ποιέω, στάσις from the root *to stand*, βούλευσις (*deliberation*) from βουλεύω. Note also in this unit the word ἰσχύς, which provides the root for the adj. ἰσχυρός, previously learned: -ρος and -ερος are common adjectival suffixes, seen also in, for instance, πονηρός (πόνος), βλαβερός (βλάπτω, root βλαβ-), φοβερός (φόβος), αἰσχρός (αἶσχος).

nouns in ι or υ (variant stems)

δύναμις, δυνάμεως, f.	power; authority; capacity, ability [dynamic]
ποίησις, ποιήσεως, f.	creation, production; writing of poetry; poem
πόλις, πόλεως, f.	city; citadel [metropolis]
στάσις, στάσεως, f.	position, standing; party (with political interests), faction; party strife, discord [apostasy]
ὕβρις, ὕβρεως, f.	violence, insolence; assault, rape [hybristic]
ἄστυ, ἄστεως, n.	town
πῆχυς, πήχεως, m.	forearm, arm; cubit (a unit of measure equal to average length from elbow to tip of middle finger)

nouns in υ (pure stems)

ἰσχύς, ἰσχύος, f.	strength
ἰχθύς, ἰχθύος, m. or f.	fish [ichthyologist]
σῦς, συός or ὗς, ὑός, m. or f.	swine, hog

nouns in ευ, αυ, ου

βασιλεύς, βασιλέως, m.	king [Basil]
βοῦς, βοός, m. or f.	ox, cow [Euboea]
γραῦς, γρᾱός, f.	old woman
ἱερεύς, ἱερέως, m.	priest, sacrificer

ἱππεύς, ἱππέως, m.	cavalryman; (pl.) the cavalry
ναῦς, νεώς, f.	ship [naumachy]
φονεύς, φονέως, m.	murderer

irregular nouns

γυνή, γυναικός, f.	woman; lady; wife[1] [gynecology]
υἱός (ὑός), υἱοῦ or υἱέος, m.	son
χείρ, χειρός, f.	hand [surgeon, chiropractor]

pronoun/adjective

αὐτός, αὐτή, αὐτό	self; him, her, it, them; the same, the very [tautology, autocrat]

EXERCISES

I. Reading.

1. οὗτοι μὲν ὑπὸ τῶν βαρβάρων ἀπέθανον.[2] ἐπεὶ [after] δὲ τούτους ἐκποδὼν [adv.: out of the way] ἐποιήσατο ὁ βασιλεύς, δεινὰ μετὰ ταῦτα τῇ πόλει ἐγένετο· ὧν ὅδε αἴτιός ἐστιν· αὐτὸς γὰρ ἔπεισε τὸν βασιλέα ἐπὶ τὴν Ἑλλάδα ἐλθεῖν.

2. καὶ ὁ Ἀγησίλαος τριήρη παρεσκεύασε καὶ Καλλίαν ἐκέλευσε ἀπαγαγεῖν τὴν παῖδα, αὐτὸς δ᾽ ἀπῆλθεν [compound of ἀπο-] εἰς τὴν ἱερὰν πόλιν, ἐν ᾗ ᾤκει ὁ τῆς βαρβάρου θεᾶς ἱερεύς. ἀπεῖχε δ᾽ αὕτη στάδια δέκα ἀπὸ τοῦ βασιλέως ἄστεως, ἐν αὐτῇ δ᾽ ἦν ποταμὸς μικρῶν ἰχθύων πλήρης [adj., nom. sing. masc.: full of + gen.].

3. ὁ πλούσιος τάς τε βοῦς καὶ τὰς σῦς τῷ υἱῷ αὐτίκα ἐπιτρέψειν ἔφη, ἀλλὰ τὰς ἵππους οὐκ ἐξεῖναι.

4. ἄλλοι ἄλλους τρόπους ἐπαινοῦσιν.

5. τῶν τειχῶν τὸ μὲν ἕτερον τοῖς ἱππεῦσι φυλάττειν παρεκελεύσατο, τοῦτο δ᾽ αὐτὸς καὶ οἱ πεζοὶ ἐφύλαττον.

6. οὕτως οὐχ ὑπὸ τῶν πολεμίων μόνον [adv.: only], ἀλλὰ καὶ ὑπὸ τούτων τῶν πολιτῶν ἐπεβουλεύεσθε [from ἐπιβουλεύω = plot against] καὶ ἀγαθόν τι πρᾶξαι ἐκωλύεσθε. καὶ ὑμᾶς [you, acc. pl.] ἡγοῦντο τῶν τῆς πόλεως κακῶν ἐπιθυμεῖν ἀπαλλαγῆναι [compl. inf., to be rid of + gen. τῶν κακῶν] καὶ περὶ τῶν ἄλλων πραγμάτων οὐκ ἐνθυμήσεσθαι [fut. inf., feel concern]. τὴν γὰρ δημοκρατίαν λύειν ἔμελλον.

---

1. Just as ἀνήρ implies male traits and social roles, so γυνή implies traits, roles, and stereotypes connected with females.

2. As the ὑπό-phrase shows, ἀποθνῄσκω is here equivalent to a passive verb, *be put to death*.

II. Render into Greek.

1. For that day the cavalry guarded the camp, but on the next day they rode against the enemy, for they believed they would easily defeat them.
2. Strife and violence are harmful to a city in the same way: each is responsible <u>for the death of good men</u> [use articular inf.].
3. We begged the king to entrust these affairs to the women themselves.
4. The old men said that the women must obey the laws, while the old women said that the men <u>had proven themselves</u> [use appropriate tense of γίγνο-μαι] responsible for terrible evils to the city.

Consonant-Declension Adjectives;
Personal Pronouns

1. *Consonant-declension Adjectives with Two Endings*. One of the two major groups of consonant-declension adjectives features consonant-declension inflection in all genders. Like the vowel-declension adjectives with two endings, these adjectives have a common masc./fem. form and a separate neuter, and again only the nom. acc. voc. actually show distinction between masc./fem. and neuter, the gen. and dat. being the same in all genders. There are two types:

a. *Stems in σ*. The two nominative forms end in -ης, -ες, and declension is similar to that of τριήρης and γένος (U15.3).

Ex. ἀληθής, ἀληθές, *"true"*   stem: ἀληθε(σ)-

		masc./fem.	neuter
sing.	nom.	ἀληθής	ἀληθές
	gen.	ἀληθοῦς	ἀληθοῦς
	dat.	ἀληθεῖ	ἀληθεῖ
	acc.	ἀληθῆ	ἀληθές
	voc.	ἀληθές	ἀληθές
(dual	n. a. v.	ἀληθεῖ	ἀληθεῖ)
	(g. d.	ἀληθοῖν	ἀληθοῖν)
plur.	n. v.	ἀληθεῖς	ἀληθῆ
	gen.	ἀληθῶν	ἀληθῶν
	dat.	ἀληθέσι(ν)	ἀληθέσι(ν)
	acc.	ἀληθεῖς	ἀληθῆ

b. *Stems in ν*. The two nominative forms end in -ων, -ον, and declension is similar to that of δαίμων (U15.1).

161

Ex.   σώφρων, σῶφρον, *"prudent"*   stem: σωφρον-

		masc./fem.	neuter
sing.	nom.	σώφρων	σῶφρον
	gen.	σώφρονος	σώφρονος
	dat.	σώφρονι	σώφρονι
	acc.	σώφρονα	σῶφρον
	voc.	σῶφρον	σῶφρον
(dual	n. a. v.	σώφρονε	σώφρονε)
	(g. d.	σωφρόνοιν	σωφρόνοιν)
plur.	n. v.	σώφρονες	σώφρονα
	gen.	σωφρόνων	σωφρόνων
	dat.	σώφροσι(ν)	σώφροσι(ν)
	acc.	σώφρονας	σώφρονα

2. *Consonant-declension Adjectives with Three Endings.* The other major group of consonant-declension adjectives shows consonant-declension inflection in the masculine and neuter, but has a separate feminine with short-alpha-declension endings. (The fem. stem consists of the masc. stem plus suffix semivocalic iota [y], which combines with the preceding syllable in euphonic change.) There are three main types:

a. *Stems in υ.* The nominative endings are -υς, -εια, -υ, and declension of the masc. and neuter is similar to that of πῆχυς and ἄστυ (U21.2a).

Ex.   ἡδύς, ἡδεῖα, ἡδύ, *"pleasant"*   stems: ἡδυ-/ἡδε-, fem. ἡδει-

		masc.	fem.	neuter
sing.	nom.	ἡδύς	ἡδεῖα	ἡδύ
	gen.	ἡδέος	ἡδείας	ἡδέος
	dat.	ἡδεῖ	ἡδείᾳ	ἡδεῖ
	acc.	ἡδύν	ἡδεῖαν	ἡδύ
	voc.	ἡδύ	ἡδεῖα	ἡδύ
(dual	n. a. v.	ἡδέε	ἡδεία	ἡδέε)
	(g. d.	ἡδέοιν	ἡδείαιν	ἡδέοιν)
plur.	n. v.	ἡδεῖς	ἡδεῖαι	ἡδέα
	gen.	ἡδέων	ἡδειῶν	ἡδέων
	dat.	ἡδέσι(ν)	ἡδείαις	ἡδέσι(ν)
	acc.	ἡδεῖς	ἡδείας	ἡδέα

Note that, unlike the similar nouns, these adjectives have -εος in the masc./neuter gen. sing. Furthermore, in the adjectives there is no contraction in the gen. sing. -εος, gen. pl. -εων, and neuter pl. nom. acc. -εα. Also note that the feminine of consonant-declension adjectives (of all types) always has the circumflex on the gen. pl. (from -άων), thus behaving like a-declension nouns and unlike the fem. of vowel-declension adjectives.

b. *Stems in ν.* Various nom. forms are found, and the declension of the masc. and neuter is generally similar to that of δαίμων (U15.1). Note that the fem. has eta-type inflection (gen. and dat. sing.) because the stem ends in ν.

Ex. μέλᾱς, μέλαινα, μέλᾰν, *"black"*
        stems: μελᾰν-, fem. μελαιν- (from μελᾰνγ-)

		masc.	*fem.*	*neuter*
sing.	nom.	μέλᾱς	μέλαινα	μέλαν
	gen.	μέλανος	μελαίνης	μέλανος
	dat.	μέλανι	μελαίνῃ	μέλανι
	acc.	μέλανα	μέλαιναν	μέλαν
	voc.	μέλαν	μέλαινα	μέλαν
(dual	n. a. v.	μέλανε	μελαίνα	μέλανε)
	(g. d.	μελάνοιν	μελαίναιν	μελάνοιν)
plur.	n. v.	μέλανες	μέλαιναι	μέλανα
	gen.	μελάνων	μελαινῶν	μελάνων
	dat.	μέλασι(ν)	μελαίναις	μέλασι(ν)
	acc.	μέλανας	μελαίνας	μέλανα

c. *Stems in ντ.* Various nom. forms are found, and the declension of the masc. and neuter is generally similar to that of γέρων or γίγας (U14.3b).

Ex. χαρίεις, χαρίεσσα, χαρίεν, *"graceful"*
        stems: χαριεντ-, fem. χαριεσσ- (from χαριεντγ-)

		masc.	*fem.*	*neuter*
sing.	nom.	χαρίεις	χαρίεσσα	χαρίεν
	gen.	χαρίεντος	χαριέσσης	χαρίεντος
	dat.	χαρίεντι	χαριέσσῃ	χαρίεντι
	acc.	χαρίεντα	χαρίεσσαν	χαρίεν
	voc.	χαρίεν	χαρίεσσα	χαρίεν
(dual	n. a. v.	χαρίεντε	χαριέσσα	χαρίεντε)
	(g. d.	χαριέντοιν	χαριέσσαιν	χαριέντοιν)
plur.	n. v.	χαρίεντες	χαρίεσσαι	χαρίεντα
	gen.	χαριέντων	χαριεσσῶν	χαριέντων
	dat.	χαρίεσι(ν)	χαριέσσαις	χαρίεσι(ν)
	acc.	χαρίεντας	χαριέσσας	χαρίεντα

Note that the feminine has eta-type inflection (gen. and dat. sing.) because the stem ends in σ.

3. *Declension and Use of* πᾶς. A very important and common consonant-declension adjective with ντ-stem is πᾶς, πᾶσα, πᾶν, *all*. The stems are masc./neut. πᾰντ-, fem. πᾱσ- (from παντυ-).

		masc.	fem.	neuter
sing.	nom.	πᾶς	πᾶσα	πᾶν[1]
	gen.	παντός	πάσης	παντός
	dat.	παντί	πάσῃ	παντί
	acc.	πάντα	πᾶσαν	πᾶν
	voc.	πᾶς	πᾶσα	πᾶν
	(dual lacking)			
plur.	n. v.	πάντες	πᾶσαι	πάντα
	gen.	πάντων	πασῶν	πάντων
	dat.	πᾶσι(ν)	πάσαις	πᾶσι(ν)
	acc.	πάντας	πάσας	πάντα

Note that the feminine has eta-type inflection (gen. and dat. sing.) because the stem ends in σ. Note also the accentuation of the masc./neuter gen. and dat. pl. (not following the usual rule for monosyllabic stems).

The most common use of πᾶς is in the predicate position with a noun that has the definite article; it then means "all" or "the whole":

πᾶσα ἡ πόλις   *the whole city*
οἱ πολῖται πάντες   *all the citizens*

When used with a noun that lacks the article, πᾶς may mean "any" or "every" or "all (conceivable)":

πᾶσα πόλις   *every city*
πάντες πολῖται   *all (conceivable) citizens*

In the attributive position πᾶς emphasizes totality or entirety:

τὸ πᾶν πλῆθος   *the entire multitude*
ἡ πᾶσα Σικελία   *the whole of Sicily*

4. *Adverbs from Consonant-declension Adjectives.* Adverbs are formed from consonant-declension adjectives in the same way as for vowel-declension adjectives (U12.1). The ending -ως is added to the stem as it occurs in the masc. gen. pl., and the adverb has the same accentuation as that form.

---

1. The long vowel of neuter πᾶν is anomalous; some other dialects have the expected πᾰν (πάν), and the short alpha is sometimes seen in compound ἄπαν in Attic poets.

Ex.   ἀληθής   ἀληθῶς

  σώφρων   σωφρόνως

  ἡδύς   ἡδέως

  χαρίεις   χαριέντως

  πᾶς   πάντως

5. *Personal Pronouns of the First and Second Persons.* For personal pronouns in general, review U21 Prelim. The oblique cases of αὐτός serve as the third-person pronoun in classical Attic. Here is the declension of the pronouns of the first and second persons:

		1st person	1st person unemphatic	2nd person	2nd person unemphatic
sing.	nom.	ἐγώ		σύ	
	gen.	ἐμοῦ	μου	σοῦ	σου
	dat.	ἐμοί	μοι	σοί	σοι
	acc.	ἐμέ	με	σέ	σε
(dual	n. a.	νώ		σφώ)	
	(g. d.	νῷν		σφῷν)	
Plur.	nom.	ἡμεῖς		ὑμεῖς	
	gen.	ἡμῶν		ὑμῶν	
	dat.	ἡμῖν		ὑμῖν	
	acc.	ἡμᾶς		ὑμᾶς	

The singular unemphatic forms (oblique cases only) are enclitic, and these are in fact the more commonly used forms. Unemphatic pronouns tend to come second in their clause or phrase. The nominative forms (sing. and plural) are used only when the subject is emphatic; otherwise the personal ending of the verb suffices.

  Ex.   τί μοι λέξεις;   *What will you say to me?*

  τὸν μὲν πατέρα μου ἐπήνεσας, ἐμὲ δ᾽ οὔ.
  You praised my father, but not me.

  ἐγὼ τὸν ποιητὴν ἐπαινῶ, ὑμεῖς δὲ τὸν ῥήτορα.
  I praise the poet, you praise the orator.

Note that when a personal pronoun is used in the possessive genitive, it takes predicate position (outside the article–noun group), as in the second example above (τὸν πατέρα μου).

WHAT TO STUDY AND DO

1. Learn the inflectional patterns of consonant-declension adjectives.

2. Learn the personal pronouns of the first and second persons.
3. Learn the vocabulary of this unit.
4. Do the exercises of this unit.

VOCABULARY

noun

τύχη, τύχης, f.   fate; chance; fortune (good, bad, or neutral);
                                    happening, event   [Tyche]

consonant-declension adjectives: sigma-stems

ἀληθής, ἀληθές   true, genuine; truthful
ἀσθενής, ἀσθενές   without strength, weak   [myasthenia]
ἀσφαλής, ἀσφαλές   steadfast; safe, secure; trustworthy
δυστυχής, δυστυχές   unlucky, unfortunate
εὐγενής, εὐγενές   well-born; noble, noble-minded   [eugenics]
εὐτυχής, εὐτυχές   lucky, fortunate
πλήρης, πλῆρες   full, full of (+ gen.)
σαφής, σαφές   sure, reliable; clear, distinct
ψευδής, ψευδές   lying, false, untrue   [pseudonym]

consonant-declension adjectives: nu-stems with two endings

ἄφρων, ἄφρον   senseless, foolish
εὐδαίμων, εὔδαιμον   blessed with a good δαίμων; fortunate, happy;
                                    wealthy   [eudaemonism]
σώφρων, σῶφρον   of sound mind; prudent; self-controlled; temperate,
                                    chaste

consonant-declension adjectives: upsilon-stems

βαθύς, βαθεῖα, βαθύ   deep, high   [bathyscaph]
βαρύς, βαρεῖα, βαρύ   heavy   [barometer]
βραχύς, βραχεῖα, βραχύ   short; small   [brachylogy, brachistochrone]
γλυκύς, γλυκεῖα, γλυκύ   sweet, pleasant, delightful   [glycerine]
ἡδύς, ἡδεῖα, ἡδύ   pleasant, welcome; glad, pleased
ἥμισυς, ἡμίσεια, ἥμισυ   half   [hemisphere][1]

consonant-declension adjectives: nu-stem with three endings

μέλας, μέλαινα, μέλαν   black, dark   [melanin]

---

1. ἥμισυς may be used as an attributive adjective (e.g., αἱ ἡμίσειαι νῆες = "half (of) the ships")
or it may be used as a substantive (with article) accompanied by the partitive genitive (e.g., αἱ
ἡμίσειαι τῶν νεῶν [the gender and number of the substantive ἥμισυς are the same as those of
the word that expresses the whole]).

consonant-declension adjectives: ντ-stems

πᾶς, πᾶσα, πᾶν   all, every, the whole   [pantomime]
      ἅπᾱς, ἅπᾱσα, ἅπᾱν   all, the whole   (strengthened form of πᾶς)
χαρίεις, χαρίεσσα, χαρίεν   graceful, beautiful, elegant; clever

possessive adjectives (1st and 2nd person)[1]

ἐμός, ἐμή, ἐμόν   my, mine
σός, σή, σόν   your, yours (sing.)
ἡμέτερος, ἡμετέρα,   our, ours
   ἡμέτερον
ὑμέτερος, ὑμετέρα,   your, yours (plural)[2]
   ὑμέτερον

EXERCISES

I. Render into Greek.

1. of these weak cattle
2. a certain city (acc.) full of strife
3. toward the foolish thieves
4. for a short time
5. all women (nom.)
6. in the presence of the elegant king
7. of the blessed priest
8. of heavy misfortune
9. the entire strength (acc.) of this town
10. in accordance with the true account
11. by means of some steadfast measure
12. my unfortunate sons (nom.)
13. into a deep river full of sweet water
14. concerning your false victory
15. for ten prudent old women
16. black ships (nom.)
17. Our life is pleasant.
18. Half the soldiers died.
19. Your daughter did not arrive.
20. on our behalf

---

1. Use of the possessive adjective (ὁ ἐμὸς πατήρ) is stylistically more formal than use of the possessive gen. of the personal pronoun (ὁ πατήρ μου), which is informal and colloquial.
2. Hint for avoiding confusion between ἡμεῖς and ὑμεῖς or ἡμέτερος and ὑμέτερος: associate *we* with the long *e*/η, associate *you* with the Greek *u*/υ.

II. Reading: Herakles at the Crossroads.

ἐβουλεύετό ποτε ὁ Ἡρακλῆς περὶ τοῦ βίου ὧδέ πως· "τί χρὴ ποιεῖν;
αἱρήσομαι τὴν δι' ἀρετῆς ὁδόν, ἢ [or] τὴν ἑτέραν:" γυναῖκες δὲ δύο [two]
πρὸς αὐτὸν ἦλθον, ἡ μὲν [supply participle being] σώφρων καὶ εὐγενής, ἡ δὲ
χαρίεσσα ἀλλὰ πονηρά. ἔπειθον δὲ τὸν ἄνδρα ἐν μέρει· αὕτη μὲν "ἐμὲ" ἔφη
"φίλην ποιήσασθαί σε χρή· τὴν γὰρ ἡδεῖάν τε καὶ ῥᾳδίαν ὁδὸν ἄξω σε, καὶ
τὰ μὲν γλυκέα πάντα ἕξεις, τὰ δὲ χαλεπὰ πάντα φεύξῃ." καὶ ὁ Ἡρακλῆς "ὦ
γύναι," ἔφη "ὄνομά σοι τί ἐστιν;" ἡ δὲ "οἱ μὲν ἐμοὶ φίλοι" ἔφη "καλοῦσί με
Εὐδαιμονίαν [happy prosperity], οἱ δ' ἄλλοι Κακίαν [vice]." ἡ δ' ἑτέρα γυνὴ
εἶπεν· "ἡ ὁδὸς ἣν ἐγώ σε ἑλέσθαι φημὶ δεῖν οὔτε βραχεῖα οὔτ' ἀσφαλὴς
οὔτε ῥᾳδία. ἀλλ' οὐκ ἔξεστι ἄνδρα ἀληθῶς καλὸν καὶ ἀγαθὸν γενέσθαι ἄνευ
[without + gen.] πόνων. χαλεπὰ γὰρ τὰ καλά, ἀλλ' ἐπαινέσουσί σε πάντες
οἱ ἄνθρωποι καὶ πάντες οἱ θεοί." ταύτῃ δὲ τὸ ὄνομα ἦν Ἀρετή.

III. Render into Greek.

1. It is necessary for all of our hoplites to exercise themselves; for this makes
    them strong in hand and brave in spirit.[1]
2. The old women said that the man was rich, ugly, and difficult, while his
    wife was graceful and pleasant.
3. The general did all these good deeds to the city, but he was put to death by
    you because of the wicked orators who made false accusations against him.

_____

1. Hint: for *in hand* and *in spirit* review U17.

MI-Verbs: Present System

1. *μι-Verbs*. In classical Attic a limited number of basic verbs form the present and/or aorist systems by adding personal endings directly to the tense stem without intervening theme vowel or tense vowel. These verbs form the second major conjugational class in Greek (alongside the ω-verbs) and are called *athematic* ("without theme vowel") verbs or μι-verbs (from the primary personal ending of the 1st person sing.). You have already learned two μι-verbs which feature slightly irregular inflection: εἰμί (U10) and φημί (U20).

2. *Personal Endings*. The personal endings are readily apparent in μι-verbs, and those used in the active are slightly different from those you have learned for the thematic conjugation, while the middle or middle/passive personal endings are *exactly* the same.

MI-VERB PERSONAL ENDINGS

		primary active	*primary middle/passive*	*secondary active*	*secondary middle/passive*
sing.	1st	-μι	-μαι	-ν	-μην
	2nd	-ς	-σαι	-ς	-σο
	3rd	-σι(ν)	-ται	—	-το
(dual	2nd	-τον	-σθον	-τον	-σθον)
	(3rd	-τον	-σθον	-την	-σθην)
plur.	1st	-μεν	-μεθα	-μεν	-μεθα
	2nd	-τε	-σθε	-τε	-σθε
	3rd	-ᾱσι(ν)	-νται	-σαν	-ντο

The active infinitive ending for μι-verbs is -ναι (with the accent always on the syllable preceding -ναι); the middle infinitive ending is -σθαι (with the accent on *A* in the present and on *P* in the aorist).

3. *The Major μι-Verbs*. The four most common μι-verbs are τίθημι, ἵημι, ἵστημι, and δίδωμι. All have present stems derived from the verb root

with iota-reduplication (defined in U19.7b). It is also characteristic that the present stem of these verbs has two forms: a strong, long-vowel form in the singular of the active, and a normal, short-vowel form in the other forms (plural of the active, all middle/passive forms; infinitive and participles).

verb root	present stem[1]
θε-	τιθη-, τιθε-
ἑ-	ἱη-, ἱε-
στᾰ-	ἱστη- [non-Attic-Ionic ἱστᾱ-], ἱστᾰ-
δο-	δω-, δο-

PARADIGMS

τίθημι, "place"   pres. act. inf. τιθέναι   pres. m/p inf. τίθεσθαι

		pres. act.	pres. m/p	imperf. act.	imperf. m/p
s.	1st	τίθημι	τίθεμαι	ἐτίθην	ἐτιθέμην
	2nd	τίθης	τίθεσαι	ἐτίθεις	ἐτίθεσο
	3rd	τίθησι(ν)	τίθεται	ἐτίθει	ἐτίθετο
(d.	2nd	τίθετον	τίθεσθον	ἐτίθετον	ἐτίθεσθον)
	(3rd	τίθετον	τίθεσθον	ἐτιθέτην	ἐτιθέσθην)
pl.	1st	τίθεμεν	τιθέμεθα	ἐτίθεμεν	ἐτιθέμεθα
	2nd	τίθετε	τίθεσθε	ἐτίθετε	ἐτίθεσθε
	3rd	τιθέᾱσι(ν)	τίθενται	ἐτίθεσαν	ἐτίθεντο

Note: the 2nd and 3rd sing. imperf. act. are explained as from *ἐτίθεες, *ἐτίθεε, with endings borrowed from ω-conjugation and contracted.

ἵημι, "let go, throw"   pres. act. inf. ἱέναι   pres. m/p inf. ἵεσθαι

		pres. act.	pres. m/p	imperf. act.	imperf. m/p
s.	1st	ἵημι	ἵεμαι	ἵην	ἱέμην
	2nd	ἵης	ἵεσαι	ἵεις	ἵεσο
	3rd	ἵησι(ν)	ἵεται	ἵει	ἵετο
(d.	2nd	ἵετον	ἵεσθον	ἵετον	ἵεσθον)
	(3rd	ἵετον	ἵεσθον	ἱέτην	ἱέσθην)
pl.	1st	ἵεμεν	ἱέμεθα	ἵεμεν	ἱέμεθα
	2nd	ἵετε	ἵεσθε	ἵετε	ἵεσθε
	3rd	ἱᾶσι(ν)	ἵενται	ἵεσαν	ἵεντο

1. τιθε- from *θιθε- by Grassmann's law (U19.7d); the original root of ἵημι was *yε-, which became *hε-, forming *(h)ι(h)ε-; ἱστα- is from *(σ)ιστα-.

Note: the 3rd pl. pres. act. is a contraction of *ἱέᾱσι(ν); the 2nd and 3rd sing. imperf. act. are explained as from *ἵεες, *ἵεε, with endings borrowed from ω-conjugation and contracted. In Attic the initial iota is usually long in the present (and of course always long when augmented in the imperfect); in Homeric Greek the initial iota is short, unless augmented.

ἵστημι, *"make stand"*   pres. act. inf. ἱστάναι   pres. m/p inf. ἵστασθαι

		pres. act.	*pres. m/p*	*imperf. act.*	*imperf. m/p*
s.	1st	ἵστημι	ἵσταμαι	ἵστην (ῑ)	ἱστάμην (ῑ)
	2nd	ἵστης	ἵστασαι	ἵστης	ἵστασο
	3rd	ἵστησι(ν)	ἵσταται	ἵστη	ἵστατο
(d.	2nd	ἵστατον	ἵστασθον	ἵστατον	ἵστασθον)
	(3rd	ἵστατον	ἵστασθον	ἱστάτην	ἱστάσθην)
pl.	1st	ἵσταμεν	ἱστάμεθα	ἵσταμεν	ἱστάμεθα
	2nd	ἵστατε	ἵστασθε	ἵστατε	ἵστασθε
	3rd	ἱστᾶσι(ν)	ἵστανται	ἵστασαν	ἵσταντο

Note: the 3rd pl. pres. act. is a contraction of *ἱστάᾱσι(ν).

δίδωμι, *"give"*   pres. act. inf. διδόναι   pres. m/p inf. δίδοσθαι

		pres. act.	*pres. m/p*	*imperf. act.*	*imperf. m/p*
s.	1st	δίδωμι	δίδομαι	ἐδίδουν	ἐδιδόμην
	2nd	δίδως	δίδοσαι	ἐδίδους	ἐδίδοσο
	3rd	δίδωσι(ν)	δίδοται	ἐδίδου	ἐδίδοτο
(d.	2nd	δίδοτον	δίδοσθον	ἐδίδοτον	ἐδίδοσθον)
	3rd	δίδοτον	δίδοσθον	ἐδιδότην	ἐδιδόσθην)
pl.	1st	δίδομεν	διδόμεθα	ἐδίδομεν	ἐδιδόμεθα
	2nd	δίδοτε	δίδοσθε	ἐδίδοτε	ἐδίδοσθε
	3rd	διδόασι(ν)	δίδονται	ἐδίδοσαν	ἐδίδοντο

Note: the sing. imperf. act. forms are explained as from *ἐδίδοον, *ἐδίδοες, *ἐδίδοε, with endings borrowed from ω-conjugation and contracted.

4. *Verbs in -νυμι.* Another group of μι-verbs has present stem with suffix νυ (or ννυ after a vowel) and shows no reduplication: for example, δείκνυμι (δεικ-), ῥήγνυμι (ῥηγ-), κεράννυμι (κερα-). Note that in these verbs the υ is long in the *singular* present active and imperfect active forms, short in all the other forms (compare the major μι-verbs).

| **Ex.** | δείκνυμι, *"show"* | | infinitives: δεικνύναι, δείκνυσθαι | |
| | *pres. act.* | *pres. m/p* | *imperf. act.* | *imperf. m/p* |

		pres. act.	*pres. m/p*	*imperf. act.*	*imperf. m/p*
s.	*1st*	δείκνῡμι	δείκνυμαι	ἐδείκνῡν	ἐδεικνύμην
	2nd	δείκνῡς	δείκνυσαι	ἐδείκνῡς	ἐδείκνυσο
	3rd	δείκνῡσι(ν)	δείκνυται	ἐδείκνῡ	ἐδείκνυτο
(*d.*	*2nd*	δείκνυτον	δείκνυσθον	ἐδείκνυτον	ἐδείκνυσθον)
	(*3rd*	δείκνυτον	δείκνυσθον	ἐδεικνύτην	ἐδεικνύσθην)
pl.	*1st*	δείκνυμεν	δεικνύμεθα	ἐδείκνυμεν	ἐδεικνύμεθα
	2nd	δείκνυτε	δείκνυσθε	ἐδείκνυτε	ἐδείκνυσθε
	3rd	δεικνύᾱσι(ν)	δείκνυνται	ἐδείκνυσαν	ἐδείκνυντο

5. εἶμι, *"to go."* The Greek verb "to go" has slightly irregular μι-verb inflection. The stems used in the present are εἰ- (augmented ᾐ-), εἰε- (augmented ᾐε-), ἰ-, and ἰε-. The present active infinitive is ἰέναι.

		pres. act.	*imperf. act.*		
s.	*1st*	εἶμι	ᾖα	or	ᾔειν
	2nd	εἶ	ᾔεισθα	or	ᾔεις
	3rd	εἶσι(ν)	ᾔειν	or	ᾔει
(*d.*	*2nd*	ἴτον	ᾖτον)		
	(*3rd*	ἴτον	ᾔτην)		
pl.	*1st*	ἴμεν	ᾖμεν		
	2nd	ἴτε	ᾖτε		
	3rd	ἴᾱσι(ν)	ᾖσαν	or	ᾔεσαν

In Attic prose εἶμι and its compounds normally have a future meaning in the present indicative (and in indirect discourse transformations of the present ind.): εἶμι = *I am going, I' ll go*. In the imperfect ind. and in the other moods the tenses of εἶμι have normal meaning. The most commonly used forms to express *to go* (simple verb and compounds of it) in Attic are thus: present ἔρχομαι, imperfect ᾖα, future εἶμι, aorist ἦλθον.[1]

Note that some forms of εἶμι can be confused with similar or identical forms of εἰμί or ἵημι unless close attention is paid to breathing, accent, and presence or absence of iota subscript: ἱέναι = *to throw* vs. ἰέναι = *to go*; εἰσί = *they are* vs. εἶσι = *he' ll go*; ἦσαν = *they were* vs. ᾖσαν = *they went*; the form εἶ may be either *you (s.) are* or *you (s.) will go* (context will usually make clear which translation to use).

---

1. Imperfect ἠρχόμην in Attic prose is always from ἄρχω rather than ἔρχομαι; the future ἐλεύσομαι is much rarer than εἶμι.

6. *Other Tenses of μι-Verbs*. Verbs that have athematic conjugation in the present system have ordinary ω-conjugation in the future, as is obvious from the future principal parts; in the aorist some have athematic conjugation and some have regular weak aorist in -σα. You must learn the principal parts to know what kind of aorist each verb has. Athematic aorist conjugation will be treated in the next unit (for now, simply learn the principal parts).

WHAT TO STUDY AND DO

1. Learn the inflectional patterns of the μι-verbs presented above.
2. Learn the vocabulary of this unit.
3. Do the exercises of this unit.

VOCABULARY

μι-verbs

δίδωμι, δώσω, ἔδωκα	give; (pres. + imperf.) offer; grant, allow [antidote, apodosis]
ἀποδίδωμι (ἀπο)	give back, return; pay; (mid.) sell
μεταδίδωμι (μετα)	give a part of, give a share of (+ gen. of thing shared)
παραδίδωμι (παρα)	give over, hand over; surrender, deliver over
προδίδωμι (προ)	give in advance; (more commonly) give up, betray, abandon
ἵημι, ἥσω, -ἧκα[1]	let go; throw, hurl; utter (words); (mid.) hasten, rush
ἀφίημι (ἀπο)	send forth, send away; release, set free; leave alone, neglect
ἐφίημι (ἐπι)	send on, against; let go, yield; (mid.) command, give orders; (mid.) aim at, long for (+ gen.)
προσίημι (προς)	let come to; (more commonly mid.) let come to oneself, admit
ἵστημι, στήσω, ἔστησα and ἔστην	(act. and 1st aor., transitive) make stand, set up; cause to stand, stop, check
	(pass. and 2nd aor., intrans.) be placed, be set up, stand; stand still, halt [hypostasis, rheostat]
ἀφίστημι (ἀπο)	(trans.) put out of the way; cause to revolt; (intrans.) keep (oneself) away from, apart from; revolt from (+ ἀπό + gen.)

---

1. The hyphen indicates that this form occurs only in compounds in Attic prose (the simple form is found in poetry).

ἐφίστημι (ἐπι)	(trans.) set upon, set in charge of; cause to stop; (intrans.) stand upon, by, against; be in charge of (+ dat.)
καθίστημι (κατα)	(trans.) set down; set in order; appoint; establish; (intrans.) set oneself down, in order; settle; become; be established
τίθημι, θήσω, ἔθηκα	set, place, put; set up, establish; bring to pass; make, cause [thesis, hypothesis]
ἀνατίθημι (ἀνα)	set up as an offering, dedicate [anathema]
ἐπιτίθημι (ἐπι)	place upon; add to; (mid.) make an attempt upon, attack (+ dat.) [epithet]
κατατίθημι (κατα)	put down; pay down; (mid.) lay aside, store up; put an end to; put away in a safe place
συντίθημι (συν)	put together; (mid.) make an agreement with (+ dat. of person), agree on, conclude (a pact, etc.) [synthetic]
δείκνῦμι, δείξω, ἔδειξα	show, point out [deictic]
ἀποδείκνῦμι (ἀπο)	display, make known; appoint, proclaim, create [apodeictic, apodictic]
ἐπιδείκνῦμι (ἐπι)	exhibit, display; show, point out, prove [epideictic]
ζεύγνῦμι, ζεύξω, ἔζευξα	yoke, join together [zeugma]
ῥήγνῦμι, ῥήξω, ἔρρηξα[1]	break, shatter [hemorrhage]
εἶμι	go, will go [ion]
ἄπειμι (ἀπο)	go away
ἔξειμι (ἐκ)	go out

EXERCISES

I. Translate the following forms precisely, and for any ten give a complete identification.

1. ἐπιδεῖξαι	10. ἵστησι	19. ἴμεν
2. παραδίδως	11. δώσειν	20. ἐρρήγνυτο
3. ἀφήσουσι	12. ἀνετίθει	21. ἀπεδείκνυσο
4. ἐφίεις	13. ζεύγνυνται	22. δείκνυς
5. ἀπιέναι	14. ἐρρήγνυ	23. καταθήσετε
6. καθίστατο	15. ἐξῄεσαν	24. παραδίδομεν
7. ἀφιέναι	16. ἐπιτίθεμαι	25. ἐφίεμαι
8. εἶσι	17. προδιδόασι	26. καταστήσουσι
9. μεταδίδοτε	18. ἐδίδους	27. μεταδίδωσι

---

1. Verbs which begin with rho double the rho when augmented with epsilon (ἐρρ-).

28. ἴῃς
29. ἐφίστασαι
30. προδίδοσθαι
31. προσίεντο
32. ἀποδίδοσθαι

33. ἀφίσταμαι
34. τίθης
35. ἐδιδόμην
36. ἵενται
37. δίδως

38. ἐφιστᾶσι
39. συντίθεσθαι
40. ἔξιτε
41. ἐζεύγνυν
42. ἐπετίθεις

II. Render into Greek.

1. they will go
2. we were setting free
3. you (s.) pay down
4. to shatter (pres.)
5. it was being set up
6. you (pl.) are betraying
7. about to make an agreement
8. to shatter (aor.)
9. they were giving a share of
10. we are yoking
11. he appoints
12. to go away (pres.)

13. it was being yoked
14. she is admitting
15. I revolt from
16. you (pl.) attack
17. they prove
18. you (s.) were breaking
19. you (s.) will go away
20. we aim at
21. we hurl
22. it is being placed
23. I was selling
24. they cause to stand

III. Reading.

1. οἱ μὲν σύμμαχοι ἀφίστανται ἀφ᾽ ἡμῶν, οἱ δὲ πολέμιοι ἐπιτίθενται τοῖς τείχεσιν ἡμῶν, οἱ δ᾽ ἡμέτεροι στρατηγοὶ προδιδόασι τὰς πόλεις, ἀλλ᾽ ὑμεῖς οἱ πολῖται οὐ προσίεσθε τοὺς περὶ τῆς εἰρήνης ἀγγέλους.

2. οἱ μὲν ἄφρονες ἀεὶ εὐτυχεῖς ἔσεσθαι ἡγοῦνται, οἱ δὲ σώφρονες τὰ τῶν ἀνθρώπων οὔποτ᾽ ἀσφαλῆ νομίζουσιν.

3. ὁ Θηραμένης ἀνεπήδησεν [jumped up] ἐπὶ τὸν βωμὸν [altar] καὶ εἶπεν· "ἐγώ, ὦ ἄνδρες, ἡγοῦμαι δεῖν μὴ τῷ Κριτίᾳ ἐξεῖναι ἐμὲ ἀποκτεῖναι, ἀλλὰ κατὰ τοῦτον τὸν νόμον ὃν οὗτοι ἔγραψαν περὶ τῶν ἐν τῷ καταλόγῳ [register (of citizens)] καὶ ὑμῖν καὶ ἐμοὶ τὴν κρίσιν [legal judgment] εἶναι. καὶ τοῦτο μὲν δῆλόν ἐστιν, ὅτι [that] οὐδέν [adv., not at all] με ὠφελήσει ὅδε ὁ βωμός, ἀλλὰ βούλομαι καὶ τοῦτο ἐπιδεῖξαι, ὅτι [that] οὗτοι οὐ μόνον [only] εἰσὶ περὶ ἀνθρώπους ἄδικοι, ἀλλὰ καὶ περὶ θεοὺς ἀνόσιοι."

MI-Verbs: Athematic Aorists

---

1. *Aorist of μι-Verbs.* The aorist systems of the μι-verbs that you have learned contain forms derived from various origins. (1) Some forms are straightforwardly athematic forms (called strong aorist or "second" aorist); that is, secondary μι-verb personal endings are added directly to the simplest form of the verb root (with augment added in the indicative): for example, ἔστην (from στη-), inf. στῆναι. In many cases, athematic aorists of this type have intransitive or quasi-passive meanings (e.g., ἔστην, *I stood*, ἔβην, *I walked*, ἑάλων, *I was captured*). (2) Some forms (in Attic, normally the singular active forms only) have weak-aorist α-endings added to a stem that has the suffix κ (e.g., ἔθηκα, *I placed*, ἔδωκα, *I gave*). (3) Some forms are true weak (first) aorist forms with suffix σ (e.g., ἔστησα, *I caused to stand* [from στη- + σ-], inf. στῆσαι; ἔδειξα, *I showed*).

2. *Aorist of the Major μι-Verbs*

(SECOND) AORIST ACTIVE

		τίθημι "place"	ἵημι "let go"	δίδωμι "give"	ἵστημι "stand"
stems:		θε-, θηκ-	ἑ-, ἡκ-	δο-, δωκ-	στη-
infinitive:		θεῖναι	ἀφεῖναι	δοῦναι	στῆναι
s.	1st	ἔθηκα	ἀφῆκα	ἔδωκα	ἔστην
	2nd	ἔθηκας	ἀφῆκας	ἔδωκας	ἔστης
	3rd	ἔθηκε(ν)	ἀφῆκε(ν)	ἔδωκε(ν)	ἔστη
(d.	2nd	ἔθετον	ἀφεῖτον	ἔδοτον	ἔστητον)
	(3rd	ἐθέτην	ἀφείτην	ἐδότην	ἐστήτην)
pl.	1st	ἔθεμεν	ἀφεῖμεν	ἔδομεν	ἔστημεν
	2nd	ἔθετε	ἀφεῖτε	ἔδοτε	ἔστητε
	3rd	ἔθεσαν	ἀφεῖσαν	ἔδοσαν	ἔστησαν

176

(SECOND) AORIST MIDDLE

		τίθημι "place"	ἵημι "let go"	δίδωμι "give"
stem:		θε-	ἑ-	δο-
infinitive:		θέσθαι	ἀφέσθαι	δόσθαι
s.	1st	ἐθέμην	ἀφείμην	ἐδόμην
	2nd	ἔθου[1]	ἀφεῖσο	ἔδου
	3rd	ἔθετο	ἀφεῖτο	ἔδοτο
(d.	2nd	ἔθεσθον	ἀφεῖσθον	ἔδοσθον)
	(3rd	ἐθέσθην	ἀφείσθην	ἐδόσθην)
pl.	1st	ἐθέμεθα	ἀφείμεθα	ἐδόμεθα
	2nd	ἔθεσθε	ἀφεῖσθε	ἔδοσθε
	3rd	ἔθεντο	ἀφεῖντο	ἔδοντο

Notes: (1) In Attic ἵστημι has no athematic aorist middle (see next paragraph). (2) The aorist of ἵημι is shown in a compound since the simple verb is not used in the aorist in Attic prose; recall that the accent cannot precede the first preverb (augment [U16.3, at end]), hence the accentuation of ἀφῆκα, etc.; the ει of the aor. ind. represents augmented ε (recall that a consonant has been lost from this root). The aor. act. inf. of ἵημι differs from the pres. act. inf. of εἰμί only in the breathing: contrast ἀφεῖναι = *to let go* (aor.) with ἀπεῖναι = *to be absent* (pres.). (3) The aorist active infinitives of τίθημι, ἵημι, δίδωμι are derived from forms with alternative ending -έναι, with contraction.

3. *The Two Aorists of* ἵστημι. The verb ἵστημι and its compounds have two aorists:[2] a transitive weak (first) aorist, causative in meaning, sharing the transitive meanings of the present, imperfect, and future active; and an intransitive strong (second) aorist, sharing the intransitive or quasi-passive meanings of the present, imperfect, and future middle/passive.

Ex. τοῦτον κατεστήσαμεν κριτήν.   (trans. 1st aor.)
We appointed this man judge.
(We caused this man to be established as judge.)

οὗτος κριτὴς κατέστη.   (intrans. 2nd aor.)
This man became (was appointed, was established as) judge.

---

1. From *ἔθε(σ)ο, with contraction; likewise ἔδου from *ἔδο(σ)ο.

2. Note that the 3rd pl. aor. act. ind. forms of ἵστημι are identical in appearance, though derived from different combinations of elements: 1st aorist ἔστησαν from augment ἐ- plus tense stem στησ- (= root στη- + weak aorist suffix σ) plus tense vowel α plus personal ending ν; 2nd aorist ἔστησαν from augment ἐ- plus tense stem στη- plus personal ending σαν.

There is no second aorist middle, but the first aorist middle is found:

> οἱ ᾿Αθηναῖοι τὸν Δημοσθένη κατεστήσαντο στρατηγόν.
> *The Athenians appointed Demosthenes as general for themselves.*

4. *Other Athematic Aorists.* A few verbs which are ω-verbs in the present system have athematic (second) aorist conjugation (in the active only, no middle). The secondary personal endings are added to the simplest form of the verb root, with augment added. These aorists, like ἔστην, are usually intransitive or passive in sense (but ἔγνων is transitive).[1] Four aorists of this kind are found in Attic prose:

		ἁλίσκομαι "be captured"	βαίνω "go, walk"	γιγνώσκω "get to know"	δύω "enter, sink"
aor. stem:		ἁλω-	βη-	γνω-	δῡ-
aor. infin.:		ἁλῶναι	βῆναι	γνῶναι	δῦναι
s.	1st	ἑάλων	ἔβην	ἔγνων	ἔδῡν
	2nd	ἑάλως	ἔβης	ἔγνως	ἔδῡς
	3rd	ἑάλω	ἔβη	ἔγνω	ἔδῡ
(d.	2nd	ἑάλωτον	ἔβητον	ἔγνωτον	ἔδῡτον)
	(3rd	ἑαλώτην	ἐβήτην	ἐγνώτην	ἐδύτην)
pl.	1st	ἑάλωμεν	ἔβημεν	ἔγνωμεν	ἔδῡμεν
	2nd	ἑάλωτε	ἔβητε	ἔγνωτε	ἔδῡτε
	3rd	ἑάλωσαν	ἔβησαν	ἔγνωσαν	ἔδῡσαν

Note that the aorist of ἁλίσκομαι has a passive translation in English, *I was captured*, etc., despite the active personal endings. There are also forms of this aorist with the initial syllables contracted: ἥλων, ἥλως, etc.

WHAT TO STUDY AND DO

1. Learn the aorist inflections presented above.
2. Learn the vocabulary of this unit.
3. Do the exercises of this unit.

---

1. There is also a transitive 1st aorist of δύω found in Attic prose (ἔδῡσα, *caused to enter or sink*); in poetry and outside Attic one may also meet transitive 1st aorists ἔβησα, *caused to go*, and (ἀν)έγνωσα, *caused to realize*.

VOCABULARY

nouns

βασιλεία, βασιλείας, f. kingdom, dominion; kingship, monarchy
ἐλευθερία, ἐλευθερίας, f. freedom, liberty
ἡσυχία, ἡσυχίας, f. quiet, rest, calm

adjectives

ἥσυχος, ἥσυχον quiet, calm, inactive [Hesychast]
πικρός, πικρά, πικρόν sharp, pungent; bitter, painful; spiteful, mean
[picrate]

verbs

ἁλίσκομαι, ἁλώσομαι, be captured, be seized [used as passive of αἱρέω]
    ἑάλων (or ἥλων)
βαίνω, -βήσομαι, -ἔβην walk, step, go [basis]
    ἀναβαίνω (ἀνα) go up; board (a ship), mount (a horse); go inland
        [anabasis]

        διαβαίνω (δια) step across; go over, cross [diabetes]
        καταβαίνω (κατα) step down; dismount; go down to the sea from
        inland [katabasis]

        παραβαίνω (παρα) go beside; overstep, transgress, violate
        [parabasis]

        συμβαίνω (συν) come together; come to an agreement, come to
        terms; (impersonal) come to pass, happen
ἀναγιγνώσκω (ἀνα) read (aloud), recite (from a written document)
διαγιγνώσκω (δια) know apart, distinguish; determine, decide (a suit)
    [diagnosis]

δύω (poetic δύνω), -δύσω, (intrans. and non-causal, including 2nd aor.) enter;
    -ἔδυσα and ἔδυν [ῡ in all get into (clothes, armor); sink into the sea, set (of
    three stems] sun, stars)
    (trans. and causal, including 1st aor.) cause to enter,
    cause to sink (more commonly in compounds)
    [ecdysiast]
        ἀποδύω (ἀπο) (act. and 1st aor.) strip off (someone else's armor
        or clothes)
        (mid. and 2nd aor.) take off (one's own clothes),
        undress
        καταδύω (κατα) (intrans. and 2nd aor.) set (of sun); plunge into
        (causal 1st aor.) cause to sink (ships)

EXERCISES

I.   Translate precisely.

1. διέβησαν	15. ἐξίασι	29. προεῖντο
2. ἀπέδοσθε	16. ἐφέσθαι	30. μετέδοτε
3. ἐπιθέσθαι	17. ἀναγνῶναι	31. ἦσαν
4. ἀπέδυσας	18. ἴτε	32. ἀνέθηκας
5. ἀποδοῦναι	19. ἀλῶναι	33. δεικνύναι
6. ἐφῆκε	20. παραβήσεσθαι	34. γνώσονται
7. συμβῆναι	21. ἀπέδωκας	35. συνθεῖναι
8. ἐπεστήσατε	22. καθίστη	36. ἥλωτε
9. κατέθηκα	23. συνέβαινον	37. κατεστήσαμεν
10. ἀπέδυς	24. ἁλίσκονται	38. ἐπέστη
11. κατέστην	25. παρέβης	39. ἐπέθου
12. διέγνω	26. ἔγνωσαν	40. παρέδοτο
13. ἀποστῆσαι	27. κατέδυ	41. διεγιγνώσκομεν
14. ἑάλωμεν	28. ἐπέθηκε	42. συνθέσθαι

II.   Render into Greek.

1. Seven ships sank.
2. We sank ten triremes.
3. you (pl.) attacked
4. to betray (aor.)
5. we became [give two versions]
6. they were being captured
7. to let come to oneself (aor.)
8. you (pl.) will cross
9. That young man aimed at being chaste.
10. you (s.) were attacking
11. they boarded
12. you (pl.) read aloud (aor.)
13. we handed over
14. you (s.) caused to revolt
15. They were all captured.
16. he transgressed
17. The king's wife undressed.
18. we did not recognize

III.   Reading.

1. ἐν ἐκείνῳ τῷ πολέμῳ ἄλλα τε δεινὰ ἐγένετο ἐν ταῖς μάχαις καὶ ᾽Αλκαῖος ὁ ποιητὴς αὐτὸς μὲν ἐξέφυγε,[1] τὴν δ᾽ ἀσπίδα ἔλιπεν, οἱ δ᾽ ᾽Αθηναῖοι αὐτὴν ἔλαβον καὶ τοῖς θεοῖς ἀνέθεσαν.

2. οἵδε μὲν ἐκ παντὸς τρόπου [by every conceivable means] βούλονταί με τῇ δίκῃ ἁλῶναι, ὑμεῖς δ᾽ οὐ παράγεσθε τοῖς ψευδέσι λόγοις ἀλλ᾽ ἀεὶ ζη-τεῖτε διαγνῶναι τοὺς ἀληθῶς δικαίους καὶ τοὺς ἀδίκους.

3. καταβήσεσθαι μέλλω, ὦ ἄνδρες δικασταί, ἀλλὰ πρότερον βούλομαι ὀλίγα [a few (words)] ἑκατέροις εἰπεῖν, τοῖς τ᾽ ἐξ ἄστεως καὶ τοῖς ἐκ

---

1. Compound of ἐκ-: guess the meaning.

Πειραιῶς·[1] ἐλπίζω γὰρ ὑμᾶς παραδείγματα [as examples] ἕξειν τὰς συμφορὰς αἳ ὑμῖν διὰ τούτων ἐγένοντο καὶ τὴν ψῆφον δικαίως καὶ σοφῶς οἴσειν· οἱ μὲν ἐξ ἄστεως χαλεπῶς ἤρχεσθε ὑπὸ τούτων καὶ διὰ τούτους ἀδελφοῖς [brothers] καὶ υἱέσι καὶ πολίταις πόλεμον ἐπολεμεῖτε.[2] οἱ δ᾽ ἐκ Πειραιῶς ἐξεπέσετε[3] ἐκ τῆς πατρίδος καὶ οὐ βραχὺν χρόνον ἐδεῖσθε πάντων, καὶ χρημάτων καὶ φίλων, ἀλλὰ τέλος κατήλθετε[4] εἰς τὴν Ἀττικήν.

4. οὐχ οὗτοι τούς τε πολεμίους ἰσχυροὺς ποιοῦσι καὶ τοὺς φίλους προδιδόασιν, οἳ ἐχθροὺς [enemies] κωλύουσι πολλοὺς [many, numerous] ποιεῖσθαι, ἀλλὰ ἐκεῖνοι, οἳ ἀδίκως τε χρήματα ἀφαιροῦνται [take away: ἀπο + αἱρέω] καὶ τοὺς δικαίους ἀποκτείνουσιν.

---

1. Peiraieus, Πειραιεύς, gen. Πειραιῶς, was and is the port town of Athens. In 404/3 the Athenians were forced into civil war by the actions of the "Thirty Tyrants," right-wing extremists who were installed as a puppet regime by the Lacedaemonians at the end of the Peloponnesian War (referred to in this adapted extract of an oration of Lysias as "these men"). The two sides in the strife eventually held Peiraieus and the town (Athens) respectively.

2. πολεμέω = wage war with + dat.

3. Compound of ἐκ-: guess the meaning.

4. Compound of κατα-: guess the meaning.

Adjectives with Variant Stems; Numerals; Reflexive and Reciprocal Pronouns; Result Constructions

---

1. *Adjectives with Variant Stems.* Two frequently used adjectives are inflected in Attic with two different stems, one using consonant-declension endings (in masc. and neut. nom. and acc. sing.), the other using vowel-declension endings (in fem. and all other cases of masc. and neut.).

a. πολύς, πολλή, πολύ, *"much, many"*   stems: πολυ-, πολλ-[1]

		masc.	*fem.*	*neut.*
sing.	nom.	πολύς	πολλή	πολύ
	gen.	πολλοῦ	πολλῆς	πολλοῦ
	dat.	πολλῷ	πολλῇ	πολλῷ
	acc.	πολύν	πολλήν	πολύ
		(no dual)		
plur.	nom.	πολλοί	πολλαί	πολλά
	gen.	πολλῶν	πολλῶν	πολλῶν
	dat.	πολλοῖς	πολλαῖς	πολλοῖς
	acc.	πολλούς	πολλάς	πολλά

b. μέγας, μεγάλη, μέγα, *"great, large"*   stems: μεγα-, μεγαλ-

		masc.	*fem.*	*neut.*
sing.	nom.	μέγας	μεγάλη	μέγα
	gen.	μεγάλου	μεγάλης	μεγάλου
	dat.	μεγάλῳ	μεγάλῃ	μεγάλῳ
	acc.	μέγαν	μεγάλην	μέγα

---

1. In poetry forms from both stems are found in all cases (the consonant stem has alternative form πολε-; cf. βαρύς); in Ionic all the forms are vowel-declension: πολλός, πολλή, πολλόν.

		masc.	fem.	neut.
(dual	n. a.	μεγάλω	μεγάλα	μεγάλω)
	(g. d.	μεγάλοιν	μεγάλαιν	μεγάλοιν)
plur.	nom.	μεγάλοι	μεγάλαι	μεγάλα
	gen.	μεγάλων	μεγάλων	μεγάλων
	dat.	μεγάλοις	μεγάλαις	μεγάλοις
	acc.	μεγάλους	μεγάλας	μεγάλα

2. *Numerals.* The cardinal numbers *one, two, three, four* are inflected as adjectives; the remaining cardinal numbers (through 200) are *indeclinable*, that is, they are used in all the cases and genders with no variation in form. Corresponding to each cardinal is an ordinal adjective (*first, second, third*, etc.); all of these have vowel-declension inflection -os, -η, -ον (except δεύτερος, which has alpha-feminine δευτέρα). There are also numerical adverbs (*once, twice, thrice, four times*, etc.); from *four times* on these all have the suffix -άκις, found also in πολλάκις, *many times, often*, and ὀλιγάκις, *few times, rarely*.

cardinal		ordinal		adverb	
one	εἷς, μία, ἕν	1st	πρῶτος	once	ἅπαξ
two	δύο	2nd	δεύτερος	twice	δίς
three	τρεῖς, τρία	3rd	τρίτος	thrice	τρίς
four	τέτταρες, τέτταρα	4th	τέταρτος	4 times	τετράκις
five	πέντε	5th	πέμπτος	5 times	πεντάκις
six	ἕξ	6th	ἕκτος	6 times	ἑξάκις
seven	ἑπτά	7th	ἕβδομος	7 times	ἑπτάκις
eight	ὀκτώ	8th	ὄγδοος	8 times	ὀκτάκις
nine	ἐννέα	9th	ἔνατος	9 times	ἐνάκις
ten	δέκα	10th	δέκατος	10 times	δεκάκις
eleven	ἕνδεκα	11th	ἑνδέκατος	11 times	ἑνδεκάκις
twelve	δώδεκα	12th	δωδέκατος	12 times	δωδεκάκις

The declension of the first four cardinals is as follows:

"*one*": masc./neut. stem ἑν-; short-vowel fem. stem μῐ-

		masc.	fem.	neut.
sing.	nom.	εἷς	μίᾰ	ἕν
	gen.	ἑνός	μιᾶς	ἑνός
	dat.	ἑνί	μιᾷ	ἑνί
	acc.	ἕνα	μίᾰν	ἕν

"no one": a compound of οὐδέ and εἷς, sometimes found written separately; the accent of the compound is the same as that of simple εἷς except in nom. sing. masc.; masc./neut. stem οὐδεν-; short-vowel fem. stem οὐδεμι-.

		masc.	*fem.*	*neut.*
sing.	*nom.*	οὐδείς	οὐδεμία	οὐδέν
	gen.	οὐδενός	οὐδεμιᾶς	οὐδενός
	dat.	οὐδενί	οὐδεμιᾷ	οὐδενί
	acc.	οὐδένα	οὐδεμίαν	οὐδέν

Exactly similar is the declension of μηδείς, used in clauses and phrases which require negative μή instead of οὐ.[1]

"two": nom. acc. δύο, gen. dat. declined δυοῖν or indeclinable δύο; used with both dual and plural nouns.

"three"

		masc./fem.	*neut.*
plur.	*nom.*	τρεῖς	τρία
	gen.	τριῶν	τριῶν
	dat.	τρισί(ν)	τρισί(ν)
	acc.	τρεῖς	τρία

"four"[2]

		masc./fem.	*neut.*
plur.	*nom.*	τέτταρες	τέτταρα
	gen.	τεττάρων	τεττάρων
	dat.	τέτταρσι(ν)	τέτταρσι(ν)
	acc.	τέτταρας	τέτταρα

3. *Reflexive and Reciprocal Pronouns*

a. A *reflexive* pronoun is one which refers back to the subject of its clause. Because of this relationship with the subject, the reflexive pronoun itself occurs only in the oblique (objective) cases, never in the nominative (subjective) case. The English reflexive pronouns are *myself, ourselves, yourself, yourselves, himself, herself, itself, themselves* (the same forms as those used as intensive pronouns in apposition to noun or pronoun).

---

1. Plural forms are occasionally found (cf. English *nobodies*): οὐδένες, οὐδένων, οὐδέσι, οὐδένας; μηδένες, μηδένας.
2. The non-Attic and Koine form is τέσσαρες, τέσσαρα.

Ex.   <u>She</u> *talks to* <u>herself</u> *out loud.*

<u>You</u> *should be ashamed of* <u>yourselves</u>.

In Greek, what is translated into English as a reflexive action may often be expressed by the middle voice (U11.1); for instance,

ἡγεμόνα αὐτὸν εἵλοντο.

They chose him as leader <u>for themselves</u>.

But Greek also has reflexive pronouns, and reflexive actions may be expressed with an active verb and reflexive pronouns. In Attic there is both a *direct* reflexive (one which has the subject of its own clause as antecedent) and an *indirect* reflexive, that is, a reflexive within an indirect statement or subordinate clause that refers back to the subject of the main clause of the complex sentence. Because of a difference of idiom, the Greek indirect reflexive will normally appear in English as a plain personal pronoun:

Ex.   <u>They</u> *thought that the general would give* <u>them</u> *the prizes.*

The commonest reflexive, normally used directly and occasionally indirectly, consists of personal pronoun stem (or pronoun, in 1st and 2nd person plural) strengthened by emphatic αὐτός.

		first person: "myself, ourselves"		*second person: "yourself, yourselves"*	
		masc.	*fem.*	*masc.*	*fem.*
s.	g.	ἐμαυτοῦ	ἐμαυτῆς	σεαυτοῦ (σαυτοῦ)	σεαυτῆς (σαυτῆς)
	d.	ἐμαυτῷ	ἐμαυτῇ	σεαυτῷ (σαυτῷ)	σεαυτῇ (σαυτῇ)
	a.	ἐμαυτόν	ἐμαυτήν	σεαυτόν (σαυτόν)	σεαυτήν (σαυτήν)
pl.	g.	ἡμῶν αὐτῶν	ἡμῶν αὐτῶν	ὑμῶν αὐτῶν	ὑμῶν αὐτῶν
	d.	ἡμῖν αὐτοῖς	ἡμῖν αὐταῖς	ὑμῖν αὐτοῖς	ὑμῖν αὐταῖς
	a.	ἡμᾶς αὐτούς	ἡμᾶς αὐτάς	ὑμᾶς αὐτούς	ὑμᾶς αὐτάς

		third person: "himself, herself, itself, themselves"		
		masc.	*fem.*	*neuter.*
sing.	gen.	ἑαυτοῦ (αὐτοῦ)	ἑαυτῆς (αὐτῆς)	ἑαυτοῦ (αὐτοῦ)
	dat.	ἑαυτῷ (αὐτῷ)	ἑαυτῇ (αὐτῇ)	ἑαυτῷ (αὐτῷ)
	acc.	ἑαυτόν (αὐτόν)	ἑαυτήν (αὐτήν)	ἑαυτό (αὐτό)
pl.	gen.	ἑαυτῶν (αὐτῶν)	ἑαυτῶν (αὐτῶν)	ἑαυτῶν (αὐτῶν)
	dat.	ἑαυτοῖς (αὐτοῖς)	ἑαυταῖς (αὐταῖς)	ἑαυτοῖς (αὐτοῖς)
	acc.	ἑαυτούς (αὐτούς)	ἑαυτάς (αὐτάς)	ἑαυτά (αὐτά)

The alternative, contracted forms for the second person singular and third person singular and plural reflexives are shown in parentheses. Note that the contracted forms αὑτοῦ, etc., are distinguishable from the oblique cases of αὐτός only by the breathing sign.[1] The third plural reflexive may also be expressed by a combination of the third plural personal pronoun σφεῖς (rare in classical Attic) with αὐτός: gen. σφῶν αὐτῶν; dat. σφίσιν αὐτοῖς or αὐταῖς; acc. σφᾶς αὐτούς or αὐτάς; neuter σφέα αὐτά.

Ex.   πρὸς ἑαυτὸν λέγει . . .
He says to himself . . .

οὕτως ὠφελήσετε ὑμᾶς αὐτούς.
In this way you will help yourselves.

ταῦτα τὰ χρήματα ἡμῖν αὐτοῖς διέδομεν.
We distributed this money among ourselves.

The *indirect* reflexive of the third person is sometimes expressed in Attic by the old personal pronoun of the third person, which survived in other dialects and in poetry, but was replaced by oblique cases of αὐτός in classical Attic. The forms are as follows (enclitic forms in parentheses):

	sing.		*plur. masc./fem.*		*plur. neuter*	
gen.	οὗ	(οὑ)	σφῶν		σφῶν	
dat.	οἷ	(οἱ)	σφίσι(ν)	(σφισι[ν])	σφίσι(ν)	(σφισι[ν])
acc.	ἕ	(ἑ)	σφᾶς	(σφας)	σφέα	(σφεα)

Ex.   ὁ Δαρεῖος ἐβούλετό οἱ τοὺς παῖδας παρεῖναι.
Darius wanted his sons to be with him(self).

   b. A *reciprocal* pronoun is used to refer to the persons involved in a reciprocal action, that is, one in which one person or group acts upon another person or group and is in turn acted upon by that other person or group. In English the compound pronouns *each other* and *one another* serve this function. In Greek a reciprocal action may be conveyed simply by the middle voice (U11.2), but there is also a reciprocal pronoun, ἀλλήλων. This pronoun is ultimately derived from a compound phrase in which ἄλλος appeared twice, both in the nominative and in an oblique case. The reciprocal pronoun is declined only in the (dual and) plural and only in the oblique cases, as shown on the next page.

---

1. Note also the difference between nom. αὐτός or αὐτή and αὑτός, *the same man* (from ὁ αὐτός by crasis), or αὑτή, *the same woman* (from ἡ αὐτή by crasis), and αὕτη, *this woman*.

RECIPROCAL PRONOUN

		masc.	*fem.*	*neut.*
(*dual*	*gen., dat.*	ἀλλήλοιν	ἀλλήλαιν	ἀλλήλοιν)
	(*acc.*	ἀλλήλω	ἀλλήλα	ἀλλήλω)
plural	*gen.*	ἀλλήλων	ἀλλήλων	ἀλλήλων
	dat.	ἀλλήλοις	ἀλλήλαις	ἀλλήλοις
	acc.	ἀλλήλους	ἀλλήλας	ἄλληλα

Ex. ἀλλήλους ἀδικοῦσιν.
They are wronging each other.

4. *Result Constructions.* A result construction expresses one (subordinate) action as the result of another action (the main action, which expresses the cause or antecedents of the result). In English a result is normally expressed by an infinitive phrase introduced by *so as to, in such a way as to, enough to, sufficient to,* or the like, or by a *that*-clause, usually anticipated in the main clause by the use of *so* or *such.*

Ex. *They are so foolish as to expect a miracle.*
They are foolish enough to be tricked by anyone.
They are so foolish that everyone tricks them.
They are such fools that everyone can trick them.

In Greek there are two kinds of result contructions:

a. *Actual* result construction: ὥστε (or ὡς) with the indicative (or sometimes another finite verb form, such as imperative). When the result is emphasized as an *actual event*, it is expressed in a clause, normally containing the indicative and introduced by ὥστε = *and so, and thus, so that,* and often anticipated in the antecedent or main clause by the use of οὕτω (or ἱκανός, *sufficient,* or the like). An actual result clause in Greek may or may not be separated from its main or antecedent clause by a comma or semicolon; in the English translation there may be no punctuation, or a comma or period, depending on how closely the resulting action is tied to the antecedent action.

Ex.
οὕτως ἄφρονές ἐστε, ὥστε ἐλπίζετε τὸν Φίλιππον φίλιον γενήσεσθαι.
You are so foolish that you (actually) expect that Philip will become friendly.
οὕτως ἄδικοι ἐγένοντο, ὥστε πολίτας ἀπέκτειναν ἀκρίτους.
They proved to be so unjust that they put citizens to death without a trial.

μέγα δύναται ὁ βασιλεύς· ὥστε ζητεῖτε [imperative] πεῖσαι αὐτὸν ὑμᾶς ὠφελεῖν.
The king has great power. So seek to persuade him to aid you.

The negative in actual result clauses is normally οὐ:

χαλεπός ἐστιν· ὥστ᾽ οὐκ ἐπείσαμεν αὐτὸν τὴν πόλιν ὠφελῆσαι.
He is a harsh man, and thus we did not persuade him to aid the city.

b. *Natural* result contruction: ὥστε (or ὡς) with the infinitive. When the result is emphasized as a potential or natural consequence of the cause or antecedent action instead of as an actual event, it is expressed by ὥστε with the infinitive. The subject of the infinitive of result is in the acc. if it differs from the subject of the finite verb of the sentence and is left unexpressed if it is the same. The negative with the infinitive of result is μή. In this construction the cause and the result are very tightly connected and the greater emphasis falls on the antecedent action or state of being, stressing that it is one that is likely to have a certain consequence (thus punctuation in Greek is either absent or a comma and in English is usually absent). The infinitive of result does not assert that the result actually took place on any specific occasion, although actual occurrence is often implied by the context. Actual occurrence would instead be asserted by the indicative in the actual result construction.

Ex.
οὕτως ἄφρονές ἐστε ὥστε ῥᾳδίως ἀδικεῖσθαι ὑπὸ πάντων.
You are so foolish that you are easily wronged by everyone.
 [note omission of subject of ἀδικεῖσθαι, same as that of ἐστε]

οὕτω χαλεποί εἰσιν οἱ Ἀθηναῖοι ὥστε μήποτε ῥᾳδίως πείθεσθαι τοῖς ἀγγέλοις.
The Athenians are so difficult that they never easily trust messengers.
 [note negative μήποτε]

ὁ ῥήτωρ ἐστὶ μέγας, ὥστε πάντας ἰδεῖν τὴν κεφαλήν.
The speaker is tall enough so that everyone sees his head.
 [note πάντας subject acc. of ἰδεῖν]

WHAT TO STUDY AND DO

1. Learn the declension and use of the adjectives, numerals, and pronouns presented above.
2. Study result constructions.
3. Learn as vocabulary the numerals and pronouns presented above as well as the words given below.
4. Do the exercises of this unit.

VOCABULARY[1]

nouns

κεφαλή, κεφαλῆς, f.	head [encephalitis]

adjectives

ἄκριτος, ἄκριτον	undecided; unjudged, without trial
μέγας, μεγάλη, μέγα	large, tall; great, mighty [megalomania, megabyte]
Λακεδαιμόνιος, -μονία, -μόνιον	Lacedaemonian [official term for the inhabitants of Laconia, the chief city of which was Sparta; sometimes loosely translated as *Spartan*]
οἱ Λακεδαιμόνιοι	the Lacedaemonians, the Spartans
ὀλίγος, ὀλίγη, ὀλίγον	little, small; few [oligarchy]
οἱ ὀλίγοι	oligarchs, oligarchical party
ὀλιγάκις	few times, rarely, seldom
πολύς, πολλή, πολύ	much, many [polychromatic]
οἱ πολλοί	the multitude, the greater number [hoi polloi]
πολλάκις	often, many times

verbs

διαδίδωμι (δια)	hand over; distribute
δύναμαι, δυνήσομαι[2]	be able, be strong enough (+ inf.); have power (frequently with internal acc., e.g., μέγα δύνασθαι, to have great power)

conjunctions

ὥστε	so as, so that, that (of result)
ὡς	so that

EXERCISES

I. Reading.

1. οὔποτε ἀσφαλῆ τὰ μεγάλα.
2. πρῶτος[3] ηὕρου ταύτην τὴν τιμήν.
3. ἄφρων ἐστὶν οὗτος, ὃς ἑαυτῷ δοκεῖ πάντα δύνασθαι.

---

1. Note the many English derivatives of Greek numerals: e.g., hendiadys, deuterium, Deuteronomy, tritium, triad, tetrahedron, tetralogy, pentagon, hebdomadal, hendecasyllabic, Dodecanese.

2. This verb is a passive deponent μι-verb; for present-system conjugation (similar to ἵσταμαι) see Appendix 3: Paradigms. The aorist (passive) will be learned later.

3. In Greek idiom, when πρῶτος agrees with the subject of a verb X, the sense is "be the first to X."

4. ὁ Πεισίστρατος βασιλέα τῶν Ἀθηναίων τρὶς ἑαυτὸν κατέστησε· δὶς γὰρ ἐξέπεσεν,[1] ἀλλὰ τέλος διὰ μεγάλων πόνων κύριος [having power over + gen.] ἀπάντων κατέστη.

5. πολλοὺς λίθους ἔβαλλον οἱ βάρβαροι, ὥστ᾽ ἔδει ἕκαστον τῶν Ἑλλήνων φυλάττεσθαι καὶ ὑπὲρ τῆς κεφαλῆς τὴν ἀσπίδα ἀνέχειν.[2]

6. ὁ μὲν πατὴρ φίλιός τε καὶ χαρίεις ἦν ὥσθ᾽ ὑπὸ πάντων φιλεῖσθαι, τῶν δὲ δύο ὑέων ἑκάτερος ἑκάτερον πολλὰ κακὰ λέγει ὥσθ᾽ ὑπὸ μηδενὸς ἐπαινεῖσθαι.

7. ὁ μὲν Σωκλῆς οὐ δίκαιον ἡγεῖσθαι ἔφη τοὺς Λακεδαιμονίους βασιλείας καθιστάναι εἰς τὰς πόλεις, οἱ δ᾽ ἄλλοι πάντες πρῶτον μὲν εἶχον ἐν ἡσυχίᾳ ἑαυτούς, ἔπειτα δ᾽ ἅπας τις[3] αὐτῶν φωνὴν ἔρρηξε [let loose his voice = broke into speech] καὶ ᾑρεῖτο τὴν ἐκείνου γνώμην. καὶ οὕτως ἐκέλευον οἱ σύμμαχοι τοὺς Λακεδαιμονίους μηδὲν ποιεῖν δεινὸν περὶ πόλιν Ἑλληνικήν.

8. ὁ Ἀριστοφάνης ἀεὶ ἐπολιτεύετο καὶ τιμῆς ἐφίετο. ὥστε τότε μετὰ Εὐνόμου νηὶ ἀπῆλθεν εἰς τὴν Σικελίαν· ἤλπιζε γὰρ πεῖσαι τὸν Διονύσιον [Dionysius, tyrant of Syracuse] κηδεστὴν [kinsman by marriage] μὲν γενέσθαι Εὐαγόρᾳ [Euagoras, ruler of Cyprus], πολέμιον δὲ Λακεδαιμονίοις, φίλον δὲ καὶ σύμμαχον τῇ πόλει τῇ ὑμετέρᾳ. καὶ πολλοὶ κίνδυνοι [dangers] ἦσαν πρὸς τὴν θάλατταν καὶ τοὺς πολεμίους, ἀλλὰ ὅμως [nevertheless] ταῦτα ἔπραττε, καὶ τέλος ἔπεισε Διονύσιον μὴ πέμψαι τριήρεις ἃς τότε παρεσκευάσατο Λακεδαιμονίοις.

II. Render into Greek.

1. Will the thieves be clever enough to conceal any of their many unjust deeds from the others?

2. Wise men say that human beings ought to help one another, and so we do this.

3. We seem to ourselves to be so virtuous that no one surpasses us.

4. By the fact that [use articular infinitive] you fled, fellow soldiers, you made the battle bitter for yourselves and sweet for the enemy.

5. For four days the sailors were able to prevent the hoplites from boarding (the ship), but on the fifth day a few fell ill, so that it was necessary for them to surrender themselves.

---

1. ἐκ- compound: guess the meaning.
2. ἀνα- compound: guess the meaning.
3. The idiom πᾶς τις or ἅπας τις is a strengthened form of πᾶς, meaning "every single one (no matter who)."

Participles: Formation and Declension

PRELIMINARIES

A *participle* is a verbal adjective and is one of the non-finite forms of the verb. Like such finite forms as the indicative, the participle has such features as tense and voice and the ability to govern objects and be modified by adverbs. Unlike finite forms, however, the participle carries no distinction of person and cannot form the predicate of a clause. As an adjective, a participle modifies (and in inflected languages agrees with) a noun or pronoun, expressed or implied.

In English, participles vary according to tense and voice. There are two simple forms, the active in *-ing* and the (past) passive, which ends in *-ed* for regular verbs and is otherwise formed for irregular verbs (the third principal part of an English verb is its past participle). English supplies other participles by using compound forms with the auxiliaries *being, having,* and *been*.

> present active: *seeing, helping*
> present passive: *being seen, being helped*
> past active: *having seen, having helped*
> past passive: *seen, having been seen; helped, having been helped*

In Greek, participles, like infinitives, may be formed from any tense stem in all available voices. For the tenses you know so far, therefore, one can form present active, present middle/passive, future active, future middle, aorist active, and aorist middle participles.

∷

1. *Active Participles*. Most active participles (and the aorist passive participle, to be learned later) are formed by the addition of the consonant-stem suffix $\nu\tau$ to the tense stem plus theme vowel or tense vowel, if any. The masc. and neuter forms have $\nu\tau$-stem declension, but (as in consonant-declension adjectives with three endings) the feminine has an additional suffix (semivocalic iota = y, leading to euphonic changes) and short-alpha declension.

a. *ω-Verb Participles in* -ων, -ουσα, -ον. In the present active, future active, and strong aorist active, -ντ- is added to tense stem plus theme vowel ο. The masc./neuter stem thus ends in -οντ- and the declension is like that of γέρων (U14.3b). Euphonic changes produce a fem. stem ending in -ουσ-. Since participles are adjectives, their accent is persistent, not recessive. For the present and future, the accent is persistent on the final syllable of the tense stem, but in the strong aorist, by contrast, the accent is persistent on the theme vowel that precedes the participial suffix (cf. the treatment of strong aorist infinitives: ἀγαγεῖν vs. present ἄγειν). In present or future stems with -έω contraction, the ε of the stem contracts with the theme vowel ο to form ου, except in the nom. sing. masc., where -έων produces -ῶν.

verb	tense stem		participle	masc./neut. part. stem
ἄγω	pres.	ἀγ-	ἄγων, ἄγουσα ἄγον	ἄγοντ-
	fut.	ἀξ-	ἄξων, ἄξουσα ἄξον	ἄξοντ-
	2nd aor.	ἀγαγ-	ἀγαγών, ἀγαγοῦσα, ἀγαγόν	ἀγαγόντ-
μένω	pres.	μεν-	μένων, μένουσα, μένον	μένοντ-
	fut.	μενε-	μενῶν, μενοῦσα, μενοῦν	μενοῦντ-
ποιέω	pres.	ποιε-	ποιῶν, ποιοῦσα, ποιοῦν	ποιοῦντ-
	fut.	ποιησ-	ποιήσων, ποιήσουσα, ποιῆσον	ποιήσουντ-
εἶδον	2nd aor.	ἰδ-	ἰδών, ἰδοῦσα, ἰδόν	ἰδόντ-

DECLENSION: PRESENT OR FUTURE, UNCONTRACTED

		masc.	fem.	neut.
sing.	n. v.	ἄγων	ἄγουσα	ἄγον
	g.	ἄγοντος	ἀγούσης	ἄγοντος
	d.	ἄγοντι	ἀγούσῃ	ἄγοντι
	a.	ἄγοντα	ἄγουσαν	ἄγον
(dual	n. a. v.	ἄγοντε	ἀγούσα	ἄγοντε)
	(g. d.	ἀγόντοιν	ἀγούσαιν	ἀγόντοιν)
plur.	n. v.	ἄγοντες	ἄγουσαι	ἄγοντα
	g.	ἀγόντων	ἀγουσῶν	ἀγόντων
	d.	ἄγουσι(ν)	ἀγούσαις	ἄγουσι(ν)
	a.	ἄγοντας	ἀγούσας	ἄγοντα

DECLENSION: PRESENT OR FUTURE, CONTRACTED

		masc.	*fem.*	*neut.*
sing.	*n. v.*	μενῶν	μενοῦσα	μενοῦν
	g.	μενοῦντος	μενούσης	μενοῦντος
	d.	μενοῦντι	μενούσῃ	μενοῦντι
	a.	μενοῦντα	μενοῦσαν	μενοῦν
(dual	*n. a. v.*	μενοῦντε	μενούσα	μενοῦντε)
	(g. d.	μενούντοιν	μενούσαιν	μενούντοιν)
plur.	*n. v.*	μενοῦντες	μενοῦσαι	μενοῦντα
	g.	μενούντων	μενουσῶν	μενούντων
	d.	μενοῦσι(ν)	μενούσαις	μενοῦσι(ν)
	a.	μενοῦντας	μενούσας	μενοῦντα

DECLENSION: STRONG AORIST ACTIVE

		masc.	*fem.*	*neut.*
sing.	*n. v.*	λιπών	λιποῦσα	λιπόν
	g.	λιπόντος	λιπούσης	λιπόντος
	d.	λιπόντι	λιπούσῃ	λιπόντι
	a.	λιπόντα	λιποῦσαν	λιπόν
(dual	*n. a. v.*	λιπόντε	λιποῦσα	λιπόντε)
	(g. d.	λιπόντοιν	λιπούσαιν	λιπόντοιν)
plur.	*n. v.*	λιπόντες	λιποῦσαι	λιπόντα
	g.	λιπόντων	λιπουσῶν	λιπόντων
	d.	λιποῦσι(ν)	λιπούσαις	λιποῦσι(ν)
	a.	λιπόντας	λιπούσας	λιπόντα

b. *Weak Aorist Active Participles in* -ᾱs, -ᾱσα, -αν. In the weak aorist active, -ντ- is added to tense stem plus tense vowel α. The masc./neuter stem thus ends in -αντ- and the declension is like that of γίγᾱς (U14.3b). Euphonic changes produce a fem. stem ending in -ᾱσ-. The accent is persistent on the final syllable of the tense stem.

verb	tense stem	participle	masc./neut. part. stem
λύω	λυσ-	λύσᾱς, λύσᾱσα, λῦσαν	λύσᾰντ-
πέμπω	πεμψ-	πέμψᾱς, πέμψᾱσα, πέμψαν	πέμψᾰντ-
μένω	μειν-	μείνᾱς, μείνᾱσα, μεῖναν	μείνᾰντ-

DECLENSION: WEAK AORIST ACTIVE

		masc.	fem.	neut.
sing.	n. v.	λύσᾱς	λύσᾱσα	λῦσαν
	g.	λύσαντος	λυσάσης	λύσαντος
	d.	λύσαντι	λυσάσῃ	λύσαντι
	a.	λύσαντα	λύσασαν	λῦσαν
(dual	n. a. v.	λύσαντε	λυσάσα	λύσαντε)
	g. d.	λυσάντοιν	λυσάσαιν	λυσάντοιν)
plur.	n. v.	λύσαντες	λύσασαι	λύσαντα
	g.	λυσάντων	λυσασῶν	λυσάντων
	d.	λύσᾱσι(ν)	λυσάσαις	λύσᾱσι(ν)
	a.	λύσαντας	λυσάσας	λύσαντα

c. *μι-Verb Participles*: in μι-verbs the participial suffix is added directly to the tense stem, which already ends in a vowel. Euphonic changes in the fem. produce stems endings in -ᾱσ-, -εισ-, -ουσ-, -ῡσ-. The accent of athematic participles is persistent on the final vowel of the stem. Full declensional patterns for participles of these kinds are given in the Appendix 3: Paradigms.

δίδωμι	present active part.	διδούς, διδοῦσα, διδόν
	masc./neut. stem	διδόντ-; dat. pl. διδοῦσι(ν)
	aorist active part.	δούς, δοῦσα, δόν
	masc./neut. stem	δόντ-; dat. pl. δοῦσι(ν)
ἵστημι	present active part.	ἱστάς, ἱστᾶσα, ἱστάν
	masc./neut. stem	ἱστάντ-; dat. pl. ἱστᾶσι(ν)
	aorist active part.	στάς, στᾶσα, στάν
	masc./neut. stem	στάντ-; dat. pl. στᾶσι(ν)[1]
τίθημι	present active part.	τιθείς, τιθεῖσα, τιθέν
	masc./neut. stem	τιθέντ-; dat. pl. τιθεῖσι(ν)
	aorist active part.	θείς, θεῖσα, θέν
	masc./neut. stem	θέντ-; dat. pl. θεῖσι(ν)
ἵημι	present active part.	ἱείς, ἱεῖσα, ἱέν
	masc./neut. stem	ἱέντ-; dat. pl. ἱεῖσι(ν)
(compounds	aorist active part.	(ἀφ)είς, (ἀφ)εῖσα, (ἀφ)έν
only)	masc./neut. stem	(ἀφ)έντ-; dat. pl. (ἀφ)εῖσι(ν)
δείκνυμι	present active part.	δεικνύς, δεικνῦσα, δεικνύν
	masc./neut. stem	δεικνύντ-; dat. pl. δεικνῦσι(ν)

---

1. Similar is poetic present active part. of φημί: φάς, φᾶσα, φάν, stem φάντ-, dat. pl. φᾶσι(ν); but in prose the participle φάσκων from φάσκω is used instead.

εἰμί	present active part.	ὤν, οὖσα, ὄν
	masc./neut. stem	ὀντ-; dat. pl. οὖσι(ν)
εἶμι	present active part.	ἰών, ἰοῦσα, ἰόν
	masc./neut. stem	ἰόντ-; dat. pl. ἰοῦσι(ν)
βαίνω	aorist active part.	βάς, βᾶσα, βάν
	masc./neut. stem	βάντ-; dat. pl. βᾶσι(ν)
ἁλίσκομαι	aorist active part.	ἁλούς, ἁλοῦσα, ἁλόν
	masc./neut. stem	ἁλόντ-; dat. pl. ἁλοῦσι(ν)
γιγνώσκω	aorist active part.	γνούς, γνοῦσα, γνόν
	masc./neut. stem	γνόντ-; dat. pl. γνοῦσι(ν)
δύω	aorist active part.	δύς, δῦσα, δύν
	masc./neut. stem	δύντ-; dat. pl. δῦσι(ν)

2. *Middle/Passive Participles.* All middle/passive or middle participles have the suffix -μενος, -μένη, -μενον. This is added to the tense stem plus theme vowel ο in present, future, and strong aorist; to tense stem with tense vowel α in weak aorist; or directly to the tense stem in μι-verbs. In contract verbs in -έω the final ε of the stem contracts with theme vowel ο to produce ου before the suffix. The accent is persistent on the syllable preceding the suffix. The declension of middle/passive participles is like that of eta-feminine vowel-declension adjectives such as ἀγαθός, -ή, -όν.

verb	tense and voice	participle
πέμπω	pres. mid./pass.	πεμπόμενος, -η, -ον
	fut. mid.	πεμψόμενος, -η, -ον
	weak aor. mid.	πεμψάμενος, -η, -ον
ἄγω	pres. mid./pass.	ἀγόμενος, -η, -ον
	fut. mid.	ἀξόμενος, -η, -ον
	strong aor. mid.	ἀγαγόμενος, -η, -ον
ἀγγέλλω	pres. mid./pass.	ἀγγελλόμενος, -η, -ον
	fut. mid.	ἀγγελούμενος, -η, -ον
	weak aor. mid.	ἀγγειλάμενος, -η, -ον
ποιέω	pres. mid./pass.	ποιούμενος, -η, -ον
	fut. mid.	ποιησόμενος, -η, -ον
	weak aor. mid.	ποιησάμενος, -η, -ον
δίδωμι	pres. mid./pass.	διδόμενος, -η, -ον
	fut. mid.	δωσόμενος, -η, -ον
	aor. mid.	δόμενος, -η, -ον
ἵστημι	pres. mid./pass.	ἱστάμενος, -η, -ον
	fut. mid.	στησόμενος, -η, -ον
	weak aor. mid.	στησάμενος, -η, -ον

ἵημι	pres. mid./pass.	ἱέμενος, -η, -ον
	fut. mid.	ἡσόμενος, -η, -ον
(compounds)	aor. mid.	(ἀφ)έμενος, -η, -ον
τίθημι	pres. mid./pass.	τιθέμενος, -η, -ον
	fut. mid.	θησόμενος, -η, -ον
	aor. mid.	θέμενος, -η, -ον
δείκνυμι	pres. mid./pass.	δεικνύμενος, -η, -ον
	fut. mid.	δειξόμενος, -η, -ον
	weak aor. mid.	δειξάμενος, -η, -ον

3. *Identification of Participles.* When asked to identify a participial form, the student should supply *seven* items: case, number, gender, tense, voice, the word *participle*, and the first principal part of the verb from which the form comes. For example, a complete identification of μαχεσαμένους is acc. pl. masc. aor. mid. participle of μάχομαι.

WHAT TO STUDY AND DO

1. Study the formation and declension of participles.
2. Learn the vocabulary of this unit.
3. Do the exercises of this unit.

VOCABULARY

ω-verbs

ἁρπάζω, ἁρπάσομαι, ἥρπασα	snatch away, carry off; seize [Harpy]
ἐσθίω, fut. ἔδομαι, ἔφαγον	eat [esophagus, anthropophagy]
καίω or κάω, καύσω, ἔκαυσα	kindle; set on fire, burn [caustic]
κρίνω [ῑ], κρῐνέω, ἔκρῑνα	pick out, choose; decide, judge [crisis]
πίνω [ῑ], fut. πίομαι or πιέομαι [ῐ], ἔπῐον	drink [symposium]
στρέφω, στρέψω, ἔστρεψα	turn, twist [strophe, catastrophe]
τέμνω, τεμέω, ἔτεμον (or poetic ἔταμον)	cut [anatomy, atom]
τρέφω, θρέψω, ἔθρεψα[1]	bring up, rear (children); nourish, maintain; cherish [atrophy, dystrophy]

---

1. The root is θρεφ-, and Grassmann's law (U19.5) operates in the present stem to produce τρεφ-.

ὑπισχνέομαι, ὑποσχήσομαι,   undertake (to do, + compl. inf.); promise, profess (+
ὑπεσχόμην[1]   indirect discourse inf.)

EXERCISES

I. Give the three nominative singular forms of the participle of the indicated
tense and voice:

1. fut. mid. of μάχομαι
2. aor. act. of βάλλω
3. pres. m/p of βούλομαι
4. pres. act. of παρατίθημι
5. aor. mid. of ἐπιδείκνυμι
6. fut. act. of νοσέω

7. aor. act. of ἐκδύω
8. fut. act. of νομίζω
9. pres. m/p of ἐφίημι
10. pres. act. of ἔξειμι
11. fut. mid. of παραβαίνω
12. aor. mid. of ἐπιτίθημι

II. Write the designated form of the participle of the indicated verb.

1. nom. s. m. fut. mid. of ἁρπάζω
2. gen. s. f. aor. act. of τέμνω
3. dat. s. m. pres. m/p of τρέφω
4. acc. s. m. fut. act. of διαδίδωμι
5. nom. pl. f. aor. mid. of γίγνομαι
6. gen. pl. n. pres. act. of ῥήγνυμι
7. dat. pl. m. fut. mid. of πάσχω
8. acc. pl. f. aor. act. of κόπτω
9. nom. s. n. pres. m/p of ἐπαινέω
10. gen. s. m. fut. act. of καλέω
11. dat. s. f. aor. mid. of μάχομαι
12. acc. s. n. pres. act. of δοκέω
13. nom. pl. m. fut. mid. of ἄγω
14. gen. pl. f. aor. act. of ἄρχω
15. dat. pl. n. pres. m/p of γράφω
16. dat. s. n. pres. m/p of πυνθάνομαι

17. nom. s. m. fut. mid. of ἡγέομαι
18. gen. s. f. aor. act. of ἀποθνῄσκω
19. acc. pl. m. aor. act. of ἀπέχω
20. acc. s. m. fut. act. of βλάπτω
21. acc. pl. m. aor. act. of διαβαίνω
22. gen. pl. n. pres. act. of οἰκέω
23. dat. pl. m. fut. mid. of ἀφίημι
24. acc. pl. f. aor. act. of εἶδον
25. nom. s. n. pres. m/p of γίγνομαι
26. gen. s. m. fut. act. of ἀποκτείνω
27. dat. s. f. aor. mid. of καθίστημι
28. acc. s. n. pres. act. of νομίζω
29. nom. pl. m. fut. mid. of εἰμί
30. gen. pl. f. aor. act. of τίθημι
31. dat. pl. n. pres. m/p of ποιέω
32. nom. pl. f. aor. mid. of
παρακελεύομαι

III. Identify completely the following participial forms.

1. ἐσομένη
2. φευξομέναις
3. ἐξιόντι
4. σπεισαμένου
5. τάττουσι
6. ἀφέντα

7. ποιούντων
8. ἐνεγκοῦσα
9. τιθέμενα
10. δῦσι
11. πεῖσον
12. βαλοῦσι

13. ὑπισχνουμένη
14. φαγόντα
15. καυσουσῶν
16. ἐφιστάντι
17. ἐροῦντας
18. ὄντα

---

1. The present stem of this deponent is a byform of ἔχω: stem σχ- has iota-reduplication and
nasal suffix added, *σισχνε- —> *ἰσχνε- —> ἰσχνε- (again by Grassmann's law).

19. παραγαγόντι	23. στάντας	27. ἀφικομένου
20. σχόντος	24. λείψουσαν	28. φιλήσας
21. ὠφελήσαντα	25. στήσασαι	29. ἀποδόμεναι
22. δουσῶν	26. λαβόντες	30. πυθομένους

IV. Reading: The fifth-century historian Herodotus discusses theories on the flooding of the Nile (adapted passage).

ἀλλ᾽ Ἑλλήνων μέν τινες, οἳ <u>ἐπίσημοι</u> ἐβούλοντο γενέσθαι σοφίαν, ἔλεξαν περὶ τοῦ ὕδατος τούτου τρεῖς <u>ὁδούς</u>, ὧν τὰς μὲν δύο οὐκ ἄξιον εἰπεῖν <u>εἰ μὴ</u> διὰ βραχέων. τούτων ἡ ἑτέρα μὲν τοὺς <u>ἐτησίας</u> ἀνέμους φησὶν εἶναι αἰτίους τοῦ <u>πληθύειν</u> τὸν ποταμόν (κωλύειν γὰρ τοὺς ἀνέμους εἰς θάλατταν <u>ἐκρεῖν</u> τὸν Νεῖλον). πολλάκις δ᾽ ἐτησίαι μὲν οὐκ <u>ἔπνευσαν</u>, ὁ δὲ Νεῖλος τὸ αὐτὸ ποιεῖ. ἡ δ᾽ ἑτέρα <u>ἀνεπιστημονεστέρα</u> ἐστίν, ἣ ἀπὸ τοῦ <u>Ὠκεανοῦ</u> φησι <u>ῥεῖν</u> αὐτόν, τὸν δ᾽ Ὠκεανὸν περὶ πᾶσαν <u>γῆν</u> ῥεῖν. ἡ δὲ τρίτη τῶν ὁδῶν πολὺ <u>ἐπιεικεστάτη</u> ἐστίν, ἀλλὰ ψευδής· λέγει γὰρ οὐδ᾽ αὕτη οὐδέν· τὸν γὰρ Νεῖλόν φησι ῥεῖν ἀπὸ <u>τηκομένης</u> <u>χιόνος</u>.

ἀλλ᾽ <u>ἐπεὶ</u> δεῖ τὴν ἐμαυτοῦ γνώμην περὶ τούτου ἀποδείξασθαι, λέξω διὰ τί μοι δοκεῖ πληθύειν ὁ Νεῖλος ὑπὸ τὸ <u>θέρος</u>· τὴν χειμερινὴν ὥραν ὁ ἥλιος ἐκ τῆς ἀρχαίας ὁδοῦ ὑπὸ τῶν <u>χειμώνων</u> <u>ἀπελαύνεται</u> καὶ ἔρχεται πρὸς τὰ <u>ἄνω</u> τῆς <u>Λιβύης</u>. καὶ ὁ Νεῖλος <u>μόνος</u> οὕτως <u>ἕλκεται</u> ὑπὸ τοῦ ἡλίου ὥστε τοῦτον τὸν χρόνον ὀλίγῳ ὕδατι ῥεῖν, τὸ δὲ θέρος μετὰ πάντων τῶν ἄλλων ποταμῶν <u>ἴσον</u> ἕλκεται καὶ <u>πλέονι</u> ὕδατι ῥεῖ.

Underlined Words

ἀνεπιστημονέστερος = *less*
  scientific
ἄνω = (adv.) *upward*; τὰ ἄνω = *the*
  inland parts
ἀπελαύνω = *drive away*
γῆ, γῆς, f. = *earth*
εἰ μή = *except, if not*
ἐκρέω = *flow out*
ἕλκω = *draw*, (here) *cause to*
  evaporate
ἐπεί = *since*
ἐπιεικέστατος = *most reasonable*
ἐπίσημος = *notable*
ἐτησίαι, -ῶν, m. = *Etesian (annual)*
  winds (blowing from north to
  south in the Aegean and eastern
  Mediterranean)

θέρος, θέρους, n. = *summer*
ἴσος, ἴση, ἴσον = *equal* (here neuter
  acc. as adv.)
Λιβύη, Λιβύης, f. = *Africa*
μόνος, μόνη, μόνον = *alone*
ὁδός = (here) *way of explaining*
πλέονι = dat. s. neut. *more*
πληθύω = *be full, become full*
πνέω, aor. ἔπνευσα = *blow*
ῥέω = *flow*
τηκόμενος = *melting*
χειμερινός, -ή, -όν = *stormy*
χειμών, χειμῶνος, m. = *(winter)*
  storm
χιών, χιόνος, f. = *snow*
ὥρα, ὥρας, f. = *season*
Ὠκεανός, -οῦ, m. = *Ocean*

Uses of the Participle I

1. *Tenses of the Participle.* The Greek participle is found in all four of the major tense-systems: present, future, and aorist (presented in U26), and the perfect (to be learned in U37). In most constructions, the participle (like the infinitive) conveys by its tense a distinction in verbal aspect (U20) rather than a distinction in time. Again like the infinitive, the participle does have time meaning when it is used in an indirect discourse transformation representing an indicative of direct speech (U28.2).

The *present* participle conveys the aspect of the present stem, that is, continuous or repeated action. In practice, it most often refers to an action contemporaneous with the action of the main verb of the sentence and is usually translated in English by a present participle (*Xing, being Xed*). But in the proper context, the present participle may refer to an action antecedent to or subsequent to that of the main verb; for example, a Greek present participle may be translated into English as an imperfect:

τοὺς τότε παρόντας οὐ παραδώσει.
He will not surrender those who <u>were present</u> at that time.

The present participle may also have *conative* force (U20.2).

The *future* participle conveys will or intention or purpose and so looks to the future. Just as the future indicative stands outside the aspect system of the present, aorist, and perfect, so does the future participle.

The *aorist* participle conveys the aspect of the aorist stem, that is, simple occurrence or completion of an action. In practice, it most often refers to an action antecedent to that of the main verb of the sentence and is usually translated in English by a past participle (*having Xed, having been Xed*). In the proper context, however, the aorist participle may refer to an action contemporaneous with or subsequent to the action of the main verb. The aorist participle sometimes has *ingressive* force (U20.3).

The *perfect* participle conveys the aspect of completed action with permanent result in the present. The difference between aorist and perfect is seen in the contrast between οἱ ἀποθανόντες ἐν τῇ μάχῃ = *those who died in the battle* (referring to a particular occasion) and οἱ τεθνηκότες (perfect part.) = *those who have died, the dead* (in general). Consider also δείξω αὐτὸν δῶρα εἰληφότα (from λαμβάνω) = *I'll show that he is guilty of having taken bribes* (more or less, *has taken bribes and is now in the state of having done so*).

2. *Attributive Participle.* There are three broad classifications of the uses of the Greek participle. The first to be considered is the *attributive* use. Like any other adjective form, the participle may be used as an attribute of a noun, that is, as a modifier that helps identify or qualify the noun without (primarily) asserting something about the noun. In English the attributive use of the participle is somewhat limited, and in English idiom attributive relative clauses (those not set off by commas) are usually the equivalent of an attributive participle:

> the *dancing* women
> the *expended* cartridge
> the man *who came into the room*   (clause instead of participle)[1]

In Greek the attributive participle is very common (more common than the relative clause). The participle falls within the article–noun group and agrees with the noun in gender, number, and case:

> αἱ ὀρχούμεναι γρᾶες
> *the dancing old women, the old women who are dancing*
>
> ὁ ἀνὴρ ὁ εἰσελθών
> *the man who came in*
>
> ὁ πρόσθεν ἄρξας στρατηγός
> *the general who held office previously*

3. *Attributive Participle as Substantive.* Like any other adjectival form, the attributive participle may be used without an expressed noun as a substantive. The article (which is usually present, but may be absent in poetry or when the substantive is indefinite) and the participle itself convey gender, number, and case, so that the person or thing referred to is clear to the listener or reader. The substantival use of the attributive participle is extremely common in Greek, and many attributive relative clauses in English are most idiomatically rendered into Greek as article and participle:

ἡ εἰσελθοῦσα	*the woman who came in*
ὁ ἄρχων	*the ruler, the officeholder*
τὰ λεγόμενα	*the things that are said*

---

1. Contrast the equivalent German idiom, with the attributive participle: *der in das Zimmer kommende Mann* = *the man who is coming into the room.*

ὁ φεύγων [τὴν δίκην]   *the defendant (the man fleeing the suit)*
ὁ διώκων [τὴν δίκην]   *the plaintiff (the man pursuing the suit)*
οἱ ἐν τῇ πόλει ὑπὸ τῶν τριάκοντα ἀποθανόντες
those who were put to death in the city by the Thirty Tyrants

4. *Circumstantial Participle.* The other two main uses of the participle involve its use in predicate position, outside the article–noun group. In this position, the participle asserts something about the noun it modifies and is therefore equivalent to a (subordinate) clause containing a finite-verb predicate. The main predicative use of the participle is called *circumstantial* because, in modifying its noun, the participle describes the circumstances under which that noun is involved in the action of the main verb of the sentence. The circumstantial participle may agree with the subject, the direct or indirect object, the object of a preposition, or any other noun or pronoun expressed or implied in the sentence. In English it is often more idiomatic to use a dependent clause (temporal, concessive, causal, conditional, etc.) or a prepositional phrase with a gerund (verbal noun in *-ing*) than to use a circumstantial participle; but Greek idiom often favors the circumstantial participle over an equivalent subordinate clause. Note the following examples:

a. temporal (expressing time)

ἔκοψε τὸν δικαστὴν ἐξερχόμενον.
He struck the juryman as (when, while) he was coming out.

φυγὼν τοὺς βαρβάρους ὑπὸ τῶν Ἀθηναίων ἑάλω.
Having fled from (after fleeing from) the foreigners, he was captured by the Athenians.

b. concessive (Greek participles with concessive force are often, but not always, marked as such by the use of the particle καίπερ preceding the participle or participial phrase.)

καίπερ νοσῶν χαλεπὴν νόσον εἰς τὴν ἀγορὰν ἦλθε.
Although he was ill with a serious disease, he came to the agora.

c. causal (Greek participles with causal force are often, but not always, marked as such by the use of the particle ὡς preceding the participle or participial phrase.)

τὸν γέροντα ὡς προδιδόντα τὴν πόλιν ἐξέβαλον.
They drove the old man into exile because he was trying to betray the city.

d. conditional

ἀσπίδας μεγάλας ἔχοντες ῥᾳδίως μαχούμεθα.
Having large shields (if we have large shields), we'll fight easily.

Choosing which kind of meaning to give to a circumstantial participle when translating it into English requires close attention to the context: in the proper context, the example just given could be causal (*Because we have large shields, we'll fight easily*). In some cases the exact force may be uncertain.

5. *Absolute Participle Constructions*. Occasionally, in English, Greek, and other languages, the noun with which the circumstantial participle agrees has no grammatical function in its sentence (it is not subject, object, or anything else). In such a case, the noun-participle phrase forms an *absolute* construction (absolute because the noun is free of grammatical connection).

> *The general having fled*, the soldiers surrendered themselves to the king.
> *This being the case*, they made a truce.
> (Compare Latin ablative absolute: *His rebus factis* nuntios mittunt.)

In Greek the most common form of absolute construction is the *genitive absolute*: both the noun (the subject of the participial action) and the circumstantial participle are in the genitive case, the genitive has no other function in the sentence, and the phrase may have temporal, concessive, causal, or conditional meaning. The most idiomatic English translation is often a subordinate clause.

> τοῦ στρατηγοῦ φυγόντος, οἱ στρατιῶται ἑαυτοὺς τῷ βασιλεῖ παρέ-
> δοσαν.
> *After the general fled, the soldiers surrendered themselves to the king.*
> τούτων οὕτως ἐχόντων ἐσπείσαντο.
> *This being the case, they made a truce.*
> τῶν γυναικῶν ἐν τῷ στρατοπέδῳ οὐσῶν οἱ ἄνδρες καλῶς μαχοῦνται.
> *If the women are in the camp, the men will fight well.*

Less common than the genitive absolute is the *accusative absolute*. This is the normal construction when an impersonal expression is involved: the participle of the impersonal verb appears in its neuter singular form, and the subject substantive of the phrase is usually either an expressed or implied infinitive or a noun clause (rarely a neuter pronoun).

> δέον πείθεσθαι τοῖς σοφοῖς τῶν ἀφρόνων ἀκούουσιν.
> *It being necessary to obey the wise, they pay heed to the fools.*
> (or *Although they ought to obey the wise, they pay heed to the fools.*)
> οὐδεὶς τὸ κακὸν αἱρήσεται ἐξὸν τὸ ἀγαθόν.
> *No one will choose the bad when it is possible to choose the good.*
> (note that infinitive αἱρεῖσθαι or ἑλέσθαι is understood with ἐξόν.)

ἄλλο τι δόξαν ὁ Δημοσθένης τὸ στράτευμα ἀπῆγε.
Something else having been decided (having seemed best), Demosthenes led the army back.

A second use of the accusative absolute is with noun and personal-verb participle introduced by ὡς or ὥσπερ = *as if, in the belief that.*

ὑμᾶς ἐξαιτήσονται, ὡς ἐκεῖνον πολλῶν ἀγαθῶν ἀλλ᾽ οὐ πολλῶν κακῶν αἴτιον γενόμενον.
They will beg you for a pardon, just as if that man had been responsible for many good things and not for many evils.

6. *Future Participle Expressing Purpose.* The principal use of the future participle (apart from indirect discourse: U28.2) is as a circumstantial participle expressing purpose or intention. In this use the participle is often introduced by ὡς.

ἔπεμψαν ἱππέας ἀγγελοῦντας τὴν νίκην.
They sent cavalrymen to announce the victory.

οὐκ ἤλθομεν ὡς τῷ βασιλεῖ πολεμήσοντες.
We have not come with the intention of waging war against the king.

7. *Negation of Participles.* Participles are negated by either οὐ or μή, usually with a clear distinction in meaning.

The negative οὐ is used when the participle refers to a fact, a specific event, or an actual occurrence, for example, with participles that have causal or concessive meaning and attributive participles used as substantives when a definite person or thing is meant.

οὐκ ἔχων χρήματα ὁ γέρων δῶρα οὐκ οἴσει.
Because (in fact) he does not have money, the old man will not bring gifts.

ἐπῃνέσαμεν τοὺς οὐ φυγόντας ἐν τῇ μάχῃ.
We praised those who did not (in fact) flee during the (specific) battle.

The negative μή is used when the participle refers to an action that is conditional or generic, for example, with participles that have conditional meaning and attributive participles used as substantives when an indefinite person (thing) or a class of people (things) is meant.

μὴ ἔχων χρήματα ὁ γέρων δῶρα οὐκ οἴσει.
If he doesn't have any money, the old man will not bring gifts.

οἱ μὴ φεύγοντες ἐν τῇ μάχῃ καλοὶ πολῖταί εἰσιν.
Those who do not flee in (any) battle are fine citizens.

ὁ μὴ νοσῶν
any man who is not sick, whoever is not sick

WHAT TO STUDY AND DO

1. Study the uses of the attributive and circumstantial participle.
2. Learn the vocabulary of this unit.
3. Do the exercises of this unit.

VOCABULARY

noun

στράτευμα, -εύματος, n.	army

numerals

εἴκοσι(ν)	twenty [icosahedron]
τριάκοντα	thirty
τετταράκοντα	forty
πεντήκοντα	fifty [Pentecost]
ἑξήκοντα	sixty
ἑβδομήκοντα	seventy
ὀγδοήκοντα	eighty
ἐνενήκοντα	ninety
ἑκατόν	hundred [hecatomb, Hecatompedon, hectoliter]

adverbs/particles

καίπερ	(usually with participle) although
ὡς	(with participle, marking causal or purposive meaning) as, as if, in the belief that, on the ground that
ὥσπερ	as, as if, just as if
πρόσθεν	(of place) before, in front of (occasionally governs gen. like a preposition); (of time) before, formerly

verbs

διώκω, διώξομαι or rarely διώξω, ἐδίωξα	pursue, chase, drive; (law) sue, prosecute
ἐξαιτέω (ἐκ)	ask for from (+ double acc.); (mid.) demand for oneself; (mid.) beg off, appeal for pardon
ἔχω + adverb	be in a certain condition or state
καλῶς ἔχω	be well
κακῶς ἔχω	be in bad shape, feel bad [cachexia]
οὕτως ἔχω	be in this state, be this way
ὀρχέομαι, ὀρχήσομαι, ὠρχησάμην	dance [orchestra]

πάρειμι (παρα + εἰμί) be by, be present

  τὸ παρόν that which is at hand, the present circumstance or time

  τὰ παρόντα present circumstances, the present state of affairs

ἄπειμι (ἀπο + εἰμί) be away, be distant, be absent

πολεμέω, πολεμήσω, make war, make war against (+ dat.)
  ἐπολέμησα

EXERCISES

I. Render into Greek. Use participles wherever possible instead of relative clauses or temporal clauses.

1. At the command of the general [use absolute participle construction], everyone marched along the river, keeping on guard.
2. Those who killed my father will <u>pay the penalty</u> [idiom: δίκην διδόναι].
3. Having left town, she went down to the sea.
4. He who is not willing to learn is sick in the soul.
5. Although he made all these promises, he did nothing.
6. Turning about [use middle], the army came to a halt.
7. A deep sleep held those who drank a lot.
8. While we were pursuing those who had crossed the river, the Athenians burned the tents and seized the horses.
9. We believe the foreigner, although he is reporting many terrible things.
10. They will be unable to equip triremes because they are not rich.

II. Reading.

1. οἱ ἄφρονες τῶν ἀνθρώπων τὰ παρόντα ἀφέντες τὰ ἀπόντα διώκουσιν.
2. τῶν ἀρχόντων πειθόντων, οἱ πολῖται εἰρήνην ἐποιήσαντο πρὸς τοὺς φεύγοντας.
3. καίπερ πολλῶν ἱππέων ἐπιτιθεμένων, τοὺς ἀποθανόντας ἀνειλόμεθα. [1]
4. ὑπέσχετο ταῦτα ποιήσειν ὁ Δημοσθένης, ψευδῶς λέγων.
5. δέον τρέφειν τὸν θρέψαντα ἐπὶ γήρως, οἱ πολλοὶ οὐκ ἐθέλουσιν.
6. τίς δυνήσεται νίκην φέρειν ἐν τῷ ἀγῶνι, μὴ μέγας καὶ ἰσχυρὸς ὤν;
7. ὁ βασιλεὺς Κῦρον συλλαμβάνει[2] ὡς ἀποκτενῶν.

---

1. Compound of ἀνα- (and what verb?); the meaning here is *take up (bodies) for burial.*
2. Compound of συν- (and what verb?); the meaning here is *arrest.*

8. [Parody of a funeral epigram, ascribed to Simonides][1]

πολλὰ πιὼν καὶ πολλὰ φαγὼν καὶ πολλὰ κάκ᾿ εἰπὼν
ἀνθρώπους κεῖμαι Τιμοκρέων Ῥόδιος.

9. ἐγὼ δέ, ὦ ἄνδρες Ἀθηναῖοι, οὐ τὴν αὐτὴν γνώμην ἔχω περὶ ἑκατέρων·
τούτους μέν, οἳ ἐλευθερίας καὶ τοῦ δικαίου ἐπιθυμοῦντες καὶ τοὺς νόμους
ἰσχύειν [to be strong, to be valid] βουλόμενοι καὶ τοὺς ἀδικοῦντας
μισοῦντες [hating] τῶν ὑμετέρων κινδύνων [dangers] μετέσχον [had a
share of, + gen.], οὐ πονηροὺς νομίζω εἶναι πολίτας· ἐκείνων δέ, οἳ
κατελθόντες[2] ἐν δημοκρατίᾳ τὸ μὲν ὑμέτερον πλῆθος ἀδικοῦσι, τοὺς δὲ
ἰδίους [personal, own] οἴκους [households] ἐκ τῶν ὑμετέρων μεγάλους
ποιοῦσι, μάλα ἰσχυρῶς δεῖ κατηγορεῖν, ὥσπερ τῶν τριάκοντα.

---

1. κάκ᾿ in the first line is κακὰ elided; it is conventional to place an acute accent on *P* when a
final vowel with a grave is elided. κεῖμαι in the second line is *(here) I lie (buried)*. Τιμοκρέων is
a man's name (nom. case); Ῥόδιος is a proper adjective, *Rhodian, of Rhodes*. The epigram is
written in the elegiac couplet: the first line is a dactylic hexameter (the meter used in Homer);
the second line is actually two shorter dactylic units. Greek meter is quantitative, that is, based
on the length of syllables. The scheme of this couplet is

$$- \cup \cup - - - - \cup \cup - - - \cup \cup - -$$

$$- - - - - \quad - \cup \cup - \cup \cup -$$

2. Compound of κατα- (and what verb?); the meaning here is *return from exile (to one's native
city)*.

Uses of the Participle II; *οἶδα*

1. *Supplementary Participle.* The third major use of the Greek participle is its *supplementary* use. With certain verbs, a participle in predicate position agreeing with the subject or direct object completes the idea of the verb, which would otherwise be vague or incomplete. The supplementary participle is found with several well-defined classes of verbs.

a. with *τυγχάνω, λανθάνω, φθάνω.* In sentences containing *τυγχάνω* (*happen, be just now*), *λανθάνω* (*escape notice, be unobserved*), or *φθάνω* (*anticipate, be before [someone or something]*) the important word is the sup-plementary participle agreeing with the subject. Note that English translations of these constructions must often be other than literal in order to convey the meaning of the Greek.

> *ἐτύγχανε πίνων.*
> [Lit.: *Drinking, he happened to be.*]
> *He happened to be drinking* or *He was by chance drinking*
>   or *He was just then drinking.*

> *ὀρχούμεναι ἔτυχον.*
> [Lit.: *Dancing, the women happened to be.*]
> *The women happened to be dancing*
>   or *The women were just then dancing.*

> *ὁ κλὼψ ἔλαθεν ἁρπάσας τὰ χρήματα.*
> [Lit.: *Having snatched the money, the thief escaped notice (was unseen).*]
> *The thief snatched the money without being seen.*

> *ἀπελθὼν ἔλαθε τοὺς φύλακας.*
> [Lit.: *Going away, he escaped the notice of the guards.*]
> *He went away without being noticed by the guards*
>   or *The guards didn't notice him go away.*

> *ἐλανθάνομεν ἡμᾶς αὐτοὺς σοφοὶ ὄντες.*
> [Lit.: *Being wise, we escaped our own notice.*]
> *We didn't realize that we were wise*
>   or *We were wise without realizing it.*

φθάνουσι τοὺς πολεμίους λαβόντες τὸ ἄκρον.
[Lit.: *Having captured the summit, they anticipate the enemy.*]
They captured the summit ahead of the enemy.

b. with verbs meaning *begin, continue, cease*, or the like:

ἄρξομαι τοὺς πατέρας ἐπαινῶν.
I'll begin (by) praising our fathers.

οἱ γέροντες μανθάνοντες διαμένουσιν.
Old men continue learning (or *continue to learn*).

παύσομαι λέγων.
I'll stop talking.

τοῦτον ἔπαυσαν προδιδόντα τὴν πόλιν.
They stopped him from betraying the city
    or *They stopped his betraying the city.*

c. with verbs of emotion:

χαίρω ταῦτα ἀκούων.
I enjoy hearing these things.

οἱ φιλόσοφοι ἀεὶ μανθάνοντες ἥδονται.
Lovers of wisdom take pleasure in constantly learning.

ἀδικούμενοι οἱ ἄνθρωποι ὀργίζονται.
People get angry at being treated unjustly.

d. with verbs meaning *do well, do ill, behave rightly, behave wrongly,
surpass, be inferior*, or the like:

καλῶς ἐποίησεν οὕτω τελευτήσας τὸν βίον.
He did well in ending his life thus.

ἁμαρτάνετε νομίζοντες τοῦτο καλόν.
You err in believing that this is a noble thing.

e. with verbs meaning *permit, endure, put up with*, or the like:

οὐκ ἀνέξεσθε ταῦτα ἀκούοντες.
You will not endure hearing these things
    or *You won't put up with listening to this.*

τοὺς συμμάχους οὐ περιοψόμεθα ἀδικουμένους.
We will not (watch without concern and) permit our allies to be wronged.

2. *Supplementary Participle Expressing Indirect Discourse.* The second
of the Greek indirect discourse constructions (U20.6–7) to be learned employs
the supplementary participle, either in agreement with the object of a verb or

in agreement with the subject of the verb if the subject of the indirect statement is the same as the subject of the main verb.

Verbs meaning *know, be ignorant, learn, remember, forget, show, prove, announce, appear*, or the like may take the supplementary participle to express indirect discourse. (Most of these verbs may also take a noun clause, the construction to be learned in U33.) In this construction the participle always has the same tense (or tense stem: present part. for imperfect ind. of direct discourse) and same voice as the verb of the direct statement.

direct	ὁ ἄγγελος ἀφίξεται.
	The messenger will arrive.
indirect	ἔγνωσαν τὸν ἄγγελον ἀφιξόμενον.
	They realized the messenger would arrive.
direct	ταῦτα εἶπεν ὁ στρατηγός.
	The general said these things.
indirect	ἀγνοεῖτε ταῦτα εἰπόντα τὸν στρατηγόν;
	Don't you know that the general said these things?
direct	ὁ Φίλιππος ἡμᾶς ἀδικεῖ.
	Philip wrongs us.
indirect	δείξω τὸν Φίλιππον ἡμᾶς ἀδικοῦντα.
	I'll show that Philip is wronging us.

Note that in the above examples the subject of the direct form becomes the accusative direct object and the finite verb becomes the participle of same tense and voice agreeing with the accusative noun. In the following examples, the main verb is passive or consists of copula and predicate adjective: the subject may be unexpressed, and the participle is in the nominative, agreeing with the subject. Greek idiom favors personal verbs in these constructions, but English idiom prefers an impersonal verb with *it* followed by a *that*-clause.

direct	ὁ Φίλιππος ἡμᾶς ἀδικεῖ.
	Philip wrongs us.
indirect	ὁ Φίλιππος ἐδείκνυτο ἡμᾶς ἀδικῶν.
	Philip was being shown to be wronging us
	or *It was being shown that Philip wrongs us.*
direct	οἱ Ἀθηναῖοι ἐνίκησαν.
	The Athenians won.
indirect	οἱ Ἀθηναῖοι ἀγγέλλονται νικήσαντες.
	The Athenians are reported to have won
	or *It is reported that the Athenians won.*
direct	ἐπιβουλεύομεν τῷ βασιλεῖ.
	We are plotting against the king.

indirect   φανεροὶ ἦμεν ἐπιβουλεύοντες τῷ βασιλεῖ.
             It was obvious that we were plotting against the king.
             [Lit.: *We were obvious, plotting against the king.*]

3. *Supplementary Participle with Verbs of Perception.* Verbs meaning *see, hear, learn of,* or the like may take either a supplementary participle expressing actual perception or a supplementary participle of indirect discourse. When the physical act of perception is denoted, the English translation cannot accurately use a *that*-clause, and some of the verbs of perception (ἀκούω, πυνθάνομαι, and sometimes αἰσθάνομαι) take a genitive rather than accusative object.

εἶδον τὸν στρατηγὸν ἀποθνῄσκοντα.
They saw (with their own eyes) the general dying.

ἠκούσατε ἐμοῦ λέγοντος ταῦτα.
You heard (with your own ears) me saying this.

When indirect discourse is denoted, it is the proposition rather than the action that is perceived: the English translation is then a *that*-clause, and the verbs ἀκούω and πυνθάνομαι take an accusative object.

ἠκούσατε αὐτὸν εἰπόντα ταῦτα.
You heard (via the report of others) <u>that</u> he said this.

ἀκούομεν τὸν Σωκράτην σοφὸν ὄντα.
We hear <u>that</u> Socrates is wise.

ἐπύθοντο τοὺς πλείστους ἀποφυγόντας.
They learned <u>that</u> most had escaped.

4. *Negation of Supplementary Participles.* The principle described in U27.7 applies to supplementary participles as well. Most supplementary participles refer to an actual event and use the negative οὐ. Thus οὐ is used with supplementary participles expressing indirect discourse and with those accompanying verbs of emotion, where the participle may be considered to express cause.

5. *Predicate Nouns and Adjectives after Participles.* Since the participle is a verb form, it may have any of the complements found with the other forms of the verb, including (for the copula and verbs of similar meaning) predicate noun or predicate adjective. As usual, the predicate noun or adjective must agree with its "subject" noun, and in a participial phrase this "subject" may be in any case.

οὐκ ἀγνοῶ χαλεπὸς ὤν.
I am not unaware that I am obstinate.
    [suppl. part. ind. disc. with same subject as main verb: nom.]

οἱ πλεῖστοι τῶν δοκούντων σοφῶν εἶναι
the majority of those who seem to be wise
    [attrib. part. as substantive: gen.]

πείθονται τῷ Δημοσθένει ὡς στρατηγῷ ὄντι.
They obey Demosthenes because he is general.
    [circumstantial part.: dat.]

6. *The Verb* οἶδα. From the same root as the aorist εἶδον there exists the irregular verb οἶδα, which is perfect in form but present in meaning (*know*). The stem appears in several forms, including οἰδ-, εἰδ- (augmented ᾐδ-), ἰσ-, and augmented ᾐσ-. The infinitive is εἰδέναι, the participle εἰδώς.[1] The pluperfect is equivalent to an imperfect in meaning. Here is the conjugation in the indicative:

		perfect	*pluperfect*
sing.	*1st*	οἶδα	ᾔδη (ᾔδειν)
	2nd	οἶσθα	ᾔδησθα (ᾔδεις)
	3rd	οἶδε(ν)	ᾔδει(ν)
(dual	*2nd*	ἴστον	ᾔδετον)
	(3rd	ἴστον	ᾐδέτην)
plur.	*1st*	ἴσμεν	ᾔδεμεν or ᾖσμεν
	2nd	ἴστε	ᾔδετε or ᾖστε
	3rd	ἴσᾱσι(ν)	ᾔδεσαν or ᾖσαν

The two singular pluperfect forms in parentheses are found in Attic from about 350 B.C.E. on.

WHAT TO STUDY AND DO

1. Study the uses of the supplementary participle.
2. Study the conjugation of οἶδα.
3. Learn the vocabulary of this unit.
4. Do the exercises of this unit.

---

1. Declension of perfect participles to be learned later, in U37.

VOCABULARY

verb

ἐπιβουλεύω (ἐπι)   plot against (+ dat.)

verbs that sometimes take a supplementary participle

ἀγνοέω, ἀγνοήσω, ἠγνόησα   not perceive, be ignorant, be unaware of   [agnostic]

ἁμαρτάνω, ἁμαρτήσομαι,   miss the mark, fail of hitting or having (+ gen.); err,
   ἥμαρτον   make a mistake (+ part.)   [hamartia]

ἀνέχω (ἀνα)   hold up; (intrans.) rise up; (mid.) bear up, endure, put
                      up with (+ part.)

διαμένω (δια)   continue, persist, last

διατελέω, διατελέω,   continue; persevere, live
   διετέλεσα (δια)

ἐλέγχω, ἐλέγξω, ἤλεγξα   cross-examine; put to the test; prove; refute
                     [elenchus]

    ἐξελέγχω   prove; convict, refute

ἐπίσταμαι, ἐπιστήσομαι (a   know how to (+ inf.); know, understand
   deponent μι-verb)[1]   [epistemology]

ἥδομαι   enjoy, take pleasure (+ dat. or + part.)

λανθάνω, λήσω, ἔλαθον   escape notice, be unobserved   [Lethe]

οἶδα (inf. εἰδέναι), fut. εἴσομαι   know

ὀργίζομαι, ὀργιέομαι   grow angry, be (made) angry (sometimes + dat. of
                     person or thing)

   (rare) ὀργίζω, (no fut.   make angry
   act.), ὤργισα

παύω, παύσω, ἔπαυσα   stop (someone else or something); (mid.) stop
                     (oneself), cease   [pause]

περιοράω, περιόψομαι,   look over; overlook; look on while doing nothing,
   περιεῖδον[2] (περι)   permit

τυγχάνω, τεύξομαι, ἔτυχον   happen to be (+ part.); happen (of events); succeed;
                     meet with, hit upon (+ gen.); obtain (+ gen.)

φθάνω, φθήσομαι, ἔφθασα   anticipate, be ahead of (+ part.)
   or ἔφθην[3]

adjective

ἄκρος, ἄκρα, ἄκρον   topmost, outmost, inmost; highest   [acrostics,
                     acrophobia]

---

1. Conjugated in present system like δύναμαι (cf. Appendix 3: Paradigms).

2. Conjugation of the present system will be learned in the next unit.

3. Conjugated like ἔβην, ἔστην. In this verb there is no difference in meaning between the strong and the weak aorists.

τὸ ἄκρον	peak, summit; farthest point
ἀκρόπολις,	upper city, citadel, acropolis
ἀκροπόλεως, f.	

EXERCISES

I. Sentences for reading.

1. κακῶς ἐποιήσατε περιϊδόντες ταύτας ὑπὸ τῶν ἄλλων γυναικῶν ἀδικουμένας.
2. τίς φθήσεται τοὺς βαρβάρους ἀναβὰς ἐπὶ τὴν ἀκρόπολιν;
3. ταῦτα εἰπὼν οὐκ ἁμαρτήσῃ.
4. ὁ νεανίας κακῶς ἔχει· οὔποτε γὰρ ἀνέχεται δεύτερος ὤν.
5. ταῦτα τὰ χρήματα κρύψαντα αὐτὸν ῥᾳδίως ἐλέγξω.
6. ἔτυχε γυμναζόμενος ἐκείνῃ τῇ ἡμέρᾳ.
7. οὐκ οἶσθα τὸν θάνατον παύσοντα καὶ τοὺς καλῶς πράττοντας καὶ τοὺς μή;

II. Reading: Lysias, in praise of Athenians who died in war, cites examples of just and brave behavior from legendary history (adapted passage).

Ἀδράστου καὶ Πολυνείκους ταῖς Θήβαις ἐπιθεμένων καὶ οὐ καλῶς πραξάντων ἐν τῇ μάχῃ, τῶν Θηβαίων κωλυόντων θάπτειν τοὺς νεκρούς, οἱ Ἀθηναῖοι, ἡγησάμενοι ἐκείνους μὲν ἀποθανόντας δίκην ἱκανὴν δοῦναι, τούτους δ᾽ ἐξαμαρτάνειν εἰς τοὺς θεούς, πρῶτον μὲν πέμψαντες ἀγγέλους ἐδέοντο αὐτῶν δοῦναι τῶν νεκρῶν ἀναίρεσιν· οὐ δυνάμενοι δὲ τούτων τυχεῖν ἐστράτευσαν ἐπ᾽ αὐτούς, οὐδεμιᾶς διαφορᾶς πρότερον πρὸς Θηβαίους οὔσης, ἡγούμενοι δεῖν τοὺς ἀποθανόντας τῶν νομιζομένων τυχεῖν. τὸ δὲ δίκαιον ἔχοντες σύμμαχον ἐνίκων μαχόμενοι καὶ πᾶσι τὴν ἑαυτῶν ἀρετὴν ἐπεδείξαντο.

ὑστέρῳ δὲ χρόνῳ, ἐπεὶ Ἡρακλῆς ἀπέθανεν, οἱ τούτου παῖδες φεύγοντες Εὐρυσθέα ἐξηλαύνοντο ὑπὸ πάντων τῶν Ἑλλήνων, αἰσχυνομένων μὲν τοῖς ἔργοις, φοβουμένων δὲ τὴν Εὐρυσθέως δύναμιν. ἀφικομένων τῶν παίδων εἰς τήνδε τὴν πόλιν καὶ ἐξαιτουμένου αὐτοὺς Εὐρυσθέως, οἱ Ἀθηναῖοι οὐκ ἠθέλησαν παραδοῦναι. ἐπιστρατευόντων δὲ τῶν Ἀργείων, οὐκ ἐγγὺς τῶν δεινῶν γενόμενοι μετέγνωσαν, ἀλλὰ τὴν αὐτὴν γνώμην εἶχον καὶ δεύτερον ἐνίκων μαχόμενοι.

Underlined Words

Ἄδραστος, -ου, m. = *Adrastus,*
  king of Argos who helped his son-
  in-law Polynices (son of Oedipus)
  mount the campaign of "the Seven
  against Thebes" against P.'s
  brother Eteocles

αἰσχύνομαι = *feel ashamed at* (+
  dat.)

ἀναίρεσις, -εως, f. = *picking up (of
  bodies)*

Ἀργεῖοι, -ων, m. = *Argives*

διαφορά, -ᾶς, f. = *disagreement*

ἐγγύς = (adv.) *near, close to* (+ gen.)

ἐνίκων = *they were victorious* (3rd
  pl. imperfect act. of νικάω)

ἐξαμαρτάνω = *commit a sin*

ἐξελαύνω = *drive out*

ἐπεί = *when, after*

ἐπιστρατεύω = *go on campaign
  against*

Εὐρυσθεύς, -έως, m. = *Eurystheus,*
  king of Tiryns and Argos, who
  persecuted Heracles and H.'s
  children

ἱκανός, -ή, -όν = *sufficient* (here
  with δίκην = *penalty*)

θάπτω = *bury*

Θῆβαι, -ῶν, f. = *Thebes*

Θηβαῖοι, -ων, m. = *Thebans*

μεταγιγνώσκω = *change one's mind*

νεκρός, -οῦ, m. = *dead body*

νομιζομένων (neut. part. as
  substantive) = *the customary
  (funeral) rites*

Πολυνείκης, -ους, m. = *Polynices*

στρατεύω = *go on a military
  campaign*

Contract Verbs in -άω and -όω; Further Uses of the Genitive and Dative

1. *Verbs in -άω.* Recall that in Attic there are three kinds of ω-verbs that show contraction in the present system (U13.1). Verbs in -άω and -όω are less common than those in -έω, which the student learned in U13. The Attic contractions which are relevant to the present system of verbs in -άω are:

$$a + \epsilon \longrightarrow \bar{a} \qquad\qquad a + o \longrightarrow \omega \qquad\qquad a + \omega \longrightarrow \omega$$

$$a + \epsilon\iota \text{ (gen.)} \longrightarrow \mathring{a} \qquad a + o\upsilon \text{ (sp.)} \longrightarrow \omega \qquad a + \eta \longrightarrow \mathring{a}$$

$$a + \epsilon\iota \text{ (sp.)} \longrightarrow \bar{a}$$

Fuller general schemes for contraction are set out in Appendix 1. The distinction between "genuine" and "spurious" ει is based on linguistic history (explained in Unit 1, page 10, footnote 2): the ει of the 2nd and 3rd singular active ending is "genuine" (and so the iota continues to appear in the contracted form); the ει of the active infinitive ending is "spurious" (the result of contraction), and so the iota does not appear in the contraction with α. [1]

In the paradigm of ὁράω (= *see*: stem ὁρα- + o/ε) shown on the next page, the uncontracted form is illustrated in parentheses next to the contracted form which results from it in Attic. The augmented stem for the imperfect of ὁράω is unusual in that it has *double* augmentation: both the addition of initial ε and lengthening of o to ω, yielding the imperfect stem ἑώρα- + o/ε. Other verbs in -άω have normal augmentation (e.g., imperfect stem ἐτιμα- from τιμάω). To understand the *accentuation*, review the rule given in U13.2 for accentuation of contracted verbs.

---

1. In the sequence α + ε + ε, contraction takes place first between α and the first ε, producing ᾱ + ε, which yields ᾱ.

PRESENT SYSTEM OF VERBS IN -άω

		pres. active ind.		pres. middle/passive ind.	
sing.	1st	(ὁράω)	ὁρῶ	(ὁράομαι)	ὁρῶμαι
	2nd	(ὁράεις)	ὁρᾷς	(ὁράῃ)	ὁρᾷ
	3rd	(ὁράει)	ὁρᾷ	(ὁράεται)	ὁρᾶται
[dual	2nd	(ὁράετον)	ὁρᾶτον	(ὁράεσθον)	ὁρᾶσθον]
	[3rd	(ὁράετον)	ὁρᾶτον	(ὁράεσθον)	ὁρᾶσθον]
plur.	1st	(ὁράομεν)	ὁρῶμεν	(ὁραόμεθα)	ὁρώμεθα
	2nd	(ὁράετε)	ὁρᾶτε	(ὁράεσθε)	ὁρᾶσθε
	3rd	(ὁράουσι)	ὁρῶσι(ν)	(ὁράονται)	ὁρῶνται

present act. inf. ὁρᾶν; present m/p inf. ὁρᾶσθαι

present act. participle ὁρῶν, ὁρῶσα, ὁρῶν, m/n stem ὁρωντ- [dat. pl. ὁρῶσι(ν)]

present m/p participle ὁρώμενος

		imperf. active ind.		imperf. middle/passive ind.	
sing.	1st	(ἑώραον)	ἑώρων	(ἑωραόμην)	ἑωρώμην
	2nd	(ἑώραες)	ἑώρας	(ἑωράου)	ἑωρῶ
	3rd	(ἑώραε)	ἑώρα	(ἑωράετο)	ἑωρᾶτο
[dual	2nd	(ἑωράετον)	ἑωρᾶτον	(ἑωράεσθον)	ἑωρᾶσθον]
	[3rd	(ἑωραέτην)	ἑωράτην	(ἑωραέσθην)	ἑωράσθην]
plur.	1st	(ἑωράομεν)	ἑωρῶμεν	(ἑωραόμεθα)	ἑωρώμεθα
	2nd	(ἑωράετε)	ἑωρᾶτε	(ἑωράεσθε)	ἑωρᾶσθε
	3rd	(ἑώραον)	ἑώρων	(ἑωράοντο)	ἑωρῶντο

2. *Verbs in* -όω. The Attic contractions which are relevant to the present system of verbs in -όω are as follows:

$$o + \epsilon \longrightarrow ov \text{ (sp.)} \qquad o + o \longrightarrow ov \text{ (sp.)} \qquad o + \omega \longrightarrow \omega$$
$$o + \epsilon\iota \text{ (gen.)} \longrightarrow o\iota \qquad o + ov \text{ (sp.)} \longrightarrow ov \text{ (sp.)} \qquad o + \eta \longrightarrow o\iota$$
$$o + \epsilon\iota \text{ (sp.)} \longrightarrow ov \text{ (sp.)}$$

Fuller general schemes for contraction are set out in Appendix 1. The distinction between "genuine" and "spurious" ου is based on linguistic history (explained Unit 1, page 11, footnote 2): the ου of the 3rd plural active ending is "spurious" (the result of compensatory lengthening), as is that of the 2nd singular middle (the result of contraction). In the case of genuine and spurious ει, the iota again appears in the contraction only when the ει is genuine (2nd

and 3rd sing. active; not in the infinitive).[1] In the following paradigm of δηλόω
(= *reveal*: stem δηλο- + ο/ε), the uncontracted form is illustrated in
parentheses next to the contracted form which results from it in Attic.

PRESENT SYSTEM OF VERBS IN -όω

		pres. active ind.		*pres. middle/passive ind.*	
sing.	1st	(δηλόω)	δηλῶ	(δηλόομαι)	δηλοῦμαι
	2nd	(δηλόεις)	δηλοῖς	(δηλόῃ)	δηλοῖ
	3rd	(δηλόει)	δηλοῖ	(δηλόεται)	δηλοῦται
[dual	2nd	(δηλόετον)	δηλοῦτον	(δηλόεσθον)	δηλοῦσθον]
	[3rd	(δηλόετον)	δηλοῦτον	(δηλόεσθον)	δηλοῦσθον]
plur.	1st	(δηλόομεν)	δηλοῦμεν	(δηλοόμεθα)	δηλούμεθα
	2nd	(δηλόετε)	δηλοῦτε	(δηλόεσθε)	δηλοῦσθε
	3rd	(δηλόουσι)	δηλοῦσι(ν)	(δηλόονται)	δηλοῦνται

present act. inf. δηλοῦν; present m/p inf. δηλοῦσθαι

present act. participle δηλῶν, δηλοῦσα, δηλοῦν, m/n stem δηλουντ- [dat. pl.
δηλοῦσι(ν)]

present m/p participle δηλούμενος

		imperf. active ind.		*imperf. middle/passive ind.*	
sing.	1st	(ἐδήλοον)	ἐδήλουν	(ἐδηλοόμην)	ἐδηλούμην
	2nd	(ἐδήλοες)	ἐδήλους	(ἐδηλόου)	ἐδηλοῦ
	3rd	(ἐδήλοε)	ἐδήλου	(ἐδηλόετο)	ἐδηλοῦτο
[dual	2nd	(ἐδηλόετον)	ἐδηλοῦτον	(ἐδηλόεσθον)	ἐδηλοῦσθον]
	[3rd	(ἐδηλοέτην)	ἐδηλούτην	(ἐδηλοέσθην)	ἐδηλούσθην]
plur.	1st	(ἐδηλόομεν)	ἐδηλοῦμεν	(ἐδηλοόμεθα)	ἐδηλούμεθα
	2nd	(ἐδηλόετε)	ἐδηλοῦτε	(ἐδηλόεσθε)	ἐδηλοῦσθε
	3rd	(ἐδήλοον)	ἐδήλουν	(ἐδηλόοντο)	ἐδηλοῦντο

3. *Futures in -άω.* A few verbs whose stems end in α lose the suffix σ in
the future and have α-contraction in the future conjugation, with endings and
accentuation exactly like those of presents such as ὁράω. Like the futures in
-έω (νομιέω, καλέω), these futures in -άω are called "Attic futures" (U18.6).
Futures with α-contraction are found for ἐλαύνω (fut. ind. ἐλῶ, ἐλᾷς, etc.; fut.
inf. ἐλᾶν, fut. part. ἐλῶν, ἐλῶσα, ἐλῶν) and for all verbs in -αννυμι (e.g.,

---

1. In the sequence ο + ε + ε, contraction takes place first between ο and the first ε, producing ου
(sp.) + ε, which yields ου (sp.).

σκεδάννυμι = *scatter*, fut. ind. σκεδῶ, fut. inf. σκεδᾶν, fut. part. σκεδῶν; likewise for κρεμάννυμι = *hang*, πετάννυμι = *spread*).

4. *Further Uses of the Genitive Case* (Review U10.5 for basic uses of the genitive.)

a. *Genitive Limiting Nouns* (cf. possessive, partitive, subjective, objective)

(1) *Genitive of Quality or Description.* A genitive phrase in the predicate may describe, or denote the quality of, the subject.

> ταῦτα πολλῶν πόνων ἐστίν.
> *These things require much toil.*
> [Lit.: *These things are of much toil.*]
>
> ὁ γέρων χαλεποῦ τρόπου ὤν . . .
> *the old man, being of a harsh disposition, . . .*

(2) *Genitive of Material.* The genitive may denote the material or contents of which a noun is composed.

> κρήνη ἡδέος ὕδατος
> *a spring of sweet water*

(3) *Genitive of Measure.* The genitive may denote the size or degree of a thing.

> ὀκτὼ σταδίων τεῖχος
> *a wall eight stades long, a wall of eight stades [in length]*
>
> πέντε ἡμερῶν σιτία
> *food for five days*

b. *Genitive with Verbs*

(1) The *partitive genitive* is used with verbs when the action affects only a part of the object. The partitive genitive is especially common with verbs of *sharing* (often compounds of μετα-):

> μεταδιδόναι τῶν σιτίων
> *to give a share of the food*
>
> μετέχειν τῆς τιμῆς
> *to have a share of the honor*

verbs of *touching* or *holding*:

> ἔχεσθαι τῆς χειρὸς αὐτοῦ
> *to hold on to his hand*

verbs of *filling*:

> οὐκ ἐμπλήσετε τὴν θάλατταν τριήρων;
> *Will you not fill the sea with ships?*

verbs of *aiming at* or *desiring*:

> ἐπιθυμεῖν τῶν ἀγαθῶν
> *to desire what is good*

verbs of *reaching* or *obtaining*:

> σπονδῶν ἔτυχον.
> *They obtained a truce.*

verbs of *remembering*, *forgetting*, or *neglecting*:

> βούλομαι ὑμᾶς ἀναμνῆσαι τῶν παρόντων πραγμάτων.
> *I want to remind you of the difficulties at hand.*

verbs of *ruling* or *being leader of*:

> ὁ Ξέρξης τῶν βαρβάρων βασιλεύει.
> *Xerxes is king of the foreigners.*

(2) *Genitive of Separation*. With verbs meaning *cease, release, fail, be distant from, lack, be in need of*, and the like, the genitive denotes separation.

> ἀπέχομεν τῆς πόλεως δύο στάδια.
> *We are two stades distant from the city.*

> παύσαντες αὐτὸν τῆς στρατηγίας
> *having removed him from the office of general*

> χρημάτων οὐκ ἀπορήσομεν.
> *We shall not be at a loss for money*
> or *We shall not lack money.*

(3) The genitive may express *price* or *value*.

> ἀπέδοτο τὴν ἵππον δύο ταλάντων.
> *He sold the mare for two talents.*

(4) The *genitive of cause* is used with many verbs of emotion, especially those meaning *wonder at, admire, praise, blame*, or the like.

> ζηλῶ αὐτὸν τῆς ἀρετῆς.
> *I admire him for (because of) his virtue.*

(5) The *genitive of distinction or comparison* is used with verbs meaning *differ, surpass, be inferior* as well as with comparative adjectives and adverbs (to be learned in the next unit).

> διαφέρει τῶν ἄλλων.
> *He differs from (is superior to) the others.*

(6) *Genitive with Compound Verbs.* The genitive is used with compounds of ἀπο-, προ-, ὑπερ-, ἐπι-, and κατα- when the compound verb has the meaning of the simple verb plus the preposition separated from it: for instance, κατηγορέω = *speak against* + gen., ὑπερμάχομαι = *fight on behalf of* + gen.

c. *Genitive with Adjectives.* The genitive may also depend on various adjectives corresponding in meaning to verbs which take the genitive.

χώρα θηρίων πλήρης	*a land full of wild beasts*
μνήμων τῶν πόνων	*mindful of the toil*

d. *Genitive of Time Within Which.* The genitive denotes the time within which an action takes place.

ἡμέρας   *during daytime, by day*

ταῦτα ὄψεσθε γιγνόμενα δέκα ἡμερῶν.
You will see these things happening within ten days.

The distinctions between the three time constructions in Greek may be clarified by thinking of a time line: the dative identifies a single point on the line (or else views a stretch of the line as a single unit); the accusative identifies a particular stretch of the line and emphasizes its extent from a beginning to an end; the genitive identifies a stretch of the line but refers indefinitely to some point or points between the indicated limits.

5. *Further Uses of the Dative* (For basic uses of the dative case, review U10.6).

a. The dative is used with a wide variety of verbs and adjectives having meanings of the following kinds:

(1) *Help, injure, please, displease, be friendly, be hostile,* and the like:

ταῦτα ἀρέσκει τῷ πλήθει.
These things please the multitude.

ἐμοὶ ὀργίζονται.	*They are angry at me.*
φίλιοι τῷ βασιλεῖ	*friendly to the king*

(2) *Meet, approach, yield:*

ἀπήντησαν αὐτοῖς οἱ στρατηγοί.
The generals came up to them (met them face to face).

(3) *Obey, serve, trust:*

πείθεσθαι τῷ ἄρχοντι	*to obey the ruler*
τῷ βασιλεῖ δουλεύειν	*to be a slave to the king*

(4) *Be like, be equal*:

> στράτευμα ἴσον τῷ τῶν ᾿Αθηναίων
> *an army equal to that of the Athenians*

b. The instrumental dative is used with expressions of comparison (including comparative adjectives) to denote the *degree of difference* (*by how much?*).

> ὀλίγῳ σοφώτερος ἐγένετο.
> *He became a little wiser (wiser by a little).*

c. The instrumental dative of an abstract substantive may express manner or accompanying circumstance (*dative of manner*).

> | πολλῇ βοῇ | *with loud shouting* |
> | τῇ ἀληθείᾳ | *in truth* |
> | σπουδῇ | *in haste* or *zealously* |
> | ἔργῳ, λόγῳ | *in deed, in word* |

d. The *comitative dative* is used to denote the persons or things which accompany or take part in an action.

(1) *Dative of (Friendly or Hostile) Association*

> | διαλέγεσθαι ἀλλήλοις | *to converse with each other* |
> | μάχεσθαι πολλοῖς | *to fight with (against) many* |

(2) *Dative of Military Accompaniment*

> ἐξελαύνει τῷ στρατεύματι παντί.
> *He marches forth with his entire army.*

e. *Locative Dative.* Place or position is normally denoted in prose by the dative with a preposition; in poetry the dative alone may be used. In prose the dative (or surviving locative case) of a proper name may be used without a preposition to indicate place.

> ᾿Αθήνησι, Πυθοῖ, Σαλαμῖνι
> *at Athens, at Pytho (= Delphi), at Salamis*

f. *Dative with Compound Verbs.* The dative is often used with verbs compounded in συν-, ἐν-, ἐπι-, παρα-, περι-, προσ-, or ὑπο- when the preposition in the compound conveys a sense which normally governs the dative.

> ἐπιτίθεσθαι τοῖς πολεμίοις
> *to attack the enemy (to place oneself upon, against the enemy)*

συναδικεῖν τοῖς ἄλλοις
to commit wrong together with the others

g. *Dative of Agent*. This use is confined to passives of the perfect stem or the passive verbal adjective, both to be learned later (U37.7, U42.6).

WHAT TO STUDY AND DO

1. Learn the inflection of verbs in -άω and -όω.
2. Study the uses of the genitive and dative.
3. Learn the vocabulary of this unit.
4. Do the exercises of this unit.

VOCABULARY

Vocabulary-building Hints. Note that many verbs in -άω and -όω are denominatives, that is, formed from noun or adjective roots. Thus τιμάω from the a-stem noun τιμή, νικάω from νίκη, τελευτάω from τελευτή; δηλόω from the o-stem adjective δῆλος, ζηλόω from the o-stem noun ζῆλος.

Also note that in forming the future and aorist (and other) principal parts of such verbs, the vowel of the stem is lengthened before the tense suffix (as was true of most verbs in -έω): τιμήσω (Attic η for ā in τιμάσω), ἐδήλωσα.

nouns

κρήνη, κρήνης, f.	well, spring [Hippocrene]
σῖτος, σίτου, m. (sing. only);	grain; bread; food, provisions [parasite]
pl. σῖτα, σίτων, n.	
σιτίον, σιτίου, n.	grain, bread; food, provisions
σπονδή, σπονδῆς, f.	drink-offering; (pl.) truce, treaty
τάλαντον, ταλάντου, n.	balance, weighing scale; unit of weight (talent), and hence a sum of money (gold or silver)[1]

adjectives

ἴσος, ἴση, ἴσον	equal [isosceles, isobar]
ἴσως	equally; probably, perhaps
μνήμων, μνῆμον (gen. μνήμονος)	mindful, remembering, unforgetting [mnemonic]

---

1. The standards of weight and monetary units in ancient Greece varied according to locale. In classical Athens, weight and money were measured in obols (ὀβολοί), drachmas (δραχμαί: the drachma is the unit of modern Greek currency), minae (μναῖ), and talents (τάλαντα), with 6 obols = 1 drachma; 100 drachmas = 1 mina; 60 minae = 1 talent. The Attic drachma was 4.37 grams.

verbs

ἀπορέω, ἀπορήσω, ἠπόρησα	be without means or resources; be at a loss, be in doubt; lack [aporia, aporetic]
βασιλεύω, βασιλεύσω, ἐβασίλευσα	be king; (inceptive aor.) became king
δηλόω, δηλώσω, ἐδήλωσα	render manifest; reveal, disclose, show
ζηλόω, ζηλώσω, ἐζήλωσα	vie with, emulate; admire, praise (+ acc. of person + gen. of cause) [zealot]
μετέχω (μετα)	partake of, have a share of or in (+ gen.)
μιμνῄσκω or μιμνήσκω, μνήσω, ἔμνησα (poetic in active)	remind, call to mind (+ acc. of person + gen. of thing); (mid./pass.) remember (+ gen. or + acc.), make mention of (+ gen.) [amnesia, amnesty]
ἀναμιμνῄσκω or ὑπομιμνῄσκω (used in prose instead of simple verb)	
νῑκάω, νῑκήσω, ἐνίκησα [ῑ]	win; conquer
ὁράω, ὄψομαι, εἶδον	see [panorama]
πίμπλημι or ἐμπίμπλημι, ἐμπλήσω, ἐνέπλησα[1]	fill (+ gen. of thing)
σκεδάννῡμι, -σκεδάω, -εσκέδασα[2]	scatter, disperse
τελευτάω, τελευτήσω, ἐτελεύτησα	accomplish; bring to an end; end one's life, die; (pres. act. part. agreeing with subject of sentence, as if an adverb) finally
τῑμάω, τῑμήσω, ἐτίμησα [ῑ]	honor, esteem
φαίνω, φανέω, ἔφηνα	bring to light, reveal; show forth, display; (pass.) come to light, appear; (with inf.) appear (seem) to be doing X; (with suppl. part.) be clearly, obviously, openly doing X [phenomenon]
φέρω + adverb	bear, endure in a certain manner
χαλεπῶς φέρω	bear with difficulty, be annoyed (+ suppl. part.)

EXERCISES

I. Identify completely and translate precisely each form.

1. ἐτελευτῶμεν	4. ἑωρῶμεν	7. μετασχήσειν
2. ἐζηλοῦντο	5. σκεδαννύασι	8. ἀνέμνησας
3. τιμῶνται	6. τιμώσαις	9. ἀναμνήσας

---

1. Outside the present, the compound is preferred in prose; conjugated in the present system like ἵστημι.

2. Outside the present, compounds such as διασκεδάννυμι are preferred in prose.

10. ἐνίκα
11. ὁρᾶσθαι
12. ἐμπίμπλησι
13. σκεδῶν
14. ἐλᾷς
15. ἐνεπίμπλης
16. ἴσμεν
17. φανεῖ
18. περιόψεσθε
19. ζηλοῦσθαι

20. ἀποροῦντι
21. τελευτώμενον
22. ἐτίμων
23. ἐδηλοῦ
24. ἁρπάσῃ
25. ἐπίστασθαι
26. δηλοῖ
27. τιμᾶν
28. ἠπόρει
29. ζηλούμενοι

30. νικᾶτε
31. ὁρῶ
32. ἐνεπίμπλαμεν
33. σκεδῶμεν
34. τελευτήσειν
35. φῆναι
36. εἴσονται
37. ἔσονται
38. ὀργιουμέναις
39. ἐπαύσατο

II. Write in Greek.

1. to emulate (pres. & aor.)
2. to bring to an end (pres. & aor.)
3. masc. dat. pl. pres. act. part. of "win"
4. the things being made manifest (nom.)
5. they used to fill
6. we are being emulated
7. you (s.) were seeing
8. gen. s. fem. pres. m/p part. of "honor"
9. to scatter (pres. & aor.)
10. acc. pl. masc. fut. act. part. of "have a share of"
11. you (pl.) remembered
12. they were emulating
13. to be conquered
14. you (s.) used to see
15. we are being honored
16. we'll march
17. she gave a share of
18. I had a share of
19. about to suffer
20. to drink (pres. & aor.)

III. Reading.

1. τρισὶ δ᾽ ἡμέραις ὕστερον τὴν ἑαυτῶν ἀρετὴν αὖθις ἐδήλωσαν ὠφελοῦντες τοὺς ἀποροῦντας σιτίων.
2. οὐ μνήμονες ὄντες, ὦ ἄνδρες στρατιῶται, φαίνεσθε οὔτε τῶν τότε γενομένων οὔτε τῶν νῦν μελλόντων γενήσεσθαι.
3. οὕτω δεινὸς λέγειν ἦν οὗτος ὁ πονηρὸς ὥστε φαίνεσθαι ἄξιος εἶναι ἀρχῆς.
4. πρῶτον μὲν ἡσυχίαν ἦγεν ὁ γέρων ταῦτα ὁρῶν πραττόμενα ὑπὸ τῶν ἐπιβουλευόντων τοῖς ἄρχουσιν, τελευτῶν δὲ τοῖς πολίταις πάντα ἀπέδειξεν ὡς παύσων τὴν στάσιν.

5. τῶν Θηβαίων οὐκ ἐξερχομένων[1] εἰς μάχην, οἱ Ἀθηναῖοι διετέλουν τεῖχος μακρῶν λίθων ποιοῦντες, τέτταρα στάδια ἀπέχον τῶν τοῦ ἄστεως τειχῶν.

6. οἱ τοῦ βασιλέως στρατιῶται τὸ μὲν πλῆθος ἴσοι εἰσὶ τοῖς Ἕλλησι, τὴν δ᾽ ἀρετὴν οὔ.[2]

7. οὐ ῥᾳδίως ἤνεγκεν ὁ Πενθεὺς ἀκούων πάσας τὰς γυναῖκας τὸν ἀπὸ τῆς Λυδίας [Lydia (a country in Asia Minor)] ἐλθόντα θεὸν τιμώσας.

8. πρότερον μὲν ἐνόμιζον ἐξεῖναι τῷ βουλομένῳ, ἡσυχίαν ἄγοντι, μήτε δίκας ἔχειν μήτε πράγματα· νῦν δὲ πάντα συμβαίνει παρ᾽ ἐλπίδα καὶ εἰς δεινὸν ἀγῶνα καθίσταμαι.

9. ἀγνοῶ τίνι ποτὲ[3] γνώμῃ χρώμενοι [making use of, + dat.] οἱ Λακε- δαιμόνιοι καιομένην τὴν Ἑλλάδα περιορῶσιν, ἡγεμόνες ὄντες τῶν Ἑλλήνων οὐκ ἀδίκως καὶ διὰ τὴν ἔμφυτον [inborn] ἀρετὴν καὶ διὰ τὴν τῶν πρὸς τὸν πόλεμον ἐπιστήμην [knowledge, expertise].

---

1. Compound of ἐκ/ἐξ; guess the meaning.

2. Note that a proclitic receives an acute accent when it precedes a pause at a mark of punctuation, as here.

3 When ποτε is attached to an interrogative, it adds emphasis: τίς/τί ποτε; = *who/what in the world?*

UNIT THIRTY

Comparison of Adjectives and Adverbs

---

1. *Comparison of Adjectives*. Recall that adjectives have three degrees (U7, Prelim. A): the positive, the comparative, and the superlative. The Greek comparative adjective may be translated in English as "more X" or simply "rather X" or "quite X." The Greek superlative may be translated in English as "most X" or simply "very X."

There are two methods of forming comparatives and superlatives in Greek, as in English. One is to modify the positive form of an adjective with the comparative and superlative adverbs μᾶλλον = *more* or μάλιστα = *most*. These adverbs must be used with most participles and may be used with other adjectives:

φιλῶν	μᾶλλον φιλῶν	μάλιστα φιλῶν
loving	*more loving*	*most loving*
εὔελπις	μᾶλλον εὔελπις	μάλιστα εὔελπις
hopeful	*more hopeful*	*most hopeful*

2. *Comparison with Suffixes*. The second method of forming comparatives and superlatives is by adding suffixes to the adjective stem (just as is done in English with *-er* and *-est*). There are two sets of suffixes in Greek.

a. *-τερος and -τατος*. Most vowel-declension adjectives and many consonant-declension adjectives use the comparative suffix *-τερος* and the superlative suffix *-τατος*. For vowel-declension adjectives, the suffix is usually added to the stem plus masc./neut. stem vowel *o*. If the previous syllable is metrically light (contains a short vowel followed by no consonant or by only one consonant), then the stem vowel is lengthened to ω before the suffix. (This occurs because Greek tends to avoid a long succession of short or light syllables.) For consonant-declension adjectives, the suffix is usually added to the masc./neut. stem. The comparative and superlative are declined like normal three-ending vowel-declension adjectives (fem. sing. in *ā* for com-

226

parative, in η for superlative). The accent of comparative and superlative is persistent on the syllable preceding the suffix.

πονηρός   πονηρότερος   πονηρότατος
   (long vowel η: omicron retained)

πικρός   πικρότερος   πικρότατος
   (short vowel ι, but two consonants: omicron retained)

ἄξιος   ἀξιώτερος   ἀξιώτατος
   (short vowel ι, no consonant: omega as link vowel)

χαλεπός   χαλεπώτερος   χαλεπώτατος
   (short vowel ε, one consonant: omega as link vowel)

ἀληθής (stem ἀληθεσ-)   ἀληθέστερος   ἀληθέστατος

βαρύς (stem βαρυ-)   βαρύτερος   βαρύτατος

Some adjectives form comparative and superlative from a modified stem: for instance, γεραιός = *aged* produces γεραίτερος, γεραίτατος; and εὐδαίμων produces εὐδαιμονέστερος, εὐδαιμονέστατος. The student will become familiar with such irregularities only through experience in reading Greek texts and through use of a good lexicon.

    b. *-ιων and -ιστος.* Some adjectives of both declensions and many adjectives with irregular comparison (due to use of different roots or different forms of a root in the different degrees) use the comparative suffix *-ῑων* (neuter *-ῑον*, gen. sing. *-ῑονος*; no separate fem.) and the superlative suffix *-ιστος, -η, -ον.* An alternative form of *-ῑων* features semivocalic iota instead of vowel *ῑ*: thus the suffix is *-yων*, which produces phonetic changes that eliminate the semivocalic iota. The adjective stem used with these suffixes often loses its final vowel or an adjectival suffix like *-ρο-*. The accent falls as far back as the length of *U* permits: thus masc. καλλίων, ἐλάττων, but neuter κάλλιον, ἔλαττον.

    Here are the major adjectives using these suffixes:

positive	comparative	superlative
ἡδύς (ἡδ-)	ἡδίων, ἥδιον	ἥδιστος, -η, -ον
ταχύς (ταχ-)	θάττων, θᾶττον[1]	τάχιστος
αἰσχρός (αἰσχ-)	αἰσχίων, αἴσχιον	αἴσχιστος
ἐχθρός (ἐχθ-)	ἐχθίων, ἔχθιον	ἔχθιστος

---

1. Non-Attic θάσσων, θᾶσσον. Note that the τ of ταχύς is due to dissimilation by Grassmann's law (just as in τρέφω vs. θρέψω). θάττων derives from a form of the root in which initial θ remains and phonetic changes produce ττ and compensatory lengthening of α.

positive	comparative	superlative
ἀγαθός = good, brave, capable, excellent	ἀμείνων, ἄμεινον	ἄριστος[1]
ἀγαθός = good, virtuous	βελτίων, βέλτιον	βέλτιστος
ἀγαθός = good, mighty, strong	κρείττων, κρεῖττον[2]	κράτιστος
κακός = bad	κακίων, κάκιον	κάκιστος
κακός = bad, lowly, mean	χείρων, χεῖρον	χείριστος
κακός = bad	ἥττων, ἧττον[3] = inferior, weaker; less, fewer	(ἥκιστος [rare])
καλός	καλλίων, κάλλιον	κάλλιστος
μέγας (μεγ-)	μείζων, μεῖζον	μέγιστος
μικρός = small	μικρότερος	μικρότατος
μικρός = small, few	ἐλάττων, ἔλαττον[4]	ἐλάχιστος
ὀλίγος	ὀλείζων, ὄλειζον	ὀλίγιστος
πολύς	πλείων or πλέων, πλέον[5]	πλεῖστος
ῥᾴδιος (ῥᾳ- or ῥᾱ-)	ῥᾴων, ῥᾷον	ῥᾷστος

3. *Declension of Comparatives in -ῑων or -ων.* These are declined like normal nu-stems, such as σώφρων (U22.1b), but in the acc. sing. masc./fem. and the nom. and acc. pl. of all genders there are alternative forms. These shorter forms are based on a stem that lacks the ν (as in the dative plural), and the ο of the stem contracts with the case ending (the acc. pl. m./f. form is borrowed from the nom.). The shorter forms are more colloquial than the regular forms. Here is the declension of καλλίων as an example:

		masc./fem.	neuter
sing.	nom.	καλλίων	κάλλιον
	gen.	καλλίονος	καλλίονος
	dat.	καλλίονι	καλλίονι
	acc.	καλλίονα or καλλίω	κάλλιον
	voc.	κάλλιον	κάλλιον
(dual	n. a. v.	καλλίονε	καλλίονε)
	(g. d.	καλλιόνοιν	καλλιόνοιν)

---

1. The superlative is from the same root seen in ἀρετή.
2. Non-Attic κρείσσων; the root is a byform of κρατ-, as in κράτος and κρατέω; again phonetic changes produce ττ and compensatory lengthening (ει).
3. Non-Attic ἥσσων.
4. Non-Attic ἐλάσσων.
5. There is an alternative form πλεῖν for the neut. sing. nom. acc. πλέον.

		masc./fem.	*neuter*
plur.	*n. v.*	καλλίονες or καλλίους	καλλίονα or καλλίω
	gen.	καλλιόνων	καλλιόνων
	dat.	καλλίοσι(ν)	καλλίοσι(ν)
	acc.	καλλίονας or καλλίους	καλλίονα or καλλίω

4. *Comparison of Adverbs.* As we have seen in U12.1 and U22.4, the positive degree of most adverbs has the ending -ως. The *comparative adverb* is supplied by the *neuter singular accusative* of the comparative adjective (an instance of the adverbial accusative: U17.3e). The *superlative adverb* is supplied by the *neuter plural accusative* of the superlative adjective.

positive	*comparative*	*superlative*
πικρῶς, *bitterly*	πικρότερον, *more bitterly*	πικρότατα, *most bitterly*
ῥᾳδίως, *easily*	ῥᾷον, *more easily*	ῥᾷστα, *most easily*
πολύ, *much*	πλέον, *to a greater degree, more*	πλεῖστα, *to the highest degree, most*
μάλα, *very*	μᾶλλον, *more*	μάλιστα, *most*

5. *Comparative Expressions*

a. With ἤ = *than*. The Greek equivalent of English *than* is ἤ. Like *than*, ἤ introduces (in theory) a comparative clause, most of which may be suppressed, leaving the items compared in the same construction (that is, in the same case).

    Ex.   ὁ Δημοσθένης κρείττων ἢ ὁ Σωκράτης.
Demosthenes is stronger than Socrates (is) [strong].

                ὁ στρατηγὸς θᾶττον ἔφυγεν ἢ οἱ ἄλλοι.
The general fled more quickly than the others (fled).

                ὑμῖν ῥᾷον πιστεύσουσιν ἢ ἡμῖν.
They will trust you more readily than (they will trust) us.

                ὑμῖν ῥᾷον πιστεύσουσιν ἐκεῖνοι ἢ ἡμεῖς.
They will trust you more readily than we (will) [trust you].

b. With the genitive of comparison (cf. U29.4b5). The second element of comparison may, in most cases, be expressed in the genitive case without ἤ.

    Ex.   ὁ Δημοσθένης κρείττων τοῦ Σωκράτους.
Demosthenes is stronger than Socrates (is) [strong].

                ὁ στρατηγὸς θᾶττον τῶν ἄλλων ἔφυγεν.
The general fled more quickly than the others (fled).

τὸν δίκαιον μᾶλλον τοῦ ἀδίκου ἐπαινῶ.
I praise the just man more than the unjust man.

The genitive of comparison is on the whole more common than the use of ἤ, but it is avoided in contexts where the presence of other genitives would cause ambiguity or an unpleasant piling up of genitive forms:

οἱ δυστυχεῖς πλειόνων εὐεργεσιῶν ἢ οἱ εὐτυχεῖς δέονται.
The unfortunate need more benefactions than the fortunate.
[εὐεργεσιῶν is gen. with δέονται, so gen. of comp. is avoided]

τῶν χρημάτων μᾶλλον ἢ τῆς τιμῆς ἐπιθυμεῖ.
He craves money more than honor.
[χρημάτων is gen. with ἐπιθυμεῖ, so gen. of comp. is avoided]

6. *Degree of Difference.* Recall (from U29.5b) that the *degree of difference* with a comparative expression may be expressed by the dative.

πολλῷ σοφώτερος   *wiser by far (by much)*

ὁ βασιλεὺς τρισὶν ἡμέραις ὕστερον τοῦ ἀγγέλου ἀφίκετο.
The king arrived three days later (later by three days) than the messenger.

Some common adverbial modifiers of comparatives are, however, adverbial accusatives of neuter adjectives or pronouns:

πολὺ σοφώτερος *much wiser (wiser by far)*

οὐδὲν καλλίων   *no more beautiful, not at all more beautiful*

7. *Partitive Genitive with Superlatives.* The partitive genitive (U10.5b) is often used with a superlative to express the class among which the noun excels:

δεινότατος λέγειν τῶν Ἀθηναίων
most clever at speaking among (of) the Athenians

8. *Strengthened Superlative.* A superlative may be strengthened by placing ὡς or ὅτι in front of it, producing the meaning "as X as possible." This usage results from ellipsis of the verb "is possible" in a clause introduced by ὡς or ὅτι. (The same function is occasionally served by relative adverb ᾗ, or in poetry by ὅσον or ὅπως.)

ὅτι τάχιστα   *as swiftly as possible*

βουλόμεθα ὡς ἄριστοι γενέσθαι.
We want to prove ourselves to be as brave as possible.

9. *Identification of Comparative or Superlative.* To identify a comparative or superlative adjective fully, give its gender, number, and case, its

nominative forms, the word *comparative* or *superlative* as appropriate, and the nom. sing. masc. of the positive adjective from which it comes, and tell what noun it modifies.

WHAT TO STUDY AND DO

1. Study the comparison of adjectives and adverbs.
2. Study the inflection of comparatives in -ιων or -ων.
3. Learn as vocabulary for this unit both the comparatives and superlatives presented in 2b above and the remaining words listed below.
4. Do the exercises of this unit.

VOCABULARY

adjectives

γεραιός, γεραιά, γεραιόν (comp. γεραίτερος, sup. γεραίτατος)	old, aged; revered
εὔελπις, εὔελπι (stem εὔελπιδ-, m./f. acc. sing. εὔελπιν)	hopeful, cheerful
ἐχθρός, ἐχθρά, ἐχθρόν	hated, hateful; hostile
ὁ ἐχθρός	enemy (in personal or interstate relations)
παλαιός, παλαιά, παλαιόν (comp. παλαίτερος, sup. παλαίτατος [less often παλαιότερος, -ότατος])	old, ancient [palaeontology, palaeolithic]
τὸ παλαιόν	(adv. acc.) in the old days, formerly
πάλαι	(adv.) long ago
ταχύς, ταχεῖα, ταχύ	swift, quick [tachygraphy]
τάχα	(adv.) quickly; perhaps
χρηστός, χρηστή, χρηστόν	useful, serviceable; good, honest, worthy [chrestomathy]

adverb

μάλα; comp. μᾶλλον, sup. μάλιστα	very; more; most

conjunction

ἤ	or; than
ἤ . . . ἤ . . .	either . . . or . . .

verbs

δουλεύω, δουλεύσω,   be a slave or servant; serve (+ dat.)
  ἐδούλευσα

πιστεύω, πιστεύσω,   trust, put faith in (+ dat.)
  ἐπίστευσα

στρατεύω, στρατεύσω,   carry out a military campaign, wage war; (mid.) carry
  ἐστράτευσα   out a campaign, march (on campaign)

χράω, χρήσω, ἔχρησα[1]   (of a god) proclaim an oracle; (mid.) (of a person)
                             consult an oracle

      χράομαι, χρήσομαι,   use, employ (+ dat.); experience (a condition) (+
        ἐχρησάμην   dat.)

EXERCISES

I.   Write in Greek.
1.   with better judgment
2.   in the worst manner
3.   more easily
4.   the uppermost parts (dat.)
5.   from the truer account
6.   to the worthiest women
7.   the safer way (acc.)
8.   the most unjust (acc.) of Cyrus's
     soldiers

9.   of the wisest teacher
10. of a certain wealthier man
11. most clearly
12. more money (nom.)
13. the largest city (dat.)
14. as useful as possible (neut. n. s.)
15. the sweetest thing (acc.) of all
16. more shamefully, most
     shamefully

II. Render into Greek.

1.   We are not unaware that young men are swifter than old men.
2.   It is reported that you are angry at many of the orators, but most of all at
     Demosthenes.
3.   The thieves did not notice that the ship they had snatched was becoming
     filled with water.
4.   Upon deliberation, it seemed better to the Greeks to send the strongest part
     of their army toward the sea so as to conceal their number [= multitude]
     from the foreigners for as long a time as possible.

---

1. Despite the dictionary form, this verb is actually treated in Attic as a contract verb with η in
place of ᾱ (and ῃ in place of ᾳ). For example, the present active is conjugated χρῶ, χρῇς, χρῇ,
etc.; the middle (which is far more common, in the sense *use*) is χρῶμαι, χρῇ, χρῆται,
χρώμεθα, χρῆσθε, χρῶνται. For a full paradigm of the present system, see Appendix 3:
Paradigms.

III. Reading: Xenophon, *Anabasis* 5.5.7–10 (slightly adapted): Having escaped from the midst of the Persian king's territory and reached the coast of the Black Sea, the army of Greek mercenaries is still having difficulties and uses force in order to obtain food and supplies. Representatives of the natives come to protest.

ἐν τούτῳ ἔρχονται ἐκ <u>Σινώπης</u> <u>πρέσβεις</u>, φοβούμενοι περὶ τῶν <u>Κοτυωριτῶν</u> τῆς τε πόλεως[1] (ἦν γὰρ ἐκείνων καὶ φόρον ἐκείνοις ἔφερον οἱ Κοτυωρῖται) καὶ περὶ τῆς χώρας (ἤκουον γὰρ αὐτὴν <u>δῃουμένην</u>). καὶ ἐλθόντες εἰς τὸ στρατόπεδον ἔλεγον (<u>προηγόρει</u> δὲ Ἑκατώνυμος δεινὸς νομιζόμενος εἶναι λέγειν)· "ἔπεμψεν ἡμᾶς, ὦ ἄνδρες στρατιῶται, ἡ τῶν <u>Σινωπέων</u> πόλις ἐπαινέσοντάς τε ὑμᾶς <u>ὅτι</u> νικᾶτε Ἕλληνες ὄντες βαρβάρους, ἔπειτα δὲ καὶ[2] <u>συνησθησομένους</u> ὅτι διὰ πολλῶν τε καὶ δεινῶν, <u>ὡς</u> ἡμεῖς ἠκούσαμεν, πραγμάτων <u>σεσωσμένοι</u> πάρεστε. <u>ἀξιοῦμεν</u> δέ, Ἕλληνες ὄντες καὶ αὐτοί, ὑφ' ὑμῶν ὄντων Ἑλλήνων ἀγαθὸν μέν τι πάσχειν, κακὸν δὲ μηδέν· οὐδὲ γὰρ ἡμεῖς ὑμᾶς οὐδὲν <u>πώποτε</u> <u>ὑπήρξαμεν</u> κακῶς ποιοῦντες. Κοτυωρῖται δὲ οὗτοί εἰσιν ἡμέτεροι <u>ἄποικοι</u>, καὶ τὴν χώραν ἡμεῖς αὐτοῖς ταύτην παρέδομεν βαρβάρους <u>ἀφελόμενοι</u>."

Underlined Words

ἀξιόω = *think proper, expect* (+ complem. inf.)

ἄποικοι = *colonists, emigrants from a mother city*

ἀφελόμενοι = ἀπο- compound (of what verb?); here *take away* (+ double acc.)

δῃόω = *plunder*

Κοτυωρῖται, -ῶν, m. = *inhabitants of Kotyora* (a subject colony of Sinope)

ὅτι (here) = *because*

πρέσβεις, -εων, m. = *ambassadors*

προηγορέω = *be spokesman*

πώποτε = *ever yet*

σεσωσμένοι = perf. mid. part. *having saved yourselves, having safely come through*

Σινωπεῖς, -έων, m. = *people of Sinope*

Σινώπη, -ης, f. = *Sinope*, a Greek city on the Black Sea

συνησθησομένους = fut. pass. (deponent) part. *rejoice with* (+ dat. of person, *you*, understood)

ὑπάρχω = *take the initiative, begin* (+ suppl. part.)

ὡς = *as*

---

1. πόλεως is the object of περὶ and Κοτυωριτῶν is possessive gen. with πόλεως; as τε shows, χώρας is also the object of περὶ, but the preposition is redundantly repeated before it because of the intervening parenthetic clause.
2. Note that ἔπειτα δὲ καὶ answers the τε after ἐπαινέσοντας; this is less formal, but more expressive than τε . . . τε . . . or τε . . . καὶ . . .

The Subjunctive

1. *The Subjunctive Mood.* Recall (from U8 Prelim.) that Greek has four finite moods. So far, we have dealt exclusively with the indicative mood, which is for assertions of fact and appears in most independent clauses and in some dependent clauses. In this and the next two units, the two subordinate moods, the subjunctive and optative, are presented. The subjunctive expresses mere assumption or possibility (as opposed to assertion) and is more often used in subordinate-clause constructions than in independent clauses (hence its name in Greek, ὑποτακτική, and Latin, *subiunctivus*, "subjoined"). The Greek subjunctive occurs in the three tense systems which express aspect (the present, the aorist, and the perfect) and always has aspect meaning rather than time meaning. In all its tenses the subjunctive has the same *primary* personal endings (like those seen in the present and future indicative), but in Attic it is distinguished from the indicative by the use of lengthened theme vowel ω/η (in place of ο/ε of the indicative). When the primary endings are added to the lengthened theme vowel, the following subjunctive endings are produced:

		active	middle/passive	
sing.	1st	-ω	-ωμαι	
	2nd	-ῃς	-ῃ	[from -η(σ)αι]
	3rd	-ῃ	-ηται	
(dual	2nd	-ητον	-ησθον)	
	(3rd	-ητον	-ησθον)	
plur.	1st	-ωμεν	-ωμεθα	
	2nd	-ητε	-ησθε	
	3rd	-ωσι(ν)	-ωνται	

2. *Conjugation of the Subjunctive*

a. *Present Active Subjunctive.* The active personal endings are added to the present stem (e.g., ἄγ-). If the present stem ends in ε (e.g., ποιέω or τίθημι), the ε disappears in contraction, but the accent falls on the resulting contracted vowel. If the present stem ends in α (e.g., ὁράω), the contractions of α with the lengthened theme vowel turn out to be the same as those in the indicative (so -άω verbs look the same in indicative and subjunctive). If the present stem in ο (e.g., δηλόω), the resulting contractions are ο + ω —> ω, ο + η —> ω, ο + ῃ —> οι (so -όω verbs look the same in the singular only of ind. and subj.). The contractions found in δίδωμι are similar, but ο + η —> ῳ. In all the subjunctives involving contraction, the contracted vowel has the circumflex accent. Here are six examples showing the five possible patterns:

ἄγω	ποιέω	τίθημι	ὁράω	δηλόω	δίδωμι
stem ἀγ-	*stem* ποιε-	*stem* τιθε-	*stem* ὁρα-	*stem* δηλο-	*stem* διδο-
ἄγω	ποιῶ	τιθῶ	ὁρῶ	δηλῶ	διδῶ
ἄγῃς	ποιῇς	τιθῇς	ὁρᾷς	δηλοῖς	διδῷς
ἄγῃ	ποιῇ	τιθῇ	ὁρᾷ	δηλοῖ	διδῷ
(ἄγητον	ποιῆτον	τιθῆτον	ὁρᾶτον	δηλῶτον	διδῶτον)
(ἄγητον	ποιῆτον	τιθῆτον	ὁρᾶτον	δηλῶτον	διδῶτον)
ἄγωμεν	ποιῶμεν	τιθῶμεν	ὁρῶμεν	δηλῶμεν	διδῶμεν
ἄγητε	ποιῆτε	τιθῆτε	ὁρᾶτε	δηλῶτε	διδῶτε
ἄγωσι(ν)	ποιῶσι(ν)	τιθῶσι(ν)	ὁρῶσι(ν)	δηλῶσι(ν)	διδῶσι(ν)

Other present active subjunctives: ἵημι —> ἱῶ, ἵστημι —> ἱστῶ, φημί —> φῶ (all three like τιθῶ); εἰμί —> ὦ, ᾖς, ᾖ, (ἦτον, ἦτον,) ὦμεν, ἦτε, ὦσι(ν); and (both without any contraction) εἶμι —> ἴω, δείκνυμι —> δεικνύω.

b. *Present Middle/Passive Subjunctive.* The primary middle/passive endings are added to the present stem. Contractions, if any, occur in the same way as in the active. Here are examples showing the five possible patterns:

ἄγω	ποιέω	ὁράω	δηλόω	δίδωμι
ἄγωμαι	ποιῶμαι	ὁρῶμαι	δηλῶμαι	διδῶμαι
ἄγῃ	ποιῇ	ὁρᾷ	δηλοῖ	διδῷ
ἄγηται	ποιῆται	ὁρᾶται	δηλῶται	διδῶται
(ἄγησθον	ποιῆσθον	ὁρᾶσθον	δηλῶσθον	διδῶσθον)
(ἄγησθον	ποιῆσθον	ὁρᾶσθον	δηλῶσθον	διδῶσθον)
ἀγώμεθα	ποιώμεθα	ὁρώμεθα	δηλώμεθα	διδώμεθα
ἄγησθε	ποιῆσθε	ὁρᾶσθε	δηλῶσθε	διδῶσθε
ἄγωνται	ποιῶνται	ὁρῶνται	δηλῶνται	διδῶνται

Other present mid/pass. subjunctives: τίθημι —> τιθῶμαι, ἵημι —> ἱῶμαι, ἵστημι —> ἱστῶμαι (all three like ποιῶμαι); δείκνυμι —> δεικνύωμαι (without any contraction); δύναμαι —> δύνωμαι, ἐπίσταμαι —> ἐπίστωμαι (both without contraction).

c. *Aorist Active Subjunctive.* The active endings are added to the aorist stem (whether strong or weak aorist). Athematic aorists feature contractions which are the same as seen in the present of the same verbs. Here are examples showing the four possible patterns:

πράττω	λείπω	τίθημι	δίδωμι
stem πραξ-	stem λιπ-	stem θε-	stem δο-
πράξω	λίπω	θῶ	δῶ
πράξῃς	λίπῃς	θῇς	δῷς
πράξῃ	λίπῃ	θῇ	δῷ
(πράξητον	λίπητον	θῆτον	δῶτον)
(πράξητον	λίπητον	θῆτον	δῶτον)
πράξωμεν	λίπωμεν	θῶμεν	δῶμεν
πράξητε	λίπητε	θῆτε	δῶτε
πράξωσι(ν)	λίπωσι(ν)	θῶσι(ν)	δῶσι(ν)

Other aorist active subjunctives: ἵημι —> -ῶ (compounds only), ἵστημι —> στῶ, βαίνω —> βῶ, φθάνω —> φθῶ (all four like θῶ); γιγνώσκω —> γνῶ, ἁλίσκομαι —> ἁλῶ (both like δῶ); δύω —> δύω (without contraction).

d. *Aorist Middle Subjunctive.* The middle/passive endings are added to the aorist stem (whether strong or weak aorist). For athematic aorists the contractions are the same as in the aorist active. Here are examples showing the four possible patterns:

πράττω	λείπω	τίθημι	δίδωμι
πράξωμαι	λίπωμαι	θῶμαι	δῶμαι
πράξῃ	λίπῃ	θῇ	δῷ
πράξηται	λίπηται	θῆται	δῶται
(πράξησθον	λίπησθον	θῆσθον	δῶσθον)
(πράξησθον	λίπησθον	θῆσθον	δῶσθον)
πραξώμεθα	λιπώμεθα	θώμεθα	δώμεθα
πράξησθε	λίπησθε	θῆσθε	δῶσθε
πράξωνται	λίπωνται	θῶνται	δῶνται

Other aorist middle subjunctives: ἵημι —> -ῶμαι (compounds only, like θῶμαι).

3. *Independent Uses of the Subjunctive.* Although the subjunctive is predominantly used in subordinate clauses, it does have several uses in independent clauses. These uses may be classified broadly as either "imperatival" (issuing a command or recommendation for future action: uses a and b

below) or "prospective" (looking to an action that might take place in the future or to a proposition that might be ascertained as true in the future: uses c and d below). Since the subjunctive expresses assumption or possibility or command rather than assertion, the negative is normally μή rather than οὐ. The choice of tense depends on the aspect of the action.

a. *Hortatory Subjunctive.* The first person plural (and less often the first person singular) subjunctive may express a proposal of action or an exhortation:

> νῦν ἴωμεν καὶ ἀκούσωμεν τοῦ ἀνδρός.
> *Let us go now and hear the man.*
>
> μὴ φοβώμεθα.
> *Let us not be afraid.*

b. *Prohibitions.* The second or third person subjunctive (normally aorist) with μή may express a prohibition, that is, a negative command. (A negative command with present aspect usually is expressed instead with the imperative: U40.)

> μὴ ποιήσητε ταῦτα.
> *Do not do this.*
>
> μηδεὶς ἡγήσηται τὸν Φίλιππον φίλον.
> *Let no one consider Philip a friend.*

c. *Doubtful Assertions and Emphatic Denials.* The subjunctive with μή may express a doubtful assertion ("Perhaps . . ." or "I suspect . . .") or, with μὴ οὐ, a doubtful denial ("Perhaps . . . not . . ."). On the other hand, the aorist subjunctive with οὐ μή (note the order) expresses a strong denial.

> μὴ τοῦτο ᾖ ὃ ἐζητοῦμεν.
> *Perhaps this is what we were seeking.*
>
> μὴ οὐκ ὀρθῶς ἔχῃ ταῦτα.
> *I suspect that these things are not correct.*
>
> οὐ μὴ δείξῃ ἀναίτιος ὢν τῶν κακῶν.
> *He will <u>never</u> show that he is free of blame for the bad things.*

d. *Deliberative Subjunctive.* The subjunctive may be used in questions in which one is asking what one *is to do* or wondering what *is to happen.*

> εἴπωμεν ἢ σιγῶμεν;
> *Shall we speak or keep silent?*
>
> τί πάθω;
> *What is to happen to me?* [Lit.: *What am I to experience?*]

4. *Dependent Uses of the Subjunctive*. Again in these uses the subjunctive has a prospective or imperatival or generalizing force that differs from the force of assertion carried by the indicative. The principal dependent uses are:

   a. Purpose clauses (see §6 below).
   b. Object clauses with verbs of fearing (see §7 below).
   c. Present general conditions and relative clauses with present general conditional force (to be presented in U34).
   d. Future more vivid conditions and relative clauses with future more vivid conditional force (to be presented in U34).
   e. Temporal clauses introduced by conjunctions meaning *before* or *until* (to be presented in U39).

5. *Sequence of Moods*. In a complex sentence, the tense or mood of the verb in the subordinate clause is often influenced by the tense of the verb in the main clause. For instance, in English one says *He says the man will come* but *He said the man would come*: the modal *would* is used in place of *will* because the leading verb (the verb of the main clause) is in a past tense. This change reflects a regular *sequence of tenses* in English.[1] Ancient Greek has a similar *sequence of moods*, depending again on the tense of the leading verb. A primary tense tends to be accompanied by an indicative or subjunctive (which has primary personal endings) in subordinate clauses of certain kinds, while a secondary tense instead tends to be accompanied by an optative in the same kinds of subordinate clause (as the student will see in the next unit, the optative has secondary personal endings). Put in its most general form, the rule for the sequence of moods may be stated thus:

> In a complex sentence in which the subordinate clause is a purpose clause, an object clause of fearing, an indirect-statement noun clause with ὅτι or ὡς, an indirect question, or the protasis of a general condition (or relative clause with general conditional force), (1) if the leading verb is in a primary tense (*primary sequence*), then the verb of the subordinate clause must be in the subjunctive or indicative (as the particular construction requires), but (2) if the leading verb is in a secondary tense (*secondary sequence*), then the verb of the subordinate clause *may* be instead in the optative.

Note that the sequence of moods in Greek is for most constructions a tendency or option rather than a rigid rule.

---

1. For students who know Latin, the relatively strict sequence of tenses which applies to the use of the Latin subjunctive is a comparable phenomenon: *iubet ut abeat*, but *iussit ut abiret*.

6. *Purpose Clauses*. Clauses denoting purpose (*that, in order that, so that*; also in English translation *in order to* with infinitive; negative also *lest* [somewhat archaic]) contain the subjunctive in primary sequence and either the optative or the subjunctive in secondary sequence. In Attic prose the following conjunctions may introduce a purpose clause (also sometimes called a *final clause*): (positive) ἵνα, ὅπως, ὡς; (negative) ἵνα μή, ὅπως μή, ὡς μή, μή.[1]

> primary sequence: subjunctive mandatory
> τοὺς σοφοὺς δοκοῦντας εἶναι ἐξελέγχει ἵνα <u>μανθάνῃ</u> τι.
> *He cross-examines those who seem to be wise <u>in order to learn something</u>.*

> secondary sequence: optative optional (to be learned in U32)
> φύλακας συνέπεμψεν ὅπως μὴ <u>λάθοιεν</u> ἀπελθόντες
> or φύλακας συνέπεμψεν ὅπως μὴ <u>λάθωσιν</u> ἀπελθόντες.
> *He sent along guards <u>in order that they not go away secretly</u>.*

7. *Object Clauses with Verbs of Fearing*

a. Clauses denoting a *fear about a future event* or about a present event the occurrence of which is unascertained contain the subjunctive in primary sequence, the optative or subjunctive in secondary sequence. Such clauses are introduced by μή when positive, by μὴ οὐ when negative.[2]

> primary sequence: subjunctive mandatory
> φοβούμεθα μὴ ὁ βασιλεὺς ἡμῖν ἐπιθῆται.
> *We are afraid that the king may attack us.*
>
> φοβούμεθα μὴ οἱ σύμμαχοι οὐκ ἔλθωσιν εἰς καιρόν.
> *We fear that the allies may not come in time.*

> secondary sequence: optative optional
> ἐφοβοῦντο μὴ ὁ βασιλεὺς ἐπιθεῖτο.
> or ἐφοβοῦντο μὴ ὁ βασιλεὺς ἐπιθῆται.
> *They were afraid that the king might attack.*

b. Clauses denoting a *fear referring to a past event* or to a present, ascertained event contain the indicative, introduced by μή or μὴ οὐ. This is a rare idiom in Greek, though the corresponding English idiom is fairly common as an apologetic or polite form of expression.

---

1. In poetry and a few prose writers the modal particle ἄν is sometimes used with the subjunctive (and rarely the optative) in purpose clauses with ὡς or ὅπως.
2. The dependent (hypotactic) fear-clause derives from an original coordinate (paratactic) construction: *We are afraid. Let the king not attack us.* ——> *We are afraid that the king may attack us.*

φοβούμεθα μὴ ἀμφοτέρων ἅμα ἡμαρτήκαμεν. (perfect ind.)
We fear that we have (actually) failed of both objects at once.

Note that verbs of fearing may also take a complementary infinitive when the
sense is *fear to do X.*

οὐ φοβεῖται τῷ βασιλεῖ ἐπιβουλεύειν.
He is not afraid to plot against the king.

WHAT TO STUDY AND DO

1. Learn the patterns of subjunctive conjugation.
2. Study the independent and dependent uses of the subjunctive.
3. Learn the vocabulary of this unit.
4. Do the exercises of this unit.

VOCABULARY

verbs

ἡττάομαι, ἡττήσομαι (no aor. mid.)[1]	be less, be inferior; be defeated, be defeated by (+ gen. of person)
σιγάω, σιγήσομαι, ἐσίγησα	be silent; (transitive) keep secret

nouns

ἆθλος, ἄθλου, m.	contest (of war or sports) [athletics, decathlon]
ἆθλον, ἄθλου, n.	prize (of a contest)
γάμος, γάμου, m.	wedding, wedding feast; marriage [polygamy]
δεῖπνον, δείπνου, n.	meal
δοῦλος, δούλου, m.	slave (male) [hierodule]
δούλη, δούλης, f.	slave (female)
ἑταῖρος, ἑταίρου, m.	comrade, companion
ἑταίρα, ἑταίρας, f.	woman companion; courtesan
καιρός, καιροῦ, m.	right measure, right degree; time, season, opportunity; critical moment, crisis
ὀργή, ὀργῆς, f.	mood, temperament; anger, wrath [orgasm]
πίστις, πίστεως, f.	trust, faith; assurance, pledge
τρόπαιον, τροπαίου, n.[2]	trophy, victory monument

adjectives

ἀμφότερος, ἀμφοτέρα, ἀμφότερον	each of two, both
ἀναίτιος, ἀναιτία, ἀναίτιον	guiltless, without blame or responsibility
θῆλυς, θήλεια, θῆλυ	female; soft, delicate [thelitis, epithelium]

---

1. Non-Attic ἡσσάομαι.
2. In older Attic also τροπαῖον.

ὀρθός, ὀρθή, ὀρθόν   straight; upright; correct   [orthodox, orthogonal]
πιστός, πιστή, πιστόν   trustworthy, faithful

conjunctions

ἵνα, ὅπως, or ὡς   in order that (+ subj. or opt. of purpose)

EXERCISES

I. Write in Greek the following subjunctive forms.

1. 3rd s. aor. act. "be silent"
2. 2nd pl. pres. pass. "be defeated"
3. 2nd s. aor. act. "be a slave"
4. 3rd s. pres. act. "be at a loss"
5. 3rd pl. pres. m/p "cross-examine"
6. 1st s. aor. mid. "attack"
7. 2nd s. pres. m/p "revolt from"
8. 1st pl. aor. act. "long for"
9. 1st s. pres. m/p "prevent"
10. 1st pl. pres. mid. "carry out a campaign"
11. 2nd s. pres. act. "go"
12. 3rd pl. aor. mid. "arrive"
13. 1st s. aor. mid. "call"
14. 2nd s. aor. act. "lead away"
15. 3rd s. pres. act. "be ill"
16. 3rd s. aor. act. "go up"
17. 2nd pl. pres. m/p "be able"
18. 3rd pl. aor. act. "make"
19. 1st pl. pres. act. "be willing"
20. 1st pl. pres. m/p "make a truce"

II. Identify each form completely.

1. παράσχωσι
2. ἀναγιγνώσκηται
3. ἀπῇς
4. ἕλωνται
5. ἀφῇς
6. βασιλεύσητε
7. δεικνύωμεν
8. δηλώσῃ
9. διαμένωσι
10. διώκῃ
11. δύνωνται
12. ἐξαιτήσησθε
13. παραβῆτε
14. κρύπτῃ
15. κρατῇ
16. μείνω
17. παραγάγῃ
18. ἡττῶνται
19. ἀγγείλωμεν
20. αἱρῆται
21. ἀκούητε
22. ὑπομιμνήσκῃς
23. ἀπίωσιν
24. ἁρπαζώμεθα
25. ἄρξῃ
26. ἀφιστῶσι
27. δείξησθε
28. ἡγῆται
29. ἐπιτρέψητε
30. πύθωμαι

III. Render into Greek.

1. Do not betray your city, men of Athens.
2. They fear that the children may not trust the slaves.
3. It is better to fill the sea with triremes in order to prevent the enemy ships from attacking the city.
4. Let no one ever remind us of those critical times.
5. *Never* will you (s.) demonstrate that you are more just than the others.
6. How am I to praise this man in the manner he deserves [= worthily]?

IV. Sentences for reading

1. τίνας δικαιότερον βλάψω ἢ τοὺς ἐμὲ ἀδικήσαντας;

2. οἱ Ἕλληνες παυσάμενοι ἀλλήλοις πολεμοῦντες εἰρήνην συντίθενται ὅπως ὁ βασιλεὺς μὴ ῥᾳδίως κρατήσῃ ἁπάντων.
3. μήποτε ἡττώμεθα τοῦ θήλεος γένους, ἄνδρες ὄντες.
4. καίπερ πίστιν δόντες τε καὶ λαβόντες, φοβούμεθα μὴ οἱ Θηβαῖοι οὐ πιστοὶ ὦσιν.
5. τῆς πόλεως μὴ καλῶς πραττούσης, μὴ δόξητε ὀργίζεσθαι τοῖς ἀναιτίοις, ἀλλὰ τοῖς μὴ ὀρθῶς βουλευομένοις.
6. διωκόντων τῶν ἱππέων τοὺς φεύγοντας, ὁ στρατηγὸς τοὺς ὁπλίτας ἔχων τρόπαιον ἔστησεν ἵνα πᾶσιν ἐπιδείξῃ τὸ ἑαυτοῦ στράτευμα κρεῖττον τοῦ πολεμίου ὄν.

V. Reading: Xenophon, *Memorabilia* 1.1.18–19 (slightly adapted): an example of Socrates' justice and courage.

ἐπιθυμήσαντός ποτε τοῦ <u>δήμου</u> παρὰ τοὺς νόμους μιᾷ ψήφῳ τοὺς <u>ἀμφὶ</u> Θράσυλλον καὶ Ἐρασινίδην ἀποκτεῖναι πάντας, Σωκράτης, <u>βουλευτὴς</u> ὢν καὶ τότε <u>ἐπιστάτης</u> ἐν τῷ δήμῳ γενόμενος, οὐκ ἠθέλησεν <u>ἐπιψηφίσαι</u>, καίπερ ὀργιζομένου μὲν αὐτῷ τοῦ δήμου, πολλῶν δὲ καὶ <u>δυνατῶν</u> ἀπει- λούντων· ἀλλὰ <u>περὶ πλείονος ἐποιήσατο εὐορκεῖν</u> ἢ <u>χαρίσασθαι</u> τῷ δήμῳ παρὰ τὸ δίκαιον καὶ φυλάξασθαι τοὺς ἀπειλοῦντας. <u>καὶ γὰρ ἐπιμελεῖσθαι</u> θεοὺς ἐνόμιζεν ἀνθρώπων, οὐχ <u>ὃν τρόπον</u> οἱ πολλοὶ νομίζουσιν· οὗτοι μὲν γὰρ οἴονται τοὺς θεοὺς τὰ μὲν εἰδέναι, τὰ δ' οὐκ εἰδέναι· Σωκράτης δὲ πάντα μὲν ἡγεῖτο θεοὺς εἰδέναι, τά τε λεγόμενα καὶ πραττόμενα καὶ τὰ <u>σιγῇ</u> βουλευόμενα, <u>πανταχοῦ</u> δὲ παρεῖναι καὶ <u>σημαίνειν</u> τοῖς ἀνθρώποις περὶ τῶν <u>ἀνθρωπείων</u> πάντων.

Underlined Words

ἀμφί = (prep. with acc.) *associated with* [Thrasyllus and Erasinides were two members of the Board of Generals accused of failing to take adequate steps to rescue the Athenians whose ships had sunk during the victorious sea battle at Arginusae in 406]

ἀνθρώπειος, -α, -ον = *human*

ἀπειλέω = *threaten*

βουλευτής, -οῦ, m. = *member of the Council (of 500 at Athens)*

δῆμος, δήμου, m. = *(common) people, Assembly (of all adult male Athenian citizens)*

δυνατός, -ή, -όν = *powerful*

ἐπιμελέομαι = *have concern for* (+ gen.)

ἐπιστάτης, -ου, m. = *chairman, presiding officer (of a meeting of the Assembly)*

ἐπιψηφίζω = *put (a measure) to a vote*

εὐορκέω = *abide by one's oath* [to abide by lawful procedures]

καὶ γάρ = *and in fact, for indeed*

ὃν τρόπον = adv. acc. *in the way in which*

πανταχοῦ = *everywhere*

περὶ πλείονος ποιεῖσθαι = *consider to be of greater importance* [+ inf. or noun object]

σημαίνω = *give signs*

σιγή, -ῆς, f. = *silence*

χαρίζομαι = *oblige* (+ dat.)

The Optative

1. *The Optative Mood.* The third of the four finite moods of Greek to be learned is the optative (Latin *optativus*, Greek εὐκτική, "of wishing"), which occurs in the three tense systems which express aspect (present, aorist, and perfect) and also (rarely, and only for indirect-discourse transformations) in the future and future perfect. The optative may be used both independently to express a wish or a potentiality (as opposed to a fact or assertion conveyed by the indicative) and in a variety of subordinate constructions.

2. *Conjugation of the Optative.* The mark of the optative mood is the mood vowel iota, which is added to the theme vowel (*o*) or to the tense vowel (e.g., *a* in the weak aorist act. and mid.). An alternative form of the mood suffix is *-ιη-*, used in athematic inflection. The optative has *secondary* personal endings, except for first person singular forms in *-οιμι* and *-αιμι*, where *-μι* is the primary ending used with athematic verbs; the third plural active ending has the variant form *-εν*.

a. *Optative in* οι: this pattern is found in uncontracted presents, uncontracted futures, and strong aorists.

Ex. ἄγω, stem ἀγ- + *o* + *ι* —> ἀγοι-

present active opt.	*present m/p opt.*
ἄγοιμι	ἀγοίμην
ἄγοις	ἄγοιο [ἄγοι(σ)ο]
ἄγοι	ἄγοιτο
(ἄγοιτον	ἄγοισθον)
(ἀγοίτην	ἀγοίσθην)
ἄγοιμεν	ἀγοίμεθα
ἄγοιτε	ἄγοισθε
ἄγοιεν	ἄγοιντο

Conjugated with the same endings are the future active opt. ἄξοιμι, future middle opt. ἀξοίμην, strong aor. act. opt. ἀγάγοιμι, strong aor. mid. opt. ἀγαγοίμην.

Accentuation: note that the final οι of the 3rd sing. act. opt. counts as long for the purpose of accentuation. Hence, optative κτείνοι with acute on *P* as opposed to nom. pl. noun οἶκοι with circumflex on *P*.

b. *Optative in* αι: this pattern is found in weak aorists, and is basically like the above but with αι for οι. In Attic, however, the alternative forms of the 2nd and 3rd sing. and 3rd pl. act. are usually used instead of the forms in αι.

Ex.   λύω, stem λυσ- + α + ι ——> λυσαι-

aorist active opt.		aorist middle opt.
λύσαιμι		λυσαίμην
λύσειας	or λύσαις	λύσαιο [λύσαι(σ)ο]
λύσειε(ν)	or λύσαι	λύσαιτο
(λύσαιτον		λύσαισθον)
(λυσαίτην		λυσαίσθην)
λύσαιμεν		λυσαίμεθα
λύσαιτε		λύσαισθε
λύσειαν	or λύσαιεν	λύσαιντο

Accentuation: note that the final αι of the 3rd sing. act. opt. counts as long for the purpose of accentuation. Hence, aor. optative κτείναι with acute on *P* as opposed to aor. inf. κτεῖναι with circumflex on *P*.

c. *Optative of* μι-*verbs*. The present optative and strong aorist optative of athematic verbs have the mood vowel iota added directly to the tense stem, forming a diphthong (ει, αι, or οι) with the final vowel of that stem. The alternative mood suffix -ιη- is found instead of simple iota in the singular forms of the present active and aorist active. Forms with -ιη- occur occasionally in other active forms (e.g., τιθείημεν for τιθεῖμεν), and such forms are more common than iota-forms in the 2nd and 3rd pl. active of monosyllabic stems (athematic aorists, and present of εἰμί and φημί). The regular secondary personal endings are used (-ν for the 1st sing. active; 3rd plur. in its variant form -εν).

The paradigms on the next page show the three possible patterns for the present. The aorists are similar except for the 2nd and 3rd pl. active (commonly -είημεν for -εῖμεν, -είητε for -εῖτε, -αίημεν for -αῖμεν, etc.). For full paradigms of the aorists of these verbs and of the present or aorist of other μι-verbs, see Appendix 3: Paradigms.

OPTATIVE OF MI-VERBS

present active			*present middle/passive*		
τιθείην	ἱσταίην	διδοίην	τιθείμην	ἱσταίμην	διδοίμην
τιθείης	ἱσταίης	διδοίης	τιθεῖο[1]	ἱσταῖο	διδοῖο
τιθείη	ἱσταίη	διδοίη	τιθεῖτο	ἱσταῖτο	διδοῖτο
(τιθεῖτον	ἱσταῖτον	διδοῖτον	τιθεῖσθον	ἱσταῖσθον	διδοῖσθον)
(τιθείτην	ἱσταίτην	διδοίτην	τιθείσθην	ἱσταίσθην	διδοίσθην)
τιθεῖμεν	ἱσταῖμεν	διδοῖμεν	τιθείμεθα	ἱσταίμεθα	διδοίμεθα
τιθεῖτε	ἱσταῖτε	διδοῖτε	τιθεῖσθε	ἱσταῖσθε	διδοῖσθε
τιθεῖεν	ἱσταῖεν	διδοῖεν	τιθεῖντο	ἱσταῖντο	διδοῖντο

Like τιθείην (τιθείμην) are inflected present ἱείην (ἱείμην) and aorists θείην (θείμην) and (ἀφ)είην (ἱάφ]είμην) (compounds only).[2]

The optative of εἰμί is similar to that of τίθημι, but the plural forms often have stem εἰη-. The inflection is εἴην, εἴης, εἴη, (εἴητον or εἶτον, εἰήτην or εἴτην,) εἴημεν or εἶμεν, εἴητε or εἶτε, εἴησαν or εἶεν.

Like ἱσταίην are inflected present φαίην and aorists σταίην, βαίην, and φθαίην; and like ἱσταίμην, presents δυναίμην and ἐπισταίμην (except that these have regular recessive accentuation, e.g., δύναιο, ἐπίσταιτο).

Like διδοίην are inflected aorists δοίην, γνοίην, and ἀλοίην. And like διδοίμην is inflected aorist middle δοίμην.

The present optative of verbs in -νυμι and of εἰμι and the aorist optative of δύω follow the ω-verb pattern: δεικνύοιμι, ἴοιμι, δύοιμι. (For the 1st sing. of εἰμι the alternative athematic form ἰοίην is occasionally found.)

Accentuation: note that the accent of athematic-verb optatives normally does not precede the diphthong containing the mood vowel iota.[3]

d. Optatives of contract verbs are presented in the next unit.

3. *Independent Uses of the Optative.* There are two independent constructions using the optative.

a. *Optative of wish*, using the optative without modal particle (further details in §4).

---

1. As usual, this is from *τιθεῖ(σ)ο.

2. By analogy with ω-verbs, there are variant forms which show theme vowel o in place of the root vowel ε: e.g., τιθοῖτο for τιθεῖτο, ἐπιθοῖντο for ἐπιθεῖντο, προοῖσθε for προεῖσθε (from προίημι), ἀφίοιεν for ἀφιεῖεν, ἀφίοιτε for ἀφιεῖτε.

3. This is the teaching of ancient grammarians, confirmed by modern experts. But for ἵστημι the medieval manuscripts normally and printed editions often present forms with regular recessive accentuation like ἵσταιτο.

b. *Potential Optative.* The optative accompanied by the modal particle ἄν expresses a possibility, probability, or any softened form of assertion or opinion. The negative is οὐ. Appropriate English translations use modal helpers like *may, might, would,* etc. The potential optative may also be used in subordinate clauses of various kinds.

ἡδέως ἂν ὑμῖν λέγοιμι.   *I would gladly tell you.*

οὐδεὶς ἂν τὴν πόλιν προδοίη.   *No one would betray the city.*
  [the speaker views the act as improbable or impossible]

οὕτως ἄφρων ἐστὶν ὥστε πᾶς τις αὐτὸν ῥᾳδίως ἂν λάθοι ἀδικῶν.
He is so foolish that anyone at all would easily wrong him without his realizing it.   [potential optative used in a result clause]

4. *Expressions of Wish.* In Attic Greek the construction with which a wish is expressed depends on whether (a) the wish is for some future object or event (or an event in the present which is viewed as still attainable) or (b) the wish is for some object or event unattainable in the present or unattained in the past.

a. *Future or possible wishes* are expressed either by the optative alone or by the optative introduced by εἴθε or εἰ γάρ, and the negative is μή.

μὴ γένοιτο.   *May it not (now or in the future) happen!*

εἴθε τὸ στράτευμα ἀφίκοιτο.   *May the army arrive!*

εἰ γὰρ ὁ παῖς σωφρονεῖν μανθάνοι.   *May the boy learn to be temperate!*

b. *Unattainable or unattained wishes* (wishes impossible of realization) are expressed by the imperfect or aorist indicative introduced by εἴθε or εἰ γάρ, and the negative is μή. The imperfect refers to what is wished for but *is not now the case*:

εἴθε παρῆν ὁ Δημοσθένης.
Would that Demosthenes were present now (but he isn't).

The aorist refers to a past wished-for occurrence that *was not the case or did not occur*:

εἰ γὰρ ὁ παῖς σωφρονεῖν ἔμαθεν.
Would that the boy had learned to be temperate (but he didn't).

An alternative method of expressing an unattainable wish is the use of strong aorist ὤφελον (from ὀφείλω = *owe*) with a complementary infinitive (present inf. for present wish, aorist inf. for past wish):

ὤφελε παρεῖναι ὁ Δημοσθένης.
Would that Demosthenes were present now (but he isn't).

ὤφελον σωφρονεῖν μαθεῖν.
I wish I had learned to be temperate (but I didn't).

5. *Dependent Uses of the Optative.* Many of the dependent uses of the optative correspond to those of the subjunctive, with the optative replacing the subjunctive after a secondary-tense leading verb by the sequence of moods (U31.5). The major dependent uses are:

a. The optative may replace the subjunctive in purpose clauses in secondary sequence (U31.6).
b. The optative may replace the subjunctive in object clauses with verbs of fearing in secondary sequence (U31.7).
c. Past general conditions and relative clauses with past general conditional force (U34.4b).
d. Future less vivid conditions and relative clauses with future less vivid conditional force (U34.5c).
e. Temporal clauses introduced by *before* or *until* (U39).
f. Indirect-discourse noun clauses introduced by ὅτι or ὡς in secondary sequence (U33).
g. Indirect questions in secondary sequence (U33).
h. Subordinate clauses in indirect discourse in secondary sequence (U38.2).

Remember that (outside of the indirect-discourse uses) the tenses of the optative have aspect meaning, not time meaning.

WHAT TO STUDY AND DO

1. Learn the patterns of optative conjugation.
2. Study the potential optative and constructions expressing wish.
3. Learn the vocabulary of this unit.
4. Do the exercises of this unit.

VOCABULARY

compounds of verbs previously learned

ἀναιρέω (ἀνα)	take up, pick up; make away with, destroy, kill
ἀποκρίνω (ἀπο)	separate, set apart; (mid.) answer, reply
διαβάλλω (δια)	throw or carry across; set at variance; discredit, attack the character of, slander [diabolical, devil]
διαλέγομαι (δια)	(passive deponent) converse with (+ dat.) [dialectic]

ἐπιλανθάνομαι (ἐπι)   (middle deponent) forget, lose thought of (+ gen.)
καταλείπω (κατα)   leave behind, abandon
παραινέω (παρα)   exhort, advise (+ dat. of person + inf.)   [paraenetic]
συγγιγνώσκω (συν)   agree with; acknowledge; excuse, pardon (+ dat. of
                                  person + acc. or dat. of thing)
συμβουλεύω (συν)   advise, counsel (+ dat. of person); (mid.) consult with
                                  (+ dat. of person)
συμφέρω (συν)   bring together; (more commonly intrans.) be
                                  advantageous, beneficial, or useful
          συμφέρει   (impersonal) it is expedient, advantageous (+ inf.)
ὑπακούω (ὑπο)   listen to, heed, obey (+ gen.); reply to (+ dat.)
ὑπολαμβάνω (ὑπο)   take up; understand, interpret; assume; reply, rejoin
ὑπομένω (ὑπο)   await; endure, stand up under

new verbs

ἀπολογέομαι, ἀπολογήσομαι,   speak in defense, defend oneself   [apology]
  ἀπελογησάμην
ὁμολογέω, ὁμολογήσω,   agree with, say the same thing as (+ dat.)
  ὡμολόγησα   [homologous]
ὀφείλω, ὀφειλήσω,   owe; be obliged to (+ inf.); (strong aor. only, with
  ὠφείλησα and ὤφελον   complem. inf.) would that . . . (to express
                                  unattainable wish)
σωφρονέω, σωφρονήσω,   be of sound mind; be temperate, moderate, etc.
  ἐσωφρόνησα

adverbs

ἄν   (postpositive modal particle used with the
                                  subjunctive in certain dependent constructions and
                                  with the potential optative and potential indicative
                                  in independent or dependent constructions)
ἄγαν   very much; too much
ἅλις   sufficiently, enough
ἅμα   at once, at the same time; (+ dat.) at the same time
                                  with   [hamadryad, hamacratic]
ἐγγύς   near; (+ gen.) next to, near
λίαν   very, exceedingly
πάλιν   back, backwards; again   [palindrome]
σχεδόν   roughly speaking, about, almost
αὔριον   tomorrow
τήμερον (non-Attic σήμερον)   today
χθές   yesterday

EXERCISES

I. Give a complete identification of each form.

1. διαβαίην	11. συνενέγκοισθε	21. ἐπιλήσονται
2. σωφρονήσωσι	12. ἐπιθῶνται	22. καταλείπουσαι
3. ὁμολογώμεθα	13. ἀποδοῖτο	23. παραινέσειας
4. ὑπομείναιμεν	14. ἀπίοιμεν	24. συγγνῶναι
5. ὑπολάβοι	15. ἀπολογουμένης	25. διήνεγκε
6. γνοίητε	16. ἀνέλοιτο	26. ἀφείη
7. ὑπακούσαι	17. ἀποκριναίμην	27. μεταδοῖεν
8. ὑπακοῦσαι	18. διαβάλλῃς	28. φθῶμεν
9. δουλεύητε	19. δύναιο	29. τεύξοισθε
10. συμβουλεύσειας	20. διελέγετο	30. θρέψαι

II. Render into Greek. (By convention, *may* is used to render subordinate Greek subjunctives and *might* is used to render subordinate optatives. In this exercise, therefore, in subordinate clauses treat *may* as subj. and *might* as opt.)

1. in order that he may use
2. lest they might go on campaign
3. Let him not become silent.
4. May you (s.) never forget.
5. Am I to go or to stay?
6. in order that I might reply
7. Let us take counsel together.
8. lest she might not be graceful
9. May the gods grant this.
10. Do not promise anything.

III. Render into Greek.

1. Let us be silent in order that the poet may surpass his accusers by defending himself as well as possible.
2. The king was afraid that Cyrus might plot against the other generals. And so he exhorted them to be on their guard.
3. Would that the army were present! May it arrive tomorrow!

IV. Reading sentences.

1. Πυθοῖ[1] ὁ Ἀπόλλων [Apollo] ἔχρη τοῖς Ἕλλησιν· "μηδὲν ἄγαν."

2. τοῖς παρὰ τοῦ Κροίσου [Croesus] χρωμένοις ἀπεκρίνατο ὁ θεὸς ὧδε· "ἀνάγκη τῷ Κροίσῳ τὸν Ἅλυν [Halys] ποταμὸν διαβάντι καταλύειν [destroy] μεγάλην ἀρχήν." καὶ ταῦτα ἀκούσας ὁ Κροῖσος κρατήσειν αὐτὸς τῶν πολεμίων ᾤετο, οὐ καλῶς ὑπολαβών. καὶ οὐ φοβούμενος μὴ ἁμαρτάνοι τῇ ἑαυτοῦ γνώμῃ πιστεύων, ἐστρατεύσατο ἐπὶ τοὺς Πέρσας [Persians] ἵνα τούτους νικήσας ἁπάσης τῆς Ἀσίας [Asia] ἄρχοι. ἀλλ' ἄλλως συνέβη· ἡττῶνταί τε γὰρ οἱ Λυδοὶ [Lydians] καὶ ἁλίσκονται ὅ τε Κροῖσος καὶ ἡ γυνὴ καὶ τὰ παιδία. ἁλοὺς δὲ τάδε πρὸς ἑαυτὸν ἔφη· "εἴθε

---

1. Cf. U29.5e.

μήποτε διέβην τὸν ῞Αλυν. καὶ νῦν τί πάθωμεν; δουλεύωμεν τοῖς
Πέρσαις; οὐ δεινὸν τοῖς δυστυχέσιν ἀποθανεῖν, ἀλλ᾽ εἴθε μὴ οἱ Πέρσαι
τὴν κεφαλὴν ἀποτέμοιεν."[1]

V. Reading: Plato, *Protagoras* 324d–325a (adapted): Protagoras the sophist is
trying to explain to Socrates how political virtue differs from other arts but can
nevertheless be taught.

῎Ετι λείπεται ἡ <u>ἀπορία</u> ἣν ἀπορεῖς περὶ τῶν ἀνδρῶν τῶν ἀγαθῶν, τί
<u>δήποτε</u> οἱ ἄνδρες οἱ ἀγαθοὶ τὰ μὲν ἄλλα τοὺς αὑτῶν ὑεῖς <u>διδάσκουσιν</u> ἃ
διδασκάλων <u>ἔχεται</u> καὶ σοφοὺς ποιοῦσιν, ἐκείνην δὲ τὴν ἀρετὴν ἣν αὐτοί
εἰσιν ἀγαθοὶ οὐδενὸς βελτίους ποιοῦσιν. καὶ περὶ τούτου, ὦ Σώκρατες,
<u>οὐκέτι μῦθόν</u> σοι ἐρῶ ἀλλὰ λόγον. ὧδε γὰρ δεῖ νομίζειν· ἔστιν τι ἓν ἢ οὐκ
ἔστιν, οὗ ἀνάγκη πάντας τοὺς πολίτας μετέχειν, <u>εἴπερ</u> μέλλει πόλις εἶναι;
ἐν τούτῳ γὰρ αὕτη λύεται ἡ ἀπορία ἣν σὺ ἀπορεῖς ἢ <u>ἄλλοθι οὐδαμοῦ</u>. <u>εἰ</u> μὲν
γὰρ <u>ἔστιν</u>, τοῦτο τὸ ἕν ἐστιν οὐ <u>τεκτονικὴ</u> οὐδὲ <u>χαλκεία</u> οὐδὲ <u>κεραμεία</u>,
ἀλλὰ <u>δικαιοσύνη</u> καὶ <u>σωφροσύνη</u> καὶ τὸ ὅσιον εἶναι. καὶ <u>συλλήβδην</u> ἓν αὐτὸ
<u>προσαγορεύω</u> εἶναι ἀνδρὸς ἀρετήν.

Underlined Words

ἄλλοθι οὐδαμοῦ = *nowhere else, in no
other place*
ἀπορία, -ας, f. = *difficulty, puzzlement*
δήποτε = (emphatic adverb intensifying
interrogative) *(why) in the world*
διδάσκω = *teach* (+ dir. object of person
+ internal acc. of the thing taught)
δικαιοσύνη, -ης, f. = *justice,
righteousness*
εἰ = *if*
εἴπερ = *if in fact*
ἔτι = (adv.) *still*
ἔχεται = *attaches to, falls within the
realm of* (+ gen.)

κεραμεία, -ας, f. = *art of ceramics*
μῦθος, -ου, m. = *tale, story, fable*
οὐκέτι = *no longer*
προσαγορεύω = *call (by a certain
name)* [αὐτὸ is the object,
συλλήβδην ἓν may be taken in
apposition to it, and ἀρετήν is
predicate noun]
συλλήβδην = *taken all together*
σωφροσύνη, -ης, f. = *moderation, self-
control*
τεκτονική, -ης, f. = *carpentry*
χαλκεία, -ας, f. = *bronzeworking*

---

1. Compound of ἀπο-: guess the meaning.

Optative of Contract Verbs; Indirect Discourse with ὅτι; Indirect Questions and Indirect Interrogative

1. *Optative of Contract Verbs.* Tense stems in -άω, -έω, -όω feature contraction of the stem vowel with the -οι- of the optative: $a + οι —> ῳ, ε + οι —> οι, ο + οι —> οι$. Thus verbs in -έω and -όω have the same endings in the optative. In addition the optative *active* has two possible forms, those based on -οιμι conjugation and those based on suffix -ιη- (as seen in μι-verb optatives, U32.2c). The -ιη- suffix is more usual in the singular; the standard suffix is more usual in the dual and plural. In the following paradigm of the active, the common form is given first and the rarer form is shown beside it in brackets.

PRESENT ACTIVE OPTATIVE

verbs in -έω		verbs in -όω		verbs in -άω	
φιλοίην	[φιλοῖμι]	δηλοίην	[δηλοῖμι]	ὀρῴην	[ὀρῷμι]
φιλοίης	[φιλοῖς]	δηλοίης	[δηλοῖς]	ὀρῴης	[ὀρῷς]
φιλοίη	[φιλοῖ]	δηλοίη	[δηλοῖ]	ὀρῴη	[ὀρῷ]
(φιλοῖτον	[φιλοίητον]	δηλοῖτον	[δηλοίητον]	ὀρῷτον	[ὀρῴητον])
(φιλοίτην	[φιλοιήτην]	δηλοίτην	[δηλοιήτην]	ὀρῴτην	[ὀρῳήτην])
φιλοῖμεν	[φιλοίημεν]	δηλοῖμεν	[δηλοίημεν]	ὀρῷμεν	[ὀρῴημεν]
φιλοῖτε	[φιλοίητε]	δηλοῖτε	[δηλοίητε]	ὀρῷτε	[ὀρῴητε]
φιλοῖεν	[φιλοίησαν]	δηλοῖεν	[δηλοίησαν]	ὀρῷεν	[ὀρῴησαν]

Like ὀρῴην is inflected the optative of futures in -άω, such as fut. act. opt. ἐλῴην from ἐλαύνω, σκεδῴην from σκεδάννυμι, etc.

Like φιλοίην is inflected the optative of futures in -έω, such as fut. act. opt. ἀγγελοίην from ἀγγέλλω, νομιοίην from νομίζω, etc.

The optative in -οίην as seen in φιλοίην is also the normal Attic form of the aorist active optative of the simple verb ἔχω: σχοίην, σχοίης, etc., like φιλοίην, except that the 3rd pl. is always σχοῖεν. On the other hand, the aorist active optative in compounds of ἔχω has the regular conjugation -σχοιμι, -σχοις, etc. (e.g., παράσχοιμι).

PRESENT MIDDLE/PASSIVE OPTATIVE

verbs in -έω	verbs in -όω	verbs in -άω
φιλοίμην	δηλοίμην	ὁρῴμην
φιλοῖο	δηλοῖο	ὁρῷο
φιλοῖτο	δηλοῖτο	ὁρῷτο
φιλοῖσθον	δηλοῖσθον	ὁρῷσθον
φιλοίσθην	δηλοίσθην	ὁρῴσθην
φιλοίμεθα	δηλοίμεθα	ὁρῴμεθα
φιλοῖσθε	δηλοῖσθε	ὁρῷσθε
φιλοῖντο	δηλοῖντο	ὁρῷντο

Like φιλοίμην is inflected the optative of futures in -έομαι, such as fut. mid. opt. πεσοίμην from πίπτω.

2. *Indirect Discourse with ὅτι or ὡς.* The third of the three indirect-discourse constructions of Greek is the use of a noun clause introduced by ὅτι or ὡς = *that, the fact that* (cf. U20.6–7, U28.2). This construction is common with verbs of saying (λέγω, εἶπον regularly; only occasionally φημί), announcing (ἀγγέλλω), knowing (γιγνώσκω, οἶδα), intellectual perception (ἀκούω, αἰσθάνομαι, μανθάνω, etc.), and emotion (θαυμάζω, ὀργίζομαι), and with impersonal expressions like δῆλόν ἐστιν ὅτι, φανερὸν ὅτι, etc. Many of these verbs and expressions may also take the supplementary participle of indirect discourse. The noun-clause construction is rare with verbs of thinking or believing, which (like φημί) usually take the infinitive of indirect discourse.

Indirect-discourse noun clauses follow the general rule for the sequence of moods (U31.5). After a main verb in a primary tense, the verb of the indirect statement retains the mood and voice and tense it had in the direct form (but the person of the verb may be changed):

direct: ὁ βασιλεὺς οὐκ εἰς καιρὸν ἀφίκετο.
             The king didn't arrive in time.
indirect: λέγω ὅτι ὁ βασιλεὺς οὐκ εἰς καιρὸν ἀφίκετο.
             I say that the king didn't arrive in time.
direct: ἀεὶ τιμήσομεν τὸν ποιητήν.
             We'll always honor the poet.
indirect: λέγουσιν ὅτι τὸν ποιητὴν ἀεὶ τιμήσουσιν.
             They say they'll always honor the poet.

After a main verb in a secondary tense, the verb of the indirect statement may either (a) be left unchanged in mood or (b) be changed to the same tense and voice of the optative. Note, however, that imperfects and pluperfects of direct discourse are usually left in the indicative and only rarely changed to the optative of the same tense stem (present or perfect). Furthermore, indicatives denoting unreality (to be learned in U36) are left unchanged.

direct: ὁ βασιλεὺς εἰς καιρὸν ἀφίξεται.
           The king will come in time.
indirect: εἶπον ὅτι ὁ βασιλεὺς εἰς καιρὸν ἀφίξεται (or ἀφίξοιτο).
           I said that the king would arrive in time.
direct: ἐστρατεύσαντο ἐπὶ τοὺς Ἀθηναίους.
           They went on campaign against the Athenians.
indirect: ἠκούσατε ὡς ἐστρατεύσαντο (or στρατεύσαιντο) ἐπὶ τοὺς
           Ἀθηναίους.
           You heard that they went (or had gone) on campaign against the Athenians.
direct: αἱ γυναῖκες ὀρχοῦνται.
           The women are dancing.
indirect: ἐπυθόμεθα ὅτι αἱ γυναῖκες ὀρχοῦνται (or ὀρχοῖντο).
           We learned that the women were dancing.
direct: αἱ γυναῖκες ὠρχοῦντο.
           The women were dancing.
indirect: ἐπυθόμεθα ὅτι αἱ γυναῖκες ὠρχοῦντο.
           We learned that the women were dancing (when something or other happened).

Note that the present optative would be ambiguous in the final example above, just as the English *were dancing* is ambiguous unless some addition is made to indicate that an imperfect is intended.

3. *Indirect Questions.* Noun clauses introduced by interrogatives (such as *who, which, what, when, why, how*) are used in the same sorts of contexts as indirect statements and are called *indirect questions*.

I know <u>what you did</u>.   noun clause as object of *know*
      (direct: *What did you do?*)

<u>Why this happened</u> is unclear.   noun clause as subject of *is*
      (direct: *Why did this happen?*)

The verb in a Greek indirect question follows the general rule for the sequence of moods (U31.5). After a main verb in a primary tense, the verb of the indirect question retains the mood and voice and tense it had in the direct form (but the person of the verb may be changed). After a main verb in a secondary

tense, the verb of the indirect question may either (a) be left unchanged in
mood or, more commonly, (b) be changed to the same tense and voice of the
optative. (Again, unreal indicatives [U36] are left unchanged.) In Greek,
indirect questions also differ from direct questions in that the interrogative
word may either be in the same form found in a direct question or appear in a
modified form, the *indirect interrogative*. The indirect interrogative pronoun
ὅστις is presented in §4 below; other indirect interrogatives will be learned in
U36.

direct:	τίς σε ἀδικεῖ; *Who wrongs you?*
indirect:	οὐκ οἶδα τίς (or ὅστις) σε ἀδικεῖ. (primary)
	I don't know who is wronging you.
	οὐκ ᾔδησθα τίς (or ὅστις) σε ἀδικοίη (or ἀδικεῖ). (secondary)
	You didn't know who was wronging you.
direct	πότε ἦλθεν ὁ ἄγγελος;
	When did the messenger come?
indirect:	πότε ἦλθεν ὁ ἄγγελος ἐρωτᾷ. (primary)
	He asks when the messenger came.
	πότε ἔλθοι (or ἦλθεν) ὁ ἄγγελος ἠρώτησεν. (secondary)
	He asked when the messenger came.
direct:	πῶς φύγωμεν; [deliberative subj.]
	How are we to escape?
indirect:	ἀπορούμεν πῶς φύγωμεν. (primary)
	We are at a loss how we are to escape.
	ἠπορούμεν πῶς φύγοιμεν (or φύγωμεν). (secondary)
	We were at a loss how we were to escape.

4. *Indefinite Relative and Indirect Interrogative.* The pronoun ὅστις,
ἥτις, ὅ τι is a combination of the relative pronoun and the indefinite pronoun,
both elements of which are declined (see paradigm, next page). By origin,
ὅστις is an indefinite relative pronoun (or adjective), *whoever, whichever,
whatever*; but like other indefinite relative words in Greek, it has a second
function as well, as indirect interrogative introducing an indirect question.

The short forms given in parentheses are common in poetry and in
inscriptions, but rare in formal prose: in these only the second element is
declined. Note that the neuter pl. nom. acc. ἅττα differs from the alternative
indefinite pronoun form ἄττα (U17.1) only in its breathing. It is a modern
printing convention to show the neut. sing. nom. acc. as two separate words to
distinguish it from ὅτι = *that* (which is in fact a frozen adverbial acc. of ὅστις).
In some texts this convention is not followed, and the two uses must be
distinguished by the interpretation of the context.

INDEFINITE RELATIVE / INDIRECT INTERROGATIVE

		masc.		*fem.*	*neuter*	
sing.	nom.	ὅστις		ἥτις	ὅ τι	
	gen.	οὗτινος	(ὅτου)	ἧστινος	οὗτινος	(ὅτου)
	dat.	ᾧτινι	(ὅτῳ)	ᾗτινι	ᾧτινι	(ὅτῳ)
	acc.	ὅντινα		ἥντινα	ὅ τι	
(dual	n. a.	ὥτινε		ὥτινε	ὥτινε)	
	(g. d.	οἷντινοιν		οἷντινοιν	οἷντινοιν)	
plur.	nom.	οἵτινες		αἵτινες	ἅτινα	(ἅττα)
	gen.	ὧντινων	(ὅτων)	ὧντινων	ὧντινων	(ὅτων)
	dat.	οἷστισι(ν)	(ὅτοις)	αἷστισι(ν)	οἷστισι(ν)	(ὅτοις)
	acc.	οὕστινας		ἅστινας	ἅτινα	(ἅττα)

Accentuation: like ὅδε, ὅστις is a combination of an accented element and an enclitic element; this explains the peculiarities of accent (ἥτις, not ἧτις; ὧντινων with circumflex on apparent *A*). The accentuation is the same as that of the simple relative pronoun.

WHAT TO STUDY AND DO

1. Learn the conjugational patterns of contract-verb optatives and the inflection of ὅστις.
2. Study indirect discourse with ὅτι and indirect questions.
3. Learn the vocabulary of this unit.
4. Do the exercises of this unit.

VOCABULARY

contract verbs

αἰτιάομαι, αἰτιάσομαι [ᾱ], ἠτιᾱσάμην	accuse, censure; allege as a cause
ἀξιόω, ἀξιώσω, ἠξίωσα	think worthy, think proper; expect, claim [axiom]
ἀπαντάω, ἀπαντήσομαι, ἀπήντησα (ἀπο)	meet, encounter (+ dat.)
ἀσθενέω, ἀσθενήσω, ἠσθένησα	be weak, be ill
ἀτιμάζω, ἀτιμάσω, ἠτίμασα	fail to honor; slight; dishonor
βοηθέω, βοηθήσω, ἐβοήθησα	come to the aid of (+ dat.); come to the rescue

γαμέω, γαμέω, ἔγημα   (act.) take as wife, marry a woman; (mid.) (of male relative of bride) give in marriage, (of bride) give self in marriage, marry a man

γελάω, γελάσομαι, ἐγέλασα [ᾰ]   laugh; laugh at (+ prep. phrase or + dat.); deride (+ acc.)

δαπανάω, δαπανήσω, ἐδαπάνησα   spend; consume, use up

ἐάω, ἐάσω [ᾱ], εἴασα (imperf. aug. εἴων)   permit, allow (+ acc. + inf.); let go, dismiss

ἐράω [no act. or mid. in fut. or aor.]   be in love with, desire (+ gen.)   [Eros, Erasmus]

[Ionic εἴρομαι],[1] ἐρήσομαι, ἠρόμην   ask, inquire

ἐρωτάω, ἐρωτήσω, ἠρώτησα   ask, inquire (sometimes + acc. of person + acc. of thing)

εὐεργετέω, εὐεργετήσω, ηὐεργέτησα[2]   benefit, show kindness toward (+ acc.)

ζῶ, ζήσω, (non-Attic ἔζησα)[3]   be alive, live   [zoology]

μισέω, μισήσω, ἐμίσησα [ῑ]   hate; (ingressive aor.) conceived a hatred for [misogynist, misanthrope]

ὁρμάω, ὁρμήσω, ὥρμησα   set in motion; (intrans. act. or mid.) start off, go; rush [hormone]

πολιορκέω, πολιορκήσω, ἐπολιόρκησα   besiege   [poliorcetics]

τελέω, τελέω (or rarely τελέσω), ἐτέλεσα   fulfill, accomplish, bring to an end; pay (taxes); initiate (into religious rites); perform rites

noun

σωτηρία, σωτηρίας, f.   saftey, means of saftey, preservation; salvation

indefinite relative/indirect interrogative

ὅστις, ἥτις, ὅ τι   whoever, whatever, whichever; who, what

conjunctions

ὅτι[4]   that (introducing a noun clause); because

ὡς   that (introducing a noun clause); as, because

---

1. In Attic ἐρωτάω is used for the present system.

2. Fourth-century texts have aorist εὐεργέτησα (because ηυ had by then become the same as ευ in pronunciation).

3. Conjugated as if from *ζάω, but η or ῃ appears instead of ᾱ or ᾳ, just as with χράω. Present ind. and subj. ζῶ, ζῇς, ζῇ, ζῶμεν, ζῆτε, ζῶσι(ν); opt. ζῴην, inf. ζῆν, part. ζῶν. Imperfect ἔζων, ἔζης, ἔζη, ἐζῶμεν, ἐζῆτε, ἔζων.

4. Never elided; ὅτ᾽ = ὅτε, *when*.

prepositions

ἄνευ	(+ gen.) without
ἕνεκα	(usually placed after its noun; + gen.) on account of, as far as regards
πλήν	(+ gen.) except; (also used as conjunction) except

EXERCISES

I. Give a complete identification of each form.

1. ὁρμῴην
2. μισοῖντο
3. βοηθοῦντα
4. γαμῆται
5. πολιορκοίης
6. ἀσθενεῖν
7. ἐρωτᾷς

8. δαπανῷεν
9. ζῶσα
10. ἠτιμάζομεν
11. γελάσαι
12. ἀξιοῖμεν
13. αἰτιᾶσθαι
14. ἐρῶσιν

15. ἐρέσθαι
16. εἴα
17. εὐεργετήσητε
18. εὐεργετήσετε
19. συνέγνωσαν
20. ἀναιροίμην
21. ἀπήντων

II. Write the optative in the designated form for each of the following:

1. 3rd pl. aor. act. of μισέω
2. 1st s. fut. mid. of γελάω
3. 2nd pl. pres. m/p of γαμέω
4. 3rd pl. pres. act. of ἀπαντάω
5. 1st pl. aor. mid. of αἰτιάομαι

6. 2nd s. pres. m/p of ὁρμάω
7. 3rd s. aor. mid. of τελέω
8. 1st pl. aor. act. of αἰτέω
9. 3rd s. pres. act. of ἐράω
10. 2nd s. pres. act. of ἀτιμάζω

III.   Render the following sentences into Greek, producing as many versions as possible by choice of different indirect-discourse constructions and by choice of sequence of moods.

1. And when he arrived, he reported that the Athenians had conceived a hatred for those who were not coming to the aid of the weak.
2. Tomorrow we shall learn where we shall encounter our allies.
3. At daybreak [= at the same time with day] just about all the cavalrymen started off toward the sea, it being obvious that no one thought it proper to permit the enemy to perceive what preparations the citizens had made.

IV. Reading sentences.

1. τοῦ νεανίου ἐρομένου ἥντινα τῶν τριῶν θυγατέρων συμφέροι γῆμαι, γελῶντες ἀπεκρινάμεθα ὅτι ἀγνοοῖμεν.
2. ἐῶμεν τὸν βασιλέα πολιορκοῦντα τὸ ἄστυ διαμένειν, ἢ βοηθήσωμεν;
3. ἠρώτων οἱ στρατιῶται πῶς εὐεργετοῖεν τὸν Κῦρον, οὐκ ἐξὸν στρατεύεσθαι ἄνευ χρημάτων· οὐ γὰρ ἠξίουν πείθεσθαι στρατηγῷ ἔλαττον ἢ ὑπέσχετο δαπανῶντι.

IV. Reading: Xenophon, *Anabasis* 6.1.26–29 (abridged, but unaltered except for last sentence): Xenophon advises the army not to appoint him as its sole commander.

ἐγώ, ὦ ἄνδρες, ἥδομαι μὲν ὑφ᾽ ὑμῶν τιμώμενος, <u>εἴπερ</u> ἄνθρωπός εἰμι, καὶ χάριν ἔχω καὶ εὔχομαι δοῦναί μοι τοὺς θεοὺς αἴτιόν τινος ὑμῖν ἀγαθοῦ γενέσθαι· τὸ <u>μέντοι</u> ἐμὲ <u>προκριθῆναι</u> ὑφ᾽ ὑμῶν ἄρχοντα Λακεδαιμονίου ἀνδρὸς παρόντος οὔτε ὑμῖν μοι δοκεῖ συμφέρον εἶναι, ἀλλ᾽ ἧττον <u>ἂν</u> διὰ τοῦτο τυγχάνειν, <u>εἴ τι δέοισθε</u> παρ᾽ αὐτῶν· ἐμοί τε αὖ οὐ <u>πάνυ τι</u> νομίζω ἀσφαλὲς εἶναι τοῦτο. ὁρῶ γὰρ ὅτι καὶ τῇ πατρίδι μου οὐ πρόσθεν ἐπαύσαντο πολεμοῦντες <u>πρὶν ἐποίησαν</u> πᾶσαν τὴν πόλιν ὁμολογεῖν Λακεδαιμονίους καὶ αὐτῶν ἡγεμόνας εἶναι. . . . <u>ὃ δὲ ὑμεῖς ἐννοεῖτε,</u> ὅτι ἧττον ἂν στάσις εἴη ἑνὸς ἄρχοντος ἢ πολλῶν, εὖ <u>ἴστε</u> ὅτι ἄλλον μὲν ἑλόμενοι οὐχ εὑρήσετε ἐμὲ <u>στασιάζοντα·</u> νομίζω γὰρ ὅστις ἐν πολέμῳ ὢν στασιάζει πρὸς ἄρχοντα, τοῦτον πρὸς τὴν ἑαυτοῦ σωτηρίαν στασιάζειν· ἐμὲ δὲ ἑλόμενοι, ἴσως ἄν τινα εὕροιτε καὶ ὑμῖν καὶ ἐμοὶ ὀργιζόμενον.

Underlined Words

ἄν here adds modal (potential) force to the infinitive τυγχάνειν (which depends on an understood δοκεῖτε = *it seems to me that you . . .*)

εἴ τι δέοισθε = *if you should ask for anything* (optative in a condition)

εἴπερ = *if in fact*

ἴστε = 2nd pl. imperative from οἶδα

μέντοι = (postpositive particle) *however*

ὃ δὲ . . . ἐννοεῖτε = *and as for the notion which you have in mind*

πάνυ τι = *very much at all, really*

ποιέω = (here) *cause, compel*

πρίν = *before*

προκριθῆναι = (aor. pass. inf.) *to be selected (as X) in preference to* (+ gen. of person)

στασιάζω = *engage in strife or dissension*

UNIT THIRTY-FOUR

Simple, General, and Future Conditions

1. *Conditional Sentences.* One of the most common forms of complex sentence is the *conditional sentence*, that is, one in which the subordinate clause (the *if*-clause; the *protasis* in the traditional terminology of Greek grammar) expresses a condition and the main clause (*then*-clause,[1] or *apodosis* in traditional terminology) expresses the consequence of that condition's fulfillment. In many languages, including Greek, conditional sentences have a variety of schemes of moods (or modal auxiliaries) and tenses in the *if*-clause and *then*-clause in order to express different notions of the possibility or probability of the condition's being fulfilled and different degrees of assertiveness in the main clause. In Greek, the conditional schemes apply not only to sentences containing εἰ = *if*, but also to various relative and temporal clauses that have a force akin to that of a condition. In this unit and in U36 the most important *regular* patterns of Greek conditions will be presented. In actual Greek texts the student will later occasionally find irregular or "mixed" conditions, but these need not concern the beginner. The negative normally used in the protasis of all kinds of conditional sentences is μή.

2. *Simple Conditions.* Grammatically most obvious as well as relatively uncommon are the conditions called *simple*. In these the protasis implies nothing about the reality or probability of the apodosis. The scheme is:

protasis   *apodosis*
εἰ + indicative   indicative or any independent-clause construction

Ex.   *simple present condition*
εἰ μανθάνεις τὴν Ἑλληνικὴν γλῶτταν, καλῶς ποιεῖς.
If you are learning Greek, you are doing the right thing.

---

1. Although the word *then* is not in fact always used in an English condition, it may always be added without changing the sense; and in an artificial programming language like Pascal, the syntax *requires* that every *if* be followed by a *then*.

simple past condition

εἰ ἐξ ἀρχῆς τὰ χαλεπὰ ῥήματα ἐμάνθανες (ἔμαθες), καλῶς ἐποίεις
(ἐποίησας).

*If you were learning (learned) the difficult verbs from the beginning, you
were doing (did) the right thing.*

Simple Relative and Temporal Clauses. Clauses introduced by a relative
pronoun, relative adverb, or temporal conjunction contain the indicative when
they refer to present or past action that is asserted as a fact applying to a
specific occasion.

ὅτε ἦλθεν, δῶρα ἤνεγκεν.
When he came (on one particular occasion), he brought gifts.

οἱ στρατιῶται οἳ νῦν πάρεισι πιστότατοί εἰσιν.
The soldiers who are present now are very trustworthy.

ἐπεὶ ὁ Δαρεῖος ἐτελεύτησε, ἐβασίλευσεν ὁ Ξέρξης.
After Darius died, Xerxes became king.

3. *General Conditions.* General conditions refer indefinitely to general
truths in the present or past or to repeated or customary actions in the present
or past. (For actions that lie in the future, on the other hand, the distinction between specificity and generality is syntactically unimportant, and other distinctions are significant instead, as §4 will show.) General conditions do not assert
the occurrence of one definite act at one definite time. To express generality,
Greek uses a dependent mood in the protasis (rather than the indicative, which
asserts fact) and the present stem (present or imperfect indicative) in the apodosis to convey repeated action or general truth (the typical aspect of the
present stem). The scheme for a *present general condition* is:

protasis	*apodosis*
ἐάν (εἰ + ἄν) + subjunctive	present indicative

Ex.

ἐὰν ἔλθῃ, δῶρα φέρει.
If he (ever) comes, he brings gifts (on each occasion).

ἐὰν μὴ νοσῇ, τὰ παιδία διδάσκει.
He teaches the children (every day) unless he is ill (at any time).

Note that one can determine whether a condition is simple or general by trying
to add adverbial phrases like *on one particular occasion, at that time* (for
simple) or *ever, on each* or *any occasion* (for general) to clarify the sense.
    The scheme for a *past general condition* is:

protasis	*apodosis*
εἰ + optative	imperfect indicative

Ex.

εἰ μὴ νοσοίη, τὰ παιδία ἐδίδασκεν.
He used to teach the children (every day) unless he was ill (at any time).

εἰ τὰ δίκαια πράττοιεν, ἐτιμῶμεν αὐτούς.
If they (ever) did what was right, we (always) used to honor them.

Relative or Temporal Clauses with General Conditional Force. Clauses of these types may also follow the general conditional patterns shown above when they are indefinite or generic or refer to repeated or customary action. Relative clauses with general force are often introduced by the indefinite relative (U33.4, U36), but the simple relative may also be used. The modal particle ἄν is often combined with a conjunction: ὅταν = ὅτε + ἄν, ἐπειδάν = ἐπειδή + ἄν, etc.

Ex.   *present general force*

ὅταν (ὁπόταν) ἔλθῃ, δῶρα φέρει.
Whenever he comes, he brings gifts (on each occasion).

οἱ στρατιῶται οἵτινες ἂν παρῶσι χρήματα λαμβάνουσιν.
Whichever soldiers are present (on any occasion) receive money.

     past general force

ὅτε (ὁπότε) ἔλθοι, δῶρα ἔφερεν.
Whenever he came, he brought gifts (on each occasion).

οἱ Ἀθηναῖοι ἐξέβαλλον ὅντινα πονηρὸν νομίζοιεν.
The Athenians used to expel any man (whom, whomsoever) they considered wicked.

4. *Future Conditions.* Future conditions express suppositions (either general or particular) about the future. The supposition is considered by the speaker to be possible, but the question of fulfillment vs. non-fulfillment is not yet decided. The moods used in the protasis and apodosis depend on the speaker's attitude toward the probability of fulfillment.

a. *Future Most Vivid.* This pattern conveys strong emotion or certainty. It is a rather rare construction in prose (and should not be used in the English-Greek exercises of this book), but is found in drama and colloquial contexts. The scheme is:

protasis	*apodosis*
εἰ + future indicative	future indicative

Ex.

εἰ ταῦτα ποιήσεις, κτενῶ σε.
If you do that, I'll kill you!

b. *Future More Vivid*. In this pattern the speaker views fulfillment as relatively probable, and so the indicative is used in the apodosis; but since the occurrence of the condition is unascertained, the protasis has the subjunctive. The scheme is:

protasis   *apodosis*
ἐάν + subjunctive   future indicative[1]

Ex.

ἐὰν τὸν βασιλέα ἕλῃς, ἄρξεις ἀντ᾽ ἐκείνου.
If you capture the king, you will rule in his place.

ἐὰν ταῦτα γένηται, χαλεπῶς οἴσετε.
If that (ever) happens, you will be upset.

c. *Future Less Vivid*. In this construction the speaker views fulfillment as relatively less probable, and so the apodosis contains the potential optative (optative + ἄν) to make a cautious or softened assertion. By assimilation of mood, the protasis also contains the optative, expressing a more remote possibility than the subjunctive + ἄν in the future more vivid pattern. The English equivalent of the future less vivid pattern is usually *should-would* (also *were to X–would*). The scheme is:

protasis   *apodosis*
εἰ + optative   optative + ἄν

Ex.

εἰ τὸν βασιλέα ἕλοις, ἄρξειας ἂν ἀντ᾽ ἐκείνου.
If you should capture the king, you would rule in his place.

λέγοιμ᾽ ἂν ὑμῖν εἰ ἐθέλοιτε ἀκούειν.
I would tell you if you should be willing to listen.

Relative or Temporal Clauses with Future Conditional Force. Clauses of these types may also follow the future more vivid or less vivid conditional patterns shown above when they are indefinite or generic, or refer to the future and the apodosis also refers to the future.

Ex.   *future more vivid force*

ἀποκτενοῦσιν οἵτινες ἂν τῷ βασιλεῖ ἐπιβουλεύωσιν.
They will put to death anyone who plots (may in the future plot) against the king.

---

1. One may also find other constructions implying future time, such as an imperative or χρή (δεῖ) + infinitive.

ὅταν ἔλθῃ, δῶρα οἴσει.
When(ever) he comes, he will bring gifts.

> *future less vivid force*

οὐκ ἂν ἐμβαίνοιμι τὰ πλοῖα ἃ Κῦρος ἡμῖν δοίη.
I would not board the ships which Cyrus might give us.

ὅπου τὸ ὕδωρ ἡδὺ εἴη ἐθέλοιμεν ἂν οἰκεῖν.
Wherever the water might be sweet, we would be willing to settle.

WHAT TO STUDY AND DO

1. Study the conditional patterns presented above.
2. Learn the vocabulary of this unit.
3. Do the exercises of this unit.

VOCABULARY

nouns

ἀδελφός, ἀδελφοῦ, m.	brother [Philadelphia]
ἀδελφή, ἀδελφῆς, f.	sister
ἀριθμός, ἀριθμοῦ, m.	number [arithmetic]
ἑσπέρα, ἑσπέρας, f.	evening; the west [Hesperides]
θαῦμα, θαύματος, n.	wonder, marvel; astonishment [thaumaturgy]
κίνδυνος, κινδύνου, m.	danger, risk
νύξ, νυκτός, f.	night
οἶκος, οἴκου, m.	house, dwelling place; household [ecology, ecosystem]
οἰκία, οἰκίας, f.	building, house
ὅπλον, ὅπλου, n.	tool, implement; (pl.) arms; ship's tackle
ὄρος, ὄρους, n.	mountain, hill
πλοῖον, πλοίου, n.	ship, boat
πρέσβυς, πρέσβεως, m.	old man; elder; ambassador (plural rare except in this last sense) [presbyopia, presbyterian]
πρεσβύτερος, -α, -ον	older, elder
πρεσβύτατος, -η, -ον	oldest, eldest
πρεσβύτης, πρεσβύτου, m.	old man, ambassador

verbs

διδάσκω, διδάξω, ἐδίδαξα	instruct, teach; train (a chorus), produce (a dance or play) [didactic]
ἐμβαίνω (ἐν)	step in or upon; board (a ship)
ἥκω, ἥξω	have come, be present (pres. with meaning of perfect)

θαυμάζω, θαυμάσομαι, ἐθαύμασα	wonder at, marvel at; admire
κλέπτω, κλέψω, ἔκλεψα	steal; behave stealthily [kleptomania]
πορεύω, πορεύσω, ἐπόρευσα	make to go, convey; (more commonly middle deponent πορεύομαι) go, walk, march
τρέχω, δραμέομαι (or rarely θρέξομαι), ἔδραμον	run [trochaic, hippodrome, aerodrome]

conjunctions

εἰ	if (with ind. or opt.); whether (in indirect question)
ἐάν, contracted ἄν[1] or ἤν	if (with subj.)
εἴπερ	if in fact, if indeed; since
εἰ μή	(without an expressed verb) if not, except
ἐπεί	since, whereas; when, after
ἐπείτε	when, since
ἐπειδή (ἐπειδή + ἄν = ἐπειδάν)	when, after; since, whereas
ὅτε (elided ὅτ'; ὅτε + ἄν = ὅταν)	when (relative adverb)
ὁπότε (ὁπότε + ἄν = ὁπόταν)	(indef. rel./indirect interrogative) whenever, when

EXERCISES

I. Render into Greek.

1. The men whom(ever) Socrates examined by conversing with (them) appeared to those present to know nothing, with the result that they were angry with him.
2. If we accuse them, they will not agree with us readily.
3. When the ambassador has come, will you ask this question or not?
4. If they should leave behind their weapons and boats and flee during the night, it would be no surprise (wonder).

II. Reading sentences.

1. ὅστις ἂν πρέσβεις ἀδικῇ, εἰ μὴ αὐτίκα ἀλλὰ τέλος δίκην δίδωσιν.
2. ἐὰν οἱ τρεῖς ἀδελφοὶ λάθωσι κλέψαντες τὰ ὅπλα ἃ ἀνέθεσαν οἱ Θηβαῖοι, πλούσιοι γενήσονται καίπερ ἀνόσια πράξαντες.

---

1. This form has long alpha; it can be distinguished from the modal particle ἄν by the length of the alpha (which is apparent in verse) and by its position in its clause (ἄν = *if* is normally first in its clause, modal ἄν is postpositive and cannot be first).

3. Ἀθήνησι¹ τὸ πάλαιον ἐθαυμάζοντο οἱ δικασταὶ οἵτινες ἀκούσαντες ἀμφοτέρων τοὺς λόγους τὴν ψῆφον θεῖντο κατὰ τὸ δίκαιον καὶ κατὰ τοὺς νόμους.
4. εἰ τάχιστα δράμοις, ἴσως ἂν τὸν κίνδυνον φύγοις.
5. ἀντὶ τούτων, ἅτινα νῦν εὐεργετήσειαν, ἀπολάβοιεν ἂν χάριν καὶ ζῶντες καὶ μετὰ τὴν τελευτὴν [= end] τοῦ βίου.
6. ἐὰν ἐρῶν τῆς ἑταίρας δαπανήσῃ πολλὰ ὁ νεανίας, οὐ συνοίσει τῷ οἴκῳ ὡς ἤδη χρημάτων ἀπορούντι.
7. πρέπει ἀεὶ ποιεῖν ὅ τι ἂν παραινέσωσιν οἱ σοφοί.
8. [Cephalus narrates:] ἐπειδὴ εἰς Ἀθήνας [Athens] ἀφικόμην, κατ᾽ ἀγορὰν ἀπήντησα Ἀδειμάντῳ καὶ Γλαύκωνι· καί μου λαβόμενος [mid. = take hold of, + gen.] τῆς χειρὸς ὁ Ἀδείμαντος, "χαῖρε [greetings]," ἔφη, "ὦ Κέφαλε, καὶ εἴ του δέῃ τῶν ἐνθάδε ἃ ἡμεῖς δυνάμεθα ποιεῖν, φράζε [tell (us)]." "ἀλλά," εἶπον ἐγώ, "πάρειμι ἐπ᾽ αὐτὸ τοῦτο, δεησόμενος ὑμῶν."

III. Reading: Aristophanes, *Wealth* 489–504: the goddess of Poverty has argued in favor of the status quo (in which the god of Wealth is blind), but Chremylos justifies his proposal to restore Wealth's sight as follows.²

Chremylos

φανερὸν μὲν ἔγωγ᾽ οἶμαι γνῶναι τοῦτ᾽ εἶναι πᾶσιν ὁμοίως,	489
ὅτι τοὺς χρηστοὺς τῶν ἀνθρώπων εὖ πράττειν ἐστὶ δίκαιον,	490
τοὺς δὲ πονηροὺς καὶ τοὺς ἀθέους τούτων τἀναντία δήπου.	
τοῦτ᾽ οὖν ἡμεῖς ἐπιθυμοῦντες μόλις ηὕρομεν ὥστε γενέσθαι	
βούλευμα καλὸν καὶ γενναῖον καὶ χρήσιμον εἰς ἅπαν ἔργον.	
ἢν γὰρ ὁ Πλοῦτος νυνὶ βλέψῃ καὶ μὴ τυφλὸς ὢν περινοστῇ,	
ὡς τοὺς ἀγαθοὺς τῶν ἀνθρώπων βαδιεῖται κοὐκ ἀπολείψει,	495
τοὺς δὲ πονηροὺς καὶ τοὺς ἀθέους φευξεῖται· κᾆτα ποήσει	
πάντας χρηστοὺς καὶ πλουτοῦντας δήπου τά τε θεῖα σέβοντας.	
καίτοι τούτου τοῖς ἀνθρώποις τίς ἂν ἐξεύροι ποτ᾽ ἄμεινον;	498

Blepsidemos

οὐδείς· τούτου μάρτυς ἐγώ σοι· μηδὲν ταύτην γ᾽ ἀνερώτα.	499

1. See U29.5e.
2. The speech is written in a meter called anapaestic tetrameter catalectic. Greek meter is quantitative (based on length of syllables). The Greek anapaest is ⏑ ⏑ – ⏑ ⏑ – , but each pair of shorts can be replaced by a long, and a long can be replaced by two shorts (within certain limits). Thus an anapaestic metron can also appear as – – – – or as – ⏑ ⏑ – – or the like. The tetrameter consists of four metra, with word-end at the end of each of the first two and with the fourth metron shortened to ⏑ ⏑ – – (with no substitutions allowed). So the first two lines are scanned:

⏑ ⏑ – ⏑ ⏑ – | – – – – | – – – – ⏑ ⏑ – – ‖
⏑ ⏑ – – – – | – – – – | – – – – ⏑ ⏑ – – ‖

Chremylos

ὡς μὲν γὰρ νῦν ἡμῖν ὁ βίος τοῖς ἀνθρώποις <u>διάκειται</u>,   500
τίς ἂν οὐχ ἡγοῖτ᾽ εἶναι <u>μανίαν</u> <u>κακοδαιμονίαν</u> τ᾽ <u>ἔτι</u> μᾶλλον;
πολλοὶ μὲν γὰρ τῶν ἀνθρώπων ὄντες πλουτοῦσι πονηροί,
ἀδίκως <u>αὐτὰ</u> <u>ξυλλεξάμενοι</u>· πολλοὶ δ᾽ ὄντες <u>πάνυ</u> χρηστοὶ
πράττουσι κακῶς καὶ <u>πεινῶσιν</u> μετὰ <u>σοῦ</u> τε <u>τὰ πλεῖστα</u> <u>σύνεισιν</u>.   504

Underlined Words

489: ἔγωγε = emphatic form of ἐγώ
489: γνῶναι = epexegetic (explanatory result) infinitive with φανερὸν, *clear to understand*
489: ὁμοίως = *equally*
491: ἄθεος, -ον = *godless, wicked*
491: τἀναντία = τὰ ἐναντία, *the opposite*
491: δήπου = *surely, you'll agree*
492: take τοῦτο as object of ηὕρομεν, further explained by ὥστε = *a way so that*
492: οὖν = *so then*
492: μόλις = *with difficulty*
493: γενναῖος, -α, -ον = *noble, excellent*
493: χρήσιμος, -η, -ον = *useful*
494: νυνί = emphatic form of νῦν
494: βλέπω, aor. ἔβλεψα = *have sight, see*
494: τυφλός, -ή, -όν = *blind*
494: περινοστέω = *go around*
495: ὡς (+ acc. of person) = (preposition) *to, to the house of*
495: βαδίζω, fut. βαδιέομαι = *walk, go*
495: κοὐκ = καὶ οὐκ
495: ἀπολείψει = ἀπο- compound; guess the meaning
496: κᾆτα = καὶ εἶτα

496: ποήσει = ποιήσει (metrical shortening of diphthong οι from popular speech)
497: πλουτέω = *be wealthy, be rich*
497: θεῖος, -α, -ον = *divine*
497: σέβω = *revere, respect*
498: καίτοι = *and yet*
498: ἐξεύροι = ἐκ- compound; guess the meaning
499: μάρτυς = *witness*
499: γ᾽ (elided γε) = enclitic adding emphasis to ταύτην (i.e., Poverty)
499: ἀνερώτα (2nd sing. imperative) = *ask*
500: διάκειμαι (deponent μι-verb) = *be disposed, be arranged*
501: μανία = *madness*
501: κακοδαιμονία = *accursed misfortune*
501: ἔτι = *still, even*
503: αὐτά = *their possessions*
503: συλλέγω, aor. συνέλεξα = *gather* (ξύν is the old Attic form of σύν)
503: πάνυ = (adv.) *altogether, exceedingly*
504: πεινάω = *starve*
504: σοῦ refers to Poverty
504: τὰ πλεῖστα (adv. acc.) = *for the most part*
504: σύνειμι = *be with*

Aorist Passive and Future Passive

1. *The Last Three Principal Parts.* Up to this point the student has dealt with the first three principal parts of the Greek verb: the first person singular forms of the present active (or middle/passive for deponent), future active (or middle), and aorist active (or middle) indicative. In the traditional order of principal parts, the fourth is the first person singular perfect active indicative, the fifth is the first person singular perfect middle/passive indicative, and the sixth is the first person singular aorist passive indicative. In this book the aorist passive will be learned first (since the aorist is more commonly used than the perfect), and the perfect will soon follow in U37. From this unit on, new verbs will be presented with all six principal parts, or as many as a particular verb actually has (since deponents and some other verbs lack some tense systems). As part of the work of this and the next two units, the student should also study the remaining principal parts of the verbs learned in previous units, using the compiled list of principal parts in Appendix 2.

2. *Formation of Aorist Passive Stem.* In origin, the aorist passive developed from an intransitive "active" form, similar in formation to intransitive athematic aorists like ἔστην or ἔβην. The more primitive aorist passive stems (called "second" aorist passive) consist of a form of the verb stem plus tense vowel η (shortened to ε in the participle, subjunctive, and optative):

γράφω	stem γραφη-	princ. part ἐγράφην
βλάπτω	stem βλαβη-	princ. part ἐβλάβην

The more recent aorist passive stems (called "first" aorist passive) add a tense suffix θη (or θε) to the verb stem:

λύω	stem λυθη-	princ. part ἐλύθην
ποιέω	stem ποιηθη-	princ. part ἐποιήθην
τίθημι	stem τεθη-	princ. part ἐτέθην[1]

---

1. Note the effect of Grassmann's law: when suffix θη is added to the verb stem θε, the result is τεθη- rather than θεθη- by dissimilation of the initial aspiration.

It is necessary to learn the principal parts because the form of the aorist stem cannot always be predicted from the first principal part; but there are certain patterns that make learning the principal parts somewhat easier:

a. Insertion of σ before the suffix $\theta\eta$ (verbs in dentals or -$\zeta\omega$, some verbs in -$\acute{\epsilon}\omega$):

πείθω	ἐπείσθην
νομίζω	ἐνομίσθην
τελέω	ἐτελέσθην

b. Labial or velar plosive aspirated before $\theta\eta$ (by assimilation):

λείπω	ἐλείφθην
πράττω (πραγ-)	ἐπράχθην

c. ν dropped before $\theta\eta$:

κρίνω	ἐκρίθην

3. *Inflection of Aorist Passive.* The inflection is the same for "first" and "second" aorist passive, so these terms are only of historical interest (unlike the case of first and second aorist active or middle). Every part of the aorist passive inflection is the same as some inflectional pattern that the student has already learned. The indicative has augment and has athematic conjugation using the appropriate secondary *active* personal endings (-ν, -s, —, -$\tau o\nu$, -$\tau\eta\nu$, -$\mu\epsilon\nu$, -$\tau\epsilon$, -$\sigma\alpha\nu$): cf. ἔστην, ἔβην. The infinitive has the ending -$\nu\alpha\iota$ with the (circumflex) accent on the tense vowel η. The participle has the *active* participial suffix -$\nu\tau$-, producing the endings -$(\theta)\epsilon\acute{\iota}s$, -$(\theta)\epsilon\hat{\iota}\sigma\alpha$, -$(\theta)\acute{\epsilon}\nu$; the declension is like that of τιθείς, τιθεῖσα, τιθέν. The subjunctive has the usual *active* subjunctive personal endings, which contract with the tense vowel ϵ, so that the conjugation is like that of subj. ποιῶ or τιθῶ. The optative has the mood suffix -$\iota\eta$- or -ι- (optional in dual and plural) added to the tense vowel ϵ, so that the conjugation is like that of optative τιθείην.

Ex. aorist passive of λύω, stem λυθη- (or λυθε-)

indicative	subjunctive	optative		
ἐλύθην	λυθῶ	λυθείην		
ἐλύθης	λυθῇς	λυθείης		
ἐλύθη	λυθῇ	λυθείη		
(ἐλύθητον	λυθῆτον	λυθείητον	or	λυθεῖτον)
(ἐλυθήτην	λυθῆτον	λυθειήτην	or	λυθείτην)
ἐλύθημεν	λυθῶμεν	λυθείημεν	or	λυθεῖμεν
ἐλύθητε	λυθῆτε	λυθείητε	or	λυθεῖτε
ἐλύθησαν	λυθῶσι(ν)	λυθείησαν	or	λυθεῖεν

infinitive: λυθῆναι
participle: λυθείς, λυθεῖσα, λυθέν; m./n. stem λυθέντ-,
  dat. pl. λυθεῖσι(ν)

4. *Future Passive System.* The sixth principal part also provides the basis for the formation of the future passive system. Recall (from U18.7) that the future middle of many verbs can have a passive meaning, but some verbs have only a future passive (e.g., ἥδομαι, ἡσθήσομαι from aor. pass. ἥσθην) and others can use either form to express a future passive meaning.

The future passive stem is formed by adding -σομαι (= future suffix σ + theme vowel ο/ε + primary middle/passive personal endings) to the aorist passive stem with vowel η.[1] The indicative, infinitive, participle, and optative are inflected just like a regular future middle in -σομαι.

Ex.   future passive of λύω, stem λυθησ- + ο/ε

indicative	optative
λυθήσομαι	λυθησοίμην
λυθήσῃ	λυθήσοιο
λυθήσεται	λυθήσοιτο
(λυθήσεσθον	λυθήσοισθον)
(λυθήσεσθον	λυθησοίσθην)
λυθησόμεθα	λυθησοίμεθα
λυθήσεσθε	λυθήσοισθε
λυθήσονται	λυθήσοιντο

infinitive: λυθήσεσθαι
participle: λυθησόμενος, -η, -ον

WHAT TO STUDY AND DO

1. Study the aorist passive and future passive systems.
2. Study the principal parts of verbs learned to date (compiled in Appendix 2). Begin to learn the perfect principal parts now as well. You may wish to read "Advice on Learning Principal Parts," which precedes the list of principal parts).
3. Learn the vocabulary of this unit.
4. Do the exercises of this unit.

---

1. A future passive from a "first" aorist passive (λυθήσομαι) is called a "first" future passive, and one from a "second" aorist passive (βλαβήσομαι) is called a "second" future passive, but the distinction is insignificant.

VOCABULARY

nouns related to words learned previously

ἀδικία, ἀδικίας, f.	injustice, wrongdoing
αἰσχύνη, αἰσχύνης, f.	shame, dishonor; sense of shame
αἰτία, αἰτίας, f.	responsibility, blame; accusation; cause
ἄρχων, ἄρχοντος, m.	ruler; archon (an Athenian magistrate, one of a group of nine chosen annually)
ἀσθένεια, ἀσθενείας, f.	weakness, illness
βάθος, βάθους, n.	depth
βάρος, βάρους, n.	weight
δικαιοσύνη, δικαιοσύνης, f.	righteousness, justice
δυστυχία, δυστυχίας, f.	ill luck, ill fortune
εὐτυχία, εὐτυχίας, f.	good luck, success
ἔχθρα, ἔχθρας, f.	hatred, enmity
ζῆλος, ζήλου, m.	eager rivalry, emulation; (less commonly) jealousy [zeal]
κακία, κακίας, f.	badness; cowardice; vice
κάλλος, κάλλους, n.	beauty [calliope]
προδότης, προδότου, m.	traitor, betrayer
σωφροσύνη, σωφροσύνης, f.	prudence; moderation, temperance
τάχος, τάχους, n.	speed, swiftness [tachometer]
τάχος	(adv. acc.) swiftly
τελευτή, τελευτῆς, f.	accomplishment; end, finish; death
φυγάς, φυγάδος, m. or f.	exile; runaway, fugitive

EXERCISES

I. Write in Greek.

1. 3rd pl. aor. pass. ind. of θαυμάζω
2. dat. pl. masc. fut. pass. part. of ζηλόω
3. 2nd sing. fut. pass. ind. of σκεδάννυμι
4. 3rd sing. fut. pass. opt. of γιγνώσκω
5. 2nd pl. aor. pass. subj. of πράττω
6. acc. sing. fem. aor. pass. part. of ῥήγνυμι
7. 1st pl. aor. pass. subj. of μιμνῄσκω
8. 1st sing. aor. pass. opt. of ὁράω
9. aor. pass. inf. of τέμνω
10. 3rd sing. aor. pass. ind. of φαίνω
11. fut. pass. inf. of ἐπαινέω
12. nom. sing. neut. aor. pass. part. of βάλλω
13. aor. act. inf. of ἔχω

14. neut. s. acc. pres. act. part. of νικάω
15. 2nd s. aor. mid. opt. of ἀποδίδωμι
16. 1st pl. aor. act. subj. of λαμβάνω
17. 3rd pl. fut. pass. ind. of αἱρέω
18. 2nd pl. fut. act. ind. of ἐλπίζω
19. 3rd s. aor. pass. opt. of διώκω
20. masc. s. nom. aor. pass. part. of ἥδομαι

II. Identify each form completely.

1. ληφθῆναι	15. κρατηθείσῃ	29. ἀγγελθήσεται
2. ποιηθήσεται	16. πεισθῶσι	30. ἀνετέθη
3. διαβαλοῦμεν	17. κρυφθέν	31. ἀνετίθει
4. κωλυθήσομαι	18. ὁρμήσαιντο	32. ἀπαχθῶμεν
5. συνέγνωτε	19. ἁρπασθησόμενον	33. ἀποροίης
6. ἐνομίσθης	20. ἐλαθείη	34. ἀπέδυτε
7. ἐτάχθησαν	21. ἐφοβήθημεν	35. γνωσθῆναι
8. γῆμαι	22. ἐρρήθη	36. δειχθεῖσαι
9. αἰτιαθῆναι	23. ἡσθήσεσθαι	37. ἐδιδάχθη
10. ἀξιωθέντων	24. ἐνεπλήσθην	38. δυνηθέντα
11. πραχθῇ	25. εὑρεθήσονται	39. ὠργίσθητε
12. ἔζη	26. ζητηθεῖμεν	40. ὀργισθῆτε
13. ἐπιθεῖο	27. ἡττηθέντος	41. ἐβλήθης
14. ἠράσθην	28. μνησθῆναι	42. δηλωθήσεσθε

III. Reading: Plato, *Gorgias* 456a–c: the sophist Gorgias explains to Socrates the primacy of the art of rhetoric.

[Socrates:] ταῦτα <u>καὶ</u> θαυμάζων, ὦ Γοργία, <u>πάλαι</u> ἐρωτῶ τίς ποτε ἡ δύναμίς ἐστιν τῆς <u>ῥητορικῆς</u>. δαιμονία γάρ <u>τις</u> <u>ἔμοιγε</u> <u>καταφαίνεται</u> τὸ <u>μέγεθος</u> οὕτω <u>σκοποῦντι</u>.

[Gorgias:] <u>εἰ πάντα</u> γε <u>εἰδείης</u>, ὦ Σώκρατες, ὅτι <u>ὡς ἔπος εἰπεῖν</u> ἁπάσας τὰς δυνάμεις <u>συλλαβοῦσα</u> ὑφ᾽ αὑτῇ ἔχει. μέγα δέ σοι <u>τεκμήριον</u> ἐρῶ· πολλάκις γὰρ ἤδη <u>ἔγωγε</u> μετὰ τοῦ ἀδελφοῦ καὶ μετὰ τῶν ἄλλων <u>ἰατρῶν</u> εἰσελθὼν παρά τινα τῶν <u>καμνόντων</u> <u>οὐχὶ</u> ἐθέλοντα ἢ <u>φάρμακον</u> πιεῖν, ἢ τεμεῖν ἢ καῦσαι <u>παρασχεῖν</u> τῷ ἰατρῷ, οὐ δυναμένου τοῦ ἰατροῦ πεῖσαι, ἐγὼ ἔπεισα, οὐκ ἄλλῃ <u>τέχνῃ</u> ἢ τῇ ῥητορικῇ. φημὶ δὲ καὶ εἰς πόλιν <u>ὅποι</u> βούλῃ ἐλθόντα <u>ῥητορικὸν</u> ἄνδρα καὶ ἰατρόν, εἰ δέοι λόγῳ <u>διαγωνίζεσθαι</u> ἐν <u>ἐκκλησίᾳ</u> ἢ ἐν ἄλλῳ τινὶ <u>συλλόγῳ</u> <u>ὁπότερον</u> δεῖ αἱρεθῆναι ἰατρόν, <u>οὐδαμοῦ</u> <u>ἂν</u> φανῆναι τὸν ἰατρόν, ἀλλ᾽ αἱρεθῆναι ἂν τὸν εἰπεῖν <u>δυνατόν</u>, εἰ βούλοιτο. καὶ εἰ πρὸς ἄλλον γε <u>δημιουργὸν</u> <u>ὀντιναοῦν</u> <u>ἀγωνίζοιτο</u>, πείσειεν ἂν αὑτὸν ἑλέσθαι ὁ ῥητορικὸς μᾶλλον ἢ ἄλλος ὁστισοῦν· οὐ γὰρ ἔστιν περὶ ὅτου οὐκ <u>ἂν</u> <u>πιθανώτερον</u> εἴποι ὁ ῥητορικὸς ἢ ἄλλος ὁστισοῦν τῶν δημιουργῶν ἐν πλήθει.

Underlined Words

ἀγωνίζομαι = *contend, compete*

ἄν here makes the indirect-discourse infs. φανῆναι and αἱρεθῆναι potential in meaning

δαιμόνιος, -α, -ον = *miraculous, marvelous*

δημιουργός, -οῦ, m. = *skilled craftsman*

διαγωνίζομαι = *contend, compete*

δυνατός, -ή, -όν = *able*

ἔγωγε = emphatic form of ἐγώ

εἰ πάντα γε εἰδείης: the particle γε marks agreement in this elliptical sentence: *"Yes, <you certainly would call it marvelous> if . . . "*; εἰδείης is optative of οἶδα

ἐκκλησία, -ας, f. = *public assembly*

ἔμοιγε = emphatic form of ἐμοί

ἰατρός, -οῦ, m. = *physician*

καί is here adverbial, *indeed, in fact*

κάμνω = *be ill*

καταφαίνω = (pass.) *appear* (understood subject is ἡ ῥητορική)

μέγεθος, -ους, n. = *size, greatness* (here acc. of respect)

ὅποι = *to wherever*

ὁπότερος, -α, -ον = *which of the two*

ὁστισοῦν = *any at all* (strengthened indefinite pronoun made of ὅστις + οὖν)

οὐδαμοῦ = *nowhere*; here *would appear nowhere* is a metaphor from racing (*would make no showing at all*)

οὐχί = emphatic form of οὐ

πάλαι is used idiomatically with the present indicative to convey *I have been Xing for a long time now*

παρασχεῖν = (here) *permit, allow* (+ dat. of person + inf. [here governing τεμεῖν ἢ καῦσαι])

πιθανός, -ή, -όν = *persuasive*

ῥητορικός, -ή, -όν = (of a person) *rhetorically skilled*; (of things) *pertaining to rhetoric* (so fem. with noun τέχνη understood = *art of rhetoric*)

σκοπέω = *examine*

συλλαμβάνω = *take together, encompass*

σύλλογος, -ου, m. = *gathering*

τεκμήριον, -ου, n. = *indication, piece of evidence*

τέχνη, -ης, f. = *art, skill*

τις added to an adj. may either soften its force (*sort of . . .*) or strengthen it, as here (*quite . . .*)

φάρμακον, -ου, n. = *drug*

ὡς ἔπος εἰπεῖν = *so to speak* (idiomatic epexegetic or result infinitive)

Contrary-to-Fact Conditions; Indicative with ἄν; Correlatives

1. *Contrary-to-Fact Conditions.* Three major classes of Greek conditional sentences were presented in U34. The fourth major class is that in which the protasis expresses a supposition which the speaker knows *is not* or *was not true* and the apodosis expresses what *would be* or *would have been* the consequence (usually with the implication that the consequence did not occur). Such conditions are called *contrary-to-fact* or *unreal*. Just as secondary tenses of the indicative are used to express impossible wishes, so the secondary tenses are used in both clauses of unreal conditions, with the modal particle ἄν added in the apodosis to mark the unreality. The scheme for a *contrary-to-fact condition in present time* (English equivalent: *were* (subj.)–*would*) is:

protasis	*apodosis*
εἰ + imperfect indicative	imperfect indicative + ἄν

Ex.

εἰ παρῆν ὁ Κῦρος, μάχεσθαι ἡμῖν ἂν παρεκελεύετο.
If Cyrus <u>were</u> present [and he is not], *he <u>would</u> exhort us to fight.*

εἰ τἀληθῆ ἔλεγεν, ἐπιστεύομεν ἄν.
If he spoke (<u>were</u> speaking) the truth [and he is not], *we <u>would</u> trust him.*

The scheme for a contrary-to-fact condition in past time (English equivalent: *had–would have*) is:

protasis	*apodosis*
εἰ + aorist indicative	aorist indicative + ἄν

Ex.

εἰ οἱ βάρβαροι ἐπέθεντο, μάχεσθαι ἡμῖν ἂν παρεκελεύσατο.
If the Persians <u>had</u> attacked [but they didn't], *he <u>would have</u> exhorted us to fight.*

εἰ μὴ τἀληθῆ ἔλεξεν, πάντες ἂν ἀπέθανον. [Note μὴ as negative.]
If he had not spoken the truth [but he did], *all would have died.*

In English, the apodosis of an unreal condition may look similar to one of the future less vivid type, but the protasis will look different in correct English. If necessary, the student can remove doubts by considering the time implications of the sentence (future as opposed to present or past) and by trying to spell out the unreality of the protasis. Contrast *If Cyrus were to be present* (i.e., at the peace conference *tomorrow*) and *If Cyrus were present* (i.e., *now*, but he isn't).

2. *Indicative with* ἄν. In Attic the secondary tenses of the indicative are sometimes used with the modal particle ἄν outside of conditional sentences to express a potentiality or probability in the past (whereas the optative with ἄν expresses a potentiality in the present or future). This use is called the *past potential indicative*. Sometimes, but not always, there appears to be ellipsis (omission) of a condition. Sometimes there is the implication that the event expressed by the indicative with ἄν is not or was not the case (*unreal indicative*).

τίς γὰρ ἂν ἡγήσατο ταῦτα γενέσθαι;
Who would have thought that this would happen?

θᾶττον ἢ ὥς τις ἂν ᾤετο
more swiftly than [as] one would think (would have thought)

οὕτως ἐνικήσατε ἄν.
In that way you would have won [but in fact you didn't].   (unreal)

In a purely potential indicative, both the imperfect and the aorist commonly refer to past time; but the imperfect may refer to present time in certain idioms like ἐβουλόμην ἄν = *I should like, I should wish*. In the unreal indicative (as in contrary-to-fact conditions and impossible wishes), the imperfect usually refers to present time, the aorist to past time. Note that, in order to avoid ambiguity, if an unreal indicative of direct discourse is put into an indirect-discourse ὅτι-clause in secondary sequence, the indicative is not changed to the optative.

A further development of the past potential indicative with ἄν is the *iterative indicative* ("iterative" = "of repeated action"):

πολλάκις ἠκούσαμεν ἄν τι κακῶς ὑμᾶς βουλευσαμένους.
We often used to hear that you had planned something badly.

3. *Imperfect of Unfulfilled Obligation.* The imperfect of an impersonal expression of obligation, propriety, necessity, or the like may be used without ἄν to denote an action that was not carried out. This usage, called the *imperfect of unfulfilled obligation*, is often found in the apodosis of a contrary-to-fact condition instead of the imperfect or aorist indicative with ἄν. In this construction the infinitive is present if it refers to an action unfulfilled in

present time, normally aorist (occasionally present) if it refers to an action unfulfilled in past time.[1]

ἔδει σε ταῦτα ποιεῖν.
You ought to be doing this (now) [but you aren't].

εἰ ἐνίκησε, δίκαιον ἦν ἐπαινέσαι αὐτόν.
If he had won, it would have been just to praise him.

ἔδει σε ταῦτα ποιῆσαι.
You ought to have done this (then).

4. *Correlatives.* Certain pronouns, pronominal adjectives, and adverbs correspond to each other in form and/or meaning and are called *correlatives* because of their occasional use in pairs in main and subordinate (relative) clauses. For instance, the English pairs *where-there* and *when-then* are correlatives:

<u>*Where*</u> there is smoke, <u>*there*</u> there is fire.
<u>*When*</u> there is victory, <u>*then*</u> there is celebration.

The table on the next page presents some Greek correlatives in organized sequences. Some of the words you have already learned; others are new. Note various patterns in the table, such as the element -οιο- denoting quality; -οσο- denoting quantity; the identity of interrogatives and indefinites except for accentuation (indefinites being enclitic); π- as first letter of many interrogatives; rough breathing as initial sound of many relatives; ὁπ- as beginning of indefinite relatives.

Of the new adjectives and pronouns shown in the table, most have normal three-ending vowel-declension inflection: e.g., ποῖος, -α, -ον; ὁπότερος, -α, -ον. In τοσόσδε, τοσήδε, τοσόνδε, where the final syllable is the enclitic suffix -δε, the accent it treated as in ὅδε, ἥδε, τόδε. The declension of τοιοῦτος and τοσοῦτος, however, is irregular: as in οὗτος, the diphthong of the stem is assimilated to that of the ending, and the neuter sing. nom. acc. may have pronominal ending -ο or adjectival ending -ον (paradigm on page 277).

---

1. The impersonal verb expresses the obligation in the past; the infinitive which is its subject expresses the action without asserting its occurrence; and the context helps the reader or listener infer that the action did not occur. The combination of imperfect tense and infinitive renders ἄν superfluous.

CORRELATIVES

interrog.	indefinite (enclitic)	demonstr.	relative	indef. rel./ indirect interrog.
τίς, τί who?	τις, τι anyone	ὅδε, οὗτος, or ἐκεῖνος this, that	ὅς, ἥ, ὅ who, which	ὅστις whoever
ποῖος what sort?	ποιός of some sort	τοιόσδε or τοιοῦτος such	οἷος (such) as, the sort which	ὁποῖος of whatever sort
πόσος how much? how many?	ποσός of some quantity	τοσόσδε or τοσοῦτος so much, so many	ὅσος as much as, as many as	ὁπόσος however much or many
πότερος which of two?	πότερος any one of two	ἕτερος the other (of two)	——	ὁπότερος whichever of two
ποῦ where?	που somewhere	ἐνθάδε, ἐνταῦθα, ἐκεῖ here, there	οὗ, ἔνθα where	ὅπου wherever
πόθεν from where?	ποθεν from some place	ἐνθένδε, ἐντεῦθεν, ἐκεῖθεν from here, from there	ὅθεν whence	ὁπόθεν whencesoever
ποῖ whither? to what place?	ποι to some place	ἐνθάδε, ἐνταῦθα, ἐκεῖσε to this place, to that place	οἷ whither	ὅποι whithersoever
πῶς how?	πως somehow	ὧδε, οὕτω, ἐκείνως in this way, in that way	ὡς as, how	ὅπως how, however
πότε when?	ποτε at some time, ever	τότε then	ὅτε when	ὁπότε whenever
πῇ by which way? where?	πη in some way	τῇδε, ταύτῃ in this way, by this way	ᾗ in which way, as	ὅπη in which way, as

DECLENSION OF τοιοῦτος

		masculine	feminine	neuter
sing.	nom.	τοιοῦτος	τοιαύτη	τοιοῦτον or τοιοῦτο
	gen.	τοιούτου	τοιαύτης	τοιούτου
	dat.	τοιούτῳ	τοιαύτῃ	τοιούτῳ
	acc.	τοιοῦτον	τοιαύτην	τοιοῦτον or τοιοῦτο
(dual	n. a.	τοιούτω	τοιούτω	τοιούτω)
	(g. d.	τοιούτοιν	τοιούτοιν	τοιούτοιν)
plur.	nom.	τοιοῦτοι	τοιαῦται	τοιαῦτα
	gen.	τοιούτων	τοιούτων	τοιούτων
	dat.	τοιούτοις	τοιαύταις	τοιούτοις
	acc.	τοιούτους	τοιαύτας	τοιαῦτα

The declension of τοσοῦτος, τοσαύτη, τοσοῦτο(ν) follows the same pattern.

5. *Some Adverbs of Place.* Several adverbs of place are formed from basic roots with similar suffixes (e.g., -θεν for place from which, -σε for place to which). Here is a table of some common adverbs:

root meaning	place where	place to which	place from which
other	ἄλλοθι, ἀλλαχοῦ *elsewhere*	ἄλλοσε, ἀλλαχόσε *in another direction*	ἄλλοθεν, ἀλλα- χόθεν *from elsewhere*
both	ἀμφοτέρωθι *on both sides*	ἀμφοτέρωσε *in both directions*	ἀμφοτέροθεν *from both sides*
all	πανταχοῦ, πανταχῇ *everywhere*	πανταχόσε, πανταχοῖ *in all directions*	πανταχόθεν *from all sides*
this, the very	αὐτοῦ *in this very place*	αὐτόσε *in the same direction*	αὐτόθεν *from the same place*
home	οἴκοι *at home*	οἴκαδε *to home*	οἴκοθεν *from home*

Also derived from the root ἀλλ- = *other* are the adverb ἄλλοτε, *at another time*, and the adjective ἀλλοῖος, *of another kind*.

WHAT TO STUDY AND DO

1. Study the indicative with ἄν and the imperfect of unfulfilled obligation.
2. Study the declension of τοιοῦτος and τοσοῦτος.

3. Learn as the vocabulary of this unit any new words presented in §§4–5 above.
4. Continue to study the principal parts of the verbs learned to date, using Appendix 2.
5. Do the exercises of this unit.

EXERCISES

I. Render into Greek.

1. You ought not to be betraying the laws [as you are], gentlemen of the jury.
2. Twenty hoplites would have been captured on that day if the exiles had not come to the rescue.
3. If the guards were not present at the shrine during the night, those who lack money would quickly steal everything.

II. Reading sentences

1. πάντας μαχέσασθαι χρῆν καὶ ὑπὲρ τῶν Θηβαίων εἰ οἱ βάρβαροι τὴν πόλιν τὴν ἐκείνων ἐπολιόρκησαν.
2. τότε μὲν οὐδεὶς ἂν παρὰ τῶν πολεμίων δῶρα ἔλαβεν, νῦν δὲ πᾶς τις ζητεῖ προδότης γενέσθαι.
3. αἱ γυναῖκες τὰ παιδία καὶ τοὺς ἄνδρας οἴκοι λιποῦσαι εἰς τὸ ὄρος ἄλλαι ἄλλοθεν ἔτρεχον.
4. ὦ φίλε Φαῖδρε, ποῖ δὴ [particle adds lively tone to question] καὶ πόθεν; — παρὰ Λυσίου, ὦ Σώκρατες, τοῦ Κεφάλου, πορεύομαι δὲ πρὸς περίπατον [walk] ἔξω [outside, + gen.] τείχους.
5. περὶ παντός, ὦ παῖ, μία ἀρχὴ τοῖς μέλλουσι καλῶς βουλεύσεσθαι· εἰδέναι δεῖ περὶ οὗ ἂν ᾖ ἡ βουλή [deliberation], ἢ παντὸς ἁμαρτάνειν ἀνάγκη.
6. οὐ κελευσθεὶς οὔθ' ὑπὸ Ξενοφῶντος οὔθ' ὑπ' ἄλλου τινὸς τοῦτο ἐποίησα· ἰδόντι δέ μοι ἄνδρα ἀγαθὸν ἀγόμενον τῶν ἐμῶν στρατιωτῶν [partitive gen. with ἄνδρα] ὑπὸ Δεξίππου, ὃν ὑμεῖς ἐπίστασθε ὑμᾶς προδόντα, δεινὸν ἔδοξεν εἶναι· καὶ ἀφειλόμην [took away (by force)] τὸν ἄνδρα, ὁμολογῶ.

III. Reading: Lysias, *Oration* 1.1–3: Euphiletus is on trial for murder, having killed the adulterer Eratosthenes upon discovering him in bed with his wife.

περὶ πολλοῦ ἂν ποιησαίμην, ὦ ἄνδρες, τὸ τοιούτους ὑμᾶς ἐμοὶ δικαστὰς περὶ τούτου τοῦ πράγματος γενέσθαι, οἷοίπερ ἂν ὑμῖν αὐτοῖς εἴητε τοιαῦτα πεπονθότες· εὖ γὰρ οἶδα ὅτι, εἰ τὴν αὐτὴν γνώμην περὶ τῶν ἄλλων ἔχοιτε, ἥνπερ περὶ ὑμῶν αὐτῶν, οὐκ ἂν εἴη ὅστις οὐκ ἐπὶ τοῖς γεγενημένοις ἀγανακτοίη, ἀλλὰ πάντες ἂν περὶ τῶν τὰ τοιαῦτα ἐπιτηδευόντων τὰς ζημίας μικρὰς ἡγοῖσθε. καὶ ταῦτα οὐκ ἂν εἴη μόνον παρ' ὑμῖν οὕτως

ἐγνωσμένα, ἀλλ᾽ ἐν ἁπάσῃ τῇ Ἑλλάδι· περὶ τούτου γὰρ μόνου τοῦ
ἀδικήματος καὶ ἐν δημοκρατίᾳ καὶ ὀλιγαρχίᾳ ἡ αὐτὴ τιμωρία τοῖς
ἀσθενεστάτοις πρὸς τοὺς τὰ μέγιστα δυναμένους ἀποδέδοται, ὥστε τὸν
χείριστον τῶν αὐτῶν τυγχάνειν τῷ βελτίστῳ· οὕτως, ὦ ἄνδρες, ταύτην
τὴν ὕβριν ἅπαντες ἄνθρωποι δεινοτάτην ἡγοῦνται. περὶ μὲν οὖν τοῦ
μεγέθους τῆς ζημίας ἅπαντας ὑμᾶς νομίζω τὴν αὐτὴν διάνοιαν ἔχειν, καὶ
οὐδένα οὕτως ὀλιγώρως διακεῖσθαι, ὅστις οἴεται δεῖν συγγνώμης τυγχάνειν
ἢ μικρᾶς ζημίας ἀξίους ἡγεῖται τοὺς τῶν τοιούτων ἔργων αἰτίους.

Underlined Words

ἀγανακτέω = *be vexed at* (here with
ἐπί-phrase); here used in the
potential optative *without* ἄν (special
idiom in indefinite relative clause)

ἀδίκημα, -ατος, n. = *crime*

ἀποδέδοται = (perf. mid./pass. ind.) *has
been granted*

γεγενημένοις = (perf. part. γίγνομαι)
things that happened

διάνοια, -ας, f. = *notion, idea*

ἐγνωσμένα = (perf. part. γιγνώσκω)
judged, determined

ἐπιτηδεύω = *practice, pursue (a form
of behavior)*

ζημία, -ας, f. = *penalty*

μέγεθος, -ους, n. = *size, greatness*

μὲν οὖν = (transitional particles) *now
then*

μόνος, -η, -ον = *alone*; (neut. acc. as
adverb) *only*

ὀλιγαρχία, -ας, f. = *oligarchy* (form of
government in which a small class,
defined by wealth, holds political
power)

ὀλιγώρως διακεῖσθαι = *be of a careless
or neglectful disposition*

πεπονθότες = (perf. part. act. πάσχω)
having suffered

-περ = intensifying suffix added to
relative words, adding notion *the very
one which, exactly the one which*

περὶ πολλοῦ ποιεῖσθαι = *consider to be
of great importance* (here with
articular inf. as its object)

συγγνώμη, -ης, f. = *forgiveness, pardon*

τιμωρία, -ας, f. = *retribution, right to
vengeance*

Perfect System

1. *The Aspect of the Perfect Tense.* The perfect stem of a Greek verb conveys the aspect of completed action with a continuing or permanent result. The Greek perfect indicative thus refers to a continuing present state and is a primary tense: it lacks augment, and it governs the subjunctive in primary sequence. The aspect of the perfect is especially clear in verbs whose perfects are best translated by an English present:

ἀποθνῄσκω, *I am dying*   τέθνηκα, *I have died and am now dead =*
                                 I am dead

ἵστημι, *I cause to stand*   ἕστηκα (intransitive perfect act.), *I have*
                                 adopted a stance and am now standing
                                 = I stand

(ἀνα)μιμνήσκω, *I call to*   μέμνημαι (perfect middle), *I have called*
    mind   *to my own mind and am now remem-*
                                 bering = I remember

ὄμνυμι, *I swear an oath*   ὀμώμοκα, *I have sworn an oath and am*
                                 now bound by it = I am under oath

The aspect of the perfect is also clear in certain legalistic uses of the supplementary participle:

δείξω τοῦτον πολλά τ' ἄλλα ἠδικηκότα καὶ τάλαντον κεκλοφότα.
I'll prove that this man is guilty of doing many other wrongs and of
    stealing a talent. [literally, *is in the state of having done wrongs and of*
    having stolen]

The close association of the perfect stem with states and conditions helps explain the existence of many intransitive perfects that correspond in meaning to middle/passive present forms and intransitive aorists:

ἵσταμαι, *I am placing myself, I am standing*
    ἔστην (intransitive strong aor.), *I stood*; ἕστηκα (intransitive perfect
    act.), *I stand*

πείθομαι, *I obey, trust*
    πέποιθα (intransitive perfect), *I have placed my trust in and now trust*
    = I trust

ἀπόλλυμαι, *I am being ruined, destroyed*
ἀπόλωλα (intransitive perfect), *I have been ruined and am now ruined*
= *I am ruined, destroyed*

In early Greek the perfect referred principally to the continuing state brought about in the subject of the action: for instance, μεμάθηκα, *I have learned and now know (the lesson)*. In classical Attic, however, the use of the perfect was extended so that it could also express a permanent result affecting the object: e.g., τέθηκα, *I have placed something (and it remains in position)*, δέδωκα, *I have given something (and it remains given)*.

2. *Reduplication.* Reduplication is a modification of a verb stem in which the initial consonant (or occasionally the initial vowel plus consonant) is repeated. Reduplication with iota is found in a limited number of present stems (cf. U19.7b). Reduplication with epsilon is the regular marker of a perfect stem, but reduplication may be effected in other ways as well. (By learning the principal parts, the student need not determine in each case which variety of reduplication is relevant to each verb.)

a. If the initial sound of the verb stem is a single consonant (other than rho) or a plosive followed by nasal or liquid, the initial sound is repeated with epsilon. In accordance with Grassmann's law (U19.5), an initial aspirated plosive is reduplicated with the corresponding unaspirated voiceless plosive.

present	*perfect active*	*perfect mid./pass.*
λείπω	λέλοιπα	λέλειμμαι
τρέφω	τέτροφα	τέθραμμαι[1]
φεύγω	πέφευγα	— —

b. If the initial sound of the verb stem is a double consonant or rho, reduplication looks no different than syllabic augment. As with augment, an initial rho is doubled.

present	*perfect active*	*perfect mid./pass.*
ζητέω	ἐζήτηκα	— —
ῥίπτω	ἔρριφα	ἔρριμμαι
γιγνώσκω	ἔγνωκα	ἔγνωσμαι
(root γνω-)		

---

1. Grassmann's law applies doubly to the perfect of τρέφω: the root is in fact θρεφ-, but Grassmann's law makes this appear as τρέφω in the present and τέτροφα in the perfect active; in the perfect middle/passive, however, the aspiration at the end of the stem is lost because of other euphonic changes and so the aspirate at the beginning of the verb stem is retained (but the reduplication is still τε-).

c. If the initial sound of the verb stem is a vowel, reduplication normally looks no different than temporal augment. Since the reduplication is a preverb element, the accent cannot precede it (cf. U16.5): in short stems a circumflex will appear on the reduplicated/augmented vowel when *U* is short.

present	perfect act.	perfect mid./pass.
ἄγω	ἦχα	ἦγμαι
παράγω	παρῆχα	παρῆγμαι
εὑρίσκω	ηὕρηκα	ηὕρημαι
ἀφικνέομαι	— —	ἀφῖγμαι

d. A few verbs beginning with a vowel reduplicate the initial vowel *and* consonant and lengthen the vowel that follows reduplication. This was called "Attic reduplication" by ancient grammarians (though it occurred in other dialects as well).

present	perfect(s)	from root
ἀκούω	ἀκήκοα	ἀκο-
ὄμνυμι	ὀμώμοκα	ὀμο-
ἐλέγχω	ἐλήλεγμαι	ἐλεγχ-
φέρω	ἐνήνοχα, ἐνήνεγμαι	*ἐνοκ-, *ἐνεκ-

e. A few verbs have odd reduplication because of the disappearance of a consonant at the beginning of the root. For instance, λαμβάνω produces perfects εἴληφα and εἴλημμαι (from root *σληπ-),[1] and λαγχάνω produces εἴληχα.[2]

3. *Perfect Active System.* The fourth principal part of the Greek verb is the first person singular perfect active indicative. This form provides the stem used in generating the perfect active indicative, subjunctive, optative, imperative, infinitive, and participle, the pluperfect active indicative, and the future perfect active indicative, optative, infinitive, and participle. Many of these forms, however, are rarely or never found for any given verb.

Perfect stems may be classed in two groups. The more primitive stems have no tense suffix, and some plosive stems of this kind have their final consonant aspirated in the perfect. These perfects are called "second" perfects:

---

1. The perfect is thus derived from *σεσληπ- —> *ἐσληπ- (loss of initial sigma) —> *εἴληπ- (loss of aspiration and loss of internal sigma with initial vowel lengthened in compensation).

2. The unusual form of reduplication in this verb is due to analogy with λαμβάνω; so too perfect διείλεγμαι from διαλέγομαι.

for example, πεφευγ-, λελοιπ-; (aspirated) βεβλαφ-, πεφυλαχ-, δεδιδαχ-. The more recent stems have the tense suffix κ and are called "first" perfects: for example, λελυκ-, πεφιληκ-, μεμαθηκ- (for the addition of η, cf. future μαθήσομαι), πεπεικ- (from πείθω; for the loss of the dental before the suffix, cf. aor. ἔπεισα). Note that in verbs which show a variation of vowel grade in the different tense stems the perfect has a strong-grade form (e.g., λείπω, ἔλιπον, λέλοιπα; φεύγω, ἔφυγον, πέφευγα).

The distinction between first and second perfects is not relevant to inflection, since the same endings are used; but many of the most primitive second perfects and those second perfects which coexist with first perfects are semantically different in that they have intransitive (or sometimes virtually passive) force: for instance, transitive first perfect πέπεικα = *I have persuaded* vs. intransitive second perfect πέποιθα = *I trust*, trans. first perf. ἀπολώλεκα = *I have ruined* vs. intrans. (quasi-passive) second perf. ἀπόλωλα = *I am ruined (destroyed)*; intrans. (quasi-passive) second perf. ἔρρωγα = *I am broken* from ῥήγνυμι.

4. Inflection of Perfect Active

a. The *perfect active indicative* has tense vowel α and (basically) primary personal endings: -α, -ας, -ε, (-ατον, -ατον,) -αμεν, -ατε, -ᾱσι (the first sing. has no ending; the third sing. has vowel ε instead of α and no ending; the third plural is -ᾱσι, as for μι-verbs, from -ᾰντι).

Ex.

		2nd perfect (λείπω)	1st perfect (βουλεύω)
sing.	1st	λέλοιπα	βεβούλευκα
	2nd	λέλοιπας	βεβούλευκας
	3rd	λέλοιπε(ν)	βεβούλευκε(ν)
(dual	2nd	λελοίπατον	βεβουλεύκατον)
	(3rd	λελοίπατον	βεβουλεύκατον)
plur.	1st	λελοίπαμεν	βεβουλεύκαμεν
	2nd	λελοίπατε	βεβουλεύκατε
	3rd	λελοίπᾱσι(ν)	βεβουλεύκᾱσι(ν)

b. The *perfect active infinitive* has the ending -έναι (accent, as usual, on the syllable preceding -ναι): for example, λελοιπέναι, λελυκέναι.

c. The *perfect active participle* has masc./neuter τ-stem (suffix -ότ-) with nominatives in -ώς, -ός (recall that all other active participles are ντ-stems); the short-vowel fem. has suffix -υῖα. The accent is persistent on the vowel of the participial suffix. The full declension is shown on the next page.

DECLENSION OF PERFECT ACTIVE PARTICIPLE

		masculine	feminine	neuter
sing.	nom.	λελυκώς	λελυκυῖα	λελυκός
	gen.	λελυκότος	λελυκυίας	λελυκότος
	dat.	λελυκότι	λελυκυίᾳ	λελυκότι
	acc.	λελυκότα	λελυκυῖαν	λελυκός
(dual	n. a.	λελυκότε	λελυκυία	λελυκότε)
	(g. d.	λελυκότοιν	λελυκυίαιν	λελυκότοιν)
plur.	nom.	λελυκότες	λελυκυῖαι	λελυκότα
	gen.	λελυκότων	λελυκυιῶν	λελυκότων
	dat.	λελυκόσι(ν)	λελυκυίαις	λελυκόσι(ν)
	acc.	λελυκότας	λελυκυίας	λελυκότα

d. The *perfect active subjunctive* is found in two forms.

(1) The normal subjunctive endings -ω, -ῃς, etc., may be added to the perfect active stem: thus, λελοίπω, λελοίπῃς, etc.

(2) More commonly, a *periphrastic* ("compound-phrase") form of the subjunctive is created by using the nominative of the perfect active participle and the present subjunctive of εἰμί: thus, λελοιπὼς ὦ, plur. λελοιπότες ὦμεν, etc. (the participle will agree in gender with the subject, so with a fem. pl. subject the periphrastic form would be, e.g., 3rd pl. λελοιπυῖαι ὦσι).

e. The *perfect active optative* is found in two forms.

(1) The normal ω-verb optative endings -οιμι, -οις, etc., may be added to the perfect active stem: thus, λελοίποιμι, λελοίποις, etc.

(2) More commonly, a periphrastic form of the optative is created by using the nominative of the perfect active participle and the present optative of εἰμί: thus, λελοιπὼς εἴην, plur. λελοιπότες εἴημεν, etc. (the participle will agree in gender with the subject, so with a fem. sing. subject the periphrastic form would be, e.g., 3rd s. λελοιπυῖα εἴη).

5. *Perfect Subjunctive and Optative of* οἶδα. The irregular perfect οἶδα (U28.6) has an *e*-grade alternative stem: εἰδε- or εἰδ-. You have already learned the infinitive εἰδέναι. The participle is εἰδώς, εἰδυῖα, εἰδός; this has masc./neut. stem εἰδοτ- and normal perfect active participle declension. Also from stem εἰδε- is the subjunctive εἰδῶ, εἰδῇς, etc. (the epsilon contracts with the subj. personal endings, as in subj. of ποιέω). Likewise, the optative is conjugated like τιθείην: εἰδείην, εἰδείης, εἰδείη, (εἰδεῖτον, εἰδείτην,) εἰδεῖμεν or εἰδείημεν, εἰδεῖτε or εἰδείητε, εἰδεῖεν or εἰδείησαν.

6. *The Perfect Middle/Passive System.* The fifth principal part of the Greek verb is the first person singular perfect mid./pass. indicative. This form provides the stem used in generating the perfect mid./pass. indicative, imperative, infinitive, and participle (from which periphrastic subjunctive and optative are made), the pluperfect mid./pass. indicative, and the future perfect mid./pass. indicative, optative, infinitive, and participle. Many of these forms, however, are rarely or never found for any given verb.

The perfect middle/passive stem is a reduplicated stem and usually very similar to the perfect active stem: for example, λέλοιπα, λέλειμμαι (stem λελειπ-: note change of vowel grade); ἔρριφα, ἔρριμμαι (stem ἐρριπ-). Sometimes it is the same as that stem without active tense-suffix κ, as in vowel stems such as τετίμηκα, τετίμημαι; πεπολίτευκα, πεπολίτευμαι.

7. *Inflection of Perfect Middle/Passive.* The perfect middle/passive has inflectional endings added directly to the stem without intervening vowel. This leads to euphonic changes in the final consonant of many stems as well as in some inflectional endings. The paradigm is shown on page 287.

a. The *perfect middle/passive indicative* has primary middle endings -μαι, -σαι, -ται, etc. Because of euphonic changes, there are several patterns of inflection (illustrated in the paradigms following this section):

(1) *Stems ending in a vowel* have the endings added without changes: for example, λέλυμαι, βεβούλευμαι.
(2) *Stems with inserted σ*: verbs with present in ζ or with dental plosive stem (τ, δ, θ) and certain vowel-stem verbs have perfect mid./pass. stem in σ (ζ or dental is dropped): νομίζω, νενόμισμαι; πείθω, πέπεισμαι; τελέω, τετέλεσμαι. In conjugation, if an ending begins with σ, the resulting double σ is reduced to a single σ (thus 2nd pl. ind. νενόμισθε, inf. τετελέσθαι).
(3) *Stems ending in labial (π, β, φ) or velar (κ, γ, χ) plosive* (e.g., λέλειμμαι, πέπραγμαι) undergo euphonic assimilation (of sound or of aspiration) in most forms:

before μ, labial becomes μ (—> μμ), velar becomes γ (—> γμ)
before σθ, σ drops out and labial becomes φ (—> φθ), velar becomes χ (—> χθ)
before τ, labial becomes π (—> ππ), velar becomes κ (—> κτ)
with σ, labial combines to produce ψ, velar combines to produce ξ

(4) *Stems ending in λ* (e.g., ἤγγελμαι) have the endings added directly, but endings beginning with σθ lose the σ (as in 2nd pl. ἤγγελθε).

(5) *Stems ending in ν* have endings beginning with τ or σθ added
directly (but the σ of σθ disappears), but the ν is replaced by σ before
endings beginning with μ. The 2nd sing. form is not found. Cf.
πέφασμαι, 3rd sing. πέφανται.

Only vowel-stem perfects (type 1 above) normally form a third plural with the
ending -νται. For all other types of verb, the third plural is formed periphrastically with plural participle plus εἰσί (or ἐστί for neuters): for example,
πεπεισμένοι εἰσί, τετελεσμένα ἐστί.[1]

   b. The *perfect middle/passive infinitive* has the middle infinitive ending
-σθαι (or -θαι after a consonant, where σ drops out) and is accented on the final syllable of the stem (acute on short vowel, circumflex on long vowel):
thus, νενομίσθαι, πεποιῆσθαι.

   c. The *perfect middle/passive participle* has the middle participle ending
-μένος, -η, -ον added to the stem (with, where needed, the same euphonic
changes as for indicative endings -μαι or -μεθα). The accent of the perfect
middle/passive participle is persistent on the participial suffix -μέν-, a feature
which distinguishes the perfect participle from all other middle participles in
-μενος: for example, πεπαιδευμένος, πεφυλαγμένος.

   d. The *perfect middle/passive subjunctive* is normally formed periphrastically with the perfect middle/passive participle plus subjunctive of εἰμί: thus,
λελειμμένος ὦ, etc. A very few verbs with stem in η whose perfects are
especially common sometimes show a simple form of subjunctive: for example, from μέμνημαι = *I remember*, μεμνῶμαι, μεμνῇ, μεμνῆται, etc.; from
κέκτημαι = *I possess*, κεκτῶμαι, etc.

   e. The *perfect middle/passive optative* is normally formed periphrastically with the perfect middle/passive participle plus optative of εἰμί: thus,
λελειμμένος εἴην, etc. A very few verbs with stem in η whose perfects are
especially common sometimes show a simple form of optative: for example,
from μέμνημαι, μεμνῄμην or μεμνῴμην; from κέκτημαι, κεκτῄμην or κεκτῴ-
μην.

---

1. In poetry and a few times in early Attic prose a simple 3rd pl. form is formed with the ending
-αται (an alternative development of the ending that usually appears as -νται): τετάχαται =
τεταγμένοι εἰσί.

PERFECT MIDDLE/PASSIVE INDICATIVE, INFINITIVE, PARTICIPLE

		vowel stem λύω stem: λελῠ-	*dental plosive stem* πείθω stem: πεπεισ-	*labial plosive stem* γράφω stem: γεγραπ-
sing.	1st	λέλυμαι	πέπεισμαι	γέγραμμαι
	2nd	λέλυσαι	πέπεισαι	γέγραψαι
	3rd	λέλυται	πέπεισται	γέγραπται
(dual	2nd	λέλυσθον	πέπεισθον	γέγραφθον)
	(3rd	λέλυσθον	πέπεισθον	γέγραφθον)
plur.	1st	λελύμεθα	πεπείσμεθα	γεγράμμεθα
	2nd	λέλυσθε	πέπεισθε	γέγραφθε
	3rd	λέλυνται	πεπεισμένοι εἰσί	γεγραμμένοι εἰσί
infinitive		λελύσθαι	πεπεῖσθαι	γεγράφθαι
participle		λελυμένος	πεπεισμένος	γεγραμμένος

		velar plosive stem πράττω stem: πεπρᾱγ-	*stem in* λ ἀγγέλλω stem: ἠγγελ-	*stem in* ν φαίνω stem: πεφαν-, πεφασ-
sing.	1st	πέπραγμαι	ἤγγελμαι	πέφασμαι
	2nd	πέπραξαι	ἤγγελσαι	—
	3rd	πέπρακται	ἤγγελται	πέφανται
(dual	2nd	πέπραχθον	ἤγγελθον	πέφανθον)
	(3rd	πέπραχθον	ἤγγελθον	πέφανθον)
plur.	1st	πεπράγμεθα	ἠγγέλμεθα	πεφάσμεθα
	2nd	πέπραχθε	ἤγγελθε	πέφανθε
	3rd	πεπραγμένοι εἰσί	ἠγγελμένοι εἰσί	πεφασμένοι εἰσί
infinitive		πεπρᾶχθαι	ἠγγέλθαι	πεφάνθαι
participle		πεπραγμένος	ἠγγελμένος	πεφασμένος

8. *Dative of Agent.* The personal agent with a perfect or pluperfect passive verb form is normally expressed by the *dative of agent* (a form of the dative of interest) rather than by ὑπό + gen. (as is usual with other passives): for example, τὰ τούτοις πεπραγμένα = *the things done by these men.*

9. *Synopsis of Verb Forms.* Now that the student has learned so many
verb forms, an effective way to practice and review verbal conjugation without
writing out over a hundred forms is to give a *synopsis* of a verb in a particular
person and number. This consists of the finite forms of that person and number
in all possible tenses, voices, and moods, plus the infinitives and participles
from each tense stem. Here is an almost complete synopsis of λείπω in the
third person singular (it does not include the imperative or the pluperfect or
future perfect, which are yet to be learned).

	present system active	future system active	aorist system active	perfect system active
ind.	λείπει	λείψει	ἔλιπε	λέλοιπε
subj.	λείπῃ	—	λίπῃ	λελοίπῃ or λελοιπὼς ᾖ
opt.	λείποι	λείψοι	λίποι	λελοίποι or λελοιπὼς εἴη
inf.	λείπειν	λείψειν	λιπεῖν	λελοιπέναι
part.	λείπων	λείψων	λιπών	λελοιπώς
imp. ind.	ἔλειπε			

	present system mid./pass.	future system middle	aorist system middle	perfect system mid./pass.
ind.	λείπεται	λείψεται	ἐλίπετο	λέλειπται
subj.	λείπηται	—	λίπηται	λελειμμένος ᾖ
opt.	λείποιτο	λείψοιτο	λίποιτο	λελειμμένος εἴη
inf.	λείπεσθαι	λείψεσθαι	λιπέσθαι	λελεῖφθαι
part.	λειπόμενος	λειψόμενος	λιπόμενος	λελειμμένος
imp. ind.	ἐλείπετο			

	future system passive	aorist system passive
ind.	λειφθήσεται	ἐλείφθη
subj.	—	λειφθῇ
opt.	λειφθήσοιτο	λειφθείη
inf.	λειφθήσεσθαι	λειφθῆναι
part.	λειφθησόμενος	λειφθείς

WHAT TO STUDY AND DO

1. Learn the conjugational patterns of the perfect system.
2. Learn the vocabulary of this unit.
3. Continue to study the principal parts of the verbs learned to date.
4. Do the exercises of this unit.

VOCABULARY

verbs

ὄλλῡμι (poetic) = ἀπόλλῡμι (prose) (ἀπο), ἀπολέω, (trans. aor.) ἀπώλεσα and (intrans. aor.) ἀπωλόμην, (trans. perf.) ἀπολώλεκα and (intrans. perf.) ἀπό-λωλα — destroy, kill; lose; (mid. and intrans. aor. and perf.) perish, die

ὄμνῡμι, ὀμέομαι, ὤμοσα, ὀμώμοκα, ὀμώμομαι or ὀμώμοσμαι, ὠμόθην or ὠμόσθην — swear; swear to, swear by; swear that (+ inf.)

ῥίπτω, ῥίψω, ἔρρῑψα, ἔρρῑφα, ἔρρῑμμαι, ἐρρίφθην or ἐρρίφην [ῑ in all stems except ἐρρίφην] — throw, hurl

verbs whose perfects have present meaning

κτάομαι, κτήσομαι, ἐκτησάμην, κέκτημαι, ἐκτήθην — acquire, get; (perfect system) possess, hold, have

μιμνήσκω (already learned in U29); perfect μέμνημαι — (perfect system) remember

καλέω (already learned in U18), perfect mid./pass. κέκλημαι — (perf. mid./pass. system) have been named, be called

EXERCISES

I. Identify each form completely.

1. ὀμωμόκασι
2. ἐρριφέναι
3. μεμνημένοι
4. κέκρυπται
5. πεφύλακται
6. συμβεβηκός

7. διείλεχθε
8. ἀκηκόατε
9. δεδογμένα
10. κέκτηνται
11. ἀπολωλότα
12. ἀπολωλεκυῖαν
13. βεβλάφαμεν
14. τέταξαι
15. πέφευγε
16. τετιμημένους
17. λεληθότι
18. τεταχέναι

19. κεκλῆσθαι
20. τεθράμμεθα
21. τετράφθαι
22. τεθήκασι
23. μεμαθηκός
24. πεπραγέναι
25. πεπωκόσι
26. ἐδηδοκυιῶν
27. πεπύσμεθα
28. ὠργισμένου
29. ἐληλυθυιῶν
30. πεπιστευμέναι ὦσιν

31. ἔσπεισθε
32. πέφηνας
33. πεπομφέναι
34. πεπόνθαμεν
35. κεκτῶντο
36. τετμῆσθαι
37. ἡττήμεθα
38. νενόμικα
39. τεθαυμάκασι
40. εἴρηκα

II. Write in Greek.
  1. 2nd s. perf. act. ind. of "throw"
  2. 1st pl. perf. m/p ind. of "honor"
  3. perf. act. inf. of "hate"
  4. 3rd pl. perf. act. ind. of "think proper"
  5. 3rd pl. perf. m/p subj. of "snatch"
  6. perf. m/p inf. of "be afraid"
  7. 3rd s. perf. m/p ind. of "be called"
  8. masc. nom. pl. perf. act. part. of "find"
  9. 3rd s. perf. act. opt. of "learn"
  10. fem. dat. pl. perf. m/p part. of "betray"
  11. 1st s. fem. perf. act. opt. of "prevent"
  12. acc. pl. neut. perf. m/p part. of "become"

III.   Write synopses of the following in all the tenses and moods you know,
including infinitives and participles:

1. αἱρέω in 3rd sing.
2. τίθημι in 2nd pl.
3. ῥίπτω in 3rd pl.
4. βουλεύω in 1st pl.

IV. Reading: Lysias, *Oration* 1.4–6 (continuation of U36, Ex. III).

ἡγοῦμαι δέ, ὦ ἄνδρες, τοῦτό με δεῖν ἐπιδεῖξαι, ὡς ἐμοίχευεν
Ἐρατοσθένης τὴν γυναῖκα τὴν ἐμὴν καὶ ἐκείνην τε διέφθειρε καὶ τοὺς
παῖδας τοὺς ἐμοὺς ᾔσχυνε καὶ ἐμὲ αὐτὸν ὕβρισεν εἰς τὴν οἰκίαν τὴν ἐμὴν
εἰσιών, καὶ οὔτε ἔχθρα ἐμοὶ καὶ ἐκείνῳ οὐδεμία ἦν πλὴν ταύτης, οὔτε
χρημάτων ἕνεκα ἔπραξα ταῦτα, ἵνα πλούσιος ἐκ πένητος γένωμαι, οὔτε
ἄλλου κέρδους οὐδενὸς πλὴν τῆς κατὰ τοὺς νόμους τιμωρίας. ἐγὼ τοίνυν ἐξ
ἀρχῆς ὑμῖν ἅπαντα ἐπιδείξω τὰ ἐμαυτοῦ πράγματα, οὐδὲν παραλείπων,
ἀλλὰ λέγων τὰ ἀληθῆ· ταύτην γὰρ ἐμαυτῷ μόνην ἡγοῦμαι σωτηρίαν, ἐὰν
ὑμῖν εἰπεῖν ἅπαντα δυνηθῶ τὰ πεπραγμένα. ἐγὼ γάρ, ὦ Ἀθηναῖοι, ἐπειδὴ
ἔδοξέ μοι γῆμαι καὶ γυναῖκα ἠγαγόμην εἰς τὴν οἰκίαν, τὸν μὲν ἄλλον

χρόνον οὕτω <u>διεκείμην</u> ὥστε μήτε <u>λυπεῖν</u> μήτε λίαν <u>ἐπ᾽ ἐκείνῃ εἶναι</u> ὅ τι ἂν ἐθέλῃ ποιεῖν, ἐφύλαττόν τε ὡς <u>οἷόν τε</u> ἦν, καὶ <u>προσεῖχον τὸν νοῦν</u> ὥσπερ <u>εἰκὸς</u> ἦν. ἐπειδὴ δέ μοι παιδίον γίγνεται, ἐπίστευον ἤδη καὶ πάντα τὰ ἐμαυτοῦ ἐκείνῃ παρέδωκα, ἡγούμενος ταύτην <u>οἰκειότητα</u> μεγίστην εἶναι.

Underlined Words

αἰσχύνω, aor. ᾔσχυνα = *dishonor, bring shame upon*

διαφθείρω, aor. διέφθειρα = *corrupt, seduce*

διάκειμαι = *be disposed* (+ adv. of manner)

εἰκός = (neut. adj., nom. s.) *reasonable*

εἰσιών = compound of εἰς: guess the meaning

ἐπ᾽ ἐκείνῃ εἶναι = *to be in her own power* (impersonal, + inf. ποιεῖν as subject)

Ἐρατοσθένης, -ους, m. = *Eratosthenes* (the man who was killed by Euphiletus, the speaker)

κέρδος, -ους, n. = *profit, financial gain*

λυπέω = *vex, cause pain or annoyance*

μοιχεύω = *commit adultery with* (a woman)

μόνος, -η, -ον = *sole, only*

οἰκειότης, -ότητος, f. = *(bond of) intimacy or friendship*

οἷόν τε = (neut. s. nom.) *possible*

παραλείπω = *omit*

πένης, πένητος, m. = *poor man* (the idiom γενέσθαι ἐκ conveys *be changed from X into Y*)

προσέχω τὸν νοῦν = *apply one's mind, pay attention*

τιμωρία, -ας, f. = *retribution, vengeance*

τοίνυν = (postpositive particle) *well then*

ὑβρίζω = *commit an outrage against, insult*

Object Clauses with Verbs of Effort; Subordinate Clauses in Indirect Discourse; Attraction

1. *Object Clauses with Verbs of Effort.* Verbs of effort govern object clauses introduced by ὅπως (negative ὅπως μή) and usually containing the future indicative in both primary and secondary sequence. Verbs of effort include those meaning *to strive* or *to bring about* (πράττω, σπουδάζω, παρα-σκευάζομαι), *to plan* (βουλεύομαι), *to take care* or *to take pains* (ἐπιμελέ-ομαι, ἐπιμέλομαι, impersonal μέλει), *to see to it that* (ὁράω, σκοπέω), or *to be on one's guard* (εὐλαβέομαι, φυλάττομαι).

Ex.

οἱ Ἀθηναῖοι πράττουσιν ὅπως μὴ ὁ Φίλιππος τῶν ἄκρων κρατήσει.

The Athenians are bringing it about that Philip will not get control of the heights.

παρεσκευάσαντο ὅπως σιτία ἕξουσιν.

They made preparations so that they would have provisions.

σκόπει [imperative] ὅπως ὡς ῥᾷστα ἄπιμεν.[1]

Consider how (see to it that) we'll depart as easily as possible.

Occasionally the future optative is used in place of the future indicative in secondary sequence:

ἐπεμέλετο ὅπως μήτε ἄσιτοι μήτε ἄποτοί ποτε ἔσοιντο.

He took care that they would never be without food or water.

Sometimes a purpose clause with the subjunctive (or optative in secondary sequence) is used with verbs of effort instead of an object clause:

ὅρα [imperative] ὅπως μή σε ἀπατήσῃ.

See to it that he doesn't deceive you.

---

1. Remember that the present ind. of εἶμι is treated as a future in Attic.

Special idiom: sometimes a ὅπως-clause with the future indicative is used without an introductory verb (that is, in ellipsis) to express an urgent warning:

ὅπως μηδενὶ ταῦτα λέξεις.
Make sure you don't tell this to anyone!

2. *Subordinate Clauses in Indirect Discourse.* When a complex sentence is transformed into an indirect statement, the main clause of the statement is expressed by whichever of the three indirect-discourse constructions (inf., part., ὅτι-clause) is appropriate with the governing verb, but the verbs of the subordinate clause(s) normally remain in finite form and are treated according to the following rules:

a. After a *primary-tense* governing verb, the subordinate-clause verbs remain unchanged in tense and mood.

direct: ἐὰν ταῦτα ποιήσῃς, μισήσω σε.   [fut. more vivid condition]
            If you do this, I'll hate you.
indirect: (inf.) ἐὰν ταῦτα ποιήσῃς, μισήσειν σέ φησιν.
            (ὅτι-clause) λέγει ὅτι ἐὰν ταῦτα ποιήσῃς, μισήσει σε.
            (part.) ἀκούομεν αὐτὸν μισήσοντά σε ἐὰν ταῦτα ποιήσῃς.
            He says (we hear) that he will hate you if you do this.

b. After a *secondary-tense* governing verb, *primary-tense* indicatives and subjunctives are usually changed to the same tense of the optative (a direct subj. with ἄν becomes an indirect opt. without ἄν), but are sometimes left unchanged.

indirect: (inf.) εἰ ταῦτα ποιήσειας, μισήσειν σε ἔφη.
            (ὅτι-clause) εἶπεν ὅτι εἰ ταῦτα ποιήσειας μισήσοι σε.
            (part.) ἠκούσαμεν αὐτὸν μισήσοντά σε εἰ ταῦτα ποιήσειας.
            He said (we heard) that he would hate you if you did (were to do, should do) this.

direct: ὁ στρατιώτης ὃν ἡ ἑταίρα φιλεῖ ἀπέθανεν ἐν τῇ μάχῃ.
            The soldier whom the courtesan loves died in the battle.
indirect: ἤγγειλαν τὸν στρατιώτην ὃν ἡ ἑταίρα φιλοίη ἀποθανόντα ἐν τῇ μάχῃ.
            They announced that the soldier whom the courtesan loves died in the battle.

c. After a *secondary-tense* governing verb, *secondary-tense* indicatives (including indicative with ἄν) and optatives remain unchanged.

direct: ὅστις ἔλθοι τοῦτο ἠρώτα.   [past gen. rel. clause]
            Whoever came always asked this question.

indirect: εἶπον ὅτι ὅστις ἔλθοι τοῦτο ἠρώτα.
            I said that whoever came always asked this question.

direct: ταῦτα ἃ ἐποιεῖτε οὐ καλά ἦν. [simple rel. clause]
            These things you were doing were not good.

indirect: οὐκ ἐνόμιζον ταῦτα ἃ ἐποιεῖτε καλά εἶναι.
            They didn't consider these things you were doing to be good.

3. *Atttraction.* It is characteristic of Greek that words referring to the same person are sometimes all expressed in the same case even though some of the words might be expected, according to strict grammar, to differ in case. This phenomenon is called *attraction*, because the case expected according to syntactic function is attracted into another case. The student has already learned some constructions which feature attraction.

a. *Attraction* of predicate nouns or adjectives *with the infinitive*. The subject of an infinitive, when expressed, is normally in the accusative, and so predicate nouns or adjectives are accusative in agreement (cf. U9.4, 10.4, 20.8). But when the subject of the infinitive is the same as the (nominative) subject of the governing verb, the subject of the infinitive is unexpressed and predicate nouns or adjectives are in the nominative by attraction: ἔφη ἀγαθὸς εἶναι. Likewise, when the subject of the infinitive is the same as a person or thing mentioned in the genitive or dative in close proximity to the infinitive (usually as gen. or dat. object of the main verb), the subject of the infinitive is usually unexpressed and predicate nouns or adjectives may either appear in the acc. or be attracted into the gen. or dat.

It is in your power (for you) to be virtuous.
ἔξεστι ὑμῖν <u>ἀγαθοὺς</u> εἶναι.   [no attraction, ὑμᾶς understood]
ἔξεστι ὑμῖν <u>ἀγαθοῖς</u> εἶναι.   [dative by attraction to ὑμῖν]

He exhorted the soldiers not to prove themselves cowards.
παρεκελεύετο τοῖς στρατιώταις μὴ <u>κακοῖς</u> γενέσθαι.

They asked Cyrus to show himself as enthusiastic as possible.
ἐδέοντο τοῦ Κύρου ὡς <u>προθυμοτάτου</u> γενέσθαι.

I beseech you to prepare yourselves, since you see that Philip is strong and you see that your allies are despondent.
δέομαι ὑμῶν παρασκευάζεσθαι, <u>ὁρῶντας</u> μὲν τὸν Φίλιππον ἰσχυρόν, <u>ὁρῶντας</u> δὲ τοὺς συμμάχους ἀθύμους ὄντας.
[no attraction: ὁρῶντας is acc. pl. masc. agreeing with the unexpressed subject of inf., ὑμᾶς]

Similarly, as already learned in U28.5, when an infinitive copula depends on a participle, a predicate noun or adjective agrees in case with the participle:

τοῖς φάσκουσι διδασκάλοις εἶναι
to those who claim they are teachers

b. *Attraction of the Relative Pronoun.* A relative pronoun normally takes its case from its construction in its own clause. But sometimes a relative is attracted into the case of its *adjacent* antecedent, especially when the relative would have been accusative and the antecedent is genitive or dative:

ἄξιοι τῆς ἐλευθερίας <u>ἧς</u> κέκτησθε
worthy of the freedom which you possess
   [unattracted relative would be ἥν, direct object of κέκτησθε]

σὺν τοῖς θησαυροῖς <u>οἷς</u> ὁ πατὴρ κατέλιπεν
together with the treasure which his father had left him
   [unattracted relative would be οὕς, direct object of κατέλιπεν]

Attraction is especially frequent when the antecedent is a (relatively unemphatic) neuter demonstrative. Indeed, the usual idiom in Greek is to omit such an antecedent and have the relative pronoun in the case which the antecedent would have had:

   He gave everyone a share of the things he had received [or *of what he had received*].
   idiomatic form: ὧν ἔλαβε πᾶσι μετέδωκε.
   fuller form: <u>τούτων</u> ἃ ἔλαβε πᾶσι μετέδωκε.
      [partitive gen. antecedent and acc. relative as direct object]

   I provide witnesses of whatever things I say.
   idiomatic form: μάρτυρας <u>ὧν</u> ἂν λέγω παρέχω.   [instead of τούτων ἃ]

   He wrongs the city in these respects in addition to the ways he wrongs individuals.
   idiomatic form: ταῦτα ἀδικεῖ τὴν πόλιν πρὸς οἷς τοὺς ἰδιώτας ἀδικεῖ.
      [instead of πρὸς τούτοις ἃ . . . ἀδικεῖ]

c. *Inverse Attraction with Relative Pronoun.* An antecedent in the nominative (or, less often, the accusative) is sometimes attracted to the case of the relative pronoun:

ἔλεγον ὅτι Λακεδαιμόνιοι ὧν δέονται <u>πάντων</u> πεπραγότες εἶεν.
They said that the Lacedaemonians had accomplished everything they needed.
   [instead of πάντα πεπραγότες εἶεν]

<u>τὸν ἄνδρα τοῦτον,</u> ὃν πάλαι ζητεῖς . . . οὗτός ἐστιν ἐνθάδε.
(Sophocles) *This man, whom you have long been seeking, . . . is here.*
   [instead of ὁ ἀνὴρ οὗτος . . . ἐστίν: note repetition of the demonstrative after the intervening clause]

A special idiom which displays inverse attraction is the use of oblique cases of
οὐδεὶς ὅστις οὐ = *everyone*, deriving from οὐδείς ἐστιν ὅστις οὐ + verb of relative clause.

> οὐδένα κίνδυνον ὅντινα οὐχ ὑπέμειναν.
> *They endured every (possible) danger.*
> [instead of fuller form οὐδείς ἐστι κίνδυνος ὅντινα οὐχ ὑπέμειναν,
> *There is no danger which they did not endure.*]

d. *Incorporation of the Antecedent.* A stylistic variation related to attraction is the incorporation of the antecedent word into the relative clause, so that
it has the same case as the relative and the relative functions as adjective instead of pronoun. Again, this is more common when the antecedent would
have been nominative or accusative (in the main clause) than when it would
have been genitive or dative.

> εἰ ἔστιν, ἣν σὺ πρότερον ἔλεγες <u>ἀρετήν</u>, ἀληθής . . .
> *if the virtue of which you were speaking before is true . . .*
> [instead of εἰ ἔστιν ἡ ἀρετή, ἣν ἔλεγες . . .]
> οὐκ ἔστιν ἥτις τοῦτ᾿ ἂν Ἑλληνὶς <u>γυνὴ</u> ἔτλη
> (Euripides) *There is no Greek woman who would have dared to do this.*
> [instead of οὐκ ἔστιν Ἑλληνὶς γυνὴ ἥτις ἂν ἔτλη]

WHAT TO STUDY AND DO

1. Study the grammatical constructions presented above.
2. Learn the vocabulary of this unit.
3. Do the exercises of this unit.

VOCABULARY

nouns

θυμός, θυμοῦ, m.	spirit; seat of courage, anger, emotion, etc. [enthymeme, thymus]
ἰδιώτης, ἰδιώτου, m.	private person (i.e., not an official or professional), individual; layman [idiot]
μάρτυς, μάρτυρος, m. or f. (dat. pl. μάρτυσι)	witness [martyr]
μισθός, μισθοῦ, m.	hire; pay, wages
τέχνη, τέχνης, f.	art, skill, craft [technical, technology]
τόξον, τόξου, n.	bow [toxic]
τοξότης, τοξότου, m.	bowman, archer

some alpha-privative and related adjectives

ἄδηλος, ἄδηλον	unseen; unknown, obscure, uncertain
ἀδύνατος, ἀδύνατον	unable, weak; impossible [adynaton]
δυνατός, δυνατή, δυνατόν	strong, able; possible
ἄθυμος, ἄθυμον	discouraged, spiritless
πρόθυμος, πρόθυμον	ready, willing, eager; bearing good will
ῥάθυμος, ῥάθυμον	easygoing, indifferent
ἄκων, ἄκουσα, ἆκον	unwilling, under constraint (when used in predicate
(masc./neut. stem ἀκοντ-)	position agreeing with subject, may be translated in English as adverb *unwillingly*)
ἑκών, ἑκοῦσα, ἑκόν (masc./neut. stem ἑκόντ-)[1]	willing (when used in predicate position agreeing with subject, may be translated in English as adverb *willingly*)
ἀνάξιος, ἀνάξιον	unworthy
ἄνομος, ἄνομον	lawless, impious [anomie, anomophyllous]
νόμιμος, νομίμη, νόμιμον	customary; lawful; legitimate
ἄποτος, ἄποτον	not drinkable; not drinking, without water or drink
ἀσαφής, ἀσαφές	indistinct, uncertain
ἄσιτος, ἄσιτον	without food
ἄτιμος, ἄτιμον	without honor; deprived of citizen rights
ἄφθονος, ἄφθονον	free from envy; (more commonly) plentiful
φθονερός, φθονερά, φθονερόν	envious, jealous

verbs

ἀθροίζω, ἀθροίσω, ἤθροισα, ἤθροικα, ἤθροισμαι, ἠθροίσθην	gather together
ἀπατάω, ἀπατήσω, ἠπάτησα, ἠπάτηκα, ἠπάτημαι, ἠπατήθην	cheat, deceive
ἐξαπατάω (ἐξ)	deceive, trick
εὐλαβέομαι, εὐλαβήσομαι, ηὐλαβήθην	beware, take care, take precautions
θύω, θύσω, ἔθυσα, τέθυκα, τέθυμαι, ἐτύθην[2]	offer by burning, sacrifice

---

1. ἑκών is in fact a strong aorist participle of a verb which survived only in this form. The non-Attic form of ἄκων is uncontracted ἀέκων, an alpha-privative compound derived from ἑκών.

2. ῡ in the first three principal parts, ῠ in the last three.

κλίνω, κλινέω, ἔκλινα,   cause to lean, slope, or lie down; (pass.) lie down,
    κέκλιμαι, ἐκλίθην or   recline   [heteroclite, clinic]
    (compounds) -εκλίνην¹
κομίζω, κομιέω, ἐκόμισα,   take care of; carry, convey; (mid.) acquire
    κεκόμικα, κεκόμισμαι,
    ἐκομίσθην
μέλω, μελήσω, ἐμέλησα,   (poetic) be a concern to (+ dat. of person); (poetic)
    μεμέληκα   take care of, care for (+ gen.)
       μέλει   (impersonal, used in prose and verse) it concerns,
                                  it is an object of concern to (+ dat. of person + inf.
                                  or + gen. of thing)
       ἐπιμέλομαι or ἐπι-   take care of, have charge of (+ gen.)
       μελέομαι, ἐπιμελ-
       ήσομαι, ἐπιμεμέ-
       λημαι, ἐπεμελήθην
σκέπτομαι, σκέψομαι,   view, examine, consider   [sceptic]
    ἐσκεψάμην, ἔσκεμμαι²
σκοπέω or σκοπέομαι   look at; examine, consider   [telescope]
σπεύδω, σπεύσω, ἔσπευσα   seek eagerly, strive (+ inf.); (intrans.) rush, hasten
σπουδάζω, σπουδάσομαι,   be serious, be earnest; be eager (+ inf.)
    ἐσπούδασα, ἐσπούδακα,
    ἐσπούδασμαι, ἐσπουδάσθην

EXERCISES

I.   Render into Greek.³

(1) And let no one of you believe that we Greeks are in a worse condition because the soldiers of Cyrus, though formerly positioned with us, have now revolted. (2) For these men are still more cowardly than the ones we have defeated. (3) For they abandoned us and fled from those men. (4) And it is much better to see those who are willing to begin a flight stationed with the enemy than (to see them) in our ranks [use sing. of τάξις, τάξεως, f.]. (5) And do not be afraid of the cavalrymen of the enemy, though they are numerous.

---

1. The ι is short by etymology and short in fut., perf., and aor. pass., but long in pres. and aor. act. (both because of compensatory lengthening in the development of the form).

2. The present is used only in poetry (prose uses σκοπέω); the other tenses serve as the remaining tenses of σκοπέω.

3. Note to instructor: loosely based on *Anab*. 3.2.17–18.

II. Reading: Thucydides, *History of the Peloponnesian War*, 1.1–2 (two lines omitted): the proem to his work.

Θουκυδίδης Ἀθηναῖος <u>συνέγραψε</u> τὸν πόλεμον τῶν <u>Πελοποννησίων</u> καὶ Ἀθηναίων, <u>ὡς</u> ἐπολέμησαν πρὸς ἀλλήλους, ἀρξάμενος <u>εὐθὺς</u> <u>καθισταμένου</u> καὶ ἐλπίσας μέγαν τε <u>ἔσεσθαι</u> καὶ <u>ἀξιολογώτατον</u> τῶν <u>προγεγενημένων</u>. . . . <u>κίνησις</u> γὰρ αὕτη μεγίστη <u>δὴ</u> τοῖς Ἕλλησιν ἐγένετο καὶ μέρει τινὶ τῶν βαρβάρων, <u>ὡς δὲ εἰπεῖν</u> καὶ ἐπὶ <u>πλεῖστον</u> ἀνθρώπων. τὰ γὰρ πρὸ αὐτῶν καὶ τὰ <u>ἔτι</u> παλαίτερα σαφῶς μὲν εὑρεῖν διὰ χρόνου πλῆθος <u>ἀδύνατα</u> ἦν, ἐκ δὲ <u>τεκμηρίων</u> ὧν ἐπὶ μακρότατον σκοποῦντί μοι πιστεῦσαι συμβαίνει οὐ μεγάλα νομίζω γενέσθαι οὔτε κατὰ τοὺς πολέμους οὔτε εἰς τὰ ἄλλα. φαίνεται γὰρ ἡ <u>νῦν Ἑλλὰς καλουμένη</u> οὐ πάλαι <u>βεβαίως</u> οἰκουμένη, ἀλλὰ <u>μεταναστάσεις</u> τε οὖσαι <u>τὰ πρότερα</u> καὶ ῥᾳδίως ἕκαστοι <u>τὴν ἑαυτῶν</u> <u>ἀπολείποντες</u> <u>βιαζόμενοι</u> ὑπό τινων αἰεὶ πλειόνων.

Underlined Words

ἀδύνατα: to be translated as if singular (ἀδύνατον ἦν εὑρεῖν); this use of the plural neuter predicate adj. is archaic. Note that the phrase τὰ γὰρ . . . παλαίτερα is thus acc., serving first as object of εὑρεῖν, then as subject of indirect-discourse inf. γενέσθαι.

αἰεί = (here) *on each occasion*

ἀξιόλογος, -ον = *noteworthy*

ἀπολείπω: compound of ἀπο-; guess the meaning

βέβαιος, -α, -ον = *secure, firm, fixed*

βιάζομαι = *be forced, be constrained*

δή = (adv.) *indeed* (emphasizes preceding adj.)

ἔσεσθαι: indirect-discourse inf. with subject τὸν πόλεμον understood from context

ἔτι = (adv.) *still, even*

εὐθύς = (adv.) *immediately, straightaway*

ἡ νῦν Ἑλλὰς καλουμένη: understand χώρα or γῆ = *land* (*the land that is now called Hellas*)

καθισταμένου: temporal genitive absolute, with noun τοῦ πολέμου understood from the context

κίνησις, -εως, f. = *movement, unrest*

μετανάστασις, -εως, f. = *migration* (with this noun and with ἕκαστοι in the next phrase, understand the verb φαίνονται to govern the supplementary participles)

Πελοποννήσιοι, -ων, m. = *Peloponnesians* (that is, the Lacedaemonians and their allies, most of whom were located in the Peloponnese [southern Greece])

πλεῖστον: supply a noun like *extent* or *portion* in translating this word

προγίγνομαι = *happen before*

συγγράφω = *compose (an account of)*

τὰ πρότερα = (adv. acc.) *previously*

τεκμήριον, -ου, n. = *indication, piece of evidence*

τὴν ἑαυτῶν: understand χώρα or γῆ = *land*

ὡς = (here) *how*

ὡς εἰπεῖν = *so to speak* (frozen idiom; epexegetic [result] infinitive)

Temporal Clauses with ἕως and the Like; πρίν; Assimilation of Mood

---

1. *Temporal Clauses with ἕως and the Like*. The conjunctions ἕως, ἔστε, μέχρι, μέχρι οὗ, ἄχρι, and ἄχρι οὗ mean *so long as*, *while* (introducing temporal clauses expressing time the same as that of the main verb) or *until* (introducing temporal clauses expressing time after that of the main verb). Many clauses introduced by these words have the same contructions as other temporal clauses (with simple, general, and future conditional force: U34), but there are also special patterns for certain types of *until*-clause.

a. Temporal clauses with ἕως, etc., referring to *definite action* in the present or past have the indicative (cf. simple conditions and simple temporal clauses with ὅτε, ἐπεί, etc.):

ἕως εἰρήνη ἦν, τῷ βασιλεῖ ἐπείθοντο.
So long as there was peace [during one specific period of time], *they obeyed the king.*

ἐκείνῃ τῇ ἡμέρᾳ ἐμάχοντο μέχρι οἱ Ἀθηναῖοι ἀπέπλευσαν.
On that day they fought until the Athenians sailed away.

b. Temporal clauses with ἕως, etc., referring to *customary or repeated action* in the present or past follow the pattern of general conditions (cf. general conditional temporal clauses with ὅτε, ἐπεί, etc.):

present time
ἕως ἂν εἰρήνη ᾖ, τῷ βασιλεῖ πείθονται.
So long as there is peace [during any number of periods of time], *they obey the king.*

ἑκάστοτε μάχονται μέχρι ἂν ὁ ἥλιος δύῃ.
They fight on each occasion until the sun sets.

past time   [not found with meaning *so long as*]
ἑκάστοτε ἐμάχοντο μέχρι ὁ ἥλιος δύοι.
They used to fight on each occasion until the sun set.

c. Temporal clauses with ἕως, etc., referring to *action in the future* usually take the construction of a future more vivid protasis, that is, subjunctive with ἄν. The main clause may have either a future indicative or, if the temporal clause expresses an *anticipated* action (*until*), a present indicative.

main clause future

ἕως ἂν εἰρήνη ᾖ, τῷ βασιλεῖ πείσονται.
So long as there is peace, they will obey the king.

μαχοῦνται μέχρι ἂν οἱ Ἀθηναῖοι ἀποπλεύσωσιν.
They will fight until the Athenians sail away.

main clause present

μένομεν ἕως ἂν ἔλθῃ ὁ ἄγγελος.
We are waiting until the messenger comes (in expectation that he will come, in anticipation that he may come).

If the main clause contains the potential optative, the temporal clause with ἕως, etc., referring to action in the future contains the optative (without ἄν: cf. future less vivid condition). This is a rare construction.

καὶ νῦν μάχοιντο ἂν μέχρι οἱ Ἀθηναῖοι ἀποπλεύσειαν.
And now they would fight (on) until the Athenians (should) sail away.

d. Temporal clauses with ἕως, etc., referring to *an action that was anticipated in the past* contain the optative (without ἄν); the main verb may be imperfect or aorist. This pattern does not correspond to any of the conditional patterns, but may be viewed as a transposition into past time of the construction illustrated under §c above (main clause present, temporal clause subj. + ἄν), with a corresponding shift of subordinate mood because of the sequence of moods.[1]

ἔμενον ἕως ἔλθοι.
They remained, waiting for him to come or
They waited in expectation that he would (might) come.

Contrast the more factual form (as in §a above):

ἔμενον ἕως ἦλθεν.
They waited until he (actually) arrived.

2. πρίν. The use of πρίν as a conjunction (= *before, until*) developed from early uses of the adverb πρίν = *before*. The usage of this word is in part

---

1. Grammarians speak of this kind of subordinate-clause optative as due to *implied indirect discourse*: that is, the writer or speaker retains the sense of expectation and non-fulfillment that is felt by those who experience the action as present; with the shift to a secondary-tense main verb, the sequence of moods applies, as for indirect discourse.

parallel to that of ἔως, etc., but is somewhat more complicated because πρίν often introduces an infinitive rather than a finite verb.

a. *πρίν with Finite Verbs.* In these constructions, the main clause is normally *negative* and a temporal adverb meaning *before* (πρόσθεν or πρότερον) is often present in it. The patterns are similar to those illustrated in §1a–d above:

definite action: indicative
οὐ πρόσθεν ἐπαύσαντο πρὶν τὴν πόλιν εἷλον.
They didn't stop until they (had) captured the city.

present general: subjunctive with ἄν
οὐ πρόσθεν παύονται πρὶν ἂν πάντας πείσωσιν.
They don't stop [on each occasion] *until they convince everyone.*

future more vivid: subjunctive with ἄν
οὐ πρότερον παύσονται πρὶν ἂν τὴν πόλιν ἔλωσιν.
They will not stop until they capture the city.

depending on clause containing optative: optative without ἄν
εἴ τις μὴ ἀνείη αὐτὸν πρὶν ἐξελκύσειεν εἰς τὸ τοῦ ἡλίου φῶς
if one should not let him go until one had dragged him into the light of the sun

anticipated action in past time: optative without ἄν
ἔπειθον αὐτοὺς μὴ ποιεῖσθαι μάχην πρὶν οἱ Ἀθηναῖοι παραγένοιντο.
They urged them not to fight (but to wait) until the Athenians should have arrived.

b. *πρίν with Infinitive.* In this construction, the main verb is normally *affirmative*, but the infinitive is sometimes found with a negative main verb; again a temporal adverb meaning *before* (πρόσθεν or πρότερον) often accompanies the main verb. The infinitive construction must be used instead of a finite-verb construction in any case where a *before-after* contrast is emphasized (that is, where in English translation *before* cannot be replaced by *until* without altering the meaning). The infinitive expresses the action absolutely and implies nothing about anticipation or actual occurrence. The infinitive with πρίν is usually aorist, but the present is used for continuing, repeated, or attempted action. The subject of the infinitive is unexpressed when it is the same as that of the main verb, accusative otherwise.

ἐμάχοντο πρὶν τοὺς Ἀθηναίους παραγενέσθαι.
They fought (at some time) before the Athenians arrived.
[not the same as *They fought until (the moment when) the Athenians arrived.*]

ἀπετράποντο εἰς τὴν πόλιν πρὶν ὑπερβαίνειν.
They turned back toward the city before attempting to scale (the wall).
  [*until* impossible since the action *scale* never occurred; present inf. to express attempt]

φοβοῦμαι μὴ πρότερόν τι πάθῃς πρὶν τέλος ἐπιθεῖναι τοῖς πραττο-
μένοις.
I fear that something may happen to you before you complete what you are doing.

3. *Assimilation of Mood.* The mood of a subordinate clause is sometimes assimilated to the mood of the clause on which it depends if the subordinate clause is an integral part of the entire thought. The most important examples of assimilation of mood involve the optative.

a. The future less vivid conditional scheme may be interpreted as an instance of assimilation. Under the influence of the potential optative in the apodosis, the unfulfilled future action expressed in the protasis is normally in the optative (instead of subj. + ἄν as in future more vivid).

b. The optative in a ἕως-clause or πρίν-clause referring to a possible future action and dependent on an optative verb is also an instance of assimilation. So in the final example under §1c the subordinate verb is assimilated in mood to the potential optative on which it depends, and in the fourth example under §2a it is assimilated to the optative of the εἰ-clause, which is a future less vivid protasis.

c. Likewise, a future condition that depends on a dependent optative is assimilated to the optative, and is more properly explained as "optative in a future condition by assimilation of mood" than as "optative in a future less vivid condition":

ἐπειδὴ Κῦρος ἐκάλει, λαβὼν ὑμᾶς ἐπορευόμην, ἵνα εἴ τι δέοιτο ὠφε-
λοίην αὐτὸν ἀνθ᾽ ὧν εὖ ἔπαθον ὑπ᾽ ἐκείνου.
When Cyrus summoned me, I came, taking you along, in order that, if he should have any need, I might aid him in return for the favors I had received from him.
  [future condition dependent on optative of purpose clause]

WHAT TO STUDY AND DO

1. Study the constructions presented above.
2. Learn the vocabulary of this unit.
3. Do the exercises of this unit.

VOCABULARY

nouns

θέρος, θέρους, n.	summer; summer harvest
πάθος, πάθους, n.	incident; experience; suffering, state, condition [pathos, pathology]
στρατός, στρατοῦ, m.	army, host
φυλακή, φυλακῆς, f.	watching, guarding; garrison
χειμών, χειμῶνος, m.	winter; storm, stormy weather
ψεῦδος, ψεύδους, n.	falsehood, lie
ὥρα, ὥρας, f.	period, season; time of day; the fitting time [hour]

verbs

ἐπιχειρέω, ἐπιχειρήσω, ἐπε-χείρησα, ἐπικεχείρηκα, ἐπικεχείρημαι, ἐπεχειρήθην (ἐπι)	put one's hand to, attempt (+ dat. or + inf.)
πειράω, πειράσω [ᾱ], ἐπείρᾱσα, πεπείρᾱκα, πε-πείρᾱμαι, ἐπειράθην [ᾱ]	(more frequently used in middle in same sense as active) make trial of (+ gen.); try (+ inf.) [pirate]
πλέω, πλεύσομαι or πλευσέομαι, ἔπλευσα, πέπλευκα, πέπλευσμαι[1]	sail, go by sea [pleopod]
ἀποπλέω (ἀπο)	sail away
προσήκω (προς)	have come; belong to, be related to (+ dat.)
προσήκει	(impersonal) it belongs to, it concerns, it is fitting (+ dat. + inf.)
ῥέω, ῥυήσομαι, ἐρρύην, ἐρρύηκα[2]	flow [rheostat, rheumatism]
συλλέγω, συλλέξω, συνέ-λεξα, συνείλοχα, συνεί-λεγμαι, συνελέγην or συνελέχθην (συν)	gather, bring together, collect [syllogism]
σῴζω, σώσω (or σῴσω), ἔσω-σα (ἔσῳσα), σέσωκα, σέ-σωμαι (σέσῳσμαι), ἐσώθην	save, keep alive; preserve; bring safely; (pass.) reach safely, arrive safely

---

1. Recall that monosyllabic verbs in -έω have contraction in present and imperfect only when the ending begins with ε or ει: cf. U13 Vocabulary, footnote 2.

2. Present and imperfect treated like δέω, πλέω (see previous note); the future principal part of this verb is actually its future passive, and the aorist principal part is its aorist passive (no middle or active forms exist in these tenses, but these passive forms have intransitive "active" translation in English).

ὑποπτεύω, ὑποπτεύσω, ὑπώπτευσα, ὑπωπτεύθην	be suspicious; suspect, hold in suspicion
φθείρω, φθερέω, ἔφθειρα, ἔφθαρκα, ἔφθαρμαι, ἐφθάρην	destroy; corrupt, bribe; seduce
διαφθείρω (δια) (also has intrans. 2nd perf. διέφθορα)	destroy utterly; corrupt, bribe; seduce; (intrans. 2nd perf.) have been ruined, destroyed
φράζω, φράσω, ἔφρασα, πέφρακα, πέφρασμαι, ἐφράσθην [ᾰ in all stems]	point out, show; tell, declare, explain [phrase, periphrastic]

adverbs, etc.

γε	(enclitic particle adding emphasis to previous word or to whole clause; sometimes untranslatable in English) at least, at any rate
δή	(postpositive particle adding emphasis to preceding word, esp. to conjunctions and pronouns) in fact, of course, certainly
καὶ δὴ καί	and in fact, and in particular
καὶ γάρ	for indeed, for in fact, and in fact
μήν	(postpositive particle adding strength to declarations) truly, surely
καὶ μήν	and what is more (introducing something new or esp. important)
ἀμφί	(preposition) (+ gen., poetic) about, for the sake of; (+ dat., poetic) on both sides of, for the sake of; (+ acc.) around, associated with (a person), occupied with (a task) [amphitheater]
ἔτι	yet, still
οὐκέτι, μηκέτι	no longer
εὐθύς	immediately, forthwith [euthynterion, euthytropic]
μόγις	with toil; scarcely, hardly
ὄπισθεν	behind; hereafter, in future; (sometimes + gen.) behind [opisthodomos]
πέλας	near; (sometimes + gen.) near
χωρίς	separately, apart; (+ gen.) without, separate from

temporal conjunctions

ἕως	until; so long as, while
ἔστε	(rare in prose) until; so long as, while
μέχρι or μέχρι οὗ	until; (also adv. or prep. + gen.) as far as, up to
ἄχρι or ἄχρι οὗ	until; (also adv. or prep. + gen.) as far as, up to
πρίν	before (+ clause or + inf.); (adverb) before, formerly

EXERCISES

I.   Render into Greek.

1. Cyrus continued to gather soldiers and money until the king suspected[1] that his brother was plotting something.
2. As long as the rivers flow into the sea, mankind will try to preserve itself.
3. May I die before any such thing happens!
4. Those who sail during the winter ought to beware that the winds do not deceive them.
5. Philip was not allowing the ambassadors to meet him until his friends should utterly ruin [= corrupt] the affairs of the city.

II. Reading: Lysias, *Oration* 12.13–15: Lysias, just arrested by order of the Thirty, has been brought to the house of Damnippus, where Theognis is guarding various detainees.

ἐν τοιούτῳ δ᾽ ὄντι μοι κινδυνεύειν ἐδόκει, ὡς τοῦ γε ἀποθανεῖν ὑπάρχοντος ἤδη. καλέσας δὲ Δάμνιππον λέγω πρὸς αὐτὸν τάδε, "ἐπιτήδειος μέν μοι τυγχάνεις ὤν, ἥκω δ᾽ εἰς τὴν σὴν οἰκίαν, ἀδικῶ δ᾽ οὐδέν, χρημάτων δ᾽ ἕνεκα ἀπόλλυμαι. σὺ οὖν ταῦτα πάσχοντί μοι πρόθυμον παράσχου τὴν σεαυτοῦ δύναμιν εἰς τὴν ἐμὴν σωτηρίαν." ὁ δ᾽ ὑπέσχετο ταῦτα ποιήσειν. ἐδόκει δ᾽ αὐτῷ βέλτιον εἶναι πρὸς Θέογνιν μνησθῆναι· ἡγεῖτο γὰρ ἅπαν ποιήσειν αὐτόν, εἴ τις ἀργύριον διδοίη. ἐκείνου δὲ διαλεγομένου Θεόγνιδι (ἔμπειρος γὰρ ὢν ἐτύγχανον τῆς οἰκίας, καὶ ᾔδειν ὅτι ἀμφίθυρος εἴη) ἐδόκει μοι ταύτῃ πειρᾶσθαι σωθῆναι, ἐνθυμουμένῳ ὅτι, ἐὰν μὲν λάθω, σωθήσομαι, ἐὰν δὲ ληφθῶ, ἡγούμην μέν, εἰ Θέογνις εἴη πεπεισμένος ὑπὸ τοῦ Δαμνίππου χρήματα λαβεῖν, οὐδὲν ἧττον ἀφεθήσεσθαι, εἰ δὲ μή, ὁμοίως ἀποθανεῖσθαι.

Underlined Words

ἀμφίθυρος, -ον =*with doors on both ends*
ἀργύριον, -ου, n. = *(silver) money*
ἔμπειρος, -ον = *experienced in,*
    knowledgeable about (+ gen.)
ἐνθυμέομαι = *ponder, consider*
ἐπιτήδειος = (here) *close acquaintance*
Θέογνις, -ιδος, m., dat. -ιδι, acc. -ιν =
    Theognis
κινδυνεύω = *take a risk*

ὁμοίως = *all the same, just the same*
οὖν = *therefore*
παράσχου = aor. mid. imperative of
    παρέχω, here *furnish me your power*
    eagerly disposed [pred. adj.] *toward*
    my salvation, or *apply your influence*
    with zeal to save me
ὑπάρχω = *be ready at hand*

---

1.   ὑποπτεύω takes the inf. construction for indirect discourse.

III. Reading: Plato, *Gorgias* 484c–e: Callicles explains to Socrates the danger of attributing too much importance to philosophy.

τὸ μὲν <u>οὖν</u> ἀληθὲς οὕτως ἔχει, γνώσῃ δέ, ἂν ἐπὶ τὰ μείζω ἔλθῃς ἐάσας ἤδη <u>φιλοσοφίαν</u>. φιλοσοφία γάρ <u>τοί</u> ἐστιν, ὦ Σώκρατες, χαρίεν, ἄν τις αὐτοῦ <u>μετρίως</u> <u>ἅψηται</u> ἐν τῇ <u>ἡλικίᾳ</u>· ἐὰν δὲ <u>περαιτέρω</u> τοῦ δέοντος <u>ἐνδιατρίψῃ</u>, <u>διαφθορὰ</u> τῶν ἀνθρώπων. ἐὰν γὰρ καὶ <u>πάνυ</u> <u>εὐφυὴς</u> ᾖ καὶ <u>πόρρω</u> τῆς ἡλικίας <u>φιλοσοφῇ</u>, ἀνάγκη πάντων <u>ἄπειρον</u> γεγονέναι ἐστὶν ὧν χρὴ <u>ἔμπειρον</u> εἶναι τὸν μέλλοντα καλὸν <u>κἀγαθὸν</u> καὶ <u>εὐδόκιμον</u> ἔσεσθαι ἄνδρα. καὶ γὰρ τῶν νόμων ἄπειροι γίγνονται τῶν κατὰ τὴν πόλιν, καὶ τῶν λόγων οἷς δεῖ χρώμενον <u>ὁμιλεῖν</u> ἐν τοῖς <u>συμβολαίοις</u> τοῖς ἀνθρώποις καὶ <u>ἰδίᾳ</u> καὶ <u>δημοσίᾳ</u>, καὶ τῶν ἡδονῶν τε καὶ ἐπιθυμιῶν τῶν <u>ἀνθρωπείων</u>, καὶ <u>συλλήβδην</u> τῶν <u>ἠθῶν</u> <u>παντάπασιν</u> ἄπειροι γίγνονται. ἐπειδὰν οὖν ἔλθωσιν εἴς τινα ἰδίαν ἢ <u>πολιτικὴν</u> <u>πρᾶξιν</u>, <u>καταγέλαστοι</u> γίγνονται, ὥσπερ γε οἶμαι οἱ πολιτικοί, ἐπειδὰν αὖ εἰς τὰς ὑμετέρας <u>διατριβὰς</u> ἔλθωσιν καὶ τοὺς λόγους, καταγέλαστοί εἰσιν.

Underlined Words

ἀνθρώπειος, -α, -ον = *human*
ἄπειρος, -ον = *inexperienced* (+ gen.)
ἅπτω, aor. ἧψα = *join*, (mid.) *touch* (+ gen.)
δημοσίᾳ = (idiomatic fem. dat. s. adv. of manner) *publicly, in public life*
διατριβή, -ῆς, f. = *pastime, pursuit*
διαφθορά, -ᾶς, f. = *ruination*
ἔμπειρος, -ον = *experienced in* (+ gen.)
ἐνδιατρίβω, aor. ἐνδιέτριψα = *spend one's time in*
εὐδόκιμος, -ον = *of good repute, famous*
εὐφυής, -ές = *innately gifted*
ἦθος, -ους, n. = (in pl.) *human character, human behavior*
ἡλικία, -ας, f. = *prime of one's youth*
ἴδιος, -α, -ον = *private*; (fem. dat. sing. as adverb) *privately, in private life*
κἀγαθὸν = καὶ ἀγαθὸν (crasis)
καταγέλαστος, -ον = *ridiculous*

μέτριος, -α, -ον = *moderate*
ὁμιλέω = *associate with* (+ dat.)
οὖν = (postpositive) *therefore*; (combined with μέν, in transitions) *now then*
παντάπασιν = (adv.) *completely*
πάνυ = (adv.) *very much, exceedingly*
περαιτέρω = (compar. adv.) *farther along*
πολιτικός, -ή, -όν = *political*
πόρρω = (adv.) *far along in* (+ gen.)
πρᾶξις, -εως, f. = *activity, action*
συλλήβδην = (adv.) *taken all together, to put it in a nutshell*
συμβόλαιον, -ου, n. = *contractual transaction*
τοι = (enclitic particle) *surely, you know*
φιλοσοφέω = *engage in philosophical pursuits*
φιλοσοφία, -ας, f. = *philosophy*

Imperative Mood

---

1. *Imperative Mood.* The fourth of the finite moods of ancient Greek is the imperative (Latin *imperativus*, Greek προστακτική, "of command"). The imperative is used to express commands in the second and third persons (for the first person, the hortatory subjunctive is available), and is found mainly in the present and aorist tenses to express the contrasting aspects associated with these stems of the verb (see §6 below). In Attic Greek no perfect active imperative forms are found, and the perfect middle/passive imperative is rare, found mainly in verbs whose perfects are common as present-tense equivalents and in third person passive imperatives in certain fixed expressions.

The English imperative of the second person is simply the present principal part of the verb with no pronoun subject expressed: *go, eat, read, study, be.* The Greek third person imperative may be translated with the English phrase *let him (her, it, them) do X.*

2. *Formation of Imperative*

a. *Thematic Verbs.* Imperatival personal endings (mainly distinct from those of the other moods) are added to the present stem plus theme vowel ο/ε and to the strong aorist stem plus theme vowel ο/ε or to the weak aorist stem plus tense vowel α (and for a few verbs directly to the middle/passive perfect stem with no intervening vowel). For the active the imperatival personal endings are: — , -τω, (-τον, -των,) -τε, -ντων; for the middle/passive, -(σ)ο, -σθω, (-σθον, -σθων,) -σθε, -σθων. The second person singular weak aorist forms have anomalous endings: -ον in the active, -αι in the middle. The accentuation of the imperative is normally recessive, but strong aorist middle -οῦ from -έ(σ)ο (with accent on theme vowel) is an exception (cf. accentuation of strong aorist inf. and part.: U19.4a, U26.1a).

Note that the third plural active imperatives happen to be identical in form to the masc./neuter gen. pl. of the active participle. Note the difference in accent and meaning between βούλευσον (2nd sing. aor. act. imper.) and βουλεῦσον (neuter nom./acc. sing. fut. act. part.); also between βούλευσαι (2nd sing. aor. mid. imper.), βουλεῦσαι (aor. act. inf.), and βουλεύσαι (3rd sing. aor. act. opt.).[1]

PRESENT ACTIVE IMPERATIVE

		βουλεύω	ποιέω	ὁράω	δηλόω
sing.	2nd	βούλευε	ποίει	ὅρᾱ	δήλου
	3rd	βουλευέτω	ποιείτω	ὁράτω	δηλούτω
(dual	2nd	βουλεύετον	ποιεῖτον	ὁρᾶτον	δηλοῦτον)
	(3rd	βουλευέτων	ποιείτων	ὁράτων	δηλούτων)
plur.	2nd	βουλεύετε	ποιεῖτε	ὁρᾶτε	δηλοῦτε
	3rd	βουλευόντων	ποιούντων	ὁρώντων	δηλούντων

PRESENT MIDDLE/PASSIVE IMPERATIVE

		βουλεύω	ποιέω	ὁράω	δηλόω
sing.	2nd	βουλεύου[2]	ποιοῦ	ὁρῶ	δηλοῦ
	3rd	βουλευέσθω	ποιείσθω	ὁράσθω	δηλούσθω
(dual	2nd	βουλεύεσθον	ποιεῖσθον	ὁρᾶσθον	δηλοῦσθον)
	(3rd	βουλευέσθων	ποιείσθων	ὁράσθων	δηλούσθων)
plur.	2nd	βουλεύεσθε	ποιεῖσθε	ὁρᾶσθε	δηλοῦσθε
	3rd	βουλευέσθων	ποιείσθων	ὁράσθων	δηλούσθων

STRONG AND WEAK AORIST IMPERATIVES

		λείπω		βουλεύω	
		active	*middle*	*active*	*middle*
sing.	2nd	λίπε	λιποῦ	βούλευσον	βούλευσαι
	3rd	λιπέτω	λιπέσθω	βουλευσάτω	βουλευσάσθω
(dual	2nd	λίπετον	λίπεσθον	βουλεύσατον	βουλεύσασθον)
	(3rd	λιπέτων	λιπέσθων	βουλευσάτων	βουλευσάσθων)
plur.	2nd	λίπετε	λίπεσθε	βουλεύσατε	βουλεύσασθε
	3rd	λιπόντων	λιπέσθων	βουλευσάντων	βουλευσάσθων

---

1. In a verb with monosyllabic stem, these distinctions may be partially or totally lost: e.g., πέμψαι (imper., inf., and opt.); λῦσαι (imper. and inf.) vs. λύσαι (opt.).

2. The 2nd sing. middle forms are based on βουλεύεσο, ποιέεσο, ὁράεσο, δηλόεσο.

Perfect imperatives: the only simple perfect imperative forms found in Attic[1] are the second and third singular middle/passive (e.g., μέμνησο, μεμνήσθω) and the second plural middle/passive (e.g., μέμνησθε). But periphrastic perfect imperatives may be formed in both active and middle/passive by using the perfect participle with the present imperative of εἰμί (presented in §4 below): e.g., λελυκὼς ἴσθι, βεβουλευμένος ἴσθι.

b. *Athematic Verbs.* Imperatival personal endings (the same as for thematic verbs except in the second singular active) are added directly to the tense stem, which normally displays its short-vowel form. The second singular active in some verbs has the personal ending -θι, in some verbs has -ς, and in the present of the major μι-verbs is formed by the addition of ε, which contracts with the stem vowel (the ε is a borrowing from the ω-verbs, as in the sing. act. imperfect forms).

PRESENT IMPERATIVES (MI-VERBS)

		τίθημι		δίδωμι	
		active	mid./pass.	active	mid./pass.
sing.	2nd	τίθει	τίθεσο	δίδου	δίδοσο
	3rd	τιθέτω	τιθέσθω	διδότω	διδόσθω
(dual	2nd	τίθετον	τίθεσθον	δίδοτον	δίδοσθον)
	(3rd	τιθέτων	τιθέσθων	διδότων	διδόσθων)
plur.	2nd	τίθετε	τίθεσθε	δίδοτε	δίδοσθε
	3rd	τιθέντων	τιθέσθων	διδόντων	διδόσθων

		ἵστημι	
		active	mid./pass.
sing.	2nd	ἵστη	ἵστασο
	3rd	ἱστάτω	ἱστάσθω
(dual	2nd	ἵστατον	ἵστασθον)
	(3rd	ἱστάτων	ἱστάσθων)
plur.	2nd	ἵστατε	ἵστασθε
	3rd	ἱστάντων	ἱστάσθων

---

1. Outside of Attic one finds, very rarely, perfect active forms like λέλυκε, λελυκέτω, λελύκετε.

AORIST IMPERATIVES (MI-VERBS)

		τίθημι		δίδωμι		ἵστημι
		active	middle	active	middle	active
s.	2nd	θές	θοῦ	δός	δοῦ	στῆθι
	3rd	θέτω	θέσθω	δότω	δόσθω	στήτω
(d.	2nd	θέτον	θέσθον	δότον	δόσθον	στῆτον)
	(3rd	θέτων	θέσθων	δότων	δόσθων	στήτων)
pl.	2nd	θέτε	θέσθε	δότε	δόσθε	στῆτε
	3rd	θέντων	θέσθων	δόντων	δόσθων	στάντων

The aorist passive, being an athematic tense, is treated in the same way as the μι-verbs; the second singular active has the ending -θι, which is changed to -τι after tense suffix -θη- in first (weak) aorist passives (by Grassmann's law).

AORIST PASSIVE IMPERATIVE

		φαίνω	λύω
		strong aor. pass.	weak aor. pass.
sing.	2nd	φάνηθι	λύθητι
	3rd	φανήτω	λυθήτω
(dual	2nd	φάνητον	λύθητον)
	(3rd	φανήτων	λυθήτων)
plur.	2nd	φάνητε	λύθητε
	3rd	φανέντων	λυθέντων

3. *Other μι-Verb Imperatives and Irregular Imperatives.* Other μι-verbs are treated similarly, but again there is variation in the second singular active ending. In addition, the third plural active ending is reduced to -των when added to a stem ending in sigma (εἰμί and οἶδα).

εἰμί: ἴσθι, ἔστω, (ἔστον, ἔστων,) ἔστε, ἔστων

εἶμι: ἴθι, ἴτω, (ἴτον, ἴτων,) ἴτε, ἰόντων

ἵημι: (like τίθημι) pres. act. ἵει, ἱέτω, etc.; pres. mid./pass. ἵεσο, ἱέσθω, etc.; aor. act. (in prose, compounds only) ἄφες, ἀφέτω, etc.; aor. mid. ἀφοῦ, ἀφέσθω, etc.

φημί: φάθι or φαθί, φάτω, (φάτον, φάτων,) φάτε, φάντων

δείκνυμι: act. δείκνῡ, δεικνύτω, etc.; mid./pass. δείκνυσο, δεικνύσθω, etc.

γιγνώσκω: (aor.) γνῶθι, γνώτω, (γνῶτον, γνώτων,) γνῶτε, γνόντων

δύω: (aor.) δῦθι, δύτω, (δῦτον, δύτων,) δῦτε, δύντων

βαίνω: (aor.) βῆθι (in compounds also -βᾶ), βήτω, (βῆτον, βήτων,)
βῆτε, βάντων

ἐπίσταμαι: 2nd s. both ἐπίστασο and ἐπίστω, otherwise like mid./pass.
of ἵστημι.

οἶδα: ἴσθι, [1] ἴστω, (ἴστον, ἴστων,) ἴστε, ἴστων

Two other verbs have irregular second singular aorist active imperative forms:
ἔχω (ἔσχον) yields σχές, and πίνω (ἔπιον) yields πῖθι.

Five strong aorists show exceptional accentuation in the second singular
active. Instead of the usual recessive accentuation, the theme vowel ε is
accented (as in 2nd aor. inf., part., and 2nd sing. mid./pass. imper.): thus, εἰπέ,
ἰδέ (from εἶδον), ἐλθέ, εὑρέ, λαβέ.

4. *Accentuation of Imperatives of Compounds*

a. Compounds of the five strong aorists with non-recessive accentuation
do have recessive accentuation: e.g., κάτειπε, ἄπελθε.

b. Since the accent of a verb cannot precede the first preverb element, a
double compound form of a monosyllabic imperative is accented on *P*
even if *U* is short (e.g., σύνεκδος from συν-εκ-δίδωμι).

c. When a prepositional prefix is disyllabic, the compound form of a
monosyllabic imperative is accented on *P* even if *U* is short: e.g.,
περίθες, ἀπόδος.

d. The accentuation of the second singular strong aorist middle imperative of thematic verbs is retained in compounds: e.g., βαλοῦ, παρα-
βαλοῦ. But in the case of monosyllabic second singular aorist middle
imperatives of the major μι-verbs, the simple-verb accent is retained with
a monosyllabic prepositional prefix, but recessive accent is found with a
disyllabic prepositional prefix: thus, from δοῦ (δίδωμι) προδοῦ but
ἀπόδου; from -οὗ (ἵημι) ἀφοῦ but from θοῦ (τίθημι) περίθου.

5. *Aspect in the Imperative.*
As for the other non-indicative moods, the
tense stems in the imperative convey distinctions of aspect rather than of time.
The present refers to an action viewed as attempted, continuous, repeated, or
customary. The aorist refers to an action viewed as unique or instantaneous.
The perfect, which is rare, refers to an action viewed as having a permanent
result.

Ex.   τίμα τὸν πατέρα σου.   *Honor thy father.*
            [stated as a general principle]

            βάλε τὸν πονηρόν.   *Stone the wretch (right now).*

---

1. 2nd sing. imper. of εἰμί and οἶδα are identical; the context makes clear which is meant.

> εἰρημένον ἔστω.   *Let it be said.*
> [implying that the statement is permanently available as public knowledge]

6. *Negation of the Imperative.* The negative with the imperative mood is μή. But the aorist imperative is very rarely negated (in prose the third person is found negated a few times, and the second person is found negated only a few times in poetry). A negative command (prohibition) with aorist aspect is normally expressed by the aorist subjunctive of prohibition (U31.3b); one with present aspect is expressed by the imperative.

Ex.	μὴ τύπτε τὸν πατέρα.	*Don't (ever) strike your father!*
	μὴ ψευδῆ λέγε.	*Don't (ever) tell lies.*
	μὴ παίσῃς τὸν πατέρα.	*Don't (right now) strike your father!*
	μὴ εἴπῃς ψευδῆ.	*Don't (on this occasion) tell lies.*

WHAT TO STUDY AND DO

1. Study the conjugational patterns of the imperative mood.
2. Learn the vocabulary of this unit.
3. Do the exercises of this unit.

VOCABULARY

number adjectives

διακόσιοι, διακόσιαι, διακόσια	two hundred
τριακόσιοι, -αι, -α	three hundred
τετρακόσιοι, -αι, -α	four hundred
πεντακόσιοι, -αι, -α	five hundred
ἑξακόσιοι, -αι, -α	six hundred
ἑπτακόσιοι, -αι, -α	seven hundred
ὀκτακόσιοι, -αι, -α	eight hundred
ἐνακόσιοι, -αι, -α	nine hundred
χίλιοι, χίλιαι, χίλια	a thousand [kilometer, kilobyte]
δισχίλιοι,	two thousand,
τρισχίλιοι, etc.	three thousand, etc.
χιλιάς, χιλιάδος, f.	a group of 1,000; a large number
μυρίος, μυρία, μυρίον	numberless, countless
μύριοι, -αι, -α (note different position of accent)	ten thousand
μυριάς, μυριάδος, f.	a group of 10,000; a countless number [myriad]

other adjectives

ἀλλότριος, ἀλλοτρία, ἀλλότριον	belonging to another; foreign; hostile, ill-disposed
ἀνδρεῖος, ἀνδρεία, ἀνδρεῖον	manly, courageous [Andrew]
γυμνός, γυμνή, γυμνόν	naked; unarmed [gymnosperm, gymnosophist]
δειλός, δειλή, δειλόν	cowardly; miserable, wretched
ἐλεύθερος, ἐλευθέρα, ἐλεύθερον	free; characteristic of a freeman
εὐρύς, εὐρεῖα, εὐρύ	wide, broad [eurygnathous]
εὖρος, εὔρους, n.	width, breadth
εὐσεβής, εὐσεβές	pious, dutiful (toward the gods or one's elders); holy
ἀσεβής, ἀσεβές	ungodly, unholy
δυσσεβής, δυσσεβές	(mainly poetic) impious, unholy
θρασύς, θρασεῖα, θρασύ	bold, rash, audacious
ἴδιος, ἰδία, ἴδιον	pertaining to oneself; private, personal; separate, distinct [idiom, idiograph]
ἱκανός, ἱκανή, ἱκανόν	sufficient, competent; suitable, adequate
μέσος, μέση, μέσον	middle, in the middle; moderate [mesolithic]
μόνος, μόνη, μόνον	alone; only, single (used in predicate position) [monotone, monarchy]
μόνον	(adv. acc.) only, solely
νέος, νέα, νέον	young; new; unexpected, strange [neolithic, neologism]
ξένος, ξένη, ξένον	foreign; strange, unusual [xenophobia]
ξένος, -ου, m.	foreigner; guest-friend; host of guest-friend
οἷός τε, οἵα τε, οἷόν τε	fit, able, possible (+ inf.)
ὅλος, ὅλη, ὅλον	whole, entire [holography]
ὅμοιος, ὁμοία, ὅμοιον	like, similar, resembling (+ dat.) [homeopathy]
παχύς, παχεῖα, παχύ	thick, stout [pachyderm]
τραχύς, τραχεῖα, τραχύ	rugged, rough [trachodon, trachyte]

verbs

ἐργάζομαι, ἐργάσομαι, ἠργασάμην, εἴργασμαι, ἠργάσθην[1]	work; work at, make; do, perform
παίω, παίσω, ἔπαισα, πέπαικα, (ἐπαίσθην rare)	strike, beat
σέβομαι (active σέβω mainly poetic)	feel awe (before the gods); revere, worship, honor

---

1. The augment of this verb is sometimes found in the spelling εἰργ- rather than ἠργ-.

εὐσεβέω	live or act piously
ἀσεβέω	live or act impiously; sin against
τίκτω, τέξομαι, ἔτεκον, τέτοκα	(of father) beget, sire; (of mother) bring into the world, give birth to; (in general) bear, produce, generate [tocodynamometer]
ὁ τεκών	father, parent
φύω, φύσω, ἔφῦσα, intrans. aor. ἔφῦν, πέφῦκα[1]	(pres., fut., weak aor. active) produce, make grow; beget; (pres. passive, intrans. strong aor., intrans. perfect) grow, be begotten, be born; (perfect with present meaning) be by nature, be by nature prone to (+ inf.) [physics, physiology]
χαίρω, χαιρήσω, κεχάρηκα, ἐχάρην [intrans.]	rejoice, be glad, delight in (+ dat. or + suppl. participle)

EXERCISES

I.   Identify completely the following verb forms.

1. τεθεῖσαι
2. ἡσθήσεσθε
3. παῖσον
4. ῥαγείης
5. κριθησόμενος
6. δραμοῖτο
7. ὁμολογηθέν
8. εἰργασμένα
9. ἀπόλαβε
10. τεκοῦσα
11. ἀποσχεῖν
12. κέκτωνται
13. λάθω
14. ἐρρύησαν
15. βουλεύσεσθε
16. μνήσθητι
17. διωξάτω
18. σκοπεῖτε
19. χαῖρε
20. εὐσέβει
21. ἴστε
22. ὡμολογηκότες ἔστων
23. βουλεῦσαι
24. πεπειράκασι
25. νικήσειας
26. ἀγαγοῦ
27. ἀπατώντων
28. κατάλιπε
29. σκέψασθε
30. πεπαυκότι
31. ἐληλεγμέναι εἰσί
32. κατάθες
33. τετελεσμένον ἔστω

II. Give the 2nd and 3rd pers. sing. and pl. imperatives of the following:

1. aor. act. of πέμπω
2. pres. m/p of γίγνομαι
3. pres. m/p of ἐπιτίθημι
4. aor. pass. of σῴζω
5. aor. mid. of παρέχω
6. aor. act. of ἀναγιγνώσκω

---

1. The strong aorist ἔφυν is conjugated like ἔδυν. The υ of the stem is generally long, but in the present may be long or short.

III. Reading: Plato, *Protagoras* 320c–321c (abridged): Protagoras uses a myth to explain to Socrates why all men are allowed to participate in political decisions, whereas technical decisions related to skilled crafts are made only by experts in those crafts.

ἦν γάρ ποτε χρόνος ὅτε θεοὶ μὲν ἦσαν, θνητὰ δὲ γένη οὐκ ἦν. ἐπειδὴ δὲ καὶ τούτοις χρόνος ἦλθεν εἱμαρμένος γενέσεως, τυποῦσιν αὐτὰ θεοὶ γῆς ἔνδον ἐκ γῆς καὶ πυρὸς μείξαντες καὶ τῶν ὅσα πυρὶ καὶ γῇ κεράννυται. ἐπειδὴ δ' ἄγειν αὐτὰ πρὸς φῶς ἔμελλον, προσέταξαν Προμηθεῖ καὶ Ἐπιμηθεῖ κοσμῆσαί τε καὶ νεῖμαι δυνάμεις ἑκάστοις ὡς πρέπει. Προμηθέα δὲ παραιτεῖται Ἐπιμηθεὺς αὐτὸς νεῖμαι, "νείμαντος δέ μου," ἔφη, "ἐπίσκεψαι." καὶ οὕτω πείσας νέμει. νέμων δὲ τοῖς μὲν ἰσχὺν ἄνευ τάχους προσῆπτεν, τοὺς δ' ἀσθενεστέρους τάχει ἐκόσμει· ... ἅτε δὴ οὖν οὐ πάνυ τι σοφὸς ὢν ὁ Ἐπιμηθεὺς ἔλαθεν αὑτὸν καταναλώσας τὰς δυνάμεις εἰς τὰ ἄλογα· λοιπὸν δὴ ἀκόσμητον ἔτι αὐτῷ ἦν τὸ ἀνθρώπων γένος, καὶ ἠπόρει ὅ τι χρήσαιτο. ἀποροῦντι δὲ αὐτῷ ἔρχεται Προμηθεὺς ἐπισκεψόμενος τὴν νομήν, καὶ ὁρᾷ τὰ μὲν ἄλλα ζῷα ἐμμελῶς πάντων ἔχοντα, τὸν δὲ ἄνθρωπον γυμνόν τε καὶ ἀνυπόδητον καὶ ἄστρωτον καὶ ἄοπλον· ἤδη δὲ καὶ ἡ εἱμαρμένη ἡμέρα παρῆν, ἐν ᾗ ἔδει καὶ ἄνθρωπον ἐξιέναι ἐκ γῆς εἰς φῶς.

Underlined Words

ἀκόσμητος -ον = *unadorned, unequipped*

ἄλογος, -ον = *without reason* (neut. pl. as substantive = *brute animals*)

ἀνυπόδητος, -ον = *without covering for the feet*

ἄοπλος, -ον = *without armor*

ἄστρωτος, -ον = *without bedding*

ἅτε δή = *particles marking the participle* ὤν *as causal*

γένεσις, -εως, f. = *birth*

γῆ, γῆς, f. = *earth* (declension: U42)

εἱμαρμένος, -η, -ον = *fated, destined* (perf. pass. part. of μείρομαι)

ἐμμελῶς ἔχειν + gen. = *be in a suitable condition with regard to, be suitably provided with*

ἔνδον = (adv.) *inside* (+ gen.)

Ἐπιμηθεύς, -έως, m. = *Epimetheus (Afterthought), brother of Prometheus*

ἐπισκέπτομαι (ἐπι) = *investigate, inspect*

ζῷον, -ου, n. = *animal*

θνητός, -ή, -όν = *mortal*

καταναλίσκω, aor. κατανήλωσα = *expend completely*

κεράννυμι = *mix, blend*

κοσμέω = *adorn, equip*

λοιπός, -ή, -όν = *remaining*

μείγνυμι, aor. ἔμειξα = *mix, combine*

νέμω, aor. ἔνειμα = *distribute, apportion*

νομή, -ῆς, f. = *distribution*

οὖν = (particle) *then, therefore, so then*

πάνυ τι = (adv.) *very much at all*

παραιτέομαι = *ask as a favor* (+ acc. of person + complementary inf.)

Προμηθεύς, -έως, m. = *Prometheus*
(Forethought), a cunning Titan who
functioned as a sort of "patron saint"
of mankind

προσάπτω (προς) = *fasten to, bestow*

προστάττω (προς) = *order, assign a
task*

πῦρ, πυρός, n. = *fire*

τυπόω = *form, mold*

τῶν ὅσα = *of those things, however
many are . . .* (τῶν here is pronominal)

χρήσαιτο with internal acc. ὅ τι = *what*
produces the idiom *what use he could
make of (a situation), how could he
cope with (a situation)*; the opt. here
represents Epimetheus's direct
deliberative question τί χρήσωμαι;

UNIT FORTY-ONE

Pluperfect and Future Perfect; Irregular Perfects

---

1. *The Greek Pluperfect.* The Greek pluperfect indicative corresponds to the Greek perfect as the Greek imperfect indicative corresponds to the Greek present: the perfect expresses an action completed in the past with permanent results in the present, while the pluperfect expresses an action completed in the deeper past with permanent results over a period of time in the more recent past. Like the imperfect, the pluperfect has only indicative forms. The Greek pluperfect is not at all common, except in those verbs whose perfects are regularly used with a present meaning. The English pluperfect *had Xed* has a different meaning (expressing an action antecedent to another action expressed in a past tense) and is more common. Note that in many cases the English pluperfect is equivalent to a Greek aorist:

When they <u>had arrived</u>, we performed the sacrifices.
ἐπεὶ ἀφίκοντο, ἐθύσαμεν.

2. *Conjugation of the Pluperfect.* The pluperfect active and middle/passive indicative are formed from the perfect active and perfect middle/passive stems with augment added at the beginning of the stem and with secondary personal endings.

a. *Pluperfect Active Indicative.* In the active the endings are mainly based on a tense vowel ε plus secondary active personal endings. In the first and second person singular, however, the endings were originally -εα, -εας, and these endings, along with the third singular -εε, suffered contraction in Attic. Pluperfects may be termed "first" or "second" depending on the form of the perfect stem (with or without suffix κ), but this distinction has no relevance to the conjugation.

On the facing page are shown the pluperfect active of λύω (perfect stem λελυκ-, augmented ἐλελυκ-), ἄγω (perfect stem ἠχ-, augment not apparent), and ἀκούω (perfect stem ἀκηκο-, augmented ἠκηκο-).

318

PLUPERFECT ACTIVE INDICATIVE

		λύω	ἄγω	ἀκούω
sing.	1st	ἐλελύκη	ἤχη	ἠκηκόη
	2nd	ἐλελύκης	ἤχης	ἠκηκόης
	3rd	ἐλελύκει(ν)	ἤχει(ν)	ἠκηκόει(ν)
(dual	2nd	ἐλελύκετον	ἤχετον	ἠκηκόετον)
	(3rd	ἐλελυκέτην	ἠχέτην	ἠκηκοέτην)
plur.	1st	ἐλελύκεμεν	ἤχεμεν	ἠκηκόεμεν
	2nd	ἐλελύκετε	ἤχετε	ἠκηκόετε
	3rd	ἐλελύκεσαν	ἤχεσαν	ἠκηκόεσαν

After about 350 B.C.E. the 1st and 2nd sing. take the form ἐλελύκειν, ἐλελύ-κεις (and to avoid ambiguity the 3rd sing. no longer takes nu-movable).[1]

b. *Pluperfect Middle/Passive Indicative.* In the middle/passive, the personal endings are added directly to the stem, and the same euphonic changes observed in the perfect middle/passive (U37.6) appear in the pluperfect as well. For all consonant stems the 3rd pl. form is periphrastic (perfect mid./pass. part. plus imperfect of εἰμί).[2]

PLUPERFECT MIDDLE/PASSIVE INDICATIVE

		vowel stem λύω stem: λελῠ-	dental plosive stem πείθω stem: πεπεισ-	labial plosive stem γράφω stem: γεγραπ-
sing.	1st	ἐλελύμην	ἐπεπείσμην	ἐγεγράμμην
	2nd	ἐλέλυσο	ἐπέπεισο	ἐγέγραψο
	3rd	ἐλέλυτο	ἐπέπειστο	ἐγέγραπτο
(dual	2nd	ἐλέλυσθον	ἐπέπεισθον	ἐγέγραφθον)
	(3rd	ἐλελύσθην	ἐπεπείσθην	ἐγεγράφθην)
plur.	1st	ἐλελύμεθα	ἐπεπείσμεθα	ἐγεγράμμεθα
	2nd	ἐλέλυσθε	ἐπέπεισθε	ἐγέγραφθε
	3rd	ἐλέλυντο	πεπεισμένοι ἦσαν	γεγραμμένοι ἦσαν

---

1. In postclassical Greek, the complete conjugation uses ει as tense vowel, so that the endings are -ειν, -εις, -ει, -ειμεν, -ειτε, -εισαν.
2. Occasionally a simple 3rd pl. form is found, such as ἐτετάχατο = τεταγμένοι ἦσαν.

		velar plosive stem	stem in λ	stem in ν
		πράττω	ἀγγέλλω	φαίνω
		stem: πεπραγ-	stem: ἠγγελ-	stem: πεφαν-, πεφασ-
sing.	1st	ἐπεπράγμην	ἠγγέλμην	ἐπεφάσμην
	2nd	ἐπέπραξο	ἤγγελσο	—
	3rd	ἐπέπρακτο	ἤγγελτο	ἐπέφαντο
(dual	2nd	ἐπέπραχθον	ἤγγελθον	ἐπέφανθον)
	(3rd	ἐπεπράχθην	ἠγγέλθην	ἐπεφάνθην)
plur.	1st	ἐπεπράγμεθα	ἠγγέλμεθα	ἐπεφάσμεθα
	2nd	ἐπέπραχθε	ἤγγελθε	ἐπέφανθε
	3rd	πεπραγμένοι ἦσαν	ἠγγελμένοι ἦσαν	πεφασμένοι ἦσαν

3. *The Future Perfect.* In English the future perfect is used to refer to an action that will be completed prior to some point in time in the future (*will have Xed*). The Greek future perfect is formed from the perfect stem and normally refers to a future state which will be the permanent result of an action completed at an earlier point in the future.

4. *Conjugation of the Future Perfect*

a. *Active.* The future perfect active indicative (subj., opt., etc.) is normally formed *periphrastically*, from perfect active participle plus future indicative (subj., opt., etc.) of εἰμί: thus, λελυκὼς ἔσομαι, *I will have released* (strictly, *I will be in the state of having released*). In Attic, there are three verbs that form a *simple* future perfect active, and they are all perfects commonly used with a present meaning (so that the Greek speakers felt as if they were forming a plain future, with -σω): from τέθνηκα, *I am dead*, fut. perf. ind. τεθνήξω, *I'll be dead (I will have died)*; from ἔστηκα, *I stand*, fut. perf. opt. ἑστήξοι (once in Plato), and from ἔοικα, *I am like*, fut. perf. ind. εἴξω, *I'll be like* (once in Aristophanes).[1]

b. *Middle/Passive.* These forms too may be formed *periphrastically*, from the perfect middle/passive participle plus the future of εἰμί: thus, λελυμένος ἔσομαι, *I'll have ransomed* or *I'll have been released* (the future perfect is more often passive in meaning than middle). But *simple* forms are also found, more commonly than for the active. The suffix -σομαι (inflected

---

1. Also, in epic κεχαρήσω from χαίρω and in the Syracusan dialect δεδοικήσω from δέδοικα.

just like future middle indicative) is added to the perfect middle stem, with lengthening of preceding vowel if the stem ends in a short vowel or with combination of the sigma with a final consonant of the stem.

Ex.   λύω, perfect middle stem λελῠ-, future perfect middle/passive indicative λελύσομαι [ῡ]

γράφω, perfect middle stem γεγραπ-, future perfect middle/ passive indicative γεγράψομαι

The future perfect mid./pass. infinitive ends in -σεσθαι, with accent on A. The most frequent infinitive of this type is μεμνήσεσθαι (= *will remember*, corresponding to present meaning of μέμνημαι = *I remember*). Only one instance of a future perfect mid./pass. participle is extant (διαπεπολεμησόμενον in Thucydides).[1] The future perfect mid./pass. optative is extant once in Plato (κεκλή-σοιτο, from κέκλημαι, a perfect with present meaning).

5. *Athematic Perfects.* ἵστημι and a few other verbs (in Attic θνῄσκω and δέδοικα) form a perfect active athematically, that is, by adding personal endings directly to a reduplicated stem without tense suffix or tense vowel. The athematic forms are found mainly in the dual and plural numbers, coexisting with regular perfect forms; in the singular the regular perfect forms are normal, and athematic forms are found only for δέδοικα. The athematic perfects are called "second," while the regular forms with κ-suffix are called "first" perfects.

a.   The perfect active system of ἵστημι is as follows:[2]

		1st perf. ind.	*2nd perf. ind.*	*1st pluperf.*	*2nd pluperf.*
sing.	*1st*	ἕστηκα		εἱστήκη	
	2nd	ἕστηκας		εἱστήκης	
	3rd	ἕστηκε(ν)		εἱστήκει	
(dual	*2nd*	ἑστήκατον	ἕστατον	εἱστήκετον	ἕστατον)
	(3rd	ἑστηκάτην	ἕστατον	εἱστηκέτην	ἑστάτην)
plur.	*1st*	ἑστήκαμεν	ἕσταμεν	εἱστήκεμεν	ἕσταμεν
	2nd	ἑστήκατε	ἕστατε	εἱστήκετε	ἕστατε
	3rd	ἑστήκᾱσι(ν)	ἑστᾶσι(ν)	εἱστήκεσαν	ἕστασαν

The infinitive is usually ἑστάναι (late classical ἑστηκέναι), the participle usually ἑστώς, ἑστῶσα, ἑστός (masc./neut. stem ἑστωτ-),[3] less commonly ἑστη-

---

1. There are a couple of other examples in non-Attic and postclassical Greek.
2. There is no augment in the 2nd pluperfect of ἵστημι; this is a very archaic feature.
3. For declension of ἑστώς (and τεθνεώς), see Appendix 3: Paradigms.

κώς, -υῖα, -ός. In the subjunctive ἑστήκω is more common than ἑστῶ, -ῇς, etc. Optative may be ἑστήκοιμι or ἑστηκὼς εἴην (in poetry also ἑσταίην). Also poetic are 2nd perfect imperative ἕσταθι, ἑστάτω, etc.

b. θνῄσκω has first perfect stem τεθνηκ- and second perfect stem τεθνᾰ-. In addition to the regular first perfect forms, the following second perfect forms are found in Attic:

> indicative: (dual τέθνατον, τέθνατον,) pl. τέθναμεν, τέθνατε, τεθνᾶ-
> σι(ν); pluperfect 3rd pl. ἐτέθνασαν
> infinitive: τεθνάναι
> participle: τεθνεώς, τεθνεῶσα, τεθνεός (masc./neut. stem τεθνεωτ-)
> optative: τεθναίην, etc.
> imperative: (poetic τέθναθι), τεθνάτω

c. δέδοικα (a perfect with present meaning, *I fear*) has second perfect forms from stem δεδι-.

> indicative: first perfect common in singular, rare in plural; second perfect
> rare in singular (δέδια, δέδιας, δέδιε), common in dual and plural
> (δέδιτον, δέδιτον, δέδιμεν, δέδιτε, δεδίᾱσι[ν])
> pluperfect: sing. ἐδεδοίκη, -ης, -ει common, pl. ἐδεδοίκεσαν less com-
> mon; sing. (late classical) ἐδεδίειν, -εις, -ει; plural ἐδέδιμεν, ἐδέδιτε,
> ἐδεδίεσαν or ἐδέδισαν
> infinitive: δεδιέναι more common than δεδοικέναι
> participle: δεδιώς, δεδιυῖα, δεδιός more common than δεδοικώς, -υῖα, -ός
> subjunctive: normally δεδοίκω (δεδίω rare)
> optative: not found
> imperative: (rare) δέδιθι

WHAT TO STUDY AND DO

1. Study the conjugations presented above.
2. Learn the vocabulary of this unit.
3. Do the exercises of this unit.

VOCABULARY

nouns

ἀνδράποδον, ἀνδραπόδου, n.	war captive sold into slavery; slave
δέος, δέους, n.	fear
ἐπιστολή, ἐπιστολῆς, f.	message, order sent by messenger; letter [epistle]

θήρα, θήρας, f.	hunting, the chase
κύκλος, κύκλου, m.	ring, circle; wheel [cycle]
κύκλῳ	(adv.) in a circle, all around
κύων, κυνός, m. or f.[1]	dog; shameless creature [cynic, cynosure]
μῆκος, μήκους, n.	length; size, greatness
νῆσος, νήσου, f.	island [Peloponnese]
οὐρανός, οὐρανοῦ, m.	heaven, the heavens, sky [Uranus]
οὐσία, οὐσίας, f.	property; (philosophy) being, essence, reality
ὀφθαλμός, ὀφθαλμοῦ, m.	eye [ophthalmologist]
πῦρ, πυρός, n.[2]	fire [pyromaniac, pyrite, empyrean]
σπουδή, σπουδῆς, f.	haste, speed; trouble, effort; regard, esteem, good will
σχολή, σχολῆς, f.	leisure, rest; talk which occupies one's leisure, learned discussion [school, scholastic]
σχολῇ	(adv.) in a leisurely way; scarcely, not at all
σῶμα, σώματος, n.	body; person [psychosomatic, chromosome]
τύραννος, τυράννου, m.	absolute ruler, tyrant [tyrannosaurus]

adjectives

ἀριστερός, ἀριστερά, ἀριστερόν	on the left, left; ominous
ἀριστερά, -ᾶς, f.	left hand
δεξιός, δεξιά, δεξιόν	on the right; fortunate; dexterous, skillful, clever
δεξιά, -ᾶς, f.	right hand
ἐναντίος, ἐναντία, ἐναντίον	opposite, opposing
οἱ ἐναντίοι	the adversary, the enemy
ἐπιτήδειος, ἐπιτηδεία, ἐπιτήδειον	made for a purpose, suitable; useful, necessary
τὰ ἐπιτήδεια	provisions
ἔσχατος, ἐσχάτη, ἔσχατον	farthest, extreme, utmost, last [eschatology]
ἕτοιμος, ἑτοίμη, ἕτοιμον	ready, prepared
θαυμάσιος, θαυμασία, θαυμάσιον	wonderful, marvelous, admirable
θαυμαστός, θαυμαστή, θαυμαστόν	wonderful, marvelous, admirable
ὑγιής, ὑγιές	healthy, sound; (of statements or persons) wise, good
ὑψηλός, ὑψηλή, ὑψηλόν	high, lofty [hypsography, hypsicephalic]
φοβερός, φοβερά, φοβερόν	causing fear, fearful; regarded with fear or dread

---

1. Vocative κύον, dat. pl. κυσί(ν).
2. This word is not found in the plural.

verbs

ἀλλάττω, ἀλλάξω, ἤλλαξα,   change, alter; exchange (+ gen. of thing received in
ἤλλαχα, ἤλλαγμαι,   return); (mid.) take in exchange (+ gen. of thing
ἠλλάχθην and ἠλλάγην[1]   given in return)   [allagite]

δέδοικα or δέδια (perfects   fear
with present meaning),
(poetic fut. δείσομαι),
ἔδεισα

ἔοικα (perf. with present   be like, look like (+ dat.); seem likely, seem probable
meaning), fut. (perf.) εἴξω[2]   (+ inf.)

στέλλω, (poetic στελέω),   make ready, fit out; send, dispatch
ἔστειλα, -έσταλκα,
ἔσταλμαι, ἐστάλην

    ἐπιστέλλω (ἐπι)   send a message; order, command (+ dat. or acc. +
inf.)

EXERCISES

I.   Identify each form completely.

1. ἠθροίκεσαν
2. ὠμωμόκει
3. ἀλλάξησθε
4. πεπαύσομαι
5. εἴργαστο
6. γεγραμμένα
7. ἠλήλεγκτο

8. ἐδέδειξο
9. δεδοικέναι
10. ἐπεσταλκυῖαν
11. ἀφεῖναι
12. ἀπιέναι
13. τέθναμεν
14. ἀφεστάναι

15. γνῶθι
16. ἐβεβήκη
17. ἐληλυθέναι
18. ἔοικας
19. κεκλήσεται
20. γεγυμνασμέναι
    ἔσονται

II.   Write the following Greek forms.

1. masc. s. gen. pres. act. part. of φαίνω
2. 2nd s. aor. mid. subj. of ὑπισχνέομαι
3. perf. m/p inf. of ὁράω
4. fem. dat. pl. perf. m/p part. of τέμνω
5. 1st pl. pres. act. opt. of τελέω
6. 3rd s. pluperf. act. ind. of συντίθημι
7. neut. s. nom. aor. pass. part. of ῥίπτω
8. 2nd pl. fut. act. opt. of διασκεδάννυμι

---

1. Non-Attic ἀλλάσσω.

2. In poetry an athematic 1st pl. form ἔοιγμεν is found, and in poetry and prose the 3rd pl. is sometimes εἴξασι, sometimes ἐοίκασι. The infinitive is ἐοικέναι or rarely εἰκέναι; the participle ἐοικώς or εἰκώς, -υῖα, -ός. For the pluperfect one finds both forms from ἐῴκη and the 3rd s. ἤκειν.

9. aor. pass. inf. of προδίδωμι
10. masc. pl. acc. fut. act. part. of πολεμέω
11. 1st s. aor. act. opt. of ἐμπίμπλημι
12. fem. s. dat. pres. m/p part. of ὀρχέομαι
13. 2nd s. pluperf. act. ind. of ἁμαρτάνω
14. 1st pl. fut. perf. m/p ind. of μιμνῄσκω
15. 3rd pl. pluperf. act. ind. of δέδοικα
16. 2nd pl. pluperf. m/p ind. of βάλλω
17. 1st s. pluperf. m/p ind. of ἁρπάζω
18. 3rd s. pres. act. imperat. of ἐπιστέλλω
19. 3rd pl. neuter pluperf. m/p ind. of ἀγγέλλω
20. aor. mid. inf. of κόπτω

III. Render into Greek.[1]

(1) In response to [= with regard to] these things Xenophon stood up and spoke on behalf of the soldiers: (2) "We have come, gentlemen of the embassy, having with difficulty saved our bodies and our arms. (3) For it was not possible to carry our possessions and to fight the enemy at the same time. (4) And wherever we go and do not have a marketplace, we take what is necessary, not in arrogance [use dat. of manner] but by necessity."

IV. Reading: Plato, *Protagoras* 321c–322b (abridged; continued from U40).

ἀπορίᾳ οὖν σχόμενος ὁ Προμηθεὺς ἥντινα σωτηρίαν τῷ ἀνθρώπῳ εὕροι, κλέπτει Ἡφαίστου καὶ Ἀθηνᾶς τὴν ἔντεχνον σοφίαν σὺν πυρί— ἀμήχανον γὰρ ἦν ἄνευ πυρὸς αὐτὴν κτητήν τῳ ἢ χρησίμην γενέσθαι—καὶ οὕτω δὴ δωρεῖται ἀνθρώπῳ. τὴν μὲν οὖν περὶ τὸν βίον σοφίαν ἄνθρωπος ταύτῃ ἔσχεν, τὴν δὲ πολιτικὴν οὐκ εἶχεν· ἦν γὰρ παρὰ τῷ Διί. . . . ἐπειδὴ δὲ ὁ ἄνθρωπος θείας μετέσχε μοίρας, πρῶτον μὲν διὰ τὴν τοῦ θεοῦ συγγένειαν ζῴων μόνον θεοὺς ἐνόμισεν, καὶ ἐπεχείρει βωμούς τε ἱδρύεσθαι καὶ ἀγάλματα θεῶν· ἔπειτα φωνὴν καὶ ὀνόματα ταχὺ διηρθρώσατο τῇ τέχνῃ, καὶ οἰκήσεις καὶ ἐσθῆτας καὶ ὑποδέσεις καὶ στρωμνὰς καὶ τὰς ἐκ γῆς τροφὰς ηὕρετο. οὕτω δὴ παρεσκευασμένοι κατ᾽ ἀρχὰς ἄνθρωποι ᾤκουν σποράδην, πόλεις δὲ οὐκ ἦσαν· ἀπώλλυντο οὖν ὑπὸ τῶν θηρίων διὰ τὸ πανταχῇ αὐτῶν ἀσθενέστεροι εἶναι, καὶ ἡ δημιουργικὴ τέχνη αὐτοῖς πρὸς μὲν τροφὴν ἱκανὴ βοηθὸς ἦν, πρὸς δὲ τὸν τῶν θηρίων πόλεμον ἐνδεής— πολιτικὴν γὰρ τέχνην οὔπω εἶχον, ἧς μέρος πολεμική—ἐζήτουν δὴ ἀθροίζεσθαι καὶ σῴζεσθαι κτίζοντες πόλεις· ὅτ᾽ οὖν ἀθροισθεῖεν, ἠδίκουν ἀλλήλους ἅτε οὐκ ἔχοντες τὴν πολιτικὴν τέχνην, ὥστε πάλιν σκεδαννύμενοι διεφθείροντο.

---

1. Note to instructor: loosely based on *Anab.* 5.5.13 and 16.

Underlined Words

ἄγαλμα, -ματος, n. = *statue, image*

Ἀθηνᾶ, -ᾶς, f. = *Athena*, goddess of wisdom and crafts (declension: U42)

ἀμήχανος, -ον = *impossible*

ἀπορία, -ας, f. = *puzzlement, uncertainty what to do*

ἅτε = particle marking the participle ἔχοντες as causal

βοηθός, -όν = (adj. as substantive) *assistant, helper*

βωμός, -οῦ, m. = *altar*

γῆ, γῆς, f. = *earth* (declension: U42)

δημιουργικός, -ή, -όν = *pertaining to the crafts*

διαρθρόω (δια) = *divide up by joints, articulate*

Διί = dat. of Ζεύς, Διός, m., *Zeus*, the chief god

δωρέομαι = *make a gift, give a gift*

ἐνδεής, -ές = *lacking, deficient*

ἔντεχνος, -ον = *artistic, relating to craftsmanship*

ἐσθής, ἐσθῆτος, f. = *clothing*

ζῷον, -ου, n. = *animal*

Ἥφαιστος, -ου, m. = *Hephaestus*, god of fire and metallurgy

θεῖος, -α, -ον = *divine, godly*

ἱδρύω = *establish*; (mid.) *found, dedicate*

κτητός, -ή, -όν = *capable of being acquired or possessed*

κτίζω = *found, establish*

οἴκησις, -εως, f. = *dwelling*

οὖν = (postpositive particle) *therefore, then*

οὔπω = *not yet*

πολεμικός, -ή, -όν = *related to war*

πολιτικός, -ή, -όν = *political*

σποράδην = (adv.) *scattered here and there*

στρωμνή, -ῆς, f. = *bedding*

συγγένεια, -ας, f. = *kinship*

σχόμενος: recall that ἔχω is the only verb in Attic prose whose aorist "middle" form can be used as a passive (U19.6)

τροφή, -ῆς, f. = *nourishment*

ὑπόδεσις, -εως, f. = *footwear*

χρήσιμος, -η, -ον = *useful*

Contract-Vowel Declension; Attic Declension; Verbal Adjectives in -τός and -τέος

1. *O-Declension Nouns with Contraction.* A few o-declension nouns have stems ending in *-oo-* or *-εo-*, and these suffer contraction in Attic. The relevant contractions are as follows:

$o + o \longrightarrow ou$ (sp.)	$o + ou$ (sp.) $\longrightarrow ou$ (sp.)	$o + \omega \longrightarrow \omega$
$o + \omega \longrightarrow \omega$	$o + \epsilon \longrightarrow ou$ (sp.)	$o + oι \longrightarrow oι$
$\epsilon + o \longrightarrow ou$ (sp.)	$\epsilon + ou \longrightarrow ou$ (sp.)	$\epsilon + \omega \longrightarrow \omega$
$\epsilon + \omega \longrightarrow \omega$	$\epsilon + oι \longrightarrow oι$	$\epsilon + a \longrightarrow \bar{a}$

The accentuation is in general in accordance with the rule given in U13.2. But compounds retain the accentuation of the nominative throughout (e.g., περί-πλου despite uncontracted περιπλόου), and the nom. acc. voc. dual of uncompounded words has acute (e.g., νώ instead of νῶ from νόω).

Ex.	uncontracted:	νόος	περίπλοος	κάνεον
		"mind"	*"voyage around"*	*"basket"*
sing.	nom.	νοῦς	περίπλους	κανοῦν
	gen.	νοῦ	περίπλου	κανοῦ
	dat.	νῷ	περίπλῳ	κανῷ
	acc.	νοῦν	περίπλουν	κανοῦν
	voc.	νοῦ	περίπλου	κανοῦν
(dual	n. a. v.	νώ	περίπλω	κανώ)
	(g. d.	νοῖν	περίπλοιν	κανοῖν)
plur.	n. v.	νοῖ	περίπλοι	κανᾶ
	gen.	νῶν	περίπλων	κανῶν
	dat.	νοῖς	περίπλοις	κανοῖς
	acc.	νοῦς	περίπλους	κανᾶ

2. *A-Declension Nouns with Contraction.* A few a-declension nouns have stems ending in -εα- or -αα-, and these suffer contraction in Attic. In all of the contractions in these nouns, the ε or α is simply absorbed in the following vowel, and the endings turn out to be exactly the same as for uncontracted a-declension nouns, except that all forms have circumflex accent on the ending. Some contract nouns are also exceptions to the general rule about the treatment of original long alpha in Attic (e.g., συκέη has η after ε, μνάα has α after α).

Ex.

	uncontracted:	γέη	συκέη	μνάα	Ἑρμέης
		"earth"	*"fig tree"*	*"mina"*	*"Hermes"*
sing.	*nom.*	γῆ	συκῆ	μνᾶ	Ἑρμῆς
	gen.	γῆς	συκῆς	μνᾶς	Ἑρμοῦ
	dat.	γῇ	συκῇ	μνᾷ	Ἑρμῇ
	acc.	γῆν	συκῆν	μνᾶν	Ἑρμῆν
	voc.	γῆ	συκῆ	μνᾶ	Ἑρμῆ
(dual	*n. a. v.*		συκᾶ	μνᾶ	Ἑρμᾶ)
	(g. d.		συκαῖν	μναῖν	Ἑρμαῖν)
plur.	*n. v.*		συκαῖ	μναῖ	Ἑρμαῖ
	gen.		συκῶν	μνῶν	Ἑρμῶν
	dat.		συκαῖς	μναῖς	Ἑρμαῖς
	acc.		συκᾶς	μνᾶς	Ἑρμᾶς

3. *Contract Adjectives.* Most vowel-declension adjectives with masculine stem in -εο- or -οο- have contracted inflection. The masculine and neuter are like contract o-declension nouns, and the fem. is like contract a-declension nouns (stems in -οο- form the feminine from a stem in -εα- rather than from the expected -οα-). Regardless of the accentuation of the uncontracted form of the adjective, the contracted forms of a simple adjective have circumflex on U in all cases and numbers (except acute on nom. acc. voc. dual masc. and neuter); contracted forms of compound adjectives retain the accentuation of the nom. sing. throughout (e.g., εὔνους, εὔνου, etc.).

As an example, the declension of χρυσοῦς, *golden* (uncontracted χρύσεος, χρυσέα, χρύσεον) is shown at the top of the next page. The same pattern applies to ἀργύρεος, "of silver," contracted ἀργυροῦς, ἀργυρᾶ, ἀργυροῦν, except that the fem. singular has alpha instead of eta (ἀργυρᾶ, ἀργυρᾶς, ἀργυρᾷ, ἀργυρᾶν). Note also that in compound adjectives, the neuter plural nom. acc. ends in -οα without contraction (e.g., εὔνοα, ἄπλοα).

CONTRACT-DECLENSION ADJECTIVE

		masc.	*fem.*	*neuter*
sing.	n. v.	χρυσοῦς	χρυσῆ	χρυσοῦν
	gen.	χρυσοῦ	χρυσῆς	χρυσοῦ
	dat.	χρυσῷ	χρυσῇ	χρυσῷ
	acc.	χρυσοῦν	χρυσῆν	χρυσοῦν
(dual	n. a. v.	χρυσώ	χρυσᾶ	χρυσώ)
	(g. d.	χρυσοῖν	χρυσαῖν	χρυσοῖν)
plur.	n. v.	χρυσοῖ	χρυσαῖ	χρυσᾶ
	gen.	χρυσῶν	χρυσῶν	χρυσῶν
	dat.	χρυσοῖς	χρυσαῖς	χρυσοῖς
	acc.	χρυσοῦς	χρυσᾶς	χρυσᾶ

4. *Attic Declension.* A few nouns in Attic have nom. sing. in -εώς and have the vowel omega in all endings, replacing the o or ου found in regular o-declension nouns. The -εως ending is the product of quantitative metathesis (as seen in Attic also in πόλεως for πόληος and νεώς for νηός [from ναῦς]). Declension of this kind was termed "Attic" because in Koine such nouns took a non-Attic/Ionic form, ending in -αος. The term was also applied to other nouns showing omega in the case endings, even though these nouns are of different origin. In both kinds of ω-nouns the accent of the nominative singular is retained in all other cases (including acute on gen. and dat. for a noun accented on *U*). A paradigm showing the most common nouns of the Attic declension is shown on the upper half of the next page .

5. *Other Nouns in -ως.* There are a few other nouns which have nominative in -ως. (1) αἰδώς is a consonant-declension sigma-stem with strong-grade vowel in nom. and normal-grade vowel in the other cases, which also lose intervocalic sigma. No other common noun in Attic has this pattern, but it is found in some feminine proper names, such as Σαπφώ, Λητώ, which have nom. in -ω but are otherwise declined like αἰδώς. (2) ἥρως is also a consonant-declension noun,[1] but the consonant which has disappeared is vau instead of sigma and the long vowel omega is found throughout the declension. Among the few other nouns declined in this way are πάτρως = *paternal uncle* and μήτρως = *maternal uncle.*

The paradigm for αἰδώς and ἥρως is shown on the lower half of the next page.

---

1. The alternative gen. form ἥρω is by assimilation to the Attic-declension pattern.

ATTIC DECLENSION NOUNS

		"temple" (Doric ναός, Ionic νηός)	*"people"* (Doric λαός, Ionic ληός)	*"dawn"*[1] (Ionic ἠώς, gen. ἠοῦς)	*"hare"* (epic λαγωός, gen. λαγωοῦ)
sing.	*nom.*	νεώς	λεώς	ἕως	λαγώς
	gen.	νεώ	λεώ	ἕω	λαγώ
	dat.	νεῴ	λεῴ	ἕῳ	λαγῴ
	acc.	νεών	λεών	ἕω	λαγών
					or λαγώ
(dual	*n. a. v.*	νεώ			λαγώ)
	(g. d.	νεῴν			λαγῴν)
plur.	*n. v.*	νεῴ	λεῴ		λαγῴ
	gen.	νεών	λεών		λαγών
	dat.	νεῴς	λεῴς		λαγῴς
	acc.	νεώς	λεώς		λαγώς

NOUNS IN -ως

		"shame"	*"hero"*
sing.	*n. v.*	αἰδώς	ἥρως
	gen.	αἰδοῦς	ἥρωος or ἥρω
	dat.	αἰδοῖ	ἥρωϊ or ἥρῳ
	acc.	αἰδῶ	ἥρωα or ἥρω
(dual	*n. a. v.*		ἥρωε)
	(g. d.		ἡρώοιν)
plur.	*n. v.*		ἥρωες or ἥρως
	gen.		ἡρώων
	dat.		ἥρωσι(ν)
	acc.		ἥρωας or ἥρως

6. *Adjectives of the Attic Declension.* A few adjectives in Attic have masc. and neuter forms in -εως, -εων following the pattern of the Attic-declension nouns. Again, quantitative metathesis or contraction lies behind the Attic

---

1. The noun "dawn" is in origin a consonant-declension σ-stem, with sigma lost between vowels in cases other than the nom. (e.g., *ἠόσος —> ἠοῦς); but in Attic it is partly assimilated to the omega-stem pattern. The accusative has the original consonant-declension ending (cf. Ionic ἠώ from *ἠόα) and has not been assimilated to the ω-declension ending -ων, based on o-declension -ον. The Attic version of the noun "hare" may be viewed as a contraction of the epic version, but the alternative accusative sing. form shows assimilation to the pattern of ἕως.

forms. Two important examples are ἵλεως (epic ἵλαος), *propitious*, and πλέως (epic πλεῖος), *full*. Note retention of the original acute on A despite the long U in the Attic form (as in πόλεως).

		"propitious"		"full"		
		masc./fem.	*neuter*	*masc.*	*fem.*	*neuter*
s.	*nom.*	ἵλεως	ἵλεων	πλέως	πλέᾱ	πλέων
	gen.	ἵλεω	ἵλεω	πλέω	πλέᾱς	πλέω
	dat.	ἵλεῳ	ἵλεῳ	πλέῳ	πλέᾳ	πλέῳ
	acc.	ἵλεων	ἵλεων	πλέων	πλέᾱν	πλέων
(d.	*n. a. v.*	ἵλεω	ἵλεω	πλέω	πλέᾱ	πλέω)
(g. d.	ἵλεῳν	ἵλεῳν	πλέῳν	πλέαιν	πλέῳν)
pl.	*n. v.*	ἵλεῳ	ἵλεα	πλέῳ	πλέαι	πλέᾰ
	gen.	ἵλεων	ἵλεων	πλέων	πλέων	πλέων
	dat.	ἵλεῳς	ἵλεῳς	πλέῳς	πλέαις	πλέῳς
	acc.	ἵλεως	ἵλεα	πλέως	πλέᾱς	πλέᾰ

7. *Verbal Adjectives in -τός and -τέος.* In addition to the very frequently used participle, many Greek verbs also possess one or two less commonly used verbal adjectives formed by the addition of the suffixes -τός, -τή, -τόν and -τέος, -τέᾱ, -τέον to a form of the verb stem (often the form apparent in the aorist passive). To ascertain whether one or both of these verbal adjectives exist for a given verb, one must consult a good Greek dictionary.

The verbal adjectives in -τός denote possibility or are equivalent to a perfect passive participle.[1]

Ex.   κρύπτω   —>   κρυπτός, *hidden*
             ὁράω   —>   ὁρᾱτός, *visible*
             φιλέω   —>   φιλητός, *loved, capable of being loved*

Verbal adjectives in -τέος, on the other hand, denote necessity.

Ex.   λέγω   —>   λεκτέος, *to be said, that must be said*
             πράττω   —>   πρᾱκτέος, *to be done, that must be done*

The verbal adjective in -τέος is only rarely used as an attributive or predicate adjective agreeing with a noun (and then only when the corresponding verb is transitive and governs the acc.). Its most common use is in the neuter singular nominative (occasionally in early Attic neut. pl. nom.) in combination with ἐστί (or with ἐστί understood) to express obligation or necessity. In this con-

---

1. Note that the suffix is etymologically the same as the standard suffix *-tus* used in the formation of Latin past passive participles.

struction the verbal adjective may govern an object in the acc., gen., or dat. (whichever is appropriate to the corresponding verb). In either usage, the agent, if expressed, must be put in the dative of agent without a preposition (cf. U37.7).

personal constuction:

ὁ ποταμὸς ἡμῖν ἐστι διαβατέος.
The river is to be crossed by us.
= *We must cross the river.*

τὰ πρακτέα, *the things which must be done*

impersonal construction:

τῷ ἀδικοῦντι δοτέον δίκην.
The wrongdoer must pay the penalty.
[δίκην is acc. obj. of the verbal adj.]

ἡμῖν σύμμαχοι ἀγαθοί, οὓς οὐ παραδοτέα τοῖς ᾿Αθηναίοις.
We have good allies, whom we must not surrender to the Athenians.

τῶν παιδίων ἐπιμελητέον.
One must take care of the children.
[παιδίων gen. obj. of the verbal adj.]

WHAT TO STUDY AND DO

1. Study the declensional patterns presented above and the use of verbal adjectives.
2. Learn the vocabulary of this unit.
3. Do the exercises of this unit.

VOCABULARY

nouns

αἰδώς, αἰδοῦς, f.	awe; sense of shame; respect for others
ἄργυρος, ἀργύρου, m.	silver [argyrocephalous]
γῆ, γῆς, f.	earth, land, country [geology]
῾Ερμῆς, ῾Ερμοῦ, m.	the god Hermes (Roman Mercury); herm (pillar surmounted by a bust, usually with male genitals on the pillar, set up by the door to ward off evil)
ἕως, ἕω, f.	dawn; the east [Eohippus]
Ζεύς, gen. Διός (dat. Διί, acc. Δία, voc. Ζεῦ), m.	Zeus (chief god of the Hellenic pantheon; Roman Jupiter)

ἥρως, ἥρωος, m.	hero, i.e., an epic warrior from the Age of Heroes and/or a cult figure with powers for good and evil worshipped at a hero shrine or tomb
κανοῦν, κανοῦ, n.[1]	basket
λαγώς, λαγώ, m.	hare [lagophthalmus, lagopodous]
μνᾶ, μνᾶς, f.	mina (a unit of weight and currency, = 100 drachmai = 1/60 talent)[2]
νεώς, νεώ, m.[3]	temple; inner shrine of a temple [pronaos]
νοῦς, νοῦ, m.[4]	mind; sense; intellect [noumenal]
νοῦν ἔχειν	be sensible, be reasonable
προσέχειν τὸν νοῦν	pay attention to (+ dat.)
πλοῦς, πλοῦ, m.	voyage
περίπλους, περίπλου, m.	circumnavigation [periplus]
σίδηρος, σιδήρου, m.	iron
σῦκον, σύκου, n.	fig [sycophant]
συκῆ, συκῆς, f.[5]	fig tree
χαλκός, χαλκοῦ, m.	copper, bronze; weapon made of bronze [chalcograph]
χρυσός, χρυσοῦ, m.	gold [chryselephantine]

adjectives

ἄπλους, ἄπλουν [ἄπλοος]	not navigable; (ships) not seaworthy
ἁπλοῦς, ἁπλῆ, ἁπλοῦν [ἁπλόος]	single; simple, straightforward [haplography]
διπλοῦς, διπλῆ, διπλοῦν [διπλόος]	double, twofold [diploma]
ἀργυροῦς, ἀργυρᾶ, ἀργυροῦν [ἀργύρεος]	of silver
εὔνους, εὔνουν [εὔνοος]	well-disposed, friendly
δύσνους, δύσνουν [δύσνοος]	ill-disposed, disaffected
ἵλεως, ἵλεων[6]	(esp. of gods) propitious, gracious; kindly [hilarity]
πλέως, πλέα, πλέων	full, filled (+ gen.)
χαλκοῦς, χαλκῆ, χαλκοῦν [χάλκεος]	of copper, of bronze

---

1. Non-Attic κάνεον.
2. See U29 Vocabulary.
3. Non-Attic ναός.
4. Non-Attic νόος.
5. Non-Attic συκέα, συκέη.
6. Non-Attic ἵλαος.

χρυσοῦς, χρυσῆ, χρυσοῦν   of gold
  [χρύσεος]

verbs

νοέω, νοήσω, ἐνόησα, νενό-   perceive; apprehend; think, deem (+ inf. of ind.
  ηκα, νενόημαι, ἐνοήθην   disc.); intend (+ inf.)   [noetic]
          διανοέομαι   intend, be minded to (+ inf.); think, suppose (+ inf.
                                    of ind. disc.); be disposed

adverb/particle

οὖν   (postpositive) therefore, then

EXERCISES

I.   Identify each form completely.

1. ἐδέδιμεν   8. δραμοῦνται   15. σύγγνωθι
2. ἀφέστασαν   9. σιγήσατε   16. ὀμωμοκέναι
3. τετροφότες   10. ὠφελεῖν   17. ἐπεπαύκη
4. τεύξεσθαι   11. ὀφελεῖν   18. πορευθεῖσι
5. φανείην   12. τετελευτημένα ἦν   19. νενικῆσθαι
6. ἐζεῦχθαι   13. ἔλεγξον   20. εἰδῆτε
7. ἐρωτῴη   14. φυλακτέος   21. διανοῇ

II. Write the following forms in Greek.

1. 3rd pl. pres. m/p subj. of ὀργίζομαι
2. pres. act. inf. of ὄμνυμι
3. neut. pl. gen. perf. act. part. of μισέω
4. 2nd s. aor. pass. subj. of κλέπτω
5. 1st pl. perf. m/p ind. of καταλείπω
6. masc. s. acc. aor. act. part. of ζεύγνυμι
7. 3rd s. pres. act. subj. of ἐπιδείκνυμι
8. fut. pass. inf. of διώκω
9. fem. pl. acc. fut. pass. part. of διδάσκω
10. 2nd pl. aor. pass. opt. of διαβάλλω
11. 1st sing. fut. mid. ind. of ἀφίστημι
12. 3rd pl. (masc.) pluperf. m/p ind. of ἀγνοέω

III. Render into Greek.[1]

(1) And now, when we came to Hellenic cities, in that one, on the one hand, (for they provided us a marketplace) we had what was necessary and, in return for the ways in which they honored us, we aided them. (2) We harmed their enemies, as much as we were able to, whichever enemies they themselves led us against. (3) But these people, who you say are yours, are themselves to blame if we have taken anything from them. (4) For they were not friendly to us, neither receiving [deponent δέχομαι] us within [εἴσω] nor sending a marketplace outside [ἔξω].

IV. Reading: Plato, *Protagoras* 322c–323a (continued from U41).

Ζεὺς οὖν δείσας περὶ τῷ γένει ἡμῶν μὴ ἀπόλοιτο πᾶν, Ἑρμῆν πέμπει ἄγοντα εἰς ἀνθρώπους αἰδῶ τε καὶ δίκην, ἵν᾽ εἶεν πόλεων <u>κόσμοι</u> τε καὶ <u>δεσμοὶ</u> φιλίας <u>συναγωγοί</u>. ἐρωτᾷ οὖν Ἑρμῆς Δία τίνα οὖν τρόπον δοίη δίκην καὶ αἰδῶ ἀνθρώποις· "<u>πότερον</u> ὡς αἱ τέχναι <u>νενέμηνται</u>, οὕτω καὶ ταύτας νείμω; νενέμηνται δὲ ὧδε· εἷς ἔχων <u>ἰατρικὴν</u> πολλοῖς ἱκανὸς ἰδιώταις, καὶ οἱ ἄλλοι <u>δημιουργοί</u>· καὶ δίκην δὴ καὶ αἰδῶ οὕτω θῶ ἐν τοῖς ἀνθρώποις, ἢ ἐπὶ πάντας νείμω;" "ἐπὶ πάντας," ἔφη ὁ Ζεύς, "καὶ πάντες μετεχόντων· οὐ γὰρ ἂν γένοιντο πόλεις, εἰ ὀλίγοι αὐτῶν μετέχοιεν ὥσπερ ἄλλων τεχνῶν· καὶ νόμον γε θὲς παρ᾽ ἐμοῦ τὸν μὴ δυνάμενον αἰδοῦς καὶ δίκης μετέχειν <u>κτείνειν</u> ὡς νόσον πόλεως." οὕτω δή, ὦ Σώκρατες, καὶ διὰ ταῦτα οἵ τε ἄλλοι καὶ Ἀθηναῖοι, ὅταν μὲν περὶ ἀρετῆς <u>τεκτονικῆς</u> ἢ λόγος ἢ ἄλλης τινὸς <u>δημιουργικῆς</u>, ὀλίγοις οἴονται <u>μετεῖναι</u> <u>συμβουλῆς</u>, καὶ ἐάν τις <u>ἐκτὸς</u> ὢν τῶν ὀλίγων συμβουλεύῃ, οὐκ ἀνέχονται, ὡς σὺ φής—εἰκότως, ὡς ἐγώ φημι—ὅταν δὲ εἰς συμβουλὴν <u>πολιτικῆς</u> ἀρετῆς ἴωσιν, ἣν δεῖ <u>διὰ</u> <u>δικαιοσύνης</u> πᾶσαν ἰέναι καὶ σωφροσύνης, εἰκότως ἅπαντος <u>ἀνδρὸς</u> ἀνέχονται, ὡς παντὶ προσῆκον ταύτης γε μετέχειν τῆς ἀρετῆς ἢ μὴ εἶναι πόλεις.

Underlined Words

ἀνδρός: gen. depending on ἀνέχονται = *put up with (listening to)*

δεσμός, δεσμοῦ, m. = *bond*

δημιουργικός, -ή, -όν = *relating to the crafts*

δημιουργός, -οῦ, m. = *craftsman*

διὰ δικαιοσύνης . . . ἰέναι καὶ σωφροσύνης = *involve justice and moderation* (idiomatic phrase with διά + gen. of abstract noun with verb of motion)

---

1. Note to instructor: loosely based on *Anab.* 5.5.14 and 19.

εἰκότως = *reasonably* (adv. formed
    from participle of ἔοικα)
ἐκτός = (adv. + gen.) *outside of*
ἰατρική, -ῆς, f. = *physician's skill*
κόσμος, -ου, m. = *arrangement,*
    organization
κτείνω = simple form of ἀποκτείνω,
    kill
μετεῖναι = inf. of impersonal μέτεστι,
    there is a share of (+ partitive gen.
    and dat. of possession)
νέμω, aor. ἔνειμα, perf. m/p νενέμημαι
    = *distribute*

πολιτικός, -ή, -όν = *political*
πότερον = (adv. acc.) *whether*
    (introduces an alternative question;
    often, as here, not to be translated
    into English; here the alternative "or
    some other way" is implied but not
    expressed)
συμβουλή, -ῆς, f. = *deliberation,*
    debate
συναγωγός, -όν = *unifying, bringing*
    together
τεκτονικός, -ή, -όν = *related to*
    carpentry or building

Table of Contractions

This is a guide to the most frequent vowel contractions in Attic Greek, applicable to contract verbs and contract nouns and adjectives.

For the distinction between "genuine" and "spurious" $\epsilon\iota$ or ov, see page 10, note 2, and page 11, note 2.

$a + a$			$\epsilon + a$		$\eta + \iota$	
$\bar{a} + a$	$\bar{a}$		$\epsilon + \bar{a}$	η	$\eta + a\iota$	
$a + \bar{a}$			$\epsilon + \eta$		$\eta + \epsilon\iota$ gen	η
					$\eta + \eta$	
$a + \iota$	$a\iota$		$\epsilon + a\iota$	η		
$a + a\iota$			$\epsilon + \eta$		$\eta + \eta$	
					$\eta + \epsilon$	η
$\bar{a} + \iota$	α		$\epsilon + \epsilon$	$\epsilon\iota$ sp	$\eta + \epsilon\iota$ sp	
$a + \alpha$			$\epsilon + \epsilon\iota$ sp			
					$\eta + o\iota$	ω
$a + \epsilon$			$\epsilon + \iota$	$\epsilon\iota$ gen		
$a + \eta$	$\bar{a}$		$\epsilon + \epsilon\iota$ gen		$o + \epsilon$	
$a + \epsilon\iota$ sp					$o + \epsilon\iota$ sp	
			$\epsilon + o$	ov sp	$o + o$	ov sp
$a + \epsilon\iota$ gen	α		$\epsilon + o\iota$	$o\iota$	$o + ov$ sp	
$a + \eta$						
			$\epsilon + v$	ϵv	$o + \epsilon\iota$ gen	
$a + o$					$o + o\iota$	$o\iota$*
$a + ov$ sp	ω		$\epsilon + \omega$	ω	$o + \eta$	
$a + \omega$						
			$\epsilon + \omega$	ω	$o + \eta$	ω
$a + o\iota$	ω				$o + \omega$	
					$o + \omega$	ω

*NOTE: in the present and aorist subjunctive of $\delta\ell\delta\omega\mu\iota$, $o + \eta \,-> \omega$ instead of $o\iota$ (as if from $\omega + \eta$: cf. the aorist subjunctive of $\gamma\iota\gamma\nu\acute{\omega}\sigma\kappa\omega$ and $\acute{a}\lambda\acute{\iota}\sigma\kappa\omega\mu\alpha\iota$).

APPENDIX TWO

Verb List

Advice on Learning Principal Parts. Although some Greek verbs exhibit such irregularity in the formation of their principal parts that *ad hoc* memorization is the only reliable method of mastery, there are several patterns of formation that do apply to a large number of verbs. Awareness of these patterns may assist students in learning the principal parts of verbs presented in this book and in recognizing the dictionary forms of new verbs they meet in reading. In addition to the endings shown in the following patterns, remember that the 3rd and 6th principal parts (aorist) will of course have augment and the 4th and 5th principal parts (perfect) will of course have reduplication.

I.   Vowel verbs.
Pattern: *-ω, -σω, -σα, -κα, -μαι, -θην*
Examples:
(regular) θύω, κωλύω, λύω; παύω; βουλεύω, πιστεύω, πολιτεύω
(some parts lacking) βασιλεύω, δουλεύω, πορεύω, στρατεύω, ὑποπτεύω, φύω
Cf. also ἀκούω (fut. mid.; -σθην in aor. pass.; irreg. perfect); καίω (parts other than
       present based on καυ-); κελεύω (-σμαι, -σθην in perf. m/p and aor. pass.); παίω
       (-σθην in aor. pass.)

II.   Verbs in *-έω*.
Pattern: *-έω, -ήσω, -ησα, -ηκα, -ημαι, -ήθην*
Examples:
(regular) ἀγνοέω, ἀδικέω, αἰτέω, ἀπορέω, ἐπιχειρέω, εὐεργετέω, κατηγορέω,
       κρατέω, μισέω, νοέω, οἰκέω, ὁμολογέω, ποιέω, πολεμέω, φιλέω, ὠφελέω
(some parts lacking) ἀπολογέομαι, ἀσθενέω, βοηθέω, ἐπιθυμέω, εὐλαβέομαι,
       ζητέω, ἡγέομαι, νοσέω, ὀρχέομαι, πολιορκέω, σωφρονέω, φοβέω
Cf. αἱρέω (2nd aor. εἷλον, aor. pass. -έθην); also verbs in which ε of stem is not
       lengthened to η: ἐπαινέω (η in perf. m/p; -έσθην in aor. pass.), καλέω (some
       parts from κλη-), τελέω (-εσμαι, -έσθην in perf. m/p and aor. pass.)

III.   Verbs in *-άω*.
Pattern: *-άω, -ήσω, -ησα, -ηκα, -ημαι, -ήθην*
       or after stem ending in ε, ι, ρ:
       -άω, -άσω [ᾱ], *-āσα, āκα, -āμαι, -άθην* [ᾱ]

338

Examples:
(regular) ἀπατάω, δαπανάω, ἐρωτάω, νικάω, ὁρμάω, τελευτάω, τιμάω
Cf. σιγάω (future middle)
(with ᾱ for η) αἰτιάομαι, ἐάω, πειράω
(some parts lacking) ἀπαντάω, ἡττάομαι, κτάομαι, χράω/χράομαι

IV. Verbs in -όω.
Pattern: **-όω, -ώσω, -ωσα, -ωκα, -ωμαι, -ώθην**
Examples: ἀξιόω, δηλόω, ζηλόω

V. Verbs in -άζω.
Pattern: **-άζω, -άσω, -ασα, -ακα, -ασμαι, -άσθην** [ᾰ in all stems]
Examples:
(regular) ἀτιμάζω, γυμνάζω, δικάζω, φράζω
(with future middle -άσομαι) ἁρπάζω, θαυμάζω, σπουδάζω
(perf. act. lacking) παρασκευάζω

VI. Verbs in -ίζω.
Pattern: **-ίζω, -ιέω, -ισα, -ικα, -ισμαι, -ίσθην**
Examples:
(regular) κομίζω, νομίζω
(some parts lacking) ἐλπίζω, ὀργίζω/ὀργίζομαι
Cf. ἀθροίζω (future ἀθροίσω)

VII. Labial plosive verbs.
Pattern: **-πτω/-πω/-φω, -ψω, -ψα, -φα, -μμαι, -φθην** or 2nd aorist
    -πην/-βην/-φην
Examples:
(regular) βλάπτω, κλέπτω, κόπτω, ῥίπτω; πέμπω, τρέπω; γράφω, τρέφω
(some parts lacking) κρύπτω, σκέπτομαι, στρέφω
Cf. λείπω (2nd aorist; no aspiration in perfect)

VIII. Velar plosive verbs.
Pattern: **-ττω/-γω/-χω/-κω, -ξω, -ξα, -χα/-γα, -γμαι, -χθην/-γην**
Examples:
(regular) ἀλλάττω, πλήττω, πράττω, τάττω, φυλάττω; συλλέγω; ἄρχω
(some parts lacking) διώκω, ἥκω; διαλέγομαι, λέγω, φεύγω; ἐλέγχω, εὔχομαι
Cf. ἄγω (2nd aorist); also (with additional present-stem suffixes) ἀφικνέομαι,
    δείκνυμι, διδάσκω, δοκέω, ζεύγνυμι, ῥήγνυμι

IX. Dental plosive verbs.
Pattern: **-θω/-δω, -σω, -σα, -κα, -σμαι, -σθην**
Examples:
(regular) πείθω
(some parts missing) σπεύδω
Cf. ἥδομαι, σπένδω

X. Liquid verbs. In these verbs, present-tense suffix produces double lambda or
    compensatory lengthening of vowel (to αι or ει or ῑ) before rho or nu; future has
    normal vowel but epsilon-contract conjugation without sigma; aorist lacks sigma
    but has compensatory lengthening (to αι or ει or ῑ).
Patterns: -λλω, -λέω, -ιλα, -λκα, -λμαι, -λθην
           -ίνω, -νέω, -ινα, -κα, -ιμαι/-σμαι, -νθην/-νην
           -ίρω, -ρέω, -ιρα, -ρκα, -ρμαι, -ρθην/-ρην
Examples (most with various irregularities): ἀγγέλλω, ἀποκτείνω, βάλλω (some
    parts from stem βλη-), κλίνω, κρίνω, μένω, στέλλω, φαίνω, φθείρω

This is an alphabetical list of the verbs learned in all the unit vocabularies
with all their principal parts. The number preceding each verb indicates the
unit in which the verb is learned; refer to that unit for full definitions. Principal
parts that occur only in compounds in Attic prose are preceded by a hyphen.
Principal parts that are unattested in Attic prose but are found in poetry are
shown in parentheses. Compound verbs are cross-referenced to the simple
verb: remember that ἐ- augment in the aorist or ἐ- reduplication in the perfect
may cause elision of the final vowel of a disyllabic prepositional prefix, and
any change in aspiration may also affect the prefix (e.g., ἀποδίδωμι, ἀπέδωκα;
ἐπιστέλλω, ἐπέσταλκα; ἀπέχω, ἀφέξω or ἀποσχήσω).

19	ἀγγέλλω	ἀγγελέω	ἤγγειλα	ἤγγελκα	ἤγγελμαι	ἠγγέλθην
28	ἀγνοέω	ἀγνοήσω	ἠγνόησα	ἠγνόηκα	ἠγνόημαι	ἠγνοήθην
8	ἄγω	ἄξω	ἤγαγον	ἦχα	ἦγμαι	ἤχθην
13	ἀδικέω	ἀδικήσω	ἠδίκησα	ἠδίκηκα	ἠδίκημαι	ἠδικήθην
38	ἀθροίζω	ἀθροίσω	ἤθροισα	ἤθροικα	ἤθροισμαι	ἠθροίσθην
13	αἱρέω	αἱρήσω	εἷλον (stem ἑλ-)	ᾕρηκα	ᾕρημαι	ᾑρέθην
11	αἰσθάνομαι	αἰσθήσομαι	ᾐσθόμην	——	ᾔσθημαι	——
16	αἰτέω	αἰτήσω	ᾔτησα	ᾔτηκα	ᾔτημαι	ᾐτήθην
33	αἰτιάομαι	αἰτιάσομαι [ᾱ]	ᾐτιᾱσάμην	——	ᾐτίᾱμαι	ᾐτιάθην [ᾱ]
11	ἀκούω	ἀκούσομαι	ἤκουσα	ἀκήκοα	——	ἠκούσθην
24	ἁλίσκομαι	ἁλώσομαι	ἑάλων or ἥλων (stem ἁλω-)	ἑάλωκα or ἥλωκα	——	
41	ἀλλάττω	ἀλλάξω	ἤλλαξα	ἤλλαχα	ἤλλαγμαι	ἠλλάχθην and ἠλλάγην
28	ἁμαρτάνω	ἁμαρτήσο- μαι	ἥμαρτον	ἡμάρτηκα	ἡμάρτημαι	ἡμαρτήθην
24	ἀναβαίνω: see βαίνω					
24	ἀναγιγνώσκω: see γιγνώσκω					
32	ἀναιρέω: see αἱρέω					

29	ἀναμιμνήσκω: see μιμνήσκω				
23	ἀνατίθημι: see τίθημι				
28	ἀνέχω: see ἔχω				
33	ἀξιόω	ἀξιώσω	ἠξίωσα	ἠξίωκα	ἠξίωμαι	ἠξιώθην
16	ἀπάγω: see ἄγω				
33	ἀπαντάω	ἀπαντήσο-μαι	ἀπήντησα	ἀπήντηκα	——	——
38	ἀπατάω	ἀπατήσω	ἠπάτησα	ἠπάτηκα	ἠπάτημαι	ἠπατήθην
27	ἄπειμι: see εἰμί				
23	ἄπειμι: see εἶμι				
16	ἀπέχω: see ἔχω				
23	ἀποδείκνυμι: see δείκνυμι				
23	ἀποδίδωμι: see δίδωμι				
24	ἀποδύω: see δύω				
8	ἀποθνήσκω	ἀποθανέο-μαι	ἀπέθανον	τέθνηκα	——	——
32	ἀποκρίνω: see κρίνω				
11	ἀποκτείνω	ἀποκτενέω	ἀπέκτεινα	ἀπέκτονα	——	——
37	ἀπόλλῡμι	ἀπολέω	ἀπώλεσα and ἀπωλόμην	ἀπολώλεκα and ἀπόλωλα	——	——
32	ἀπολογέ-ομαι	ἀπολογή-σομαι	ἀπελογη-σάμην	——	ἀπολελό-γημαι	——
39	ἀποπλέω: see πλέω				
29	ἀπορέω	ἀπορήσω	ἠπόρησα	ἠπόρηκα	ἠπόρημαι	ἠπορήθην
26	ἁρπάζω	ἁρπάσομαι	ἥρπασα	ἥρπακα	ἥρπασμαι	ἡρπάσθην
8	ἄρχω	ἄρξω	ἦρξα	ἦρχα	ἦργμαι	ἤρχθην
40	ἀσεβέω	——				
33	ἀσθενέω	ἀσθενήσω	ἠσθένησα	ἠσθένηκα	——	——
33	ἀτιμάζω	ἀτιμάσω	ἠτίμασα	ἠτίμακα	ἠτίμασμαι	ἠτιμάσθην
23	ἀφίημι: see ἵημι				
13	ἀφικνέομαι	ἀφίξομαι	ἀφῑκόμην	——	ἀφῖγμαι	
23	ἀφίστημι: see ἵστημι				
24	βαίνω	-βήσομαι	-ἔβην	βέβηκα	-βέβαμαι	-ἐβάθην
10	βάλλω	βαλέω	ἔβαλον	βέβληκα	βέβλημαι	ἐβλήθην
29	βασιλεύω	βασιλεύσω	ἐβασίλευσα	——		
9	βλάπτω	βλάψω	ἔβλαψα	βέβλαφα	βέβλαμμαι	ἐβλάβην and ἐβλάφθην
33	βοηθέω	βοηθήσω	ἐβοήθησα	βεβοήθηκα	βεβοήθη-μαι	
11	βουλεύω	βουλεύσω	ἐβούλευσα	βεβούλευ-κα	βεβούλευ-μαι	ἐβουλεύ-θην
11	βούλομαι[1]	βουλήσο-μαι	——	——	βεβούλη-μαι	ἐβουλήθην
33	γαμέω	γαμέω	ἔγημα	γεγάμηκα	γεγάμημαι	——

---

1. In postclassical Attic, this verb often has "double augmentation," that is, imperfect ἠβουλόμην, aorist ἠβουλήθην.

33	γελάω	γελάσομαι [ᾰ]	ἐγέλᾰσα	——	——	ἐγελάσθην
11	γίγνομαι	γενήσομαι	ἐγενόμην	γέγονα	γεγένημαι	ἐγενήθην
19	γιγνώσκω	γνώσομαι	ἔγνων (U24)	ἔγνωκα	ἔγνωσμαι	ἐγνώσθην
8	γράφω	γράψω	ἔγραψα	γέγραφα	γέγραμμαι	ἐγράφην
11	γυμνάζω	γυμνάσω	ἐγύμνασα	γεγύμνακα	γεγύμνασ- μαι	ἐγυμνάσ- θην
33	δαπανάω	δαπανήσω	ἐδαπάνησα	δεδαπάνη- κα	δεδαπάνη- μαι	ἐδαπανή- θην
41	[δέδοικα]¹	(δείσομαι)	ἔδεισα	δέδοικα or δέδια	——	——
23	δείκνῡμι	δείξω	ἔδειξα	δέδειχα	δέδειγμαι	ἐδείχθην
13	δέω	δεήσω	ἐδέησα	δεδέηκα	δεδέημαι	ἐδεήθην
9	δεῖ	δεήσει	ἐδέησε	——		
29	δηλόω	δηλώσω	ἐδήλωσα	δεδήλωκα	δεδήλωμαι	ἐδηλώθην
24	διαβαίνω: see βαίνω					
32	διαβάλλω: see βάλλω					
24	διαγιγνώσκω: see γιγνώσκω					
25	διαδίδωμι: see δίδωμι					
32	διαλέγομαι [cf. λέγω]	διαλέξομαι	——	——	διείλεγμαι	διελέχθην and διελέγην
28	διαμένω: see μένω					
42	διανοέομαι: see νοέω					
28	διατελέω: see τελέω					
17	διαφέρω: see φέρω					
39	διαφθείρω: see φθείρω					
34	διδάσκω	διδάξω	ἐδίδαξα	δεδίδαχα	δεδίδαγμαι	ἐδιδάχθην
23	δίδωμι	δώσω	ἔδωκα	δέδωκα	δέδομαι	ἐδόθην
11	δικάζω	δικάσω	ἐδίκασα	δεδίκακα	δεδίκασμαι	ἐδικάσθην
27	διώκω	διώξομαι or rarely διώξω	ἐδίωξα	δεδίωχα	——	ἐδιώχθην
13	δοκέω	δόξω	ἔδοξα	——	δέδογμαι	-εδόχθην
9	δοκεῖ	δόξει	ἔδοξε	——	δέδοκται	
30	δουλεύω	δουλεύσω	ἐδούλευσα	δεδούλευκα	——	——
25	δύναμαι²	δυνήσομαι	——	——	δεδύνημαι	ἐδυνήθην
24	δύω [ῠ]	-δύσω [ῡ]	-έδῡσα and ἔδῡν	-δέδῡκα	-δέδῠμαι	-εδύθην [ῠ]
33	ἐάω	ἐάσω [ᾱ]	εἴᾱσα	εἴᾱκα	εἴᾱμαι	εἰάθην [ᾱ]
8	ἐθέλω	ἐθελήσω	ἠθέλησα	ἠθέληκα	——	
19	εἶδον: see ὁράω					
10	εἰμί	ἔσομαι	——	——	——	
23	εἶμι	(for other tenses parts of ἔρχομαι are used)				
19	εἶπον: see ἐρέω					

---

1. Perfect with present meaning; no present in Attic.

2. In late classical or postclassical Attic, this verb often has "double augmentation," that is, imperfect ἠδυνάμην, aorist ἠδυνήθην.

33	[εἴρομαι] (Ionic)	ἐρήσομαι	ἠρόμην	——	——	——
8	ἐλαύνω	ἐλάω (U29)	ἤλασα	-ελήλακα	ἐλήλαμαι	ἠλάθην
28	ἐλέγχω	ἐλέγξω	ἤλεγξα	——	ἐλήλεγμαι (stem ἐληλεγχ-)	ἠλέγχθην
19	ἐλπίζω	ἐλπιέω	ἤλπισα	——	——	ἠλπίσθην
34	ἐμβαίνω: see βαίνω					
29	ἐμπίμπλη- μι	ἐμπλήσω	ἐνέπλησα	ἐμπέπληκα	ἐμπέπλησ- μαι	ἐνεπλήσ- θην
27	ἐξαιτέω: see αἰτέω					
38	ἐξαπατάω: see ἀπατάω					
23	ἔξειμι: see εἰμι					
28	ἐξελέγχω: see ἐλέγχω					
9	ἔξεστι	ἔξεσται	——	——	——	——
41	ἔοικα[1]	εἴξω	——	——	——	——
16	ἐπαινέω	ἐπαινέσω	ἐπήνεσα	ἐπήνεκα	ἐπήνημαι	ἐπηνέσθην
28	ἐπιβουλεύω: see βουλεύω					
23	ἐπιδείκνῡμι: see δείκνῡμι					
16	ἐπιθῡμέω	ἐπιθῡμήσω	ἐπεθύμησα [ῡ]	ἐπιτεθύμη- κα [ῡ]	——	——
32	ἐπιλανθάνομαι: see λανθάνω					
38	ἐπιμέλομαι or ἐπιμελέομαι	ἐπιμελή- σομαι	——	——	ἐπιμεμέ- λημαι	ἐπεμελή- θην
28	ἐπίσταμαι	ἐπιστήσο- μαι	——	——	——	ἠπιστήθην
41	ἐπιστέλλω: see στέλλω					
23	ἐπιτίθημι: see τίθημι					
8	ἐπιτρέπω: see τρέπω					
39	ἐπιχειρέω	ἐπιχειρήσω	ἐπεχείρησα	ἐπικεχεί- ρηκα	ἐπικεχεί- ρημαι	ἐπεχειρή- θην
33	ἐράω	(ἐρασθήσο- μαι)	——	——	——	ἠράσθην
40	ἐργάζομαι	ἐργάσομαι	ἠργασάμην·	——	εἴργασμαι	ἠργάσθην
19	[no present in Attic]	ἐρέω	εἶπον (stem εἰπ-)	εἴρηκα	εἴρημαι	ἐρρήθην
11	ἔρχομαι	ἐλεύσομαι	ἦλθον (stem ἐλθ-)	ἐλήλυθα	——	——
33	ἐρωτάω	ἐρωτήσω	ἠρώτησα	ἠρώτηκα	ἠρώτημαι	ἠρωτήθην
26	ἐσθίω	ἔδομαι	ἔφαγον	ἐδήδοκα	-ἐδήδεσμαι	ἠδέσθην
33	εὐεργετέω	εὐεργετή- σω	ηὐεργέτη- σα[2]	ηὐεργέτη- κα	ηὐεργέτη- μαι	ηὐεργετή- θην
38	εὐλαβέο- μαι	εὐλαβήσο- μαι	——	——	——	ηὐλαβήθην

---

1. Perfect with present meaning; no present in Attic.

2. Verbs in ευ-, like εὐεργετέω and εὑρίσκω, will be found in some texts without the augmentation or reduplication to ηυ-: e.g., aorist εὗρον, perfect εὐεργέτηκα. This is a reflection of 4th-century Attic spelling, the result of the loss of distinction between the sounds ευ and ηυ.

10	εὑρίσκω	εὑρήσω	ηὗρον[1]	ηὕρηκα	ηὕρημαι	ηὑρέθην
40	εὐσεβέω	——	——	——	——	——
17	εὔχομαι	εὔξομαι	ηὐξάμην	——	ηὖγμαι	——
23	ἐφίημι: see ἵημι					
23	ἐφίστημι: see ἵστημι					
8	ἔχω	ἕξω and σχήσω	ἔσχον	ἔσχηκα	-έσχημαι	——
23	ζεύγνῡμι	ζεύξω	ἔζευξα	——	ἔζευγμαι	ἐζύγην [ῠ] and ἐζεύχθην
29	ζηλόω	ζηλώσω	ἐζήλωσα	ἐζήλωκα	ἐζήλωμαι	ἐζηλώθην
16	ζητέω	ζητήσω	ἐζήτησα	ἐζήτηκα	——	ἐζητήθην
33	ζῶ	ζήσω	[non-Attic ἔζησα]	——	——	——
16	ἡγέομαι	ἡγήσομαι	ἡγησάμην	——	ἥγημαι	-ηγήθην
28	ἥδομαι	ἡσθήσομαι	——	——	——	ἥσθην
34	ἥκω	ἥξω	——	——	——	
31	ἡττάομαι	ἡττήσομαι	——	——	ἥττημαι	ἡττήθην
34	θαυμάζω	θαυμάσομαι	ἐθαύμασα	τεθαύμακα	τεθαύμασμαι	ἐθαυμάσθην
38	θύω [ῠ]	θύσω [ῠ]	ἔθῡσα	τέθῠκα	τέθῠμαι	ἐτύθην [ῠ]
23	ἵημι	ἥσω	-ἧκα	-εἷκα	-εἷμαι	-εἵθην
23	ἵστημι	στήσω	ἔστησα and ἔστην	ἕστηκα (cf. U41)	ἕσταμαι	ἐστάθην
23	καθίστημι: see ἵστημι					
26	καίω or κάω	καύσω	ἔκαυσα[2]	-κέκαυκα	κέκαυμαι	ἐκαύθην
18	καλέω	καλέω	ἐκάλεσα	κέκληκα	κέκλημαι	ἐκλήθην
24	καταβαίνω: see βαίνω					
24	καταδύω: see δύω					
32	καταλείπω: see λείπω					
23	κατατίθημι: see τίθημι					
17	κατηγορέω	κατηγορήσω	κατηγόρησα	κατηγόρηκα	κατηγόρημαι	κατηγορήθην
9	κελεύω	κελεύσω	ἐκέλευσα	κεκέλευκα	κεκέλευσμαι	ἐκελεύσθην
34	κλέπτω	κλέψω	ἔκλεψα	κέκλοφα	κέκλεμμαι	ἐκλάπην
38	κλίνω [ῑ]	κλῑνέω	ἔκλῑνα	——	κέκλῐμαι	ἐκλίθην or -εκλίνην [ῐ]
38	κομίζω	κομιέω	ἐκόμισα	κεκόμικα	κεκόμισμαι	ἐκομίσθην
9	κόπτω	κόψω	ἔκοψα	-κέκοφα	κέκομμαι	-εκόπην
13	κρατέω	κρατήσω	ἐκράτησα	κεκράτηκα	κεκράτημαι	ἐκρατήθην
26	κρίνω [ῑ]	κρῑνέω	ἔκρῑνα	κέκρῐκα	κέκρῐμαι	ἐκρίθην [ῐ]
17	κρύπτω	κρύψω	ἔκρυψα	——	κέκρυμμαι	ἐκρύφθην
37	κτάομαι	κτήσομαι	ἐκτησάμην	——	κέκτημαι	ἐκτήθην

1. See previous note.
2. Aorist participle also κέας.

16	κωλύω [ῡ]	κωλύσω [ῡ]	ἐκώλῡσα	κεκώλῡκα	κεκώλῡμαι	ἐκωλύθην [ῡ]
8	λαμβάνω	λήψομαι	ἔλαβον	εἴληφα	εἴλημμαι	ἐλήφθην
28	λανθάνω	λήσω	ἔλαθον	λέληθα	-λέλησμαι	——
8	λέγω	λέξω	ἔλεξα	——	λέλεγμαι	ἐλέχθην
8	λείπω	λείψω	ἔλιπον	λέλοιπα	λέλειμμαι	ἐλείφθην
8	λύω [ῡ]	λύσω [ῡ]	ἔλῡσα	λέλῠκα	λέλῠμαι	ἐλύθην [ῠ]
18	μανθάνω	μαθήσομαι	ἔμαθον	μεμάθηκα	——	——
11	μάχομαι	μαχέομαι	ἐμαχεσά- μην		μεμάχημαι	——
18	μέλλω[1]	μελλήσω	ἐμέλλησα	——	——	——
38	μέλω	μελήσω	ἐμέλησα	μεμέληκα	——	——
8	μένω	μενέω	ἔμεινα	μεμένηκα	——	——
23	μεταδίδωμι: see δίδωμι					
29	μετέχω: see ἔχω					
29	μιμνῄσκω or μιμνήσκω	μνήσω	ἔμνησα (poetic in act.)	——	μέμνημαι	ἐμνήσθην
33	μῑσέω	μῑσήσω	ἐμίσησα [ῑ]	μεμίσηκα [ῑ]	μεμίσημαι [ῑ]	ἐμῑσήθην
29	νῑκάω	νῑκήσω	ἐνίκησα [ῑ]	νενίκηκα [ῑ]	νενίκημαι [ῑ]	ἐνῑκήθην
42	νοέω	νοήσω	ἐνόησα	νενόηκα	νενόημαι	ἐνοήθην
18	νομίζω	νομιέω	ἐνόμισα	νενόμικα	νενόμισμαι	ἐνομίσθην
13	νοσέω	νοσήσω	ἐνόσησα	νενόσηκα	——	——
28	οἶδα	εἴσομαι	——	——	——	——
13	οἰκέω	οἰκήσω	ᾤκησα	ᾤκηκα	ᾤκημαι	ᾠκήθην
11	οἴομαι or οἶμαι	οἰήσομαι	——	——	——	ᾠήθην
37	ὄλλῡμι (poetic): see ἀπόλλῡμι (prose)					
37	ὄμνῡμι	ὀμέομαι	ὤμοσα	ὀμώμοκα	ὀμώμομαι or ὀμώμοσμαι	ὠμόθην or ὠμόσθην
32	ὁμολογέω	ὁμολογήσω	ὡμολόγη- σα	ὡμολόγηκα	ὡμολόγη- μαι	ὡμολογή- θην
29	ὁράω	ὄψομαι	εἶδον (stem ἰδ-)	ἑόρακα or ἑώρακα	ἑώραμαι or ὦμμαι (stem ὠπ-)	ὤφθην
28	ὀργίζομαι	ὀργιέομαι	——	——	ὤργισμαι	ὠργίσθην
28	ὀργίζω	——	ὤργισα	——		
33	ὁρμάω	ὁρμήσω	ὥρμησα	ὥρμηκα	ὥρμημαι	ὡρμήθην
27	ὀρχέομαι	ὀρχήσομαι	ὠρχησά- μην	——	——	——
32	ὀφείλω	ὀφειλήσω	ὠφείλησα and ὤφελον	ὠφείληκα	——	ὠφειλήθην
40	παίω	παίσω	ἔπαισα	πέπαικα	——	ἐπαίσθην

---

1. This verb sometimes shows "double augmentation," that is, imperfect ἤμελλον, aorist ἠμέλλησα.

24	παραβαίνω: see βαίνω					
16	παράγω: see ἄγω					
23	παραδίδωμι: see δίδωμι					
32	παραινέω: see (ἐπ)αινέω					
11	παρακελεύομαι: see κελεύω (middle forms)					
11	παρασκευ-άζω	παρασκευ-άσω	παρεσκεύ-ασα	——	παρεσκεύ-ασμαι	παρεσκευ-άσθην
27	πάρειμι: see εἰμί					
16	παρέχω: see ἔχω					
10	πάσχω	πείσομαι	ἔπαθον	πέπονθα	——	
28	παύω	παύσω	ἔπαυσα	πέπαυκα	πέπαυμαι	ἐπαύθην
8	πείθω	πείσω	ἔπεισα	πέπεικα and πέποιθα	πέπεισμαι	ἐπείσθην
39	πειράω	πειράσω [ᾱ]	ἐπείρᾱσα	πεπείρᾱκα	πεπείρᾱμαι	ἐπειρᾱθην [ᾱ]
8	πέμπω	πέμψω	ἔπεμψα	πέπομφα	πέπεμμαι	ἐπέμφθην
28	περιοράω	περιόψο-μαι	περιεῖδον	——	——	——
29	πίμπλημι: see ἐμπίμπλημι					
26	πίνω [ῑ]	πίομαι or πιέομαι [ῐ]	ἔπῐον	πέπωκα	-πέπομαι	-επόθην
18	πίπτω	πεσέομαι	ἔπεσον	πέπτωκα	——	——
30	πιστεύω	πιστεύσω	ἐπίστευσα	πεπίστευ-κα	πεπίστευ-μαι	ἐπιστεύ-θην
39	πλέω	πλεύσομαι or πλευσέομαι	ἔπλευσα	πέπλευκα	πέπλευσ-μαι	——
17	-πλήττω	-πλήξω	-έπληξα	πέπληγα	πέπληγμαι	ἐπλήγην and -επλάγην
13	ποιέω	ποιήσω	ἐποίησα	πεποίηκα	πεποίημαι	ἐποιήθην
27	πολεμέω	πολεμήσω	ἐπολέμησα	πεπολέμη-κα	πεπολέμη-μαι	ἐπολεμή-θην
33	πολιορκέω	πολιορκή-σω	ἐπολιόρκη-σα	——	-πεπολιόρ-κημαι	ἐπολιορκή-θην
11	πολῑτεύω	πολῑτεύσω	ἐπολίτευ-σα [ῑ]	πεπολίτευ-κα [ῑ]	πεπολίτευ-μαι [ῑ]	ἐπολῑτεύ-θην
34	πορεύω	πορεύσω	ἐπόρευσα		πεπόρευμαι	ἐπορεύθην
10	πράττω [ᾱ]	πράξω [ᾱ]	ἔπρᾱξα	πέπρᾱγα and πέπρᾱχα	πέπρᾱγμαι	ἐπράχθην [ᾱ]
9	πρέπει	——	——	——	——	
23	προδίδωμι: see δίδωμι					
39	προσήκω: see ἥκω					
23	προσίημι: see ἵημι					
11	πυνθάνομαι	πεύσομαι	ἐπυθόμην	——	πέπυσμαι	
39	ῥέω	ῥυήσομαι	——	ἐρρύηκα	——	ἐρρύην
23	ῥήγνῡμι	ῥήξω	ἔρρηξα	-έρρωγα	——	ἐρράγην [ᾰ]

37	ῥίπτω [ῐ]	ῥίψω [ῑ]	ἔρρῑψα	ἔρρῑφα	ἔρρῑμμαι	ἐρρίφθην or ἐρρίφην [ῐ]
40	σέβομαι	——	——	——	——	
31	σιγάω	σιγήσομαι	ἐσίγησα	σεσίγηκα	σεσίγημαι	ἐσιγήθην
29	σκεδάννῡμι	-σκεδάω	-εσκέδασα		ἐσκέδασμαι	ἐσκεδάσ- θην
38	σκέπτομαι	σκέψομαι	ἐσκεψάμην	——	ἔσκεμμαι	
38	σκοπέω or σκοπέομαι		(for other tenses, parts of σκέπτομαι are used)			
11	σπένδω	σπείσω	ἔσπεισα	——	ἔσπεισμαι	
38	σπεύδω	σπεύσω	ἔσπευσα	——		——
38	σπουδάζω	σπουδάσο- μαι	ἐσπούδασα	ἐσπούδακα	ἐσπούδασ- μαι	ἐσπουδάσ- θην
41	στέλλω	(στελέω)	ἔστειλα	-έσταλκα	ἔσταλμαι	ἐστάλην
30	στρατεύω	στρατεύσω	ἐστράτευ- σα	ἐστράτευκα	ἐστράτευ- μαι	——
26	στρέφω	στρέψω	ἔστρεψα	——	ἔστραμμαι	ἐστρέφθην or ἐστράφην
32	συγγιγνώσκω: see γιγνώσκω					
39	συλλέγω	συλλέξω	συνέλεξα	συνείλοχα	συνείλεγ- μαι	συνελέγην or συνελέχθην
24	συμβαίνω: see βαίνω					
32	συμβουλεύω: see βουλεύω					
32	συμφέρω: see φέρω					
23	συντίθημι: see τίθημι					
39	σῴζω	σώσω or σῴσω	ἔσωσα or ἔσῳσα	σέσωκα	σέσωμαι or σέσῳσμαι	ἐσώθην
32	σωφρονέω	σωφρονή- σω	ἐσωφρόνη- σα	σεσωφρό- νηκα	σεσωφρό- νημαι	——
9	τάττω	τάξω	ἔταξα	τέταχα	τέταγμαι	ἐτάχθην
29	τελευτάω	τελευτήσω	ἐτελεύτη- σα	τετελεύτη- κα	τετελεύτη- μαι	ἐτελευτή- θην
33	τελέω	τελέω (or rarely τελέσω)	ἐτέλεσα	τετέλεκα	τετέλεσμαι	ἐτελέσθην
26	τέμνω	τεμέω	ἔτεμον or (ἔταμον)	-τέτμηκα	τέτμημαι	ἐτμήθην
23	τίθημι	θήσω	ἔθηκα	τέθηκα	τέθειμαι	ἐτέθην
40	τίκτω	τέξομαι	ἔτεκον	τέτοκα	——	——
29	τῑμάω	τῑμήσω	ἐτίμησα [ῑ]	τετίμηκα [ῑ]	τετίμημαι [ῑ]	ἐτῑμήθην
16	τρέπω	τρέψω	ἔτρεψα and ἔτραπον[1]	τέτροφα	τέτραμμαι	ἐτρέφθην and ἐτράπην

---

1. The second aorist is poetic and intransitive in sense; in prose the second aorist middle is used with the intransitive meaning "fled."

26	τρέφω	θρέψω	ἔθρεψα	τέτροφα	τέθραμμαι	ἐτράφην (rarely ἐτρέφθην)
34	τρέχω	δραμέομαι (or rarely θρέξομαι)	ἔδραμον	-δεδράμηκα	-δεδράμη- μαι	——
28	τυγχάνω	τεύξομαι	ἔτυχον	τετύχηκα	——	——
12	τύπτω	τυπτήσω	——	——	——	——
32	ὑπακούω: see ἀκούω					
26	ὑπισχνέ- ομαι	ὑποσχήσο- μαι	ὑπεσχόμην	——	ὑπέσχημαι	——
32	ὑπολαμβάνω: see λαμβάνω					
32	ὑπομένω: see μένω					
29	ὑπομιμνήσκω: see μιμνήσκω					
39	ὑποπτεύω	ὑποπτεύσω	ὑπώπτευσα	——	——	ὑπωπτεύ- θην
29	φαίνω	φανέω	ἔφηνα	πέφηνα	πέφασμαι	ἐφάνην (or rarely ἐφάνθην)
8	φέρω	οἴσω	ἤνεγκον and ἤνεγκα (stem ἐνεγκ-)	ἐνήνοχα	ἐνήνεγμαι	ἠνέχθην
8	φεύγω	φεύξομαι and φευξέομαι	ἔφυγον	πέφευγα	——	——
20	φημί	φήσω	ἔφησα	——	——	——
28	φθάνω	φθήσομαι	ἔφθασα or ἔφθην	——	——	——
39	φθείρω	φθερέω	ἔφθειρα	ἔφθαρκα and -έφθορα	ἔφθαρμαι	ἐφθάρην
13	φιλέω	φιλήσω	ἐφίλησα	πεφίληκα	πεφίλημαι	ἐφιλήθην
13	φοβέω	φοβήσω	ἐφόβησα		πεφόβημαι	ἐφοβήθην
39	φράζω	φράσω	ἔφρασα	πέφρακα	πέφρασμαι	ἐφράσθην
16	φυλάττω	φυλάξω	ἐφύλαξα	πεφύλαχα	πεφύλαγ- μαι	ἐφυλάχθην
40	φύω [ῡ or ῠ]	φύσω [ῡ]	ἔφυσα and ἔφυν	πέφῡκα	——	——
40	χαίρω	χαιρήσω	——	κεχάρηκα	——	ἐχάρην
30	χράομαι	χρήσομαι	ἐχρησάμην	——	κέχρημαι	ἐχρήσθην
30	χράω	χρήσω	ἔχρησα	——	——	ἐχρήσθην
9	χρή	χρῆσται[1]	——	——		
13	ὠφελέω	ὠφελήσω	ὠφέλησα	ὠφέληκα	ὠφέλημαι	ὠφελήθην

---

1. Contraction of χρὴ ἔσται. Cf. present infinitive χρῆναι (= χρὴ εἶναι), imperfect χρῆν (= χρὴ ἦν) or ἐχρῆν.

APPENDIX THREE

Paradigms

NOUNS

O-DECLENSION (U3)[1]

		masc./fem.	neuter
sing.	nom.	ἄνθρωπος	ἔργον
	gen.	ἀνθρώπου	ἔργου
	dat.	ἀνθρώπῳ	ἔργῳ
	acc.	ἄνθρωπον	ἔργον
	voc	ἄνθρωπε	ἔργον
dual	n. a. v.	ἀνθρώπω	ἔργω
	g. d.	ἀνθρώποιν	ἔργοιν
plur.	n. v.	ἄνθρωποι	ἔργᾰ
	gen.	ἀνθρώπων	ἔργων
	dat.	ἀνθρώποις	ἔργοις
	acc.	ἀνθρώπους	ἔργᾰ

A-DECLENSION (U4–U5)

long-vowel fem.		short-vowel fem.		masc.	
χώρᾱ	γνώμη	ὑγίειᾰ	θάλαττᾰ	νεανίᾱς	στρατιώτης
χώρᾱς	γνώμης	ὑγιείᾱς	θαλάττης	νεανίου	στρατιώτου
χώρᾳ	γνώμῃ	ὑγιείᾳ	θαλάττῃ	νεανίᾳ	στρατιώτῃ
χώρᾱν	γνώμην	ὑγίειᾰν	θάλαττᾰν	νεανίᾱν	στρατιώτην
χώρᾱ	γνώμη	ὑγίειᾰ	θάλαττᾰ	νεανίᾱ	στρατιῶτᾰ
χώρᾱ	γνώμᾱ	ὑγιείᾱ	θαλάττᾱ	νεανίᾱ	στρατιώτᾱ
χώραιν	γνώμαιν	ὑγιείαιν	θαλάτταιν	νεανίαιν	στρατιώταιν
χῶραι	γνῶμαι	ὑγίειαι	θάλατται	νεανίαι	στρατιῶται
χωρῶν	γνωμῶν	ὑγιειῶν	θαλαττῶν	νεανιῶν	στρατιωτῶν
χώραις	γνώμαις	ὑγιείαις	θαλάτταις	νεανίαις	στρατιώταις
χώρᾱς	γνώμᾱς	ὑγιείᾱς	θαλάττᾱς	νεανίᾱς	στρατιώτᾱς

---

1. The cases in all noun, adjective, and participle paradigms will be in the order of this table; the markings of number and case will not be repeated.

CONSONANT DECLENSION (U14–15, U21)

plosive stems (U14)

κλώψ	φύλαξ	χάρις	ἀσπίς	Ἑλλάς
κλωπός	φύλακος	χάριτος	ἀσπίδος	Ἑλλάδος
κλωπί	φύλακι	χάριτι	ἀσπίδι	Ἑλλάδι
κλῶπᾰ	φύλακᾰ	χάριν	ἀσπίδᾰ	Ἑλλάδᾰ
κλώψ	φύλαξ	χάρι	ἀσπί	Ἑλλάς
κλῶπε	φύλακε	χάριτε	ἀσπίδε	Ἑλλάδε
κλωποῖν	φυλάκοιν	χαρίτοιν	ἀσπίδοιν	Ἑλλάδοιν
κλῶπες	φύλακες	χάριτες	ἀσπίδες	Ἑλλάδες
κλωπῶν	φυλάκων	χαρίτων	ἀσπίδων	Ἑλλάδων
κλωψί(ν)	φύλαξι(ν)	χάρισι(ν)	ἀσπίσι(ν)	Ἑλλάσι(ν)
κλῶπᾰς	φύλακᾰς	χάριτᾰς	ἀσπίδᾰς	Ἑλλάδᾰς

ντ-stems (U14) / neuter τ-stems (U14)

γέρων	γίγᾱς	ὀδούς	πρᾶγμα	τέρας
γέροντος	γίγαντος	ὀδόντος	πράγματος	τέρατος
γέροντι	γίγαντι	ὀδόντι	πράγματι	τέρατι
γέροντᾰ	γίγαντᾰ	ὀδόντᾰ	πρᾶγμα	τέρας
γέρον	γίγᾰν	ὀδούς	πρᾶγμα	τέρας
γέροντε	γίγαντε	ὀδόντε	πράγματε	τέρατε
γερόντοιν	γιγάντοιν	ὀδόντοιν	πραγμάτοιν	τεράτοιν
γέροντες	γίγαντες	ὀδόντες	πράγματα	τέρατα
γερόντων	γιγάντων	ὀδόντων	πραγμάτων	τεράτων
γέρουσι(ν)	γίγᾱσι(ν)	ὀδοῦσι(ν)	πράγμασι(ν)	τέρασι(ν)
γέροντᾰς	γίγαντᾰς	ὀδόντᾰς	πράγματα	τέρατα

liquid and nasal stems (U15)

ῥήτωρ	δαίμων	ἀγών	ἅλς
ῥήτορος	δαίμονος	ἀγῶνος	ἁλός
ῥήτορι	δαίμονι	ἀγῶνι	ἁλί
ῥήτορᾰ	δαίμονᾰ	ἀγῶνᾰ	ἅλᾰ
ῥῆτορ	δαῖμον	ἀγών	— —
ῥήτορε	δαίμονε	ἀγῶνε	ἅλε
ῥητόροιν	δαιμόνοιν	ἀγώνοιν	ἁλοῖν
ῥήτορες	δαίμονες	ἀγῶνες	ἅλες
ῥητόρων	δαιμόνων	ἀγώνων	ἁλῶν
ῥήτορσι(ν)	δαίμοσι(ν)	ἀγῶσι(ν)	ἁλσί(ν)
ῥήτορᾰς	δαίμονᾰς	ἀγῶνᾰς	ἅλᾰς

irregular ρ-stems (U15)

πατήρ	μήτηρ	θυγάτηρ	ἀνήρ
πατρός	μητρός	θυγατρός	ἀνδρός
πατρί	μητρί	θυγατρί	ἀνδρί
πατέρα	μητέρα	θυγατέρα	ἄνδρα
πάτερ	μῆτερ	θύγατερ	ἄνερ
πατέρε	μητέρε	θυγατέρε	ἄνδρε
πατέροιν	μητέροιν	θυγατέροιν	ἀνδροῖν
πατέρες	μητέρες	θυγατέρες	ἄνδρες
πατέρων	μητέρων	θυγατέρων	ἀνδρῶν
πατράσι(ν)	μητράσι(ν)	θυγατράσι(ν)	ἀνδράσι(ν)
πατέρας	μητέρας	θυγατέρας	ἄνδρας

σ-stems (U15)   ### irregular (U21)

τριήρης	γένος	γέρας	γυνή	χείρ
τριήρους	γένους	γέρως	γυναικός	χειρός
τριήρει	γένει	γέραι or γέρᾳ	γυναικί	χειρί
τριήρη	γένος	γέρας	γυναῖκᾰ	χεῖρᾰ
τριῆρες	γένος	γέρας	γύναι	χείρ
τριήρει	γένει	γέρᾱ	γυναῖκε	χεῖρε
τριήροιν	γενοῖν	γερῷν	γυναικοῖν	χεροῖν
τριήρεις	γένη	γέρᾱ	γυναῖκες	χεῖρες
τριήρων	γενῶν	γερῶν	γυναικῶν	χειρῶν
τριήρεσι(ν)	γένεσι(ν)	γέρασι(ν)	γυναιξί(ν)	χερσί(ν)
τριήρεις	γένη	γέρᾱ	γυναῖκᾰς	χεῖρᾰς

stems in ι or υ (U21)

πόλις	πῆχυς	ἄστυ	ἰχθύς or -ῦς
πόλεως	πήχεως	ἄστεως	ἰχθύος
πόλει	πήχει	ἄστει	ἰχθύϊ
πόλιν	πῆχυν	ἄστυ	ἰχθύν
πόλι	πῆχυ	ἄστυ	ἰχθύ
πόλει	πήχει	ἄστει	ἰχθύε
πολέοιν	πηχέοιν	ἀστέοιν	ἰχθύοιν
πόλεις	πήχεις	ἄστη	ἰχθύες
πόλεων	πήχεων	ἄστεων	ἰχθύων
πόλεσι(ν)	πήχεσι(ν)	ἄστεσι(ν)	ἰχθύσι(ν)
πόλεις	πήχεις	ἄστη	ἰχθῦς

stems in ευ, αυ, ου (U21)

ἱππεύς	γραῦς	ναῦς	βοῦς
ἱππέως	γρᾱός	νεώς	βοός
ἱππεῖ	γρᾱΐ	νηΐ	βοΐ
ἱππέᾱ	γραῦν	νῆα	βοῦν
ἱππεῦ	γραῦ	ναῦ	βοῦ
ἱππῆ	γρᾶε	νῆε	βόε
ἱππέοιν	γρᾱοῖν	νεοῖν	βοοῖν
ἱππῆς or -εῖς	γρᾶες	νῆες	βόες
ἱππέων	γρᾱῶν	νεῶν	βοῶν
ἱππεῦσι(ν)	γραυσί(ν)	ναυσί(ν)	βουσί(ν)
ἱππέᾱς	γραῦς	ναῦς	βοῦς

NOUNS WITH CONTRACTION (U42)

o-declension			*a-declension*			
νοῦς	περίπλους	κανοῦν	γῆ	συκῆ	μνᾶ	Ἑρμῆς
νοῦ	περίπλου	κανοῦ	γῆς	συκῆς	μνᾶς	Ἑρμοῦ
νῷ	περίπλῳ	κανῷ	γῇ	συκῇ	μνᾷ	Ἑρμῇ
νοῦν	περίπλουν	κανοῦν	γῆν	συκῆν	μνᾶν	Ἑρμῆν
νοῦ	περίπλου	κανοῦν	γῆ	συκῆ	μνᾶ	Ἑρμῆ
νώ	περίπλω	κανώ		συκᾶ	μνᾶ	Ἑρμᾶ
νοῖν	περίπλοιν	κανοῖν		συκαῖν	μναῖν	Ἑρμαῖν
νοῖ	περίπλοι	κανᾶ		συκαῖ	μναῖ	Ἑρμαῖ
νῶν	περίπλων	κανῶν		συκῶν	μνῶν	Ἑρμῶν
νοῖς	περίπλοις	κανοῖς		συκαῖς	μναῖς	Ἑρμαῖς
νοῦς	περίπλους	κανᾶ		συκᾶς	μνᾶς	Ἑρμᾶς

ATTIC DECLENSION AND NOUNS IN -ως (U42)

Attic declension				*nouns in -ως*		
νεώς	λεώς	ἕως	λαγώς	αἰδώς	ἥρως	
νεώ	λεώ	ἕω	λαγώ	αἰδοῦς	ἥρωος	or ἥρω
νεῴ	λεῴ	ἕῳ	λαγώ	αἰδοῖ	ἥρωϊ	or ἥρῳ
νεών	λεών	ἕω	λαγών or λαγώ	αἰδῶ	ἥρωᾰ	or ἥρω
νεώ	— —	— —	λαγώ	— —	ἥρωε	
νεῴν	— —	— —	λαγών	— —	ἡρώοιν	
νεῴ	λεῴ	— —	λαγώ	— —	ἥρωες	or ἥρως
νεών	λεών	— —	λαγών	— —	ἡρώων	
νεῴς	λεῴς	— —	λαγώς	— —	ἥρωσι(ν)	
νεώς	λεώς	— —	λαγώς	— —	ἥρωᾰς	or ἥρως

ADJECTIVES

VOWEL-DECLENSION ADJECTIVES WITH THREE ENDINGS (U7)

with fem. in -ā			*with fem. in -η*		
masc.	*fem.*	*neuter*	*masc.*	*fem.*	*neuter*
ἄξιος	ἀξία	ἄξιον	ἀγαθός	ἀγαθή	ἀγαθόν
ἀξίου	ἀξίας	ἀξίου	ἀγαθοῦ	ἀγαθῆς	ἀγαθοῦ
ἀξίῳ	ἀξίᾳ	ἀξίῳ	ἀγαθῷ	ἀγαθῇ	ἀγαθῷ
ἄξιον	ἀξίαν	ἄξιον	ἀγαθόν	ἀγαθήν	ἀγαθόν
ἄξιε	ἀξία	ἄξιον	ἀγαθέ	ἀγαθή	ἀγαθόν
ἀξίω	ἀξία	ἀξίω	ἀγαθώ	ἀγαθά	ἀγαθώ
ἀξίοιν	ἀξίαιν	ἀξίοιν	ἀγαθοῖν	ἀγαθαῖν	ἀγαθοῖν
ἄξιοι	ἄξιαι	ἄξιᾰ	ἀγαθοί	ἀγαθαί	ἀγαθά
ἀξίων	ἀξίων	ἀξίων	ἀγαθῶν	ἀγαθῶν	ἀγαθῶν
ἀξίοις	ἀξίαις	ἀξίοις	ἀγαθοῖς	ἀγαθαῖς	ἀγαθοῖς
ἀξίους	ἀξίας	ἄξιᾰ	ἀγαθούς	ἀγαθάς	ἀγαθά

VOWEL-DECLENSION ADJECTIVES WITH TWO ENDINGS (U9)

masc./fem.	*neuter*
ἄδικος	ἄδικον
ἀδίκου	ἀδίκου
ἀδίκῳ	ἀδίκῳ
ἄδικον	ἄδικον
ἄδικε	ἄδικον
ἀδίκω	ἀδίκω
ἀδίκοιν	ἀδίκοιν
ἄδικοι	ἄδικᾰ
ἀδίκων	ἀδίκων
ἀδίκοις	ἀδίκοις
ἀδίκους	ἄδικᾰ

CONSONANT-DECLENSION ADJECTIVES (U22)

with two endings				
masc./fem.	*neuter*		*masc./fem.*	*neuter*
ἀληθής	ἀληθές		σώφρων	σῶφρον
ἀληθοῦς	ἀληθοῦς		σώφρονος	σώφρονος
ἀληθεῖ	ἀληθεῖ		σώφρονι	σώφρονι
ἀληθῆ	ἀληθές		σώφρονᾰ	σῶφρον
ἀληθές	ἀληθές		σῶφρον	σῶφρον

masc./fem.	neuter	masc./fem.	neuter
ἀληθεῖ	ἀληθεῖ	σώφρονε	σώφρονε
ἀληθοῖν	ἀληθοῖν	σωφρόνοιν	σωφρόνοιν
ἀληθεῖς	ἀληθῆ	σώφρονες	σώφρονᾰ
ἀληθῶν	ἀληθῶν	σωφρόνων	σωφρόνων
ἀληθέσι(ν)	ἀληθέσι(ν)	σώφροσι(ν)	σώφροσι(ν)
ἀληθεῖς	ἀληθῆ	σώφρονᾰς	σώφρονᾰ

with three endings

stems in υ   /   stems in ν

masc.	fem.	neuter	masc.	fem.	neuter
ἡδύς	ἡδεῖᾰ	ἡδύ	μέλας	μέλαινᾰ	μέλαν
ἡδέος	ἡδείᾱς	ἡδέος	μέλανος	μελαίνης	μέλανος
ἡδεῖ	ἡδείᾳ	ἡδεῖ	μέλανι	μελαίνῃ	μέλανι
ἡδύν	ἡδεῖᾰν	ἡδύ	μέλανᾰ	μέλαινᾰν	μέλαν
ἡδύ	ἡδεῖᾰ	ἡδύ	μέλαν	μέλαινᾰ	μέλαν
ἡδέε	ἡδείᾱ	ἡδέε	μέλανε	μελαίνᾱ	μέλανε
ἡδέοιν	ἡδείαιν	ἡδέοιν	μελάνοιν	μελαίναιν	μελάνοιν
ἡδεῖς	ἡδεῖαι	ἡδέα	μέλανες	μέλαιναι	μέλανᾰ
ἡδέων	ἡδειῶν	ἡδέων	μελάνων	μελαινῶν	μελάνων
ἡδέσι(ν)	ἡδείαις	ἡδέσι(ν)	μέλασι(ν)	μελαίναις	μέλασι(ν)
ἡδεῖς	ἡδείας	ἡδέα	μέλανᾰς	μελαίνᾱς	μέλανᾰ

stems in ντ

masc.	fem.	neuter	masc.	fem.	neuter
χαρίεις	χαρίεσσᾰ	χαρίεν	πᾶς	πᾶσᾰ	πᾶν
χαρίεντος	χαριέσσης	χαρίεντος	παντός	πάσης	παντός
χαρίεντι	χαριέσσῃ	χαρίεντι	παντί	πάσῃ	παντί
χαρίεντᾰ	χαρίεσσᾰν	χαρίεν	πάντᾰ	πᾶσᾰν	πᾶν
χαρίεν	χαρίεσσᾰ	χαρίεν	πᾶς	πᾶσᾰ	πᾶν
χαρίεντε	χαριέσσᾱ	χαρίεντε			
χαριέντοιν	χαριέσσαιν	χαριέντοιν			
χαρίεντες	χαρίεσσαι	χαρίεντᾰ	πάντες	πᾶσαι	πάντᾰ
χαριέντων	χαριεσσῶν	χαριέντων	πάντων	πασῶν	πάντων
χαρίεσι(ν)	χαριέσσαις	χαρίεσι(ν)	πᾶσι(ν)	πάσαις	πᾶσι(ν)
χαρίεντᾰς	χαριέσσᾱς	χαρίεντᾰ	πάντᾰς	πάσᾱς	πάντᾰ

VOWEL-DECLENSION ADJS. WITH CONTRACTION (U42)

masc.	fem.	neuter
χρυσοῦς	χρυσῆ	χρυσοῦν
χρυσοῦ	χρυσῆς	χρυσοῦ
χρυσῷ	χρυσῇ	χρυσῷ
χρυσοῦν	χρυσῆν	χρυσοῦν
χρυσώ	χρυσᾶ	χρυσώ
χρυσοῖν	χρυσαῖν	χρυσοῖν
χρυσοῖ	χρυσαῖ	χρυσᾶ
χρυσῶν	χρυσῶν	χρυσῶν
χρυσοῖς	χρυσαῖς	χρυσοῖς
χρυσοῦς	χρυσᾶς	χρυσᾶ

masc.	fem.	neuter	masc./fem.	neuter
ἀργυροῦς	ἀργυρᾶ	ἀργυροῦν	εὔνους	εὔνουν
ἀργυροῦ	ἀργυρᾶς	ἀργυροῦ	εὔνου	εὔνου
ἀργυρῷ	ἀργυρᾷ	ἀργυρῷ	εὔνῳ	εὔνῳ
ἀργυροῦν	ἀργυρᾶν	ἀργυροῦν	εὔνουν	εὔνουν
ἀργυρώ	ἀργυρᾶ	ἀργυρώ	εὔνω	εὔνω
ἀργυροῖν	ἀργυραῖν	ἀργυροῖν	εὔνοιν	εὔνοιν
ἀργυροῖ	ἀργυραῖ	ἀργυρᾶ	εὔνοι	εὔνοἄ
ἀργυρῶν	ἀργυρῶν	ἀργυρῶν	εὔνων	εὔνων
ἀργυροῖς	ἀργυραῖς	ἀργυροῖς	εὔνοις	εὔνοις
ἀργυροῦς	ἀργυρᾶς	ἀργυρᾶ	εὔνους	εὔνοἄ

ADJECTIVES WITH ATTIC DECLENSION (U42)

masc./fem.	neuter	masc.	fem.	neuter
ἵλεως	ἵλεων	πλέως	πλέᾱ	πλέων
ἵλεω	ἵλεω	πλέω	πλέᾱς	πλέω
ἵλεῳ	ἵλεῳ	πλέῳ	πλέᾳ	πλέῳ
ἵλεων	ἵλεων	πλέων	πλέᾱν	πλέων
ἵλεω	ἵλεω	πλέω	πλέᾱ	πλέω
ἵλεων	ἵλεων	πλέων	πλέαιν	πλέων
ἵλεῳ	ἵλεᾰ	πλέῳ	πλέαι	πλέᾰ
ἵλεων	ἵλεων	πλέων	πλέων	πλέων
ἵλεως	ἵλεως	πλέως	πλέαις	πλέως
ἵλεως	ἵλεᾰ	πλέως	πλέᾱς	πλέᾰ

PRONOUNS AND PRONOUN/ADJECTIVES

ARTICLE (U6)

masc.	fem.		neut.
ὁ	ἡ		τό
τοῦ	τῆς		τοῦ
τῷ	τῇ		τῷ
τόν	τήν		τό
τώ	τώ	(or τά)	τώ
τοῖν	τοῖν	(or ταῖν)	τοῖν
οἱ	αἱ		τά
τῶν	τῶν		τῶν
τοῖς	ταῖς		τοῖς
τούς	τάς		τά

PERSONAL PRONOUNS (U22)

1st sing.	(unem-phatic)	1st dual	1st plur.	2nd sing.	(unem-phatic)	2nd dual	2nd plur.
ἐγώ		νώ	ἡμεῖς	σύ		σφώ	ὑμεῖς
ἐμοῦ	μου	νῷν	ἡμῶν	σοῦ	σου	σφῷν	ὑμῶν
ἐμοί	μοι		ἡμῖν	σοί	σοι		ὑμῖν
ἐμέ	με		ἡμᾶς	σέ	σε		ὑμᾶς

THIRD PERSON (OBLIQUE CASES) AND INTENSIVE (ALL CASES) (U21)

αὐτός	αὐτή	αὐτό
αὐτοῦ	αὐτῆς	αὐτοῦ
αὐτῷ	αὐτῇ	αὐτῷ
αὐτόν	αὐτήν	αὐτό
αὐτώ	αὐτώ	αὐτώ
αὐτοῖν	αὐτοῖν	αὐτοῖν
αὐτοί	αὐταί	αὐτά
αὐτῶν	αὐτῶν	αὐτῶν
αὐτοῖς	αὐταῖς	αὐτοῖς
αὐτούς	αὐτάς	αὐτά

DEMONSTRATIVE PRONOUNS (U13)

ὅδε	ἥδε	τόδε	οὗτος	αὕτη	τοῦτο
τοῦδε	τῆσδε	τοῦδε	τούτου	ταύτης	τούτου
τῷδε	τῇδε	τῷδε	τούτῳ	ταύτῃ	τούτῳ
τόνδε	τήνδε	τόδε	τοῦτον	ταύτην	τοῦτο

demonstrative pronouns (dual and plural)

τώδε	τώδε	τώδε	τούτω	τούτω	τούτω
τοῖνδε	τοῖνδε	τοῖνδε	τούτοιν	τούτοιν	τούτοιν
οἵδε	αἵδε	τάδε	οὗτοι	αὗται	ταῦτα
τῶνδε	τῶνδε	τῶνδε	τούτων	τούτων	τούτων
τοῖσδε	ταῖσδε	τοῖσδε	τούτοις	ταύταις	τούτοις
τούσδε	τάσδε	τάδε	τούτους	ταύτας	ταῦτα

ἐκεῖνος	ἐκείνη	ἐκεῖνο
ἐκείνου	ἐκείνης	ἐκείνου
ἐκείνῳ	ἐκείνῃ	ἐκείνῳ
ἐκεῖνον	ἐκείνην	ἐκεῖνο
ἐκείνω	ἐκείνω	ἐκείνω
ἐκείνοιν	ἐκείνοιν	ἐκείνοιν
ἐκεῖνοι	ἐκεῖναι	ἐκεῖνα
ἐκείνων	ἐκείνων	ἐκείνων
ἐκείνοις	ἐκείναις	ἐκείνοις
ἐκείνους	ἐκείνας	ἐκεῖνα

INTERROGATIVE AND INDEFINITE PRONOUN/ADJECTIVE (U15, U17)

τίς		τί		τις		τι	
τίνος	(τοῦ)	τίνος	(τοῦ)	τινός	(του)	τινός	(του)
τίνι	(τῷ)	τίνι	(τῷ)	τινί	(τῳ)	τινί	(τῳ)
τίνα		τί		τινά		τι	
τίνε		τίνε		τινέ		τινέ	
τίνοιν		τίνοιν		τινοῖν		τινοῖν	
τίνες		τίνα		τινές		τινά	(ἄττα)
τίνων		τίνων		τινῶν		τινῶν	
τίσι(ν)		τίσι(ν)		τισί(ν)		τισί(ν)	
τίνας		τίνα		τινάς		τινά	(ἄττα)

RELATIVE AND INDEFINITE RELATIVE PRONOUNS (U12, U33)

ὅς	ἥ	ὅ	ὅστις		ἥτις		ὅ τι	
οὗ	ἧς	οὗ	οὗτινος	(ὅτου)	ἧστινος		οὗτινος	(ὅτου)
ᾧ	ᾗ	ᾧ	ᾧτινι	(ὅτῳ)	ᾗτινι		ᾧτινι	(ὅτῳ)
ὅν	ἥν	ὅ	ὅντινα		ἥντινα		ὅ τι	
ὥ	ὥ	ὥ	ᾧτινε		ᾧτινε		ᾧτινε	
οἷν	οἷν	οἷν	οἷντινοιν		οἷντινοιν		οἷντινοιν	
οἵ	αἵ	ἅ	οἵτινες		αἵτινες		ἅτινα	(ἄττα)
ὧν	ὧν	ὧν	ὧντινων	(ὅτων)	ὧντινων		ὧντινων	(ὅτων)
οἷς	αἷς	οἷς	οἷστισι(ν)	(ὅτοις)	αἷστισι(ν)		οἷστισι(ν)	(ὅτοις)
οὕς	ἅς	ἅ	οὕστινας		ἅστινας		ἅτινα	(ἄττα)

REFLEXIVE PRONOUNS (U25)

1st pers. masc.	1st pers. fem.	2nd pers. masc.	2nd pers. fem.
ἐμαυτοῦ	ἐμαυτῆς	σεαυτοῦ (σαυτοῦ)	σεαυτῆς (σαυτῆς)
ἐμαυτῷ	ἐμαυτῇ	σεαυτῷ (σαυτῷ)	σεαυτῇ (σαυτῇ)
ἐμαυτόν	ἐμαυτήν	σεαυτόν (σαυτόν)	σεαυτήν (σαυτήν)
ἡμῶν αὐτῶν	ἡμῶν αὐτῶν	ὑμῶν αὐτῶν	ὑμῶν αὐτῶν
ἡμῖν αὐτοῖς	ἡμῖν αὐταῖς	ὑμῖν αὐτοῖς	ὑμῖν αὐταῖς
ἡμᾶς αὐτούς	ἡμᾶς αὐτάς	ὑμᾶς αὐτούς	ὑμᾶς αὐτάς

3rd pers. masc.	3rd pers. fem.	3rd pers. neuter.
ἑαυτοῦ (αὑτοῦ)	ἑαυτῆς (αὑτῆς)	ἑαυτοῦ (αὑτοῦ)
ἑαυτῷ (αὑτῷ)	ἑαυτῇ (αὑτῇ)	ἑαυτῷ (αὑτῷ)
ἑαυτόν (αὑτόν)	ἑαυτήν (αὑτήν)	ἑαυτό (αὑτό)
ἑαυτῶν (αὑτῶν)	ἑαυτῶν (αὑτῶν)	ἑαυτῶν (αὑτῶν)
ἑαυτοῖς (αὑτοῖς)	ἑαυταῖς (αὑταῖς)	ἑαυτοῖς (αὑτοῖς)
ἑαυτούς (αὑτούς)	ἑαυτάς (αὑτάς)	ἑαυτά (αὑτά)

INDIRECT REFLEXIVE (3RD PERSON) (U25)

	sing.		plur. masc./fem.		plur. neuter	
gen.	οὗ	(οὑ)	σφῶν		σφῶν	
dat.	οἷ	(οἱ)	σφίσι(ν)	(σφισι[ν])	σφίσι(ν)	(σφισι[ν])
acc.	ἕ	(ἑ)	σφᾶς	(σφας)	σφέα	(σφεα)

RECIPROCAL PRONOUN (U25)

		masc.	fem.	neuter
dual	gen. dat.	ἀλλήλοιν	ἀλλήλαιν	ἀλλήλοιν
	acc.	ἀλλήλω	ἀλλήλα	ἀλλήλω
plur.	gen.	ἀλλήλων	ἀλλήλων	ἀλλήλων
	dat.	ἀλλήλοις	ἀλλήλαις	ἀλλήλοις
	acc.	ἀλλήλους	ἀλλήλας	ἄλληλα

τοιοῦτος (τοσοῦτος) (U36)

τοιοῦτος	τοιαύτη	τοιοῦτον	or τοιοῦτο
τοιούτου	τοιαύτης	τοιούτου	
τοιούτῳ	τοιαύτῃ	τοιούτῳ	
τοιοῦτον	τοιαύτην	τοιοῦτον	or τοιοῦτο

τοιούτω	τοιούτω	τοιούτω
τοιούτοιν	τοιούτοιν	τοιούτοιν
τοιοῦτοι	τοιαῦται	τοιαῦτα
τοιούτων	τοιούτων	τοιούτων
τοιούτοις	τοιαύταις	τοιούτοις
τοιούτους	τοιαύτας	τοιαῦτα

VERBS

Ω-VERBS: PRESENT SYSTEM ACTIVE[1]

indicative	subjunctive	optative	imperative	imperf. ind.
βουλεύω	βουλεύω	βουλεύοιμι		ἐβούλευον
βουλεύεις	βουλεύῃς	βουλεύοις	βούλευε	ἐβούλευες
βουλεύει	βουλεύῃ	βουλεύοι	βουλευέτω	ἐβούλευε(ν)
βουλεύετον	βουλεύητον	βουλεύοιτον	βουλευέτον	ἐβουλευέτον
βουλεύετον	βουλεύητον	βουλευοίτην	βουλευέτων	ἐβουλευέτην
βουλεύομεν	βουλεύωμεν	βουλεύοιμεν		ἐβουλεύομεν
βουλεύετε	βουλεύητε	βουλεύοιτε	βουλεύετε	ἐβουλεύετε
βουλεύουσι(ν)	βουλεύωσι(ν)	βουλεύοιεν	βουλευόντων	ἐβούλευον

infinitive: βουλεύειν
participle: βουλεύων, βουλεύουσα, βουλεῦον

Ω-VERBS: PRESENT SYSTEM MIDDLE-PASSIVE

indicative	subjunctive	optative	imperative	imperf. ind.
βουλεύομαι	βουλεύωμαι	βουλευοίμην		ἐβουλευόμην
βουλεύῃ (or -ει)	βουλεύῃ	βουλεύοιο	βουλεύου	ἐβουλεύου
βουλεύεται	βουλεύηται	βουλεύοιτο	βουλευέσθω	ἐβουλεύετο
βουλεύεσθον	βουλεύησθον	βουλεύοισθον	βουλεύεσθον	ἐβουλεύεσθον
βουλεύεσθον	βουλεύησθον	βουλευοίσθην	βουλευέσθων	ἐβουλευέσθην
βουλευόμεθα	βουλευώμεθα	βουλευοίμεθα		ἐβουλευόμεθα
βουλεύεσθε	βουλεύησθε	βουλεύοισθε	βουλεύεσθε	ἐβουλεύεσθε
βουλεύονται	βουλεύωνται	βουλεύοιντο	βουλευέσθων	ἐβουλεύοντο

infinitive: βουλεύεσθαι
participle: βουλευόμενος, -η, -ον

---

1. For finite forms of verbs, the listing is consistently in the order 1st, 2nd, 3rd singular; 2nd, 3rd dual; 1st, 2nd, 3rd plural; but person/number labels are omitted.

FUTURE SYSTEM

active indicative	active optative	middle indicative	middle optative
βουλεύσω	βουλεύσοιμι	βουλεύσομαι	βουλευσοίμην
βουλεύσεις	βουλεύσοις	βουλεύσῃ (or -ει)	βουλεύσοιο
βουλεύσει	βουλεύσοι	βουλεύσεται	βουλεύσοιτο
βουλεύσετον	βουλεύσοιτον	βουλεύσεσθον	βουλεύσοισθον
βουλεύσετον	βουλευσοίτην	βουλεύσεσθον	βουλευσοίσθην
βουλεύσομεν	βουλεύσοιμεν	βουλευσόμεθα	βουλευσοίμεθα
βουλεύσετε	βουλεύσοιτε	βουλεύσεσθε	βουλεύσοισθε
βουλεύσουσι(ν)	βουλεύσοιεν	βουλεύσονται	βουλεύσοιντο

active infinitive:	βουλεύσειν
middle infinitive:	βουλεύσεσθαι
active participle:	βουλεύσων, βουλεύσουσα, βουλεῦσον
middle participle:	βουλευσόμενος, -η, -ον

passive indicative	passive optative
βουλευθήσομαι	βουλευθησοίμην
βουλευθήσῃ (or -ει)	βουλευθήσοιο
βουλευθήσεται	βουλευθήσοιτο
βουλευθήσεσθον	βουλευθήσοισθον
βουλευθήσεσθον	βουλευθησοίσθην
βουλευθησόμεθα	βουλευθησοίμεθα
βουλευθήσεσθε	βουλευθήσοισθε
βουλευθήσονται	βουλευθήσοιντο

passive infinitive:	βουλευθήσεσθαι
passive participle:	βουλευθησόμενος, -η, -ον

STRONG (2ND) AORIST SYSTEM ACTIVE

indicative	subjunctive	optative	imperative
ἤγαγον	ἀγάγω	ἀγάγοιμι	
ἤγαγες	ἀγάγῃς	ἀγάγοις	ἄγαγε
ἤγαγε(ν)	ἀγάγῃ	ἀγάγοι	ἀγαγέτω
ἠγάγετον	ἀγάγητον	ἀγάγοιτον	ἀγάγετον
ἠγαγέτην	ἀγάγητον	ἀγαγοίτην	ἀγαγέτων
ἠγάγομεν	ἀγάγωμεν	ἀγάγοιμεν	
ἠγάγετε	ἀγάγητε	ἀγάγοιτε	ἀγάγετε
ἤγαγον	ἀγάγωσι(ν)	ἀγάγοιεν	ἀγαγόντων

infinitive:	ἀγαγεῖν
participle:	ἀγαγών, ἀγαγοῦσα, ἀγαγόν

STRONG (2ND) AORIST SYSTEM MIDDLE

indicative	subjunctive	optative	imperative
ἠγαγόμην	ἀγάγωμαι	ἀγαγοίμην	
ἠγάγου	ἀγάγῃ	ἀγάγοιο	ἀγαγοῦ
ἠγάγετο	ἀγάγηται	ἀγάγοιτο	ἀγαγέσθω
ἠγάγεσθον	ἀγάγησθον	ἀγάγοισθον	ἀγάγεσθον
ἠγαγέσθην	ἀγάγησθον	ἀγαγοίσθην	ἀγαγέσθων
ἠγαγόμεθα	ἀγαγώμεθα	ἀγαγοίμεθα	
ἠγάγεσθε	ἀγάγησθε	ἀγάγοισθε	ἀγάγεσθε
ἠγάγοντο	ἀγάγωνται	ἀγάγοιντο	ἀγαγέσθων

infinitive: ἀγαγέσθαι
participle: ἀγαγόμενος, -η, -ον

WEAK (1ST) AORIST SYSTEM ACTIVE

indicative	subjunctive	optative	imperative
ἐβούλευσα	βουλεύσω	βουλεύσαιμι	
ἐβούλευσας	βουλεύσῃς	βουλεύσειας or βουλεύσαις	βούλευσον
ἐβούλευσε(ν)	βουλεύσῃ	βουλεύσειε(ν) or βουλεύσαι	βουλευσάτω
ἐβουλεύσατον	βουλεύσητον	βουλεύσαιτον	βουλεύσατον
ἐβουλευσάτην	βουλεύσητον	βουλευσαίτην	βουλευσάτων
ἐβουλεύσαμεν	βουλεύσωμεν	βουλεύσαιμεν	
ἐβουλεύσατε	βουλεύσητε	βουλεύσαιτε	βουλεύσατε
ἐβούλευσαν	βουλεύσωσι(ν)	βουλεύσειαν or βουλεύσαιεν	βουλευσάντων

infinitive: βουλεῦσαι
participle: βουλεύσας, βουλεύσασα, βουλεῦσαν

WEAK (1ST) AORIST SYSTEM MIDDLE

indicative	subjunctive	optative	imperative
ἐβουλευσάμην	βουλεύσωμαι	βουλευσαίμην	
ἐβουλεύσω	βουλεύσῃ	βουλεύσαιο	βούλευσαι
ἐβουλεύσατο	βουλεύσηται	βουλεύσαιτο	βουλευσάσθω
ἐβουλεύσασθον	βουλεύσησθον	βουλεύσαισθον	βουλεύσασθον
ἐβουλευσάσθην	βουλεύσησθον	βουλευσαίσθην	βουλευσάσθων
ἐβουλευσάμεθα	βουλευσώμεθα	βουλευσαίμεθα	
ἐβουλεύσασθε	βουλεύσησθε	βουλεύσαισθε	βουλεύσασθε
ἐβουλεύσαντο	βουλεύσωνται	βουλεύσαιντο	βουλευσάσθων

infinitive: βουλεύσασθαι
participle: βουλευσάμενος, -η, -ον

AORIST SYSTEM PASSIVE

indicative	subjunctive	optative	imperative
ἐβουλεύθην	βουλευθῶ	βουλευθείην	
ἐβουλεύθης	βουλευθῇς	βουλευθείης	βουλεύθητι
ἐβουλεύθη	βουλευθῇ	βουλευθείη	βουλευθήτω
ἐβουλεύθητον	βουλευθῆτον	βουλευθείητον or -θεῖτον	βουλεύθητον
ἐβουλευθήτην	βουλευθῆτον	βουλευθειήτην or -θείτην	βουλευθήτων
ἐβουλεύθημεν	βουλευθῶμεν	βουλευθείημεν or -θεῖμεν	
ἐβουλεύθητε	βουλευθῆτε	βουλευθείητε or -θεῖτε	βουλεύθητε
ἐβουλεύθησαν	βουλευθῶσι(ν)	βουλευθείησαν or -θεῖεν	βουλευθέντων

infinitive: βουλευθῆναι

participle: βουλευθείς, βουλευθεῖσα, βουλευθέν

PERFECT SYSTEM ACTIVE

1st perf. ind.	2nd perf. ind.	subj. (simple)	subj. (periphrastic form)
λέλυκα	λέλοιπα	λελοίπω	λελοιπὼς ὦ or λελοιπυῖα ὦ
λέλυκας	λέλοιπας	λελοίπῃς	λελοιπὼς (-υῖα) ᾖς
λέλυκε	λέλοιπε(ν)	λελοίπῃ	λελοιπὼς (-υῖα, -ὸς) ᾖ
λελύκατον	λελοίπατον	λελοίπητον	λελοιπότε (-υία) ἦτον
λελύκατον	λελοίπατον	λελοίπητον	λελοιπότε (-υία) ἦτον
λελύκαμεν	λελοίπαμεν	λελοίπωμεν	λελοιπότες (-υῖαι) ὦμεν
λελύκατε	λελοίπατε	λελοίπητε	λελοιπότες (-υῖαι) ἦτε
λελύκᾱσι(ν)	λελοίπᾱσι(ν)	λελοίπωσι(ν)	λελοιπότες (-υῖαι) ὦσι(ν) or λελοιπότα ᾖ

opt. (simple form)	opt. (periphrastic form)	imperative
λελοίποιμι	λελοιπὼς (-υῖα) εἴην	
λελοίποις	λελοιπὼς (-υῖα) εἴης	λελοιπὼς (-υῖα) ἴσθι
λελοίποι	λελοιπὼς (-υῖα, -ὸς) εἴη	λελοιπὼς (-υῖα, -ὸς) ἔστω
λελοίποιτον	λελοιπότε (-υία) εἴητον	λελοιπότε (-υία) ἔστον
λελοιποίτην	λελοιπότε (-υία) εἰήτην	λελοιπότε (-υία) ἔστων
λελοίποιμεν	λελοιπότες (-υῖαι) εἶμεν	
λελοίποιτε	λελοιπότες (-υῖαι) εἶτε	λελοιπότες (-υῖαι) ἔστε
λελοίποιεν	λελοιπότες (-υῖαι) εἶεν or λελοιπότα εἴη	λελοιπότες (-υῖαι) ἔστων or λελοιπότα ἔστω

perfect active infinitive: λελοιπέναι

perfect active participle: λελοιπώς, λελοιπυῖα, λελοιπός

PERFECT SYSTEM: M/P INDICATIVE, INFINITIVE, PARTICIPLE

	vowel stem	*dental plosive stem*	*labial plosive stem*
ind.	λέλυμαι	πέπεισμαι	γέγραμμαι
	λέλυσαι	πέπεισαι	γέγραψαι
	λέλυται	πέπεισται	γέγραπται
	λέλυσθον	πέπεισθον	γέγραφθον
	λέλυσθον	πέπεισθον	γέγραφθον
	λελύμεθα	πεπείσμεθα	γεγράμμεθα
	λέλυσθε	πέπεισθε	γέγραφθε
	λέλυνται	πεπεισμένοι (-αι) εἰσί or πεπεισμένα ἐστί	γεγραμμένοι (-αι) εἰσί or γεγραμμένα ἐστί
inf.	λελύσθαι	πεπεῖσθαι	γεγράφθαι
part.	λελυμένος, -η, -ον	πεπεισμένος, -η, -ον	γεγραμμένος, -η, -ον

	velar plosive stem	*stem in* λ	*stem in* ν
ind.	πέπραγμαι	ἤγγελμαι	πέφασμαι
	πέπραξαι	ἤγγελσαι	— — —
	πέπρακται	ἤγγελται	πέφανται
	πέπραχθον	ἤγγελθον	πέφανθον
	πέπραχθον	ἤγγελθον	πέφανθον
	πεπράγμεθα	ἠγγέλμεθα	πεφάσμεθα
	πέπραχθε	ἤγγελθε	πέφανθε
	πεπραγμένοι (-αι) εἰσί or πεπραγμένα ἐστί	ἠγγελμένοι (-αι) εἰσί or ἠγγελμένα ἐστί	πεφασμένοι (-αι) εἰσί or πεφασμένα ἐστί
inf.	πεπρᾶχθαι	ἠγγέλθαι	πεφάνθαι
part.	πεπραγμένος, -η, -ον	ἠγγελμένος, -η, -ον	πεφασμένος, -η, -ον

PERFECT SYSTEM: M/P SUBJUNCTIVE, OPTATIVE, IMPERATIVE

subjunctive	*optative*	*imperative*
λελυμένος (-η) ὦ	λελυμένος (-η) εἴην	
λελυμένος (-η) ᾖς	λελυμένος (-η) εἴης	λελυμένος (-η) ἴσθι
λελυμένος (-η, -ον) ᾖ	λελυμένος (-η, -ον) εἴη	λελυμένος (-η, -ον) ἔστω
λελυμένω (-α) ἦτον	λελυμένω (-α) εἴητον	λελυμένω (-α) ἔστον
λελυμένω (-α) ἦτον	λελυμένω (-α) εἰήτην	λελυμένω (-α) ἔστων
λελυμένοι (-αι) ὦμεν	λελυμένοι (-αι) εἶμεν	
λελυμένοι (-αι) ἦτε	λελυμένοι (-αι) εἶτε	λελυμένοι (-αι) ἔστε
λελυμένοι (-αι) ὦσι(ν)	λελυμένοι (-αι) εἶεν	λελυμένοι (-αι) ἔστων
or λελυμένα ᾖ	or λελυμένα εἴη	or λελυμένα ἔστω

PERFECT SYSTEM: M/P SUBJ., OPT., IMPER. (RARE SIMPLE FORM)

subjunctive	optative		imperative
μεμνῶμαι	μεμνῄμην or	μεμνῴμην	
μεμνῇ	μεμνῇο	μεμνῷο	μέμνησο
μεμνῆται	μεμνῇτο	μεμνῷτο	μεμνήσθω
μεμνῆσθον	μεμνῇσθον	μεμνῷσθον	
μεμνῆσθον	μεμνῄσθην	μεμνῴσθην	
μεμνώμεθα	μεμνῄμεθα	μεμνῴμεθα	
μεμνῆσθε	μεμνῇσθε	μεμνῷσθε	μέμνησθε
μεμνῶνται	μεμνῇντο	μεμνῷντο	

PLUPERFECT ACTIVE AND MIDDLE/PASSIVE INDICATIVE

active	middle-passive vowel stem	dental plosive stem	labial plosive stem
ἐλελύκη	ἐλελύμην	ἐπεπείσμην	ἐγεγράμμην
ἐλελύκης	ἐλέλυσο	ἐπέπεισο	ἐγέγραψο
ἐλελύκει(ν)	ἐλέλυτο	ἐπέπειστο	ἐγέγραπτο
ἐλελύκετον	ἐλέλυσθον	ἐπέπεισθον	ἐγέγραφθον
ἐλελυκέτην	ἐλελύσθην	ἐπεπείσθην	ἐγεγράφθην
ἐλελύκεμεν	ἐλελύμεθα	ἐπεπείσμεθα	ἐγεγράμμεθα
ἐλελύκετε	ἐλέλυσθε	ἐπέπεισθε	ἐγέγραφθε
ἐλελύκεσαν	ἐλέλυντο	πεπεισμένοι (-αι) ἦσαν	γεγραμμένοι (-αι) ἦσαν
		or πεπεισμένα ἦν	or γεγραμμένα ἦν

middle-passive velar plosive stem	stem in λ	stem in ν
ἐπεπράγμην	ἠγγέλμην	ἐπεφάσμην
ἐπέπραξο	ἤγγελσο	———
ἐπέπρακτο	ἤγγελτο	ἐπέφαντο
ἐπέπραχθον	ἤγγελθον	ἐπέφανθον
ἐπεπράχθην	ἠγγέλθην	ἐπεφάνθην
ἐπεπράγμεθα	ἠγγέλμεθα	ἐπεφάσμεθα
ἐπέπραχθε	ἤγγελθε	ἐπέφανθε
πεπραγμένοι (-αι) ἦσαν	ἠγγελμένοι (-αι) ἦσαν	πεφασμένοι (-αι) ἦσαν
or πεπραγμένα ἦν	or ἠγγελμένα ἦν	or πεφασμένα ἦν

FUTURE PERFECT INDICATIVE

active	middle-passive		
λελυκὼς (-υῖα) ἔσομαι	λελύσομαι	or	λελυμένος (-η) ἔσομαι
λελυκὼς (-υῖα) ἔσῃ	λελύσῃ		λελυμένος (-η) ἔσῃ
λελυκὼς (-υῖα, -ὸς) ἔσται	λελύσεται		λελυμένος (-η, -ον) ἔσται
λελυκότε (-υία) ἔσεσθον	λελύσεσθον		λελυμένω ἔσεσθον
λελυκότε (-υία) ἔσεσθον	λελύσεσθον		λελυμένω ἔσεσθον
λελυκότες (-υῖαι) ἐσόμεθα	λελυσόμεθα		λελυμένοι (-αι) ἐσόμεθα
λελυκότες (-υῖαι) ἔσεσθε	λελύσεσθε		λελυμένοι (-αι) ἔσεσθε
λελυκότες (-υῖαι) ἔσονται	λελύσονται		λελυμένοι (-αι) ἔσονται
or λελυκότα ἔσται			or λελυμένα ἔσται

future perfect middle-passive infinitive: λελύσεσθαι
future perfect middle-passive participle: λελυσόμενος, -η, -ον

ATHEMATIC PERFECTS (U41)

ἵστημι *(in addition to forms from* ἕστηκα*)*

indicative	subjunctive	opt. (poetic)	imper. (poetic)	pluperfect
	ἑστῶ	ἑσταίην		
	ἑστῇς	ἑσταίης	ἕσταθι	
	ἑστῇ	ἑσταίη	ἑστάτω	
ἕστατον	ἑστῆτον	ἑσταῖτον	ἕστατον	ἕστατον
ἕστατον	ἑστῆτον	ἑσταίτην	ἑστάτων	ἑστάτην
ἕσταμεν	ἑστῶμεν	ἑσταῖμεν		ἕσταμεν
ἕστατε	ἑστῆτε	ἑσταῖτε	ἕστατε	ἕστατε
ἑστᾶσι(ν)	ἑστῶσι(ν)	ἑσταῖεν	ἑστάντων	ἕστασαν

infinitive: ἑστάναι
participle: ἑστώς, ἑστῶσα, ἑστός (masc./neut. stem ἑστωτ-)

θνῄσκω *(in addition to forms from* τέθνηκα*)*

indicative	subjunctive	opt. (poetic)	imperative	pluperfect
		τεθναίην		
	not found	τεθναίης	τέθναθι (poetic)	
		τεθναίη	τεθνάτω	
τέθνατον		τεθναῖτον		
τέθνατον		τεθναίτην		
τέθναμεν		τεθναῖμεν		
τέθνατε		τεθναῖτε		
τεθνᾶσι(ν)		τεθναῖεν		ἐτέθνασαν

infinitive: τεθνάναι
participle: τεθνεώς, τεθνεῶσα, τεθνεός (masc./neut. stem τεθνεωτ-)

δέδια *(in addition to forms from* δέδοικα*)*

indicative	subj. (rare)	optative	imperative	pluperfect
δέδια	δεδίω			ἐδεδίειν
δέδιας	δεδίῃς	not found	δέδιθι	ἐδεδίεις
δέδιε(ν)	δεδίῃ			ἐδεδίει
δέδιτον	δεδίητον			
δέδιτον	δεδίητον			
δέδιμεν	δεδίωμεν			ἐδέδιμεν
δέδιτε	δεδίητε			ἐδέδιτε
δεδίᾱσι(ν)	δεδίωσι(ν)			ἐδεδίεσαν
				or ἐδέδισαν

> infinitive: δεδιέναι
> participle: δεδιώς, δεδιυῖα, δεδιός

PRESENT SYSTEM OF CONTRACT Ω-VERBS[1]

VERBS IN -έω: ACTIVE

indicative	subjunctive	optative[2]		imperative	imperf. ind.
ποιῶ	ποιῶ	(ποιοῖμι) or	ποιοίην		ἐποίουν
ποιεῖς	ποιῇς	(ποιοῖς)	ποιοίης	ποίει	ἐποίεις
ποιεῖ	ποιῇ	(ποιοῖ)	ποιοίη	ποιείτω	ἐποίει
ποιεῖτον	ποιῆτον	ποιοῖτον	(ποιοίητον)	ποιεῖτον	ἐποιεῖτον
ποιεῖτον	ποιῆτον	ποιοίτην	(ποιοιήτην)	ποιείτων	ἐποιείτην
ποιοῦμεν	ποιῶμεν	ποιοῖμεν	(ποιοίημεν)		ἐποιοῦμεν
ποιεῖτε	ποιῆτε	ποιοῖτε	(ποιοίητε)	ποιεῖτε	ἐποιεῖτε
ποιοῦσι(ν)	ποιῶσι(ν)	ποιοῖεν	(ποιοίησαν)	ποιούντων	ἐποίουν

> infinitive: ποιεῖν
> participle: ποιῶν, ποιοῦσα, ποιοῦν

VERBS IN -έω WITH MONOSYLLABIC STEM: ACTIVE

indicative	subjunctive	optative	imperative	imperf.
πλέω	πλέω	πλέοιμι		ἔπλεον
πλεῖς	πλέῃς	πλέοις	πλεῖ	ἔπλεις
πλεῖ	πλέῃ	πλέοι	πλείτω	ἔπλει

---

1. Future system with contract conjugation (such as -έω contraction in νομιῶ, ἀγγελῶ, and -άω contraction in ἐλῶ, σκεδῶ) has the same endings for indicative, optative, infinitive, and participle (no subjunctive or imperative in the future).

2. Less common forms in parentheses.

active of verbs in -έω with monosyllabic stem (dual and plural)

indicative	subjunctive	optative	imperative	imperf.
πλεῖτον	πλέητον	πλέοιτον	πλεῖτον	ἐπλεῖτον
πλεῖτον	πλέητον	πλεοίτην	πλείτων	ἐπλείτην
πλέομεν	πλέωμεν	πλέοιμεν		ἐπλέομεν
πλεῖτε	πλέητε	πλέοιτε	πλεῖτε	ἐπλεῖτε
πλέουσι(ν)	πλέωσι(ν)	πλέοιεν	πλεόντων	ἔπλεον

> *infinitive:* πλεῖν
> *participle:* πλέων, πλέουσα, πλέον

VERBS IN -έω: MIDDLE-PASSIVE

indicative	subjunctive	optative	imperative	imperf. ind.
ποιοῦμαι	ποιῶμαι	ποιοίμην		ἐποιούμην
ποιῇ	ποιῇ	ποιοῖο	ποιοῦ	ἐποιοῦ
ποιεῖται	ποιῆται	ποιοῖτο	ποιείσθω	ἐποιεῖτο
ποιεῖσθον	ποιῆσθον	ποιοῖσθον	ποιεῖσθον	ἐποιεῖσθον
ποιεῖσθον	ποιῆσθον	ποιοίσθην	ποιείσθων	ἐποιείσθην
ποιούμεθα	ποιώμεθα	ποιοίμεθα		ἐποιούμεθα
ποιεῖσθε	ποιῆσθε	ποιοῖσθε	ποιεῖσθε	ἐποιεῖσθε
ποιοῦνται	ποιῶνται	ποιοῖντο	ποιείσθων	ἐποιοῦντο

> *infinitive:* ποιεῖσθαι
> *participle:* ποιούμενος, -η, -ον

VERBS IN -έω WITH MONOSYLLABIC STEM: MIDDLE-PASSIVE

indicative	subjunctive	optative	imperative	imperf. ind.
δέομαι	δέωμαι	δεοίμην		ἐδεόμην
δέῃ	δέῃ	δέοιο	δέου	ἐδέου
δεῖται	δέηται	δέοιτο	δείσθω	ἐδεῖτο
δεῖσθον	δέησθον	δέοισθον	δεῖσθον	ἐδεῖσθον
δεῖσθον	δέησθον	δεοίσθην	δείσθων	ἐδείσθην
δεόμεθα	δεώμεθα	δεοίμεθα		ἐδεόμεθα
δεῖσθε	δέησθε	δέοισθε	δεῖσθε	ἐδεῖσθε
δέονται	δέωνται	δέοιντο	δείσθων	ἐδέοντο

> *infinitive:* δεῖσθαι
> *participle:* δεόμενος, -η, -ον

VERBS IN -άω: ACTIVE

indicative	subjunctive	optative			imperative	imperf.
ὁρῶ	ὁρῶ	(ὁρῷμι)	or	ὁρῴην		ἑώρων
ὁρᾷς	ὁρᾷς	(ὁρῷς)		ὁρῴης	ὅρα	ἑώρας
ὁρᾷ	ὁρᾷ	(ὁρῷ)		ὁρῴη	ὁράτω	ἑώρα
ὁρᾶτον	ὁράτον	ὁρῷτον		(ὁρῴητον)	ὁράτον	ἑωρᾶτον
ὁρᾶτον	ὁράτον	ὁρῴτην		(ὁρῳήτην)	ὁράτων	ἑωράτην
ὁρῶμεν	ὁρῶμεν	ὁρῷμεν		(ὁρῴημεν)		ἑωρῶμεν
ὁρᾶτε	ὁρᾶτε	ὁρῷτε		(ὁρῴητε)	ὁρᾶτε	ἑωρᾶτε
ὁρῶσι(ν)	ὁρῶσι(ν)	ὁρῷεν		(ὁρῴησαν)	ὁρώντων	ἑώρων

infinitive: ὁρᾶν
participle: ὁρῶν, ὁρῶσα, ὁρῶν

VERBS IN -άω WITH η IN CONTRACTION: ACTIVE

indicative	subjunctive	optative	imperative	imperf.
χρῶ	χρῶ	χρῴην		ἔχρων
χρῇς	χρῇς	χρῴης	χρῇ	ἔχρης
χρῇ	χρῇ	χρῴη	χρήτω	ἔχρη
χρῆτον	χρῆτον	χρῷτον	χρῆτον	ἐχρῆτον
χρῆτον	χρῆτον	χρῴτην	χρήτων	ἐχρήτην
χρῶμεν	χρῶμεν	χρῷμεν		ἐχρῶμεν
χρῆτε	χρῆτε	χρῷτε	χρῆτε	ἐχρῆτε
χρῶσι(ν)	χρῶσι(ν)	χρῷεν	χρώντων	ἔχρων

infinitive: χρῆν
participle: χρῶν, χρῶσα, χρῶν

VERBS IN -άω: MIDDLE-PASSIVE

indicative	subjunctive	optative	imperative	imperf.
ὁρῶμαι	ὁρῶμαι	ὁρῴμην		ἑωρώμην
ὁρᾷ	ὁρᾷ	ὁρῷο	ὁρῶ	ἑωρῶ
ὁρᾶται	ὁρᾶται	ὁρῷτο	ὁράσθω	ἑωρᾶτο
ὁρᾶσθον	ὁρᾶσθον	ὁρῷσθον	ὁρᾶσθον	ἑωρᾶσθον
ὁρᾶσθον	ὁρᾶσθον	ὁρῴσθην	ὁράσθων	ἑωράσθην
ὁρώμεθα	ὁρώμεθα	ὁρῴμεθα		ἑωρώμεθα
ὁρᾶσθε	ὁρᾶσθε	ὁρῷσθε	ὁρᾶσθε	ἑωρᾶσθε
ὁρῶνται	ὁρῶνται	ὁρῷντο	ὁράσθων	ἑωρῶντο

infinitive: ὁρᾶσθαι
participle: ὁρώμενος, -η, -ον

VERBS IN -άω WITH η IN CONTRACTION: MIDDLE-PASSIVE

indicative	*subjunctive*	*optative*	*imperative*	*imperf.*
χρῶμαι	χρῶμαι	χρώμην		ἐχρώμην
χρῇ	χρῇ	χρῷο	χρῶ	ἐχρῶ
χρῆται	χρῆται	χρῷτο	χρήσθω	ἐχρῆτο
χρῆσθον	χρῆσθον	χρῷσθον	χρῆσθον	ἐχρῆσθον
χρῆσθον	χρῆσθον	χρῷσθην	χρήσθων	ἐχρήσθην
χρώμεθα	χρώμεθα	χρώμεθα		ἐχρώμεθα
χρῆσθε	χρῆσθε	χρῷσθε	χρῆσθε	ἐχρῆσθε
χρῶνται	χρῶνται	χρῷντο	χρήσθων	ἐχρῶντο

infinitive: χρῆσθαι
participle: χρώμενος, -η, -ον

VERBS IN -όω: ACTIVE

indicative	*subjunctive*	*optative*		*imperative*	*imperf.*
δηλῶ	δηλῶ	(δηλοῖμι) or	δηλοίην		ἐδήλουν
δηλοῖς	δηλοῖς	(δηλοῖς)	δηλοίης	δήλου	ἐδήλους
δηλοῖ	δηλοῖ	(δηλοῖ)	δηλοίη	δηλούτω	ἐδήλου
δηλοῦτον	δηλῶτον	δηλοῖτον	(δηλοίητον)	δηλοῦτον	ἐδηλούτον
δηλοῦτον	δηλῶτον	δηλοίτην	(δηλοιήτην)	δηλούτων	ἐδηλούτην
δηλοῦμεν	δηλῶμεν	δηλοῖμεν	(δηλοίημεν)		ἐδηλοῦμεν
δηλοῦτε	δηλῶτε	δηλοῖτε	(δηλοίητε)	δηλοῦτε	ἐδηλοῦτε
δηλοῦσι(ν)	δηλῶσι(ν)	δηλοῖεν	(δηλοίησαν)	δηλούντων	ἐδήλουν

infinitive: δηλοῦν
participle: δηλῶν, δηλοῦσα, δηλοῦν

VERBS IN -όω: MIDDLE-PASSIVE

indicative	*subjunctive*	*optative*	*imperative*	*imperf.*
δηλοῦμαι	δηλῶμαι	δηλοίμην		ἐδηλούμην
δηλοῖ	δηλοῖ	δηλοῖο	δηλοῦ	ἐδηλοῦ
δηλοῦται	δηλῶται	δηλοῖτο	δηλούσθω	ἐδηλοῦτο
δηλοῦσθον	δηλῶσθον	δηλοῖσθον	δηλοῦσθον	ἐδηλοῦσθον
δηλοῦσθον	δηλῶσθον	δηλοίσθην	δηλούσθων	ἐδηλούσθην
δηλούμεθα	δηλώμεθα	δηλοίμεθα		ἐδηλούμεθα
δηλοῦσθε	δηλῶσθε	δηλοῖσθε	δηλοῦσθε	ἐδηλοῦσθε
δηλοῦνται	δηλῶνται	δηλοῖντο	δηλούσθων	ἐδηλοῦντο

infinitive: δηλοῦσθαι
participle: δηλούμενος, -η, -ον

MI-VERBS

τίθημι: PRESENT SYSTEM ACTIVE

indicative	subjunctive	optative	imperative	imperf.
τίθημι	τιθῶ	τιθείην		ἐτίθην
τίθης	τιθῇς	τιθείης	τίθει	ἐτίθεις
τίθησι(ν)	τιθῇ	τιθείη	τιθέτω	ἐτίθει
τίθετον	τιθῆτον	τιθεῖτον	τίθετον	ἐτίθετον
τίθετον	τιθῆτον	τιθείτην	τιθέτων	ἐτιθέτην
τίθεμεν	τιθῶμεν	τιθεῖμεν		ἐτίθεμεν
τίθετε	τιθῆτε	τιθεῖτε	τίθετε	ἐτίθετε
τιθέᾱσι(ν)	τιθῶσι(ν)	τιθεῖεν	τιθέντων	ἐτίθεσαν

infinitive: τιθέναι
participle: τιθείς, τιθεῖσα, τιθέν

τίθημι: PRESENT SYSTEM MIDDLE-PASSIVE

indicative	subjunctive	optative	imperative	imperf.
τίθεμαι	τιθῶμαι	τιθείμην		ἐτιθέμην
τίθεσαι	τιθῇ	τιθεῖο	τίθεσο	ἐτίθεσο
τίθεται	τιθῆται	τιθεῖτο	τιθέσθω	ἐτίθετο
τίθεσθον	τιθῆσθον	τιθεῖσθον	τίθεσθον	ἐτίθεσθον
τίθεσθον	τιθῆσθον	τιθείσθην	τιθέσθων	ἐτιθέσθην
τιθέμεθα	τιθώμεθα	τιθείμεθα		ἐτιθέμεθα
τίθεσθε	τιθῆσθε	τιθεῖσθε	τίθεσθε	ἐτίθεσθε
τίθενται	τιθῶνται	τιθεῖντο	τιθέσθων	ἐτίθεντο

infinitive: τίθεσθαι
participle: τιθέμενος, -η, -ον

τίθημι: AORIST SYSTEM ACTIVE

indicative	subjunctive	optative	imperative
ἔθηκα	θῶ	θείην	
ἔθηκας	θῇς	θείης	θές
ἔθηκε(ν)	θῇ	θείη	θέτω
ἔθετον	θῆτον	θεῖτον	θέτον
ἐθέτην	θῆτον	θείτην	θέτων
ἔθεμεν	θῶμεν	θείημεν or θεῖμεν	
ἔθετε	θῆτε	θείητε or θεῖτε	θέτε
ἔθεσαν	θῶσι(ν)	θεῖεν	θέντων

infinitive: θεῖναι
participle: θείς, θεῖσα, θέν

τίθημι: AORIST SYSTEM MIDDLE

indicative	subjunctive	optative	imperative
ἐθέμην	θῶμαι	θείμην	
ἔθου	θῇ	θεῖο	θοῦ
ἔθετο	θῆται	θεῖτο	θέσθω
ἔθεσθον	θῆσθον	θεῖσθον	θέσθον
ἐθέσθην	θῆσθον	θείσθην	θέσθων
ἐθέμεθα	θώμεθα	θείμεθα	
ἔθεσθε	θῆσθε	θεῖσθε	θέσθε
ἔθεντο	θῶνται	θεῖντο	θέσθων

infinitive: θέσθαι
participle: θέμενος, -η, -ον

ἵημι: PRESENT SYSTEM ACTIVE

indicative	subjunctive	optative	imperative	imperfect ind.
ἵημι	ἱῶ	ἱείην		ἵην
ἵης	ἱῇς	ἱείης	ἵει	ἵεις
ἵησι(ν)	ἱῇ	ἱείη	ἱέτω	ἵει
ἵετον	ἱῆτον	ἱεῖτον	ἵετον	ἵετον
ἵετον	ἱῆτον	ἱείτην	ἱέτων	ἱέτην
ἵεμεν	ἱῶμεν	ἱεῖμεν		ἵεμεν
ἵετε	ἱῆτε	ἱεῖτε	ἵετε	ἵετε
ἱᾶσι(ν)	ἱῶσι(ν)	ἱεῖεν	ἱέντων	ἵεσαν

infinitive: ἱέναι
participle: ἱείς, ἱεῖσα, ἱέν

ἵημι: PRESENT SYSTEM MIDDLE-PASSIVE

indicative	subjunctive	optative	imperative	imperfect ind.
ἵεμαι	ἱῶμαι	ἱείμην		ἱέμην
ἵεσαι	ἱῇ	ἱεῖο	ἵεσο	ἵεσο
ἵεται	ἱῆται	ἱεῖτο	ἱέσθω	ἵετο
ἵεσθον	ἱῆσθον	ἱεῖσθον	ἵεσθον	ἵεσθον
ἵεσθον	ἱῆσθον	ἱείσθην	ἱέσθων	ἱέσθην
ἱέμεθα	ἱώμεθα	ἱείμεθα		ἱέμεθα
ἵεσθε	ἱῆσθε	ἱεῖσθε	ἵεσθε	ἵεσθε
ἵενται	ἱῶνται	ἱεῖντο	ἱέσθων	ἵεντο

infinitive: ἵεσθαι
participle: ἱέμενος, -η, -ον

ἵημι: AORIST SYSTEM ACTIVE

indicative	subjunctive	optative	imperative
(ἀφ)ῆκα	(ἀφ)ῶ	(ἀφ)είην	
(ἀφ)ῆκας	(ἀφ)ῇς	(ἀφ)είης	(ἀφ)ές
(ἀφ)ῆκε(ν)	(ἀφ)ῇ	(ἀφ)είη	(ἀφ)έτω
(ἀφ)εῖτον	(ἀφ)ῆτον	(ἀφ)εῖτον	(ἀφ)έτον
(ἀφ)είτην	(ἀφ)ῆτον	(ἀφ)είτην	(ἀφ)έτων
(ἀφ)εῖμεν	(ἀφ)ῶμεν	(ἀφ)εῖμεν	
(ἀφ)εῖτε	(ἀφ)ῆτε	(ἀφ)εῖτε or (ἀφ)είητε	(ἀφ)έτε
(ἀφ)εῖσαν	(ἀφ)ῶσι(ν)	(ἀφ)εῖεν or (ἀφ)είησαν	(ἀφ)έντων

infinitive: (ἀφ)εῖναι
participle: (ἀφ)είς, (ἀφ)εῖσα, (ἀφ)έν

ἵημι: AORIST SYSTEM MIDDLE

indicative	subjunctive	optative	imperative
(ἀφ)είμην	(ἀφ)ῶμαι	(ἀφ)είμην	
(ἀφ)εῖσο	(ἀφ)ῇ	(ἀφ)εῖο	(ἀφ)οῦ
(ἀφ)εῖτο	(ἀφ)ῆται	(ἀφ)εῖτο	(ἀφ)έσθω
(ἀφ)εῖσθον	(ἀφ)ῆσθον	(ἀφ)εῖσθον	(ἄφ)εσθον
(ἀφ)είσθην	(ἀφ)ῆσθον	(ἀφ)είσθην	(ἀφ)έσθων
(ἀφ)είμεθα	(ἀφ)ώμεθα	(ἀφ)είμεθα	
(ἀφ)εῖσθε	(ἀφ)ῆσθε	(ἀφ)εῖσθε	(ἄφ)εσθε
(ἀφ)εῖντο	(ἀφ)ῶνται	(ἀφ)εῖντο	(ἀφ)έσθων

infinitive: (ἀφ)έσθαι
participle: (ἀφ)έμενος, -η, -ον

δίδωμι: PRESENT SYSTEM ACTIVE

indicative	subjunctive	optative	imperative	imperf. ind.
δίδωμι	διδῶ	διδοίην		ἐδίδουν
δίδως	διδῷς	διδοίης	δίδου	ἐδίδους
δίδωσι(ν)	διδῷ	διδοίη	διδότω	ἐδίδου
δίδοτον	διδῶτον	διδοῖτον	δίδοτον	ἐδίδοτον
δίδοτον	διδῶτον	διδοίτην	διδότων	ἐδιδότην
δίδομεν	διδῶμεν	διδοῖμεν		ἐδίδομεν
δίδοτε	διδῶτε	διδοῖτε	δίδοτε	ἐδίδοτε
διδόᾱσι(ν)	διδῶσι(ν)	διδοῖεν	διδόντων	ἐδίδοσαν

infinitive: διδόναι
participle: διδούς, διδοῦσα, διδόν

δίδωμι: PRESENT SYSTEM MIDDLE-PASSIVE

indicative	subjunctive	optative	imperative	imperf. ind.
δίδομαι	διδῶμαι	διδοίμην		ἐδιδόμην
δίδοσαι	διδῷ	διδοῖο	δίδοσο	ἐδίδοσο
δίδοται	διδῶται	διδοῖτο	διδόσθω	ἐδίδοτο
δίδοσθον	διδῶσθον	διδοῖσθον	δίδοσθον	ἐδίδοσθον
δίδοσθον	διδῶσθον	διδοίσθην	διδόσθων	ἐδιδόσθην
διδόμεθα	διδώμεθα	διδοίμεθα		ἐδιδόμεθα
δίδοσθε	διδῶσθε	διδοῖσθε	δίδοσθε	ἐδίδοσθε
δίδονται	διδῶνται	διδοῖντο	διδόσθων	ἐδίδοντο

infinitive: δίδοσθαι
participle: διδόμενος, -η, -ον

δίδωμι: AORIST SYSTEM ACTIVE

indicative	subjunctive	optative	imperative
ἔδωκα	δῶ	δοίην	
ἔδωκας	δῷς	δοίης	δός
ἔδωκε(ν)	δῷ	δοίη	δότω
ἔδοτον	δῶτον	δοῖτον	δότον
ἐδότην	δῶτον	δοίτην	δότων
ἔδομεν	δῶμεν	δοίημεν or δοῖμεν	
ἔδοτε	δῶτε	δοίητε	δότε
ἔδοσαν	δῶσι(ν)	δοῖεν or δοίησαν	δόντων

infinitive: δοῦναι
participle: δούς, δοῦσα, δόν

δίδωμι: AORIST SYSTEM MIDDLE

indicative	subjunctive	optative	imperative
ἐδόμην	δῶμαι	δοίμην	
ἔδου	δῷ	δοῖο	δοῦ
ἔδοτο	δῶται	δοῖτο	δόσθω
ἔδοσθον	δῶσθον	δοῖσθον	δόσθον
ἐδόσθην	δῶσθον	δοίσθην	δόσθων
ἐδόμεθα	δώμεθα	δοίμεθα	
ἔδοσθε	δῶσθε	δοῖσθε	δόσθε
ἔδοντο	δῶνται	δοῖντο	δόσθων

infinitive: δόσθαι
participle: δόμενος, -η, -ον

ἵστημι: PRESENT SYSTEM ACTIVE

indicative	subjunctive	optative	imperative	imperf. ind.
ἵστημι	ἱστῶ	ἱσταίην		ἵστην [ῑ]
ἵστης	ἱστῇς	ἱσταίης	ἵστη	ἵστης
ἵστησι(ν)	ἱστῇ	ἱσταίη	ἱστάτω	ἵστη
ἵστατον	ἱστῆτον	ἱσταῖτον	ἵστατον	ἵστατον
ἵστατον	ἱστῆτον	ἱσταίτην	ἱστάτων	ἱστάτην
ἵσταμεν	ἱστῶμεν	ἱσταῖμεν		ἵσταμεν
ἵστατε	ἱστῆτε	ἱσταῖτε	ἵστατε	ἵστατε
ἱστᾶσι(ν)	ἱστῶσι(ν)	ἱσταῖεν	ἱστάντων	ἵστασαν

> infinitive: ἱστάναι
> participle: ἱστάς, ἱστᾶσα, ἱστάν

ἵστημι: PRESENT SYSTEM MIDDLE-PASSIVE

indicative	subjunctive	optative	imperative	imperf. ind.
ἵσταμαι	ἱστῶμαι	ἱσταίμην		ἱστάμην [ῑ]
ἵστασαι	ἱστῇ	ἱσταῖο	ἵστασο	ἵστασο
ἵσταται	ἱστῆται	ἱσταῖτο	ἱστάσθω	ἵστατο
ἵστασθον	ἱστῆσθον	ἱσταῖσθον	ἵστασθον	ἵστασθον
ἵστασθον	ἱστῆσθον	ἱσταίσθην	ἱστάσθων	ἱστάσθην
ἱστάμεθα	ἱστώμεθα	ἱσταίμεθα		ἱστάμεθα
ἵστασθε	ἱστῆσθε	ἱσταῖσθε	ἵστασθε	ἵστασθε
ἵστανται	ἱστῶνται	ἱσταῖντο	ἱστάσθων	ἵσταντο

> infinitive: ἵστασθαι
> participle: ἱστάμενος, -η, -ον

ἵστημι: STRONG (INTRANSITIVE) AORIST SYSTEM ACTIVE

indicative	subjunctive	optative	imperative
ἔστην	στῶ	σταίην	
ἔστης	στῇς	σταίης	στῆθι
ἔστη	στῇ	σταίη	στήτω
ἔστητον	στῆτον	σταῖτον	στῆτον
ἐστήτην	στῆτον	σταίτην	στήτων
ἔστημεν	στῶμεν	σταίημεν	
ἔστητε	στῆτε	σταίητε	στῆτε
ἔστησαν	στῶσι(ν)	σταῖεν	στάντων

> infinitive: στῆναι
> participle: στάς, στᾶσα, στάν

δύναμαι (ἐπίσταμαι): PRESENT SYSTEM MIDDLE-PASSIVE

indicative	subjunctive	optative	imperative	imperf. ind.
δύναμαι	δύνωμαι	δυναίμην		ἐδυνάμην
δύνασαι, δύνᾳ, or	δύνῃ	δύναιο	ἐπίστασο or	ἐδύνω
δύνῃ			ἐπίστω	(ἠπίστω or
(ἐπίστασαι or ἐπίστᾳ)				ἠπίστασο)
δύναται	δύνηται	δύναιτο	ἐπιστάσθω	ἐδύνατο
δύνασθον	δύνησθον	δύναισθον	ἐπίστασθον	ἐδύνασθον
δύνασθον	δύνησθον	δυναίσθην	ἐπιστάσθων	ἐδυνάσθην
δυνάμεθα	δυνώμεθα	δυναίμεθα		ἐδυνάμεθα
δύνασθε	δύνησθε	δύναισθε	ἐπίστασθε	ἐδύνασθε
δύνανται	δύνωνται	δύναιντο	ἐπιστάσθων	ἐδύναντο

> infinitive: δύνασθαι (ἐπίστασθαι)
> participle: δυνάμενος, -η, -ον (ἐπιστάμενος, -η, -ον)

δείκνῡμι: PRESENT SYSTEM ACTIVE

indicative	subjunctive	optative	imperative	imperf. ind.
δείκνῡμι	δεικνύω	δεικνύοιμι		ἐδείκνῡν
δείκνῡς	δεικνύῃς	δεικνύοις	δείκνῡ	ἐδείκνῡς
δείκνῡσι(ν)	δεικνύῃ	δεικνύοι	δεικνύτω	ἐδείκνῡ
δείκνυτον	δεικνύητον	δεικνύοιτον	δείκνυτον	ἐδείκνυτον
δείκνυτον	δεικνύητον	δεικνυοίτην	δεικνύτων	ἐδεικνύτην
δείκνυμεν	δεικνύωμεν	δεικνύοιμεν		ἐδείκνυμεν
δείκνυτε	δεικνύητε	δεικνύοιτε	δείκνυτε	ἐδείκνυτε
δεικνύᾱσι(ν)	δεικνύωσι(ν)	δεικνύοιεν	δεικνύντων	ἐδείκνυσαν

> infinitive: δεικνύναι
> participle: δεικνύς, δεικνῦσα, δεικνύν

δείκνῡμι: PRESENT SYSTEM MIDDLE-PASSIVE

indicative	subjunctive	optative	imperative	imperf. ind.
δείκνυμαι	δεικνύωμαι	δεικνυοίμην		ἐδεικνύμην
δείκνυσαι	δεικνύῃ	δεικνύοιο	δείκνυσο	ἐδείκνυσο
δείκνυται	δεικνύηται	δεικνύοιτο	δεικνύσθω	ἐδείκνυτο
δείκνυσθον	δεικνύησθον	δεικνύοισθον	δείκνυσθον	ἐδείκνυσθον
δείκνυσθον	δεικνύησθον	δεικνυοίσθην	δεικνύσθων	ἐδεικνύσθην
δεικνύμεθα	δεικνυώμεθα	δεικνυοίμεθα		ἐδεικνύμεθα
δείκνυσθε	δεικνύησθε	δεικνύοισθε	δείκνυσθε	ἐδείκνυσθε
δείκνυνται	δεικνύωνται	δεικνύοιντο	δεικνύσθων	ἐδείκνυντο

> infinitive: δείκνυσθαι
> participle: δεικνύμενος, -η, -ον

εἰμί (BE): PRESENT SYSTEM AND FUTURE

pres. ind.	pres. subj.	pres. optative			imperat.	imperf.	fut.
εἰμί	ὦ	εἴην				ἦ or ἦν	ἔσομαι
εἶ	ᾖς	εἴης			ἴσθι	ἦσθα	ἔσῃ
ἐστί(ν)	ᾖ	εἴη			ἔστω	ἦν	ἔσται
ἐστόν	ἦτον	εἶτον	or	εἴητον	ἔστον	ἦστον	ἔσεσθον
ἐστόν	ἦτον	εἴτην		εἰήτην	ἔστων	ἤστην	ἔσεσθον
ἐσμέν	ὦμεν	εἶμεν		εἴημεν		ἦμεν	ἐσόμεθα
ἐστέ	ἦτε	εἶτε		εἴητε	ἔστε	ἦτε or ἦστε	ἔσεσθε
εἰσί(ν)	ὦσι(ν)	εἶεν		εἴησαν	ἔστων	ἦσαν	ἔσονται

> infinitives: εἶναι, (fut.) ἔσεσθαι
> participles: ὤν, οὖσα, ὄν, (fut.) ἐσόμενος, -η, -ον

εἰμι (GO): PRESENT SYSTEM

ind.	subj.	opt.	imperat.	imperfect		
εἶμι	ἴω	ἴοιμι or ἰοίην		ᾖα	or	ᾔειν
εἶ	ἴῃς	ἴοις	ἴθι	ᾔεισθα		ᾔεις
εἶσι(ν)	ἴῃ	ἴοι	ἴτω	ᾔειν		ᾔει
ἴτον	ἴητον	ἴοιτον	ἴτον	ᾖτον		
ἴτον	ἴητον	ἰοίτην	ἴτων	ᾔτην		
ἴμεν	ἴωμεν	ἴοιμεν		ᾖμεν		
ἴτε	ἴητε	ἴοιτε	ἴτε	ᾖτε		
ἴᾱσι(ν)	ἴωσι(ν)	ἴοιεν	ἰόντων	ᾖσαν		ᾔεσαν

> infinitive: ἰέναι
> participle: ἰών, ἰοῦσα, ἰόν

φημί: PRESENT SYSTEM

ind.	subj.	opt.	imperat.	imperf.
φημί	φῶ	φαίην		ἔφην
φής	φῇς	φαίης	φάθι or φαθί	ἔφησθα or ἔφης
φησί(ν)	φῇ	φαίη	φάτω	ἔφη
φατόν	φῆτον	φαῖτον	φάτον	ἔφατον
φατόν	φῆτον	φαίτην	φάτων	ἐφάτην
φαμέν	φῶμεν	φαῖμεν or φαίημεν		ἔφαμεν
φατέ	φῆτε	φαίητε	φάτε	ἔφατε
φᾱσί(ν)	φῶσι(ν)	φαῖεν or φαίησαν	φάντων	ἔφασαν

> infinitive: φάναι
> participle: (poetic) φάς, φᾶσα, φάν

βαίνω: AORIST SYSTEM ACTIVE

indicative	subjunctive	optative	imperative
ἔβην	βῶ	βαίην	
ἔβης	βῇς	βαίης	βῆθι or -βᾱ
ἔβη	βῇ	βαίη	βήτω
ἔβητον	βῆτον	βαίητον or βαῖτον	βῆτον
ἐβήτην	βῆτον	βαιήτην or βαίτην	βήτων
ἔβημεν	βῶμεν	βαίημεν or βαῖμεν	
ἔβητε	βῆτε	βαίητε	βῆτε
ἔβησαν	βῶσι(ν)	βαῖεν	βάντων

infinitive: βῆναι
participle: βάς, βᾶσα, βάν

γιγνώσκω: AORIST SYSTEM ACTIVE

indicative	subjunctive	optative	imperative
ἔγνων	γνῶ	γνοίην	
ἔγνως	γνῷς	γνοίης	γνῶθι
ἔγνω	γνῷ	γνοίη	γνώτω
ἔγνωτον	γνῶτον	γνοίητον or γνοῖτον	γνῶτον
ἐγνώτην	γνῶτον	γνοιήτην or γνοίτην	γνώτων
ἔγνωμεν	γνῶμεν	γνοίημεν or γνοῖμεν	
ἔγνωτε	γνῶτε	γνοίητε	γνῶτε
ἔγνωσαν	γνῶσι(ν)	γνοῖεν	γνόντων

infinitive: γνῶναι
participle: γνούς, γνοῦσα, γνόν

ἁλίσκομαι: AORIST SYSTEM

indicative		subjunctive	optative	imperative
ἑάλων or	ἥλων	ἁλῶ	ἁλοίην	
ἑάλως	ἥλως	ἁλῷς	ἁλοίης	not found
ἑάλω	ἥλω	ἁλῷ	ἁλοίη	
ἑάλωτον	ἥλωτον	ἁλῶτον	dual not found	
ἑαλώτην	ἡλώτην	ἁλῶτον		
ἑάλωμεν	ἥλωμεν	ἁλῶμεν	plural not found	
ἑάλωτε	ἥλωτε	ἁλῶτε		
ἑάλωσαν	ἥλωσαν	ἁλῶσι(ν)		

infinitive: ἁλῶναι
participle: ἁλούς, ἁλοῦσα, ἁλόν

δύω: AORIST SYSTEM ACTIVE

indicative	subjunctive	optative	imperative
ἔδῡν	δύω	δύοιμι	
ἔδῡς	δύῃς	δύοις	δῦθι
ἔδῡ	δύῃ	δύοι	δύτω
ἔδῡτον	δύητον	δύοιτον	δῦτον
ἐδύτην	δύητον	δυοίτην	δύτων
ἔδῡμεν	δύωμεν	δύοιμεν	
ἔδῡτε	δύητε	δύοιτε	δῦτε
ἔδῡσαν	δύωσι(ν)	δύοιεν	δύντων

infinitive: δῦναι
participle: δύς, δῦσα, δύν

οἶδα: PERFECT SYSTEM

ind.	subj.	optative		imper.	pluperfect ind.	
οἶδα	εἰδῶ	εἰδείην			ᾔδη or ᾔδειν	
οἶσθα	εἰδῇς	εἰδείης		ἴσθι	ᾔδησθα	ᾔδεις
οἶδε(ν)	εἰδῇ	εἰδείη		ἴστω	ᾔδειν	ᾔδει
ἴστον	εἰδῆτον	εἰδεῖτον		ἴστον	ᾔδετον	
ἴστον	εἰδῆτον	εἰδείτην		ἴστων	ᾐδέτην	
ἴσμεν	εἰδῶμεν	εἰδεῖμεν or εἰδείημεν			ᾔδεμεν	ᾖσμεν
ἴστε	εἰδῆτε	εἰδεῖτε	εἰδείητε	ἴστε	ᾔδετε	ᾖστε
ἴσᾱσι(ν)	εἰδῶσι(ν)	εἰδεῖεν	εἰδείησαν	ἴστων	ᾔδεσαν	ᾖσαν

future (perfect) indicative: εἴσομαι
infinitive: εἰδέναι
participle: εἰδώς, εἰδυῖα, εἰδός

DECLENSION OF PARTICIPLES IN -ντ-

PARTICIPLES IN -ων, -ουσα, -ον *(present and future, uncontracted)*			PARTICIPLES IN -ῶν, -οῦσα, -οῦν *(present and future, -έω or -όω contraction)*		
masc.	*fem.*	*neuter*	*masc.*	*fem.*	*neuter*
ἄγων	ἄγουσα	ἄγον	μενῶν	μενοῦσα	μενοῦν
ἄγοντος	ἀγούσης	ἄγοντος	μενοῦντος	μενούσης	μενοῦντος
ἄγοντι	ἀγούσῃ	ἄγοντι	μενοῦντι	μενούσῃ	μενοῦντι
ἄγοντα	ἄγουσαν	ἄγον	μενοῦντα	μενοῦσαν	μενοῦν
ἄγοντε	ἀγούσα	ἄγοντε	μενοῦντε	μενούσα	μενοῦντε
ἀγόντοιν	ἀγούσαιν	ἀγόντοιν	μενούντοιν	μενούσαιν	μενούντοιν
ἄγοντες	ἄγουσαι	ἄγοντα	μενοῦντες	μενοῦσαι	μενοῦντα
ἀγόντων	ἀγουσῶν	ἀγόντων	μενούντων	μενουσῶν	μενούντων
ἄγουσι(ν)	ἀγούσαις	ἄγουσι(ν)	μενοῦσι(ν)	μενούσαις	μενοῦσι(ν)
ἄγοντας	ἀγούσας	ἄγοντα	μενοῦντας	μενούσας	μενοῦντα

PARTICIPLES IN -ῶν, -ῶσα, -ῶν *(present and future active, -άω contraction)*			PARTICIPLES IN -ών, -οῦσα, -όν *(strong aorist active [thematic verbs] and present active of εἰμί and εἶμι)*		
ὁρῶν	ὁρῶσα	ὁρῶν	λιπών	λιποῦσα	λιπόν
ὁρῶντος	ὁρώσης	ὁρῶντος	λιπόντος	λιπούσης	λιπόντος
ὁρῶντι	ὁρώσῃ	ὁρῶντι	λιπόντι	λιπούσῃ	λιπόντι
ὁρῶντα	ὁρῶσαν	ὁρῶν	λιπόντα	λιποῦσαν	λιπόν
ὁρῶντε	ὁρώσα	ὁρῶντε	λιπόντε	λιπούσα	λιπόντε
ὁρώντοιν	ὁρώσαιν	ὁρώντοιν	λιπόντοιν	λιπούσαιν	λιπόντοιν
ὁρῶντες	ὁρῶσαι	ὁρῶντα	λιπόντες	λιποῦσαι	λιπόντα
ὁρώντων	ὁρωσῶν	ὁρώντων	λιπόντων	λιπουσῶν	λιπόντων
ὁρῶσι(ν)	ὁρώσαις	ὁρῶσι(ν)	λιποῦσι(ν)	λιπούσαις	λιποῦσι(ν)
ὁρῶντας	ὁρώσας	ὁρῶντα	λιπόντας	λιπούσας	λιπόντα

PARTICIPLES IN -ας, -ᾶσα, -αν
(weak aorist active)

λύσας	λύσασα	λῦσαν
λύσαντος	λυσάσης	λύσαντος
λύσαντι	λυσάσῃ	λύσαντι
λύσαντα	λύσασαν	λῦσαν
λύσαντε	λυσάσα	λύσαντε
λυσάντοιν	λυσάσαιν	λυσάντοιν
λύσαντες	λύσασαι	λύσαντα
λυσάντων	λυσασῶν	λυσάντων
λύσασι(ν)	λυσάσαις	λύσασι(ν)
λύσαντας	λυσάσας	λύσαντα

PARTICIPLES IN -άς, -ᾶσα, -άν
(μι-verb active)

ἱστάς	ἱστᾶσα	ἱστάν
ἱστάντος	ἱστάσης	ἱστάντος
ἱστάντι	ἱστάσῃ	ἱστάντι
ἱστάντα	ἱστᾶσαν	ἱστάν
ἱστάντε	ἱστάσα	ἱστάντε
ἱστάντοιν	ἱστάσαιν	ἱστάντοιν
ἱστάντες	ἱστᾶσαι	ἱστάντα
ἱστάντων	ἱστασῶν	ἱστάντων
ἱστᾶσι(ν)	ἱστάσαις	ἱστᾶσι(ν)
ἱστάντας	ἱστάσας	ἱστάντα

PARTICIPLES IN -είς, -εῖσα, -έν

μι-verb present or aorist active			aorist passive (all verbs)		
τιθείς	τιθεῖσα	τιθέν	λυθείς	λυθεῖσα	λυθέν
τιθέντος	τιθείσης	τιθέντος	λυθέντος	λυθείσης	λυθέντος
τιθέντι	τιθείσῃ	τιθέντι	λυθέντι	λυθείσῃ	λυθέντι
τιθέντα	τιθεῖσαν	τιθέν	λυθέντα	λυθεῖσαν	λυθέν
τιθέντε	τιθεῖσα	τιθέντε	λυθέντε	λυθεῖσα	λυθέντε
τιθέντοιν	τιθείσαιν	τιθέντοιν	λυθέντοιν	λυθείσαιν	λυθέντοιν
τιθέντες	τιθεῖσαι	τιθέντα	λυθέντες	λυθεῖσαι	λυθέντα
τιθέντων	τιθεισῶν	τιθέντων	λυθέντων	λυθεισῶν	λυθέντων
τιθεῖσι(ν)	τιθείσαις	τιθεῖσι(ν)	λυθεῖσι(ν)	λυθείσαις	λυθεῖσι(ν)
τιθέντας	τιθείσας	τιθέντα	λυθέντας	λυθείσας	λυθέντα

PARTICIPLES IN -ούς, -οῦσα, -όν
(μι-verb active)

διδούς	διδοῦσα	διδόν
διδόντος	διδούσης	διδόντος
διδόντι	διδούσῃ	διδόντι
διδόντα	διδοῦσαν	διδόν
διδόντε	διδοῦσα	διδόντε
διδόντοιν	διδούσαιν	διδόντοιν
διδόντες	διδοῦσαι	διδόντα
διδόντων	διδουσῶν	διδόντων
διδοῦσι(ν)	διδούσαις	διδοῦσι(ν)
διδόντας	διδούσας	διδόντα

PARTICIPLES IN -ύς, -ῦσα, -ύν
(μι-verb active)

δεικνύς	δεικνῦσα	δεικνύν
δεικνύντος	δεικνύσης	δεικνύντος
δεικνύντι	δεικνύσῃ	δεικνύντι
δεικνύντα	δεικνῦσαν	δεικνύν
δεικνύντε	δεικνῦσα	δεικνύντε
δεικνύντοιν	δεικνύσαιν	δεικνύντοιν
δεικνύντες	δεικνῦσαι	δεικνύντα
δεικνύντων	δεικνυσῶν	δεικνύντων
δεικνῦσι(ν)	δεικνύσαις	δεικνῦσι(ν)
δεικνύντας	δεικνύσας	δεικνύντα

DECLENSION OF PERFECT ACTIVE PARTICIPLES

PARTICIPLES IN -ώς, -υῖα, -ός (MOST VERBS)

λελοιπώς	λελοιπυῖα	λελοιπός
λελοιπότος	λελοιπυίας	λελοιπότος
λελοιπότι	λελοιπυίᾳ	λελοιπότι
λελοιπότα	λελοιπυῖαν	λελοιπός
λελοιπότε	λελοιπυία	λελοιπότε
λελοιπότοιν	λελοιπυίαιν	λελοιπότοιν
λελοιπότες	λελοιπυῖαι	λελοιπότα
λελοιπότων	λελοιπυιῶν	λελοιπότων
λελοιπόσι(ν)	λελοιπυίαις	λελοιπόσι(ν)
λελοιπότας	λελοιπυίας	λελοιπότα

PARTICIPLES IN -ώς, -ῶσα, -ός
(SOME ATHEMATIC PERFECTS)

ἑστώς	ἑστῶσα	ἑστός
ἑστῶτος	ἑστώσης	ἑστῶτος
ἑστῶτι	ἑστώσῃ	ἑστῶτι
ἑστῶτα	ἑστῶσαν	ἑστός
ἑστῶτε	ἑστώσα	ἑστῶτε
ἑστώτοιν	ἑστώσαιν	ἑστώτοιν
ἑστῶτες	ἑστῶσαι	ἑστῶτα
ἑστώτων	ἑστωσῶν	ἑστώτων
ἑστῶσι(ν)	ἑστώσαις	ἑστῶσι(ν)
ἑστῶτας	ἑστώσας	ἑστῶτα

Greek-English Glossary

This glossary contains all the words assigned to be learned in the units and their vocabulary lists. The number in parentheses after each word indicates the unit in which it was assigned; if the number is preceded by U, the word is presented within the unit itself rather than in the vocabulary list of the unit. English equivalents are given selectively here; for more information about meanings and grammatical usage, refer to the fuller entry in the unit vocabulary indicated.

ἀγαθός, -ή, -όν (7) — good, well-born, brave

ἄγαν (32) — very much, too much

ἀγγέλλω (19) — bear a message, announce

ἄγγελος, -ου, m. (3) — messenger, herald

ἀγνοέω (28) — not perceive, be unaware of

ἀγορά, -ᾶς, f. (4) — place of assembly; marketplace

ἄγω (8) — lead, carry

ἀγών, ἀγῶνος, m. (15) — contest, struggle

ἀδελφή, -ῆς, f. (34) — sister

ἀδελφός, -οῦ, m. (34) — brother

ἄδηλος, -ον (38) — unseen, uncertain

ἀδικέω (13) — be unjust, do wrong

ἀδικία, -ας, f. (35) — injustice

ἄδικος, -ον (9) — unjust

ἀδύνατος, -ον (38) — unable; impossible

ἀεί or αἰεί (12) — always

ἀθάνατος, -ον (9) — undying, immortal

Ἀθηναῖος, -α, -ον (10) — Athenian; (m. pl. as noun) the Athenians

ἆθλον, -ου, n. (31) — prize

ἆθλος, -ου, m. (31) — contest

ἀθροίζω (38) — gather together

ἄθυμος, -ον (38) — discouraged, spiritless

αἰδώς, αἰδοῦς, f. (42) — awe, shame, respect

αἰεί or ἀεί (12) — always

αἱρέω (13) — take, seize; (mid.) choose, elect

αἰσθάνομαι (11) — perceive, understand

αἰσχίων, αἴσχιστος (U30) — more shameful, most shameful

αἰσχρός, -ά, -όν (7) — ugly; shameful, base

αἰσχύνη, -ης, f. (35) — shame, dishonor

αἰτέω (16) — ask for

αἰτία, -ας, f. (35) — blame, cause

αἰτιάομαι (33) — accuse; allege as a cause

αἴτιος, -α, -ον (10) — responsible (for), cause of (+ gen.)

ἀκούω (11) — hear

ἄκριτος, -ον (25) — unjudged, without trial

ἀκρόπολις, -εως, f. (28) — upper city, citadel

ἄκρος, -α, -ον (28) — topmost, outmost; highest; (n. as noun) peak, summit

ἄκων, ἄκουσα, ἆκον (38) — unwilling, under constraint

ἀλήθεια, -ας, f. (5) — truth; truthfulness

ἀληθής, -ές (22) — true, truthful

ἅλις (32) — enough

ἀλίσκομαι (24) — be captured, be seized

ἀλλά (U12) — but, but rather

ἀλλάττω (41) — change, exchange; (mid.) take in exchange

ἀλλαχόθεν (U36) — from elsewhere

ἀλλαχόσε (U36) — in another direction

ἀλλαχοῦ (U36) — elsewhere

ἀλλήλων (U25) — each other, one another

ἄλλοθεν (U36) — from elsewhere

ἄλλοθι (U36) — elsewhere

ἀλλοῖος (U36) — of another kind

ἄλλος, -η, -ο (19) — another, other

ἄλλοσε (U36) — in another direction

ἄλλοτε (U36) — at another time

ἀλλότριος (40) — belonging to another; hostile

ἅλς, ἁλός, m. (15) — salt; (f.) sea

ἅμα (32) — at once, at the same time (with) (+ dat.)

ἁμαρτάνω (28) — miss the mark; err, make a mistake

ἀμείνων, -ον (U30) — better (comp. of ἀγαθός)

ἀμφί (39) — (+ gen.) about; (+ dat.) around; (+ acc.) around

ἀμφότερος, -α, -ον (31) — each of two, both

ἀμφοτέρωθεν (U36) — from both sides

ἀμφοτέρωθι (U36) — on both sides

ἀμφοτέρωσε (U36) — in both directions

ἄν (32) — (modal particle: see U32, U34, U36)

ἀνά (U12) — (+ acc.) up (along), throughout

ἀναβαίνω (24) — go up, mount, go inland

ἀναγιγνώσκω (24) — read aloud, recite

ἀνάγκη, -ης, f. (10) — force, constraint, necessity; (as impersonal verb) it is necessary (+ inf.)

ἀναιρέω (32) — take up; destroy, kill

ἀναίτιος, -ον (31) — guiltless, without blame

ἀναμιμνήσκω (29) — remind, call to mind; (mid./pass.) remember, make mention of

ἀνάξιος, -ον (38) — unworthy (+ gen.)

ἀνατίθημι (23) — set up as offering, dedicate

ἀνδράποδον, -ου, n. (41) — slave

ἀνδρεῖος, -α, -ον (40) — manly, courageous

ἄνεμος, -ου, m. (3) — wind

ἄνευ (33) — without (+ gen.)

ἀνέχω (28) — hold up; (mid.) bear up, endure (+ part.)

ἀνήρ, ἀνδρός, m. (15) — man, warrior, husband

ἄνθρωπος, -ου, m. (3) — human being, man

ἄνομος, -ον (38) — lawless, impious

ἀνόσιος, -ον (9) — unholy, profane

ἀντί (U12) — (+ gen.) instead of, in return for

ἄξιος, -α, -ον (7) — worth; worthy (of) (+ gen.)

ἀξιόω (33) — think proper, expect

ἀπάγω (16) — lead away, arrest

ἀπαντάω (33) — meet (+ dat.)

ἅπαξ (U25) — once

ἅπας, ἅπασα, ἅπαν (22) — all, the whole

ἀπατάω (38) — cheat, deceive

ἄπειμι (27) [εἰμί] — be away, be absent

ἄπειμι (23) [εἶμι] — go away

ἀπέχω (16) — hold off; be distant from

ἄπλους, -ουν (42) — not navigable, not seaworthy

ἁπλοῦς, -ῆ, -οῦν (42) — single, simple

ἀπό (U6) — (+ gen.) away from, from

ἀποδείκνυμι (23) — display, make known; appoint

ἀποδίδωμι (23) — give back, pay; (mid.) sell

ἀποδύω (24) — strip off; (mid., 2nd aor.) take off (own clothes)

ἀποθνήσκω (8) — die

ἀποκρίνω (32) — separate; (mid.) reply

ἀποκτείνω (11) — kill, put to death

ἀπόλλυμι (37) — destroy, kill; (mid., intrans. forms) perish, die

ἀπολογέομαι (32) — speak in defense, defend oneself

ἀποπλέω (39) — sail away

ἀπορέω (29) — be without resources, be at a loss, lack

ἄποτος, -ον (38) — not drinkable; without drink

ἄργυρος, -ου, m. (42) — silver

ἀργυροῦς, -ᾶ, -οῦν (42) — of silver

ἀρετή, -ῆς, f. (4) — excellence; valor; virtue

ἀριθμός, -οῦ, m. (34) — number

ἀριστερά, -ᾶς, f. (41) — left hand

ἀριστερός, -ά, -όν (41) — on the left, ominous

ἄριστος (U30) — best (superl. of ἀγαθός)

ἁρπάζω (26) — snatch away, seize

(τὸ) ἀρχαῖον (U17) — formerly, in the old days

ἀρχαῖος, -α, -ον (16) — ancient, old

ἀρχή, -ῆς, f. (4) — beginning; rule, office; realm

ἄρχω (8) — begin; rule, be leader of (+ gen.)

ἄρχων, -οντος, m. (35) — ruler, archon

ἀσαφής, -ές (38) — indistinct, unclear

ἀσεβέω (40) — act impiously, sin against

ἀσεβής, -ές (40) — ungodly, unholy

ἀσθένεια, -ας, f. (35) — weakness, illness

ἀσθενέω (33) — be weak, be ill

ἀσθενής, -ές (22) — weak

ἄσιτος, -ον (38) — without food

ἀσπίς, -ίδος, f. (14) — shield

ἄστυ, ἄστεως, n. (21) — town

ἀσφαλής, -ές (22) — steadfast; safe, secure

ἀτιμάζω (33) — fail to honor, dishonor

ἄτιμος, -ον (38) — without honor

αὖ (12) — again, in turn

αὖθις (12) — again, in turn

αὔριον (32) — tomorrow

αὐτίκα (12) — at once, immediately

αὐτόθεν (U36) — from the same place

αὐτός, -ή, -ό (21) — self; (obl. cases) him, her, it, them; (with art.) the same

αὐτόσε (U36) — in the same direction

αὐτοῦ (U36) — in this very place

ἄφθονος, -ον (38) — free from envy; plentiful

ἀφίημι (23) — send forth; release; leave alone

ἀφικνέομαι (13) — arrive (at), reach

ἀφίστημι (23) — cause to revolt; (pass. and 2nd aor.) keep apart from, revolt from

ἄφρων, ἄφρον (22) — senseless, foolish

ἄχρι (39) — until; (+ gen.) up to

βάθος, -ους, n. (35) — depth

βαθύς, -εῖα, -ύ (22) — deep, high

βαίνω (24) — walk, step, go

βάλλω (10) — throw, strike

βάρβαρος, -ον (9) — foreign; (pl. as noun) foreigners, Persians

βάρος -ους, n. (35) — weight

βαρύς, -εῖα, -ύ (22) — heavy

βασιλεία, -ας, f. (24) — kingdom; kingship

βασιλεύς, -έως, m. (21) — king

βασιλεύω (29) — be king

βέλτιστος (U30) — best (superl. of ἀγαθός)

βελτίων (U30) — better (comp. of ἀγαθός)

βιβλίον, -ου, n. (3) — book

βίος, -ου, m. (3) — life, livelihood

βλαβερός, -ά, -όν (16) — harmful

βλάπτω (9) — harm, damage

βοηθέω (33) — come to the aid of (+ dat.)

βούλευμα, -ατος, n. (14) — plan, resolution

βουλεύω (11) — plan; (mid.) take counsel, deliberate

βούλομαι (11) — want, desire, wish

βοῦς, βοός, m. or f. (21) — ox, cow

βραχύς, -εῖα, -ύ (22) — short, small

γαμέω (33) — marry (a wife); (mid.) give (daughter) in marriage, marry (a husband)

γάμος, -ου, m. (31) — wedding (feast), marriage

γάρ (U12) — for, because (postpositive)

καὶ γάρ — for indeed, and in fact

γε (39) — at least, at any rate (postpositive)

γελάω (33) — laugh (at), deride

γένος, γένους, n. (15) — race, offspring; class, kind

γεραιός, -ά, -όν (30) — old, revered

γεραίτερος, γεραίτατος (30) — older, oldest

γέρας, γέρως, n. (15) — gift of honor, privilege

γέρων, -οντος, m. (14) — old man

γέφυρα, -ας, f. (5) — bridge

γῆ, γῆς, f. (42) — earth, country

γῆρας, γήρως, n. (15) — old age

γίγας, -αντος, m. (14) — giant

γίγνομαι (11) — come into being, become

γιγνώσκω (19) — get to know; perceive; think, judge

γλυκύς, -εῖα, -ύ (22) — sweet, pleasant

γλῶττα, -ης, f. (5) — tongue; language

γνώμη, -ης, f. (4) — faculty of judgment; opinion

γράμμα, -ατος, n. (14) — line, picture, writing

γραῦς, γραός, f. (21) — old woman

γράφω (8) — write

γυμνάζω (11) — train, exercise; (mid.) be in training

γυμνός, -ή, -όν (40) — naked, unarmed

γυνή, γυναικός, f. (21) — woman, wife

δαίμων, -μονος, m. or f. (15) — divinity; one's destiny, lot

δαπανάω (33) — spend, consume

δέ (U12) — and, but (postpositive)

δέδοικα/δέδια (41) — fear

δεῖ (9) — it is necessary (+ inf.)

δείκνυμι (23) — show, point out

δειλός, -ή, -όν (40) — cowardly, wretched

δεινός, -ή, -όν (16) — terrible; wondrous; clever, skillful

δεῖπνον, -ου, n. (31) — meal

δεῖται (13) — there is need of (+ dat. of person, gen. of thing)

δέκα (17) — ten

δεκάκις (U25) — ten times

δέκατος, -η, -ον (U25) — tenth

δεξιά, -ᾶς, f. (41) — right hand

δεξιός, -ά, -όν (41) — on the right; fortunate; skillful

δέομαι (13) — be in need of (+ gen.); beg, ask for (+ gen.)

δέος, -ους, n. (41) — fear

δεσπότης, -ου, m. (5) — master; absolute ruler

δεύτερος, -α, -ον (U25) — second

δέω (13) — lack, be in need of (+ gen.)

δή (39) — in fact, certainly (postpositive)

καὶ δὴ καί — and in fact, and in particular

δῆλος, -η, -ον (7) — clear, manifest

δηλόω (29) — render manifest, show

δημοκρατία, -ας, f. (4) — democracy

Δημοσθένης, -ους, m. (15) — Demosthenes

διά (U6) — (+ gen.) through, by; (+ acc.) by aid of, on account of

διαβαίνω (24) — go over, cross

διαβάλλω (32) — throw across; set at variance; slander

διαγιγνώσκω (24) — distinguish; decide

διαδίδωμι (25) — distribute

διακόσιοι, -αι, -α (40) — two hundred

διαλέγομαι (32) — converse with (+ dat.)

διαμένω (28) — continue, persist

διανοέομαι (42) — intend; think; be disposed

διατελέω (28) — continue, persevere

διαφέρω (17) — carry across; differ, excel (+ gen.)

διαφθείρω (39) — destroy utterly, corrupt, seduce

διδάσκαλος, -ου, m. (17) — teacher, trainer

διδάσκω (34) — instruct, teach

δίδωμι (23) — give, offer, grant

δικάζω (11) — serve as judge or juror; (mid.) plead a case

δίκαιος, -α, -ον (7) — just

δικαιοσύνη, -ης, f. (35) — righteousness, justice

δικαστής, -οῦ, m. (5) — juryman, judge

δίκη, -ης, f. (4) — justice; lawsuit; punishment

διπλοῦς, -ῆ, -οῦν (42) — double, twofold

δίς (U25) — twice

δισχίλιοι, -αι, -α (40) — two thousand

διώκω (27) — pursue, chase; prosecute

δοκεῖ (9) — it seems good, best (+ inf.)

δοκέω (13) — seem; think

δόξα, -ης, f. (5) — opinion, reputation

δουλεύω (30) — be a slave, serve (+ dat.)

δούλη, -ης, f. (31) — slave (female)

δοῦλος, -ου, m. (31) — slave

δραμ(ε)- — aor./fut. of *run* (34)

δύναμαι (25) — be able, be strong (enough) (+ inf.); have power

δύναμις, -εως, f. (21) — power, ability

δυνατός, -ή, -όν (38) — strong, able; possible

δύο (U25) — two

δύσνους, -ουν (42) — ill-disposed

δυσσεβής, -ές (40) — impious, unholy

δυστυχής, -ές (22) — unlucky, unfortunate

δυστυχία, -ας, f. (35) — ill luck, ill fortune

δύω (24) — enter, sink, set; cause to enter, cause to sink

δώδεκα (U25) — twelve

δωδεκάκις (U25) — twelve times

δωδέκατος, -η, -ον (U25) — twelfth

δῶρον, -ου, n. (3) — gift

ἐάν, ἄν, ἤν (34) — if (with subj.)

ἑαυτοῦ (U25) — himself, herself, itself (reflexive)

ἐάω (33) — permit, allow; dismiss

ἑβδομήκοντα (27) — seventy

ἕβδομος, -η, -ον (U25) — seventh

ἐγγύς (32) — near; next to (+ gen.)

ἐγώ (U22) — I

ἔδομαι — fut. of *eat* (26)

ἐθέλω (8) — be willing, wish

εἰ (34) — if (with ind. or opt.)

εἰδέναι (U28) — inf. of οἶδα, know

εἶδον (19) — saw (cf. ὁράω)

εἴκοσι (27) — twenty

εἷλον	aor. of αἱρέω (13)	Ἑλλάς, -άδος, f. (14)	Greece
εἰ μή (34)	if not, except	Ἕλλην, -ηνος, m. (15)	a Greek man
εἰμί (10)	be		
εἶμι (23)	go, will go	ἐλπίζω (19)	expect, hope (for)
εἴπερ (34)	if in fact, since	ἐλπίς, -ίδος, f. (14)	hope, expectation
εἶπον (19)	said		
εἰρήνη, -ης, f. (10)	peace; peace treaty	ἐμαυτοῦ (U25)	myself (reflexive)
εἰς or ἐς (U6)	(+ acc.) into, to, toward	ἐμβαίνω (33)	step upon, board
εἷς, μία, ἕν (U25)	one	ἐμός, ἐμή, ἐμόν (22)	my, mine
εἴσομαι	fut. of οἶδα (28)	ἐμπίμπλημι (29)	fill
εἶτα (12)	then, next; therefore	ἐν (U6)	(+ dat.) in, within, on, at, among
ἐκ or ἐξ (U6)	(+ gen.) out of, forth from	ἐνάκις (U25)	nine times
ἕκαστος, -η, -ον (19)	each (of more than two)	ἐνακόσιοι, -αι, -α (40)	nine hundred
ἑκάστοτε (19)	on each occasion	ἐναντίος, -α, -ον (41)	opposite, opposing; (m. pl. as noun) the adversary
ἑκάτερος, -α, -ον (19)	each of two		
ἑκατόν (27)	hundred		
ἐκεῖ (13)	there, in that place	ἔνατος, -η, -ον (U25)	ninth
ἐκεῖθεν (U36)	from there	ἕνδεκα (U25)	eleven
ἐκεῖνος, -η, -ο (U13)	that; the former	ἑνδεκάκις (U25)	eleven times
ἐκείνως (U36)	in that manner	ἑνδέκατος, -η, -ον (U25)	eleventh
ἐκεῖσε (U36)	to that place		
ἕκτος, -η, -ον (U25)	sixth	ἐνεγκ-	aor. of φέρω (8)
ἑκών, ἑκοῦσα, ἑκόν (38)	willing	ἕνεκα (33)	on account of (+ gen.)
ἐλ-	aor. of αἱρέω (13)	ἐνενήκοντα (27)	ninety
ἐλάττων (U30)	smaller, fewer	ἔνθα (U36)	where
ἐλαύνω (8)	drive; ride, march	ἐνθάδε (12)	here, there
ἐλάχιστος (U30)	smallest, fewest	ἐνθένδε (U36)	from here
ἐλέγχω (28)	cross-examine; prove; refute	ἐννέα (U25)	nine
		ἐνταῦθα (U36)	in this place, to this place
ἐλευθερία, -ας, f. (24)	freedom, liberty	ἐντεῦθεν (U36)	from this place
ἐλεύθερος, -α, -ον (40)	free	ἐξ or ἐκ (U6)	(+ gen.) out of, forth from
ἐλεύσομαι	fut. of ἔρχομαι (11)	ἕξ (U25)	six
ἐλθ-	aor. of ἔρχομαι (11)	ἐξαιτέω (27)	ask for from; (mid.) appeal for pardon
		ἑξάκις (U25)	six times

ἐξακόσιοι, -αι, -α (40)   six hundred

ἔξειμι (23)   go out

ἐξελέγχω (28)   prove, convict

ἔξεστι (9)   it is permitted, it is possible (+ inf.)

ἐξήκοντα (27)   sixty

ἔοικα (41)   be like, look like; seem probable

ἐπαινέω (16)   approve, praise

ἐπεί (34)   since, when, after

ἐπειδή (34)   when, after, since

ἔπειτα (12)   then, next; therefore

ἐπείτε (34)   when, since

ἐπί (U6)   (+ gen.) upon; (+ dat.) upon, over; next to; in addition to; (+ acc.) onto, up to, toward; against

ἐπιβουλεύω (28)   plot against (+ dat.)

ἐπιδείκνυμι (23)   exhibit, show, prove

ἐπιθυμέω (16)   long for, desire (+ gen.)

ἐπιθυμία, -ας, f. (10)   desire, yearning

ἐπιμέλομαι or ἐπιμελέομαι (38)   take care of, have charge of (+ gen.)

ἐπιορκία, -ας, f. (10)   perjury

ἐπίσταμαι (28)   know (how to), understand

ἐπιστέλλω (41)   send a message, order

ἐπιστολή, -ῆς, f. (41)   message, letter

ἐπιτήδειος, -α, -ον (41)   suitable; useful, necessary; (n. pl. as noun) provisions

ἐπιτίθημι (23)   place upon, add to; (mid.) attack (+ dat.)

ἐπιτρέπω (8)   turn over to, entrust

ἐπιχειρέω (39)   attempt (+ dat. or inf.)

ἑπτά (17)   seven

ἑπτάκις (U25)   seven times

ἑπτακόσιοι, -αι, -α (40)   seven hundred

ἐράω (33)   be in love with (+ gen.)

ἐργάζομαι (40)   work, make, do

ἔργον, -ου, n. (3)   work, action, deed

ἐρέω (19)   will say

ἐρήσομαι (33)   will ask

ἔρις, -ιδος, f. (14)   strife, quarrel

Ἑρμῆς, -οῦ, m. (42)   Hermes, herm

ἔρχομαι (11)   come, go

ἐρωτάω (33)   ask, inquire

ἐς or εἰς (U6)   (+ acc.) into, to, toward

ἐσθίω (26)   eat

ἑσπέρα, -ας, f. (34)   evening, the west

ἔστε (39)   until, so long as

ἔσχατος, -η, -ον (41)   farthest, last

ἑταίρα, -ας, f. (31)   woman companion; courtesan

ἑταῖρος, -ου, m. (31)   comrade, companion

ἕτερος, -α, -ον (19)   one of two, the other of two

ἔτι (39)   yet, still

ἕτοιμος, -η, -ον (41)   ready, prepared

ἔτος, ἔτους, n. (15)   year

εὖ (12)   well

εὐγενής, -ές (22)   well-born, noble

εὐδαίμων, -ον (22)   fortunate, happy

εὔελπις, εὔελπι (30) — hopeful, cheerful

εὐεργετέω (33) — benefit, show kindness toward

εὐθύς (39) — immediately

εὐλαβέομαι (38) — beware, take care

εὔνους, -ουν (42) — well-disposed, friendly

εὑρίσκω (10) — find (out), discover

εὗρος, -ους, n. (40) — width, breadth

εὐρύς, -εῖα, -ύ (40) — wide, broad

εὐσεβέω (40) — live or act piously

εὐσεβής, -ές (40) — pious, holy

εὐτυχής, -ές (22) — lucky, fortunate

εὐτυχία, -ας, f. (35) — good luck, success

εὐχή, -ῆς, f. (17) — prayer, vow

εὔχομαι (17) — pray (for); boast

ἐφίημι (23) — send against; set free; (mid.) command; aim at, long for (+ gen.)

ἐφίστημι (23) — set in charge of, cause to stop; (pass. and 2nd aor.) stand upon; be in charge of (+ dat.)

ἐχθίων, ἔχθιστος (U30) — more hated, most hated

ἔχθρα, -ας, f. (35) — hatred, enmity

ἐχθρός, -ά, -όν (30) — hated; hostile; (m. as noun) enemy

ἔχω (8) — have, hold; (27) (with adverb) be in a certain condition

ἕως [conj.] (39) — until, so long as

ἕως, ἕω, f. (42) — dawn, the east

ζεύγνυμι (23) — yoke, join together

Ζεύς, Διός, m. (42) — Zeus

ζῆλος, -ου, m. (35) — emulation, jealousy

ζηλόω (29) — emulate, praise

ζητέω (16) — seek; examine

ζῶ (33) — be alive, live

ἤ (30) — or, than; either/or

ᾗ (U36) — in which way, as

ἡγεμών, -όνος, m. (16) — leader, guide

ἡγέομαι (16) — lead, guide (+ dat.); rule (+ gen.); consider, think

ἤδη (12) — already; immediately; actually, now

ἡδίων, ἥδιστος (U30) — more pleasant, most pleasant

ἥδομαι (28) — enjoy, take pleasure (+ dat. or + part.)

ἡδονή, -ῆς, f. (4) — pleasure

ἡδύς, -εῖα, -ύ (22) — pleasant, welcome; glad

ἥκιστος (U30) — worst, least

ἥκω (33) — have come

ἦλθον — aor. of ἔρχομαι (11)

ἥλιος, -ου, m. (3) — sun

ἡμεῖς (22) — we

ἡμέρα, -ας, f. (4) — day

ἡμέτερος, -α, -ον (22) — our, ours

ἥμισυς, -εια, -υ (22) — half

ἠρόμην (33) — asked

ἥρως, ἥρωος, m. (42) — hero

ἡσυχία, -ας, f. (24) — quiet, rest, calm

ἥσυχος, -ον (24) — quiet, calm

ἡττάομαι (31) — be inferior, be defeated (+ gen.)

ἥττων (U30) — worse, less

θάλαττα, -ης, f. (5) — sea

θάνατος, -ου, m. (3) — death

θάττων (U30) — swifter

θαῦμα, -ατος, n. (34) — wonder, marvel

θαυμάζω (34) — wonder at, admire

θαυμάσιος, -α, -ον (41) — wonderful, marvelous, admirable

θαυμαστός, -ή, -όν (41) — wonderful, marvelous, admirable

θεά, -ᾶς, f. (4) — goddess

θεός, -οῦ, m. or f. (3) — god, divinity

θέρος, -ους, n. (39) — summer, summer harvest

θῆλυς, -εια, -υ (31) — female; soft, delicate

θήρ, θηρός, m. (16) — wild animal

θήρα, -ας, f. (41) — hunting

θηρίον, -ου, n. (16) — wild animal

θρασύς, -εῖα, -ύ (40) — bold, rash

θυγάτηρ, -τρός, f. (15) — daughter

θυμός, -οῦ, m. (38) — spirit; seat of emotion

θύρα, -ας, f. (4) — door

θύω (38) — offer by burning, sacrifice

θώραξ, -ακος, m. (14) — breastplate; trunk

ἴδιος, -α, -ον (40) — pertaining to oneself; personal; distinct

ἰδιώτης, -ου, m. (38) — private person, layman

ἱερεύς, -έως, m. (21) — priest

ἱερός, -ά, -όν (7) — holy; (n. as noun) shrine; (pl.) offerings; omens; rites

ἵημι (23) — let go, hurl; (mid.) hasten, rush

ἱκανός, -ή, -όν (40) — sufficient, suitable

ἵλεως, -εων (42) — propitious, kindly

ἵνα (31) — in order that

ἱππεύς, -έως, m. (21) — cavalryman

ἵππος, -ου, m. or f. (3) — horse; (f.) mare

ἴσος, -η, -ον (29) — equal

ἵστημι (23) — make stand, stop; (pass. and 2nd aor.) be placed, stand; stand still

ἰσχυρός, -ά, -όν (17) — strong, violent

ἰσχύς, -ύος, f. (21) — strength

ἴσως (29) — equally; perhaps

ἰχθύς, -ύος, m. or f. (21) — fish

καθίστημι (23) — set down; establish, appoint; (pass. and 2nd aor.) become, be established

καί (U12) — and; (adv.) even

καίπερ (27) — (with participle) although

καιρός, -οῦ, m. (31) — right measure; opportunity; critical moment

καίω (26) — kindle, burn

κακία, -ας, f. (35) — badness, vice

κακίων, κάκιστος (U30) — worse, worst

κακός, -ή, -όν (7) — bad, evil; low-born

κακῶς ἔχω (27) — be in bad shape, feel bad

καλέω (18) — call, summon; call by name

καλλίων, κάλλιστος (U30) — more beautiful, finer; most beautiful, finest

κάλλος, -ους, n. (35) — beauty

καλός, -ή, -όν (7) — beautiful; fine, noble

καλῶς ἔχω (27) — be well

κανοῦν, -οῦ, n. (42) — basket

κατά (U12) — (+ gen.) down from, against; (+ acc.) down along, in accordance with

καταβαίνω (24) — step down, dismount, go down toward the sea

καταδύω (24) — set; cause to sink

καταλείπω (32) — leave behind

κατατίθημι (23) — put down; (mid.) lay aside, store up

κατηγορέω (17) — speak against, accuse (+ gen.)

κελεύω (9) — order, command

κεφαλή, -ῆς, f. (25) — head

κίνδυνος, -ου, m. (34) — danger, risk

κλέπτω (34) — steal

κλίνω (38) — cause to lean; (pass.) lie down

κλώψ, κλωπός, m. (14) — thief

κοινός, -ή, -όν (16) — common, public; (n. as noun) public authority, state; (pl.) public funds, public affairs

κομίζω (38) — take care of; carry; (mid.) acquire

κόπτω (9) — strike, chop, beat

κρατέω (13) — be strong; rule over (+ gen.); conquer

κράτιστος (U30) — best, strongest (superl. of ἀγαθός)

κράτος, -ους, n. (15) — strength, power

κρείττων (U30) — better, stronger (comp. of ἀγαθός)

κρήνη, -ης, f. (29) — well, spring

κρίνω (26) — pick out; decide, judge

κριτής, -οῦ, m. (5) — judge (in contest), umpire

κρύπτω (17) — hide, conceal

κτάομαι (37) — acquire; (perf.) possess, have

κύκλος, -ου, m. (41) — circle, wheel; (dat. as adv.) in a circle, all around

κύων, κυνός, m. or f. (41) — dog; shameless creature

κωλύω (16) — prevent

λαγώς, λαγώ, m. (42) — hare

Λακεδαιμόνιος, -α, -ον (25) — Lacedaemonian, Spartan; (m. pl. as noun) the Lacedaemonians, the Spartans

λαμβάνω (8) — take, grasp; receive

λανθάνω (28) — escape notice, be unobserved (+ participle)

λέγω (8) — say, recount

λείπω (8) — leave, abandon

λέων, -οντος, m. (14) — lion

λίαν (32) — very, exceedingly

λίθος, -ου, m. (10) — stone; (f.) magnet, crystal

λόγος, -ου, m. (3) — word, speech; account; reason

λύω (8) — loosen, release

μακρός, -ά, -όν (7) — long, tall, large

μάλα (12) — very, exceedingly

μάλιστα (30) — very much, most

μᾶλλον (30) — more, rather

μανθάνω (18) — learn, understand

μάρτυς, -υρος, m. or f. (38) — witness

μάχη, -ης, f. (10) — battle, combat

μάχομαι (11) — fight

μέγας, μεγάλη, μέγα (25) — large, tall, great

μέγιστος (U30) — largest, greatest

μείζων (U30) — larger, greater

μέλας, -αινα, -αν (22) — black, dark

μέλλω (18) — be destined to; be about to; delay (+ inf.)

μέλω (38) — be a concern to; (impersonal) it concerns (+ dat. + inf. or gen. of thing)

μέν (U12) — (emphatic postpositive particle anticipating a contrast with δέ)

μένω (8) — remain; wait for

μέρος, -ους, n. (15) — share, part

μέσος, -η, -ον (40) — middle, in the middle

μετά (U6) — (+ gen.) among, with; (+ acc.) in pursuit of, after

μεταδίδωμι (23) — give a share of (+ gen.)

μετέχω (29) — partake of (+ gen.)

μέτρον, -ου, n. (3) — measure; moderate amount

μέχρι (39) — until; up to (+ gen.)

μή (9) — not

μηδέ (18) — and not, but not; not even

μηδείς, μηδεμία, μηδέν (U25) — no one, nothing

μηκέτι (39) — no longer

μῆκος, -ους, n. (41) — length, size, greatness

μήν (39) — truly, surely (postpositive)

καὶ μήν — and what is more

μήποτε (17) — never

μήτε (18) — neither/nor

μήτηρ, μητρός, f. (15) — mother

μικρός, -ά, -όν (7) — small, little

μιμνῄσκω (29) — remind, call to mind; (mid./pass.) remember, make mention of

μισέω (33) — hate

μισθός, -οῦ, m. (38) — hire, pay, wages

μνᾶ, μνᾶς, f. (42) — mina

μνήμων, μνῆμον (29) — mindful

μόγις (39) — with toil, scarcely

μοῖρα, -ας, f. (5) — portion; destiny

μόνος, -η, -ον (40) — alone, only, single; (acc. s. neut. adv.) only, solely

μυριάς, -άδος, f. (40) — group of 10,000

μύριοι, -αι, -α (40) — ten thousand

μυρίος, -α, -ον (40) — numberless

ναῦς, νεώς, f. (21) — ship

ναύτης, -ου, m. (5) — sailor

νεανίας, -ου, m. (5) — young man

νέος, -α, -ον (40) — young, new; unexpected

νεώς, νεώ, m. (42) — temple, inner shrine

νῆσος, -ου, f. (41) — island

νικάω (29) — win, conquer

νίκη, -ης, f. (4) — victory

νοέω (42) — perceive; think; intend

νομίζω (18) — have as a custom; believe, think

νόμιμος, -η, -ον (38) — customary, lawful

νόμος, -ου, m. (3) — custom, law

νοσέω (13) — be sick

νόσος, -ου, f. (3) — sickness, disease

νοῦς, νοῦ, m. (42) — mind, sense
   νοῦν ἔχειν — be sensible
   προσέχειν τὸν νοῦν — pay attention to (+ dat.)

νῦν (12) — now, presently

νύξ, νυκτός, f. (34) — night

ξένος, -η, -ον (40) — foreign, strange; (m. as noun) foreigner, guest-friend or host

ὁ, ἡ, τό (U6) — the

ὀγδοήκοντα (27) — eighty

ὄγδοος, -η, -ον (U25) — eighth

ὅδε, ἥδε, τόδε (U13) — this, that; the following

ὁδός, -οῦ, f. (3) — road, way; journey

ὀδούς, ὀδόντος, m. (14) — tooth

ὅθεν (U36) — whence

οἷ (U36) — whither

οἶδα (28) — know

οἴκαδε (U36) — homewards, (to) home

οἰκέω (13) — inhabit; manage; dwell

οἰκία, -ας, f. (34) — building, house

οἴκοθεν (U36) — from home

οἴκοι (U36) — at home

οἶκος, -ου, m. (34) — house, household

οἴομαι or οἶμαι (11) — think, believe

οἷος (U36) — as, the sort which

οἷός τε, οἵα τε, οἷόν τε (40) — fit, able, possible (+ inf.)

οἴσω — fut. of φέρω (8)

ὀκτάκις (U25) — eight times

ὀκτακόσιοι, -αι, -α (40) — eight hundred

ὀκτώ (17) — eight

ὀλείζων (U30) — fewer

ὀλιγάκις (25) — few times, seldom

ὀλίγιστος (U30) — fewest

ὀλίγος, -η, -ον (25) — little, few; (m. pl. as noun) oligarchs

ὄλλυμι (37) — destroy, lose

ὅλος, -η, -ον (40) — whole, entire

ὄμνυμι (37) — swear

ὅμοιος, -α, -ον (40) — like, similar (+ dat.)

ὁμολογέω (32) — agree with (+ dat.)

ὄνομα, -ατος, n. (17) — name

ὅπη (U36) — in which way, as

ὄπισθεν (39) — behind (+ gen.); in future

ὁπλίτης, -ου, m. (5) — heavy-armed soldier

ὅπλον, -ου, n. (34) — tool; (pl.) arms

ὁπόθεν (U36) — whence(soever)

ὅποι (U36) — whither(soever)

ὁποῖος (U36) — of whatever sort

ὁπόσος (U36) — however much, however many

ὁπότε (34) — whenever

ὁπότερος (U36) — whichever of two

ὅπου (U36) — where(ver)

ὅπως (31, U36) — in order that; (+ fut.) that (U38); how, however

ὁράω (29) — see

ὀργή, -ῆς, f. (31)   mood; anger

ὀργίζομαι (28)   grow angry;
     (rarely active)
     make angry

ὀρθός, -ή, -όν (31)   straight; correct

ὁρμάω (33)   set in motion; start
     off

ὄρνις, -ιθος, m. or   bird; omen
   f. (14)

ὄρος, -ους, n. (34)   mountain

ὀρχέομαι (27)   dance

ὅς, ἥ, ὅ (U12)   who, which, that

ὅσιος, -α, -ον (9)   hallowed; pious

ὅσος (U36)   as much as, as
     many as

ὅστις, ἥτις, ὅ τι   who(ever),
   (33)   what(ever),
     which(ever)

ὅτε (34)   when

ὅτι (33)   that (indirect
     discourse);
     because

οὗ, οὑ [pron.]   himself, herself,
   (U25)   itself (indirect
     reflexive)

οὗ [adv.] (U36)   where

οὐ, οὐκ, οὐχ (8)   not

οὐδέ (18)   and not, but not;
     not even

οὐδείς, οὐδεμία,   no one, nothing
   οὐδέν (U25)

οὐκ (8)   not

οὐκέτι (39)   no longer

οὖν (42)   therefore, then
     (postpositive)

οὔποτε (17)   never

οὐρανός, -οῦ, m.   heaven, sky
   (41)

οὐσία, -ας, f. (41)   property; being,
     essence

οὔτε (18)   neither/nor

οὗτος, αὕτη,   this, the nearer; the
   τοῦτο (U13)   latter; the
     foregoing

οὕτω(ς) (13)   in this manner,
     thus, so;

     (27) (with ἔχω)
     be in this state,
     be this way

οὐχ (8)   not

ὀφείλω (32)   owe, be obliged to;
     (strong aor. +
     inf.) would
     that . . .

ὀφθαλμός, -οῦ, m.   eye
   (41)

ὄψομαι   fut. of *see* (19)

παθ-   aor. of πάσχω (10)

πάθος, -ους, n.   incident,
   (39)   experience,
     suffering

παιδεία, -ας, f. (4)   education, training

παιδίον, -ου, n.   child
   (3)

παῖς, παιδός, m.   child, boy, girl;
   or f. (16)   slave

παίω (40)   strike, beat

πάλαι (30)   long ago

παλαιός, -ά, -όν   old, ancient; (n.
   (30)   adv. acc., with
     τό) in the old
     days

παλαίτερος,   older, oldest
   παλαίτατος
   (30)

πάλιν (32)   back, backwards;
     again

πανταχῇ (U36)   everywhere

πανταχόθεν (U36)   from all sides

πανταχοῖ (U36)   in all directions

πανταχόσε (U36)   in all directions

πανταχοῦ (U36)   everywhere

παρά (U6)   (+ gen.) from the
     side of; (+ dat.)
     by the side of;
     (+ acc.) to the
     side of; beside;
     past, beyond

παράγω (16)   lead by; lead astray

παραβαίνω (24)   go beside;
     transgress

παραδίδωμι (23)   hand over,
              surrender

παραινέω (32)   advise (+ dat.)

παρακελεύομαι   exhort, encourage
   (11)   (+ dat.)

παρασκευάζω (11)   prepare, provide;
              (mid.) make
              preparations

πάρειμι (27)   be present

παρέχω (16)   furnish, supply

τὸ παρόν   that which is at
              hand; the
              present time;
              (pl.) the present
              state of affairs

πᾶς, πᾶσα, πᾶν   all, every; the
   (22)   whole

πάσχω (10)   experience, suffer

πατήρ, πατρός,   father
   m. (15)

πατρίς, -ίδος, f.   fatherland
   (14)

παύω (28)   stop; (mid.) cease

παχύς, -εῖα, -ύ   thick, stout
   (40)

πεζός, -ή, -όν (7)   on foot, on land;
              (m. as s. or pl.
              noun) infantry,
              footsoldiers

πείθω (8)   persuade, urge;
              (mid.) obey,
              trust, believe (+
              dat.) (U11)

πεῖρα, -ας, f. (5)   trial, attempt

πειράω or   make trial of (+
   πειράομαι (39)   gen.), try (+ inf.)

πείσομαι   fut. of πάσχω or
              fut. mid. of
              πείθω

πέλας (39)   near (+ gen.)

πέμπτος, -η, -ον   fifth
   (U25)

πέμπω (8)   send

πεντάκις (U25)   five times

πεντακόσιοι, -αι,   five hundred
   -α (40)

πέντε (U25)   five

πεντήκοντα (27)   fifty

περί (U12)   (+ gen.) about,
              above; (+ dat.)
              around, about;
              (+ acc.) around,
              concerning

περιοράω (28)   look over;
              overlook; permit

περίπλους, -ου,   circumnavigation
   m. (42)

πεσ(ε)-   aor./fut. of *fall* (18)

πῇ (U36)   by which way?
              where?

πη (U36)   in some way

πῆχυς, -εως, m.   forearm, arm
   (21)

πικρός, -ά, -όν   sharp, bitter, mean
   (24)

πίμπλημι (29)   fill

πίνω (26)   drink

πίπτω (18)   fall

πιστεύω (30)   trust (+ dat.)

πίστις, -εως, f.   trust, faith, pledge
   (31)

πιστός, -ή, -όν   trustworthy,
   (31)   faithful

πλεῖστος, -η, -ον   most, greatest,
   (10)   largest; (m. pl.
              as noun) the
              majority

πλείων or πλέων   more
   (U30)

πλέω (39)   sail, go by sea

πλέως, πλέα,   full, filled
   πλέων (42)

πληγή, -ῆς, f. (17)   blow, stroke

πλῆθος, -ους, n.   multitude; the
   (15)   masses; size

πλήν (33)   except (+ gen.)

πλήρης, πλῆρες   full (of) (+ gen.)
   (22)

πλήττω (17)   strike

πλοῖον, -ου, n.   ship, boat
   (34)

πλοῦς, πλοῦ, m. (42) — voyage

πλούσιος, -α, -ον (7) — wealthy, rich; (pl. noun) rich men

πλοῦτος, -ου, m. (6) — wealth, riches

πόθεν (U36) — from where?

ποθέν (U36) — from some place

ποῖ (U36) — whither?

ποι (U36) — to some place

ποιέω (13) — make, do

ποίημα, -ατος, n. (14) — product; poem

ποίησις, -εως, f. (21) — creation; writing of poetry

ποιητής, -οῦ, m. (5) — maker; poet

ποῖος (U36) — what sort?

ποιός (U36) — of some sort

πολεμέω (27) — make war (against) (+ dat.)

πολέμιος, -α, -ον (7) — hostile; (m. pl. as noun) the enemy

πόλεμος, -ου, m. (3) — war

πολιορκέω (33) — besiege

πόλις, -εως, f. (21) — city

πολιτεύω (11) — be a citizen; (mid.) participate in politics

πολίτης, -ου, m. (5) — citizen

πολλάκις (25) — often, many times

πολύς, πολλή, πολύ (25) — much, many; (m. pl. as noun) the multitude

πονηρός, -ά, -όν (7) — worthless; evil, base

πόνος, -ου, m. (6) — hard work, toil; suffering

πορεύω (33) — convey; (mid.) go, walk, march

πόσος (U36) — how much/many?

ποσός (U36) — of some quantity

ποταμός, -οῦ, m. (6) — river

πότε (17) — when?

ποτέ (17) — at any time, ever; (strengthening an interrogative) ever, in the world

πότερος (U36) — which of two?; any one of two

ποῦ (17) — where?

που (17) — somewhere, anywhere; to some degree, perhaps

πούς, ποδός, m. (17) — foot

πρᾶγμα, -ατος, n. (14) — deed; event; thing; (pl.) trouble

πράττω (10) — accomplish, do; fare

πρέπει (9) — it is fitting (+ inf.)

πρέσβυς, -εως, m. (34) — old man, ambassador

πρεσβύτερος, πρεσβύτατος (34) — older, oldest

πρεσβύτης, -ου, m. (34) — old man, ambassador

πρίν (39) — before; formerly

πρό (U12) — (+ gen.) in front of, in defense of, before

προδίδωμι (23) — give up, betray

προδότης, -ου, m. (35) — traitor

πρόθυμος, -ον (38) — ready, eager; bearing good-will

πρός (U6) — (+ gen.) from, proceeding from; (+ dat.) near, beside; in addition to; (+ acc.) to, toward; against; regarding προσήκω (39) — belong to, be related to (+ dat.); (impersonal) it is fitting

πρόσθεν (27) — before, in front of (+ gen.); previously

προσίημι (23) — let come to; (mid.) let come to oneself

πρότερος, -α, -ον (10) — former, previous

πρῶτος, -η, -ον (U25) — first

πυνθάνομαι (11) — learn (by inquiry), inquire

πῦρ, πυρός, n. (41) — fire

πῶς (17) — how?

πως (17) — somehow, in any way, at all

ῥᾴδιος, -α, -ον (9) — easy

ῥᾴθυμος, -ον (38) — easygoing, indifferent

ῥᾷστος (U30) — easiest

ῥᾴων (U30) — easier

ῥέω (39) — flow

ῥήγνυμι (23) — break, shatter

ῥήτωρ, -ορος, m. (15) — speaker, orator

ῥίπτω (37) — throw, hurl

σαφής, -ές (22) — sure, reliable; clear

σεαυτοῦ (U25) — yourself (sing. reflexive)

σέβομαι (40) — feel awe, revere

σιγάω (31) — be silent, keep secret

σίδηρος, -ου, m. (42) — iron

σιτίον, -ου, n. (29) — grain, bread, food

σῖτος, -ου, m. (but pl. n. σῖτα) (29) — grain, bread, food

σκεδάννυμι (29) — scatter, disperse

σκέπτομαι (38) — view, examine

σκηνή, -ῆς, f. (4) — tent; stage

σκοπέω (38) — look at, examine

σός, σή, σόν (22) — your, yours (sing.)

σοφία, -ας, f. (17) — cleverness, skill; wisdom

σοφός, -ή, -όν (7) — skilled, clever, wise

σπένδω (11) — pour a libation; (mid.) make a truce

σπεύδω (38) — seek eagerly, strive; hasten

σπονδή, -ῆς, f. (29) — drink offering; (pl.) truce, treaty

σπουδάζω (38) — be serious, be eager

σπουδή, -ῆς, f. (41) — haste; effort; regard

στάδιον, -ου, n. (also m. in pl.) (17) — stade (1/8 mile); race course

στάσις, -εως, f. (21) — position; faction, party strife

στέλλω (41) — make ready; send

στενός, -ή, -όν (17) — narrow, confined

στράτευμα, -ατος, n. (27) — army

στρατεύω (30) — wage war; (mid.) march on campaign

στρατηγός, -οῦ, m. (6) — general

στρατιά, -ᾶς, f. (4) — army

στρατιώτης, -ου, m. (5) — soldier

στρατόπεδον, -ου, n. (17) — camp (of army)

στρατός, -οῦ, m. (39) — army, host

στρέφω (26) — turn, twist

σύ (U22) — you (sing.)

συγγιγνώσκω (32) — agree with; acknowledge; pardon (+ dat.)

συκῆ, -ῆς, f. (42) — fig tree

σῦκον, -ου, n. (42) — fig

συλλέγω (39) — gather, collect

συμβαίνω (24) — come together; (impersonal) happen

συμβουλεύω (32) — advise; (mid.) consult with (+ dat.)

σύμμαχος, -ον (9) — allied with; (m. pl. as noun) allies

συμφέρω (32) — bring together; be advantageous; (impers.) it is expedient

συμφορά, -ᾶς, f. (4) — event; misfortune

σύν (U6) — (+ dat.) with

συντίθημι (23) — put together; (mid.) make an agreement, agree on

σῦς, συός, m. or f. (21) — swine, hog

σχεδόν (32) — about, almost

σχολή, -ῆς, f. (41) — leisure; learned discussion

σχολῇ — (dat. as adv.) in a leisurely way; scarcely, not at all

σῴζω (39) — save, preserve; (pass.) reach safely

Σωκράτης, -ους, m. (15) — Socrates

σῶμα, -ατος, n. (41) — body, person

σωτηρία, -ας, f. (33) — safety, preservation

σωφρονέω (32) — be temperate, moderate, chaste

σωφροσύνη, -ης, f. (35) — moderation, temperance

σώφρων, σῶφρον (22) — prudent, temperate, chaste

τάλαντον, -ου, n. (29) — balance; talent (unit of weight or money)

τάττω (9) — marshal; arrange

ταύτῃ (U36) — in this way, by this way

τάχα (30) — quickly; perhaps

τάχιστος (U30) — swiftest

τάχος, -ους, n. (35) — speed, swiftness; (adv. acc.) swiftly

ταχύς, -εῖα, -ύ (30) — swift, quick

τε (U12) — and (postpositive)

τεῖχος, -ους, n. (15) — wall

τεκών, -όντος, m. (40) — father, parent

τελευτάω (29) — accomplish, end; die

τελευτή, -ῆς, f. (35) — end, death

τελέω (33) — fulfill, bring to an end

τέλος, -ους, n. (15) — fulfillment, end; (pl.) rites, taxes; (U17) (acc. sing. as adv.) finally, at last

τέμνω (26) — cut

τέρας, -ατος, n. (14) — portent, monster

τέταρτος, -η, -ον (U25) — fourth

τετράκις (U25) — four times

τετρακόσιοι, -αι, -α (40) — four hundred

τετταράκοντα (27) — forty

τέτταρες, -α (U25) — four

τέχνη, -ης, f. (38) — art, skill, craft

τῇδε (U36) — in this way, by this way

τήμερον (32) — today

τί (U17) — (adv. acc.) why?

τίθημι (23) — place, put; make, cause

τίκτω (40) — beget; give birth to; produce

τιμάω (29) — honor, esteem

τιμή, -ῆς, f. (4) — honor, esteem

τίς, τί (15) — who?, which?, what?

τις, τι (17) — anyone, someone, anything, something; (adj.) any, some, (a) certain

τοιόσδε (U36) — such

τοιοῦτος, τοιαύτη, τοιοῦτο(ν) (U36) — such

τόξον, -ου, n. (38) — bow

τοξότης, -ου, m. (38) — archer

τοσόσδε (U36) — so much, so many

τοσοῦτος, τοσαύτη, τοσοῦτο(ν) (U36) — so much, so many

τότε (12) — then, at that time

τράπεζα, -ης, f. (5) — table; bank

τραχύς, -εῖα, -ύ (40) — rugged, rough

τρεῖς, τρία (U25) — three

τρέπω (16) — turn, change; put to flight

τρέφω (26) — rear, nourish, cherish

τρέχω (34) — run

τριάκοντα (27) — thirty

τριακόσιοι, -αι, -α (40) — three hundred

τριήρης, -ους, f. (15) — trireme

τρίς (U25) — thrice

τρισχίλιοι, -αι, -α (40) — three thousand

τρίτος, -η, -ον (U25) — third

τρόπαιον, -ου, n. (31) — trophy, victory monument

τρόπος, -ου, m. (6) — turn; way, manner; character; (adv. acc. with adj.) in X manner

τυγχάνω (28) — happen to be (+ part.); happen; succeed; meet with, obtain (+ gen.)

τύπτω (12) — strike, beat

τύραννος, -ου, m. (41) — absolute ruler, tyrant

τύχη, -ης, f. (22) — fate, chance, fortune, event

ὕβρις, -εως, f. (21) — violence, insolence

ὑγίεια, -ας, f. (5) — health, soundness

ὑγιής, -ές (41) — healthy; wise

ὕδωρ, ὕδατος, n. (14) — water

υἱός, υἱοῦ or υἱέος, m. (21) — son

ὑμεῖς (U22) — you (pl.)

ὑμέτερος, -α, -ον (22) — your, yours (pl.)

ὑός, ὑοῦ or ὑέος, m. (21) — son

ὑπακούω (32) — listen to, obey (+ gen.); reply (+ dat.)

ὑπέρ (U12) — (+ gen.) over, above, concerning; (+ acc.) over, across, beyond

ὑπισχνέομαι (26) — undertake, promise (+ inf.)

ὕπνος, -ου, m. (6) — sleep

ὑπό (U12) — (+ gen.) (from) under; by (of personal agent with passive

ὑπό
(continued)

verb); (+ dat.) under (the power of); (+ acc.) under, during

ὑπολαμβάνω (32) understand, assume; reply

ὑπομένω (32) await, endure

ὑπομιμνήσκω (29) remind, call to mind; (mid./pass.) remember, make mention of

ὑποπτεύω (39) suspect

ὗς, ὑός, m. or f. (21) swine, hog

ὕστερος, -α, -ον (10) latter, later, next

ὑψηλός, -ή, -όν (41) high, lofty

φαγ- aor. of *eat* (26)

φαίνω (29) reveal, display; (pass.) come to light, appear

φάλαγξ, -αγγος, f. (14) line of battle; line of hoplites

φανερός, -ά, -όν (16) visible, manifest

φέρω (8) bear, carry; endure; (29) (+ adv.) bear in a certain manner

φεύγω (8) flee, be in exile

φημί (U20) say

φθάνω (28) anticipate, be ahead of (+ participle)

φθείρω (39) destroy, corrupt, seduce

φθονερός, -ά, -όν (38) envious, jealous

φθόνος, -ου, m. (6) envy, jealousy

φιλέω (13) love, like

φιλία, -ας, f. (4) friendship

φίλιος, -α, -ον (7) friendly; beloved

φίλος, -η, -ον (7) beloved, dear; (as m. or f. noun) friend

φοβερός, -ά, -όν (41) fearful, feared

φοβέω (13) frighten; (mid./pass.) be afraid (of)

φόβος, -ου, m. (6) fear

φονεύς, -έως, m. (21) murderer

φόρος, -ου, m. (17) payment, tribute

φράζω (39) point out, tell, explain

φυγάς, -άδος, m. or f. (35) exile, runaway

φυγή, -ῆς, f. (4) flight; exile

φυλακή, -ῆς, f. (39) watching; garrison

φύλαξ, -ακος, m. (14) guard, sentinel

φυλάττω (16) guard, watch for; (mid.) be on one's guard

φύω (40) produce, beget; (pass. and intrans. forms) grow, be born; (perf.) be by nature, be by nature prone to (+ inf.)

φωνή, -ῆς, f. (4) sound; voice

φῶς, φωτός, n. (14) light

χαίρω (40) rejoice, delight in (+ dat.)

χαλεπός, -ή, -όν (7) difficult, hard; harsh

χαλεπῶς φέρω (29) bear with difficulty, be annoyed

χαλκός, -οῦ, m. (42) — copper, bronze; weapon of bronze

χαλκοῦς, -ῆ, -οῦν (42) — of copper or bronze

χαρίεις, -ίεσσα, -ίεν (22) — graceful, elegant; clever

χάρις, -ιτος, f. (14) — grace; favor; gratitude

χειμών, -ῶνος, m. (39) — winter; storm

χείρ, χειρός, f. (21) — hand

χείρων, χείριστος (U30) — worse, worst

χθές (32) — yesterday

χιλιάς, -άδος, f. (40) — group of 1,000

χίλιοι, -αι, -α (40) — one thousand

χράομαι (30) — use, experience (+ dat.)

χράω (30) — proclaim an oracle; (mid.) consult an oracle

χρή (9) — it is necessary (+ inf.)

χρῆμα, -ατος, n. (17) — thing, matter; (pl.) property, money

χρηστός, -ή, -όν (30) — useful, good

χρόνος, -ου, m. (6) — time, period of time

χρυσός, -οῦ, m. (42) — gold

χρυσοῦς, -ῆ, -οῦν (42) — of gold

χώρα, -ας, f. (4) — space; land, country

χωρίς (39) — separately, apart; (+ gen.) without

ψευδής, -ές (22) — lying, false

ψεῦδος, -ους, n. (39) — falsehood, lie

ψῆφος, -ου, f. (3) — pebble; vote

ψυχή, -ῆς, f. (4) — life; soul

ὦ (18) — (particle with vocatives) o! (or left untranslated)

ὧδε (13) — in this way, so very

ὥρα, -ας, f. (39) — period, season; time of day; fitting time

ὡς (25, 27, 31, 33, U36) — so that (result); (with part.) as if, on the ground that; (+ subj./ opt.) in order that; (indirect discourse) that; as, because; how

ὥσπερ (27) — (just) as if, as

ὥστε (25) — so that, so as, that (result)

ὠφελέω (13) — help, aid

English-Greek Glossary

This glossary contains words used in all English-to-Greek word, phrase, and sentence exercises of this book. Each Greek word is cross-referenced by a number in parentheses to the unit vocabulary in which the word is introduced. For full information on inflection and correct usage of words, consult the vocabulary list in the indicated unit.

abandon, καταλείπω (32)

able: be able, δύναμαι (25)

about, (= concerning) περί + gen. (U12); (= roughly) σχεδόν (32)

about to (may be used as rough translation of future inf.); be about to, μέλλω (18)

accordance: in accordance with, κατά + acc. (U12)

account, λόγος (3)
on account of, διά + acc. (U6)

accusation: make an accusation against, κατηγορέω + gen. (17)

accuse, κατηγορέω (17)

accuser, ὁ κατηγορῶν (17)

acquire, aorist of ἔχω (8)

action, πρᾶγμα (14)

addition: in addition to, ἐπί + dat. or πρός + dat. (U6)

admit (to oneself, to one's presence), προσίεμαι (23)

affair, πρᾶγμα (14); or use neuter adj. or demonstrative

afraid: be afraid, φοβέομαι (13)

after, μετά + acc.

against (march, fight, war against), πρός + acc. (U6) or ἐπί + acc. (U6) or κατά + gen. (U12) (or gen. alone with κατα-compound verb)

agree (= have same opinion), ὁμολογέω (32)

agreement: make an agreement, συντίθεμαι (23)

aid, ὠφελέω (13)
come to the aid of, βοηθέω (33)

aim at, ἐφίεμαι + gen. (23)

all, πᾶς, ἅπας (22)

allow, ἐάω (33)

ally, σύμμαχος (10)

along (e.g., a road): use acc. of space over which (U17)

alongside, παρά + dat. or acc. (U6)

already, ἤδη (12)

although, καίπερ (27) with circumstantial participle

always, ἀεί (12)

ambassador, πρεσβύτης (34), in pl. also πρέσβεις (34)

among, ἐν + dat. or παρά + dat. (U6)

and, καί, τε (U12)

angry: be angry, ὀργίζομαι (28)

announce, ἀγγέλλω (19)

another: one another, ἀλλήλων (U25)

any, τις, τι (17)

anything, τι (17)
not ... anything, οὐδέν, μηδέν (25)

appear, φαίνομαι (29)

appoint, καθίστημι (23)

arrange, τάττω (9)
arms, ὅπλα (34)
army, στρατιά (4), στράτευμα (27),
στρατός (39)
arrive, ἀφικνέομαι (13)
arrogance, ὕβρις (21)
as, ὡς (27)
as long as, ἕως (39)
as much as, ὅσον (36)
as a result of, ἐκ + gen. (U6)
as X as possible, ὡς or ὅτι +
superlative (30)
ask (for), αἰτέω (16)
ask (a question), ἐρωτάω (33),
ἐρήσομαι (34)
at the same time with, ἅμα + dat. (32)
Athenian, Ἀθηναῖος (10)
Athens: men of Athens, Ἀθηναῖοι
(10)
attack, ἐπιτίθεμαι (23)
await, μένω (8)
away from, ἀπό + gen. (U6)

bad, κακός (7), πονηρός (7)
base, κακός (7), αἰσχρός (7)
battle, μάχη (10)
be, εἰμί (10)
be a slave, δουλεύω (30)
be able, δύναμαι (25)
be afraid, φοβέομαι (13)
be at a loss, ἀπορέω (29)
be defeated, ἡττάομαι (31)
be distant from, ἀπέχω (16)
be in training, γυμνάζομαι (11)
be on guard, φυλάττομαι (16)
be present, πάρειμι (27)
be sick, νοσέω (13)
be silent, σιγάω (31)
be willing, ἐθέλω (8)
bear, φέρω (8)
beast, θήρ (16), θηρίον (16)
beautiful, καλός (7)
because: use causal circumstantial
participle (with ὡς); or conjunction
ὅτι or ὡς (33)
because of, διά + acc. (U6)

become, γίγνομαι (11), καθίσταμαι
(23)
befit, πρέπει (9)
before, πρίν (39)
beg, δέομαι + gen. (13)
begin, ἄρχω or ἄρχομαι + gen. or +
inf. or participle (8)
beginning, ἀρχή (4)
behalf: on behalf of, ὑπέρ or πρό +
gen. (U12)
believe (a proposition), νομίζω (18),
οἴομαι (11), ἡγέομαι (16)
believe (trust) (a person), πείθομαι +
dat. (8, U11)
belong to: use gen. of possession in
predicate with copula
beloved, φίλος (7)
beside (of extension), παρά + acc.
(U6); (of location), ἐπί, πρός,
παρά + dat. (U6)
betray, προδίδωμι (23)
better, βελτίων, ἀμείνων, κρείττων
(U30)
beware, εὐλαβέομαι (38)
beyond, παρά + acc. (U6)
bird, ὄρνις (14)
bitter, πικρός (24)
black, μέλας (22)
blame: (adj.) to blame, αἴτιος (10)
blessed, εὐδαίμων (22)
blow, πληγή (17)
board (a ship), ἀναβαίνω (24)
boat, πλοῖον (34)
body, σῶμα (41)
book, βιβλίον (3)
both . . . and, καὶ . . . καὶ,
. . . τε(. . .)καὶ, . . . τε . . . τε
(U12)
brave, ἀγαθός (7)
break, ῥήγνυμι (24)
breastplate, θώραξ (14)
bridge, γέφυρα (5)
bring, φέρω (8)
bring to an end, τελευτάω (29)
brother, ἀδελφός (34)
burn, καίω (26)

but, δέ, ἀλλά (U12)
by (of personal agent with passive
  verb), ὑπό + gen. (U12)
by means of, διά + gen. (U6), or dat.
  without preposition (U10)

call, καλέω (18); be
  called, κέκλημαι (37)
camp, στρατόπεδον (17)
campaign: carry out a
  campaign, στρατεύομαι (30); go on
  campaign, στρατεύω (30)
capture, αἱρέω (13); be
  captured, ἁλίσκομαι (24)
carry, φέρω (8)
carry out a campaign, στρατεύομαι
  (30)
case: plead a case, δικάζομαι (11)
cattle, (plur. of) βοῦς (21)
cause to revolt, ἀφίστημι (23)
cause to stand, ἵστημι (23)
cavalry (= cavalrymen), ἱππῆς (21)
certain: a certain (one), τις, τι (17)
character, τρόπος (6)
characteristic: it is characteristic
  of, use gen. of possession in
  predicate with copula
chaste, σώφρων (22)
child, παιδίον (3), παῖς (16)
choose, αἱρέομαι (13)
chorus trainer, διδάσκαλος (17)
citizen, πολίτης (5)
city, πόλις (21)
clear, δῆλος (7), φανερός (16)
clever, σοφός (7)
cling to, ἔχομαι + gen. (U11)
come, ἔρχομαι (11), ἀφικνέομαι (13);
  have come, ἥκω (34); let come (to
  oneself), προσίεμαι (23)
come to a halt, ἐφίσταμαι (23)
come to the aid of, βοηθέω (33)
come to the rescue, βοηθέω (33)
command, κελεύω (9)
conceal, κρύπτω (17)
conceived hatred, (ingressive aor. of)
  μισέω (33)

concerning, περί + gen. (U12)
condition: be in X condition, ἔχω +
  adv. (27)
conquer, κρατέω (13), νικάω (29)
consecrated, ἱερός (7)
contest, ἀγών (15)
continue, διαμένω, διατελέω (28)
converse with, διαλέγομαι (32)
corrupt, διαφθείρω (39)
counsel: take counsel
  together, συμβουλεύομαι (32)
country, χώρα (4)
cowardly, κακός (7), δειλός (40)
critical time, καιρός (31)
cross, διαβαίνω (24)
cross-examine, ἐλέγχω (28)
custom: have as a custom, νομίζω
  (18)
Cyrus, Κῦρος, -ου, m.

damage, βλάπτω (9)
daughter, θυγάτηρ (15)
day, ἡμέρα (4)
death, θάνατος (3); be put to
  death, ἀποθνῄσκω (8)
deceive, (ἐξ)ἀπατάω (38)
deed, ἔργον (3); do good (bad)
  deeds, ἀγαθὰ (κακὰ) ποιεῖν (U17)
deep, βαθύς (22)
defeat, κρατέω + gen. or acc. (13),
  νικάω (28); be defeated, ἡττάομαι
  (31)
defend oneself, ἀπολογέομαι (32)
deliberate, βουλεύομαι (11)
deliberation: upon deliberation, use
  participle of βουλεύομαι (11)
democracy, δημοκρατία (4)
demonstrate, ἀποδείκνυμι,
  ἐπιδείκνυμι (23)
Demosthenes, Δημοσθένης (15)
desire, ἐπιθυμία (10); βούλομαι (11),
  ἐπιθυμέω (16)
destroy utterly, διαφθείρω (39)
die, ἀποθνῄσκω (8)
different, ἄλλος (19)
difficult, χαλεπός (7)

difficulty: with difficulty, χαλεπῶς
(7), μόγις (39)
discover, εὑρίσκω (10)
disease, νόσος (3)
disgraceful, αἰσχρός (7)
distant: be distant from, ἀπέχω (16)
divinity (esp. tutelary), δαίμων (15)
do, πράττω (10), ποιέω (13); may
also be auxiliary verb in English
present emphatic, not separately
translated in Greek (U8)
door, θύρα (4)
down, κατά (U12), or expressed by
κατα-prefix in compound verb
dreadful, δεινός (16)
drink, πίνω (26)
duration, use acc. of time (U17)
during, ὑπό + acc., κατά + acc. (U12),
ἐν + dat. (U6); also gen. of time
without preposition (U29)
dwell, οἰκέω (13)

each (one) of more than two, ἕκαστος
(19)
each (one) of two, ἑκάτερος (19)
earlier, πρότερος (10)
easy, ῥᾴδιος (9)
education, παιδεία (4)
elegant, χαρίεις (22)
embassy, see ambassadors
emulate, ζηλόω (29)
encounter, ἀπαντάω (33)
end, τέλος (15); bring to an
end, τελευτάω (29)
endure, φέρω (8)
enemy, (adj.) πολέμιος; (noun) οἱ
πολέμιοι (7)
enough: enough to, use result
construction with ὥστε (U25)
entire, πᾶς, ἅπας (22)
entrust, ἐπιτρέπω (8)
envy, φθόνος (6)
equip, παρασκευάζω (11)
even, καί (U12); not even, οὐδέ,
μηδέ (18)
event, πρᾶγμα (14), συμφορά (4)

ever, ποτέ (17)
everyone, πᾶς, ἅπας (22)
everything, πάντα (22)
evil, κακός (7)
examine, ἐλέγχω (28)
exceedingly, μάλα (12)
excel, διαφέρω (17)
exercise (oneself), γυμνάζομαι (11)
exhort, παρακελεύομαι (11)
exile, (condition) φυγή (4); (person)
φυγάς (35)
eye: in the eyes of, use dat. of
reference (U9) or παρά + dat. (U6)

fact: the fact that, use articular
infinitive (U9) or ὅτι-clause (U33)
faculty of judgment, γνώμη (4)
fall, πίπτω (18)
fall ill, (ingressive aor. of) νοσέω (13)
false, ψευδής (22)
fare, πράττω + adv. (10)
fate, μοῖρα (5)
father, πατήρ (15)
fatherland, πατρίς (14)
favor, χάρις (14)
fear, φόβος (6); φοβέομαι (13)
fellow: fellow soldiers (citizens,
etc.), not separately translated into
Greek, or use ἄνδρες in apposition
few, ὀλίγοι (25)
fifth, πέμπτος (U25)
fight, μάχομαι (11)
fill, (ἐμ)πίμπλημι (29)
find, εὑρίσκω (10)
fine, καλός (7)
flee, φεύγω (8)
flee from, φεύγω + acc. (8)
flight, φυγή (4)
flow, ῥέω (39)
following: the following, ὅδε (U13)
foolish, ἄφρων (22)
foot, πούς (17)
footsoldiers, πεζοί (7)
for, (conj.) γάρ (U12); (prep.) often
expressed by dative without prep.;

(duration of time) use acc. without prep. (U17)

foreigner, βάρβαρος (9)

forget, ἐπιλανθάνομαι (32)

former: the former (vs. the latter), ἐκεῖνος (U13)

formerly, πρόσθεν (27)

four, τέτταρες (U25)

free: set free, ἀφίημι (23)

friend, φίλος (7)

friendly, φίλιος (7)

friendship, φιλία (4)

from, ἀπό, ἐκ, πρός, παρά + gen. (U6)

full (of), πλήρης (+ gen.) (22)

furnish, παρέχω (16)

gather, συλλέγω (39), ἀθροίζω (38)

general, στρατηγός (6)

gentlemen (voc.), ἄνδρες (15)

giant, γίγας (14)

gift, δῶρον (3)

give, δίδωμι (23)

give a share of, μεταδίδωμι (23)

go, ἔρχομαι (11), εἶμι (23)

go away, ἄπειμι (23)

go down to the sea, καταβαίνω (24)

go on campaign, στρατεύω (30)

go up, ἀναβαίνω (24)

god, θεός (3)

goddess, θεά (4)

good, ἀγαθός (7)

graceful, χαρίεις (22)

grant, δίδωμι (23)

gratitude, χάρις (14)

Greece, Ἑλλάς (14)

Greek (man), Ἕλλην (15)

guard, φυλάττω (16); φύλαξ (14); be on one's guard, keep on one's guard, φυλάττομαι (16)

guide, ἡγεμών (16); ἡγέομαι + dat. (16)

half, ἥμισυς (22)

halt, ἐφίσταμαι (23)

hand, χείρ (21); on the one hand . . . , on the other hand, μὲν . . . δὲ (U12)

hand over, παραδίδωμι (23)

handsome, καλός (7)

happen, γίγνομαι (11), τυγχάνω (28)

hard: hard work, πόνος (6)

harm, do harm, βλάπτω (9), κακὸν (κακὰ) ποιεῖν (+ acc.) (U17)

harmful, βλαβερός (16)

harsh, χαλεπός (7)

hate, μισέω (33)

hatred: conceived hatred (for), (ingressive aor. of) μισέω (33)

have, ἔχω (8)

have a share of, μετέχω (29)

have as a custom, νομίζω (18)

he, (subject of verb expressed by 3rd pers. sing. ending of verb)

health, ὑγίεια (5)

hear, ἀκούω (11)

heavy, βαρύς (22)

Hellenic, Ἑλληνικός, -ή, -όν

help, ὠφελέω (13), βοηθέω (33)

her, (oblique cases of) αὐτή (21); (as possessive) gen. αὐτῆς, or unemphatic possessive may be expressed by article alone (U7)

him, (oblique cases of) αὐτός (21)

himself, herself, itself, (intensive) αὐτός (21); (reflexive) ἑαυτοῦ (αὑτοῦ) (U25)

hinder, κωλύω (16)

his, possessive gen. αὐτοῦ, or unemphatic possessive may be expressed by article alone (U7)

hold, ἔχω (8)

hold office, ἄρχω (8)

holy, ἱερός (7)

honor, τιμή (4); τιμάω (29)

hope, ἐλπίς (14); ἐλπίζω (19)

hoplite, ὁπλίτης (5)

horse, ἵππος (3)

hostile, πολέμιος (7)

house: in the house of, παρά + dat. (U6)

how, πῶς (17)

human being, ἄνθρωπος (3)

hurl, ἵημι (23)
husband, ἀνήρ (15)

I, (unemphatic subject expressed by
1st pers. sing. ending of verb);
(emphatic) ἐγώ (U22)
if, εἰ, ἐάν (34)
ill: be ill, νοσέω (13)
immortal, ἀθάνατος (9)
impossible: it is impossible, οὐκ
ἔξεστι (9)
in, ἐν + dat. (U6)
in order to, in order that, ἵνα, ὅπως,
ὡς + subjunctive (U31)
indict, γράφομαι (U11)
inhabit, οἰκέω (13)
inquire, πυνθάνομαι (11)
into, εἰς + acc. (U6)
it, (oblique cases of) αὐτό (21);
unemphatic subject expressed by 3rd
pers. sing. ending of verb

jealousy, φθόνος (6)
judge, (in a contest) κριτής (5); (in a
law court) δικαστής (5)
judge, serve as judge, δικάζω (11)
judgment, γνώμη (4)
juror, δικαστής (5)
jury: gentlemen of the jury
(voc.), ἄνδρες δικασταί
juryman, δικαστής (5)
just, δίκαιος (7)
just about, σχεδόν (32)
justice, δίκη (4)

keep: keep on one's
guard, φυλάττομαι (16)
kill, ἀποκτείνω (11)
king, βασιλεύς (21)
know, οἶδα (28)

lack, ἀπορέω (29), δέομαι (13)
land, χώρα (4)
large, μακρός (7)
law, νόμος (3)
lawsuit, δίκη (4); participate in a
lawsuit, δικάζομαι (11)

lead, ἄγω (8); (= be leader
of), ἄρχω (8)
lead astray, παράγω (16)
lead away, ἀπάγω (16)
leader, ἡγεμών (16); be leader
of, ἄρχω (8)
learn, μανθάνω (18)
learn by inquiry, πυνθάνομαι (11)
leave, λείπω (8)
leave behind, καταλείπω (32)
lest, μή + subj. or opt. (U31)
let, (English auxiliary verb used in
constructions equivalent to Greek
hortatory subj., subj. of prohibition,
and 3rd person imperative, U31, U40)
let come (to oneself), προσίεμαι (23)
libation: pour a libation, σπένδω (11)
life, βίος (3)
light, φῶς (14)
like, φιλέω (13)
lion, λέων (14)
long, μακρός (7), (of time) πολύς
(25); long for, ἐφίεμαι (23); as long
as, ἕως (39)
loosen, λύω (8)
loss: be at a loss, ἀπορέω (29)
lot: a lot (adv.), πολύ (25)
love, φιλέω (13)

majority: the majority, plural of
πλεῖστος (10) in appropriate gender,
with article
make, ποιέω (13)
make a promise, ὑπισχνέομαι
make a truce, σπένδομαι (11)
make an accusation, κατηγορέω (17)
make an agreement, συντίθεμαι (23)
make manifest, δηλόω (29)
make preparations, παρασκευάζομαι
(11)
man, (*qua* human being) ἄνθρωπος
(3); (*qua* male person) ἀνήρ (15);
(generically, with an adj.) use adj.
alone
manifest: make manifest, δηλόω (29)
mankind, οἱ ἄνθρωποι (3)

manner, τρόπος (6) (adv. acc. idiom, U17); or use adverb of manner

many, πολύς (25)

march, ἐλαύνω (8)

mare, ἡ ἵππος (3)

marketplace, ἀγορά (4)

marry, ἄγομαι (U11)

marshal, τάττω (9)

master, δεσπότης (5)

matter, πρᾶγμα (14); or use neuter demonstrative or adjective alone

means: by means of, διά + gen. (U6); dat. without preposition (U10)

measure, μέτρον (3)

meet, ἀπαντάω (33)

messenger, ἄγγελος (3)

misfortune, συμφορά (4)

mislead, παράγω (16)

moderation, σωφροσύνη (35)

money, χρήματα (17)

monster, τέρας (14)

more, use comparative form (U30); (adv.) μᾶλλον (30); (of quantity) πλέων (U30)

most, (of quantity) πλεῖστος (10); (adv.) μάλιστα (30), or use superlative form (U30)

mother, μήτηρ (15)

much, (adv.) πολύ (25); as much as, ὅσον (U36)

multitude, πλῆθος (15)

must, use impersonal δεῖ, χρή (9)

my, ἐμός (22); or possessive gen. ἐμοῦ/μου

narrow, στενός (17)

necessary: be necessary, δεῖ or χρή (9); what is necessary, τὰ ἐπιτήδεια (41)

necessity, ἀνάγκη (10)

need: be in need of, δέομαι + gen. (13)

neither . . . nor, οὔτε . . . οὔτε, μήτε . . . μήτε (18)

never, οὔποτε, μήποτε (17)

next, (= later, following) ὕστερος (10)

next to, ἐπί, παρά, πρός + dat. (U6)

night, νύξ (34)

no one, οὐδείς, μηδείς (U25)

noble, καλός (7)

nor, *see* neither

not, (with ind., with inf. of indirect statement, with expression of particulars) οὐ (8); (with inf., imperative, subj., opt., in conditional clauses, in expressions with generic meaning) μή (9)

nothing, οὐδέν, μηδέν (25)

notice, ὁράω (29), αἰσθάνομαι (11); not notice, use λανθάνω (28)

now, νῦν (12)

numerous, πολύς (25)

oath: being under oath, use perf. part. of ὄμνυμι (37)

obey, πείθομαι + dat. (U11)

obvious, δῆλος (7), φανερός (16)

of, (use some type of gen., e.g., possessive, objective, U7)

office, ἀρχή (4); hold office, ἄρχω (8)

old: old man, γέρων (14); old woman, γραῦς (21)

omen, ὄρνις (14)

on, ἐν + dat. (U6), ἐπί + gen. (U6)

on (. . .) day, use dat. of time without preposition (U10)

on account of, διά + acc. (U6)

one: (pronoun) (the) one, (as subject of impersonal verb or antecedent of relative clause) unexpressed in Greek; sometimes expressed by adj. with article or by demonstrative; the one . . . the other, ὁ μὲν . . . ὁ δὲ (U12)

one another, ἀλλήλων (25)

one's, expressed by article alone (cf. *his, her*)

opinion, γνώμη (4), δόξα (5)

or, ἤ (30)

orator, ῥήτωρ (15)

order, κελεύω (9); in order to, ἵνα,
ὅπως, ὡς + subj. (U31)
other, ἄλλος (19); the one . . . the
  other, ὁ μὲν . . . ὁ δὲ (U12); some
  . . . the others, οἱ μὲν . . . οἱ δὲ
  (U12)
ought, use impersonal δεῖ, χρή (9)
our, ἡμέτερος (22), or possessive gen.
  ἡμῶν (U22)
ourselves, ἡμῶν αὐτῶν (U25)
out of, ἐκ + gen. (U6)
outside, ἔξω

part, μέρος (15)
participate: participate in
  politics, πολιτεύομαι (11);
  participate in a lawsuit, δικάζομαι
  (11)
pay: pay down, κατατίθημι (23); pay
  the penalty, δίκην διδόναι
peace, peace treaty, εἰρήνη (10)
pebble, ψῆφος (3)
pelt, βάλλω (10)
penalty: pay the penalty, δίκην
  διδόναι
people, (without adj.) see man; (with
  adj. or demonstrative) unexpressed in
  Greek
perceive, αἰσθάνομαι (11)
perish, ἀπόλλυμι (37)
perjury, ἐπιορκία (10)
permit, ἐάω (33)
permitted: it is permitted, ἔξεστι (9)
Persians, οἱ βάρβαροι (9)
persuade, πείθω (8)
phalanx, φάλαγξ (14)
Philip, Φίλιππος, -ου, m.
piece of writing, γράμμα (14)
pious, ὅσιος (9)
plan, βούλευμα (14)
plead (a case), δικάζομαι (11)
pleasant, ἡδύς (22)
pleasure, ἡδονή (4)
plot (against), ἐπιβουλεύω (+ dat.)
  (28)
poem, ποίημα (14)

poet, ποιητής (5)
politics: participate in
  politics, πολιτεύομαι (11)
portent, τέρας (14)
portion, μοῖρα (5), μέρος (15)
position, (esp. troops) τάττω (9)
possessions, χρήματα (17)
possible, δυνατός (38); it is
  possible, ἔξεστι (9); as X as
  possible, ὡς or ὅτι with superlative
  (U30)
pour: pour a libation, σπένδω (11)
power, κράτος (15)
praise, ἐπαινέω (16)
pray, εὔχομαι (17)
prayer, εὐχή (17)
preparations: make
  preparations, παρασκευάζομαι (11)
presence: in the presence of, παρά +
  dat. (U6)
present: be present, πάρειμι (27)
preserve, σῴζω (39)
prevent, κωλύω (16)
priest, ἱερεύς (21)
privilege, γέρας (15)
produce, ποιέω (13)
promise, ὑπισχνέομαι (26)
proper: think proper, ἀξιόω (33)
prove, ἐπιδείκνυμι (23), ἐλέγχω (28)
provide, παρέχω (16)
prudent, σώφρων (22)
pursue, διώκω (27)
pursuit: in pursuit of, μετά + acc. (U6)
put: be put to death, ἀποθνῄσκω (8)

quickly, ταχέως (30), τάχος (35)

race, γένος (15)
ranks, τάξις, τάξεως, f.
ransom, λύομαι (U11)
read aloud, ἀναγιγνώσκω (24)
readily, ῥᾳδίως (9)
reason, λόγος (3)
receive, δέχομαι
recognize, γιγνώσκω (19)
regard: in regard to, πρός + acc. (U6)

regarding, εἰς, πρός + acc. (U6)
release, λύω (8)
remain, μένω (8)
remember, ἀπο-/ὑπομιμνῄσκομαι (29), μέμνημαι (U37)
remind, ἀπο-/ὑπομιμνῄσκω (29)
reply, ἀποκρίνομαι (32)
report, ἀγγέλλω (19)
reputation, δόξα (5)
rescue: come to the rescue, βοηθέω (33)
resolve, use impersonal δοκεῖ ("it seems best") + dat. (9)
response: in response to, πρός + acc.
responsible (for), αἴτιος + gen. (10)
result: as a result of, ἐκ + gen. (U6); with the result that, ὥστε (25)
return: in return for, ἀντί + gen. (U12)
revolt (from), ἀφίσταμαι (23); cause to revolt, ἀφίστημι (23)
rich, πλούσιος (7)
ride, ἐλαύνω (8)
righteousness, δικαιοσύνη (35)
river, ποταμός (6)
road, ὁδός (3)
ruin utterly, διαφθείρω (39)
rule, ἀρχή (4); ἄρχω + gen. (8)
rule over, κρατέω + gen. (13)

safe, ἀσφαλής (22)
sail, πλέω (39)
sailor, ναύτης (5)
same: the same, ὁ αὐτός, ἡ αὐτή, τὸ αὐτό (21); at the same time, ἅμα (32)
save, σῴζω (39)
say, λέγω (8), φημί (20), εἶπον (19)
scatter, σκεδάννυμι (29)
sea, θάλαττα (5); go down to the sea, καταβαίνω (24)
see, εἶδον (19), ὁράω (29)
seek, ζητέω (16)
seem, δοκέω (13)
seize, αἱρέω (13), ἁρπάζω (26)
sell, ἀποδίδομαι (23)
send, πέμπω (8)

sentinel, φύλαξ (14)
serve as judge, δικάζω (11)
set: set free, ἀφίημι (23); set up, ἀνατίθημι (23)
seven, ἑπτά (17)
shameful, αἰσχρός (7)
share: give a share of, μεταδίδωμι (23); have a share of, μετέχω (29)
shatter, ῥήγνυμι (23)
she, (subject of verb expressed by 3rd pers. sing. ending of verb)
shield, ἀσπίς (14)
ship, ναῦς (21)
short, βραχύς (22)
shrine, ἱερόν (7)
sick: be sick, νοσέω (13)
sickness, νόσος (3)
silent: be silent, σιγάω (31); become silent, use ingressive aor. of σιγάω (31)
sink, καταδύω (24)
slave, δοῦλος (31); be a slave, δουλεύω (30)
sleep, ὕπνος (6)
small, μικρός (7)
snatch, ἁρπάζω (26)
so, οὕτω(ς) (13); and so, use result construction (U25)
so as to, ὥστε (U25)
Socrates, Σωκράτης (15)
soldier, στρατιώτης (5)
some, τις, τι (17)
some ... others, οἱ μὲν ... οἱ δὲ (U12)
somebody, τις, τι (17)
somehow, πως (17)
something, τι (17)
son, υἱός (21)
soul, ψυχή (4)
speak, λέγω (8), εἶπον (19), φημί (U20)
speaker, ῥήτωρ (15)
spirit, ψυχή (4)
stand, ἵσταμαι (23); cause to stand, ἵστημι (23)
stand up, ἀνίσταμαι (23)

start off, ὁρμάω (33)

station, τάττω (9)

stay, μένω (8)

steadfast, ἀσφαλής (22)

steal, κλέπτω (34)

still, ἔτι (39)

stone, ψῆφος (3), λίθος (10)

story, λόγος (3)

strength, ἰσχύς (21)

strife, ἔρις (14); (of political factions) στάσις (21)

strike, κόπτω (9)

strong, ἰσχυρός (17)

such, τοιοῦτος (U36)

suffer, πάσχω (10)

suit, δίκη (4)

summon, καλέω (18)

sun, ἥλιος (3)

suppose, οἴομαι (11)

surpass, διαφέρω (17)

surprise, θαῦμα (34)

surrender, παραδίδωμι (23)

suspect, ὑποπτεύω (39)

swear, ὄμνυμι (37)

sweet, γλυκύς (22)

swift, ταχύς (30)

table, τράπεζα (5)

take, λαμβάνω (8)

take counsel together, συμβουλεύομαι (32)

task, ἔργον (3)

teacher, διδάσκαλος (17)

tell, λέγω (8)

temple, ἱερόν (7)

ten, δέκα (17)

tent, σκηνή (4)

terrible, δεινός (16)

terrify, φοβέω (13)

than, ἤ (30); or use gen. of comparison

that: that, those (demonstrative) ἐκεῖνος, ὅδε (U13); (conj., introducing noun clause), ὅτι, ὡς (33); (conj., clause of effort, etc.), ὅπως (38); (of result, = "so

that"), ὥστε (25); at that time, τότε (12)

the, ὁ, ἡ, τό (U6)

their, possessive gen. αὐτῶν (21); or unemphatic possessive may be expressed by article alone (U7)

them, (oblique cases, plural of) αὐτός (21)

themselves, (intensive) αὐτοί (21); (reflexive) ἑαυτῶν (αὑτῶν) (U25)

they, (subject of verb expressed by 3rd pers. pl. ending of verb)

thief, κλώψ (14)

thing, χρῆμα (17); or use neuter adj. or demonstrative without noun

think, νομίζω (18), οἴομαι (11), ἡγέομαι (16)

think proper, ἀξιόω (33)

this, these, οὗτος, αὕτη, τοῦτο (U13)

though, καίπερ with circumstantial participle (27)

throughout, διά + acc. (U6)

throw, βάλλω (10)

time, χρόνος (6); critical time, καιρός (31); at that time, τότε (12); at the same time, ἅμα (32)

to, (with indirect object) dat. without preposition (U8)

today, τήμερον (32)

toil, πόνος (6)

tomorrow, αὔριον (32)

tongue, γλῶττα (5)

tooth, ὀδούς (14)

toward, εἰς, πρός + acc. (U6)

town, ἄστυ (21)

training: be in training, γυμνάζομαι (11)

transgress, παραβαίνω (24)

trireme, τριήρης (15)

truce: make a truce, σπένδομαι (11)

true, ἀληθής (22)

trust, πιστεύω (30)

truth, ἀλήθεια (5)

try, πειράω, πειράομαι (39)

turn, turn about, τρέπω (16), στρέφω (26)

twenty, εἴκοσι (27)

ugly, αἰσχρός (7)

umpire, κριτής (5)

unable: be unable, οὐ δύναμαι (25)

unaware: be unaware, ἀγνοέω (28); cf. also λανθάνω (28)

undress, ἀποδύομαι (24)

unfortunate, δυστυχής (22)

unjust, ἄδικος (9)

until, ἕως, μέχρι, ἄχρι (39)

unwilling: be unwilling, οὐκ ἐθέλω (8)

up, ἀνά (U12)

upon, ἐπί + gen. (U6)

uppermost, ἄκρος (28)

urge, πείθω (8)

use, χράομαι + dat. (30)

used to X, use imperfect tense

useful, χρηστός (30)

valor, ἀρετή (4)

victory, νίκη (4)

violence, ὕβρις (21)

virtue, ἀρετή (4)

virtuous, ἀγαθός (6)

voice, φωνή (4)

vote, ψῆφος (3)

wall, τεῖχος (15)

want, βούλομαι (11)

war, πόλεμος (3)

water, ὕδωρ (14)

way, ὁδός (3); (= "manner"), τρόπος (6); in X way (manner), adv. acc. τρόπον with adj. (U17)

we, us, (oblique cases and nom. as emphatic subject) ἡμεῖς (22); unemphatic subject expressed by 1st pers. pl. ending of verb

weak, ἀσθενής (22)

wealth, πλοῦτος (6)

wealthy, πλούσιος (7)

weapons, ὅπλα (34)

well, εὖ (12)

what, τίς, τί (U15)

when, (relative) ὅτε, ὅταν, ἐπεί, ἐπειδή, ἐπειδάν (34)

where, (interrogative) ποῦ (17); (ind. interrog./indef. rel.) ὅπου (36)

wherever, ὅπου (36); to wherever, ὅποι (36)

which, (interrogative) τίς, τί (U15); (relative) ὅς, ἥ, ὅ (U12)

whichever, ὅστις (33)

while, (English complex sentence with *while*-clause is often equivalent to Greek compound sentence with μέν . . . δέ [U12])

who, whom, (interrogative) τίς, τί (U15); (relative) ὅς, ἥ, ὅ (U12)

whoever, ὅστις (33)

wicked, κακός, πονηρός (7)

wife, γυνή (21)

willing: be willing, ἐθέλω (8)

win, νικάω (29); win something for oneself, φέρομαι (U11)

wind, ἄνεμος (3)

winter, χειμών (39)

wisdom, σοφία (17)

wise, σοφός (7)

wish, ἐθέλω (8)

with, σύν + dat., μετά + gen. (U6); dat. of means or manner without preposition (U10, U29)

within, εἴσω

woman, γυνή (21)

wonder, θαῦμα (34)

wondrous, δεινός (16)

word, λόγος (3)

work, ἔργον; hard work, πόνος (6)

worse, κακίων, χείρων (U30)

worst, κάκιστος, χείριστος (U30)

worthless, πονηρός (7)

worthy (of), ἄξιος (+ gen.) (7)

write, γράφω (8)

writing, piece of writing, γράμμα (14)

wrong: do wrong, ἀδικέω (13)

Xenophon, Ξενοφῶν, Ξενοφῶντος, m.

year, ἔτος (15)

yoke, ζεύγνυμι (23)

you, (oblique cases and nom. as emphatic subject) sing. σύ, pl. ὑμεῖς (U22); unemphatic subject expressed by 2nd. pers. ending of verb

young man, νεανίας (5)

your, sing. σός, pl. ὑμέτερος (22); or use possessive gen. σοῦ (σου), ὑμῶν (U22)

yourselves, ὑμῶν αὐτῶν (U25)

Index

Greek words are indexed separately following the end of the index of English terms.